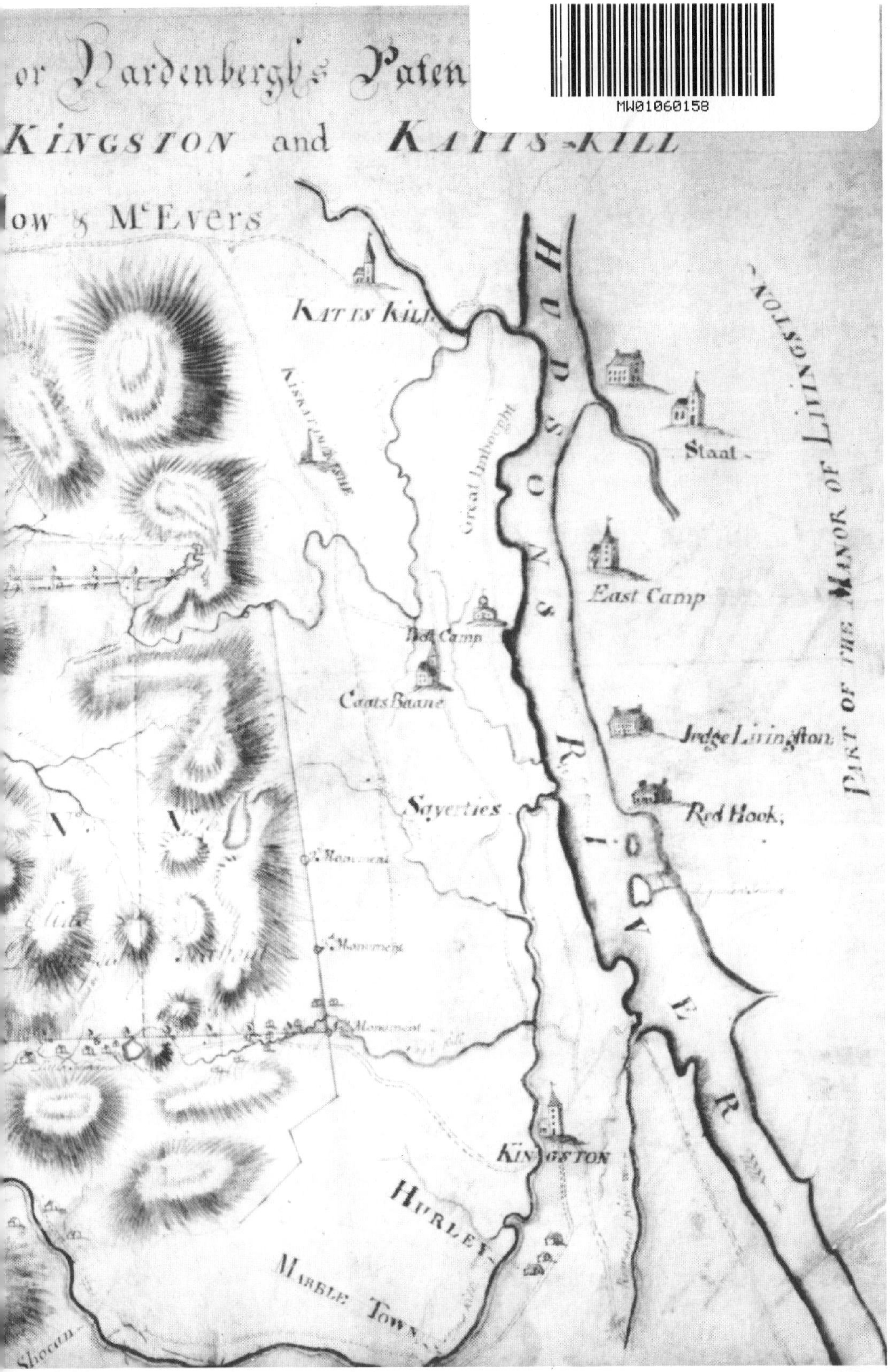

or Hardenbergh's Paten

KINGSTON and KATTS-KILL

ow & McEvers

MW01060158

KATTS KILL

NISKATHA KILL

Great Imboght

HOSSUNH RIVER

Staat

East Camp

PART OF THE MANOR OF LIVINGSTON

Red Camp

Coats Baane

Judge Livingston.

Red Hook,

Sayerties

S. Monument

S. Monument

Monument

KINGSTON

RIVER

HURLEY

MARBLE TOWN

Shoan

WOODSTOCK

History of an American Town

Also by Alf Evers

THE CATSKILLS
From Wilderness to Woodstock

WOODSTOCK

HISTORY OF AN AMERICAN TOWN

Alf Evers

THE OVERLOOK PRESS
WOODSTOCK · NEW YORK

First published in 1987 by:
The Overlook Press
Lewis Hollow Road
Woodstock, New York 12498

Copyright © 1987 Alf Evers

All Rights Reserved. No part of this publication may be reproduced or transmitted in
any form or by any means, electronic or mechanical, including photocopy, recording,
or any information or storage and retrieval system now known or to be invented,
without permission in writing from the publisher, except by a reviewer who wishes to
quote brief passages in connection with a review written for inclusion in a magazine,
newspaper or broadcast.

Library of Congress Cataloging in Publication Data

Evers, Alf.
    Woodstock: History of an American Town

Includes index.
1.Woodstock (N.Y.)   —History.   I. Title.
F129.W85E94   1986   974.7'34   86-16461
ISBN 0-87951-983-5

Printed in the United States of America

CONTENTS

ACKNOWLEDGMENTS

Like all town histories, this book is the result of cooperation between the people of the town and the author. Many hundreds of Woodstock people have given me bits of information, fresh ideas and encouragement during the almost twenty years that the book has been in the making. I am grateful to them all although I can name only a few. Among these sharers in this history were Victor Lasher, Elizabeth Clough, Charles Herrick, Cy Keegan, Robert Lasher, George and Stanley Shultis, Sherman Short, Jean Lasher Gaede, Harriet and Elsie Goddard, Sam Wiley, Edward L. Chase, Jan Van De Bogart, Peter Whitehead, Martin Comeau and John and Mable Kingsbury. I am grateful also to Woodstock people of the past who helped me by leasing or buying land or by making wills thereby getting bits of their lives set down in the Ulster County records. I am grateful to the succession of Woodstock town clerks who so faithfully kept the town's records as well as to the writers of Woodstock "items" for the Ulster County newspapers for more than a century. I owe much to the bookkeepers of the town's glass factories and stores and to those who have preceded me in putting Woodstock history into print, notable among them, Anita M. Smith in her *Woodstock, History and Hearsay,* and the authors of Woodstock materials in early gazetteers and county histories.

Many people outside of Woodstock have helped me put this history together. My sister Elisabeth helped by finding references to Woodstock in obscure printed sources. The librarians of the New York State Library at Albany, the New York Public Library and the Library of the New-

York Historical Society, whose massive collection of Livingston family papers shed needed light on Woodstock's eighteenth and early nineteenth century history, all gave their help cheerfully and efficiently.

Woodstock officials and the members of the Woodstock Historical Society have made my self-imposed task easier by choosing me as Town Historian and longtime trustee and president of the Society thereby giving me an official position from which research might continue. The trustees of the Bar College Center appointed me a fellow that enabled me to test ideas and approaches in inter-generational seminars.

My three children, Jane, Barbro and Christopher and my nine grandchildren supported me by their belief that I was doing something worthwhile in writing a history of Woodstock.

I want to express my gratitude to those who helped turn my attention to local history many years ago—to psychologist Margaret K. Smith who first convinced me that local history has a value, to Ralph LeFevre my Sunday School teacher and the author of a solid history of the town of New Paltz, N.Y. to Byron Terwilliger, an oldtime country school teacher with whom I explored old cemeteries and rummaged among accumulations of old Ulster papers.

For the past four years my grandaughter Mary James has given me almost daily help and mental stimulation—for this I am deeply grateful.

And finally I thank Sue Pilla, Geddy Sveikauskas and the others on the staff of the *Woodstock Times* for making it possible for this history to become so largely a hometown production and to appear serially in their paper and to Deborah Baker, my editor in the book's final stages, for getting my manuscript over many obstacles to the printer.

ALF EVERS
May 1987

WOODSTOCK

History of an American Town

1

A VERY QUICK LOOK AT WOODSTOCK

Every inhabited place on this earth owes its character to a combination of its living organisms and inanimate things such as its soil, rock, water, air and position on our globe—and to its distance from the equator and its height above the sea. No place exists by itself alone. No place remains static. Each changes continually in ways that are sometimes subtle and sometimes obvious, in accordance with natural laws and human behavior.

In writing accounts of small towns it has long been customary to begin by describing the physical features of the town and placing it in relationship to its neighbors. There is no better way of grasping the size, shape and physical character of the town of Woodstock in the county of Ulster and the state of New York than by climbing Overlook Mountain and looking down from its top.

With its massive supporting ridges Overlook Mountain fills the northeast corner of the town. It rises to 3150 feet above the tidal waters of the Hudson River, which flows by some ten miles to the east on its way to join the Atlantic Ocean a hundred miles to the south. Overlook's summit forms a natural observation platform from which Woodstock's seventy-plus square miles of mountains, hills, valleys, plains, streams and lakes may be taken in with a single sweeping glance. From the platform, and especially from the steel tower which rises above it, the boundaries which set Woodstock apart from the rest of the world may be traced.

It would be impossible to follow the sixty miles or so of Woodstock's perimeter on wheels. The boundaries climb cliffs, push through dense forests, and cross lakes and streams. To follow the boundaries on foot would take a good hiker several days. As far as I know, no one has recently undertaken this rugged hike. But even a lazy man or woman standing on top of Overlook may send his eyes racing along Woodstock's boundaries and make the entire circuit in a minute or two.

A good starting point for this sixty-mile hike by eye is roundish, forest-encircled Echo Lake, about two miles to the north and about a thousand feet below Overlook's summit. Some eleven miles westward along the base of the Indian Head range the line disappears behind Alderbark Mountain. Pick it up again after it finishes making a left turn and emerges from behind Alderbark. Follow it as it moves on a little below the plateau-like top of Mount Tremper and glides behind a cone-shaped mountain to the south—this is Mount Tobias.

Up to this point a topographical map may have made things easy. Thanks to compromises of hard-fought boundary disputes of long ago the line now moves on and zigs and zags, jigs and jogs, keeping well away from the northern edge of the Ashokan Reservoir gleaming to the southeast. Once past the reservoir, however, the line executes a bold foray out of the Catskill Mountains and into the lowland towns of Kingston and Ulster. The result on the map appears to jut out like a beard from the corner of the main mass of Woodstock. Oldtimers have been heard to call this part of town "the chin whisker of Woodstock." The whisker resulted from the attempt by politicians of the 1870s to influence voting results through gerrymandering.

Once it has defined the whisker, the Woodstock boundary line returns to simplicity. It moves northeastward, getting ever closer to the base of Overlook Mountain and passing out of sight behind one of the mountain's huge shoulders. It staggers irregularly for a moment before turning westward and splashing into the water close to the northern shore of Echo Lake.[1]

An observer on the highest ledges of Overlook can easily understand how the land within the Woodstock boundaries has been carved into its present shape. The mountains below form a projecting part of the eastern edge of the Alleghany Plateau, the softer parts of which have been worn away by the forces of frost, glacial ice, moving water and gravity. Rocks rolling along their streambeds have cut Woodstock valleys deep into the plateau, leaving mountains like

2

Overlook towering above. Retreating ice sheets have left boulders, gravel and clay, heaped up in some places, spread out in others, and forming the natural dams which made possible Cooper Lake, Yankeetown Pond, Echo Lake and Mead's Pond.

The long process of shaping and reshaping Woodstock has not yet come to an end and will not do so as long as our earth endures. Every once in a while a dramatic natural event like a flood or a land slip reminds Woodstock people that their town is subject to changes which have deeper roots than the changes brought about by a town election or the invention of a new gadget for making transportation faster or housework easier.

One such event occurred at ten a.m. on October 12, 1831 at the cliff on Overlook Mountain long known from the dignified profile it presents as the Minister's Face. Just why a great mass of rock fell away from the Minister's Face that day is not altogether certain. There had been no heavy rains to prompt it. Two more fundamental factors may have been at work. Overlook Mountain is close to the fault which runs along Woodstock's eastern boundaries, thought to be a southward continuation of one beginning in Canada known as Logan's Line; rock beneath the surface along this line sometimes slips, producing local tremors sufficiently strong to dislodge already weakened masses of rock and earth. And the rocks which form the Minister's Face are structurally weak. There are great variations in the strength of the layers of sandstone and shale which form the Catskill Mountains. The Minister's Face is the result of the crumbling over many, many years of a mass of weak rock jutting out from Overlook.

The rock fall of 1831 was spectacular enough to be described thus in a Kingston newspaper: "Trees eighteen inches in diameter were flattened, as the great mass of rock fell down . . . . A chasm sixty feet in width, resembling . . . . the bed of a rapid stream . . . . " appeared below. According to the Ulster *Palladium* of October 26, 1831, "The noise," reported the paper, "resembled heavy thunder, or rather the deep-toned sounds of an approaching earthquake, and was distinctly heard at a distance of six miles. For some minutes afterward the sides of the mountain were enveloped in smoke like the effects from the discharge of heavy artillery."

Seen from the top of Overlook on a summer day the color of Woodstock is leaf-green. Trees seem to cover the landscape. They fill many valleys, they swarm up mountainsides, they find footholds among the lichen-covered ledges of Overlook's summit, and there they become dwarfed and twisted in winter by wind and ice. But trees form only one part of the network of living things which thrives on the soil of Woodstock. Low native plants—ferns, mountain laurel, wintergreen, trailing arbutus and many others—grow on the mountainsides. Near the roads which follow the valleys plants from Europe—clovers, grasses, ox-eyed daisies and similar Old-World plants—enliven the landscape with their blossoms each summer. Mosses cling to shady rocks, mushrooms dot the forest floor, cattails and pond lilies stand or float on Yankeetown Pond or Echo Lake, algae multiply in stagnant waters, organisms like bacteria fill the soil and float in the air. Each plant struggles to increase in the parts of the town where living conditions suit it best.

The living things of Woodstock, like living things everywhere, exist in a state of mingled interdependence and conflict. Animals breathe the oxygen given off by plants, plants thrive on the waste products of animals and on their dead bodies. Humans working their valley gardens pull up the crabgrass which crowds in and threatens the well-being of their roses, radishes and petunias. Deer and porcupines crop the tips of young trees high on Woodstock mountains. On every square inch of the town interdependence and conflict form essential parts of life.

So too it is with those living things which have the power of moving. Some, like chipmunks and chickadees, are met in both the valleys and the mountains. Others, like bears, varying hare and rattlesnakes, seldom leave the mountains. Human beings, except for occasional hunters or hikers, are confined to the valleys because they can live there in greater physical comfort and travel to their jobs more quickly and with less effort. Few Woodstock people live at an altitude above one thousand feet, the very highest dwellings are located at about two thousand feet.

Seen from the summit of Overlook the effects of over two centuries of human occupancy are almost invisible. Long ridges and tall trees hide the valley floors where neat housing developments stand and where churches, playing fields, schools, roads and houses abound. Woodstock by some act of magic seems to retain the appearance of the days when human beings formed no part of the town's community of living things.

To those who have learned to read the story the landscape tells, however, evidence of human occupancy can be found in the soil, the rocks and the water, and even in the trees themselves. The cutting and

4

burning of the primeval forest has destroyed the cap of balsam fir and spruce which once crowned Overlook as it still crowns Indian Head Mountain, its neighbor to the north. Fire-resistant oaks have taken the place of more tender sugar maples, beeches, hemlocks and other trees on many slopes. Squares of young pine trees mark mountainside fields long ago abandoned as erosion carried off the once-fertile soil. The chestnut trees which formerly grew to great size and vigor on sunny slopes have succumbed to a disease brought by human agency from China—their places have been taken by oaks, hemlocks and other trees.

A stranger looking down from the top of Overlook on a summer day would not suspect that close to 7000 people live year round among the trees and behind the ridges below or that on a weekend the town's population is often multiplied several times. He would not suspect that the green expanse beneath him is the site of a famous art colony where painters, sculptors, writers, musicians and craftspeople have gathered since the early years of the twentieth century. The stranger would probably accept on faith a belief that Indians had once been active in Woodstock, for the Indians' presence is felt throughout America. He would have to go down Overlook if he wanted to discover signs of the Indians. But he could surely find them. These signs are still visible and they can tell us much about the Indians and how they related to the Woodstock society of living and inanimate things of their time.[2]

2

THE INDIANS
OF WOODSTOCK

Sometimes a hiker or hunter on the southeastern side of Overlook Mountain takes shelter from a storm under an overhanging ledge. If the storm holds him captive long enough for boredom to set in and if he knows something of the past of Overlook he may amuse himself in a simple way. He may call up in his imagination the people who have taken shelter beneath the same ledge before him. And these people are numerous. Woodstock boys getting their first awed taste of contact with the power of a mountainside thunderstorm, hunters of Civil War days, others wearing the buckskin jackets of Colonial times, and—most appealing of all— the Indians who were the first human beings to struggle up the sides of Overlook.

This happened several thousand years after the last American glaciation, known as the Wisconsin, retreated some twelve thousand years ago and vegetation and animal life began returning to the mountain. The pioneer or Paleo-Indians who had roamed the valley below Overlook in search of game once the glacier retreated are unlikely to have climbed the mountain. It was as yet too barren to have anything of value to them.[1]

In the spring of 1952 a young man plowing his garden in Lewis Hollow on the southeastern side of the mountain turned up a flint spearpoint. He took the spearpoint to experts in New York State archeology, who declared that the bit of flint had probably been shaped some time between 3500 and 1300 B.C. It belonged to what is known as the Archaic Hunting, Fishing and Gathering Stage of Indian culture. This stage preceded the one which marked Indian life in the days when the first European sailors moved up the Hudson River and made contact with its Indians. By that time the growing of corn, beans and squash, the use of the bow and arrow, and the making of pottery had brought the culture of the local Indians a little closer to that of the Europeans.

One spearpoint found near the surface of a mountainside does not prove anything, for such an object might have reached its point of discovery in any of a number of ways. But when added to other bits of evidence the Lewis Hollow spearpoint does suggest that Indian hunters were active on Overlook long before the birth of Christ. At the time of the first settlement of the Hudson Valley by white people the Indians whom they began displacing belonged to a large and widespread family, all of whom spoke dialects of a language we know as Algonkian.

Much of the Catskill Mountains, including Woodstock, formed part of the hunting grounds of Algonkian-speaking Indians living year-round on the banks of the Esopus Creek in Kingston, Hurley and Saugerties, and so called the Esopus Indians. They lived in what is called the Woodland Stage of Indian culture. They used dome-shaped dwellings of overlapping sheets of bark secured to a framework of saplings made fast in the ground; sometimes these dwellings were elongated to serve several related families. Within, woven mats of the soft inner bark of basswood and other trees or of grass served as beds or couches. A small pit in the center held the fire; smoke escaped as best it could through an opening in the roof. Clothing was largely made of deerskin as the Indians had no cloth. Personal ornaments were made from shells, stones, the teeth and claws of animals, or dyed porcupine quills.

The Indian women tended the crops grown near their dwellings, using hoes made of stone or the shoulderblades of deer. Each fall they stored their harvest of corn in pits lined with mats. In the intervals of their agricultural and household work they accompanied their men on work trips to gather and prepare the necessities of life available at certain seasons. So they travelled in summer, perhaps in dugout canoes, to the point at which the Esopus Creek pours into the Hudson. There the freshwater mussels or clams that abounded were prepared for winter use. In the fall or winter the work parties followed well-worn trails to Woodstock, where deer, bear and turkey and chestnut, beechnuts and acorns, could be found. The Indians gathered these staple foods for their immediate use and also carried some back to their valley homes.

The women worked at preparing food and clothing from the animals killed by their mates. They kept fires burning for warmth and cooking in their "rock houses" while the men pursued bear and deer. The men may have used the Indian method known as "fire hunting," which involved setting fires in the dry spring or autumn woods in order to drive game animals toward places where they could be more easily killed. Such fires would have altered the vegetational makeup of Woodstock by favoring grasses and oaks and lessening the numbers of more sensitive trees such as beeches and basswood; once grass and brush sprang up on fire-ravaged areas, a more favorable environment would exist for deer.[2]

Indian paths leading from the Esopus Creek to the Overlook hunting grounds may still be traced. One such path follows the Sawkill from the Indian settlement close to the point at which the Sawkill joins the Esopus Creek. The path moved upward through the present hamlet of Sawkill and that of Zena and so on to the rock houses or shelters located up to an elevation of about one thousand feet on Overlook Mountain, with a few on Ohayo Mountain. The shelters were formed when softer strata of rock eroded and left harder rock layers projecting above. The early Dutch called such shelters "jagd houses," which meant hunting houses—and that is exactly what they were.

Some Indians who lived on the fertile plains near Kingston made their way to Woodstock over a trail which followed the route now known as the Waghkonk Road, past a spot still called the Indian Spring, and then joined the Sawkill trail. Waghkonk, or Awaghkonk, is a genuine Algonkian Indian name, meaning "at or near a mountain." The name was used in old records to locate land near the base of Overlook Mountain—later the name was restricted to Zena. It first appears in official records in 1702 as Anguagekonk.[3]

Another part of Woodstock has a traditional name derived not from the Indians' language but from that of the early white settlers. It is the Indian Orchard. This spot close to the Beaverkill and the present Shandaken-Woodstock boundary line was recorded in May 1844 by surveyor Henry Ramsay as he followed the Woodstock boundary northward. Ramsay set up a stake and a pile of stones to mark the town line in "a small clearing called Indian Orchard, fine land, very gentle N.W. aspect," he wrote in his notebook.[4]

Indian Orchard is a not uncommon American place name usually given to the site of an Indian camp or settlement at which Indians had planted the seeds of European apples and had left old trees behind when they moved on. Woodstock's Indian Orchard may have been a camp site of Indians who travelled a trail leading from their Esopus Creek lowlands along the upper course of the creek and across the Catskills at Pine Hill to the Delaware Valley. At what is known today as Mount Tremper, a branch trail led along the Beaverkill to Lake Hill. This trail was still being referred to in early Woodstock records as "the footpath." [5]

Until Europeans began settling in the Hudson Valley, Indian visits to their Woodstock camps and rock shelters continued to follow their traditional patterns. But after white settlement began in Kingston changes became inevitable. For a time the Indian cornfields and clusters of domed houses lingered along the Esopus, mixed more and more with Dutch plantations of wheat. Conflict between whites and Indians grew more frequent. Indians shot the Dutch peoples' hogs and cows which wandered into their cornfields. Brandy received by the Indians in return for beaver pelts, beans and venison stirred them to ever more intense resentment against the Dutch settlers.

The Dutch coveted the fine Esopus lowlands. These lands, they said, were the most fertile in the entire province of New Netherland, and because the Indians had kept them almost treeless by cultivation and fire they were "ready for the plow." Governor Stuyvesant himself owned land along the Esopus and did his best to help push the unwilling Indians back into the hilly and mountainous lands to the west.

In 1660 the first of the Esopus Wars ended in defeat for the Indians. The second in 1663 shook their society to its foundations. In December of that year, during discussions leading to an armistice, it was reported that "the Esopus savages are obliged to make their living by the chase as they have no corn and every one with his prisoner [these were Dutch men, women and children captured during the war] is scattered here and there. . . ." The Indians were "deprived of all means of subsistence through the destruction of their corn" by Dutch soldiers who pulled up growing corn and burned the corn stored in Indian pits for the winter. It is likely that the Woodstock rock shelters became Indian retreats at this time and that Indians lived on the shore of Cooper Lake.[6]

Until a few years ago some old Woodstock people remembered

hearing from their parents or grandparents of Indians living at Echo Lake and of an old Indian doctor doing business in the hamlet of Woodstock. But the link of rock shelters with the Indians left no marks in local lore. It was not until the 1890s that a wave of interest in the old Indian inhabitants of Woodstock was aroused by a discovery made at Cooper Lake and led young people to rummage in the old rock shelters in search of traces of Indians.

Six years after the Cooper Lake discovery the Pine Hill *Sentinel* of July 29, 1899 had this to say:

> Many of the summer guests in the Catskills frequently visit Lake Hill these days to see a curiously engraved stone there owned by Rufus Van Debogart. The stone was found at the bottom of Cooper's Lake when it was cleaned. It is five feet long, two and one half feet wide and weighs seven hundred pounds. The engraving, it is believed, is the work of Indians. It is also evident that the engraving was not quite finished. Perhaps the Indians were disturbed during the work by foes, and hurled the stone into the lake. This is the accepted theory. Mr. Van Debogart has had many offers for the stone, from $25 in cash to a $75 threshing machine. He says he wants $100 cash for it.

The engraving mentioned by the *Sentinel* consisted of groups of small lens-shaped depressions which seemed to any ordinarily imaginative eye to have been cut into the stone with the purpose of conveying a message. But this was not all the pale gray stone had to offer. It seemed to have been shaped into boldly curved forms which suggested the waves of the sea, an Indian woman, a baby's head and a variety of animals. When R. Lionel De Lisser discussed the stone in his *Picturesque Ulster* of 1897 he ignored the engravings and laid stress instead on "the grotesque heads and forms supposed to have been the work of the aborigines."

Descriptions of the stone were sent to experts on the American Indian with inconclusive results. Some accepted it as an unusual but genuine example of "pictographic art," and others expressed a guarded doubt. In 1931 Bruno Louis Zimm, sculptor, craftsman and scholarly student of Woodstock history, described the markings on the stone as "a series of chisel cuts." He expressed regret at not having been able to turn up any information about "the mysterious, unnamed people who fashioned this strange stone." Zimm added that "the authorities I have consulted are unable . . . to help; and assign it to the same group as that mysterious Dighton Stone found at Bristol, Mass., some time before 1680, which set the entire scientific world agog in its endeavor to connect it with a known historic period." [7]

For more than half a century interest in the Lake Hill Stone continued strong. Rufus Van De Bogart displayed it on his lawn, where many visitors stared at it year after year—but no one was willing to pay Van De Bogart his hundred dollars. At the same time the stone did much to focus attention on Woodstock as an Indian site. It stimulated collectors of Indian artifacts to visit Woodstock rock shelters and to hunt for worked flint on the shores of Cooper Lake. Collecting "Indian relics" had been a popular hobby ever since early nineteenth-century poets, painters and novelists had used Indians as romantic figures. By the time the Lake Hill Stone was discovered good Indian artifacts had acquired a small value in cash and collections of them were on display in museums.

In 1917 an archeologist named Max Schrabisch excavated five Indian rock shelters on the southeastern side of Overlook and two on Ohayo Mountain. He found that one shelter on Overlook was far larger than the others and showed signs of the presence of many Indians over a long period. He also found that other diggers had preceded him there. One, whom Schrabisch described as "a curio hunter," had been the most industrious—he had made off with many arrow points, a flint drill, "a bone awl, a worked deer bone, a bear claw and a muskrat tooth," among other objects. Schrabisch, as he dug to the deepest levels, found bones of deer, bear, raccoon, wild turkey and other animals; he found, besides much worked flint, shells of the freshwater mussel, much broken pottery, parts of clay pipes, several thin pieces of copper perforated as if to be used as ornaments, the brass hilt of a dagger.[8]

Schrabisch's digging was interrupted by an accusation that he was a German spy—he had come to Woodstock shortly after the United States joined the First World War. But even had he dug without interruption he may have destroyed more than he discovered. For the many refinements in archeology which are in wide use today were unknown to him. He did not record the levels at which artifacts were found, nor did he study their context. His industrious digging made radio-carbon dating, which might have given us a chronology of Indian trips to the Woodstock shelters, unlikely. The artifacts which he took away from Woodstock have disappeared, probably sold during Schrabisch's poverty-filled old age. The lists of objects which Schrabisch found suggest many centuries of use. They tell us that Indians used the shelters for some time after the white traders arrived and furnished them with such things as clay pipes and European daggers. They tell us what animals the Indians hunted and ate.

By 1970 Rufus Van De Bogart had long since died and his son William, who inherited the Lake Hill Stone, was old and in poor health. William left Woodstock to live with relatives across the Hudson River in Dutchess County. And before he left he presented the Senate House Museum in Kingston with the stone. Curator Herbert H. Cutler consulted Dr. William A. Ritchie, New York State Archeologist and leading authority on the state's prehistoric Indians. Dr. Ritchie got the opinions of geologists and other experts and then proceeded to demolish all claims of the Lake Hill Stone to Indian associations. The stone was a piece of dolomitic limestone which contained many small areas of lower magnesium carbonate content. These areas had dissolved, leaving behind the "multiple pittings" which seemed to so many observers to have been cut by Indians. The stone was entirely a natural production, although an unusually interesting one worthy of exhibit. The stone was too hard to have been shaped or carved by any tool known to Woodstock's prehistoric Indians.[9]

Not everyone accepts the Ritchie explanation. There are Woodstock people who still believe that some day the stone which has been the object of so much speculation for three-quarters of a century will be proved to have been given its present form if not by Indians then by European immigrants of long ago. Every upsurge of interest in theories of the presence in America of Bronze Age Celts or Phoenicians has been followed by a renewal of interest in the Lake Hill Stone. And in spite of the Ritchie explanation this is likely to continue even if the stone's former location deep in the mud of a lake bottom and the failure of its pattern of little pits to suggest any known system of conveying information present formidable barriers to proof that it carries a message devised by human hands and brain.

The persistence of belief in the Indian association of the Lake Hill Stone grows in part out of the nineteenth-century American urge to romanticize their country's Indian background. The Lake Hill Stone was not alone in adding touches to the romanticized picture of the old Indian hunters of Woodstock. With the ending of the Civil War Woodstock became a promising center of summer life for urban people, and in response the friends of the new Overlook Mountain House felt the need to provide the kind of Indian lore and legend which was being pushed by rival summer hotels in the Catskills. In 1873 "The Traditions of the Overlook" appeared as a small booklet. It contained a tongue-in-cheek account of the naming of a number of features of the top of Overlook to an accompaniment of champagne and whimsical speeches in which the mountain was called "the Mount Sinai of the aborigines" and its summit was celebrated as the scene of Indian war dances and divine appearances.[10]

In the 1870s no one could take "The Traditions" very seriously. The booklet, after stirring a good deal of amusement, was forgotten. Yet the traces of its Indian references remained in Woodstock's consciousness to surface now and then in altered and embellished form. As Woodstock became an art colony after 1902 oldtimers told the new people that Indians had once held ceremonies on the mountaintop. They weren't sure how they had acquired this information, it was something that "everybody knew." The young people known as hippies and flower children who flocked to Woodstock in the 1960s seized on the Indian associations of Overlook, which they accepted as the Indians' "sacred mountain," and an elaborate local Indian cult evolved.[11]

In spite of all efforts at romanticizing local Indians, the Indian rock shelters of Woodstock remain the town's major reminder of the days when Woodstock was part of the hunting grounds of the Esopus Indians. The largest of the shelters, forty feet long by about twelve feet deep, is an impressive one. The great mass of rock above, the quiet woods around, the cool of the shelter's interior, all work together to make almost visible the Indians of long ago, the women crouched over their cooking fires at the rear of the shelter, the children playing among the dry leaves outside, the dogs lying in the sun, the men mending their hunting gear.

Just how long ago the last party of Indians used the great shelter will probably never be known. Not only did the Esopus Wars of 1660 and 1663 severely damage their society, but alcohol and epidemics of diseases brought by the Europeans from which the Indians had no protection also lessened their numbers and their vigor. Woodstock traditions tell of Indians living in small groups in Woodstock as recently as a century ago. Martin MacDaniel used to speak of the pre-Civil War days when his parents were young and "there were Indians at Echo Lake." But these and other Indians who came and went in Woodstock may not have been descendants of the Esopus people— they could very well have wandered from as far away as Canada. Such Indians often travelled from place to place making and selling baskets and wooden household objects and working as harvest hands.

Before 1700 Woodstock Indians play no part in the recorded

history of the town; but soon after they began to leave traces of their presence in the records of Ulster County. That happened when white men first gave signs of wanting something which belonged to the Indians who had for so long used Woodstock as hunting grounds and refuge. What the white men wanted was the Indians' land. The first step on record which began changing Woodstock from an Indian to a white man's possession took place on March 12, 1702.

3

THE WHITES ADVANCE ON INDIAN WOODSTOCK

From the beginning of their settlement the people of Esopus—now called Kingston—had been pushing, expanding and overflowing into the up-country. They had pushed up the valleys of the Wallkill and Rondout Creek and taken over the fertile riverside flatlands cleared and cultivated by Indian effort and now ready for the most profitable of all crops—wheat.

By 1678 New York was exporting sixty thousand bushels of wheat per year, largely to the West Indies; prices were high, demand was brisk. Nowhere in America did wheat grow more luxuriantly than on these riverside flatlands within easy reach of the Esopus settlers. Some settlers were drawn to the neighborhood they were soon calling the Brabant, in memory of Nord Brabant in Holland, where mixtures of low flatlands, marshes and slow-winding streams suggested the name to Brabant-born Esopus settlers.

The vicinity had another attraction which appealed very strongly to the Esopus Dutch. A stream soon to be known as the Sagh Kill or Sawkill entered the Esopus at the Brabant. It had its beginnings in Woodstock's Echo and Cooper Lakes, and made its way downward through a valley marked by a succession of flatlands suited to farming and by rough and rocky stretches of streams. The waterfalls, when properly harnessed, were able to turn sawmill wheels which would produce boards and beams for home use and export, or grind the grain grown on Brabant and Sawkill valley fields. The Hudson River nearby provided cheap transportation to market of both wheat and timber.[1]

In 1664 the province of New York came under British rule. But life along the Esopus Creek continued much as in Dutch days. In 1670 and 1671 Governor Lovelace, officially recognizing the growing interest in the Brabant-Sawkill vicinity, made the first grants of land there. An innship (a collection of dwelling houses) was planned for the neighborhood in order that those working the land and cutting the forests to the north and west might live close together for protection against the sometimes-restless Indians. Captain Thomas Chambers, the lord of nearby Foxhall Manor, proposed two dwelling houses "within Two Musquett Shot of the said Innship." [2]

By the 1690s the innship had come into being, and William Legg was operating a sawmill well up the Sawkill above the constriction in the valley known to the plain-speaking Dutch as the Aasegat or asshole. The demand for timber and for land capable of producing good crops of wheat was increasing year by year. A further push up the Sawkill was soon under way, and by 1700 what would one day become Woodstock was being eyed with speculative interest.

As the push from Esopus intensified, Indians were still using their old rock shelters on the side of Overlook Mountain, and had established camps on the shore of Cooper Lake and perhaps Yankeetown Pond. And it is likely they were growing corn and other crops on Sawkill Valley flatlands above the upper limit of the white man's possessions.[3]

By 1702 several speculators were maneuvering to get hold of the lands to which some of the Esopus Indians had retreated. The first group to make an appearance in the old records was led by merchant and Indian trader Johannis Hardenbergh. On March 12, 1702 Hardenbergh petitioned New York governor Nanfan for permission to buy from the Indians some lands, now part of Woodstock. He described these lands as those "called by the Indians by the name of Sakowonorkonk and Pogkandkonk lying to the northwest of the Town of Kingston upon a certain creek called Sawkill." These lands, as later records made clear, were not on the Sawkill at all but lay along the Beaverkill below the point at which the stream emerges from Mink Hollow; they include the flatlands at the present hamlets of Lake Hill and Willow.

Permission to buy was granted. Hardenbergh, however, allowed the year during which the permission was valid to go by without acting. On the same day Hardenbergh had made his petition Albert

16

Rosa of Kingston also asked permission to buy land in what is now Woodstock. The land he wanted, Rosa stated, was "called by ye Indians by ye name of Anguagekonk, lying to ye northwest of Kingston, upon a certain creek called Sawkill, westerly above William Legg's sawmill, and near ye high mountains which lands are in ye hands of ye Indian proprietors who are willing to sell to your Petitioner." Rosa's petition was written in the same handwriting as Hardenbergh's. Obviously the two were working together.[4]

Other hopeful acquirers were at work, too, and before long the results came to the surface. In 1704 a group of nine men living and farming in Hurley to the southwest of Esopus petitioned the new governor who had succeeded Nanfan in May 1702, asking him to authorize a survey of lands adjoining Hurley to the north.[5]

The new governor with whom the Hurley people dealt was as bizarre as any character in American colonial history. He was Edward, Viscount Cornbury, a cousin of Queen Anne, a nephew of King James II and a grandson of the great Earl of Clarendon, who had been prime minister and Lord Chancellor of England. When William of Orange had invaded England, Cornbury had joined him and so betrayed his uncle, King James. William rewarded Cornbury by appointing him governor of New York and New Jersey. And Cornbury proceeded to astonish New Yorkers not only by his arrogance and greed but also by his way of parading around New York dressed as a woman.

The Hurley men gave the governor a reasonable explanation for wanting the land for which they were asking. Hurley's riverside fields could not be surpassed for the growing of wheat, but Hurley farmers lacked the extensive woodlands and pasture they needed to carry on the kind of well-rounded farming which promised the greatest longterm profits. Firewood in the days when it was the only household fuel was needed in enormous quantities; cattle, horses, hogs and sheep needed ample pasturelands. Hurley was fitted into a small triangle between Kingston and Marbletown as it had been set up after the Esopus Wars. It did not have the extensive wild lands which were attached to the territories of its two neighbors.[6]

In a number of agreements, deeds and other documents over the first three-quarters of the eighteenth century the Hurley nine and their heirs made it plain that they were not trying to speculate in land but had a genuine desire to protect themselves against future shortages of firewood, pasture and other necessities of their society. They repeated that the lands for which they asked in 1704 were to be kept "uncultivated" and to "remain forever in Commons for Wood, Pasturage and Drift of Cattle." The only exceptions to this intention were "Arable Lands, Creeks for Mills, and such like cases." Lands like these might be sold by the nine or their heirs.

Even before the petition of the Hurley men had been acted upon, a candidate for buying "Arable Lands and Creeks for Mills" came forward to take steps toward buying Woodstock real estate. The candidate was a speculator on an immense scale. He was Hendrickus, or Henry, Beekman, justice of the peace and a member of the Provincial Assembly, a man loaded down with official honors and determined positively to gorge himself on land. On August 6, 1705 Beekman executed a deed (now known only through a copy) by which four Esopus Indians conveyed to him for a payment of a hundred pounds the best agricultural lands in Woodstock and the right to much of the Sawkill. The lands were in two pieces of five hundred acres each. One lay on both sides of the Sawkill between Awaghkonk and the site of the present hamlet of Woodstock. The other included the flatlands of Lake Hill and Willow on both sides of the Beaverkill.

The Indians with whom Beekman came to terms were the earliest to be recorded by name as being connected to Woodstock, and therefore deserve to be remembered. They were Sam Hees (who may have been given the Dutch family name of Voorhees, sometimes spelled V. Hees); Hendrick Hekan, whose Indian name is given in the deed as Kackaweerimin; and Hekan's sisters, Geertasd and Casay. Nothing beyond their names is known at present about Hees and Geertasd and Casay. All four were probably descended from chiefs of their group. Geertasd and Casay, although of their people's upper class, are likely to have worked like the other Indian women of their vicinity at planting, hoeing, making clothing and carrying burdens when forming part of the work groups.[7]

While we know nothing of Hees, Geertasd and Casay, of Hendrick Hekan we know a great deal, enough to make it possible for us to visualize him as an individual human being who may once have called Woodstock home. Under numerous variations of both his Indian and English names he turns up now and then in the Ulster records of his time; he was one of the "lesser sachems" of the Esopus who signed renewals of the treaty of peace following the Esopus Wars. By 1712 the center of Esopus Indian life had moved westward to the East Branch of the Delaware River at Papakunk, now Margaretville, where Hekan farmed. In his later years he spoke with pride of the hard cider he made of apples grown in his own orchard. By the late 1730s he was described as grayheaded but still active, and the "chief Chesan" (sachem) of the "Dallaware and Esopus Indians." He made his mark on a deed to land in the upper Delaware Valley in 1746. On May 1, 1751 two Indians named Amoucht and Wesany were referred to as "both sons of Hendryck Heckan, deceased." No one can say whether Hekan, his sisters and Sam Hees once lived in the Sawkill Valley or used the rock shelters on the side of Overlook Mountain. But it is likely that they did, and so may have been among the last of the early historic Indians to live in Woodstock.[8]

What we can say for certain is that the four Indians of the Beekman deed played a part in setting down in 1705 Indian names for the various parts of the Sawkill and Beaverkill valleys in Woodstock. These were not place names as we know them but descriptive ones. Westward of Anguagekonk lay Coteskakunk, which probably included the site of the present hamlet of Woodstock; Cooper Lake was "a great lake or pond known by the name of Opdondsase"; after that the description takes up at "a kreek that comes out of the mountains [at the entrance of Mink Hollow] to a place called pagkanagkinck on Booth syds of sd Kreek as far down as the land goes and also forder down sdkill or Krieck to a trackt of Land Called sac:in:darow. . . ." The flat lands of Lake Hill and Willow are apparently meant by these two names, variants of those used by Johannis Hardenbergh in 1702. The land conveyed by the four Indians then moves on down the Beaverkill to its junction with "the great kill that runs to Assokant" [this is the Esopus Creek] and so passes out of Woodstock.[9]

On July 18, 1706 Johannis Hardenbergh re-entered the picture, asking permission of the governor to buy from the Esopus Indians "a small tract vacant land." This sounds modest enough, but what Hardenbergh was actually working up to was a grant of a million and a half acres, including most of the region of the Catskill Mountains and overlapping the claims of Cornelis Cool and Henry Beekman. Very quickly Hardenbergh got a deed from an Esopus sachem named Nanisinos or Nisinos. A period of struggle between the opposing sides followed. By April 20, 1708 the governor and his council had arrived at a decision. They gave Hardenbergh what he had asked for.

And no wonder. For Hardenbergh had acquired seven equal partners, some of them very close to Governor Cornbury. One was the governor's secretary, Peter Fauconnier. Two others were Thomas Wenham, a member of Cornbury's council, and May Bickley, his attorney general (neither appeared in the letters patent but hid behind substitutes). A final secret member of Hardenbergh and Company, as the group was called, was surveyor general Augustine Graham, whose share was not claimed until 1729 and only then by his son and heir James. A persistent tradition still maintains that Cornbury himself had a share in the Hardenbergh Patent, but so cleverly concealed that it has never been discovered.[10]

By way of an attempt to quiet Cornelis Cool and his group from Hurley, the governor's council asked the Hardenbergh patentees to sell them a tract of land sufficient for Hurley's pasture and firewood needs. This was done. For a payment of sixty pounds the Hurley people were sold a vaguely described tract of land cut from the Hardenbergh Patent. The parcel included much of Woodstock. Beekman's land bought from the Indians in 1705 formed part of it.

Several not-very-successful tries at clearing up the confusion of titles were made. On November 29, 1714 Cool and his people deeded to Beekman for a consideration of fifteen pounds the two five-hundred-acre tracts Beekman had bought from the four Indians, one at Coteskakunk and the other at Pagkanagkinck. The Hurley people retained their right to "Cutt, break and Rive and carry away all sorts of Wood and Stone from any part of the above granted two parcels of land that is not in fence. . . ." At the same time the two parcels were claimed by the Hardenbergh patentees as part of their grant. The confusion was indeed deep in the valleys of the Sawkill and Beaverkill. And it was deepened by an angry dispute over the boundaries of Albert Rosa's land at Anguagkonk.

As Hardenbergh, Cool and Beekman engaged in hot competition for land, the push of Kingston people up the valley of the Sawkill continued. Another sawmill appeared above William Legg's. Fine white pines, the best and most valuable timber, were picked out of the ancient forest high up the valley above the mills. As firewood became scarce close to the Hudson Valley settlements, the Kingston trustees, aroused by the cutting of hardwood to be shipped down the Hudson to New York from their commons, passed ordinances to prevent this activity. On the last day of December 1720 the trustees passed a resolution aimed at preventing Albert and Evert Rosa from cutting wood inside the commons line near Anguagkonk.

The western boundary of the land granted to Kingston in 1687 had never been determined with accuracy. Now the Hardenbergh patentees were taking advantage of this to push their own claim eastward across what Kingston people believed to be their line. Johannis Hardenbergh leased land at what is now Zena to at least one settler, and protested when his tenants' fences were broken down by Kingston people who claimed the land. Hardenbergh and his fellow patentees took the matter to court, where it smoldered year after year. Henry Beekman died in 1716. The vast landholdings he left, including his claim to much valley land in Woodstock, remained divided among his heirs. That may be why the Beekman claim lay dormant for forty years after the deed from Cornelis Cool had given it substance.[11]

By then most of the Indians had been driven from the hills and valleys of Woodstock. The demand for forest products and tillable land was making the place attractive. Yet only a few settlers appeared, in part because of the persistent clash of claims to the land. And there were other reasons as well.

4

ON THE EVE OF
WHITE SETTLEMENT

For more than a half century after
Sam Hees, Hendrick Hekan, Geertasd, Casay and Nanisinos gave up
their rights to ownership of Woodstock, wars between the British and
the French, who held Canada, plagued the North American continent
and made settlement in frontier places like Woodstock an uneasy
business. Even during periods of peace, like the one between the
ending of Queen Anne's War in 1713 and the beginning of King
George's War in 1740, rumors of plots and raids by the French and
their Iroquois Indian allies made people who might otherwise have
moved farther up the Sawkill Valley hesitate.

Until the French yielded what is now Canada to Britain in 1763,
bands of militiamen from the Hudson Valley roamed at intervals
among the Catskills in search of enemies. Trappers and hunters came
and went in the upper valleys of the Sawkill and the Beaverkill.
Though some probably put together cabins and settled down for a
while as squatters, the farthest outpost of serious settlement remained
along Woodstock's eastern border.[1]

Even if fear of death at the hands of raiding Indians or
Frenchmen had not chilled the enthusiasm of prospective settlers,
doubts as to the legality of the title to the land would have. They
would have been especially doubtful about the validity of the
Hardenbergh Patent, whose sharers had the most conspicuous claim to
Woodstock. By the 1740s nearly all the original Hardenbergh

patentees were dead and a multitude of heirs had taken over. The heirs held the patent in common and no part of it could be sold or leased without the consent of all these widely scattered men and women. Each passing year made the division of the Patent among its sharers more difficult, and lessened their energy in defending their title against assaults from neighboring landowners. The market value of a one-eighth share in the million and a half acres of the Patent had sunk to three hundred York pounds—a York pound had not much more than half the value of a pound sterling.

The low value of the Patent was due not only to the multiplicity of its owners but also to the dubious character of its original granting. But all this only helped stimulate men with a speculative itch into taking chances on its future. By 1741 two of these men were accumulating shares in the Patent. The leader of the two was Robert Livingston, and like his associate Gulian Verplanck he was a merchant in the city of New York. Both had profited from the colonial wars between British and French and were already landowners on a large scale. As he bought his way into the Patent, Livingston was taking a long step toward making possible the delayed settlement of the flatlands of the Sawkill and Beaverkill Valleys.

By the 1740s Robert Livingston was the owner of the imposing mansion called Clermont, on the east bank of the Hudson. Around the house, with its fine view of Overlook Mountain, lay the thirteen-thousand-acre estate which had come to Livingston from his father, the first of many American Robert Livingstons.

The elder Robert Livingston was among the most aggressively acquisitive men of his time. His concentration on acquiring property led him to becoming the rich lord of Livingston Manor. It was from the southern end of the manor that the Clermont estate was sliced following the elder Livingston's death in 1728, the rest of the manor going to old Robert's eldest son, Philip.[2]

Robert Livingston of Clermont was, according to family tradition, tall. His face was described as "remarkable for its regular beauty of feature." It beamed "with . . . benevolence and intelligence . . . " Robert's manners were elegant and he had a seemingly boundless fund of energy, optimism and enthusiasm. He had been educated in the Livingstons' native Scotland, and had studied law in London. By the time he returned from Europe in the 1720s he was ready to embark upon a career as a merchant. His business activities brought him the capital he invested in the Patent.[3]

Through the 1740s Livingston's energy triggered a succession of actions aimed at pulling the Hardenbergh Patent out of its torpor and preparing it for taking an active place in the world. A first step was a survey of the land, which was then partitioned among the descendants of the original holders of shares. There were boundary disputes to be settled—that with Kingston was finally arbitrated in 1746. In 1749 a map and survey of the Patent were ready, and partition had been made of all except for the disputed northwestern part.[4]

Surveyor Ebenezer Wooster had divided the Patent into Great Lots. Number 8, which included the lands along the Sawkill and Beaverkill and which Henry Beekman had bought from the Indians in 1705, was among the Great Lots which fell to Livingston. Great Lot 26, which took in Overlook Mountain, went to the heirs of Thomas Wenham, the member of Lord Cornbury's council who had slipped into the Patent behind a straw man. Great Lot 25, which ran northward from a little foothold on Cooper Lake through Mink Hollow and on to the Schohariekill Valley, became the property of the heirs of Captain Benjamin Fanueil. Great Lot 24, containing part of Willow and Silver Hollow, fell to Robert Livingston's fellow in land speculation, Gulian Verplanck.

Livingston and Verplanck lost no time in trying to put new settlers on their lands. In 1749 the two made an agreement to advertise in Scotland in the hope of luring settlers to their shares in the Patent. King George's War had come to an end the previous year in a none-too-stable compromise, and the Iroquois warriors who had raided New York settlements had quieted down. Yet the possibility of an Indian War breaking out at any time remained to hinder settlements. Even with Indian raids possible, however, plans for settlement were still being considered. A paper dating from this period headed "Method of forming such settlements upon the Frontiers as might support themselves during an Indian War" can be found among the Livingston manuscripts in the library of the New-York Historical Society. It calls for one hundred families settling on a 640-acre "Township" with a centrally located stockade, houses and gardens for settlers around it, and "plantations," "commons" and woodland beyond.

A map drawn shortly after the partition and known only from a slightly later copy lays emphasis on the streams and waterfalls at the site of the future hamlet of Woodstock. As in the 1670s in the lower Sawkill Valley, waterfalls were of crucial importance in plans for settlement because they made possible sawmills which could put trees cleared from the land to use as timber instead of wasting them in great bonfires. Later gristmills would replace sawmills as the cleared land produced crops of wheat and corn.[5]

The deed from the four Esopus Indians to Henry Beekman has importance to Woodstock history because it sets down in writing Indian names for various parts of the town. In the same way the old map has value, in part because it suggests attitudes toward streams and gives some of them names used in the Dutch-speaking days of the mid-eighteenth century. The stream which drains Lewis Hollow on the side of Overlook Mountain and joins the Sawkill at Zena is called the "fontyn kill," a New York Dutch name for a spring-fed or rushing brook. The little stream which crosses Route 212 a bit west of the Playhouse is the "hooglandts killitje." A killitje is a small brook; hooglandts means that the brook was believed to come down from the highlands or mountains—it actually begins in a swamp at the foot of Overlook.

Detailed knowledge of Woodstock's topography was scant in the 1750s, and here as elsewhere errors were not uncommon. The map gives the Sawkill a variant of its old Dutch name—it is marked Saagkill. The brook which crosses Glasco Turnpike close to the Rock City crossroads is called the "second killitje," meaning that it is the next tributary on the right upstream after the hooglandts killitje. It merges with what we know today as the Tannery Brook before joining the Sawkill.

Not only are the waterfalls of the hamlet of Woodstock indicated, but an evaluation is also made of each on the map. Just above the present country club is "a fall very good"; one above the Sawkill is "a fall but not so very good"; the fall to the south of the Tannery Brook bridge in the center of Woodstock's business district is "A verry Good fall in the mouth of ye Swamp." The low tract to the north of Woodstock's Tinker Street was obviously a swamp before settlement began.[6]

Evidence such as that shown on the 1750s map of Woodstock's water resources helps give a picture of the town as it was on the eve of settlement. Nearly all the town was covered with primeval forests, although it is likely that unusually fine white pines and cherry trees growing along the Sawkill as far up as the hamlet of Woodstock had been cut and taken downstream to the sawmills of the lower Sawkill. The mill highest above the stream about 1750, built on the

25

southeastern corner of Albert Rosa's three-hundred-acre claim, had come into the possession of Johannis Hardenbergh. It was at the spot in Zena not far to the south of Route 212 known to this day as Hardenbergh's Mill.

The vicinity of the mill, even before the arbitration agreement of 1746 had settled the boundary question, had been cleared and divided into fields. When the survey preceding the arbitration agreement was made in 1745, the line was placed between Cornelis Van Keuren's substantial stone house and his barn. According to the map made by surveyor Charles Clinton, the house was on the Hardenbergh Patent or Woodstock side of the line and the barn was in Kingston. When he went to milk his cows Van Keuren had to go all the way from Woodstock to Kingston and then had to carry the milk back to Woodstock again—so Van Keuren's predicament has been seen by a local tall-talker.[7]

The Van Keuren house and barn remained landmarks for many years. They were set down by mapmakers and mentioned in surveys such as that made by Ebenezer Wooster on which the partition of 1749 was based. The house stood firm until it was pulled down in the late 1870s and replaced by a more fashionable frame house. A few years later the gerrymandering operation of 1880 placed the site of the barn and the house together within the boundaries of Woodstock.

King George's War ended in 1748. The next period of British-French struggle in America, often known as the French and Indian War, did not get under way until 1754. The intervening years saw a good deal of activity among the proprietors of the Hardenbergh Patent, especially in what was to become Woodstock. Robert Livingston of Clermont was not the only big landowner to dream of putting settlers on his land. Another was Cornelis Tiebout, a New York businessman who was one of the group who bought the share in the Hardenbergh Patent inherited by Thomas Wenham's son John.

The group was formed of a curious mixture of New York and Hudson Valley people. They were Robert Livingston of Clermont; John Aspinwall of New York; William Alexander, who married a Livingston and was known as Lord Stirling; Philip and Catherine Livingston of Livingston Manor; Cornelis Tiebout and his brother-in-law Christian Hertell, described as a mariner but also involved in glassmaking at New Windsor; Samuel Tingley, mariner, who may have been the privateer of that name known to have operated from New York during the 1750s; and David Cox, barber. Great Lot 26 was the only part of the Wenham holdings to contain land in Woodstock. It stretched southward from the Kaaterskill to the Great Lot 8 line, which began a little south of the Van Keuren house and ran through the present business center of Woodstock across the northwestern edge of the great flats at Willow, and so to its end on the banks of the East Branch of the Delaware River at Margaretville.

In 1752 the proprietors of Great Lot 26, or at least some of them, were making an attempt to attract settlers from Germany to their recently acquired and still unpartitioned lands. Their lands in Woodstock were unsuited to settlement except for the part running along the base of Overlook Mountain and its lower slopes. As far as is known no Germans showed interest in settling there, although some did on other Wenham lots elsewhere in the Hardenbergh Patent.[8]

The Beekman claims to Coteskakunk and Paganekunk in Woodstock had lain dormant until a few months after the owners of Great Lot 26 began to try to promote settlement. It had not been until 1741, the "fourteenth Year of George II," that Henry Beekman's vast holdings were divided in equal shares among his children according to the terms of his will. The Woodstock claim went to daughter Cornelia and her husband Gilbert Livingston, a lawyer, representative in the Colonial Assembly of the Manor of Livingston, and County Clerk of Ulster. After their death the claim on Woodstock of the couple went to their children, Robert Gilbert of New York and Henry of Poughkeepsie among them. In 1753 Robert Gilbert wrote to Henry asking his "Loving Brother" to help him lay a foundation for claiming the lands deeded to their grandfather by the four Esopus Indians in 1705. "Look among Dady's papers whether you cant find the Conveyances," he suggested. If nothing could be found by that method, he proposed employing John Elting to search for them. "It is high time something should be done . . . as they are now, neither of us can expect to make anything of them," he concluded. But nothing was done, and nothing would be done for almost twenty years.[9]

In 1755 events in the French and Indian War were bringing discouragement to land speculators and to ordinary people who had been thinking of settling on frontier farms in New York. Soon the Iroquois allies of the French were burning houses and killing settlers along the frontiers. In Kingston plans were being made for building a stout blockhouse to provide a place of safety from French and Indian attacks. Local militiamen again patrolled the base of the Catskills and made their way up valleys like that of the Sawkill. But at last the course of the war changed and a succession of British victories brought hostilities to a conclusion, ending French rule over Canada.

Even before the peace treaty was signed in Paris in 1763 settlers were moving into Woodstock. Doubts about the validity of the Hardenbergh Patent were widespread. The claims of the Hurley people and of Henry Beekman's descendants were unresolved. But land was cleared thanks to the energy and optimism of Robert Livingston. Houses were built, and Woodstock began at last to change from an Indian hunting ground with a half-dozen farms in Zena to a white man's settlement.[10]

5

THE WHITES MOVE IN

Early in the spring of 1762 Robert Livingston placed his first tenant-settlers among the forests of Woodstock. The many obstacles Livingston had to overcome would have discouraged a less energetic and optimistic landowner. There was the continuing bad reputation of the Hardenbergh Patent, there were occasional rumors of a possible resumption of Indian hostilities, and there were boundary disputes which remained unsettled.

Especially troublesome was Livingston's uncertain boundary with the town of Hurley to the south. Hurley people in search of timber, firewood and pasture had been pushing with vigor across what Livingston insisted was the proper southern boundary of his lands on the southeastern part of Great Lot 8 of the Hardenbergh Patent; "they destroy it [the timber] abominably," Livingston wrote on March 1, 1762. The old Beekman claim to the bottom lands along the Sawkill and the Beaverkill did not seem threatening because Livingston's cousins to whom the claim had been handed down were not asserting it. But the line separating Great Lot 8 from Great Lot 26 to the north—that was a different story. No one disputed the validity of the line, but what annoyed Robert Livingston was that it ran so close to the settlement he planned for the Sawkill Valley.[1]

Livingston had a one-eighth share in Great Lot 26. His fellow-owners were undecided as to what to do with this lot, which they had bought from Thomas Wenham's heirs without examining it. Most of the lot was occupied by the high wall of the Catskill Mountains running northward from Overlook Mountain to the Kaaterskill Clove. Only a narrow strip at the mountains' base, scattered bits like those at the heads of Plattekill and Kaaterskill Cloves, and a broad band at the base of Overlook Mountain had promise as potential farmland.

Though there was timber in plenty on Great Lot 26, the difficulties of hauling it to market were insurmountable. As seen from the Hudson Valley and the river's east bank, the Great Lot's mountains formed an imposing sight. But sights like these had no market value. More promising were the possibilities of mineral deposits which were every now and then rumored to have been exposed at such likely spots as Overlook's crumbling Minister's Face or in the deep cuts carved into the mountain wall at the Plattekill and Kaaterskill Cloves.

The owners of Great Lot 26 sometimes tried to sell it as a whole. More often they discussed partitioning it among themselves. In 1751 they drew up a partition agreement (not to be recorded until 1764). Robert Livingston's share turned out to consist largely of Overlook Mountain's summit and untillable lands in the upper Sawkill Valley just below Echo Lake. Cornelius Tiebout was lucky enough to get the tract of gently sloping and potentially tillable land between Overlook Mountain and the northern line of Livingston's Great Lot 8. Tiebout's share of 26 even included a loop of the winding Sawkill. There was too little good land to justify an attempt at forming a settlement, Tiebout realized.[2]

Yet the good land which belonged so naturally with Robert Livingston's holdings had considerable value as material to use in bargaining and exchanging. Both men had many tracts of land scattered across the Hardenbergh Patent. By 1760 they were deep in dickering about these lands. Livingston's eagerness to own the southeastern part of Tiebout's Great Lot 26 lands was obvious enough to Tiebout, who tried to work it for all he could. Tiebout's credulousness in putting faith in rumors of mines on Livingston's cliffs and rocks on Overlook Mountain gave Livingston an excellent bargaining point.

It is not to be wondered that Tiebout and Livingston dickered in an atmosphere of mutual dislike and suspicion. The two men were very different. Tiebout was what is often called a self-made man, whose shrewdness and determination had carried him upward from small beginnings to a degree of wealth which made it possible for him to live in considerable style in Roxbury, his country house located at what is now Union Square, New York. Tiebout had no children. His only hope for carrying his name and wealth into the future was his namesake, the son of his brother-in-law Christian Hertell. His own education was limited—Livingston once referred to him as illiterate.[3]

Livingston, on the other hand, had received a good classical education. He had been a businessman, it is true; yet he owed his wealth not so much to his business as to his landed inheritance from his father. A descendant of the Scottish Earls of Callender, he could look back with satisfaction at upper-class ancestors.[4]

After a great deal of haggling, Tiebout and Livingston made a deal which involved Livingston getting a tract of twelve hundred acres beginning within lower Lewis Hollow on the side of Overlook Mountain and running down to the Great Lot 8 line at Waghkunk or Zena. A bit later Tiebout sold several tracts to the west of this one. Eventually these lands slipped easily into functioning as parts of the settlement of Woodstock, as they remain to this day.[5]

By March 1, 1762 Robert Livingston had a sawmill under construction near the site of the present Woodstock Country Club. He told his son Robert R. Livingston that he expected to have the mill finished by July. Abram Post of Saugerties, who had dined with Livingston at Clermont the day before, had reported that everything at Woodstock was going swimmingly. Post could well be regarded as an expert on Woodstock and its possiblities; he lived in nearby Saugerties and he had been sergeant in a militia unit which patrolled the eastern part of the Catskills in the vicinity of Woodstock during the 1750s in search of Frenchmen and Indians. Besides, the sergeant's relatives kept a tavern in Saugerties which was a center at which local people, farmers, woodsmen, idlers, trappers and hunters gathered and exchanged bits of information, gossip and boasts and told tales of adventure in the wilderness of the Catskills.[6]

By the time the sergeant and Robert Livingston had their optimistic talk over the dinner table, several settlers were already making a beginning as tenants not only in the neighborhood of the Livingston sawmill but also along the shore of Cooper Lake and in what is now known as Willow. Among these settlers were Henry and Thomas Shadwick (also known as Chadwick)—for a while the lake was known in their honor as Shadwick's (or Shedwick's) Lake. The Shadwicks, like Jacob Sheefer, who was making a clearing nearby, came from the Livingston country across the Hudson; like most of the

31

Livingstons' Woodstock people, they were living in a new place under their old landlord.[7]

That spring and summer of 1762 Robert Livingston's letters to his son glowed with high hopes for the future of his Woodstock venture. He was confident tenants would pour in and clear his valley lands, cut trees to feed his sawmill, and haul the resulting boards and planks to the banks of the Hudson River opposite Clermont. He hinted at the possibility of several sawmills to produce oak for shipbuilding, ash for oars, "curl'd maple" for gunstocks, and white pine siding for housebuilding. He toyed with the notion of setting up an "iron works" to use the scanty local deposits of bog iron or crude pigs of iron brought from across the Hudson.

He hoped all these activities would build up a settlement in which the clearing of land would not result in the wasteful destruction of timber all too usual in American settlements of the time. As in the Scotland and England in which Livingston had been educated, trees would be treated with respect and made to play their parts in a system of land management aimed at setting up patchworks of tilled fields in the valleys, pastures on the lower slopes of the mountains, and woodland above or on land too rocky for cultivation. Woodstock would become a kind of extension of the thirteen-thousand-acre estate of Clermont to which it was soon linked by a road beginning close to the Shadwick farm and making its way downward past Livingston's Mill all the way to the Hudson at Saugerties. During most winters, the obliging river froze sufficiently to allow the road to lead across the ice to the very door of the mansion at Clermont.[8]

It was not Livingston's intention to sell farms at Woodstock to the people he was beginning to settle on them. Instead he planned to follow the custom which prevailed at Clermont and lease the farms to tenants similar to those already established at Clermont. None of the earliest leases of Woodstock farms are known to have survived, but abstracts of a few are in existence. One of these deals with what is probably Livingston's first Woodstock lease under which the two Shadwicks took possession of a two-hundred-acre farm described as lying in "Little ShonDecan" and extending from the shore of Cooper Lake to a point well across the Beaverkill.

Much of the Shadwick farm was level as a table top. Well enough drained, yet with a lake and a creek at hand, it was probably the most desirable location in Woodstock from a farmer's point of view. That may have been why it and its surrounding flatlands had been included in the Sam Hees-William Beekman deed of 1705 under the name Pagkanagkinck; it and neighboring Sacindarow—today known as Willow—began to be known as Little ShonDecan. Big or Great Shandaken, as the name came to be spelled, lay in the Esopus Valley above the junction of the Beaverkill and the Esopus Creek. The name Shandaken is thought to mean a place of hemlock trees.[9]

Other place name changes accompanied Robert Livingston's beginning of settlement and marked the change from Indian hunting grounds and perhaps a few cabins of trappers and hunters to a settled way of life in which the Indians had little part. Occasionally through the early 1760s Robert Livingston referred to his possessions in what is now Woodstock as Waghkonck. But quickly Woodstock took over. The lake called Opdonsase in 1705 after briefly being Shadwick's Lake became Shandaken Lake. The eastern parts of Woodstock lying along the Kingston boundary continued for a long time to be called Waghkonck. The Wagonck Road, taking off from Route 28 at Stony Hollow, is the only surviving reminder of the old Indian name. Henry Beekman's Costekakunk, which perhaps included the site of the hamlet of Woodstock, was forgotten.[10]

There is no evidence presently known to tell us why Robert Livingston gave the name of Woodstock to his settlement. Two other American places had already received the same name. And in the case of one—the town of Woodstock in what is now New Hampshire—the name was probably given not directly in memory of old Woodstock in Oxfordshire but in honor of rich and young Viscount Woodstock. The first of American Woodstocks was the one now in Connecticut but originally part of Massachusetts. This town was given its name by Judge Samuel Sewall in 1690. Sewall, one of the town's proprietors, recorded the bestowal of the name in his diary in honor of Woodstock in Oxfordshire.

In his abstract of the Shadwick or Chadwick lease of 1763, Livingston surveyor and land agent William Cockburn uses the name "Woodfield" for the new settlement. Perhaps this was no more than an error, or perhaps there was a short period of trying out variations of the name. A letter written from "Claremont" by Judge Robert R. Livingston and addressed to his father, "Robert Livingston Esqr., Woodstock," on February 2, 1764 raises the possibility that the town's name rose out of an attempt to find an English name with some visual relationship to the Indian name of Waghkonk, or Wachkunk, as it was sometimes spelled. The letter begins, "Honored Sir. I am just come here and should have been very glad to have had the Pleasure of seeing you, but as I have not it gives me not a little to hear that you are hearty & well at Wachkunk . . . " The name Wachkunk is then crossed out and Woodstock written in above. The similarity of the two names as they appear in the Judge's flowing script is striking.[11]

Whatever the reasons behind the naming of Woodstock in Ulster County in the province of New York, the name was appropriate. The English Woodstock, of course, was a place with many claims to fame. It had associations with Saxon King Ethelred the Unready, with Thomas a Becket, Edward the Black Prince and Queen Elizabeth. It had been a favorite hunting place of many English kings; there Blenheim Palace had been built out of gratitude to the great soldier the Duke of Marlborough; there the manufacture of Woodstock gloves and Woodstock jewelry steel had carried the name of the place abroad. It was there that Fair Rosamund, mistress of King Henry II, lived in the supposed security of a surrounding maze which did not protect her from the bloody vengeance of Henry's Queen—or so goes a dubious but popular bit of folklore. Later Sir Walter Scott wrote an enormously admired novel called *Woodstock*. And still later Winston Churchill was born in Blenheim Palace.

In spite of all this glory the old English town retained in its name the memory of the days when it too had been newly born in a forest. Its name is derived by its historians from the Saxon "wudestoc," which means either a clearing in a wood or the stump of a tree. The town's coat of arms embellishes this theme. It shows a tree stump with three deer heads above surmounted by a crest formed of an oak tree. The shield on which the stump is shown is supported by two "savages" nearly naked, bearded and hairy and holding rough clubs.[12]

The new Woodstock, with Indians still roaming its forests and dotted with the stumps of the trees felled to supply its sawmill and to clear the land for farming, had acquired a name and a little group of first settlers. It was ready for expansion under the enthusiastic guidance of Robert Livingston.

6

SETTLERS ARRIVE AND TREES FALL

The early 1760s were not the best possible years for pushing ahead with settling Woodstock. The end of the French and Indian War had brought a period of economic unhappiness. Land values were dropping. Profits accumulated as a result of years of conflict and warfare were rapidly dwindling. Robert Livingston and his son Robert R. had done very well during the war years, but now the elder Livingston was seeing his war money melting away.

Accounts of the son for 1758 show substantial profits from privateering ventures stimulated by the war. They list hundreds of pounds received from shares in captured ships such as the Duke of Luxemburgh, "the Sally, French Prize" and "Griffiths' Prizes." Money was also spent for outfitting privateers. But by 1763 Robert Livingston had little left but vast accumulations of land and his home estate of Clermont, which provided a saleable surplus of farm products, an annual income from the rents of its tenant farmers, and food and shelter. Income was seldom received in cash. It came in the form of grain, livestock and timber which the Livingstons shipped for sale to New York on board their sloop.

For a younger son of a rich, landed American, Robert Livingston had been unusually fortunate. It was true that under the prevailing rule of primogeniture his elder brother Phillip had become not only Lord of Livingston Manor but also master of most of the land and money scraped together by their father outside the manor. Because Robert had been willed the thirteen thousand acres at Clermont, however, he had a fine base upon which to build a position to equal that of his brother—not in his own lifetime, of course, but in that of his son and of his son's descendants. Robert sometimes said he had brought up his son "to keep an estate, not to get one." He hoped Robert R. would some day preside as a securely-placed landed gentleman over Clermont and his nearby Hardenbergh Patent lands. Like many an English younger son Robert himself had gone into trade in order to assure for his son a pleasant and privileged life. Now that dream seemed threatened.[1]

The son had such a character that he could take with equanimity the blows that so upset his father. Robert R. Livingston was widely admired and loved for the sweetness of his temper and for his intelligence and ability. One friend declared that if he were to be exiled to a lonely island with only one book and one friend the book would be the Bible and the friend Robert R. Livingston. Young Livingston's wife was in every way worthy of her paragon of a husband. She was the only surviving child of Colonel Henry Beekman of neighboring Rhinebeck, one of the greatest landowners of his time and related to the earlier Henry Beekman who had dealt with the four Indians in Woodstock in 1705.

George Dangerfield in his *Chancellor Robert R. Livingston of New York 1746-1813* has written with skill and perception about this couple who were to have so decided an influence on Woodstock's future. Their marriage, Dangerfield wrote, ". . . may well have been one of convenience, the union of two adjacent estates; but like many such marriages it turned out to be a happy one. The husband was not only a man of character, but also a man with a singularly winning personality. The wife, if one can judge by a portrait painted ten years later [i.e. ten years after her marriage at eighteen] was a full-bodied Dutch beauty. A certain pietism, excessive by our standards, is to be discovered in her diaries when she was a young matron; but Livingston was pious, too; and their concern for things not of this world did not prevent them, as their surviving letters attest, from enjoying what would be considered, by any standard, a very earthy affection."[2]

When the difficulties of the early 1760s disturbed old Robert, Robert R. wrote him comforting letters. It was true enough, he agreed, that the profits of years in trade had vanished. Yet, he pointed out,

Clermont and the Hardenbergh Patent lands had survived "the wreck." Even more heartening was his father-in-law's great fortune, which seems to have remained intact. When Henry Beekman died and his estate was settled, Robert R. exulted, "I think it not improbable that I may be absolutely the richest man in the whole Government." He strongly advised his father to be satisfied with what he had and to live out his days in pleasant retirement.[3]

But old Robert would not be comforted, nor would he relax his efforts to convert his Woodstock forests into a settled and profitable adjunct to Clermont. With the help of his son he tried hard to sell more distant parts of his Hardenbergh Patent holdings in order to raise cash. In 1763 he succeeded in selling much of what is now the town of Stamford at the northwestern corner of the Patent to a group of sixty Connecticut men. Whatever cash he raised Livingston put into his Woodstock schemes. The place became a virtual obsession with him, so much so that his son sometimes became alarmed lest Woodstock swallow up Clermont and bring down his branch of the Livingston family in a spectacular crash.[4]

Few details are known of old Livingston's Woodstock projects. They appear so large and expensive in the letters written to him by his son between 1762 and 1766 as to justify the son's ever-increasing apprehension. Immersed in a euphoric cloud, Robert plunged ahead, ignoring his son's advice. Even the rumors in 1763 of a new Indian war did nothing to check his enthusiasm for pouring money and energy into his settlement at Woodstock.

He spent much time at Woodstock. The earliest letters known to have been addressed to anyone in Woodstock were from Robert R. to his father. The older Livingston had encouragement in his plans from the group of men who had gathered around him—woodsmen, nearby settlers, Saugerties men who saw the settling of Woodstock as a source of profit to their hamlet on the Hudson, which seemed certain to become the river landing for the promising new settlement. From Woodstock Livingston envisaged forest products, both raw and manufactured, iron and grain being hauled to the river and across to Clermont. It would make possible a fine way of life to future generations of Livingstons of Clermont.[5]

His son the Judge (Robert R. had become an associate judge of the Supreme Court of the province of New York in 1759) came to view his father's hopes in Woodstock with ever-greater realism. His letters contained ever more skeptical comments on the Woodstock venture. Finally in the spring of 1766 he spoke his mind plainly and bluntly. He wrote, "It is impossible for me to dissemble the Concern it gives me for it [what the Judge had learned about his father's doings in Woodstock] fully convinces me that You have a parcel of People about you who are endeavoring by the slyest & most cunning artifices leading You from one barren Project to another, to fatten themselves on your Spoils, as soon as one thing miscarries they push you on to another . . . My Dear Father you must forgive me, I must speak tho' Ruin to myself should be the Consequence . . . " Robert R. went on to knock down his father's plans for building sawmills, making oars of white ash and making iron in Woodstock, citing facts and figures to prove their economic absurdity. "[O]ur Country is too young for any large Business not managed with the utmost Economy," he wrote. He made no secret of his belief that his father's management of his Woodstock ventures was devoid of the slightest shred of economy.

The Judge had his way. Robert Livingston, then 78 years old, gave up his Woodstock dream and retired to a dignified existence at Clermont. He conveyed to his son all his Woodstock lands on January 22, 1768. Old Robert in his retirement to Clermont was much admired. Many years later his grandson, Edward Livingston, wrote a graphic account of Robert's way of life during his final years: "His figure was tall and somewhat bent, but not emaciated by age, which had marked, but had not disfigured, a face once remarkable for its regular beauty of feature, and still beaming with [the] benevolence, and intelligence, that had always illumined it. He marked the epoch at which he had retired from the world by preserving its costume—the flowing well-powdered wig, the bright brown coat, with large cuffs, and square skirts, the cut velvet waistcoat, with ample flaps, and the breeches scarcely covering the knee, the silk stockings, rolled over them with embroidered clocks, and shining square-toed shoes, fastened near the ancle with small embossed gold buckles. These were retained in his service, not to affect a singularity, but because he thought it was ridiculous, at his time of life, to allow quick successions of fashion."[6]

Edward's sister, Janet Montgomery, recalled that during the first half of the 1770s Robert "always rose at five in the morning and read without ceasing until near breakfast. The year before his death he learned the German tongue and spoke it fluently."[7]

By the time Judge Livingston took over the management of Woodstock the advance up the Sawkill Valley begun back in the 1670s had been joined by the Livingston advance from the bank of the

38

Hudson opposite Clermont at Saugerties. The advance had reached what is now Bearsville and there had moved along what is known today as the Lake Road, passing to the south of Cooper Lake and then moving down the valley of the Beaverkill to the fine flatlands of Lake Hill and Willow. The farms strung along the Sawkill and the Beaverkill were linked by a number of roads and paths. One branch of the Esopus Road began in the Brabant and followed the Sawkill upward. The road from Kingston joined the Sawkill branch at Zena and the two became the Chestnut Hill Road. The Saugerties Road tied the infant hamlet of Woodstock to Saugerties and Clermont and went on to provide a means of reaching the farms along the upper Beaverkill at Little Shandaken. From this road a rough trail followed the headwaters of the Beaverkill through Mink Hollow, penetrated Mink Hollow Notch, and found its way down the Schoharie Valley to what was later called Prattsville. Another trail or "footpath" began at the southern end of the Willow Flats and followed the Beaverkill to its junction with the Esopus Creek at what is now Mount Tremper. It is likely that these footpaths or perhaps pack horse trails followed old Indian routes.

The farms stitched together by this primitive road system owed their placement to geographic and economic factors. The process of earth sculpture which had given Woodstock its surface shape had resulted in much high, stony land unsuited to cultivation and a small amount of fertile flatlands built up by the deposit of waterborne soil along the Sawkill and the Beaverkill. On these flatlands the white settlers of the 1760s and 1770s cleared away the forest and planted their crops.

The flatlands at Awaghkonck were already occupied. Those at Little Shandaken were some five hundred feet higher and therefore had a slightly shorter growing season, but this plus their greater distance from the Hudson River was not enough to overcome the attraction of the rich, level and relatively stone-free soil. Along the Sawkill settlers took over wherever they found a desirable expanse of potential farmland. Some may have found small clearings already made by little groups of Indians evicted from their Esopus Valley homes or by white trappers and hunters who had taken to life in the woods. The ample evidence of Indian occupancy found along the shores of Cooper Lake suggests that the nearby land on which the Chadwicks were settled by 1762 may have been cleared by Indian predecessors.[8]

39

In some ways the early settlers of Woodstock did not conform to the accepted picture of American pioneers going out into the wilderness, axe on shoulder, to hew a home for themselves and their families on their own bit of the earth's surface which no one could ever take away from them. As in much of the province of New York, most Woodstock land was held by an absentee landlord who preferred the Old World way of leasing land to its tillers rather than selling it. The leases under which the earliest Woodstock pioneers held their lands were not standardized. They varied from each other very much.

Some people had no leases at all. They had simply settled on land that appealed to them without consulting the legal owner. If they seemed industrious people Robert Livingston did not disturb them. There would be plenty of time later on to prod them into accepting leases. In the meantime their work in clearing the land added to its value year by year.

Other settlers had brief lease agreements jotted down in the notebooks of land agents and owners. These usually provided for the tenant to pay the expenses of surveying his land and eventually drawing up a lease. The period of years—often five or more—during which the new farm would be in the process of partial clearing and therefore not very productive would be rent-free or subject to a very small token rent. After this period was over an annual rent of fifteen to twenty bushels of wheat per hundred acres was likely, plus three or four "good fat hens" and from one to three days' work with team for the landlord. A tenant had the right to sell his leasehold, but if he did he had to pay the landlord one-sixth of what he received.[9]

At some time during the 1760s Robert Livingston had a standard lease form printed, but no example of this form in use in present-day Woodstock has survived. Judge Livingston used one of these forms when in 1768 he agreed upon a lease with Jacob Longyear, a German weaver who had been living for ten years or more on Livingston land along the Esopus Creek in what was then part of Woodstock but is now in the town of Shandaken. This lease has an Old World air about it that seems astonishing to Americans of today. Drawn up in "the eighth year of our Sovereign Lord George ye third, by the Grace of God, of Great Britain, France and Ireland, King Defender of the Faith etc.," the lease was to remain in effect only during the lifetimes of Jacob Lanyar (Longyear), Jacob Lanyar Jr. and Johannis Lanyar—these last were old Jacob's sons. Longyear was given the use of one hundred five acres lying in "the Lothians" (this was the name the Livingstons were trying to give to the Catskills in memory of their own Scottish background) and in addition Longyear had "free House-Bote, Plow-Bote and Hay-Bote." House-Bote is an old English term for a supply of wood taken from the landlord's commons (his unleased or untilled land) and used for building or for heating the tenant's house. Plow-Bote was wood from the commons used for making or repairing farm implements. And Hay-Bote was wood from the same source put to use in fencing—hay is an old word of French origin meaning a fence or hedge.

In addition Longyear had the right of "free Commonage for commonable Cattle in the waste-Grounds (that is, the commons) of the said ROBERT LIVINGSTON . . . " This, of course, was the right to pasture his cattle. All sites for mills were reserved to Livingston. So too were any mines that might be discovered together with enough land to making working the mines possible. Longyear was required to have his grain ground at his landlord's mill provided such a mill were in operation within ten miles of his farm.

He was also required to obey all "reasonable orders" for helping lay out and keep in good condition paths and roads and for giving help in "extinguishing Fires when Burning the Woods." His rent was "a good merchantable Gammon [of bacon] of fourteen pounds," or if Longyear preferred eighteen bushels of wheat per year. If Longyear wished to sell grain he had first to offer it to his landlord. If Longyear's rent was still unpaid twenty days after it became due or if he did not take actual possession of his farm within six months after the lease was signed then the landlord might re-enter on the property and, if he wished, lease it to someone else.[10]

Between 1762 and 1775 most Woodstock tenants lived under terms like those spelled out in the Longyear lease, although these terms were often not strictly enforced. There were some exceptions. A tenant in especially good favor with his landlord might get a lease "For Ever," meaning without limit of time or lives. Such a lease agreement was made on May 1, 1771 between Judge Livingston and Peter Winne for a 109-acre farm at what is now known as Lake Hill. Winne was to pay five bushels of wheat as rent during the first three years of his lease, ten bushels for each of the next seven years, and forever afterwards twenty-one bushels per year. Like tenants for three lives Winne had the right to use but not to sell wood taken from the commons. He could sell his leasehold after getting his landlord's permission, but like Longyear he had to pay Livingson one-sixth of whatever he received. Another tenant, Samuel Ferris, whose lease took effect on the same day as Winne's, committed himself to paying his rent in cash—his farm of 112 acres cost him sixteen shillings a year during his life and that of his wife Mary.[11]

On February 16, 1773 Johannis Hubner, "Cordwainer of the Mannor of Livingston," (a cordwainer was a shoemaker, the word had orginally referred to any worker in cordovan leather) signed his lease for a Woodstock farm with Judge Livingston and agreed to pay his rent partly in cash and partly in wheat. The lease required an annual payment of "three pounds proclamation money . . . and eight bushels of good sweet merchantable winter wheat." Proclamation money, which had resulted from a government attempt at checking the continuing devaluation of the pound in relation to the plentiful Spanish reals and pieces of eight, was the safest sort of currency.

Antiquated terms like House-Bote, Plow-Bote and Hay-Bote had vanished from Woodstock leases by the early 1770s. Instead tenants like Hubner were given the right to "cut wood for fireing, fencing and building for the use of the said farm in the waste and unimproved Lands . . . adjoining the said farm while they continue waste and unimproved . . . " Judge Livingston was a good lawyer who wrote his leases in plain English which his tenants might better understand. While earlier tenants had only a twenty-day period of grace in which to pay their rent, Hubner had two years.[12]

As far as is known no Woodstock farm was sold by the Livingstons between 1762 and 1775. The great advantage to a tenant of the system of leases for three lives was that a man might start farming without capital. But early settlers must have grumbled about being tied to the soil by a lease which did not ensure that the land a man had brought into cultivation could go down to his descendants.

Something of this feeling may be reflected in a bit of folklore about one of the first sales of a Woodstock farm. In 1787 Frederick Rowe, Junior wanted to buy the Lake Hill farm settled by Henry and Thomas Chadwick. But the Livingston landlord of that time offered him no more than the usual lease for three lives. Rowe was asked to set down in the proper blank place the names of two people other than himself. And Rowe boldly wrote the names of a black slave and the Devil. The landlord knew the Devil to be immortal and refused to sign. In addition it was beneath the dignity of a Livingston of Clermont to be associated in a business deal with a black man. So the landlord got out of the predicament by selling the farm to Rowe.[13]

Another piece of folklore gives a different sort of glimpse of the feelings of Woodstock people about leases for three lives. It was reported in a garbled form by English writer Richard LeGallienne in his account of Woodstock published in 1923. "According to old Woodstock residents," LeGallienne wrote, "a man took first possession of a tract he desired by cutting down a pine tree, and when the pine tree rotted [in about fifty years] he either lost the land or acquired a lease of it for a small sum . . . " The stumps of white pine trees, reasoned LaGallienne, took longer than most others to rot after the clearing of Woodstock farms, and the fifty years during which they held out against the attacks of fungi and bacteria was exactly the length of time a lease for three lives was expected to run—if the tenants' luck was good.[14]

In fact Woodstock leases of the first two decades of settlement did not mention pine trees. But mention of that tree did turn up in many leases signed during the third decade, when tenants were forbidden to cut pine trees. These most valuable of all Woodstock trees in the marketplace were reserved to the landlord. And the association of pine tree and leases for three lives of Le Gallienne's story, if in a confused and roundabout way, was passed along from one Woodstock person to another across two centuries and on into our own days.

WOODSTOCK LIFE UNDER GEORGE THE THIRD

F or fourteen years after the first Livingston settlers appeared they were subjects of King George the Third of England. A glimpse of the daily lives of these colonial English people can be put together and understood from the traces of what they did to the land—the fields they cleared and the stone walls they built remain for us to see. What they wore and what they ate as well as what they worked at emerge from old account books. Church records tell when their babies were born and how eager they were to have their babies properly and promptly baptized. Among the vast accumulations of records of the Livingstons of Clermont are many details of payment or non-payment of rent, of some tenants who gave up and others who hung on.

Among Woodstock's earliest settlers were those who lived on the flats along the Sawkill, where the possibilities of farming were the most promising. The very earliest were tenants of Kingston in Zena or Waghkonck who later bought their farms. The houses and farms of these people—some were named Osterhoudt, Legg, Van Etten—began appearing above William Legg's sawmill even before 1700. These people formed an offshoot of Kingston or Esopus—or 'Sopus, as the town continued to be called until half a century ago. They spoke Dutch, and their culture had many other Dutch features. The songs they sang, the curses they invoked on balky horses, the church services they attended were all Dutch. Their family Bibles were Dutch. The names they gave their children—Pieter and Wilhelmus, Geesje and Annatje—were Dutch. One Waghkonck settler was Cornelis Van Keuren, of Dutch descent and probably a carpenter (it was he whose house and barn had been separated by a boundary line).[1]

In May 1760 Gerrit Newkerk bought from the heirs of Major Johannis Hardenbergh the tract in Waghkonck at the northern end of what we call Zena and long known as Hardenbergh's three hundred acres. Newkerk and his descendants lived there, not far from the Van Keuren house, for many years. His house, later owned by members of the expanding Van Etten family, is probably the one owned until the 1970s by the Baumgarten family.

At the point of junction of the Esopus or Chestnut Hill and Saugerties Roads and across the Sawkill from the lands of the Woodstock Country Club was another stone house which was mentioned in leases going back to the 1770s. Before 1773 the house was occupied by Johannis Fiero, a member of one of the German families who were to contribute much to Woodstock. Refugees from war and famine who left the banks of the Rhine and its tributaries first for England and then for the New World, these Germans were placed in the Hudson Valley in 1709 and 1710. They were expected to work out the passage and subsistence money advanced to them by Queen Anne by making pitch and tar for the Royal Navy from the valley pine trees. They settled at Germantown on the east side of the Hudson and in three villages on the west side in what is now Saugerties—the hamlet of West Camp commemorates in its name one German settlement.[2]

The refugees were not treated well. The pitch-and-tar-making project failed. The Germans were thrown back on their own resources. While they had been receiving living expenses from Queen Anne they had been exploited relentlessly. Now some of these people became tenants on Livingston Manor. Others settled in the Schoharie Valley, some made their way to the German settlements of Pennsylvania. Some remained in the neighborhood of their former camps in and around Saugerties.

Fiero was one of the Palatines, as they were often called, who found the Woodstock of pioneer days inviting. But by 1773 Fiero was gone and the farm he had tilled was leased to Johannis Hubner, the cordwainer. Hubner did not stay very long. Soon the farm was being leased by another man of German background, John Kraft or Craft. It is likely that his house served as Robert Livingston's headquarters in

Woodstock during the early 1760s, but of this there is no definite proof.

By 1774 the beginnings of settlement had been made in what is now the hamlet of Woodstock. The first house known to have been built there was that of a Newkerk—his first name is not definitely known. This house stood on a ten-acre plot within a few feet of the former Longyear-Brinkerhoff house on Rock City Road, just north of the line dividing Great Lots Eight and Twenty-Six. Ten acres is too small a piece for use as a farm. Newkerk may have intended to keep a tavern or store, for his plot was close to the falls in the Tannery Brook which before too many years would power the gristmill and sawmill which were to become the centers of the growing hamlet.

Across the Sawkill and close to the junction of the Ohayo Mountain Road and Broadview Avenue was the 69-acre farm of Peter Short, his wife Annatje Bakker (Becker) and their nine children, including sons Zacharias, Hendrick and Peter. Old Peter is believed to have been a descendant of Adam Short, an English Quaker who arrived at New Castle, Delaware on board William Penn's ship the *Welcome* on August 24, 1682. Adam's son Henry migrated to Kingston, N.Y. before 1724 and married a local girl, Gepje Winne. These two were the parents of Peter Short of Woodstock, who would play a prominent part in the life of the early settlement.[3]

On what are now known as the Bearsville Flats Ephraim Van Keuren and several others farmed. And at Bearsville Samuel Ferris and his wife, Mary Purdy, occupied a farm on "the road leading to Little Jan decan," as a record of 1771 reads. Ferris was probably a New Englander; his son Jehiel Ferris, who may have lived with him, gave "New Englant" as his birthplace when he married Margaret Sandford of New York in 1769. Both stated that they lived in Woodstock. Samuel Ferris gave a name to his locality, which was long known as Ferris or Faris Clove, the lovely valley which parallels the Lake Road as it moves from Bearsville to Cooper Lake.

Woodstock proper ended with Ferris Clove, and beyond that lay Little Shandaken and the farm of Thomas and Henry Shadwick. The Shadwicks, like Ferris, were probably of Yankee origin. A Thomas Chadwick was in trouble with the law at Livingston Manor in 1752, and perhaps this was the same man. By the late 1770s the Shadwicks seem to have left Woodstock. Their land was then being farmed by Frederick Rowe, Jr., who had formerly lived close to the eastern wall of the Catskills in what is now Saugerties. His ancestors, whose name was once spelled Rau, were Palatine Germans who had settled at West Camp.

Close to the Shadwick-Rowe farm lived German-descended Hendrick Henigar, his wife and his son Dirck. Little is known about them other than their family name in a variety of spellings. Also close by in 1771 were Peter Winne and his wife, Arriantje Van Etten, whose farm began according to an entry in a notebook of land agent William Cockburn "at the Southwest corner of a farm in possession of Hendrick Henegar." Winne was a cousin of Peter Short and a descendant of the Peter Winne who had come to Kingston before 1661 from Curacao in the West Indies. His father, also named Peter, had been a partner in the sawmill on the Plattekill just a few miles east of the Woodstock-Kingston line in what is now part of Saugerties. Arriantje Winne's people, who came from the town of Etten in the Brabant and may have been the family from whom Brabant on the Esopus took its name, were numerous along the lower Sawkill and Plattekill.[4]

As farms replaced forest on the Livingston lands in Great Lot 8, there was activity on Great Lots 24, 25 and 26, parts of which lay within the boundaries of the Woodstock of today. In 1749 Great Lot 24 had been partitioned to Gulian Verplanck, and after his death it went to his two daughters. One married Charles McEvers of New York and the other Gabriel G. Ludlow of Hempstead, Long Island. In 1774 Ludlow sold his wife's half of the Lot consisting of about twelve thousand acres to John Carle and his wife, Freelove Mitchill, also of Hempstead. Both the Carles and the Mitchills were of English descent. Freelove's family were Quakers, and her sister had married into the more elevated Ludlow family. That may help explain the sale. There is no evidence the Carles lived on their land until the late 1780s.

The part of Woodstock which lies in and around Mink Hollow and adjoins the Carle half of Great Lot 24 forms the southern end of Great Lot 25. In the 1749 partition it had gone to Captain Benjamin Faneuil, a New York merchant, shipowner and distiller who was described as "a French Protestant Refugee"—the well-known Boston building called Faneuil Hall was built by a nephew of his. After Faneuil died his heirs sold Great Lot 25 to Elias Desbrosses, a French Protestant, or Huguenot, who dealt in wines and spirits. Desbrosses, who died in 1784, is not known to have made any attempt to put settlers on his lands. However, the road or path which penetrated Mink Hollow by 1773 hints at an attempt to attract settlers. A map of

1777 shows a house standing on Desbrosses' land close to the junction of the Mink Hollow Road and the one leading from Woodstock to Little Shandaken.

By 1775 Woodstock had become a recognizably settled place, with houses and barns, ploughed fields and apple orchards not yet in bearing. Dutch was the predominant language of the place, with English and German also in use. A mixture of the three sometimes baffled outsiders. Most Woodstock people attended the church at Katsbaan in Saugerties. About ten miles away in a straight line, the church was considerably farther over the "road from Shedwick's to Sajerties," as it was marked on an early map. At this church Woodstock babies were baptized and Woodstock people married. Records of these events were kept. A few Woodstock pioneers used the Dutch church in Kingston, which could be reached by the Esopus road, the one which branched off from the Saugerties road in front of the stone house near Livingston's sawmill.[5]

Business as well as religion helped keep Woodstock pioneers from the extreme isolation which marked many new American settlements on the frontier. There were of course the ties which most Woodstock farmers had with the Livingstons of Clermont. And there were also important relationships with people like Captain Benjamin Snyder of Saugerties. Captain Snyder, a busy, energetic and versatile man, lived at Churchland in the southern part of what is now the town of Saugerties, close to Woodstock's eastern boundary.

Snyder took his Hudson River sloop on regular trips to New York, carrying country products for sale and bringing back manufactured goods and raw materials needed by Saugerties and Woodstock people. Adam Short, Peter Short's brother, sometimes helped "crewe the sloop," as Snyder put it, and made repairs on the boat. At Snyder's store in Churchland Woodstock people bought cloth and liquor, food and tools. There they paid their bills, sometimes in cash but often in the products of their farms and woodlots. Snyder's account books form the most useful source presently known to give us a picture of the daily life of Woodstock pioneers between 1768 and 1776.[6]

Snyder's books show that he played many parts in the little drama of settlement. For one thing, he acted as a banker in a society which had no banks. In theory he and his customers balanced their accounts annually, but in practice Snyder often "carried" Woodstock people for years and occasionally even advanced small sums of cash to those who had demonstrated responsibility.

It was also Snyder who surveyed the farms of Peter Short, Peter Winne, Ephriam Van Keuren, Samuel Ferris and others between 1771 and 1773. He also drew up leases. The tenants were required by the terms of their leases to pay for both these services. On December 31, 1778, for example, Snyder entered a charge of sixteen shillings in the account of Henry Henigar for surveying Henigar's farm. Peter Winne, who had much more land in his two leaseholds, paid one pound, five shillings. Peter Miller, Peter Short's son-in-law, was charged twelve shillings "for Survayen his farm and making the plan." Snyder noted that he spent one day surveying the Henigar farm and two days on the Winne job.

In 1773 William Medermick (McDermot) paid sixteen shillings for the survey of his leasehold. Just where it was in Woodstock is uncertain. The spelling of McDermot's name is a good example of the way Snyder had of setting down English words and names in a form which came as close as he could get to the way they entered his Dutch-trained ears. Wife became "waife," wine was "waine," flaxseed "flak seat," wheat "weath," an awl handle or haft became "allhaf," large became "larch," handkerchief turned into "henketsue," and so on. Snyder's phonetic spellings preserve the way of speaking of his time and place in a manner which makes it almost possible for us to recreate everyday speech of Woodstock people two centuries ago.

Snyder's house in Churchland served as a tavern where Saugerties and Woodstock men drank, occasionally ate meals together, and bought liquor to carry home. On February 28, 1771 Peter Short and Peter Winne were among thirteen men who had "drams" of liquor together. On June 6 of the same year Peter Winne shared a quart of wine with Johannis M. Snyder. Though metheglin, cider, cordials and "pons" (punch) were occasionally consumed, the staple liquor was rum, both the locally made "York rum" and the much more popular "Wastindy" (West Indies) kind. Sales of rum to take out rose during the harvest season. In August 1771 Peter Winne bought one gallon and three quarts of rum at three shillings sixpence "for his grass Bea." This was of course what was later called a "haying bee." Sales of rum for use at "beas" in March suggest the prevalence of maple-sugar bees.

Snuff was frequently bought by nearly all Snyder's Woodstock customers. But tobacco was not. Instead it appears on the credit side of some Woodstock and Saugerties accounts, which suggests it was grown locally. Snuff was probably used by women as well as men. In 1768 Peter Short's "waife" bought a "Snuf Bocks" for one shilling ninepence (1/9).[7]

Household goods were sold now and then to Woodstock people at Snyder's store. Knives, "spoans," "arten" plates, "basons" and "cops" are recorded. Bulking much larger in the Snyder accounts are materials used for making clothing. These increased in late fall and early spring. A typical sale was made to Peter Short on December 18, 1770. Short bought "8 ells Oznabruck, 11/4 Ells flannel and 1 ell ginniva." Peter Winne that same day bought "10 Bottons" and "3 Skans trad." The next day Thomas Shadwick was charged with "2 1/2 Ells of chak and 21 1/2 Ells of Carz, 8 Ells of Silk Poplin, and 1/2 Ell of 'Stoof'." His son Samuel did the buying and charged it to his father.

Needles and pins were bought at dressmaking times. So too were "pase borts" used in making bonnets. Lea Bakker, the sister of Annatje Short, seems to have lived with her sister's family. She must have been a dressmaker, for she is debited with substantial amounts of cloth and dressmaking sundries. "Everlasting," "grean frize," cambrick, shirting and other kinds of linen, "Duram" silk of various colors, "taffety," "Schillon," and many other kinds of cloth all were used by Woodstock pioneers. Joseph Lawrence of Saugerties sometimes did tailoring for these people—in 1773 he made a black coat for Peter Winne. Materials for dying were bought by Woodstock settlers—redwood and indigo were prominent and "allum" was bought for use as a mordant in the dying process. "Duch Lase" was often bought for use as trimming and sales of "bockels" and ribbons were frequent.

Often the making of a specific garment and for whom it was made were marked on Snyder's books. One such case was a sale on August 21, 1775 when Dirck Henigar, son of Hendrick Henigar of Little Shandaken, bought "1 velve Patron for a jacket 16/, and clout for the Hine parts 4/, 2 Ells of Schilloon 5/. 1 stick Mohar and 1 doz. Bottons 1/, Received this in full by his father." Stockings, woolen hats and "basseloney or other" silk or linen handkerchiefs are among the readymade items of wear charged to Woodstock people.

On May 1, 1770 Mrs. Peter Winne bought three "abc Books" for 1/6—this is the only such sale on Snyder's books. Occasional sales of a "book of wryten paper" are recorded. Sugar and tea (but no coffee) were the principal foodstuffs bought by Snyder's Woodstock customers. He also sold them pepper, salt and such things as "alispice."

A good deal of powder, flints and "Schod" went from Snyder's to Woodstock men, who now and then bought tools from him, a hammer, an awl or a scythe or "scy," as Snyder put it. This pronunciation was still used in Ulster County forty years ago. The scythes were sometimes described as long and sometimes as short; some were sold with "hafts" and some weren't. Window glass for use when houses were being built was also sold. On November 18, 1772 Peter Short was charged with "23 Squars of glass at /6-11"; sales of nails were fairly frequent.

The ways in which Woodstock purchases were paid foretells much about life in the new settlement. People in the older part of the town, like Arie Van Etten of Zena, balanced their purchases with casks of honey, with tobacco and firkins of butter, and sometimes sent consignments of these products to New York on board Snyder's sloop. Members of the Wolven family who farmed along the road between Woodstock and Saugerties were also butter and sometimes honey people. Their farms had been settled long enough to have become fairly mellow and productive.

But the lands leased by the Shorts, the Winnes and other recent Woodstock settlers were stump-littered and raw. Cattle were few and must have had none too easy a time. Peter Winne apparently bred horses for from time to time he turned one over to Benjamin Snyder in payment of his account; on January 25, 1775 he was credited with -6 for "one black hors." He also pastured horses or wintered them. This suggests that his farm at the Lake Hill-Willow flats had been cleared long enough to make good pasture possible.

Peter Short made trips for Snyder to "Pakepsy" or Loonenburg, sometimes "riding" or hauling loads of flaxseed or other merchandise. He made shingles, and sometimes Snyder took the "schingels" to New York—the earliest example of manufactured goods going to New York from Woodstock. On June 22, 1773 Snyder credited Short with 4-10-0 for three thousand shingles at 30/ per hundred. On July 20 that same year Short delivered one thousand shingles to be put on board Snyder's sloop. These shingles were probably made of the white pine trees which grew well in many parts of Woodstock, and more usually—but not always—were reserved to the landlord. Oats, corn and in 1770 three "schypel Chistnuts" helped balance Short's account.

Once in a while scrap metal such as brass or pewter derived from broken or wornout household objects was accepted by Snyder, weighed and credited to a Woodstock customer. Only rarely was a deerskin taken in payment. This suggests that Woodstock people traded their skins and furs elsewhere, for they used substantial amounts of ammunition during the cooler months. Or they may have converted the skins into clothing at home, as local traditions tell us they did.[8]

Flaxseed often appears on the credit side of Woodstock accounts. Flax was grown by most pioneers. It grew almost weed-free at first because the European field weeds which accompanied settlers from Europe had not yet become common. Some of the flax harvest was made into sheets, shirts and other articles of daily use, while fancier clothing was made from cloth bought from Ben Snyder or others. Part of the flax crop was allowed to ripen its pale-brown, shiny seeds. Flaxseed was as good as cash at any merchant's because shiploads of it were exported every year from New York to be used by Irish flax growers. Wheat, rye, oats and corn were also often traded for merchandise. Grain, flaxseed and nuts were measured for customers in Dutch schepels, one of which was equal to an English bushel and a half. But sometimes the English measure was used and was set down as a "bossel."[9]

Establishing a Woodstock farm in the 1760s and 1770s was not a quick or simple act. The first step was the exploration of the woods and the choice of a favorable spot—this was known as "making a pitch." The kinds of plants growing on the land gave clues to the quality of the soil. Chestnut oaks meant that bedrock was close to the surface. Tulip trees usually grew in deep soil. Beech and butternut testified to a good supply of moisture. Jewelweed might indicate the presence of a spring—and a good source of water was of the highest importance. Beside the Sawkill and Beaverkill and their tributaries early settlers sometimes came upon level and fertile tracts known as beaver meadows, which had resulted from the backing up of water and depositing of silt behind the dams beaver built. The fertile soils of Waghkonck and of Willow had been improved by beaver; Peter Short's farm settled by 1770 across the Sawkill from the present hamlet of Woodstock in what was called the South Settlement may have included a beaver meadow.

After a man had made his pitch he would assemble all the men and boys he could muster among his friends, family and neighbors, and set to work clearing the land. He could not hope to clear more than one to three acres his first summer. The trees were usually enormous by present-day Woodstock standards, and felling them was neither quick nor easy. In order to prevent the growth of a lusty crop of sprouts from stumps as certain kinds of trees struggled to remain alive, these trees were cut as high as possible—ash, oaks and soft maples were among the trees which sprouted most vigorously.

Logs twelve feet long were cut and rolled or pulled by oxen into heaps which were burned during a rainless spell in late summer or early fall when a sawmill was not convenient. The ashes were readily saleable and formed the settler's first cash crop from his farm. Smaller trunks and branches were burned, but enough were saved to be used in making a fence to keep animal marauders out of the crops planted among the stumps. If the trees cut were of the kinds like beech, hemlock and birch, which formed dense mats of roots close to the surface, no plowing would be attempted for several years.

Wheat would be scattered on the surface and harrowed in with a crude harrow often pulled by men. If no harrow was available a thorny bush might be pressed into service. Sometimes Indian corn was the first crop. While all this was in progress the men and boys would camp out in what was known as a "wigwam" formed of evergreen boughs, sheets of bark and logs. These shelters were inspired by those of the Indians. They were Woodstock's first homes for white people.[10]

Traditional foods included salt pork and corn meal, to which trout caught in nearby brooks were added. In the fall of the first few years a pioneer would return to his old home for the winter after beginning to work on his pitch. There was a good deal of going back and forth all year round because most settlers of the 1760s and 1770s came from no more than ten to twenty miles away. When enough land was cleared to make the beginning of farm life possible, a frame or perhaps a log house would be built with the help of neighbors and then the women and younger children of the family would move in. Grass appeared quickly among the blackened stumps, making life possible for horses and cattle. Some settlers speeded up the process of clearing by what is known as girdling. A band of bark was cut from the lower part of tree trunks. The trees, deprived of the nourishment flowing upward through the inner bark, would die.[11]

From 1762 to 1774 the number of trees in Woodstock diminished and the number of cleared fields increased. Although complete records are lacking, it seems safe to say that about fifteen farms were then in the process of formation within the limits of the present town of Woodstock. A few along the eastern border were fairly well cleared, with good barns and stone houses; the rest had perhaps ten of their sixty to one hundred acres in grain and hay. The balance consisted of primeval woods and fire-blackened semi-clearing in which grass was beginning to grow. Farms were sometimes abandoned and then taken over by squatters without the owner's permission. Until 1774, under the sober guidance of Judge Livingston, the town's population was growing. Large families of children were the rule. In spite of the persistence of leases for three lives, and in spite of discouragements like deaths from fever which led to occasional abandonment, the new settlement seemed to be headed for growth and perhaps even a modest sort of prosperity.[12]

Then, in 1774, all this changed. The violent and doubt-ridden days of the American Revolution lay ahead. Before the Revolution ended in 1783, not only did the growth of farming cease but the settlement's houses stood empty and its fields untilled, as Woodstock was virtually abandoned because of military necessity.

8

FOR OR AGAINST THE KING

Ever since the end of the Seven Years' War forces had been at work to widen the gap between King George the Third and his American subjects. Old Robert Livingston and his son had been well aware of these forces. It is unlikely, however, that they were the subject of much Woodstock discussion. The persistence of Dutch as Woodstock's everyday language imposed a barrier against the ideas and activities of the larger America and worked toward a concentration on immediate and local matters. And besides, few Woodstock people could read or write.

By 1774 Woodstock people realized that a time of crisis was drawing close. That year the Continental Congress, organized in protest against what more and more Americans regarded as British tyranny, came into being at Carpenters Hall in Philadelphia. The members of the Congress signed a Continental Association by which they pledged themselves to oppose infringements on the liberties they enjoyed as British subjects. Throughout the colonies modified copies of the Association were circulated by local committees. Committeemen urged "freemen, freeholders and inhabitants" to let the British government know that taxation without representation and other acts of oppression were almost universally opposed. The names of those who signed and those who refused to do so were made public.

Not a single man—women were not asked to sign—who lived in Woodstock is known to have signed a Woodstock Association. And only one—Frederick Rowe, Jr.—is known to have refused to sign the Kingston Association. Arie Van Etten, who lived on what was sometimes called the Van Etten Patent in Woodstock's "chin whisker" of the future, did sign the Association in Kingston. So did several members of the Wolven family, who lived on long-settled farms just across Woodstock's eastern boundary along the road to Saugerties. It may have been that a copy of the Association circulated in Woodstock was lost. But it may have been that the pledge was not circulated there in an attempt to keep the list of non-signers as short as possible. Woodstock people were known not to be eager to pledge resistance to the British government and to King George.[1]

There were understandable reasons for this. Tenants on Woodstock lands knew their absentee landlords were enthusiastic supporters of all the Continental Congress stood for. Young Robert R. Livingston, son of Judge Livingston of Clermont, sat in the Provincial Convention. Like many other substantial American landlords the Livingstons had long enjoyed a protected and privileged position. They paid no taxes on their unsettled lands, they had seats in the provincial assemblies and on the bench, they exercised political power out of all proportion to their numbers. The British parliament eyed them with misgivings and threatened to take action to curb their power. Were the taxation-without-representation measures being proposed to succeed, a tax on large landholdings could not be far off. Fear of such a tax, when added to other motivations, made great American landlords into powerful leaders and devoted supporters of the Congress and before long of the Revolution.

Things seemed very different from the point of view of many of the tenants of landlords like the Livingstons. To the landlords the advantages of resistance to the oppressive measures of parliament and king were obvious enough. To the tenants it was equally obvious that they had much to lose and nothing to gain. A triumph of the Congress could only confirm the system of leases for lives under which they lived, and King George, it was soon being said, would eventually reward his supporters with farms of their own taken from his enemies, the great American landlords.

The tenants were in an uncomfortable position. They were being pushed and pulled by two powerful parties. Many lived in a state of doubt and confusion. They found their daily lives being affected by bitter debate. Attempts at peaceful resistance eventually gave way to open and bloody conflict.

In 1775 a company of rangers of some 25 to 30 men was formed to patrol the edge of the Catskills in Woodstock and vicinity in order to give warning of the approach of armed parties of British sympathizers and Indian allies of King George. The rangers were recruited and led by Captain Elias Hasbrouck of Kingston, who would later become Woodstock's leading citizen. The rangers were billetted in the houses of the settlers. One of these billets, described as a "picket fort," was Peter Short's house close to the Sawkill and to what is now known as the Ohayo Mountain Road. This billetting did a good deal to give the Congress party a public presence in the town. The rangers' food and lodging was paid for, creating good will for their cause and making it a little easier to attract recruits from among the sons of Woodstock settlers.[2]

The rangers came and went, scouring the mountain passes and the trails that followed the Sawkill, the Beaverkill and other streams. Benjamin Snyder's books show that he was becoming less and less able to supply the needs of Woodstock people. Traffic on the Hudson River, a vital link in the defense plans of the Congress, was now irregular and sometimes hazardous for Snyder's sloop. Business at Snyder's Churchland store dwindled. Tea, sugar and other commodities bought by his Woodstock customers were no longer in stock.[3]

By June 1776 Snyder had given up his trips to New York and was using his sloop to carry saltpeter for making gunpowder from New Windsor to the landing of the powder mill set up near Clermont by old Robert Livingston. Instead of carrying country produce he carried fifty of the picked militiamen known as "minute men" to New York. There they were expected to serve in the defense of the city against imminent British attack. On July 25 Snyder sold his sloop to a secret committee of the Provincial Congress of New York for use in repelling British attempts at sailing up the Hudson and so splitting the rebellious American colonies into two weakened groups.[4]

The sloop went off to war with something made in Woodstock, its "cannoe" or lifeboat. In the fall of 1775 the old canoe on Snyder's sloop had been repaired; the following spring it was replaced by a new one that a number of local men, including Peter Short, one of his sons and his brother William, had made in Woodstock of Woodstock timber. The canoe was the only Woodstock production put to war uses, as far as is known.

Woodstock was well into a period of economic stagnation. With the market for its farm and forest products cut off, with a constant fear of Indian raids from behind the Catskills, with soldiers a daily sight on its roads and trails and with its people hopelessly divided in allegiance between King and Congress, an air of fear, suspicion and doubt hung over the settlements of Little Shandaken, Woodstock and Awaghkonck. The clearing of land came to an end. Here and there the surrounding forest took little steps toward recapturing fields and meadows. A good many names of settlers of the 1760s and 1770s disappeared forever from local records. Pending the outcome of the great struggle which might radically change the condition of their lives, most tenants refused to pay rents.[5]

By 1776 Revolutionary activity was involving Woodstock ever more deeply. The Provincial Convention was meeting in Kingston. The British had taken possession of New York and were preparing to move up the Hudson River to join the forces of Generals Burgoyne and St. Leger moving from Canada. Agents of the British were roaming the Hudson Valley promising not only farms of their own to tenants but also freedom to slaves who would fight for the King. Some young tenant farmers "went off" to join the British. Many remained at home but were classed as "disaffected." Some disaffected men joined with the Indian allies of the British to harass neighbors who were "strong Wigs" and to give shelter to British agents guiding recruits to behind the British lines.[6]

As 1776 ended enthusiasm for the cause of the King was rising rapidly among the tenants on the landed estates of the Hudson Valley. The smooth-talking British agents who were moving more freely from house to house now had the help of a network of local Tories to supply them with food, shelter, horses and vehicles. The agents were said to have carried bags of British gold which they used to buy help for the King. And according to local traditions still being kept alive, they buried their gold or hid it under the floorboards of a house when they were in danger of capture. Young men were persuaded to form armed groups and to join the British forces, known to them as "the Regulars." The success of the British in taking the city of New York and the size and power of the forces they had set in motion to take over the Hudson Valley made their triumph seem to royalist sympathizers to be inevitable.[7]

Across the Hudson in January 1777 a regiment of militiamen refused to obey orders to march to the defense of the Highlands against the British moving up the Hudson. Instead, many of them, reported Peter R. Livingston of Livingston Manor, were "daily riding about the county huzzaing for the King, and drinking his health in the taverns." In Woodstock people denounced neighbors as Tories often on the flimsiest of evidence; old friends refused to speak to each other and families were divided in their loyalties.[8]

Cornelis Newkerk, who farmed the lands along Route 212 as it enters Woodstock from Saugerties, was a Tory, although most of his relatives were active Whigs. His neighbor to the south, Wilhelmus Rowe, was also a Tory; he was the brother of Frederick Rowe, Jr. of Little Shandaken, whom many regarded as the leader among Woodstock Tories. The Van Ettens, who farmed to the south and southeast of Wilhelmus Rowe (and for whom the neighborhood known as Vandale may have been named), were deeply divided. Arie, the oldest son, was a decided Whig, but his younger brother Gisbert was a Tory; their sister Lea was the wife of Cornelis Newkerk. Westward from Cornelis Newkerk, John Croft, who had taken over the stone house and the farm once leased to cordwainer Hubner, was an active Tory.[9]

In what was becoming the hamlet of Woodstock and along both sides of the Sawkill to Bearsville sympathies were divided. The Tory side was favored by most Livingston tenants. But Peter Short, his sons and his son-in-law, Peter Miller, were prominent Whigs upon whom much Tory hostility was focussed. Only in Little Shandaken was there unanimity—the neighborhood continued to be a Tory stronghold.

Evidence for these divisions in Woodstock during the Revolutionary War can be found in the minutes of the Kingston "Committee of safety & Observation" for April 9, 1777. This committee existed to ferret out Tories and "Tory conspiracies," to persuade lukewarm Tories to give up their firearms to the Whigs, who were suffering from a shortage of weapons, and to imprison active Tories and British agents penetrating the Whig lines. Neighboring Dutchess County's committee had borne down so hard on their own Tories that many were crossing the Hudson to hide out among Tory adherents living within the Catskill Mountains. Two of these refugees, James Atwater and Daniel Wilson, had been seized and brought before the Ulster committee. The minutes of their examination and the curious incident to which their capture led are revealing.[10]

Atwater and Wilson told the committee members that they had been heading inland on "the Woodstock Road" on Saturday the fifth of April 1777. They met a stranger named William Doud (the meeting probably took place in the lower Sawkill Valley). After a bit of conversational fencing with Doud the two Dutchess men realized that all three were Tories—that "he and we were both of one mind." Atwater and Wilson told Doud that "we were in Trouble and wanted a place where to flee."

Doud proved to be immensely helpful; he was a positive mine of information about Whigs and Tories in Woodstock and its vicinity. He warned the refugees against certain "strong Wigs" like Peter Short, Peter Miller, Jeremiah Snyder (brother of Benjamin Snyder), Tobias Wynkoop and Christian Myer of Saugerties. He recommended people who might be trusted to help fellow Tories in trouble—young John and Helmur Rowe, sons of Frederick Rowe, Jr. of Little Shandaken, were among them. So too was Gisbert Van Etten. And Zachariah Snyder, the sole Tory in a large family of Whigs, could also be trusted. In February he had guided some Tories to safety at John Croft's house on the edge of the hamlet of Woodstock.

Fortified with Doud's information Atwater and Wilson continued up the Woodstock Road and called on Gisbert Van Etten. Van Etten assured them he was indeed "a friend to the King's forces." He told them of the location of two horses which they might be able to borrow to ride to Frederick Rowe's place at Little Shandaken. Van Etten said he'd had word of the whereabouts of the horses from Peter Winne, a strong Tory and a friend of Frederick Rowe.

The refugees left Van Etten's and continued toward Woodstock along the road known today as the Chestnut Hill Road. Where this road came to an end at the curve in the Sawkill a bit east of the Woodstock Country Club they arrived at John Croft's stone house. But neither Croft nor his wife was at home, their daughter said. She warned them that "The Company was there." By this Miss Croft probably meant the militia company which patrolled Woodstock and its vicinity. This unpleasant news may have caused the men to change any plan they might have had of trying to find a hideout in Little Shandaken. Instead they turned right and made for the stone house of Cornelis Newkerk close to the Kingston (now the Saugerties) border less than two miles east of Croft's.

Cornelis made no bones about the fact that he was, as he put it, "a man for the King." His boys were just as loyal as he was, said Cornelis. He could hardly keep them from going off at once "To the Regulars." He expected them to go in about eight days. His son Jacobus backed up what his father said. Soon, under the guidance of "Lieut. Snyder"—just who the lieutenant was is not clear—Atwater and Wilson found their way to Wilhelmus Rowe's house. There they met Wilhelmus' son Jacobus. Jacobus told them that his cousins John and Peter (the sons of Frederick) had been there three or four days earlier and had left their horse and "slay there, and there came another slay with three men on it, Peter and Caltus Heffer & an Englishman unknown to them then."

It was at Wilhelmus Rowe's or shortly after leaving there that Atwater and Wilson ran out of good luck. Just how and where they were captured has not been recorded—probably word of their presence had gotten around and "the Company" had tracked them down and picked up Cornelis Newkerk, William McDermot—who probably lived at or close to Newkerk's—and young Jacobus. Jacobus, the prize of the catch, was known to have intended to have joined the Regulars and was probably armed. He was put in jail. The others were held and questioned separately.

Atwater and Wilson saved their own skins by making a detailed confession about their wanderings in Woodstock in search of a hideout, implicating others. Newkerk, Van Etten and McDermot denied everything until the statement of the two Dutchess County men was read to them. Then they wilted and admitted the statement was correct.

Even after they had confessed, the situation of the three Woodstock Tories was not too serious. They had been "charged with Treasonable Discourses" with Atwater and Wilson. They had taken no anti-Whig action except in conversation. That was why they were offered a chance to regain their freedom by taking the oath sometimes called The Test. It went like this:

> I the Subscriber Do most solemnly swear that I Renounce all allegiance to the King of Great Britain that I will be a good and true Subject to the State of New York that I will to the utmost of my Power defend the said State against the Enemies thereof and that I will discover all Plots & Conspiracies against it which may come to my knowledge and Pray God Almighty so to keep me as I do faithfully and sincerely keep this Oath and Declaration.

After they had taken the oath and paid "the Cost & Expenses accrued in apprehending them" the three, now officially converted from Tories to Whigs, were released. But the troubles of Newkerk and McDermot were not over. They headed on horseback through a night of melting snow and swollen streams and arrived at a fording place known even to this day by the Dutch name of "the Rift." There, in the words of the Committee of Safety and Observation, they were "afraid to cross The Creek." They found their way to the house of Joseph Osterhoudt nearby and asked to be put up for the night. Osterhoudt took them in.

Joseph Osterhoudt was a signer of the Articles of Association, a member of the first regiment of the Ulster militia and a grandson of Abraham Hasbrouck, who was said to be the richest man in Ulster County and a financier of Whig activities. With a candle in his hand Osterhoudt led the two men to an upstairs room in which there were two beds. One, Osterhoudt indicated, was for them. He did not tell them that the other bed was occupied by a sharp-eared and inquisitive lady named Elizabeth Yeomans. She ". . . had drawn the Curtains of the bed Close Together" so that she could not be seen. "After Mr. Osterhoudt Left the Room, the said McDarmoth & Newkerk when Laid Down supposing themselves alone began to talk About The Transactions of the Day before the Committee." And Mrs. Yeomans listened.

First Newkerk said that the committee members now took him and McDermot to be "good Whigs, but my heart is the same as before." McDermot said he felt the same but that it was a good thing to have taken the oath. Then Newkerk launched into an ingenious explanation of his reasons for believing that he hadn't actually taken the oath. When it was read to him, and it was read to him more than once, he hadn't heard it because he had "stopped his ears with wool." McDermot seemed incredulous and asked where Newkerk had got the wool. He had brought it with him from home, said Newkerk, for he had expected the oath to be offered to him.

At this McDermot said regretfully that he hadn't thought so far ahead. But he too had a bit of casuistry in explanation of his own belief that he was not bound by the Whig oath. The committeemen who had examined him had asked him to swear to be true to the country, he told Newkerk, and "I could do that and free my Conscience for it is our country where we were born but the King is Ruler of the Country."

Newkerk asked McDermot if he didn't think they might be able to force the committee to return the weapons taken from them when they were Tories. Now that they were Whigs they had a right to keep the weapons. McDermot didn't think the weapons would be returned. He said he was keeping an account of the expenses he had been put to because of his arrest in the expectation of eventual repayment. He thought that Newkerk and Gisbert Van Etten should do the same.

Newkerk explained that he would keep an account if he could—but he couldn't write. Maybe his son Jacobus would do it for him, but Jacobus was still in jail and wouldn't be out until he took the test oath. Then the two talked about hanging someone, possibly the person whom they believed to have betrayed them to the Whig authorities.

For a while longer the two men talked in their bed while Mrs. Yeomans strained her ears to catch every murmur. Newkerk put into words his feelings about his sons. If he gave the boys some money as a reward for not enlisting he thought they would probably stay home. But if he did that he would "always be sorry afterwards for they [the boys] must do their Own mind."

Early the next morning Mrs. Yeomans slipped out of bed and out of the room and told Joseph Osterhoudt what she had heard. Osterhoudt dashed off at once to the house of Silvester Salisbury, a devoted Whig and captain of a military unit known as the Ulster Light Horse. He reported what Mrs. Yeomans had overheard. Very soon after, Newkerk and McDermot were in custody again. When confronted with Mrs. Yeomans' statement they "Confessed Every word."

This time no oath was offered to the prisoners. They had taken it once and there would be no second chance. Just where they were imprisoned and for exactly how long is uncertain—that summer McDermot was recorded as being a prisoner in Hurley. But a year later he and Newkerk were again free men; on July 11 of that year Newkerk bought the farm on which he had been living from Whig officer Evert Wynkoop. The conveyance was witnessed by a neighbor, William Berringer, and by William McDermot.

What happened to Newkerk's sons isn't clear. Probably they were persuaded while imprisoned to enlist in the Whig forces. That was the way young Tories often ended up. For by the late 1770s many Woodstock Tories were losing confidence and giving up loyalty to the king. The war was far from over. It was clear that the Whigs were gaining in power and the king was fading away as a possible source of rewards for loyalty. Yet a few Woodstock Tories, notably those in Little Shandaken, remained to the end fiercely loyal to King George.[11]

9

REVOLUTIONARY
TIMES

A good many stories of Revolutionary days have been kept alive in Woodstock into our own times. A few have no evidence at all to support them. One such story tells of troops of the Continental Army marching through Woodstock and up Mink Hollow into the Delaware Valley. Another is a variant of a standard wartime atrocity story often repeated in both Europe and America. An Indian member of a Tory raiding party had refused to kill a Woodstock baby smiling at him from its cradle, and a "Tory named Newkerk ran his bayonet through the infant and carried it out on the tip of his weapon." As Newkerk lay dying years later the Devil punished him by throwing him out of his bed and forcing him to die all alone in his barnyard. The Newkerk of the story may well have been meant for the Cornelis Newkerk who with William McDermot got into trouble in 1777.[1]

Other anecdotes have a great deal of corroboration in reliable records. One of these dealing with the Tories of Little Shandaken was set down in 1888 by Kingston lawyer Marius Schoonmaker in his *History of Kingston*. Schoonmaker wrote:

In one season during the Revolution a number of Tories and deserters wintered in the mountains at the west end of Woodstock at a neighborhood called "Little Shandaken." At the time there were only four or five dwellings at the settlement, occupied by Frederick Rowe and his two sons, John and Peter, and also the Carle family. Frederick Rowe was considerably advanced in age, He had one negro. The refugees were some twenty in number, and had a log hut near a dark ravine in the mountains, about three miles from the settlement. In order to procure food, whenever a snowstorm occurred they would take that night to go to the settlement and get what they wanted. They were always careful to wear their shoes wrong-end foremost and to make the track of one going into the woods instead of coming out, and again changing the shoes on returning. Rowe's negro often carried the food by order of his master, but he was a patriot and disliked the duty.

The story is given substance by a number of sources. Frederick Rowe, Jr. did indeed own a male slave. The number of houses in Little Shandaken is approximately correct, and the evidence given by Atwater and Wilson tells of Tory activities in the late winter of 1777 which may well have been related to a Tory hideout close to Little Shandaken. Documents among the papers of Governor George Clinton show it was not unusual for young men of Woodstock who had joined the Regulars to return home for the winter near their friends and families. This going into winter quarters during the dull season for military activity was permitted by British officers. Finally, the wearing of shoes (they would have been boots) backward is not as bizarre as it may sound to modern ears. The boots Americans wore during the eighteenth century were not differentiated into lefts and rights; both were alike and fitted less snugly than modern boots and shoes. Woodstock oldtimers agree that the Tory hideout was in isolated Silver Hollow, though the exact spot has never been determined.[2]

Some Woodstock Revolutionary traditions having to do with refugees fleeing to Woodstock from the Hudson Valley have a firm foundation. In 1777 the forces of General Burgoyne coming south from Canada collapsed and surrendered at Saratoga. At almost the same time a British detachment under General Vaughan managed to break through the strong defenses of the Hudson River and moved up the river from New York. Vaughan's men burned Kingston, the Livingstons' house at Clermont and two houses at Saugerties. Refugees from Kingston and Saugerties sought shelter inland. Most Kingston people went to Hurley, but Saugerties people and a few from Kingston who had relatives in Woodstock hastened there.

Among the Saugerties people were Mrs. John Brink and her young child; Brink is said to have been serving at the time with the Whig forces. Refugees often carried their most valuable portable belongings with them and so helped give rise to lore of treasures hidden away in Woodstock. Tories fleeing the Whigs are also said to have buried or otherwise hidden treasure during Revolutionary days.

One persistent story of Tory treasure is told about a farm lying on the old road to Cooper Lake. Anita M. Smith gives this version in a paper read to the Historical Society of Woodstock in 1931:

> There is an old story of Tory Treasure buried during the Revolution on a hill near Bearsville. However, none of us may ever find it, for the legend says that in order to ensure its secrecy a small negro was buried alive with it. It did create a han't. For years later two belated natives returning past the spot at night perceived a weird dog. The animal lurked around the wheels of their cart, but he was not of this earth for the thong of their whip passed right through him without interrupting his antics.

Some versions make the treasure a Whig one carried from Kingston. But whether Whig or Tory there may be some truth in the story. During the 1930s an old silver spoon and a silver snuffbox were dug up near the traditional location. And every now and then someone reports seeing a strange creature, human or animal, prowling the neighborhood by night.[3]

Woodstock's most dramatic bit of Revolutionary lore tells of Tory-Indian raids. This kind of story in its broad outlines has substantial backing in contemporary documents. For several years after the defeat of Burgoyne and the burning of Kingston Woodstock played a part in the border warfare phase of the Revolution. Stories of the raids have lingered on in tradition. The possibility that the Regulars would soon take possession of the Hudson Valley began to seem remote after the events of 1777. Instead Woodstock Tories looked with hope and the Whigs with apprehension across the Catskills to the west.[4]

Woodstock lay on the long line which separated the more settled parts of the American colonies from the back country still largely controlled by British allies among the Indians. The possibility of raids on settlements like Woodstock was constant except in winter. And every once in a while rumors that a party of Indians and white Tories was on its way to attack Woodstock went from house to house throughout the town.

The leader of the party was usually imagined to be the man who was most feared of all their enemies by Woodstock people. He was Joseph Brant, an Indian with a white man's education. Brant was a brother of Molly, Indian "wife" of Sir William Johnson, who was colonial Commissioner of Indian Affairs, and he was secretary to Sir William's successor, his nephew Guy Johnson. Brant was a devout and active layman of the Episcopalian Church and a bold and daring military leader. Around Brant crystallized much of the fear and hatred generated by the border war. He was often undeservedly portrayed in Woodstock traditions as a monster of cruelty and malevolence.[5]

A bit of lore once repeated by Woodstock people linked Brant to the Woodstock landscape. It held that Brant and his Indian scouts and raiders had maintained bases for observation and for the storing of supplies and plunder taken in raids high on the eastern escarpment of the Catskills and that a base of this kind was established on Overlook Mountain. The Overlook Cliff offers the observation point closest to the Hudson and with the most extensive view up and down the valley. Nearby is an excellent spring on a plateau well suited for use as a campsite. Some Woodstock people treasure bits of stone found on the plateau and the Overlook Cliff, believing that these are tools and carvings made by the Indians of Revolutionary times if not by their ancestors of "sacred mountain" days. On careful examination these stone relics turn out to be natural productions roughly imitating man-made ones.[6]

Although there is much evidence that Indians used a base on Round Top or High Peak Mountain a few miles to the northeast of Overlook there is nothing that points conclusively to an Overlook base. One piece of contemporary evidence that may relate to Overlook can be found in a letter written July 23, 1779 by Colonel John Butler, the boldest and most active of white British border fighters. It tells of an Indian who had known Woodstock in pre-War days and had friends there. Butler wrote: "John Rimp [better known as Renhope or Runnip] a trusty and intelligent Indian whom I sent out some time ago is returning this afternoon; he brings some Rebel newspapers which I enclose you; you will find by them that Genl. Clinton is certainly advancing up the North [the Hudson] River—he says, that he himself from the top of the Blue Mountains which lye near the River heard the Fireing and saw the smoke as of two armies engaged at Fish-Kill eighteen days ago . . . " [7]

At that time there was indeed military activity near Peekskill (the Fish-Kill of the letter is likely to have been an error). The British took Stony Point, only to have it retaken a bit later by General Anthony Wayne. A man with keen senses might have seen signs and heard sounds of the engagement at Stony Point more clearly from the Overlook Cliff than from any other point on the Blue or Catskill Mountains.

And there is another more solid piece of evidence to suggest a link of Overlook with Indian activity during the Revolution. On the

WOODSTOCK: HISTORY OF AN AMERICAN TOWN

northeast slope of the mountain close to the Woodstock town line and somewhat more than halfway up the mountain is a cave known as Jager's Cave. It is entered by a very narrow passage which leads past a precipitous drop of some twenty feet to a capacious chamber. Caves are rare among the Catskills, and that makes it seem likely that this one may well have been used, as tradition states, by Indian scouts and raiders.[8]

Some incidents of the Revolution in Woodstock have left little trace in oral tradition but have excellent documentary evidence to support them. One of these is the setting up and manning of a defensive post in the neighborhood of the Willow of our times; the place was then part of Little Shandaken. Because of its Tory settlers and its exposed position, Little Shandaken was a weak point in the Whig line of defense stretching from "Schandaken to the Eikaberg," this Eikaberg or Oak Mountain being the one in the present town of Durham. In 1778 Little Shandaken's defenses were improved. An advance post was established, probably by a stockade of logs built around an existing house, similar to that which may already have been built at Peter Short's place on the Sawkill.

There seems to be no tradition about the location of the post. Most of what we know about it is contained in a letter written from there on October 15, 1778 by Captain Jeremiah Snyder, who was in command—he lived not far away on a farm at Blue Mountain. When he took charge Snyder wrote to General George Clinton that he "found that the Company was in a bad posture of Defense in Regard to Ammunition." Snyder asked for ammunition in order that "we may be able to make some Resistance in case the enemy should make an excursion upon this Settlement, but we have at Present no intelligence of their being near this Place." His company, Snyder went on to say, consisted of "Forty-one Privates besides Serjeants & Corporals, and these I cannot Supply with three Cartirages a peice . . . " [9]

Pleas like Captain Snyder's were to be repeated over and over again as the Revolutionary War moved along. Military necessities elsewhere caused men and munitions to be withdrawn from the defense of Woodstock's frontiers. Whig morale often turned shaky when it became apparent that the War would last not a few months but years. In the first welling-up of enthusiasm for the Whig cause recruiters had made young men promises which as the war effort became more grim and demanding they could not keep.

Isaac Davis of Little Shandaken and James Winne and Samuel

Newkerk of the same place had enlisted in Captain Elias Hasbrouck's "Company of Raingers." Davis gave a clear account in a letter to General George Clinton of January 14, 1777 of how he had enlisted and why he had become dissatisfied. Hasbrouck, Davis said, had come to his "father-in-laws at Shandaken & Spooke there for his Quarters and insisted upon my Inlisting. I told him that I could not because I had a family to maintain and had to Build that fall. Then he promised me that he should be stationed at Shandaken and Should range nowhere but from a place called the Blue Mountain toward Rochester and I should have my board at my house. He promised me that he Should help me make my house done with his men and that I would have his men at any time for an afternoon Spell to Clere land. . . ."[10]

Seldom had a recruit had more attractive bait dangled before him. He could draw a soldier's pay while living at home, with his fellow soldiers helping clear his land and build his house. Davis was so thoroughly delighted with Hasbrouck's "fair promises" that he had "listed Six men who are mad at me for Deceiving them."

Very soon, Davis wrote, he realized that he had been deceived. His land lay uncleared, his house unbuilt. He himself was drafted into the Continental service and whisked far from home while his wife and two little children remained behind "with nobody to provide for them." And when his term of enlistment was up and Davis returned home he found that Hasbrouck proposed withholding much of his pay on the ground that Davis had not lived up to his commitment. But Hasbrouck's superiors ruled that Davis had indeed been deceived and had made a "Sinister contract" with Hasbrouck. Davis and others in his predicament were awarded a small bounty in the hope that they would be encouraged to re-enlist.

Davis did not re-enlist. But he remained sympathetic to the Whig side and on at least one occasion supplied information on possible enemy movements. Isaac was a son of Samuel and Elsie Davis, who lived on a farm with a site for a grist mill on the Little Beaverkill, near the point at which it ends its journey from Yankeetown Pond and merges with the Esopus Creek; his brother Jacobus had joined the Regulars, and had been captured and sentenced to death. Jacobus had been pardoned when he agreed to enlist in a Whig regiment. Isaac's brother Peter married Theodosia Ferris, daughter of Samuel and Mary Ferris of what is now Bearsville; Theodosia's Tory brother Joshua had joined the Regulars. Isaac's wife was Catharina Rowe, daughter of Tory Frederick Rowe, Jr. of Little Shandaken.

All these connections put Isaac in a position to pick up information of interest to the Whigs, and that is what he did in a warning letter of May 11, 1779. Isaac began, "These are the inteligence I Can give from the Indians after they Returned from Shandaken." The course of the war was then adding to the fear and doubt which had been part of Woodstock life since 1776. George Washington had become convinced that the only way of removing the threat of Indian and British assaults on the Hudson Valley from the west and northwest was by destroying the prosperous Indian villages to the west of the Catskills and the Delaware Valley. The British found out what was being planned against them and their allies; by way of blunting the Whig attack they stepped up border raids and made their presence felt along the line separating British and Whig held territory in New York. The year before had been marked by bloody British raids on Cherry Valley, Wyoming in Pennsylvania, and other border settlements.[11]

In the spring of 1779 similar raids were feared by Hudson Valley people; some were getting out of Kingston before the blow could strike. On May 4th a raiding party struck at the settlement of Fantinekill in Wawarsing; eleven civilians were killed. At about the same time General George Clinton received a report of "the Appearance of about 100 Indians & Tories at Great Shandeacon. They were joined at that Place by 27 Tories, chiefly Hessian Deserters, from the Convention Troops & soon after disappeared without doing any Misschief." The "Convention troops" had served under General Burgoyne and had deserted after Burgoyne's surrender at Saratoga.[12]

Clinton hastened to Kingston in response to what seemed a possible prelude to a British push across the Catskills and down the Esopus Valley. Davis' letter of May 11 confirmed the many hints of trouble which Clinton had recently received. The Indians and Tories at Shandaken, Davis wrote, ". . .was to Go to fitch Brandt with his Company to Come Down this Quarter, Burn and Distroy where Ever they Come. . . ." Davis outlined what he had heard of the British intentions and concluded with "These Informations I have Received from my wife; from Whom she has it I Dont know, But the whole to remain a Secrit."

Very quickly Clinton took action. He ordered a strengthening of defenses, including the setting up of one fort in the Boiceville of our day and another at Lackawack in the upper Rondout Valley. Late that summer the attack on the Indian settlements along the Susquehanna

River took place and Indian power was largely destroyed. Border warfare, however, continued, if on a smaller scale, and those Woodstock people who had not left for safer localities remained on the alert, especially by night, for strange sounds that might tell of a British officer or a Woodstock neighbor on the prowl disguised as an Indian.[13]

A recently arrived Scottish immigrant named Thomas Cummins came to Woodstck one night and stored several barrels of tinsmith's and japanner's tools and a mahogany bedstead in the Mill House or the one in which John Croft lived. The goods belonged to John Burch, who been obliged to given up a prosperous business in New York and later in Albany because of his Tory convictions. Cummins helped manage Burch's landholdings along the East Branch of the Delaware, where Burch supplied British raiding parties with food and recruits. Woodstock Whigs learned of the cache in the Mill House and confiscated it. Cummins was captured and his services to Britain earned him a sentence of death. His letter of September 27 1779, successfully appealing the sentence, is a touching document. He wrote that "Situated on a frontier Settlement open to the inroads of a Savage Army, unprotected by the state to which he belonged, and ignorant of the Points on which the Law defining Treason turns, your Petitioner calls an omniscient God to witness that what he did flowed from Necessity and not from Choice, and was done solely to save his Property and Life . . . " [14]

Some Tories who operated with more discretion than Cummins managed to escape arrest throughout the War. Among them was Frederick Rowe, Jr. of Little Shandaken, who operated a kind of Tory post office at his house. "I have been informed," wrote a Whig officer to General George Clinton, "of one Row, living toward the Blue Mountains behind Sopis; said Row Receives all the letters from the Enemie and does send them to the disaffected and likewise the letters directed to the Enemie are forwarded by him . . . " [15]

Young Woodstock men encouraged by their parents left their tenant farms each spring to join the forces of Colonel Butler or Brant and take part often in Indian disguise in raids on settlements along the Ulster frontier. In March of 1781 a "Party of Rascals formerly Deserted from Woodstock & Shandaken . . . arrived at Little Shandaken for the Purpose of Recruiting and watching an opportunity to Carry some good men off, and while there were Entertained by Frederick Rowe, Peter Winnen, Nicolaus Britt & others . . . " So wrote Colonel Johannis Snyder of the First Ulster County Regiment.[16]

While much of Woodstock's Revolutionary history is supported by reliable contemporary evidence and much rests on tradition, one piece seems to have resulted from nothing more than an error made many years ago. In 1838 William L. Stone's *Life of Joseph Brant* was published in two volumes. On page 64 of the second volume there is an account of the raid on Fantinekill of May 4 by "thirty of forty of Butler's Rangers." Following the flight of the raiders from Fantinekill, Stone goes on to explain, some of them "fell upon the town of Woodstock, in the neighborhood of Kingston, where they burned several houses and committed other depredations. They made a few prisonners, some of whom were carried away; while others were compelled, by the up-raised hatchet, to take an oath not to serve in arms against the King." The source given for the incident is John Almon's *Remembrancer*, a London periodical which presented among other reports of interest to the Englishman of the 1780s many accounts of the war then going on in America.

A search of the appropriate numbers of the *Remembrancer* turned up no mention of Woodstock. But it located an account of the famous Wyoming Massacre in Pennsylvania in 1779 and the statement that, following the massacre, "the enemy appeared on the mountains back of Kingston" and made raids. Neither here nor elsewhere in the *Remembrancer* is there any mention of activities in Woodstock, N.Y.; it seems very likely that William L. Stone had confused the Kingston, Pa. of Almon's report with Kingston, N.Y. The incident as given by Stone was reprinted from time to time and eventually found brief mention in one of the best of the multi-volumed histories of America published during the nineteenth century, Justin Winsor's *Narrative and Critical History of America*. There Woodstock as well as Fantinekill were said to have had "houses destroyed, cattle killed, and prisoners taken." A recent reprint of the sixth volume of the Winsor history contains the error intact.[17]

Another Revolutionary incident has all the confirmation the one reported by Stone lacks. In fact, there is so much evidence to support this story that anyone trying to track down all of it can't help becoming overwhelmed by detail, though the detail is not always in agreement. This is the story of the capture by Tories of two Woodstock men, Peter Short and Short's son-in-law Peter Miller on a Sunday in June 1780.

The capture took place at a time when Woodstock people were in a state of excitement over a Tory and Indian raid of a few weeks earlier which had resulted in the looting and burning of the house in Blue Mountain of Captain Jeremiah Snyder (the same Captain Snyder who had been in command at Little Shandaken) and his son Elias; the Captain and his son had been captured and led off to prison in Canada. The story of Short and Miller is mentioned in the letters and reports of Revolutionary officials. Related with embellishments in local histories, it has been repeated for close to two centuries by the descendants of the two men involved and by the descendants of their friends and neighbors. A historical marker was set up by the State of New York during the 1930s at the site of the capture. The marker stands a little across the Woodstock line on the soil of the town of Saugerties. And so Saugerties historians have a right to claim the story and have taken advantage of that opportunity.

Because of its human interest the story of the capture of Short and Miller is Woodstock's most popular Revolutionary incident—and likely to remain so. Among the most interesting and informative versions is the one given by Peter Short's grandson Moses, printed in the Kingston *Weekly Freeman* of April 1, 1886 under a heading which stresses the story's romantic aspects. It goes:

THE DAYS OF TORY RULE
Moses Short, of South Woodstock, Tells a Thrilling Story

In Mingo Hollow When the Times Tried Men's Souls—A Long Weary Journey—Faces Painted Black—An Indian's Intercession.

Earlier in 1886 the *Freeman* had printed an account of the Short and Miller incident and placed it in 1777 with the two men and their wives having been killed. Eighty-year-old Moses, at his home in South Woodstock, now known as Wittenberg, read the story, was outraged at what he rightly regarded as its inaccuracies, and made his feelings known. The *Freeman* dispatched a reporter to South Woodstock to interview the old man and get his "true account." And it was this account which appeared on April 1 under the newspaper's arresting headline.

Short and Miller, their wives (both named Annatje) and three children had gone to their church to have the Millers' baby baptized,

Moses Short said. The church was the one at Katsbaan. Church records bear out the story. They show that on June 18, 1780 the church's pastor, Laurentius De Ronde, baptized the Millers' son Petrus. The witnesses were Petrus Short and Annatje Bakker, his wife.

On their way home by wagon the Shorts and Millers were surprised at finding the road obstructed by a rope stretched across it. One of the men jumped down from the wagon to remove the rope, and at that moment four Tories appeared. The Tories "proceeded to cut the harness from the horses. They told the women folks to go home, and not say anything of the occurrence, for if they did, they would be killed. The Tories then placed heavy loads on the backs of Mr. Short and Mr. Miller, they taking the horses and started for Canada." This was the usual destination of Whig captives; there prison awaited them and a reward was paid to their captors.

"On arriving at the town of Hunter, Mr. Short begged the Tories to let the horses loose, so they would return to the women who would use them in working the land. One Tory being a relative of my father, prevailed on the others to let the horses go and they went safely back to South Woodstock. The journey was then resumed. Mr. Miller assisting my father across the streams with the heavy load on his back, he being sixty-four years of age. Mr. Miller was a young man and could carry his burden better. At night the Tories tied the hands of the two men behind their backs so the mosquitoes could bite them. When they laid down to rest a Tory lay between them so as to watch them and prevent an escape. Before reaching Canada the faces of the captives were painted black. One day, meeting some Indians, my father was knocked down with the breech of a musquet in the hands of one of the savages, and another attempted to shoot Mr. Miller, but fortunately the gun only snapped and his life was spared. Then a chief named John Runnet came up, and recognizing my grand father whom he knew before the war began, asked the Tories what the men had done to be made prisoners and why their faces were painted black. The Tories told the Chief that they had done nothing except they had a fort near their house, in which were 50 armed men. Runnet, the Chief, then said to the prisoners that they had been painted black so they would be killed and told them to go wash it off. He made the Tories take them to Canada, telling them to use the captives well, and if he did not he would kill them on his return from the South, where he was going to obtain prisoners."

The *Freeman* story concludes by telling how after a year of imprisonment in Canada Short was exchanged. A year after that Miller escaped and returned to Woodstock "where he and his father-in-law lived for years, neighbors to the Tories, who had captured them and caused them so much suffering."

Other accounts do not agree in detail with the one given by Moses Short and probably garbled a bit by the *Freeman's* reporter. The captured Peter Short was Moses' grandfather and not his father (his father was Peter, Jr.). The Indian who saved the lives of the two men is sometimes given as Joe DeWit—most accounts make him the John Renhope or Runnip who looked out from the top of the Blue Mountains and had taken part in the capture of Jeremiah and Elias Snyder on May 6, 1780.[18]

According to some accounts Short and Miller both escaped and Short was not exchanged—there are many other variations. A Saugerties clergyman related that as the men were captured one of the Tories snatched a high fur hat which Short was wearing that June day, put it on his own head and capered about in derision.[19]

The *Freeman's* story gives the site of Peter Short's house as South Woodstock, but this was not the case, although Moses and his father lived there. The suggestion in Moses' story that his grandfather was picked out for capture because of the "fort near his house" is a good point not mentioned in any other account. Armed men were certainly stationed at the picket fort at or close to Short's house and this gave him an importance in Tory eyes which made him well worth capturing. The *Freeman's* story does not state that the Tories who captured Short and Miller were disguised, nor that they were accompanied by genuine Indians, as was usually the case. Other accounts mention both disguises and Indians.

The *Freeman* ends its story with Short and Miller back home and living as neighbors to some of their captors of 1780. This may be borne out by an often-repeated bit of Woostock lore which has Peter, some years after his return, meeting one of his captors and suggesting that the two let bygones be bygones.

The capture of Short and Miller was the last recorded episode of the violence that marked Revolutionary days in Woodstock. The war was moving on toward its end, and deep discouragement was overtaking Woodstock Tories.

The population of Woodstock had been dwindling since 1776, due in part to fear of living on the frontier exposed to raiding and skirmishing of Whigs, Indians (real and imitation) and British. Also, official Whig policy urged and often required settlers to move back from the frontier zone to older settlements. Those who were Tories could there be of less help to the enemy and those who were Whigs would not raise grain, hay and cattle only to have them seized by the enemy. Yet because prices of agricultural production were very high many settlers returned to their farms in the spring to plant and in the late summer to harvest, leaving their houses, barns and fields unprotected in between.

The Continental Congress had been concerned by the problems posed by the continued lingering-on of settlers on the frontier and in 1778 had urged all frontier dwellers to move back, taking with them their cattle and furniture, women and children. In New York Governor Clinton had not been successful in his attempts to move settlers from the frontiers. Little Shandaken was so very "Toreyfied" as to be a continual source of difficulty.[20]

In 1781 Governor Clinton acted decisively and "ordered the Inhabitants along the Frontier to move from their places." Little Shandaken became completely deserted and many of the remaining people of Woodstock were escorted by troops to Kingston or Saugerties. Colonel Johannis Snyder of the First Ulster County Regiment reported from Kingston on April 29, 1781 that "A Party of Levies are gone this morning to guard the family of Peter Short down from Woodstock. . . ." Less than a year later, on January 3, 1782, Colonel Snyder again wrote to the Governor. His letter is one of the most informative of all documents dealing with the Revolution in Woodstock. Snyder told of a recent incident which sheds a clear light on the situation of Woodstock's Tories as the Revolution neared its end.[21]

Ever since he had evacuated the frontiers, the Colonel wrote, there had been "no trouble on our frontiers of Enemy (except that Party Burning and Plundering at Wawaarsinck) and on the Retreat of the Party five of those that had Carried of Capt. Jeremiah Snyder & others Deserted from the Party and came to Little Shandaken Expecting to find their Parents & Friends. . . ." The five men found neither parents nor friends, only empty houses and barns and pastures. There was not even a single horse or cow to welcome them. They went on past Shandaken Lake and down to Woodstock. And there too they found silence and emptiness. Only when they came to Awaghkonk did they find human beings in the shape of Lieutenant Van Deusen and his rangers, whom they managed to escape. They continued down the Sawkill Valley and came to the house of Tory Arie Van Etten. Van Etten had fled. "But hunger forced them to apply to one Hommel who lived in Van Etten's house for Victuals. Hommel being alone gave them victuals. They told Hommel they did belong to that party at Wawaarsinck and had Deserted for want of Provision and wo'd, if their Country wo'd forgive them, surrender to their Country and serve faithfull but were afraid the Country wo'd take their lives. They did not know what to do." [22]

The burning of Wawarsing on August 12, 1781 was the last border raid of the Revolution in the Catskills. The five men who deserted there must have met their disappointment at Little Shandaken and Woodstock a week or so later. By then the military phase of the Revolution was nearly over; Cornwallis' surrender at Yorktown was less than two months in the future. The end of the war found Woodstock almost a ghost town. The continuity of its development had been broken. Many problems faced the men, women and children who began trickling back to the three settlements of Woodstock, Little Shandaken and Awaghkonck.

10

WOODSTOCK
BECOMES A TOWN

I t is not always easy to form a clear picture of the flow of Woodstock history as it moves from the past to the present. Evidence on many points is scanty or contradictory. And even when there is a good deal of reliable evidence confusion is hard to avoid because so many things are happening at the same time. One such period is that between 1785 and 1810. During these twenty-five years Woodstock became an organized town, shrunk from its original enormous size to approximately its present borders, changed its absentee landlords, experienced a substantial increase in population, and saw the beginnings of industries which had important results for the town and its people.

First in time came the organization. Before the Revolution the people living in what is now Woodstock were content to get along without any organized local government. Ulster County officials had jurisdiction over them in such matters as law enforcement, land transfers and so on. As far as is known no elections were held in Woodstock. Roads were laid out and maintained by great landowners, with their tenants usually doing the pick-and-shovel work in part payment of their rents.[1]

On March 12, 1778 the New York State Legislature had taken a roundabout first step toward giving Woodstock and its neighboring settlements organization as towns. The step was said to have been taken for military reasons. But, as soon became apparent, hostilities between lowland Ulster County people and those of the Hardenbergh Patent with their differing ways of life were also at work.

Woodstock and most of the rest of the old Hardenbergh Patent lands were owned by absentee landlords, and most of the inhabitants were poor tenants or squatters. In contrast much of the rest of Ulster County in which the entire Patent was long included was a prosperous place of staid slave-owning farmers who owned their acres. Ulster County farms by Revolutionary days had often already been handed down for several generations from the original settlers to their descendants. Their farmhouses were substantial stone structures reminiscent in appearance to the homes of their Dutch and Walloon ancestors. These houses were accompanied by broad low barns of the kind known as "Dutch barns." In Woodstock, by contrast, tenants' houses were often makeshift buildings planned to last out the duration of a lease for three lives and nothing more, or they were brush-and-bark huts used in summer only.

The arrival of the Revolution intensified the doubts and suspicions which divided the well-nourished lowland farmers and the struggling Patent people. During the Revolution most of the Patent people became Tories while the lowland people, with few exceptions, turned into devoted Whigs. The two groups viewed each other with a mingling of fear and distrust. When the progress of the Revolution made advisable some kind of organization of Woodstock and its neighboring settlements, the Legislature acted in an atmosphere colored by lowland-Patent animosities.[2]

The 1778 act's title didn't hint that its final clause was of close concern to Woodstock. "An ACT for encreasing the number of assessors throughout the State," it read. The final clause read in part, "[A]s well for the purpose of assessments, as all military purposes whatsoever, the settlements of *Woodstock*, of Great and Little *Shandaken*, be and are hereby severally annexed to and made parts of the township of Hurley." The act went on to annex the settlement of Lackawack to the town of Rochester in Ulster County; Lackawack lay on the border of the Hardenbergh Patent. The principal purpose of the act was to make possible the collection of the tax the Legislature had imposed on the fathers of young men who had "gone off" to join the British forces. The tax was based on an assessment of the property of the fathers. Very few lowland Ulster fathers would be affected by the tax, but many Woodstock and Shandaken fathers would.

The attachment of Woodstock and the Shandakens took place on paper only. Hurley refused to absorb the Tory settlements into its own township. The refusal and the emotion that lay behind it are well documented by a letter written on January 11, 1781 by Hurley's supervisor, Charles D. DeWitt, to Governor George Clinton.[3]

DeWitt began by admitting that he was charged by the Legislature to see to it that an assessment was made "on Persons whose Son or Sons are gone off, to the Enemy." But, DeWitt said, there were no such persons "whish the law reaches" in Hurley. And although "the People of Woodstock, Great & Little Shandaken are by an act of the Legislature annexed to the Town of Hurley I do not find that they were ever under the command of the Captain of Hurley, or were ever considered as being within his beat. I confess it is a Pity that such notorious offenders as some of them are, should escape Taxing, and yet is fortunate for Capt. Lafever [he was the Captain of Hurley] that they are not in his Beat, as very great uneasiness and discontent hath Prevailed among the People of Hurley since that extraordinary addition to Hurley, which every Person that has the least knowledge of the situation of the three Towns can easily see, would have been better suited the two adjacent Towns.

"If some Folks in Kingston had not appeared so very officious with their assistance [insistence] to me, to Tax these men, I should perhaps not have entertained so strong a suspicion that their Design was only to forge another Rivet, to fix them fast to Hurley; and least any misrepresentations take place, I thought it my Duty to acquaint you, Sir, that in my opinion I could not call upon these people as lying within the Captain's Beat, which the Law expressly mentions."

Supervisor DeWitt gives vivid expression to the very hostile feelings of the people of Hurley, with their clean Whig record, toward the Tory-filled three Hardenbergh Patent settlements. His suspicion that Kingston people had a hand in forcing the three settlements upon Hurley may well be true. DeWitt's refusal to accept the settlements was apparently condoned. There is no known record of any attempt to compel him to carry out the provisions of the law of March 12, 1778.

Woodstock was indeed in an unhappy state as the Revolution ended, unloved by its neighbors, its pre-War settlers gone, without a town government, with squatters moving into empty cabins and skimpily tilling clearings in the hope of snatching a crop or two before they were discovered. Of all the leases and lease agreements entered into by tenants and Robert Livingston or his son Judge Robert R. in pre-War times only one survived the turmoil of the Revolution. And it should come as no surprise to learn that this was the lease (dated 1770) of Peter Short. Here as elsewhere Short behaved as if bent on asserting a claim to be Woodstock's oldest and most active and alert settler—he continued to make appearances in Woodstock history until a few years before his death in 1808.[4]

The confused state of Woodstock as the Revolution came to an end in 1783 (the treaty ending the war was not ratified until the following year) did not prevent one group of men, the trustees of Kingston, from sensing opportunity in Woodstock. The trustees recognized that the future prosperity of their town depended on their developing Kingston as a trading and shipping center for the back country, which now the war was over could be expected to fill with settlers. And these settlers, provided they were given usable roads converging on Kingston, would soon be sending their wheat, lumber, maple sugar, hay and other "country produce" to Kingston. It seemed logical that a good share of the money they received would be spent in Kingston. The action the trustees took played a part in giving Woodstock the shape it would have before very long.

After a preliminary exploration of the back country had been made the trustees decided on two roads, both of which had been in existence before the Revolution but had almost vanished during the war. One road followed the Esopus Creek westward and crossed the high Catskills at Pine Hill before swooping down upon the fertile valley of the Delaware. The other made its way through Woodstock by way of the old Esopus Road and went on to Little Shandaken. There it joined what was left of the road that back in 1773 had found its way up narrow Mink Hollow and through the pass that separates Sugarloaf and Plateau Mountains; from there it moved on to the elevated lands bordering the Schoharie Creek and eventually, it was hoped, would follow the creek toward its junction with the Mohawk. The route provided the easiest possible access from the Hudson Valley to the settlements of the valley of the Schoharie; it had few steep grades and considering the irregular topography of the Catskills was very direct.

Before 1783 was over the trustees, probably stimulated by large landowners along the route, offered a reward of two hundred pounds for "a good road that can be used with a Cart Waggon or Slay in Summer and Winter carrying loads and freights to and from Little Shandaken and the Schohary Kill or the settlements there." Very soon the route became alive with workers with axes, picks and shovels.

Whites and blacks, free men and slaves toiled together as the road moved upward from Lake Hill and then down to the banks of the Schoharie Kill. The work was financed and guided by "the Marchents of Kingston," as its backers described themselves.

Sixty-five men worked on the project. Some among them—Abraham Cole, William Castle, Hendrick Short and Peter Miller—were tenants on the Livingston lands in Woodstock. Miller was the same man who not long before had returned from captivity in Canada. Most of the workers were from Kingston. At least six were slaves whose pay went to their owners. The pay for ordinary workers was "three shillings pr. Day from the Day they shall enter until discharged, or at the Rate of four shillings pr. Day to those who may only chuse to work in fair weather." [5]

The effect on Woodstock of what was known as the "Schoharie (or Schohariekill) Road" quickly became apparent. The center of Little Shandaken (where the Mink Hollow Road takes off from Route 212) became a crossroads with a promising future. From this point a rough road already followed the Beaverkill westward across the flats at Willow and through what would soon be known as DeVall Hollow, joining the Kingston-Delaware Road in Great Shandaken at what is now the hamlet of Mount Tremper. The crossroad was centrally located in relation to the parts of the four Great Lots of the Hardenbergh Patent which were going into the making of Woodstock. By reviving the pre-war Schoharie Road the Kingston merchants had brought the sparse settlements known as Schoharie Kill into a closer relationship to the settlement of Woodstock. People considering establishing a town of Woodstock could now see the town as including Schoharie Kill and Great Shandaken linked by road to the crossroads at Little Shandaken.

Because of the promising commercial future of the Little Shandaken-Mink Hollow crossroads, Captain Elias Hasbrouck settled there. He had been not only a captain of the Revolutionary Rangers but a quartermaster of the Army as well as a Kingston merchant. Now he gave up his Kingston business and built a house at the entrance to Mink Hollow and proposed running a store and an inn there so he might take advantage of the busy traffic expected to flow over the new road.[6]

As work on the Schoharie Road went forward, the Livingston Great Lot 8 became involved in a lengthy project which would also have an effect on the shape of the town of Woodstock. The project had its origin in the desire of the heirs and assigns of the eight men and one woman who had bought the Hurley Patentee Woods back in 1709 to divide the Woods among themselves. These people, unlike earlier sharers in the Woods, did not think of the Woods as committed to remaining forever uncultivated and a source of firewood and pasture alone. Once the Revolution was over Americans had been seized by a passion for speculating in land. This probably influenced the Hurley owners of the Patentees Woods to want to partition the land so each owner might do as he or she chose. An act of the State Legislature of March 16, 1785 made easier the partitioning of lands held in common. Soon the first steps under the new act were being taken in Hurley—the final step would not be completed (after much tedious and complicated work and compromise) until 1806.[7]

First of all it was necessary to survey and mark the line dividing the Livingston lands in Great Lot 8 from the Hurley Woods. This line was identical through much of its length with the town of Woodstock-town of Hurley line which would soon come into being. William Cockburn and the two other surveyors found the line none too easy to locate. Some of the heaps of stones and marked trees which testified to former surveys could not be found. Old inhabitants were then hired to do their best to scramble over mountains and rocks in an effort to locate the lines; Peter Short, by then the oldest inhabitant of Woodstock as far as anyone knew, and Peter Miller were among those hired.

Complications resulting from the survey affected Peter's sons Zachary and Peter, Jr. Both had settled before 1786 upon what they believed to be Livingston lands near Yankeetown Pond in what is now called Wittenberg. The survey revealed that the farms of the two Shorts and a number of other settlers straddled the Livingston-Hurley line as it was then agreed upon. Adjustments were made. The Shorts and their neighbors received leases from the trustees of Hurley for those parts of their lands which lay within Hurley. The Livingston owner allowed his tenants to retain the rights in the Woodstock commons which had gone with their original lease agreements.

In the course of the boundary study and settlement the old Beekman claim to the Woodstock flatlands reached its end. After making a half-hearted effort to revive their claim, Henry Beekman's descendants realized that they had no chance of success and dropped it for good.[8]

Vigorous efforts toward creating a town of Woodstock got under way. A petition circulated among Woodstock settlers and landowners was forwarded to the State Legislature; the petitioners asked that a separate town to be called Woodstock be set up by act of Legislature. They gave compelling reasons: "They live remote from other inhabitants, and have no town officers to regulate the roads, or to compel any persons to work upon them; and they are subject to other inconveniences, by means whereof other persons are discouraged from settling among them." The new town would be formed of the three settlements of Woodstock and Great and Little Shandaken. Awaghkonck by this time was regarded as divided between Kingston and Woodstock and so was not named.[9]

On April 11, 1787 the Legislature passed "An Act to erect the settlements of Woodstock and Great and Little Shandaken, in Ulster county into a separate township." The boundaries of the town as described in the act began at "the head of Cartwrights Kill" (this was the outlet of North Lake in the present town of Hunter), then followed the Albany-Ulster county line as far as the northeastern corner of Great Lot 20 of the Hardenbergh Patent; this point was close to West Settlement in the present town of Ashland. The line then followed the Great Lot 20's eastern line "about fourteen miles" southward and continued beyond this line for "about eight miles" until it struck the northern line of Great Lot 7, owned by the descendants of Robert Livingston's partner in acquisition, Gulian Verplanck. This point on the Great Lot 7 line lay in what is now the town of Middletown in Delaware County.

From there the line followed the Great Lot 7 boundary southeasterly "about eighteen miles to the bounds of Marbletown." It crossed the "Esopus Kill," moved eastward until it struck the bounds of Kingston, which it followed northward to the head of Cartwrights Kill, the point of beginning. No new survey was made of the Woodstock boundaries. Old and sometimes debatable ones were relied on, which is why the description of the town given in the act is sometimes contradictory or vague. The Hurley-Woodstock line, which was not yet officially agreed upon, was sketched out in the most unspecific way imaginable.

The new Woodstock formed an immense town, covering at least 450 square miles. That made it larger than many a European principality or grand duchy, much larger than modern Liechtenstein with only 65 square miles. Wooodstock was far too huge a township to have any chance of functioning well. Yet under the terms of the authorizing act an attempt at functioning had to be made. The act required Woodstock people to assemble in their first town meeting on the first Tuesday in June, 1787 and then and there elect "one supervisor, one town clerk, three assessors, one collector, two constables, two overseers of the poor, three commissioners of highways, and so many overseers of the highways, fence viewers and pound masters, as to the freeholders and inhabitants of the same township, so met, shall seem necessary and convenient . . . "

The collector was the collector of taxes. The commissioners of highways had the duty of laying out and caring for highways. Each overseer was responsible for the upkeep of the highways in his own part of the town—there was no superintendent of all town highways as there is today. The fence viewers saw to it that fences were adequate to keep cattle, horses and hogs from escaping from their owners' farms and damaging the crops of neighbors. If any did escape they were caught and held by the pound masters.[10]

The first town meeting and election of Woodstock (this was the actual birthday of the town) was held at the house of Captain Elias Hasbrouck in Little Shandaken on Tuesday, June 5. The record of the meeting in the town clerk's minute book indicates that few people from outside Woodstock and Little Shandaken attended. Among the "Parsons [who] ware by Plurality of Voyces Chosen Town Officers" none were inhabitants of the outlying parts of the township. All "taxable persons" were allowed to vote, meaning that Livingston tenants, who were unable under the property qualifications of the time to vote for most officials above the town level, could vote and be elected. Elias Hasbrouck became Woodstock's first supervisor. John Rowe, son of Tory Frederick Rowe, Jr., became town clerk. The two overseers of the poor, Andries Riselar (Andrew Riseley) and Barent Lewis, were Livingston tenants.

And as might have been expected Peter Short, now seventy-one years old (according to family tradition), was elected the first of the three assessors; an assessor was required to have a good knowledge of his town and its people—and this Short had, although he was unable to read or write. Peter's son Zachary became tax collector and old Peter himself served the town double as a commissioner of highways.[11]

The organization of Woodstock had some immediate effects. It stimulated an influx of new settlers and raised the hopes for profit of large landowners. At the same time Woodstock felt the effects of difficulties which were plaguing all the United States. A period of deflation had followed the brief boom stimulated by the ending of the Revolution, enormous imports from Britain of manufactured goods had stifled American industry, and the national government was in the process of painful alterations.

In 1787, as Woodstock people were preparing for their first town meeting, a Constitutional Convention was meeting in Philadelphia—it would propose replacing the Articles of Confederation under which the nation had been operating with a new kind of government based on a written constitution. Supervisor Hasbrouck was an Anti-Federalist. He agreed with most Woodstock people in opposing adoption of the new Constitution on the ground that it gave too much power to the federal government and favored the rich.

As Hasbrouck and the rest of the original officers of Woodstock took office, the town had many obvious problems with which to grapple. Its boundaries were still vague in many places; the town was too large and unwieldy for effective government. Yet in spite of its many difficulties the place had taken a long step forward—it had become an organized and functioning town.[12]

11

MADAME LIVINGSTON TAKES OVER

All through Woodstock's colonial years the place had behaved as if determined to resist conforming to the usual image of an American settlement in the wilderness. After the Revolution, it was still not the kind of place to which a man could go to hack out a farm of his own from the forest, do as he pleased with it, and then hand it down to his descendants far into the future. Instead unusual conditions of settlement were imposed by Robert Livingston, who seemed bent on setting up in the New World the kind of landlord-dominated settlement which prevailed in the Old World and to which emigrants had fled to America to escape. Livingston's leases for three lives—with their restrictions on a tenant's freedom, their payments of rents in wheat, labor and fat hens—were antiquarian survivals, hardly in line with the new kind of society emerging in America. It was not surprising that many Woodstock tenants, conditioned by the European way of life required of them by their landlord, resisted Americanization and when the Revolution arrived displayed marked devotion to King George the Third.

For these as well as other reasons, when Woodstock began its career as an organized town in 1787 it came into a large, rich and often confusing inheritance from its colonial past. That was why many of the town's Tories did not flee to Canada and British protection as Tories did elsewhere but remained and did business as usual.

87

Various members of the Rowe family remained prominent. Not only was John Rowe elected Woodstock's first town clerk but his prosperous uncle Wilhelmus became justice of the peace (an office then conferred by county appointment). Wilhelmus was later elected supervisor and an overseer of the poor; in addition to being a farmer, he was also Woodstock's first known moneylender. And Frederick Rowe, Jr., in spite of his record of enthusiastic Tory activity, was in such good favor with the Livingstons of Clermont that they sold him outright in 1787 the farm at Lake Hill originally settled by the Chadwicks. Madame Livingston, however, retained the part touching Cooper Lake, which was expected to rise in value because the new Schohariekill Road would cross it. Rowe lived there on good terms with the neighbors who had been his mortal enemies a few years earlier. The Tory Winnes, however, lost their lease.[1]

A significant share of Woodstock's colonial inheritance grew out of its division into five parts, each with characteristics of its own. Four of these parts had been determined in 1749 when the partitioning of the Hardenbergh Patent created the divisions known as Great Lots 8, 24, 25 and 26. Each of the parts of these Great Lots in Woodstock had its own proprietor, and each proprietor had his own way of doing things.

After Woodstock became a town, the part lying in Great Lot 8 with its Livingston tenants and squatters continued to dominate. It contained by far the most land and people. The everyday language of Great Lot 8 was a dialect of Dutch, although English was making inroads. A story in the Reynolds family of Shady tells of a small son of the first Reynolds to arrive in Woodstock from New England in the 1790s. The boy had come home from school across the Great Lot 8 line on the edge of Great Lot 25 in tears. His classmates had ridiculed him because he was the only one in the school who couldn't speak Dutch. The Dutch dialect of Woodstock would have been hard to understand even for a Dutchman. It had elements of the German of the town's Palatine-descended settlers plus a bit of English added to a base of the kind of Dutch spoken in Holland a century and more earlier.[2]

Great Lot 26, to the north of the eastern part of Great Lot 8, had few inhabitants, in part because most of it was occupied by rocky Overlook Mountain and was therefore unfit for farming. Another reason for the Lot's sparse peopling was its owner. Portly, speculating Cornelius Tiebout had no children, and therefore unlike Robert

Livingston could have had no ambition to pass his lands down intact to his posterity. Upon his death in 1785, he willed his Woodstock holdings to his young widow and his nephew and namesake Cornelius Tiebout Hertell.

Tiebout had high hopes for profits from coal and other minerals he believed were hidden away on Overlook Mountain. He did not lease his lands to farmer-tenants. But when a chance came along for selling at a good price a tract of five hundred acres or so suitable for farming he took advantage of it. He made one such sale of six hundred acres, including part of the present hamlet of Woodstock, to John Read, "farmer of Rynbeck" in Dutchess County, in 1774. It is significant that Tiebout reserved rights to "coal mines and all other mines and minerals whatever . . ." [3]

Tiebout and his brother-in-law Christian Hertell were involved in speculations or investments in industrial projects. Both, Hertell especially, had been interested in a glassmaking venture at New Windsor in what is now Orange County. It is quite likely that Tiebout saw his Woodstock lands as having an industrial and mining future above all else. He may have foreseen the industrial development which would take place on his lands in the upper Sawkill Valley more than twenty years after his death.

The people his dealings brought to Woodstock were quite different from the Dutch-speaking tenant farmers of Great Lot 8. The names of John Read or Reid and James Farquharson of New York to whom Tiebout sold a five-hundred-acre farm adjoining Read's to the east, suggest a Scottish background. Farquharson, it was stated in his deed of 1775, "speedily intends to remove to and reside . . ." in Ulster County. Though there is no evidence Farquharson ever carried out his intention, evidently Read did move to his new farm. A deed of 1788 refers to him as "late of Woodstock." The outbreak of the Revolution probably kept both men from settling permanently in the town.

The relationship of owners and settlers to the land differed on Great Lots 8 and 26; it differed from both on Great Lot 25, owned by James Desbrosses, "of the City of New-York, Merchant." Here, once the rush set off by the building of the Schoharie Road was under way, Desbrosses' agents, William Cockburn and his brother James of Rhinebeck, drew up leases which called for a payment "yearly and every year forever" of one shilling per acre "to be paid in Spanish Milled Dollars, at the rate of Eight Shillings each Dollar, or so much

Current Money of the State of New-York as shall be equal in value to Spanish Milled Dollars, at Eight Shillings each Dollar. . . ." All taxes were to be paid by the tenant, as were the costs of surveying and drawing up of leases.

A Desbrosses tenant, provided he were sure of a small amount of cash income, had a far better deal than a man on Livingston land. He could cut the timber on his farm without restriction, he could build a house without the stone-walled cellar required on Great Lot 8; if he sold his leasehold he need not pay any part of what he received to his landlord. And best of all his lease ran on—provided he paid his rent—forever and might be willed to his children or to whomever he chose. A disadvantage of the Great Lot 25 land within the Woodstock of 1787 was that it was so elevated that its crops had a shorter growing season. Much of the part of Great Lot 25 lying in the Woodstock of today was in Mink Hollow, hemmed in and shadowed by mountains.[4]

Great Lot 24 was the least settled part of the new Town of Woodstock. Soon after Gabriel G. Ludlow sold his half of the Lot to John Carle in 1774, the Revolution saw Ludlow commanding a Long Island regiment which took the part of the King; after military reverses Ludlow fled to Canada. In 1779 an act of the New York State Legislature included him in a list of prominent Tories who were attainted, which meant among other things that their lands within the United States were confiscated. During the war it was on the Ludlow-Carle part of Great Lot 24 that Tories spent the winter, giving rise to much local lore. When the war ended Col. Ludlow made a claim to the British government for lands in the Hardenbergh Patent which seem to have included those he once owned in Woodstock. The claim was not allowed.

Not long after the end of the Revolution John Carle was operating a sawmill possibly at a spot on Great Lot 24 still known as Sawmill Hill. A few years later he was proprietor of a tavern on Great Lot 8 close to the Little Shandaken crossroads. But for a few years longer the Great Lot 24 part of Woodstock was without settlers except probably for a few squatters who left no marks in the records.

Great Lot 24 was described by Chancellor Robert R. Livingston to English visitor William Strickland in these words: "This tract consisting of long ranges of lofty mountains, divided by deep vallies, has hitherto been scarcely explored, has very few settlers upon any part of it [these few were beyond the present Woodstock boundaries and along the Schohariekill in what is now Hunter] and is almost in a perfect state of nature and consequently harbours most of the wild animals of this part of the continent. Dear, Elks, Bears, Wolves, Panthers, Wildcats and various other lesser animals . . . "[5]

The fifth division of Woodstock in 1787 was the southeastern corner of Great Lot 26 and much of what is now Zena in Great Lot 8, the neighborhood long known as Awaghkonck. The first settlement of Woodstock had taken place on the fertile and level flats here beside the Sawkill. Awaghkonck was the most thoroughly Dutch part of the new town. Its stone farmhouses and prosperous farmers gave it the look of being the offshoot of Kingston, which in fact it was. The most important man in Awaghkonck was Justice Wilhelmus Rowe, who also owned the old Hardenbergh grist mill which still stands beside the Sawkill.[6]

In one unusual way the colonial inheritance of Great Lot 8 differed from that of the other parts which made up Woodstock. Great Lot 8 was owned by a woman, Margaret Beekman Livingston of Clermont, who became the landlord of most Woodstock settlers as the result of a swift succession of deaths which began in July 1775. Then old Robert Livingston died at Clermont while eagerly following the beginning of conflict in the Revolution. Less than six months later, his son, Judge Livingston, unexpectedly died. About three weeks later his father-in-law, Henry Beekman, died in his house at Rhinebeck. This succession of deaths had its effect on Woodstock.

The Judge had inherited his father's landholdings, except of course for Woodstock and Clermont, which had been conveyed to him earlier. But the interval between his father's death and his own was so brief and the times were so lively that the Judge didn't get around to changing his will to take into account the enormous landholdings which as his parents' only son he had inherited. Under the rule of primogeniture which still prevailed (it would soon be ended by act of legislature), Old Robert's Hardenbergh Patent lands went to the eldest son of the Judge and his wife; he was Robert R. Livingston.

Although his father had not devised his Hardenbergh Patent lands, young Robert R. was aware that he had expressed a wish that they be divided among his ten surviving children. Accordingly, in 1779, Robert R. conveyed a share of twenty to thirty thousand acres of land in the Patent to each of his brothers and sisters and retained a share for himself.[7]

This did not leave Margaret Livingston a propertyless widow dependent on her children—far from it. Had her father, Henry

Beekman, died while the Judge was still alive Beekman's property, except for a small part devised to his second wife, would have gone to Margaret's husband, the Judge. The law of the time did not permit a married woman to own property; property she might have before her marriage or might acquire afterwards belonged to her husband. A single woman or a widow, however, might own property in the same manner as a man.

Because he died before his father-in-law, Judge Livingston had been disappointed in his hope of becoming "absolutely the richest man in the Government." His widow, in her early fifties, became owner in her own right of the lands he had dreamed of. No longer the "full-bodied Dutch beauty" of her youth, she had become a rich and powerful woman characterized by people who knew her as above all "stately." While retaining the piety of her youth she now added to it, as if in response to the difficulties of the times and the demands of her new position, an energy and a persistence in accomplishing what she wanted to do that still emanate from her letters.

She became known to her tenants on both sides of the Hudson as Madame Livingston or sometimes as The Madame, and this name persisted among the descendants of her tenants for a century and a half. She developed a sort of imperiousness not unexpected in a person of her position in life. The letters of her children mention her with a respect bordering upon awe. At the same time Madame Livingston was known to be kind in her own haughty way. She had fifteen slaves, most of whom she freed in her will, and she provided as well for the maintenance of those ex-slaves who were old. Her Woodstock tenants passed on to their descendants as late as the 1920s a warm image of the Madame; when tenants travelled from Woodstock to Clermont to pay their rents of bushels of wheat and fat hens on May Day, their horses were taken to the Clermont stables and fed, they themselves were invited into the house for a meal and a few pleasant words with Madame Livingston herself.

The Judge's widow took control of her property through the years of the Revolution. Her children were too much involved in the war to be of much help. Daughter Janet's husband, Richard Montgomery, was killed at the siege of Quebec. Her son Robert R. was deep in war work as a member of the Continental Congress, and soon he was named chancellor of New York's Court of Chancery. Son John devoted his energies to making as large as possible a profit out of the conflict. Henry Beekman Livingston was an army officer. As Margaret

Livingston's younger daughters married, they chose men involved in the war. One was surgeon-general, another quartermaster-general; son-in-law General John Armstrong served on George Washington's staff.

When the British burned Kingston in October 1777 they also burned Madame Livingston's Clermont house. A lesser woman might have been reduced to helplessness by this grim event, but not Madame Livingston. She promptly set about rebuilding the house even at a time when labor and materials were almost impossible to get, when cash was scarce and inflation rampant. Her determination had its effect and the house was rebuilt. But there was a cost in public esteem; Hudson Valley people asked why other victims of British destruction should be living in cold temporary shacks, while the great house at Clermont was rebuilt with such indecent speed during a time of war.

Madame Livingston took notice of this criticism but refused to accept it. In a letter of February 4, 1780 she wrote to her son the Chancellor, as he had come to be generally called, and told him that Morgan Lewis, husband of daughter Margaret, had gone to Albany "to dispel calumnies." Morgan Lewis was quartermaster-general of the Whig forces and so in a position to allocate labor and materials. It was being said, wrote Madame Livingston, that Morgan Lewis, in that time of bloodshed and shortages of the necessities of life, had built a large stable at Clermont. Actually it was only a matter of "a small barrack of 4 poles," a structure for protecting stacks of hay. "It is also asserted that I could not have built this house if I had not had a Quarter Master for my Son-in-Law etc. etc. These things are vexatious but they do not wound my Peace because I know they are false and orriginate in Malice and Envy."

The envy was certainly there. A growing spirit of independence led many people to regard with distaste the Livingstons' struggle to maintain their pre-War position of privilege. Madame Livingston reacted by expressing disdain. "I pray," she wrote her son the Chancellor on December 30, 1779, "for deliverance from the persecutions of the Lower Class who I foresee will be as despotic as any Prince (if not more so) in Europe." [8]

In Woodstock during the war years the lower class had paid little attention to their new landlord, Madame Livingston, and she realized that trying to collect rents and keep track of tenants on the Woodstock frontier would be a waste of effort. Much of her time was taken up with struggling with inflation and wartime taxes. "I have taken it upon me to order John [Curry] to sell yr. Horses to pay tax," she wrote to the Chancellor in the spring of 1780.[9]

John Curry was employed by Madame Livingston to take care of farm matters at Clermont and Woodstock. Neither Curry nor his employer felt that wartime Woodstock would reward any attempt at mangement. "Labour is so Immensely dear and hands so scarce that I think that you and I should Let out our farms upon shares—John [Curry] could attend to both as he does not think of Woodstock till the war is over," so Madame Livingston wrote her son.

Once the War was over Madame Livingston and her land agent William Cockburn began to think in earnest of Woodstock. The effort at settling the division line between the Town of Hurley and Madame Livingston's lands in Woodstock was one result. Although the Hurley-Livingston line coincided with the Hurley-Woodstock line nothing in the surviving records indicates that the Town of Woodstock took any part in the surveys, negotiations and disputes that marked the settlement. Once the line was settled, however, the Town of Woodstock accepted it.

While the boundary question was of great importance to Madame Livingston, another question of equal importance in her mind and of even more importance in the minds of her ten children during the decade following the ending of the Revolution was a decision as to the division of the huge landholdings she had inherited from her father and her husband. Great landowning families like the Livingstons are seldom reticent about arranging for the future of their lands after the members who hold them are gone. The Livingston children brought up the matter of the disposition of the Madame's lands from time to time, and before too long this pressure caused Madame Livingston to make a decision.

Judge Livingston had left no written statement as to what disposition he wanted his widow to make of the lands she had received from him. What evidence there is suggests he had expressed a wish that the Madame should use the lands during her lifetime and then divide them among the couple's children. He had certainly expressed a similar wish about his Hardenbergh Patent lands outside of Woodstock. A letter of December 13, 1787 written by Chancellor Livingston to his brother-in-law Dr. Thomas T. Tillotson (Tillotson had married the Chancellor's sister Margaret) explains how the division got under way. "Just before I left Clermont," the Chancellor wrote, "my mother desired me to consult with the children at New

York and with William Cockburn to agree on such a division as she should make as they seemed anxious about it we had one or two meetings & agreed upon a division on the principle we talked of to throw each division as much as possible together and to draw for the choice. . . ."

In other words, Madame Livingston's lands were to be grouped in ten convenient packages. Her children would then draw lots; whoever got number one would have first choice; number two would have second choice and so on. In his letter to Dr. Tillotson Chancellor Livingston described himself as lucky in the draw, and indeed he was for he drew number one and so could choose Woodstock.

Several years passed before the actual division of Madame Livingston's land was made. By April 1789 the winding-up of the whole matter was close enough for the Madame to write to the Chancellor with characteristic piety that "I sincerely pray that God will Bless to each of you what you have chosen."

In February 1790 Madame Livingston gave the Chancellor a deed to her Woodstock lands. These lands remained in the Chancellor's name from 1790 until his death in 1813. But while his mother lived, she reserved the right to make leases, to collect rents and to evict tenants who did not observe their agreements. She agreed, however, not to make any leases for a longer term than three lives, and, of course she could not sell or mortgage any part of the property, for she no longer owned it. In this way Chancellor Livingston was assured of becoming the absentee landlord of the most thickly settled part of Woodstock, and in this way the Livingston leases for three lives were assured of continuing as an important if anachronistic part of Woodstock life under the new republic.[10]

By 1790 Madame Livingston's Woodstock estate was taking shape after the disruptions of the War. Squatters had been offered and many had taken leases. New settlers were pouring in. Elias Hasbrouck, the supervisor of the town, was well disposed toward the Livingston family; he had served an apprenticeship with old Robert Livingston of Clermont and had named one of his sons Montgomery in honor of General Richard Montgomery, the son-in-law of Madame Livingston who had died in the siege of Quebec. Hasbrouck family tradition tells of a gold ring given by the widowed Janet Montgomery to the baby. Other Woodstock babies were named for Livingstons; little Roberts, Margarets, Phillips, Alidas and Janets appeared on Livingston lands in Woodstock, giving evidence of good will toward the Madame and her family as well as showing a desire on the part of tenants to raise their status in their world by taking more socially acceptable names than the Dutch and German ones handed down from ancestors.[11]

Twenty-five years after the death of Robert Livingston of Clermont, the Livingston lands in Woodstock appeared to be entering upon the sort of existence of which old Robert had dreamed back in the early 1760s. At Clermont an imposing leather-bound book embellished on its cover with the Livingston motto held careful records of dealings with each Woodstock tenant. There the names of participants in leases for three lives were set down often with the ages of each person; payments—or failure to pay—bushels of wheat, days of labor or fat hens by way of rent were recorded. In Woodstock itself clearings were being made and new farms established. The place was taking on the look of becoming what Robert Livingston had hoped— an extension into the wild Hardenbergh Patent of his Clermont estate where Old-World ways lingered on and tenants bowed respectfully whenever a Livingston passed by.[12]

12

LIFE IN A
DWINDLING TOWN

Until the explosive twentieth century no period in all of Woodstock history saw so much change as the first seventeen years after Woodstock's organization. This was the time of the dwindling of Woodstock from its enormous size of 1787.

First to be "set off" from the town by act of State Legislature was Middletown, which became a separate town centered around Margaretville on March 3, 1789. In 1787 Delaware County was established (prior to this much of what is now Delaware had been in Ulster). In 1798 the Town of Windham was formed out of the northern part of Woodstock territory lying beyond the present Greene County-Ulster County line. The present towns of Hunter, Jewett, Lexington and part of Prattsville were later carved from this tract. In 1800 Greene County was set up from parts of Albany and Ulster counties.

Shandaken or Big Shandaken as it had long been called continued to cling to its parent Woodstock. It would not become a separate town until 1804.

Woodstock people did not view this dwindling of their town with horror. On the contrary they welcomed it. The town as first set up had been too large to be manageable. Early town records document Woodstock people's desire for a smaller town. "At a Town Meeting Held on the first Tuesday of Apl 1796 A Sence of the Meeting Being Taken it was Unanimously Without one Dissenting Voice Voted that the Town of Woodstock Should be Divided." The following December "it was Unanimously agreed to Elect a Committee of Persons who should fix upon the Line of Division Between Woodstock and Schohary Kill." [1]

The Woodstock in which the federal census-taker of 1790 went from door to door contained an official 254 persons belonging to 53 families within the boundaries of present-day Woodstock, excluding the chin whisker. The figure for the larger Woodstock was 1025. These totals of course were not entirely accurate—census figures never are. The census taker included only people living as families. Those getting along alone were omitted, as were pioneers living part of the year in their old homes in longer-settled places and coming to Woodstock at intervals to clear land, plant and harvest crops and build houses and barns.

Excluded also, as in later censuses, was a small number of persons who simply didn't want to be counted for one reason or another. The census figure of 254 might safely be increased to about three hundred, and if we add the people of the chin whisker, which was still part of Kingston, we get a grand total of perhaps 340 people living in 1790 within the bounds of our Woodstock.

All but a few of these people were white. The names of about thirty per cent of the heads of the more than fifty families were of German origin. Dutch names were a close second, A half dozen had English names, four or five had Irish names. The Hasbroucks, Dumonds and DuBoises were descended from Huguenot refugees. Five black slaves were counted, and it is likely a few escaped slaves might have been making a hard but free living in remote hollows.

Two heads of families of the Woodstock of 1790 give room for speculation. Rachel Frenchy and Hannibal Jackson lived in or near what is now the hamlet of Woodstock. Neither appears in local church or land records. The families which they headed are given as composed of "all other free person." This must mean that the twelve persons involved were either black or Indian—we have no means of learning which. But a number of scattered bits of evidence suggest that from its earliest days Woodstock had its black settlers—Josias Smith and "Jno Pierce" or Pine are recorded as blacks having "possessions" in Mink Hollow before 1800. [2]

According to local tradition black families lived for many years beside the Sawkill along Route 212 between the intersection of Routes 375 and 212 and the Zena road. At least one of these families was still there sixty years ago. It may have been here or in the hamlet of Woodstock that the Frenchy and Jackson families were called on by the 1790 census-taker.

The neighborhood may have functioned as a little ghetto from which black workers could easily walk to employment in the homes and on the farms of the prosperous Waghkonck farmers or in the taverns springing up in the hamlet of Woodstock. To the northwest of the present business center of Woodstock a tract of land is mentioned in deeds of a few years after 1800 as "Scipio's thirty acre lot." The name Scipio was a familiar one among negro slaves—Scipio Africanus had been a well-known member of a patrician Roman family. Names like his were often given to slaves in America—another was Hannibal (the original Hannibal had been defeated by Scipio Africanus in 202 B.C.), which strengthens the likelihood that Hannibal Jackson of Woodstock was black, living on Scipio's land and possibly related to him. But there is at present no conclusive evidence for all this.

It is likely the Sawkill Valley had been a tempting escape route for fleeing Ulster County slaves far back in the past. The minutes of the Ulster County Court of Sessions for March 1, 1714/15 tell of two black men being charged with taking two horses and riding them "in the dead time of night so furr as near where Johannis Burhans lives. . . ." This was close to the point of juncture of the Sawkill and the Esopus. The two men might have been merely having a high-spirited fling, but they might also have hoped to go on up the Sawkill Valley to the freedom of what was not yet known as Woodstock.[3]

New York State before and after the Revolution had the largest number of slaves of any northern state. Efforts toward the abolition of slavery, largely made by emigrants from New England where slavery had never taken firm root, made little progress until 1799. Then the State Legislature named July 4, 1827 as the day on which all slavery would end within the state.

Under this law all children born to slaves were required to be registered with their town clerk by the parents' owners—this would help make sure that these children would be free. The first child of Woodstock slaves was registered like this in the town clerk's minute book, "Cornelis Dumond [Dumond farmed on the Bearsville Flats] has one Black Female child born November 1st 1799, called her name Susannah." The registration was not made until 1801, the tardiness suggesting the reluctance of a slave owner to accept the prospect of eventual abolition. The prospect of abolition apparently did little to discourage slavery in Woodstock—the census of 1810 showed seventeen slaves owned by Woodstock people.

Local traditions tell of Indians living on in Woodstock until well into the nineteenth century. Much tradition puts the last Indians to live in Woodstock at Echo Lake known until the 1870s as Schue's Pond. (Probably named for Teunis Schue, who was located at the eastern base of Overlook as close as any farmer could be to the Pond. Schue is said to have hunted and trapped at the Pond as far back as 1760 or so.) Wandering groups of Indians were recorded in the Hudson Valley not far from Woodstock in the 1790s. They may well have passed through the town. One such group of Indians from Stockbridge, Massachusetts camped "in a swamp" at the Livingstons' Clermont in 1794—they made and sold baskets, brooms and similar objects and moved on to join another Indian group in the Mohawk Valley.[4]

All the town's early residents were Protestants—the few who might not have been probably kept the fact quiet. It was not until 1806 that Roman Catholics were allowed to hold public office in the state. A Livingston tenant referred to as "Jacob the Jew" had lived in Woodstock before the Revolution, but he sold his leasehold and vanished.

The Katsbaan Church from which Peter Short and Peter Miller and their families had been returning when they were captured by Tories and Indians continued to serve most Woodstock people. This church, built in 1732, had gained in membership over the earlier Palatine church at West Camp. Services at Katsbaan reflected the increasingly Dutch culture of the Palatines and their children; services there were sometimes in the German Lutheran manner, but more and more often in that of the Reformed Dutch Church. A few Woodstock people with Kingston connections used Kingston's Reformed Dutch Church.

The growth of population in Woodstock and the increasing sense of forming a community of its own is suggested by records of the Katsbaan Church for 1795. Here Woodstock babies are recorded as having been baptized in their own town by the pastor of the Katsbaan Church. This suggests other religious activities as well were being held in Woodstock. By the end of the 1790s Woodstock people were discussing organizing a Dutch church of their own. Actual organization did not take place until 1805, with a Lutheran church coming into being the following year.

Long before Woodstock had churches of its own it had its taverns. During the 1790s at least six taverns were in business at the same time under proper licenses from the town. These taverns had good reason for existence; Woodstock was then, to use a phrase coined almost a century later, a "gateway to the Catskills." [5]

The Schohariekill Road of the merchants of Kingston divided beyond Mink Hollow, with one branch going on to Prattsville and the other moving eastward to the headwaters of the Schohariekill near Haines Falls. Woodstock's Commissioners of Highways had been busy since 1787 surveying and laying out roads. The principal Woodstock roads of the 1790s provided access from the Hudson Valley to what is known today as "the mountaintop" of the Schohariekill Valley—an alternate route zigzagging up the face of the Catskills from north of Palenville was built shortly after 1790. It proved hard to maintain and was not much used.

Because Woodstock lay less than a day's journey from the Hudson River on increasingly used roads to the interior it was a logical spot for taverns at which travellers might eat, drink and sleep. Prospective settlers, speculators and teamsters hauling loads of choice lumber such as white pine, cherry, curly maple and straight-grained ash all passed through Woodstock and used its taverns. And the town's taverns did more than care for travellers and their horses.

Far back in the history of the Old World, taverns had given officials trouble because they had often become centers for the amusement of local people. Typically gamblers, petty swindlers, alcoholics, prostitutes and idlers had congregated there and had often enough indulged in brawling. New World taverns from the beginning gave rise to much legislation aimed at checking the "immorality" often associated with them. In March 1788 the New York Legislature passed an act regulating in detail the taverns of the state.

Pondering the applications in December 1789 of Conradt Rightmyer for a license to conduct a tavern in Woodstock—the license was granted—town supervisor Elias Hasbrouck jotted down some of the provisions of the new law on the back of a letter, first noting that "Right Myre" would post a bond of £50 before the license could be granted. Rightmyer was not to keep "a disorderly In or thereing suffer or permit any cock fighting, gaming or playing with cards or dice or keep any billiard table or Shuffleboard, in the said tavern . . . or within any outhouse, yard or garden belonging thereunto . . ."

The law required every licensed tavernkeeper to provide at least two beds for guests, with sufficient bedding; stabling and hay for horses were also required. Though heavy penalties were provided for selling "strong or spirituous liquors" without a license, a tavernkeeper might sell "metheglin, currant wine, cherry wine or cyder" of his own making to be consumed off his premises. In addition he was required to display a sign with his name on it and to conform to many other regulations. The "sine post" noted in early road surveys as standing at Little Shandaken probably showed the location of John Carle's tavern.

Taverns were not only centers for caring for travellers and entertaining local people. They were the places in which town meetings, auction sales and other serious pieces of business took place. The reason was obvious. Taverns were the only buildings which had rooms large enough to hold any but small groups.

Woodstock tavernkeepers were often prominent men in the community. After Elias Hasbrouck died in 1791 (tradition says that he died suddenly while hunting squirrels) his widow Elizabeth kept a tavern in the house Hasbrouck had built close to the entrance to Mink Hollow—the house is no longer standing although a slightly later house, incorporating part of the earlier house and greatly altered within, and an old barn in which travellers put their horses remain. Later Richard M. Hasbrouck, the son of Elizabeth and Elias, kept the tavern close to the important Lake Hill crossroads; like his father, Richard M. served as supervisor of Woodstock.[6]

Woodstock men of the period 1787-1804 typically earned their living by a combination of farming, making a variety of wood products, and lumbering, hunting and tavernkeeping. Women cooked, baked, washed, bore and brought up children, and helped with farm work. During this time the hamlet of Woodstock became firmly established as the center of the town—its water-power resources determined that.

A 107-acre farm including the Tannery Brook falls had been sold by the Chancellor in 1789 to Issac Davis of Rhinebeck (whether the Issac Davis who had supplied military information during the Revolution is not clear). It was regarded as good policy for a landlord like Livingston to sell to an energetic and ambitious man the land on which a business and industrial center might be formed. And soon a sawmill and grist mill, a fulling and a carding mill appeared on the Davis tract. A general store, a blacksmith shop and Newkerk's tavern all stimulated the growth of the hamlet, providing income and employment.[7]

On winter days when there was little farm work to be done and on evenings through the year Woodstock men split shingles from white pine or hemlock or made barrel staves and hoops for use in New York and for export. The bark could be peeled from oak and hemlock trees most easily during the late spring and early summer. Men piled up tanbark in the woods and returned the following winter to haul it by sledge to the Woodstock tannery or to the Hudson at Saugerties or Kingston. John C. Ring had a "tan house and Tan Vats" on the Tannery Brook in the heart of the hamlet. Oldtimers used to say that "Woodstock stank" for the period of almost a century during which the tannery was in business and the refuse of the operation oozed into the brook and lay on its banks.

In 1797, Jacob Hunt, who lived close to the site of the present Woodstock Library, sold barrel staves and hoops to Hasbrouck and Janson, merchants of Kingston. His staves sold at twelve shillings per hundred, while 135 hoop-poles brought sixteen shillings and threepence. Peter Short went on making and selling wood products as he had before the Revolution; in January 1797 he bought wine, gin, sugar, chocolate, lace, an auger and a file from Hasbrouck and Janson and was credited with "117 Pipe staves" at 24 shillings per hundred; such staves were used in making casks to hold liquids. Short's son David was credited that same day with "a load of bark" worth four shillings ninepence. Most of the younger Shorts were, like David, active in lumbering. On June 11, 1793 John Brink, who operated the ferry crossing the Hudson from Saugerties to near Clermont, gave Edward Short a receipt noting that Short "has Rode" 30-inch boards "from Woodstock Mill to the North [i.e., the Hudson] River." Hundreds of similar bits of paper have survived to demonstrate the important place which lumbering had in Woodstock life—and to show how rapidly the town's forest cover was shrinking. The shrinking process was helped by widespread charcoal burning.[8]

A number of Woodstock people of the 1790s followed skilled trades or occupations. William Eltinge, who came to Woodstock from Kingston in 1790, had been a wood turner; whether he made turnings in Woodstock in addition to farming isn't known, but if he did he may have used the power of the "Wide Clove brook" which crosses the Rock City Road on the six-hundred-acre tract Eltinge bought from John Reed of Rhinebeck, who in turn had bought it from Cornelius Tiebout in 1774. Eltinge's house stood on the site of the former Krack house, now converted into apartments and shops, at the corner of Rock City Road facing the Village Green.

Blacksmiths were numerous along main roads, where they were

called upon to mend the ironwork of wagons and sledges and to shoe the horses and oxen of travellers. John Wolven carried on this trade close to the point at which Route 212 crosses the Saugerties-Woodstock line. James Bogardus worked in Little Shandaken. Benjamin P. Davis, of a family which gave three or four generations of blacksmiths to Woodstock, was among the blacksmiths of the hamlet of Woodstock. He was also an axe-maker.[9]

During Woodstock's early existence as an organized town, farming was becoming of greater importance than before the Revolution. Few farms had as much as one-third of their land cleared. Apple orchards planted before the War were now in bearing. Cider, which would later on play a larger part in Woodstock life, was beginning to be made. The first cider-mill may have been that of Andries Risely, whose farm lay on the Bearsville Flats not far west of the hamlet of Woodstock.

Field crops continued much as before the Revolution. Wheat, corn, oats, rye and flax were grown. A grist mill had appeared on the Tannery Brook by the 1790s in response to the larger local production of grain. The old Hardenbergh mill in what is now Zena had been grinding grain for some time.

Farm animals increased in number as better pasturage developed. Native American grasses had been scarce in Woodstock's primeval state, and European grasses better suited to the needs of grazing animals steadily pushed their way into the town's abandoned fields and burned-over woodlands or sprang up and gained their first footholds along the new roads. Cattle, sheep, hogs, chickens and other poultry grew in numbers, although their quality by present-day standards was low. Wire fencing had not yet appeared. Fences when there were any were made of brush, logs, uprooted stumps, stones or split rails.

A Hurley ordinance of 1801 forbids the cutting of "Chestnut, White or black oak wood before it is ten Inches [in diameter] for use in making fences." These same woods were also used in Woodstock log or rail fences. A British traveller in the part of Columbia County from which many Woodstock pioneers came was shocked at the wasteful manner in which he saw some log fences being made. Trees were felled in a way that sent them down more or less on the intended fence line, or were cut nearby, stripped of branches and rolled to the line where they rested on the earth or a little above it, soon to decay under the attacks of boring insects, fungi and bacteria. Such fences "consume immense quantities of timber," the Englishman commented with disapproval.[10]

With pasture fences so crude and makeshift, animals were forever wandering from their home grounds. To take care of these strays an elaborate system of old and new rules and customs was used. Some farmers marked their animals and recorded the marks in the town clerk's minute book. So Barent Lewis (he gave his name to Lewis Hollow in which he once lived) declared on June 28, 1795 that he "marks his Cattle, Hogs and Sheep with a piece of the Right Ear. . . ." That meant that a bit had been snipped from the ear of each animal. Philip Rick later in 1795 stated that his farm animals were marked "with a Round Hole in the right Ear."

Not every Woodstock farmer marked his animals, and this led to a good deal of confusion. Wandering cows or hogs were sometimes claimed by men who didn't actually own them. Sometimes there was room for an honest difference of opinion, especially when the animal involved had been working its way through the woods for six months and had grown in the process. Pastures were far from being the smooth, well-kept expanses of turf of later years. Most often they were no more than the uncleared or partly cleared or abandoned parts of the hills and mountainsides where cattle fed less on grass and more on the tips of the branches of brush or on the tops of recently felled trees.

When farm animals left this environment for cleared and cultivated land they could do a good deal of damage. It was to take care of this possibility that pound masters were elected each year. These officials were required to maintain enclosures in which stray animals could be held until claimed and until the damage done by the strays was ascertained and paid for. Woodstock fence viewers after 1794 had the duty of being "called out to appraise and ascertain Damages." They were paid five shillings per day for this service.[11]

The stray-animal problem was complicated by the fact that Woodstock people sometimes contracted to pasture animals from the older settlements. And if the acorn or beechnut crop were good in the fall large troops of hogs were driven from Kingston to fatten in the woods of Woodstock. This kind of pasturing had its effects on the woods. When the animals devoured young trees and low woody plants, they interfered in the natural process of forest regeneration. The pasturing of cattle from out of town on the Woodstock Commons was forbidden by town ordinance in 1808.[12]

A few references during the early years of Woodstock's existence as a town show that the townspeople had gardens in which they grew vegetables. What kinds they grew has not come down to us. But they were probably limited until garden seeds grown and packaged by the "Shaking Quakers" of New Lebanon began after 1809 to be advertised in Ulster newspapers. Though no record of plants being grown for the sake of flowers is known, it is likely that rose bushes and other ornamental plants were brought from older settlements to Woodstock as to other settlements. In 1793 Henry Van Nieukerk of Kingston advertised in the *Farmers Register* a stock of "elegant and beautiful flowers," bulbs including hyacinths, parrot and other tulips, jonquils and narcissus imported from Holland. Some of these may have found their way to Woodstock. Wild fruits, nuts, roots and leaves, their uses learned from the Indians, were gathered and eaten, but mushrooms were not known to have been touched.

Trout caught in the Sawkill and Beaverkill and the pickerel for which Cooper Lake had a fine local reputation formed an important part of Woodstock diet. So too did the meat of deer, bears, wild pigeons and squirrels shot by Woodstock men who had begun to hunt while still boys. Hunting these animals had a double purpose. Deer ate growing field crops, bears made off with young pigs or lambs, and squirrels, sometimes in enormous numbers, raided stands of ripening corn.[13]

By the 1790s Woodstock people were turning away from building the kind of stone houses whose design had been brought to the Hudson Valley by Dutch, German or Walloon ancestors. Instead they were accepting the frame buildings favored by immigrants from New England who were coming to the Hudson Valley. New Englanders had brought a tradition of frame construction with them across the Atlantic and had adapted it to American conditions. That explains in part why the stone house which once stood at the intersection of the Chestnut Hill and Route 212 was the farthest point westward of the older kind of house. And there was another reason—few tenants on lands leased for three lives felt justified in building substantial and expensive houses which they might lose when their leases "fell in." Many tenants on Livingston land lived in rough log houses. Others continued to make do with makeshift "wigwams" from which they retreated in the winter.

The more substantial wooden buildings of Woodstock's early post-Revolutionary days had frames of hewn timbers (of oak or chestnut in the earliest period, later of hemlock). These timbers were joined by mortice and tenon joints secured by oaken pegs; diagonal braces linking plates and corner posts stiffened the frame. Studs and many larger timbers were usually sawed in the local sawmills. Chimneys were of local stone, topped with brick to make flashing more effective.

In some houses crosspieces made of saplings were sprung horizontally between the studs and covered with a mixture of clay and oat straw midway between the inside plastered wall and the exterior clapboards; this was an interesting survival of Old-World mud-and-stud, wattle-and-daub and half-timber methods. Good examples of surviving houses of this kind are the Riseley house on the Bearsville Flats a little before and across Route 212 from the Jonathan Apple monument and the Lewis house at the end of the Lewis Hollow Road.

Many Woodstock houses built soon after the end of the Revolution were less well put together. Examples which have come down to our days (most have not been able to weather the years) are roughly framed with logs flattened on the upper side used as floor joists and with rafters also of round timber. In these houses as in better ones doors were of the batten kind, with clinched handmade nails used to secure the battens. Because they clinched so much better than the cut and wire nails of later times, handmade nails were saved by carpenters and used in making batten doors until the present century. Cut nails were being used after about 1815.[14]

Old inventories show that these Woodstock houses were simply furnished. The inventory of Wilhelmus Rowe's belongings made after his death in 1803 shows two pairs of andirons, pewter dishes, plates and spoons, earthenware, four chests, a cupboard, five beds with bedding worth £40, six Windsor chairs and a dozen other chairs, a looking glass, some teaspoons besides one "curled Maple table" valued at £2-8-0. Spinning wheels and weaving tackle, seven milk cows and other farm stock, harness, an ox cart and "a pleasure Sleigh," two slaves, Pompey valued at £80 and "one Negro wench named Elizabeth £40," show what a prosperous Waghkonck man possessed in his house and barn. Rowe's inventory was not complete; clothing, for example, was not included. Other Woodstock inventories show that clothing was likely to be divided among the children of a man or woman who died, but if there were no children clothing was listed.

The inventories of poorer people were less impressive. When unmarried Dennis Delaney, a laborer of Woodstock, died in 1792 he left behind goods valued by Wilhelmus Rowe and Peter Short at a bit over £25. The complete inventory included, "1 pr. oxen, 1 3 y.o. Mare, Shear and Coller, 2 ox chanes, pare old Bots [Boots], 2 do. [that is, pairs] Shous [shoes], Old Engeon [Indian] Blancket, Cloubeded Coat, 2 old Linig Sherts, 2 pare old Sockings, Coten hakerchief, flannel shirt, do. Coat, vest, pare overhols doflers [probably of duffels, a coarse woolen cloth], old silk hankerchef, pare plush Breeches, do. [that is, a pair] Lining Trowsers, old saddle, friing pan, 2 Iron wedges, 2 do. [old] wood slays, Ox Youk, one ox, Saw logs."

That is the total of Delaney's belongings [the values of each item are here omitted]. The Indian blanket was of the kind originally made in Europe to trade with the Indians. Blankets of this kind were widely used by whites. The "cloubeded" coat was made of "clouded" or spottily-colored cloth. Delaney's inventory, if it does nothing else, shows us quite plainly how Woodstock men of the poorer kind dressed in the early 1790s.[15]

Barns and other farm buildings were more numerous than houses. Not many of these buildings have come down to us. Most were allowed to deteriorate and collapse as farming came to a virtual end during the second quarter of the twentieth century.

No barn of the early type known as the Dutch barn has survived in Woodstock, but the earliest barns still standing have much of the low, broad proportions characteristic of Dutch barns. A barn of this kind is the Wigram barn now known as Parnassus Square. The central portion is not set off from the aisles by pillars into which the great anchor beams are morticed as in true Dutch barns. It is a fine example of a barn of the days when Dutch barns were giving way to what were known locally as "English barns." A few small farm buildings of early years have managed to live on into our own times. One that used its upstairs as a granary and its downstairs as a wagon shed and shop is on the old Sagendorf-Shultis place in Wittenberg.

Until 1805 Woodstock people got along without a resident doctor. For a while before that their ailments had been sometimes treated by Boaz Searle, who lived in Middletown and had patients strung out all the way from Roxbury to Woodstock. In 1805 Searle advertised that the prices of medicines were much lower than in recent years and urged patients to take advantage of this pleasant turn of events. "To the honest poor he is determined to be friendly and indulgent, He will be ready at all times to attend to the calls of patients . . . and he will be faithful to his trust . . . ," Searle advertised. He also asked those who owed him money for his services to pay up promptly.

As Searle's advertisement appeared in *The Plebeian* of Kingston, Dr. Benjamin R. Bevier was arriving in Woodstock with a brand-new degree in medicine from New York's Columbia College. Searle seems to have lacked a degree, as did the "Indian doctors" whom oldtimers say once practiced in Woodstock. Bevier's arrival came as Woodstock moved away from frontier status and was rapidly losing the roughness of a town newly emerged from the wilderness.

As Dr. Bevier started his practice, elementary schooling was struggling to become regularly established in the town. The Revolution had put an end to the meager educational efforts of the people of colonial New York. Before the war Ben Snyder and others had kept occasional school. In Kingston an Academy had been born in 1774; the children of Elizabeth and Elias Hasbrouck had attended it.[16]

A few Woodstock pioneers of Palatine German background probably learned to read but not to write under the guidance of Matthew Junck of West Camp. Junck ". . . used to teach a German School three or four months every winter. He was a very perfect good reader and singer in the German Low Dutch and English, but a very poor writer and knew no arithmetic at all," as his grandson Judge John M. Brown, born at Blue Mountain, recalled in 1823. Junck's teaching ended in 1753 when he moved to Schoharie.[17]

Ben Snyder of Churchland taught a few Woodstock children before the Revolution and immediately after, but most Woodstock children grew up unable to read or write until the State of New York set up a common school system. In 1784 Governor George Clinton had urged the Legislature to create such a system. Progress was slow and it was not until 1797 that Woodstock people, in compliance with an act of Legislature, elected their first officials charged with the duty of taking care of elementary education. That year a schoolhouse lot was marked off at the southeastern corner of Route 212 and Pine Grove Avenue. Classes were held here or elsewhere at irregular intervals while the Legislature slowly felt its way toward setting up a more regular system.

In Woodstock's early years as an organized town the poor as well as the young were matters of concern. The upheaval of the Revolution had created a few rich American families and a great many poor ones. The poor often moved about from town to town in an effort at finding a place where they could live in decency and reasonable comfort.

In 1786 the Town of Hurley, to which Woodstock then belonged (on paper, at least), passed an ordinance aimed at controlling the influx of "strangers." Strangers were forbidden to "enjoy all the benefits, Previledges, Commonages, and Liberties with the freeborn Inhabitants of the Said town without contributing toward the Support of the poor, or other Necessary or Contingent taxes of the town . . ." The strangers were specifically forbidden to cut wood or do business in the town without a license. In 1788 the State Legislature passed an act providing for the "better Settlement and Relief of the poor" which superseded ordinances like the Hurley one and placed responsibility for dealing with strangers and the needy poor entirely on the shoulders of the state's towns.

The act regularized previous practice by requiring strangers to live, work and pay rent in a town for two years before they could qualify for relief as paupers. If they became penniless during the two-year period they would be sent back, in the charge of a constable if need be, to the town from which they came.

A good later example of how this worked is given by the case of Tobias Van Dyck, who became a tenant of Robert R. Livingston in 1808, when he was forty-five and his wife Margaret was thirty-seven. By about 1820 Van Dyck was too ill to take care of his farm. He gave up the lease on his 115 acres and headed westward to try to make a living in another town. The overseers of the town, however, sent him back to Woodstock. Then eleven Woodstock men, all but one Livingston tenants, petitioned their landlord, Robert L. Livingston, asking him to allow Van Dyck, who seemed to have improved in health, a small piece of land rent-free on which he might, in the concluding words of the petition, "help him Self to a Living and we hope that the Dispenser of all good will bountifully Reward you and your petitioners will Ever pray Martin Gulneck, David Short, George Shultis Junr., Henry P. Shultis, Richard M. Hasbrouck, Philip Rick, Philip Rick Juner [sic], Isaac Eltinge [who was then supervisor of Woodstock], Peter Harder, Peter Van de Bogert."

The petition was granted and Van Dyck was given permission "to settle on a piece of Land without Rent." And there he was still living, and still in poverty, in 1834. Van Dyck's troubles were due in part to the fact that he and his wife had no children to accept responsibility for them. All the petitioners on his behalf did have children and every one is represented in the Woodstock of today by direct or collateral descendants.[18]

Early Woodstock had its little scandals, most of which have been forgotten. But one, the absconding of town constable William Hoff, became a matter of record. Whether Hoff left town to avoid paying debts or had committed some other offense we do not know, but in August 1795 "Twelve Reputable freeholders" petitioned for a special town meeting at which Benjamin Marricle was elected in Hoff's place.

The Woodstock of 1787-1804 weathered the lessening in its size without difficulty. It grew along lines which had been determined in the days before the Revolution. Each center of population had not only good land but also good sources of waterpower for saw and grist mills. While Elias Hasbrouck had been supervisor Little Shandaken seemed to be making a bid to become the central hamlet of the new town. But as the town dwindled in size the position of Little Shandaken became less central and that of the hamlet of Woodstock more so. Waghkonck remained much as it had been before the War. Settlers were gathering around the sawmill set up near the outlet of Yankeetown Pond during the 1790s. Some of these people lived on Hurley land which would not become part of Woodstock until 1853.[19]

In July 1800 word came to Woodstock tenants that their landlord, Madame Livingston, had died. In the words of her daughter Margaret, "She arose [on July 1] in her usual health and spirits, walked in her [garden and at] 9 at night she was called from the bosom of her family." The death of Madame Livingston made little practical difference to her Woodstock tenants, as her son Chancellor Robert R. Livingston took possession. During his mother's tenure the Chancellor had exerted some indirect influence on the management of Woodstock. His influence continued to be indirect, for in 1801 President Thomas Jefferson appointed him minister plenipotentiary to France.

The Chancellor set sail for France aboard the frigate *Boston* in October. He did not return until 1804. While he was away the management of his lands in Woodstock and elsewhere remained in the hands of agents who were not always energetic and vigilant in protecting the Chancellor's interest. During this period the glassmaking industry came to Woodstock and before long had a transforming effect on the town, furnishing employment to many people, bringing in new people with different ways of living and denuding mountainsides of their forests.

13

IRON AND GLASS

People new to Woodstock often ask oldtimers how it happened that glassmaking came to so remote a spot as the upper Sawkill Valley. They ask too why it was that the industry eventually vanished, leaving behind little more than glass slag gleaming in the soil, a few weatherbeaten buildings, and a good deal of local folklore about Keefe Hollow and the hamlet of Shady. Among those who have puzzled over these mysteries was Thomas Cole, the greatest figure of the Hudson River School of landscape painting.

Cole was a member of a party of twelve men and women who came to Woodstock on August 13, 1846 in order to climb Overlook Mountain and spend the night close to the mountain's summit. The party travelled in several wagons. This meant that while they were on the mountain their horses would have to be cared for in the valley. A horse, unlike an automobile, cannot be locked up and left to fare for itself.

The wagons moved through Woodstock and up the steep slope that led to the Wide Clove, where Mead's boardinghouse would be built in another twenty years. Then the wagons headed down the road to what we know as Keefe Hollow. Cole wrote in his journal, "We entered now a deep valley which lies on the Western side of the peak which it was our intention to ascend & came to some buildings, many of which were in a ruined and desolate condition. These seemed strange amid the verdant mountains that rose precipitous around &

112

broken into grander forms than usual in this range. A Glass House was formerly in operation in this secluded valley & the ruins of which might yet be seen in some heaps of stone. How a Glass House came to be established in this situation I have not yet been able to learn nor the cause of its abandonnment but when its fires ceased to burn the fires of the neighboring cottages were extinguished & the inhabitants of the vale are sheltered under two or three roofs." [1]

To Cole and his friends the ruinous glassmakers' village, enclosed on three sides by a wall of imposing mountains, was an exciting and romantic sight. And this is not surprising. Ever since glassmaking began some five thousand years ago this craft has stirred the human imagination as if it were touched by magic. How is it possible for the simple ingredients of glass to become vases and bowls, bottles and window panes? It is hardly to be wondered at that glassmakers were sometimes thought to be magicians and that the salamanders of ancient folklore were seen in the flames of glass-house furnaces.

The basic ingredients of glass made in Woodstock was silica, to which was added an alkali such as potash or soda ash. Clean sand was the source of the silica. Wood or seaweed ashes produced the alkali. The ingredients were moistened and heated.

To lower the melting point, broken glass known as "cullet" was added. The mixture, by this time called a "batch," after having been ground was put in a preheated pot or crucible already placed in a hot furnace lined with fire clay or a heat-resisting sandstone.

"Furnace tenders" fed the fire with pieces of wood four feet long and perhaps two inches in diameter. The wood had been seasoned for a year and then oven-dried to a point at which it would ignite when touched by the flame of a candle. When the batch reached a temperature of 1400 to 1500 degrees Centigrade, the melted impurities that formed a scum on the surface were skimmed off and the molten glass was ready.

Working through an opening called a "glory hole" the glassmaker thrust into the pot one end of a tube some five feet long—this was his blowpipe. The pipe was withdrawn and again dipped in the pot. This was repeated until a "gather" had formed which was neither liquid nor solid but in a soft plastic state.

The glassmaker next blew on his pipe. The gather expanded much as a soap bubble does when blown by a child. When the bubble reached the size and shape wanted (helped along by rolling on a wooden block), an iron rod called a pontil was fastened with a small gather to the end of the bubble opposite the blowpipe, and the pipe was removed. The bubble was then further shaped by a combination of swinging in the air, rolling on the arm of a "glassmaker's chair" and working with a variety of tools. From time to time as the bubble cooled and became less plastic it was reheated at the furnace. Finally the pontil was cracked off and the piece of glass, still intensely hot, was carried off by an apprentice to an annealing oven, where it could gradually cool, for rapid cooling would damage glass.

Most glass made in Woodstock was window glass made by a method generally used on the continent of Europe and called the "cylinder" method. In England "crown glass" was made by a method which involved whirling the glass bubble until it inverted and formed a disk five or six feet in diameter. Crown glass brought a higher price but required special skills and in America was seldom attempted except in Boston—an unsuccessful attempt at crown glass may have been made in Woodstock. After the maker of cylinder glass had produced an elongated bubble, he stopped his blowpipe and held the end of his bubble to the furnace. The air within the bubble expanded, and so the hot end blew out. The bubble was then shaped a bit more and cut down the side with shears; it was then placed in a "flattening oven" where it eventually became a more or less rectangular sheet of glass from which, when cool, panes might be cut with a diamond-edged tool

From this simplified account of glassmaking one thing above all should emerge: An immense amount of heat was required in order to make glass. The making of the pots (these were critical objects in glassmaking) was the first step to require heat. The pots were made of imported clay mixed with something like thirty to forty per cent of the burnt clay of broken pots. The broken pieces were first cleaned of every trace of glass which adhered to them, and were then ground into a fine powder and mixed with the fresh clay. The mixture was carefully worked up either in a mill or by treading by the feet of workmen. It was then made into rolls from which the pot was built up; the pots were probably about twenty to thirty inches in diameter and a little more in height.

Once a pot was made it was necessary to "season" it at a constant temperature and moisture for two months to a year before it was ready to be placed in a furnace for firing. As a number of pots approached completion a glass-house crew prepared for the coming "firing" or "campaign." Firewood was moved from the drying sheds into the ovens where every possible drop of moisture was driven out by heat; and batches were prepared. Then a difficult moment in the glassmaking process became imminent—the white hot pots were ready to be removed from the ovens in which they had been fired and "seated" on a "bench" in the furnace.

When the pots were ready, by day or night, the bell housed in a cupola on top of the glass house rang urgently. The workers quickly assembled. If they failed to appear they were fined.

It is easy enough to understand why glassworkers often failed to respond at pot-setting time. The work was dangerous and difficult because of the extreme heat of both pots and furnaces. To protect themselves against the heat, workers wore garments made of leather or armor of sheet metal. Masks made of metal were also worn. The pots were moved as quickly as possible from one hell-like fire to another. In relief after the task was done, glassworkers sometimes capered out of their house and delighted children by dancing in their bizarre costumes like so many demons on the street of the glassmakers' village.

Thomas Cole had wondered why a glass factory happened to come to so secluded a place as the upper Sawkill Valley. The answer is that it came there because closeness to an enormous supply of fuel was the very first consideration in choosing a site. The upper Sawkill Valley before the arrival of glassmaking was filled with a dense stand of mixed hardwoods and hemlock covering thousands of acres. That promised to supply enough fuel to keep the glass furnaces hot for half a century or so.

Second in importance to a supply of fuel was a good source for the right kind of sand. Most sand had too many impurities to be suitable. But on the shores of nearby Cooper Lake there was an area of sand deposited there as the last Ice Age went out of business which was believed at first to be excellent for making glass. Besides the availability of wood and sand there were two more favorable factors. The Hudson River with its promise of cheap and safe transportation was not too far away. And the land was reasonably priced. For all these reasons the Keefe Hollow glassmakers' village Thomas Cole saw in 1846 was built along the Sawkill.[2]

The second question which puzzled Thomas Cole was why glassmaking had been abandoned. The answer to this question can be understood only after the story of glassmaking in Woodstock with all its successes and failures and ups and downs is understood. That story probably begins in the year 1802, and it begins with as fascinating a character as ever came to Woodstock, Frederick Augustus DeZeng.

DeZeng was the second son of Baron de Zeng of Ruckerswalde-Wolkenstein and Johanna Philippa von Ponickau. Born in 1756 in Dresden, the capital of Saxony, he was trained as a soldier. He became an officer in the Guards of the King of Saxony and later took service with the Landgrave of Hesse-Cassel, seeing active service in the Landgrave's wars. When he returned to Dresden in 1776 he was appointed Hof-Juncker or Gentleman of the Chamber to the Saxony king. This was a time when some German princes maintained large armies which they hired out at so much a head to larger powers to use in war. The money raised in this way went to help the princes keep up an imposing way of life, with great palaces, parks and collections of works of art.

Young Baron de Zeng (all sons of a German nobleman used the family title) was sent in 1780 to New York with a body of the kind of troops we know as Hessians. The active part of the war was almost over and DeZeng played no part in it. Like many other Hessians he was easily persuaded to accept the new country and to remain there. He married a Quaker girl of the Lawrence family of Flushing on Long Island, was honorably discharged from his military duties, and promptly became an American citizen. By 1783 DeZeng and his wife were living in Red Hook, where the ex-Baron charmed Chancellor Livingston and his circle by his polished manners, his energy and enthusiasm, and his knowledge of all sorts of things needed to set the United States on a firm economic footing. DeZeng was knowledgeable in forestry and the use of timber (his father was "High Forest Officer" to the King of Saxony); he had skill in engineering, in ironmaking and glassmaking. And above all he was an amazingly persuasive man who had the knack of arousing enthusiasm in others, raising money and managing the many projects which seemed to pour endlessly from his imaginative mind.[3]

By 1785 DeZeng was operating a sawmill on the Little Beaverkill at what is now known as Beechford—the spot was included in Woodstock until 1804. Soon he was appointed a major of militiamen of Woodstock, Shandaken and the country to the west. The sawmill did not prove the road to wealth which the ever-hopeful DeZeng had expected. He was soon deep in canal and turnpike projects in central New York. In 1796 he was invited "by the Albany Glass Factory Concern Consisting of a number of Gentlemen of the first

Respectability and property to join them as well as to Superintend the Work . . ."

Just how long DeZeng remained with the glass factory in Albany is not known but by 1801 he was back in Ulster County, dazzling Kingston men whom he referred to as "a parcel of old Dutschmen, here before only remarcable for doing nothing" with his new project of a turnpike road to tie their village to the valley of the Delaware via the Esopus Valley, Woodstock and the Pine Hill. He soon persuaded the Dutchmen to buy 1400 shares in the turnpike. At the same time he was making rosy plans for a venture of his own—this was a glass factory on the Sawkill in Shady to be reached via the turnpike.[4]

From the beginning of his glassmaking plans DeZeng had an eye on Chancellor Livingston as a likely source of financial help for his factory. The Chancellor's lands in Woodstock adjoined the site of the proposed glass factory; if the factory were to be a success the value of the Chancellor's lands would surely be increased, his tenants might find work teaming and cutting wood for the furnaces of DeZeng's project, and Woodstock would thrive and grow. At the time the Chancellor was living at Clermont, busying himself with the agricultural and mechanical improvements which meant so much to him. Improving the breed of sheep, devising new means of fertilizing farm crops, joining with Robert Fulton in developing the steamboat, papermaking and other projects were competing with still lively political ambitions in his mind.

In 1800 newly elected President Thomas Jefferson offered the Chancellor the post of Secretary of the Navy. Livingston turned down this relatively unimportant position. But when the President appointed him minister plenipotentiary to France, a post in which his talents could have ample scope, he accepted at once. As the Chancellor was preparing to sail for France in 1801 to take up his new duties, DeZeng called on him at Clermont and told him of his glassmaking project. Though the Chancellor's response is not known, it could not have been entirely negative. After the minister had settled down in Paris, DeZeng returned to the subject in a letter dated April 8, 1802.

By that time DeZeng, with his brother-in-law John G. Clark, had bought from the heirs of Cornelius Tiebout and from Cornelius C. Roosevelt (a cousin of the family which would produce two Presidents) a tract of more than eight thousand acres which included the upper Sawkill Valley and Overlook Mountain. Enough big hardwood timber grew on this tract to keep a glass factory, greedy for fuel though it was, supplied for generations to come. DeZeng next bought the leasehold of one of the Chancellor's tenants, James Becker, whose farm lay on Cooper Lake in "a handsome Situation and very handy to the Intentet works," as DeZeng put it. Unwilling to put a valuable building on land held only under a lease agreement for three lives, DeZeng offered to buy the Becker property in fee simple.

He had underestimated the degree to which the Chancellor was wedded to his leases for three lives. The Chancellor would not sell. Neither did he take up DeZeng's offer to him of a share in the glassmaking venture which promised to produce a profit "by propre management of 30 to 40 per cent . . . anualy," and which if successful would greatly increase the value of all lands in Little Shandaken and Woodstock.

In his most persuasive manner DeZeng pointed out to the Chancellor that "Perhaps in no part of the world a better Situation in many Respects can be found for the Establishment of a Glass Factory or Factorys on any scale whatever . . ." The Chancellor may have been too much involved in the complicated negotiations which were then leading up to the Louisiana Purchase, or he may have feared that the setting up of a glass factory on the very edge of his domain might result in the kind of devastating deforestation which had followed glassmaking in Europe. And it is likely that he had less faith in the stimulating effect on glassmaking profits than did DeZeng of the recently passed increase in duties on imported glass to which DeZeng had referred in his letter of April 8, 1802.

DeZeng brought the Chancellor up to date on the progress of the Ulster and Delaware Turnpike. Work was going ahead rapidly. The route had been changed in order to save seven miles. It would not pass through the hamlets of Woodstock and Little Shandaken as originally planned. Instead it would pass through the "Hurley Woods & Yanky Town, over the Cannenbergh at Big Shandaken." The present road from Glenford via Yankeetown to Mount Tremper still follows this route. The change was made necessary if the turnpike were to compete with rival "great western roads" starting at Catskill and Newburgh. DeZeng wrote elsewhere that the new route was a matter of regret to him because now the turnpike would not pass by the site of his proposed glass works. But this was a minor setback which did nothing to diminish DeZeng's bubbling optimism for both the turnpike and the glass works.

In a letter of November 30, 1802 DeZeng again brought up the related subjects of the turnpike and his glass works. Now that the glass works were "almost totally" cut off from their logical shipping point at Kingston Landing by the change in the turnpike's route, he was planning a "good road" taking off from the Ulster and Delaware Turnpike at Yankeetown and leading via Bearsville and Woodstock to the Hudson below Saugerties. This road would eventually come into being—the Glasco Turnpike of our own day is a remnant of it.[5]

The matter of access to a shipping point on the Hudson was not the only one to give DeZeng's project trouble. He wrote that "having as yet failed in procuring good workmen from Germany &&" he had "errected a Forge, which is nearly compleated, and will be altogether out of my way by the time the Glass makers can be procured, having still some prospects to obtain them from Bohemia." He asked the Chancellor to let him know if "there is any probability of obtaining good workmen from the French Terrytory—as I would wish in preference to undertake anything else, to embark in such a manufactory" which would not only be profitable but would also bring "great advantages to our country in keeping great sums out of the hands of the English." The English at that time made most of the glass used in the United States.

DeZeng was now working to overcome the obstacle caused by the bypassing by the Ulster and Delaware Turnpike of his factory site. But there was little he could do to bring together the group of highly skilled workmen needed by a glass factory. In Europe such men were so highly valued that they were forbidden to emigrate. The rich folklore of glassmaking has many tales of European glass workers being treated to drinks by plausible secret agents of American glass factories to the point of stupor and awakening to find themselves on board ships bound for New York. As glass factories later multiplied in the United States factory managers tricked, bribed, cajoled or even forcibly kidnapped the workers of rival establishments and set them to work, grumbling but usually well paid, in their own plants.

When DeZeng had been active in the management of the glassmaking venture near Albany it had been possible to import workmen from Germany. With Napoleon now bestriding Europe, however, emigration of glass workers had become very much more difficult. DeZeng's glassmaking dreams for Woodstock's upper Sawkill valley had met obstacles which even the inventive and resourceful German could not hurdle. They remained nothing but dreams for the next seven years, until a combination of events in the outside world made glassmaking in Woodstock both attractive and possible.

In the meanwhile DeZeng set up a forge which served if nothing more to hold a space for the glassmaking operation which eventually arrived. Unfortunately not a great deal is known about the forge. It seems reasonably certain that it was located close to the point at which the stream which forms the outlet of Cooper Lake joins the Sawkill, close to where the Shady bridge now is on Route 212.

Not far above was a good dam site on the Sawkill. A grist mill and a sawmill later on used the water impounded by it. The Sawkill has torn and gouged the site in recurring floods, and the course of the stream may well have changed. In addition the City of Kingston has buried a water main across the site in order to carry Cooper Lake water to their Kingston customers. Roads and bridges nearby have been changed or washed out by floods to further confuse the trail of DeZeng's forge.

A clue to the forge may lie beneath some gentle mounds in what is now the pasture of two saddle horses. Under the mound are many pieces of red brick four inches wide and an inch and a quarter thick as well as many bits of extremely hard fire clay. Shady is full of surprises which go back to its industrial days. Until an expert in early American industries studies the upper Sawkill Valley they are likely to remain unexplained.

The piece of evidence that sheds the most light on DeZeng's forge may not, however, be found buried in the earth of Woodstock. It is an advertisement in a newspaper of 1805. The advertisement grew out of DeZeng's way of moving on with compulsive energy from one project to another. The advertisement shows that DeZeng was eager to unload his Woodstock projects. It reads in part:

Ten Thousand Acres of Land

In the town of Woodstock whereon is a new Forge and Blacksmith's shop adjoining with a store house for iron 30 by 18 feet. The Forge in complete order, and extremely well situated for timber and water, and in every respect as well calculated for doing business as any forge in the state, with a coal house, 60 by 24 feet, calculated to hold twenty thousand bushels of coal, on the same stream on which the forge stands are two Saw mills, and another contracted to be built this coming summer. Also in the course of the summer will be built within one hundred and fifty yards of the forge a new grist mill, calculated for two runs of stones. Also within about the same distance from the forge is a new two-story dwelling house with a kitchen now finishing off. Said house is very commodius and comfortable for a large family, with a store house in front now building and will be finished off complete to answer for the dry goods and grocery business. The stand will in time be very good for that business being in

120

the very centre of the town of Woodstock. Also now is building a large barn 40 by 50 feet, two stories high to be finished after the English style. With necessary houses for Bloomers, Sawyers, Millers, Colliers and other labourers. Upon the said tract are several important improvements and a never failing quantity of wood for coal and timber of various kinds for the mills . . .

The advertisement appeared in the (Kingston) *Plebeian* dated April 13, 1805. It is signed by DeZeng's partner, John G. Clark, who was in business in Kingston. Like so many other advertisements it was composed in order to make a better impression than the facts warranted. The forge is not described and does not seem to have been operating. Some of the buildings are unfinished or merely in the planned stage. The number of houses for workers is not given. The caption stresses the land rather than the forge.

It is likely then that the forge was not a large or elaborate one. Victor S. Clark in his *History of Manufactures in the United States* describes a typical forge in this way, "The forge consisted of one or more fires and tilt-hammers operated by a water-wheel. The sow of iron, weighing 60 or 70 pounds and not unlike our modern pigs, was heated, and hammered under a heavy hammer until it lost its granulated structure and was freed of dross, when it was turned over to a second crew, who with a smaller hammer 'drew' it into the bars of commerce." Bars like these were used by blacksmiths who made the hinges, horseshoes and countless other iron objects in daily use in early America. 'Bloomers' as used here were the men who produced the blooms which were hammered into bars—the blooms were rounded masses of refined iron. Colliers made the charcoal which kept the fires of the forge alive.

Somewhere in Woodstock during the next eighteen years a deposit of iron ore was worked and reduced. Only a few tons were produced, but the iron was said to have been of a high quality. The deposit was probably what is called bog iron, concentrated from iron compounds in the soil and rock by bacterial action on the margins of streams. The ore ran out and no more iron was made. What was made could well have resulted from the reduction of local ores in small quantities with no more than the forge's usual equipment. As was the case with other New York State forges of the time, partly processed iron might have been brought from a considerable distance to be finished. The most likely source were the iron fields in Columbia County close to the Connecticut border.

The advertisement in the *Plebeian* was well-phrased to arouse the attention of people ambitious either to speculate in land or form an industrial center, or both; and it stirred the imagination of a man who was just as remarkable in his own way as DeZeng. He was Stephen Stilwell, who had recently given up his hardware and jewelry business at 169 Pearl Street in the City of New York. Stilwell bought the entire DeZeng and Clark tract. After many problems the long-delayed dream of making glass in the upper Sawkill Valley eventually was realized.

14

THE GLASSMAKERS' VILLAGE ON THE SAWKILL

When Stephen Stilwell was a boy in Jamaica, Long Island during the early 1770s "he was inventive and ingenious to a degree that set all his neighbors talking." He made a little "weather house." The carved and painted man who lived there came out when the weather was fine. When it was about to rain the man ducked inside. Stilwell also made two figures, one holding a whip and the other a saw. When the wind turned the little windmill which was their motive power, one figure threatened the other with his whip and the second figure sawed a miniature log.

The boy obviously had a good share in the mechanical ingenuity which was developing in America and would later on transform its industry and agriculture. When the American Revolution came Stilwell, while not yet out of his teens, served in Long Island battles of the War and was taken prisoner by Hessian troops. After the War was over he operated one of the tide mills which were then a feature of Long Island life. His mill at Flushing was said to have been six stories tall.

In order to locate and buy wheat and deliver flour, Stillwell had a sloop in which he sailed up and down the coast. At about the same time he became partner in a jewelry and hardware business in New York and before long invented and patented the "smut cone," a mechanical device for cleaning grain of certain impurities. As a hardware dealer he was on the lookout for improved and ingenious gadgets of all sorts. When the French portraitist St. Memin came to New York with the "physionotrace," a mechanical device for taking portraits, Stilwell's store on Pearl Street became his agency.

Late in 1800 Stilwell and his partner William DeForest advertised that they wanted "to decline the Hardware and Jewellers business" and offered their establishment for sale. It was a good time to give up the business. The war boom in Europe which had created temporary prosperity in the United States was soon to end with the signing of the treaty of Amiens. Relations with Britain and France were worsening. Doubt and uncertainties slowed business and industry.[1]

By 1806 Stilwell had made his decision to buy DeZeng and Clark's Woodstock lands. Britain and France were interfering with neutral shipping on the high seas. The importation of manufactured goods from Europe was slowing down. American manufacturers were encouraged to expand by the lessening of competition from abroad. This trend reached a culmination in 1807 with the passing by Congress of the Embargo Act intended to cut off commercal relations and trade with Europe. The act took effect December 22, 1807. Very quickly American manufacturers began taking advantage of the opportunity which now was theirs. Factories making textiles, metal objects, glass and many other things sprang up.

Unhappily, Stephen Stilwell could not take a direct part in the upsurge of manufacturing effort. Speculating in land had been almost an obsession with him. When he sold his business in New York and his valuable mill and farms on Long Island he used much of the capital he raised in this way in unsuccessful speculations in scattered tracts of land. By 1807 he was in trouble and the sheriff of Ulster County had an eye on him.

In July 1808 thousands of acres of Stilwell's Woodstock lands were advertised "to be sold at auction August 24 at the Kingston Court House." A few months later the sheriff proposed selling Stillwell's goods and chattels at his house in Woodstock. The forge was not mentioned in the advertisements. It had not been a success and probably was not thought to have any market value.[2]

Stilwell fought back manfully against this tide of misfortune. The sheriff's sales did not take place. Instead a group of New Yorkers headed by Stephen's more cautious younger brother Samuel bought the upper half of Stephen's close to nine thousand acre tract and proposed to put a glass factory on it. In Woodstock and Ulster County the project was greeted with enthusiasm.

On August 8, 1809 Jesse Buel, editor of the Ulster *Plebeian*, published an editorial which related the proposed factory to the economic forces which were making it possible. "Among the useful establishments springing up . . . we feel a pleasure in noticing two, of no inconsiderable magnitude which are contemplated in this vicinity. One is a glass house which is to be erected in Woodstock by the Ulster Glass Manufacturing company. Sand, supposed to be suitable for making glass, is found in abundance near the site . . . [the second establishment Buel noticed was a cotton factory at Eddyville on the the Rondout Creek]." Buel added that it was a consolation "to reflect that the injustice of Europe, which aims to prostrate our prosperity, essentially contributes to encourage, invigorate and perfect these improvements."

As he launched glassmaking in Woodstock, Samuel Stilwell was a man whose opinions carried weight. He had been a member of the State Legislature a few years earlier, He was rich. He was official surveyor to the City of New York (in this capacity he helped lay out the city plan with the narrow lots and absence of open spaces which have plagued New Yorkers ever since). He was active in the Methodist Church; he and Stephen remembered attending Methodist meetings in the old rigging loft which was the birthplace of Methodism in New York.

Samuel had no trouble in getting together a solid group of New York City stockholders to finance the glassmaking plan. Isaac Wright and Sons were among them—the Wrights were shipping people who would soon form the famous Black Ball Line, first of all trans-Atlantic packets. Another investor was Peter Stuyvesant, a descendant of New York's last Dutch governor. Elisha Williams was a distinguished trial lawyer and politician. Samuel Hicks was a rich Quaker whose mercantile house of Samuel Hicks and Sons was spoken of with respect. Several men who revolved around Hicks were also stockholders, among them Hicks' son-in-law, Effingham Embree, the well-known jeweler. Alderman Jacob Mott also took shares.

Early in 1809 a committee of the State Legislature was considering Samuel Stilwell's petition for an act which would incorporate the Woodstock Glass Manufacturing Society. The petition was granted and the Society came into being on March 24, 1809 (the name of the corporation was changed to the Woodstock Glass Manufacturing Company by a legislative act of June 12, 1812).[3]

Even before the company was incorporated a beginning of

glassmaking had been made on the 4200-acre tract bought from Stephen and his wife by Samuel and his associates. The town clerk's minute book of Woodstock refers in road surveys of March 23, 1809 (just one day before incorporation) to the sawmill of the "Woodstock Glass Manufactory" and to the "Old Glass Factory near James McDonough's." The phrase "Old Glass Manufactory" has long puzzled local historians and is still without explanation. It gives strong evidence that an attempt at setting up a glass factory had already been made, perhaps by DeZeng and apparently on a site other than the one on the former Herbert Keefe farm in Keefe Hollow, where glass was being made in 1811 and continued to be made for many years.

And this is not the only mystery surrounding the beginnings of glassmaking in the upper Sawkill Valley. In March 1810 the Society petitioned the Legislature to be allowed to manufacture some product other than glass—they were not permitted under their original act of incorporation to use their capital for any purpose other than glassmaking. The act of 1812 which changed the corporation's name also suggested that there had been irregularities in the management of the Company and stated that these did not void the act of incorporation under which it operated.

The Woodstock Glass Manufacturing Society's petition to be allowed to make something else was turned down. Its backers then plunged into establishing their glass factory. By January 5, 1811 they were advertising for "five thousand cords of Furnace wood for which cash will be paid." By November of the same year they advertised window glass for sale "by the Box or single pane at the Woodstock Glass Factory . . ." In the same advertisement they added:

> Wood choppers take notice!
> Constant employ may be had at the above Fact
> ory and a liberal price given in cash
> For chopping wood by the cord or acre.

Obviously the factory was in business and was able to offer cash to workers. Active in the management of the venture was William M. Stilwell (it was he who had signed the company's advertisements). William, the oldest son of Stephen, later was to become a clergyman in the City of New York and in the Catskills. With the backing of his uncle, the Honorable Samuel, he would lead a once-famous secession from the Methodist Church. He would give his name to the sect known as the Methodist Society or the Stilwellites. But in 1811 William was using his energies on behalf of the glassmaking venture beginning to strip the upper Sawkill Valley of its primeval forests.

At the same time Stephen, rescued from disaster by the sale of a number of pieces of land, was far from idle. On January 5, 1810 he put a notice in the *Plebeian* that indicated he was taking an active part in a scheme to establish a number of industries in the upper Sawkill Valley and to construct a turnpike to connect the valley to a good landing on the Hudson River around which a bustling town known as Glasco was to be built—this was the turnpike planned earlier by DeZeng. The notice read:

PUBLIC NOTICE

Is hereby given that we the subscribers intend to present a petition to the legislature . . . at their next session, for an act of incorporation, to enable us to make a turn pike road, to commence at Hudson's River nearly opposite Red Hook Landing, at the red house near Cornelis Minklaer's in the town of Kingston, and from thence to run the most direct and convenient route, through the towns of Kingston and Woodstock, to the place contemplated for the Woodstock Glass Company manufactory, in the town of Woodstock. Dated Jan. 1810. [The date of 1809 in the first printing of the advertisement was corrected to 1810 in the next printing.]

The Embargo Acts of 1807-10 had thrown many American merchants into bankruptcy and caused debtors' prisons to overflow. It was now, however, bringing manufacturers visions of fortunes to be made in textiles, earthenwares, iron objects, glass and many other products. Events in Europe and on the high seas had stimulated the Stilwells and their associates, and they responded vigorously. Stephen Stilwell obtained an act of incorporation for the Bristol Glass, Cotton and Clay Company. The new company did not have to confine its activities to glass only. With imports of cotton from Europe cut off, enormous American demand had caused a rush to build cotton mills in many places where waterpower was available. For some years after 1807 American cotton spinners used their virtual monopoly to make good profits.

Beds of excellent clay were known to lie on and close to the Minklaer farm, mentioned in Stilwell's advertisement. The Hudson River would move bricks and other clay products to New York. Fuel to be used in brickmaking could be brought down from the upper Sawkill Valley. Three-quarters of a century later one of the brickyards on the land formerly owned by Stilwell's company was employing 250 workers and sending 25,000,000 bricks down the Hudson each year. The "Clay" in the name of the Bristol Glass, Cotton and Clay Company referred to the Glasco clay; the name of the settlement around the landing on the Hudson is said to have been a shortened form of "Glass Company," which appeared on a large sign on the company wharf.

The two corporations in the upper Sawkill Valley seem to have cooperated in many ways. The Bristol company had as directors besides Stephen Stillwell a number of men who owned land at Glasco or along the route of the proposed turnpike. These same men were the directors of the Bristol Glass, Cotton and Clay Company. They, unlike the Woodstock Glass Manufacturing Society, had no rich New Yorkers among their number. When the Glasco Turnpike came into being, both companies used it. And after the glass companies' landing was surveyed people connected with both glass factories bought lots in the hope that the place would quickly become a bustling riverside town. Its streets were given such names as Liberty, Plenty, Ontario and Albany. The large numbers of brick used in the buildings of both companies were made in Glasco.

Between 1811 and 1815 the managers and stockholders of both of Woodstock's glassmaking companies had good reason to be cheerful. The beginning of the War of 1812 briefly stimulated the demand for domestic manufactures, and the Woodstock Glass Manufacturing Society was able to declare a dividend of ten per cent.

Peace in 1815 brought with it a flood of imports from England. The booming American glass industry quickly suffered. Both the Woodstock companies had borrowed money for expansion, and were faced with repayment at a time when sales were tumbling. Notices of sheriff's sales began appearing in the Kingston newspapers. William and John Mott of New York, who had loaned the Glass Manufacturing Society fifteen thousand dollars, bought the plant and 4200 acres at a forced sale held to recover over $76,000 owed to Isaac Honfield, also of New York.[4]

The Bristol Company managed to ride out the storm, and soon Stephen Stillwell announced the factory was resuming operations. In 1816 Dr. Ebenezer Hall, who had come to Woodstock in 1813 and paid $500 for the secrets of glassmaking to George Seaman, superintendent of the Woodstock Glass Manufacturing Company, returned to become superintendent himself.[5]

The two factories staggered forward under many difficulties. The deposits of sand "on the borders of Shandaken or Row's Lake" which the factories had used under agreement with the Livingstons of Clermont proved to be not of the highest quality. As time went on, the sand became increasingly expensive to dig out. Sand had to be brought from New Jersey or near Albany by sloop and stored until needed in a sandhouse on the bank of the Hudson at Glasco.

And that was not all. A remarkable period of long winters and cold summers bedevilled farmers and manufacturers. When that was over a financial panic in 1819 brought industry to a crawl and in many cases to a halt. The panic is believed to have been among other things a result of overextension by manufacturers like those who made glass in the upper Sawkill Valley. Yet, harried by legal actions and pressures to reorganize as they were, the Woodstock factories continued to produce window glass and to a lesser extent bottles. In 1825 the Bristol Glass, Cotton and Clay Company was re-chartered as the New York Crown and Cylinder Glass Company. Its superintendent continued to be (as he had been for some years) Daniel Elliot.

That same year Spafford's *Gazetteer of New York* stated that "the Bristol and Woodstock glass manufactories are said to produce good profits and good glass." But not everyone saw the Woodstock glass factories in so cheerful a light. James Pierce, in an account of the Catskills in the *American Journal of Science* in 1823, wrote of the "Bristol glass works " that, "Window glass is the principal article manufactured, and four miles north east of this establishment in an elevated and secluded mountain valley another manufactory of glass has been erected [this, of course was that of the Woodstock Glass Company]. Sand for these manufactories is procured from Philadelphia and the sea coast, and the other materials from a distance. The advantage resulting from the cheapness of wood and soil, will not compensate for the enhanced expense incurred in transporting the ingredients of glass and the bricks, stone, lime and clay, for the furnaces and crucibles, and many of the necessaries of life, sixteen or twenty miles over mountain roads." [6]

In a few sentences of description of the Woodstock Glass Company's site and buildings, Pierce showed himself to be impressed by the same romantic quality which Thomas Cole was to feel many years later. "A small hamlet of about thirty houses has been erected adjacent to the upper or mountain glass house, on ground favorable for gardens and meadows," wrote Pierce. "North of this village an elevated, wood clad and steep mountain ranges to the westward; its wildly irregular waving summits are several miles in view." The Indian Head range of mountains is still a stirring sight as it rises beyond the Sawkill and the nearby pastures in what is known today as Keefe Hollow.

By 1837 James Pierce's gloomy prediction had been fulfilled as far as the upper glass house was concerned. It was no longer in business, perhaps a casualty of the difficult economic conditions of the 1830s which culminated in the panic of 1837. The former Bristol Glass Company, however, was doing better. Gordon's Gazetteer of 1837 credits it with a monthly production of 1500 boxes of glass and 50 employees. This factory too went out of business about 1845 after a number of ups and downs.

It was revived in 1853 under the corporate name of the Ulster County Glass Manufacturing Company. It was owned cooperatively by a group headed by lawyer Marius Schoonmaker of Kingston with Peter Reynolds as superintendent. Some local historians have speculated that its failure in 1855 was due to its worker-owners having bought too freely at the well-stocked company store. But this is unlikely to have been the factor which gave the final push to the already tottering glassmaking industry of Woodstock. Coal instead of wood had come into general use as fuel for glassmaking. The Woodstock factories could not compete with producers located near good sources of coal. Besides, the hardwood forests close to their factories had been cut and burned. Wood had to be brought at greater expense from an ever-increasing distance. They were reduced to burning hemlock or other less efficient fuels.[7]

When the taker of the New York census of 1855 visited the Ulster Glass Manufacturing Company's plant he noted it had 32 employees, real estate to the value of $1000, and tools and machinery of the same value. The cash value of its raw materials was $7353 and that of its manufactured articles—the glass on hand—$13,500. The census man had arrived just in time to be present at the end of Woodstock glassmaking.

Already the once-enormous tract of forested land owned by the two glass ventures was in the process of division and sale. In January 1849 Alfred A. Mott of New York, whose family had bought the lands of the upper glass factory at sheriff's sales, put on the market ten farms of two hundred acres each "half cleared." The farms, Mott advertised, were "well watered and are considered some of the best grass farms in the county, and are well worthy of the attention of persons engaged in the grazing business . . ."

Most of this land was bought by Christian Baehr, the German-born storekeeper who gave his name in an altered form to the hamlet of Bearsville. Peter Reynolds bought the lands owned by the Ulster County Glass Manufacturing Company. His descendants still own some of it plus the two old buildings which are believed to have housed the glass furnaces. Nearby stand a few much-altered houses, the survivors of the glassmakers' and forge-workers' cottages of the company village owned successively by DeZeng and Clark, Stephen Stilwell, the Bristol Glass, Cotton and Clay Company, the New York Crown and Cylinder Glass Company and briefly the Ulster County Glass Company.[8]

This company village once bustled with life and activity, as did its neighbor higher on the Sawkill in Keefe Hollow. Wagons loaded with casks of clay, with sand and soda, and with wooden boxes of window glass packed in hay or straw went on their way to Glasco and by sloop to New York. Glassworkers were traditionally lively and imaginative people. They were fond of music. Because their lungs were well developed and their throats affected by blowing glass, they were often singers. Glassblowers' choirs were a feature of European glass villages, tucked away as were those of Woodstock in forests.

Among the familiar personalities in the glassmaking villages were a father and son both named Lewis Edson. The elder Edson had been born in Massachusetts, where he had been known as "the great singer," as a choir master and a composer of hymn tunes (outstanding were those named Lenox, Bridgewater and Greenfield) and fuguing tunes. He and his son taught singing school over a wide area. The elder Edson had come to Woodstock about the time DeZeng set up his forge. A blacksmith and nailmaker by trade, he may well have been drawn to Woodstock to work for DeZeng or Stilwell. The younger Edson had published a book of hymns and social songs accompanied by a few pages of instructions in reading music and singing—it was called the *Social Harmonist*. He operated a sawmill in Mink Hollow and supplied the glass factories with boards for use in making packing boxes.

A notebook kept by the son and now in the music division of the New York Public Library contains many of his tunes and a few verses he is believed to have written. One, called "The Brag," belongs with the boasts which American folk heroes like Davy Crockett and Mike Fink are said to have declaimed. But there was a notable difference. Instead of boasting of skill in shooting or fighting as the "ring-tailed roarers" like Crockett did, Edson boasted of skill in a variety of arts and crafts. His verses suggest that life in the glassmakers' villages had a side that was in keeping with the way of life of present-day Woodstock. It goes:

Writing is what I do well understand
Printing is also at my own command,
Cuting down Trees, and sewing up Trousers;
Carving to me's very handy,
Marking out statues or drinking of brandy;
Stamping of muslin I do very neat,
Engraving's an Art, I have it compleat;
Staining I do it both hansome and good,
Painting by me is well understood;
Inditing is what I well understand,
He that don't b'leive may dought & be d---d.

The account books of the glasshouse store show Lewis Edson, Jr. was fond of gin as well as of brandy. He married a granddaughter of old Peter Short. The couple had several children, among them two boys whom they named for poets, Virgil and Milton. In 1819, the year of America's first big financial panic, Lewis, Jr. filed a bankruptcy petition to avoid being sent to debtor's prison. Daniel Elliot, manager of the Bristol Glass Company, assumed his debts of a little over $107 and Edson went on as before. The last sad mention of him is a notation in the Woodstock poormaster's book for February 3, 1846 of $3.00 paid "for a coffin for Lewis Edson." [9]

Lewis, Jr.'s career in Woodstock suggests the wide variety of human beings who were attracted to the town after glassmaking began. It sheds light on the human cost of economic distress (many Woodstock people were in trouble around 1819), and it makes it plain that the life of a composer of hymn tunes and a singing teacher even in a glassmakers' village was far from profitable a century and a half ago.

As a good deal of folklore suggests, there was a more cheerful side to the lives of glassmakers. Because skilled glassworkers were scarce, they were often well paid. They were long remembered for spending their money freely at the glass company store and at Woodstock's many roadside taverns. One tale collected by Anita M. Smith tells of a group of glassworkers betting on who would order the most expensive meal. The winner ordered two slices of buttered bread, put a ten-dollar bill between them, ate the sandwich and won the bet.

Stilwell family history has preserved the deeds of a black man who astonished glass village people by his feats of skill and daring. He was Jem Day, son of Stephen Stilwell's cook. Mrs. Day had been a slave who looked forward to becoming free according to New York

State law, on July 4, 1827. The Stilwells bought Mrs. Day's time up to 1827 from her former owner and took her with them when they came to Woodstock about 1803. When glassmaking began Jem sometimes demonstrated his courage and acrobatic skills by dancing on a beam above the glass furnace when it was in full blast. A fall would have meant instant death.

Stephen Stilwell used his mechanical skills to good advantage, as did his son Stephen Jr., who did a good deal of such work as grinding up the old glassmaking pots for use in making new ones. The elder Stilwell is said to have made his own false teeth and a set for his wife as well. He is also believed to have introduced Methodism to Woodstock with the help of his brother Samuel and his nephew Rev. William Stilwell. The earliest Methodist services are said to have been held in Stillwell's house, which still stands at the point where the Glasco Turnpike joins Route 212 in Shady. (Some say, however, that the Henry P. Shultis farm on the Wittenberg Road was the scene of the earliest Methodist meetings.) A number of other buildings now gone gave the intersection a busy air. One house standing close to the site of the former Shady post office was moved to Reynolds' Lane next to the Brokenshaw house, in which managers of the glass company once lived and which was for many years the Reynolds house. Across the road from the Brokenshaw house the old company store is now used as a studio. On the Sawkill not far away are the remains of the grist mill, built about 1805 and in business with a cider mill beside it well into the twentieth century.

Silas Moore Stilwell, who as a boy lived in Shady with his parents, the Stephen Stilwells, grew up to become a man of considerable fame. At various times in an active life he was a member of the legislature of Tennessee, of the Virginia House of Burgesses and of the New York State Legislature. Author of the New York State law of 1831 which abolished imprisonment for debt, he wrote much on banking reform. Having become a spiritualist he wrote a book on the subject, but it was never published.[10]

Children in the lower glassmakers' village attended school in the house now owned by the Rev. Adelmar Bryon. As in other communities of the time they were set to work at an early age. Glassmaking records show that boys worked at various tasks in the glass factories and did part-time work in something called "picking pot shells," the chipping of adhering glass away from pots which had broken after use for several months to a year in the furnaces.

Company store account books show the children probably played jews harps.

Tradition preserves memories of a peddler who came to the glassmakers from time to time with a wagonload of musical instruments. Then a man might turn in his flute and get a fiddle in return or add instruments to the collection he already had.[11]

A controversial man in early glassmaking was Dr. Ebenezer Hall. He lived in Woodstock at the same time as another Dr. Hall, Larry Gilbert Hall, who lived in the present Woodstock Library building. Though the two have been hopelessly confused in local lore, enough reliable evidence has survived to show the difference. Dr. Ebenezer was an emigrant from Scotland who turned up as a doctor in Warwick, Conn. and there persuaded his fellow townsmen to buy stock in a proposed glass factory. The doctor, according to one of those to whom he sold stock, had "a considerable share of natural powers of mind, and a particularly fascinating and alluring address, more brilliant than solid, more theoretical and visionary than practical and real . . ." and "a persuasive and flattering tongue."

Hall set up a factory and "having cast sand and salt and potash into the fire it came out glass." At this point Hall was in a pretty predicament. His theoretical understanding of glassmaking needed to be supplemented by practical knowledge and experience if he were to actually make glass in a commercial way. He hastened to Woodstock, the excellent quality of whose glassmaking products were already becoming known, for instruction in the art of making glass.

Fortified with his new knowledge Hall returned to Warwick and started up the factory. Aided by the harsh economic climate of the times, he brought the venture to failure. Local people had been persuaded to "lay aside the plough, the axe, and the spade, and to mortgage their possessions" to finance the factory. Now they drove Hall from their midst. He returned to Woodstock before long and became superintendent in the place of his teacher, George Seaman.

There were no complaints of Hall's lack of ability in managing the glass works. He also practiced medicine, took part in politics and held office as a member of what was then known as the Republican party (it later became the Democratic party). He was active in the local Lutheran Church. By the 1830s he moved on to Michigan and a career of glassmaking, politics and canal building in which he demonstrated his continued ability to persuade his fellow citizens to invest their money in enticing projects.[12]

For close to half a century Woodstock's glassmakers did much to change the town. Many of the glassblowers had worked in other American glassmaking centers and had acquired a breadth of experience of life far more varied than that of most of tenants for lives. In addition they brought to the town an interest in music and a creative spirit. Some intermarried with older local families, some members of older families became glassblowers. Joseph Higgins Short, son of glassworker Peter W. Short (whose grandfather was pioneer Peter Short), went on to blow glass in Pennsylvania and upstate New York. Other glass workers with shallower roots in Woodstock left for other more prosperous glassmaking towns.

Because glassmaking was so very hot an occupation, glass houses did not function by summer. Through the cold months of the year the two Woodstock glass houses were popular gathering places in the evening because they were the warmest places in town. Then the blowers used the "metal" left over from the day's work in making "whimsies" for their friends or making a pitcher or bowl for someone who asked. Until recently many Woodstock farmhouses had a glass cane, dipper, hat or other whimsy hanging on the parlor wall as a relic of glassmaking days. Glass turtles or other creatures were used as doorstops. People from outside Woodstock often came to the glass houses to watch the wonders of glassmaking and carry whimsies away as souvenirs.[13]

For almost fifty years Woodstock produced a large annual output of window glass and, occasional bottles and tableware. Population increased. So too did taverns, stores and churches. Supervisors and other officials came from the ranks of glass people, among them Daniel Elliot, who managed the lower glass works. Glassmaking brought the first post office to town. With other Ulster industries stimulated by the power of the Napoleonic Wars it attracted the first bank to the county in 1820. This bank closed in 1829, but in 1832 the Bank of Ulster began to function. Ever since Woodstock peoples' lives and fortunes have been affected by their county banks.

The most conspicuous and long-reaching effect on the visible landscape of Woodstock's glassmaking years was the deforestation of Woodstock's hills and mountains, often followed by forest fires which blazed among the dry branches left behind by the woodcutters. Erosion then carried away the already sparse mountainside soil or piled up gravel and stones on fertile valley fields.

With the ending of glassmaking a good source of income for

Woodstock farmers and their sons vanished. They could no longer cut wood by winter for the glass works, or transport glass, sand and other materials to and from Glasco, Saugerties and Rondout. The mid-1850s was a time of nationwide depression which made Woodstock feel the closing of the glass houses even more keenly. Attention then turned to other sources of possible income. One which will be dealt with in a later chapter was quarrying of bluestone. Another was a revival of a longtime obsession with finding and mining deposits of minerals. This obsession, which had long haunted Woodstock people, brought with it dreams of sudden wealth to be uncovered beneath the surface of the earth.

15

HUNTERS FOR GOLD, SILVER AND COAL

While Woodstock people, like the Indians before them, saw their way of living as closely related to their soil, to its bedrock, to the streams that furrowed earth and rock, and to the living things, plant and animal, which were sustained by the earth. Glassmaking, lumbering, land speculation, tanning and the making of forest products all had their sources in combinations of the earth's bounty. And underneath the earth, hidden from the eyes of most people and unthought of by the Indians, lay the possibility of fabulous wealth derived from minerals.

Dreams of mineral wealth in our own time usually take the form of visions of oil wells, or at least deposits of natural gas. Until recently it was the potential presence of gold and silver that gave rise to similar dreams. Much lore about gold and silver discoveries forms a part of Woodstock's folklore and still survives in the minds of some of its older people. Until he died some twenty years ago one of these old people was Charley Herrick, who handed some of this old lore on to me.

When I first came to live in Lewis Hollow high on the side of Overlook Mountain oldtimers told me that the ridge which hems in the hollow to the north was called the Beehive. The name didn't make sense to me. I asked Charley Herrick, who had known the Hollow from boyhood, the reason for the name. He chuckled and said I'd understand after I came to know the Beehive better. For several months I speculated about the Beehive's name. It still made no sense.

One day sheets of mist were coming and going over the face of Overlook Mountain. I had driven out of the Hollow and was heading eastward on the West Saugerties Road close to the point at which the road takes off from the old Glasco Turnpike. I looked up at Overlook and immediately understood the reason for the Beehive's name.

That morning the mist had revealed many secrets of the mountain. It had separated what had seemed an uninterrupted upward slope the day before into a series of ridges and hollows. I saw the ridge which had been my neighbor for several months against a dim background of mist; it had exactly the form of the kind of straw beehive used by Woodstock farmers of long ago, but magnified until it stood about a thousand feet high. The parallel layers of sandstone which make up the Beehive are slightly tilted toward the southwest. They correspond neatly to the spiralled rope of straw wound round and round to make an old-fashioned beehive.

Poet William Wordsworth commented on the phenomena which explained the Beehive more than a century and a half ago when he wrote of the mountains of the "Country of the Lakes" in which he lived. "Their apparent forms and colours," he wrote, "are perpetually changed by the clouds and vapours which float round them; the effect indeed of mist or haze, in a country of this character, is like that of magic . . ." The effect I had seen seemed indeed magical, yet there was a rational explanation for it. The Beehive had once been a longer ridge which had been worn down by millennia of erosion into its present rounded shape. Later I learned that several other beehives may be seen when conditions are right standing along the wall of the Catskills to the north of Overlook. Others can be found at a number of valleys within the Catskills.

When I told Charley Herrick of the dramatic revelation to me of the Beehive, he nodded. If some people had seen what I had seen, he said, they'd be up on the Beehive digging for gold. Plenty of people believe that what I'd seen was the Lord's way of showing me where a mine was. He didn't believe it, he said, but plenty of others did.

Later on I found that Charley was referring to a belief that went back to the beginning of exploration and settlement of the Catskills and had never died out, a belief that there were valuable minerals, most likely gold and silver, underground in the Catskills. From time to time God had taken action to point out the location of these deposits to selected individuals. Trees struck by lightning, rock slides or new rock surfaces revealed by flood, the magical transformations wrought by clouds and haze—all these formed part of a body of lore current in Europe in the seventeenth century and carried across the Atlantic.[1]

Early attempts at locating minerals in the Province of New York in the days of Dutch and then English rule had produced no spectacular results. But faith that the Catskills contained rich veins of minerals remained strong. There just had to be gold and silver or at least copper and coal in the Catskills, some people believed, because if not why had the Lord created the Catskills? Level valleys, these people believed, had been created for farmers to grow crops on, hillsides for pasture, rivers to hold a supply of fish for human use as well as for transportation, and mountains to hold minerals.

Overlook and its neighboring mountains had been explored for minerals as far back as the mid-1660s; in 1702 Lord Cornbury, the newly appointed British governor of the Province of New York, while travelling the Hudson River on his official barge spent some time ashore at Kingston. Soon he informed his cousin, Queen Anne, that while he was on this trip "he is come to ye knowledge of Severall Minerals in ye Mountains of Said Province (New York) & has engaged Severall Persons who will undertake to Worke those Mines, if y'r. Ma'ty shall be graciously pleased to give a grant thereof unto him, under whom they may Securely proceed on that Worke, & have ye necessary Assurances of a reasonable Profit for their Labour." The mines, Cornbury said, were in the mountains of Ulster and Albany counties—and this included those of Woodstock. Overlook because of its conspicuous position and its crumbling Minister's Face was a likely place, according to Old World miners' lore, to find minerals.

The petition by which Cornbury asked for a grant of mining rights was passed from one London official to another and was shelved without any action being taken. In the Hardenbergh Patent of 1708 all rights to the "royal metals" of gold and silver were reserved to the Crown. During the long period while the Hardenbergh Patent lay undivided and untouchable there is no known evidence of prospecting in what was to become Woodstock. On May 1, 1762, however, Robert Livingston of Clermont wrote to his son that "here is again a report that there is a mine (tho I give no credit to it)." Livingston was referring to Overlook Mountain and Cornelius Tiebout's visions of minerals there. That the hope for coal was increasing is shown by the reservation of coal mining rights in some deeds to land on Overlook as early as 1775.[2]

In 1788 dreams of gold and silver mines awakened, a likely outgrowth of the intense going-over given the Hurley-Margaret Livingston boundary. On June 27 of that year Margaret Livingston made an agreement with Aldert Smedes, a descendant of one of the Hurley Patentees and so entitled to a share in the Hurley Patentee Woods. The agreement read in part, "In consequence of the Discoverys that Aldert Smedes of Hurley shall here after make, of any Gold & Silver mines Belonging to her in the Hardenbergh Patent . . ." Smede was to have complete "Benefit" of the mines for six months, after which Madame Livingston was to have a one-fourth share of all gold or silver found "free and clear of all expense." Later that year, on December 8, William Cockburn, who had drawn up the Margaret Livingston-Aldert Smedes agreement, drafted a petition to the State Legislature on his own behalf, "that your Petitioner with much Toil and Expense has made some Discoverys of Gold & Silver ore within the County of Ulster. Your Petitioner therfor prays he may have the Exclusive Privilege of Sarching for, Diging; working, and Carrying away all such Mettles & ores, as he has or may Discover . . ."

Neither the agreement nor the petition is specific as to the location of the gold and silver discovered. That is not to be wondered at, for were their location to have been revealed it would surely have precipitated a gold rush. There is no further known evidence about the "discoveries." It is probable that iron pyrite or some other substance was mistaken for gold or silver.[3]

By the time glassmaking was being planned for the upper Sawkill Valley, American interest in coal was becoming intense. A bit earlier—in 1796—Dr. Samuel Latham Mitchill, leading New York scientist, had led an expedition which tried without success to find deposits of coal within easy reach of the Hudson River. After Stephen Stilwell got into financial trouble and had overextended himself in land speculation, he had turned hopefully to the veins of coal long said to exist on his property in Woodstock. On December 8, 1807 the *Plebeian* of Kingston printed under the caption COAL the following, "We understand that Mr. Stephen Stilwell has discovered a vein of Fossil coal near his Iron works in the town of Woodstock about 12 miles from this village [Kingston] from which sanguine expectations are induldged. The coal is found near the surface and the stratum is represented to us as being from 9 to 18 inches in thickness." [4]

Because Stilwell's once-considerable capital was tied up in land, he needed a source of money to develop his mine. He appealed to the City of New York, and the committee of New York's Common Council to which his proposition was referred brought in its report on Dec. 21, 1807. It went:

> They have submitted the Specimen of Coal produced by Stillwell to the inspection and examination of Doctor Bruce professor of mineralogy and Doctor Dewitt professor of Chemistry of the College of Physicians in this city. That those gentlemen are decidedly of opinion that the Specimen indicates the existence of a coal mine, the extent and quality of which can only be ascertained by actual exploration.
>
> From satisfactory inquiry into the character of Mr. Stillwell your Committee are perfectly assured that the Specimen of Coal offered by him has been, bona fide, taken from a mine as set forth in his petition. The expense of exploring being too great and hazardous for him to attempt alone, he proposes to raise a fund of $50000 in Shares of fifty dollars each, pledging the land on which the Mine is situate for the benefit of the Subscribers together with a right to one half of the coalmine.
>
> How far the Corporation may judge it expedient to contribute toward exploring the mine, either by subscription for a number of shares, or by an advance of a reasonable sum on such security as Mr. Stillwell can give, or by offering a premium for the first quantity of Coal amounting to [blank] Chaldrons produced from his mine, is submitted to the wisdom of the board.
>
> The Committee cannot conclude this reference without observing that it is certainly an object of the highest consequence and a duty imposed on this Board to encourage every plausible plan that may tend to produce a supply of an Article so essentially necessary for the comfort and existence of the citizens of this rapidly encreasing metropolis as mineral Coal so called to distinguish it from charcoal especially when the resource can be found within the bosom of our own State, whereby our citizens will be relieved from the uncertain dependence on foreign supplies.
>
> The Augmentation of our population exceeds, annually, the growth of Forests for Fuel, and unless additional resources be explored, this essential article of existence must bear extremely oppressive, as indeed it does at present, on the poorer classes of Society.

The members of the Common Council were not persuaded to support Stilwell's scheme by the Committee's report, despite its prediction of what a later generation would term an approaching energy crisis. They were not even won over by the fact that coal from Stilwell's Woodstock lands was burning in the grate that heated the chamber in which the report was being read.

Yet Stilwell's proposal must have been attractive, especially in the year 1807. The situation was as acute as the Committee suggested. The immense quantities of firewood needed by New Yorkers were being brought from farther and farther away at ever-increasing cost as local sources dwindled. Supplies of soft coal imported from England were becoming less and less dependable as relations between England and the United States worsened. Imports seemed about to be cut off. Though coal mines in Woodstock may have seemed attractive, the members of the Common Council apparently realized that all Stilwell had to offer was the possibility of discovering a vein, thicker and more productive than the one from which he had pried the coal he brought to New York.[5]

The failure of Stilwell's attempt to interest the Common Council in his discovery did little to discourage other Woodstock people from dreaming of becoming rich from coal. As coal came into much wider use and as methods of burning anthracite successfully were developed during the first decade of the nineteenth century, a "coal mania" seized much of the United States. In 1814 the Society for the Promotion of Useful Arts resolved "That this society deem it highly important to make researches for the discovery of Fossil Coal, and that a committee be appointed to procure pecuniary aid for this purpose . . ."

The committee was appointed and got to work. It recalled that the city of Albany had recently offered a reward of one thousand dollars for the discovery of coal nearby and urged "the corporation of the opulent city of New-York" to offer "twice or thrice" that sum for exploration and the making of borings. All this had much the look of a revival of Stephen Stilwell's proposal of 1807.

One result of the coal mania was to focus attention on Woodstock. In his 1814 pioneer gazetteer of New York, Horatio Gates Spafford, who served on the coal committee of the Society for the Promotion of the Useful Arts, devoted a good bit of his note on Woodstock to its hopes for coal. "The inhabitants are reserving coal-mines in all their transfers of land, and suppose they have found sure indications of that valuable fossil," Spafford wrote. "But I do not learn that any coal has yet been found." In the second edition of his *Gazetteer* published in 1824, Spafford was less skeptical, quoting a "highly respected correspondent" as writing "they are now boring for coal, and have obtained about 20 bushels of the anthracite species, which has been used by smiths in the vicinity and tried in New-York, and found to be of superior quality." Spafford gave it as his opinion that Woodstock "may afford the true coal, of bituminous origin, likely to exist in large fields . . ."

In 1823 James Pierce, a talented amateur scientist of Catskill, had drawn national attention to Woodstock coal in an account of the Catskills published in the sixth volume of the *American Journal of Science*. Pierce wrote:

I have observed narrow strata or seams of coal at several places in the southern part of the Catskill ridge. The widest is situated in a perpendicular ledge of gray wacke slate on the eastern face of the mountain, in the town of Woodstock, Ulster County, at an elevation of about 1000 feet above the Hudson. This seam, which has been recently explored, is eight inches wide on the surface, and is observed for some distance on the face of the ledge. The coal is stratified, and inclines with the rock at an angle of near fifteen degrees. Narrow strata of argillaceous slate, imbedded in the gray wacke ledges, form the roof and floor of the coal bed. This slate contains alum, and cubic crystals of sulphuret of iron, and sometimes presents a dark surface glistening with carburet of iron.

The coal bed, in exploring, widened to twenty-two inches; but diminishing in the interior to a narrow seam and the adjacent rock being of difficult fracture, the pursuit has been abandonned for the present. Another vein of coal is located in a higher ledge of the same mountain, and coal has been noticed to the southwest in this range for three miles. The coal of the Catskill mountain appears of a good quality for upper strata. It is light, shining and burns with a moderate flame proceeding from bitumen or sulphur.

If beds of coal of this description could be found five feet in thickness they might be penetrated without breaking the rock, and would be valuable . . . ."

Flames from spontaneous combustions, generated in beds of coal or sulphuret of iron have been seen issuing from the ledges of the Catskill mountains by neighboring inhabitants. Combustions of this character often occur in the coal districts of Europe and America.

Adjacent to and forming a threatening canopy over the entrance of the coal excavation in the mountain near Woodstock, is a rock of several tons weight. It is separated from the ledge and balanced on a narrow base of decaying alum slate by an opposite projection of equal weight. From progressive decay this base is lessening, and the rock will before long be precipitated down the steep side of the mountain . . . .[6]

The threatening canopy which James Pierce thought about to crash down the mountainside is still in place, looking every bit as threatening as it did a century and a half ago. It hangs over one of the two man-made caves in what is known to oldtimers as the Coal Mine Ledge to the west of the upper part of Lewis Hollow. The caves are about a hundred feet apart; one is about thirty and the other about twenty feet in depth. In winter, water dripping through their roofs creates ice formations which strongly suggest the stalactites of limestone caves.

Pierce, Spafford and other writers who followed them encouraged local people to turn prospector at the slightest hint. Mrs. Cora Van Aken, born close to a century ago in Shady, liked to tell of a "coal mine" on Lake Hill Mountain where, she remembered, it was possible to "pick up big lumps of coal." Grenville Quick of Willow remembers being told of a coal mine on "the Ostrander place"—coal mined there was used by local blacksmiths, who found that it would burn well when urged on by their huge bellows.

In 1932 Bruno Louis Zimm of Lewis Hollow brought together much mining lore in a paper called "Some History and Traditions of Mines in Woodstock." There Zimm told of a Pennsylvania coal miner who came to Woodstock about 1870 and with the help of some young Bearsville men worked "a vein of coal on the southern bounds of Byrdcliffe." Coal "of good size and quality was mined but not in sufficient quantities to pay." This was the story of the many other attempts at mining Woodstock coal. Coal of a sort was there right enough, but it was laid down in Devonian days when the earth's vegetation was too sparse to equal that of the later Carboniferous period which had resulted in immense coal seams such as those of Pennsylvania.[7]

By the 1860s discoveries of oil and gas were making fortunes in Pennsylvania and a fresh exploration of the Catskills got under way. On October 14, 1886 the Kingston *Weekly Freeman and Journal* told of the visit to Woodstock of "Professor Tuck" of California. "The Professor took a trip to Woodstock to see if there were any indications for oil or gas, but he found none."

In 1889 the Kingston *Weekly Leader* reported that "a large tract of land has been leased from several owners in West Woodstock by the Standard Oil Company and they will bore for oil and gas at an early date." But nothing came of this venture.

The negative findings of Professor Tuck and the Standard Oil Company did not put an end to Woodstock dreams of oil and gas riches. During the mid-1950s drilling carried on by the Dome Gas and Oil Corporation in the town of Shandaken found small quantities of gas. Stock was being bought by local people. Oil geologists appeared in Woodstock from time to time until well into the 1960s, when the excitement died down.

Though the search for gold and silver in Woodstock has produced no metal, it has spawned a rich and revealing folklore. A favorite story was well put by Bruno Zimm. It goes, "Old residents of Shady relate a tale that was often told to them by their elders, respecting a certain Mr. Newkirk, who spent considerable time in prospecting and digging on the hills and slopes west of the Lake Hill Road. Excavations still visible on the old Van De Bogart farm are pointed to as evidence and as one of the sites of Mr. Newkirk's serious labor.

"The tale runs that Mr. Newkirk's uncle, the pioneer who settled on the site of the Woodstock Valley Hotel before the Revolution, had befriended some Indians, who in return for his kindness offered to guide him to a place of precious metal. There was a stipulation, however, that he was to wear a blindfold until they reached their destination. Little was said as they wended their way, the elder Newkirk alert and intent upon registering anything in the nature of a clue as to the character of the country through which he was being guided. At one point he became aware of passing a large body of water. Shortly after this his blindfold was removed, to expose to him the mine of precious metal that glistened in the shadow of the dense woods. A short time was spent in examining the metal, after which he was again blindfolded and led over much rough and steep ground and finally released in Lewis Hollow. At the close of the Revolution he made many fruitless attempts to locate the site of the treasure, and finally becoming too old for such arduous undertakings, took his nephew into his confidence, who continued the search, but with no better success . . ." [8]

Bruno Louis Zimm was a sculptor and a well-informed amateur geologist and paleontologist whose collection of local fossils is now in the Smithsonian Institution. He believed it likely that what Newkirk saw if he saw anything gold-like was "that old deceiver, iron pyrites, commonly known as fool's gold," which Zimm had found to be of "common occurence and known discovery here." While Zimm discouraged hopes of gold or silver mines in Woodstock he raised the hopes of local coal-hunters when he explored the Lewis Hollow mine and concluded that "in our modest way we have contributed to the gradually accumulating body of evidence gathered by modern geologists to support the contention that coal may be found in workable quantities in the Devonian formation which is typical of our locality." [9]

During the nineteenth century the recurrent gold rushes which marked the period incited Woodstock men to make their way to California, Leadville or the Klondike. Those who could not leave their home town sometimes tried digging in their backyards or in the ledges of the mountain that overhung their farms. The Klondike fever of the late 1890s gave birth to what the Kingston *Argus* called a "mine craze" in Lake Hill, but after stirring the earth here and there the craze died out.

As far as is known no Woodstock prospectors ever struck it rich either at home or in California or the Klondike. But surviving letters show that some Woodstock people who went mine-hunting away from home enjoyed their adventures. On May 30, 1880 William E.

Hasbrouck, a descendant of old Elias, wrote home to his "Uncle Woolvin" from Leadville, Colorado, the scene of a recent big silver find. He was amazed at the lack of observance of Sunday, he said. "Business here is rather dull at present, the mines are on a strike there has not been mutch trouble yet only one man hurt and he only had his Ear shot off but that is a closer shave than I would [care] to have." [10]

Every once in a while the hopes for sudden wealth found beneath the surface of the Woodstock earth still soars. Once a young man found a terra-cotta statuette buried three feet beneath the surface of the hamlet of Woodstock. The statuette resembled ancient Mexican Indian work. It was Mexican indeed, but of recent manufacture for the tourist trade and had been found in a disused garbage dump into which it had been thrown after it lost an arm.

One evening an excited woman phoned me to tell me that she had found a "tourmaline mine" along the Sawkill about halfway between Shady and Bearsville. Ten minutes later I was standing beside the woman's dining table staring at an amazing collection of huge pieces—some almost as big as my head—of glittering, glowing lumps of what looked like all the rough gems of the world brought together and put on display. The gems were not less beautiful for being glass. Somehow a pocket of them had become covered with earth beside the Sawkill well below the old glass factory and had only now emerged into the light.

Oldtimers in the vicinity tell of loads of glass slag being dumped here and there in the old days just to get it out of the way. Or perhaps this was the site of an unrecorded atttempt at experimenting in glassmaking—only an archeological study of the glassmaking region of Woodstock will tell. Nearby I saw an indication of charcoal burning—a circle some fifteen feet in diameter of charred wood well covered through the efforts of the years with earth and vegetation.[11]

Woodstock people of the early nineteenth century kept busy and hopeful. They kept on the alert for chances to find minerals, to farm, to lumber and to work as teamsters on the roads that linked Hudson Valley shipping towns to the back country, and to turn out their forest products. And the Livingstons, who still owned most of Woodstock, continued as they had ever since 1762 to lease land for three lives, to do their best to collect rents but to take some satisfaction in seeing their land converted more and more from forest to fields and so increased in market value. Tenants and absentee landlords had a common interest in seeing Woodstock prosper.

16

LANDLORDS, AGENTS
AND TENANTS

Woodstock had six successive
Livingston landlords of marked individuality between the time Robert
Livingston of Clermont set up the sawmill around which the
settlement of Woodstock quickly clustered and 1850 or so. Robert of
Clermont had begun settlement with energy and enthusiasm. His son
Judge Robert R. had applied cool good sense to his task of putting
what his father had done on a practical basis. The Judge's widow,
Margaret Beekman, had imposed on Woodstock a slack but often
kindly matriarchal rule. A few months before he left for his mission in
Paris, Margaret's son the Chancellor took possession of his Woodstock
lands, but left their management to his mother.

After 1804 the Chancellor's son-in-law, Robert L. Livingston,
became increasingly responsible for the family interests in Woodstock.
The Chancellor willed these lands to Robert L.'s wife, Margaret Maria.
And after the Chancellor's death in 1813 Robert L. managed the
Woodstock lands as owner until he was declared incompetent shortly
before his death in 1844. After that Robert Livingston's sons
Montgomery and Eugene Augustus came into possession, divided their
holdings and proceeded to put nearly all of them on the market. In
this way Livingston power in Woodstock came to a virtual end.

Of all the Livingstons associated with Woodstock the most
distinguished by far was the Chancellor. He was tall and gray-eyed,
graceful in his gestures and eloquent in his speech. Strangers first

meeting him were aware at once that here was a man thoroughly conscious of his position as a Hudson Valley patrician of the very first order; before long they realized that the Chancellor's intelligence and abilities came close to matching the distinction of his social position.

The Chancellor served his state and nation in many capacities. He was delegate to the Continental Congress and member of many important Revolutionary committees. He was Secretary for Foreign Affairs. He was a member of New York's Assembly. As his state's first Chancellor he presided over the Court of Chancery. As Minister to France he played a critical part in negotiating the Louisiana Purchase, which added so greatly to the territory of the United States.[1]

Some of his contemporaries believed that the Chancellor would have risen even higher in the public life of his day—perhaps to the level of President—had it not been for the air of superiority which marked his dealings with politicians and ordinary voters. In 1798 the Chancellor had run for the governship of New York and missed election by a narrow margin. Although he had become an Anglophobe and an admirer of France, he took after his English counterparts, the peers of vast acres and influence. Like these fortunate beings, Livingston experimented with improved methods of agriculture and mechanics; he served on committees of societies devoted to improvements and was president of his state's Society for Improving Agriculture, Manufacturing and the Useful Arts.

In addition he was an enthusiastic supporter of stimulating American interest in painting and sculpture. He was involved in the founding of the New-York Academy of Fine Arts. During his five years in Paris the Chancellor had collected Gobelin tapestries, gilded French furniture, fine porcelains and old silver for use in his New York house and in the one he had built during the early 1790s close to Madame Livingston's rebuilt house. He enjoyed taking visitors on tours of his houses and pointing out the treasures of his collections.

When the Chancellor returned to the Hudson Valley in 1804 he was received with tributes to his achievement in Paris. In New York a large and impressive public dinner was eaten with apparent pleasure not only by his friends but by a surprising number of his most inveterate political enemies. Kingston declared a holiday; the Chancellor was escorted through the streets in a civic procession and was given a dinner at Bogardus Tavern. Kingston citizens had a special reason for honoring the returned Minister. After Kingston was burned by the British in 1777 he had given them a tract of

Hardenbergh Patent land as an expression of sympathy.

At Saugerties a group of citizens, including Woodstock people, determined to express their appreciation of the Chancellor's "distinguished service." Accompanied by "the company of volunteer rangers" they marched to the ferry and crossed the Hudson to Clermont. There a small cannon previously placed on the lawn was fired. The entire group sat down to an "elegant dinner," with the governor of the state, the Chancellor's brother-in-law Morgan Lewis, in attendance.[2]

The tributes to the Chancellor of 1804 and 1805 were more than an appreciation of services to his country as Minister to France. They marked the beginning of his retirement from public life. And as far as Woodstock was concerned the Chancellor's return from France and the tributes that followed stood at the beginning of a new relationship between most Woodstock people and their absentee landlord. It was at this time that the aging Chancellor gave up virtually all concern with Woodstock and turned management of his lands to his son-in-law.

For the remainder of his life the Chancellor devoted himself to projects which he hoped might simultaneously benefit himself, his descendants and the American people. During the 1790s he had experimented on the Hudson with a steamboat. In 1801 he experimented on the Seine. As the owner in partnership with Robert Fulton in 1807 of a boat powered by steam, he had the satisfaction of seeing it making a triumphant if noisy and smoky progress up the Hudson from New York, ushering in a new era in transportation.

The last years of the Chancellor's life saw him carrying to a very successful peak his experiments with improving the breed of American sheep. While in Paris he had sent home some merino sheep, distinguished for the high quality of their wool, from the royal flock at Rambouillet. After his return from Paris Clermont was the scene of a festive annual sheep-shearing comparable to similar events on some great British estates at which members of the now-famous Clermont flock were sold at high prices. Immersed in these projects the Chancellor grew old. He became ever more deaf. In 1813 he died.

As Robert L. Livingston acted the part of landlord of all of Woodstock owned by the Chancellor between 1805 and 1813, he became ruefully aware that this role was very different from the one he had played for the five years of the Chancellor's tenure as Minister to France. Then, as the Chancellor's private secretary (Robert L. was known in Paris as Colonel Livingston) and as husband of his cousin (the talented Margaret Maria, who was the dark-eyed beauty of the Clermont Livingstons), Robert L. moved in the highest circles of the gay French capital under First Consul Napoleon Bonaparte. He and his cousin Edward P. Livingston (husband of Margaret Maria's older sister Mary Stephens Livingston, who was the Chancellor's official secretary), were associated in Parisian society with rich and noble people from all over Europe. Dressed in the uniforms of aides to the Governor of New York they attended official receptions and chatted with royalty. They enjoyed opera, theater and ballet, and other public performances in which Paris was so bountiful. Robert L. wrote home about the awe with which he viewed the paintings and statues looted by Napoleon from Italy, now newly on display in Paris.

From this it was a long jump to life at Clermont with the deaf Chancellor, struggles with Woodstock tenants and attendance to business in New York. Cousin Edward P. consoled himself by plunging into politics. He became his state's lieutenant-governor and a state senator. Robert L. became tied to the Chancellor's lands and their management. He found that Woodstock tenants had come to treat Great Lot 8 as their own; not only did they fail to pay rent, but they cut timber for sale as boards, shingles and other uses at a lively rate. Robert L. tried to put a stop to this. By the time the Chancellor's estate was being wound up lawyer Charles Ruggles of Kingston could list suits and other legal proceedings against a dozen Woodstock tenants, including Shultises, Shorts, Montrosses and Gulnacks, who had "trespassed" on Livingston lands or had paid no rent since 1801 or had failed to pay the one-sixth due their landlord upon the sale of a leasehold.[3]

In the fall of 1805 Robert L. acquired a new resident agent in Woodstock, surveyor and land agent John Wigram. For a time Wigram faithfully protected Livingston interests in his town. A native of Gosport, which lies close to the great British naval base of Portsmouth, in his teens Wigram became a midshipman on the frigate *Juno* bound for New York. Life at sea did not suit young Wigram, who left his ship and before long found himself a more pleasant berth as an assistant and apprentice to William Cockburn, later a surveyor and land agent for the Clermont Livingstons.

After service to the Manor Livingstons as surveyor, manager of their iron works and in other capacities and after a period of teaching and acting as land agent for a variety of clients Wigram came to Woodstock and settled there in 1806. He and his family had moved from their former home in the town of Gallitin in Columbia County. It is a tribute to both Livingston power and Wigram's persuasiveness that Wigram was at once elected supervisor although so new to the town and so much a source of apprehension to Woodstock tenants. With its business office, the Wigram house was well placed close to the hamlet of Woodstock. It stood on the Rock City Road nearly opposite the barn now known as Parnassus Square. His house was demolished in 1894 and replaced by the large white "mansion," as it was described when first built, which still occupies the site.

Mr. and Mrs. Wigram were regarded socially as a considerable cut above most local people. They represented the gentry in Woodstock. They had their portraits painted by the well-known Hudson Valley limner Ammi Philips. Wigram is shown holding a letter addressed to him, Mrs. Wigram in her lace cap and sober gray gown holding a snuff box. When Mrs. Wigram died in 1830 at the age of eighty she was thought important enough for Maria James, the remarkable woman who served the Chancellor's sister, Mrs. Freeborn Garrettson, as domestic servant, to write an epitaph extolling her. It goes, as published in Miss James' collected poems of 1839:

> All heart could wish lies buried here,
> Of mother wife or friend sincere;
> From day to day she meekly trod
> In duty's path and serv'd her God;
> Serv'd Him by faith, who now is seen
> Without a dimming veil between.

In 1806 and 1807 Wigram set about trying to put the Livingston farms in Woodstock upon a paying basis. He studied the rent rolls of the 1790s and the Chancellor's Paris years and ferreted out discrepancies and omissions. Tenants had been permitted to deliver their rents in wheat to merchants along the Hudson, notably to Legg and Burhans at Saugerties. The merchants' records were not always of the best, the wheat delivered was sometimes not of the "sound merchantable" sort called for in a tenant's lease. Back rents had piled up for tenants who in many cases had no means of paying. Tenants were obliged to pay all taxes on their farms. When they neglected to do this the landlord had to pay or risk losing the farm.

Wigram went from tenant to tenant, checking up on these matters and making the best arrangements he could. He organized rent-paying parties in various parts of the town—at Isaac Eltinge's tavern at Yankeetown, at Jacob Montross's in Little Shandaken and at Philip Bonesteel's tavern on the edge of the hamlet of Woodstock. Tenants who could not pay were offered a note to be signed. Tenants who did not show up at the appointed time and place were notified to appear in the awesome atmosphere of Wigram's office.

Wigram's rent-collecting measures were not always harsh and unfeeling. One tenant named Frederick Wentworth, who had paid no rent since the Chancellor's departure for France, turned up at Clermont one day in February having driven from Woodstock across the ice of the Hudson with a load of charcoal which he had just made and was offering in part payment of his rent. He carried with him a note from Wigram to Robert L. Livingston.

Wentworth, Wigram explained, deserved help and sympathy: "He is a poor Honest Industrious Man has met with many Misfortunes has to maintain Father & Mother in law & his Wife has been under the Doctor's hands for some Years and has a very Indifferent farm—his boys are now coming on so as to be able to help him—he wishes to be so far favored as to have some of the Back Rent abated if you should be pleased as he say he never shall be able to recover if he is obliged to pay the whole of the arrearages—altho' so poor a man he has the Confidence of the Town & has been Collector & Constable for some Years and has performed his duty & paid the taxes [on his rented farm] faithfully."

Wentworth's charcoal was accepted for resale or use in the Livingston household, and his back rents were partly forgiven. Other tenants found Wigram to be equally reasonable. Peter Bogardus, the Little Shandaken blacksmith, turned over two oxen worth $80 to Wigram. He promised to pay a year's back rent in wheat during the winter of 1806-1807 and produced a receipt for 11¼ bushels of wheat delivered at the Legg and Van Leuven store but not credited to him during the slack bookkeeping which prevailed during the Chancellor's absence. All this left Bogardus with only about two years' back rent to pay.

Bogardus' neighbor, Daniel Sherwood, who operated a sawmill and was a justice of the peace, sent an ox worth $33 to Clermont and was then like Bogardus only two years' rent in debt. Other tenants during Wigram's period as a Livingston man paid rents in a variety of ways. One brought a load of "wild hay" to be credited to Robert L. by the glass factory store at Bristol. When old Peter Short's son David hauled two hundred and fifty pounds of maple sugar made at

Yankeetown to Clermont in April 1814, he was credited on his rent account with a little over $26.

During 1806 and 1807 Wigram performed a number of little services to earn his salary from Robert L. Before Christmas 1806, in answer to a request of Robert L.'s, he bought "two Hanches of Venison" from Richard Montgomery Hasbrouck of Little Shandaken and sent them to his employer at Clermont; both were "young, and one of them very fine, I can get no more at present." When he wrote to tell Livingston of the venison he ended his letter with the words "Wishing yourself & families many happy returns of this festive season." This is the earliest Christmas greeting known to have been set down on paper in Woodstock.

While Wigram tried to persuade tenants to pay up their debts, he was also busy making surveys of Woodstock farms—the costs as in the past to be borne by the tenants. In this way Wigram uncovered a good many errors made by earlier surveyors. Henry Heniger's farm in what is now Willow had been surveyed back in 1770 by Benjamin Snyder, who had found it to take in forty-five acres and tenants ever since had paid a rent based on this acreage. Wigram found the farm to have only thirty-five acres and the tenant of 1807 (he was Jonathan Freeman) had his rent reduced.

Wigram made a survey of the Matthew Lewis farm, which occupied the northwestern corner of the the Livingston 1200-acre tract (sometimes referred to as the 1500-acre tract) in Great Lot 26, in what is now known as Lewis Hollow. He found the line dividing this tract from the adjoining five hundred acres of Judge Jonathan Hasbrouck of Kingston (this was the lot Cornelius Tiebout had sold before the Revolution to James Farquarson) was incorrect. Wigram followed the line of marked trees dividing the Livingston-Hasbrouck tracts down the mountainside to the point at which the line struck what is now Route 212 close to the beginning of Plochmann Lane. He boxed the signs of the blazes made by Tiebout's surveyor by cutting out a piece of wood as far down as the original blaze and counting the rings of wood which had grown over the blaze year after year. As a result of Wigram's work Hasbrouck and Livingston agreed upon a more accurate boundary line which added several acres to the Livingston land.

Wigram carried on the excellent tradition of both surveying and map-making which he had learned from William Cockburn (Cockburn died in 1810 after a few years of lessened activity). Several of

Wigram's maps are still of great use to those burrowing down into the lower levels of Woodstock titles to land.[4]

Besides his activities in dealing with tenants and in surveying Wigram had another area of importance to the Woodstock of his time. He was what would later on be called a booster, ever busy with schemes for advancing the interests of Woodstock people, Robert L. Livingston and himself. He was active with Stephen Stilwell in promoting the Woodstock-Saugerties turnpike against what he described as great opposition from Kingston people who wanted very much to see Woodstock tied to Kingston rather than Saugerties. But before he committed himself to the project he wrote to Robert L. that he would push the turnpike, only "provided it meets the Chancellors and your approbation."[5]

In 1814 he helped circulate a petition to the Postmaster-General asking that a post office be set up in Woodstock. The petition said that the local population had increased and that the town had two glass factories in business. The post office was established in the hamlet of Woodstock. The first postmaster was probably Richard Keator, a bookkepper and then or later a justice of the peace. The post office had difficulties and closed. It was revived with John Wigram as postmaster in 1819. He served several terms as Woodstock's supervisor and far into old age carried on an extensive and widespread business as surveyor and land agent for a number of large New York landowners.[6]

After Wigram died in 1830 his son John S. carried on his business and became town clerk while son William practised law locally and in Saugerties and Catskill. The Rock City Road along which the Wigram farm lay was once known as Wigram Lane. Old John's three unmarried daughters lived to be ladies of marked individuality as they carried on to the end in the old house on their lane. In 1820 the Ulster County Agricultural Society awarded John Wigram a prize of $7.50 for the "best piece of carpeting made in the county and submitted at their annual fair." The carpeting had certainly been woven by Wigram's wife (she had been born Maritje Schermerhorn of Catskill) or by the daughters or by all four together, but the custom of the time gave the official credit to the man who headed the household.

Wigram farmed with the help of slaves who are said to have continued to live on after they were freed by law in 1827 exactly as they had in the days of slavery. They lived in a house of their own behind the farmhouse. One, Tom Wigram, became a notable local character. It was he who planted the great "cotton-wood" or yellow poplar tree which stood near the farmhouse and beside the road until it was taken down in the 1950s. It came to be known as the largest tree in all the town. The tree's buds each spring produced a sticky resin-like substance which Tom used in making a salve. Tom was spry until late in life in spite of having to depend on a wooden leg, made, they said, from a bit of an antique bedpost. Tom operated a little roadside stand at which he sold refreshments to summer visitors.

The three Wigram girls, after their parents died, became known for their extreme thrift. The tea they drank, for example, was brewed from free samples cadged from local storekeepers. John S., the dignified town clerk who wore a fine plug hat as he rode his horse about Woodstock, was annoyed at his sisters' refusal to pay for their tea. One day, they say, he bought a whole pound of tea, brought it home and scattered it over the family kitchen garden. "There," he said to his horrified sisters, "now grow your own tea." [7]

From time to time Robert L. Livingston visited his lands in Woodstock, Shandaken and Bushkill (now part of the town of Olive) "to settle with the tenants." He stayed at local inns, favoring Philip Bonesteel's in Woodstock, and spending four or five days on these expeditions. At the same time he kept an eye out for trespassers, whom he prosecuted with vigor. He was aware as previous Livingston landlords had been that his Hardenbergh Patent holdings were most valuable to him not from the rental income painfully extracted from tenants but from the rise in market value which might be expected to take place in the land over a long period of years. The timber too was rising in value and tempting trespassers.[8]

At the same time Robert L. was troubled by a chronic shortage of cash. The Chancellor had derived a good income from his home farm of 630 acres and especially from its flock of salable merino sheep. But the merino craze came to an end about the time the Chancellor died and sheep were less easily sold even at much lower prices. Though Livingston owned lands in the city of New York and in twenty New York townships—his lands in and adjoining Woodstock alone amounted to about 66,000 acres—his income from all this was not enormous. His Woodstock lands and those in adjoining Shandaken and Olive never produced even on paper more than a scant $2000 per year in rents.

During these years the large income which had once seemed guaranteed to the Chancellor's daughters and to Robert L.'s sister

Harriet, wife of Robert Fulton, remained. The monopoly of steamboat rights the New York Legislature had given the Chancellor and Fulton, however, was soon infringed upon and eventually found to be unconstitutional. Robert L. and his wife saw their children growing up and becoming ever more expensive to maintain. Robert L.'s thoughts turned more and more often to coaxing a better income from his lands.

He dispatched Wigram to some of his large landholdings in upstate New York with instructions to sell what he could to settlers. Because title to some of this land was shaky, the prices obtained were low. Even then buyers had to be harried by Wigram before they would make the payments agreed upon.

Among the many papers of Robert L. Livingston left behind when he died are some on which he listed the trees growing on his Woodstock lands. He copied from such authorities as Francois Michaux's *North American Sylva* the uses of each tree, apparently in an effort at arriving at a means of turning his forests to profit before they were all carried off by the timber thieves who caused him so much concern.

The establishment of the forge and glass factories just across his boundary line stimulated Robert L. to develop ambitions for similar projects. In April 1814 the New York Legislature granted a charter to the Woodstock and Saugerties General Mining and Manufacturing Company and authorized it to establish "a manufactory of cotton and wool, flax and hemp, earthen ware, glass, iron and also to apply such part of their capital for the purpose of digging for iron ore, lead and coal, as they may judge expedient, in the towns of Woodstock and Saugerties, and in other places in the counties of Ulster and Sullivan where the said company may think proper . . ." Robert L. became president and treasurer of the company. John Wigram and Rufus Briggs (miller and land agent at Clermont and later at Saugerties) were among the incorporators. The capital stock was set at eight thousand shares of fifty dollars each.

Livingston's mining and manufacturing company had come upon the scene just in time to be strangled by the recession which followed the ending in 1815 of the Napoleonic Wars. The tales of lead deposits on Livingston lands in Sullivan and western Ulster counties as well as the greatly exaggerated reports of iron and coal in Woodstock led only to disappointment. The company languished, its stock unsaleable. The sole meeting of the company's board which has left a visible trace attracted only one member besides Robert L.[9]

The bleak prospects of his new company were not the only misfortunes to affect Robert L. during the years following 1815. In 1818 his wife Margaret Maria died following giving birth to the last of her nine children, leaving her husband with the children to be reared, educated and launched into the world on a level befitting their family dignity. Hard times were approaching, nudged along by unusually bad weather for farming; in 1819 the nation's first financial panic shook the American economy.

Robert L., faced with diminishing income and expanding expenses, sat in the old Chancellor's library and struggled year after year to set down on paper schemes for extracting a better return from his lands. Several agents after Wigram had tried their hands at collecting rents from Woodstock tenants—John Elwyn and John Eldridge, himself a Livingston tenant farmer, were among them—but no one proved successful. On March 10, 1825 Robert L., determined to put greater pressure on his agents, wrote them a set of instructions: "It is *most* necessary that my business at Woodstock should be prosecuted with energy, and that your undivided attention should be paid to see my instructions executed—heretofore my property in Ulster and Sullivan has been much neglected, owing in some degree to my time having been employed on business of greater importance. It has become absolutely necessary that the rents due should be collected, but in a way not to injure the tenant but to serve him . . ." Here Robert L. explains that if "the tenant knows that his rent must be paid, he will exert himself to fullfil his engagement—he will become more industrious. . . ." All this was in line with an old Livingston belief once put in writing by Judge Robert R. Livingston that a system of landholding under which the people who tilled the soil held their land not as owners but as tenants of great landlords benefitted the workers by compelling them to work harder and so to produce more, and this greater production also benefitted the nation as whole.

Robert L. gave his agents a schedule of days on which payments of rents were to be made. Some tenants whom he listed were to be permitted to make their payments by cutting and cording hemlock wood and delivering it to an appointed agent at Kingston Landing. "I may venture to say" Robert L. wrote, "that no Landlord could under similar circumstances make a more favorable proposition."[10]

17

MAKING A LIVING
IN FORESTS, FIELDS
AND HOMES

Everything we can learn from the great mass of papers Robert L. Livingston left behind suggests he saw Woodstock as little more than a source of money to be used for the benefit of himself, his nine children and the poor relations he helped from time to time. To his tenants, of course, Woodstock had a very different meaning. It was home, with all that word implies in emotional attachment. And it was the center of the social and economic unit of which local people formed parts. Though Livingston retained some remnants of the paternal feeling toward tenants which had marked the best of Old World landlords, he made it plain that he regarded the tenants' own shiftlessness and dishonesty as responsible for most of their troubles. The tenants for their part felt that Livingston's social position and vast landholdings reflected a modest glory on them, and at the same time they blamed him and his agents for many of their troubles.

Through the first three decades of the nineteenth century Livingston and his tenants engaged in a game in which each side struggled to receive as much and give as little as possible. Changes which had taken place since the end of the Revolution had made it easier for the tenants to receive more. Even while the old leases for three lives and their payments in kind continued, by the 1820s more tenants were able to pay their rents in cash.[1]

There was more cleared land for growing grain and pasturing

cattle. The European enemies of wheat and flax arrived, erosion attacked hillside fields, and floods rolled boulders onto valley land. Yet Woodstock farmers were able to adapt by growing rye and buckwheat instead of wheat and by clearing tracts of forest to make fresh fields temporarily rich in accumulated plant food.

Drought and flood harassed the town's farmers. There is no written record of damage to soil caused by floods in this period. Yet we may assume that soil was damaged, as for example in 1818, when a great flood "carried away" Wynkoop's snuff mill on the Sawkill in Zena, later the site of the dam of Kingston Reservoir No. 1.[2]

The arrival of the two glass factories, with their opportunities for cash income from teaming and woodcutting, the opening of the Saugerties, Glasco and Ulster and Delaware Turnpikes, the establishment of a post office, the arrival of glass factory people, usually with English rather than Dutch and German traditions, and the beginning of common schools—all these helped broaden Woodstock people's view of life and enabled them to live pleasanter lives. This did not mean that the long, hard hours of work of the past were over—far from it.

As in the past Woodstock women worked endlessly at household and family responsibilities. They cooked and warmed water in fireplaces—it was not until close to the middle of the century that iron cookstoves became at all usual. Washing continued to be done on the rocks beside a stream. Slaughtering time and other events on the farm calendar brought extra work for the women and children. Soapmaking using lye derived from ashes and home-grown animal fats, drying apples, pickling, preserving and a dozen other tasks kept women in a constant whirl of work, with sewing and spinning flax or wool filling in the moments not otherwise occupied.

As clearing of the forests made more land available for pasture, the number of cows increased and butter made by the women became a valued cash crop. This was the chief way in which women were directly responsible for a part of the cash family income. The men brought in most of the cash. Though they worked at much subsistence farming, such as cutting wood for fuel, planting and harvesting, and tending to the needs of farm animals (the chickens were often in the care of the women), the men also did work which supplied the immediate cash needed if a family were to get along. Teaming and cutting wood for the glass factories, making maple sugar, hauling logs out of the woods to local sawmill and boards to the Hudson River landings, and part-time blacksmithing all supplied cash to men who were principally farmers.

Besides this there were other occupations carried on in odds and ends of time at home. These involved the use of wood from the still-large Woodstock forests, most of which belonged to Robert L. Livingston or other absentee landlords and were to be taken only by trespassing. Shingle-making, making hoop poles, cutting oak, hickory and ash into forms wanted by wheelrights and wagonmakers, making staves—all these crafts were often carried on beside the kitchen fire, with the waste wood supplying fuel.

Making shingles from hemlock and white pine kept many Woodstock men busy through the winter. Their methods were the same as those of their fathers and grandfathers in the colonial days of Woodstock. Of all early Woodstock forest crafts shingle-making had the most endurance; until the 1960s there were still a few local men who had made hemlock shingles in the old way when they were young, and could show how it was done.

In the fall the woods were searched for suitable pines or hemlocks. A "box" was cut into the trees near their bases in order to make sure that the trees were not "shaky" (in a shaky tree the annual layers of growth were not firmly attached to each other). If the tree was not shaky it was felled. A peeled sapling some eight feet high was nailed to the resulting logs in order that the logs might be found and hauled out of the woods by oxen when the winter snows lay deep. Then, working by night and in stormy weather in the farmhouse kitchen, the farmer used a tool called a froe to split the hemlock already sawed to the proper length into pieces about half an inch thick. These pieces were fastened by a clamp to what was called a shingle horse. A few swift strokes of a shaving knife tapered and smoothed the rough shingle into its final form.[3]

Shingles like these rived with the grain of the wood lasted longer than the sawed ones which came along later and which often ignored the structure of the wood. But a "shingle weaver" (this was an old name for these workers) had to work quickly and efficiently. The price he received was too low to encourage dawdling or bungling. A Woodstock man who lived in Yankeetown was long remembered for the immense numbers of shingles he made in the intervals of farm work. It was said half-seriously of Livingston tenant Hosea Wood that he made enough shingles in his lifetime to cover a roof eighteen feet wide extending from Yankeetown Pond all the way into the heart of

160

Kingston. Woodstock had more shingle-makers than most similar towns because of its many fine hemlocks and white pines and its closeness to a market via the Hudson River.

By the 1790s and even in earlier days Woodstock men had been making the parts that were sent from their town to be assembled into barrels. They and their sons continued to make barrel parts, but now at an accelerated rate. Barrels and their big brothers the hogsheads were the standard containers in which an enormous amount of merchandise was shipped. The corrugated cardboard carton and other containers of our day had not yet come into being. The demand for staves, headings and hoops was unending.

Woodstock stores—De Forest's in the hamlet of Woodstock and the stores of the two glass companies—were always glad to accept good staves in trade. Amasa Hoyt of what is now Shady usually paid his store bills in staves. On February 24, 1824 Philip Eighmey, apparently in a festive mood, bought spirits, gin, tea, tobacco and pipes at the Bristol Glass Company store. Storekeeper William Greele noted, "To be paid in staves next week." Between 1814 and 1816 William Riseley, who farmed the lands on the Bearsville Flats originally leased by his grandfather, set down in his account book many entries relating to buying staves and "riding" them to Hudson River landings.[4]

So important were barrels to the export trade of New York that the State Legislature, in the belief that this would help keep up the reputation of New York products, passed laws regulating all phases of barrel-making. Staves of the group of tougher oaks known in the lumber trade as white oaks were required for barrels and hogsheads in which whiskey and other liquids were shipped, but the more porous red oaks could be used in barrels holding the enormous quantities of flour shipped each year to Europe and the West Indies. A red oak hogshead stave—most Woodstock staves were of red oak—was required by law to be "three feet six inches long, four inches broad, including sap, and shall be three quarters of an inch thick on the edge." No stave could contain more than three wormholes. An official known as a culler was appointed to inspect all staves and headings leaving New York to see that they conformed to law. After going to Europe and the West Indies many of these barrel parts were there assembled and were often sent back to New York filled with a great variety of goods.

Higher prices were paid for staves that met the legal

requirements. In 1815 red-oak staves were fetching $34 per "thousand of twelve hundred" on the New York waterfront; the extra two hundred were said to have been needed to allow for culling. With prices so low stave-makers, like shingle-weavers, had to work swiftly and surely. But the quantity of staves made in the town shows that many did develop the needed skill and speed.[5]

Staves and headings were rived from lengths sawed from logs and then given the required shape and thickness by being clamped on a horse similar to a shingle horse and worked on with a draw knife. The law required staves to be "regularly split with the grain of the wood" to give them the greatest strength possible. Also finished on a wooden horse were the hoops used to hold barrels together. They were made of hardwood saplings two inches or so in diameter. Saplings like these of oak, ash, hickory and other woods were used. They had to be worked into hoop poles while still limber and unseasoned. After hoops were "shaved" they were tied into bundles before being marketed.

Shaving hoop poles, like making shingles and staves and headings, required swift prolonged effort, with a man turning himself into a kind of machine which repeated a few unvarying movements thousands of times in a day. At the end of a long day of bending over his horse a hoop-shaver's back and muscles were often so stiff a period of adjustment was needed before he could stand up like a normal man.

The huge demand for hoops is suggested by the advertisements which Hudson River merchants and traders placed in Ulster County newspapers. Abraham Hasbrouck of Rondout, with whom many Woodstock people had dealings, offered cash in 1813 for 10,000 hogshead hoop poles and for 12,000 "barrel" hoop poles. The making of hoop poles did not die out in Woodstock until wire hoops and machinery for making wooden ones came into use late in the nineteeth century.[6]

Many a man of old Woodstock was half-farmer and half-woodsman, wise in the many ways of turning the trees of his town to use. Old account books tell of the sale of great quantities of cordwood for fuel, and of oak, ash and hickory being sold to wheelwrights and wagonmakers. Benjamin Force, a skilled woodworker who made doors and windows for new houses, is on record as making and selling wheelbarrows and a "woolin" spinning wheel he probably made. Force also made many of the boxes in which glass was shipped from Woodstock.[7]

A man working in the woods could add to his income in a less confining way than at a horse beside the kitchen fire. One of these alternatives was peeling tanbark, or "pealing," as it was more often spelled in the old days. Because it had to be done in late spring or early summer when the bark was easily removed from hemlock or oak trees—a busy time in a farmer's fields—peeling bark had the disadvantage of not fitting too snugly into a farmer's calendar. Once cut into sheets of a standard length the pieces of bark were piled neatly and left in the woods until the snow of the following winter made it easy to enter the woods to haul the bark out with ox team and sledge.

Most Woodstock tanbark, first stripped from oak trees and later from hemlock, went to the tanneries of John Ring and of Samuel, Philip A. and John Culver on the Tannery Brook. In February 1816 the Culvers paid two dollars for sixty-four (cubic) feet of bark. They bought hides after local animals were slaughtered. They sold finished leather in the town for use by shoemakers and harnessmakers. They may have made shoes, for the glass company store records purchases of shoes from them.

The tannery remained in business under a variety of owners and managers until almost 1880, and through all these years it bought tanbark from local men. During its last years it ground bark to be used by other tanners and did no tanning of its own. Some Woodstock tanbark went to tanneries in Kingston and probably in New York.

Selling the ashes that resulted from the burning of the debris from the clearing of land had been an important source of cash in the earliest days of settlement. Less than a century ago ashes were still being taken in trade by local storekeepers. Ashes saved from the fires which served for winter warmth and year-round cooking were leached at home in order to obtain lye for soap-making. Many bushels of ashes taken to local stores were credited against purchases of food, clothing and other items. In April 1824, for example, Andrew Ryon bought "2 tin basons to be pd. in ashes." Ashes were then worth twelve and a half cents per bushel in trade.[8]

Another source of income from the forest has left hidden signs, many of which are yet to be uncovered. Every now and then someone digging in the Woodstock earth finds a layer of finely-broken charcoal beneath the surface. If he goes on digging he can reveal a circle of charcoal bits about twenty feet in diameter, the site of what used to be called a charcoal or coal pit.

Here a hard-working Woodstock man of long ago had piled up

cordwood into a domed mass and then covered the dome, except for a few very small openings at the bottom and the top, with earth and sod. The mass of thirty or forty cords of wood was ignited and the fire carefully controlled in order to keep it from going beyond smoldering. If the fire burst through the earth and sod coating it could quickly turn into a roaring blaze which would consume the entire pit.

The charcoal burner had to be on the alert day and night, ready to throw more earth on any spot where flame threatened to erupt, for the week or two it took to burn his pit. Charcoal burners usually camped out in a little hut built close to their pit and had someone handy to stand watch while they took a little sleep. If all went well the cordwood would end up reduced in bulk and weight and ready for use in blacksmith's forges, in smelting iron or for many other uses.

The forge set up by Ferdinand Augustus DeZeng in 1802 had emphasized charcoal burning in Woodstock. For more than a century afterward young men and lonely old men eager to make a little money at the cost of much effort and the loss of considerable sleep turned charcoal burners. As late as 1907 Leander Bonesteel burned a pit of charcoal on Ohayo Mountain just across the Woodstock line and camped out in a tiny log hut beside his pit.

Charcoal burning never became the large, well-organized enterprise in Woodstock that it did in neighboring Shandaken during the final decades of the nineteenth century. But in the 1820s Robert L. Livingston, well aware of his tenants' individual efforts at charcoal-making, sketched a scheme under which the tenants would make charcoal for him from those parts of his trees that were unsuited to more profitable uses. Though the scheme looked good on paper, it found the tenants, who had their own more profitable way of making charcoal in their own unorganized way, uncooperative.[9]

The sawmills of Woodstock provided a good share of the town's income while supplying boards and joists for local house and barn building. The census of 1820 tells of twelve sawmills in operation within the boundaries of Woodstock. While these mills were giving employment to Woodstock men, they were also consuming great parts of the forests which in 1820 still covered seven-eighths of the town's surface. Woodstock as a settled place had begun around a sawmill. On the earliest known map to show the settlement it is called not Woodstock but Livingston's Mill. Ever since the water wheel of the Livingston mill of about 1762 began to turn, sawmills had been at work, interrupted only by the Revolutionary War and by periods of unfavorable economic conditions.

In their leases the Livingstons had reserved the rights to all possible mill sites. They had tried to keep all sawmills on their lands under as close control and supervision as possible. When Chancellor Livingston sold the tract of land in what was becoming the hamlet of Woodstock to Isaac Davis, he had only included the excellent mill rights on the Tannery Brook in an effort to stimulate the growth of an industrial social and trading center for his Woodstock estate. This kind of sale was not unusual among the great landlords of New York State. In this case the Livingston sawmill on the Tannery Brook continued as private business. Eventually a grist mill, a tannery and a fulling mill joined it. All other mill sites on the Livingstons' Woodstock lands remained firmly in the possession of Livingstons.[10]

When a Woodstock settler cleared his land he hoped to haul suitable trees to a sawmill to be cut into the boards and "joices" to be used in building his house and barn. Because of the poor quality of early roads logs were seldom hauled more than a few miles. The records of the Livingston sawmill on the Country Club site (on which it stood before giving way to a grist mill) for 1806 and 1807, when it was run by Tunis Brizzee, show that only those tenants living within about a two-mile radius brought their logs to this sawmill. Many of these same tenants paid the two-or-three-days'-labor-with-team provision of their leases by riding loads of inch-thick boards from the mill to the house of John Brink, whose ferry went back and forth across the Hudson between Clermont and Saugerties. The lumber was made into rafts and floated when tide and wind favored across the river to Clermont.[11]

Sawmills in Woodstock were often temporary and cheaply built structures, set at mill sites close by unusually good stands of white pine or other kinds of timber in demand at the time or near lands being cleared by new settlers. Mills and millponds were very vulnerable to flooding, which often caused them to cease functioning. An example was Daniel Sherwood's mill in Little Shandaken, mentioned as active shortly after 1800. By 1814 it was ruined. That year Robert L. Livingston agreed to lease it for one year to Henry and Jacob Bogardus, who agreed to repair the mill and dam and supply a "new mill saw." Livingston was to have a third of the mill production. During that year the Bogarduses ("if the weather will admit it . . .") were to saw three hundred logs, "to get the logs from the commons & to take those that are down when they are to be had and not to permit any sawed stuff to be taken from the mill until they shall be divided by some person sent by Mr. Livingston for that purpose . . ."

A good deal of information about the sawmills is touched upon in the Bogardus-Livingston agreement; the reliance of sawmills on rainy seasons, the activities of trespassers who were scared off after they had cut down trees on the commons, the on-and-off and short-term operation of many mills, and the lack of confidence in the sawmiller's honesty in delivering the landlord's share.

Sherrod's Mill, as it was sometimes called in a way that gives a clue to the pronunciation of the name, operated on and off until the death of Esquire Sherwood, so called because of his office of Justice of the Peace, in the early 1830s. About 1820 Lewis Edson, Jr., the singing school teacher and composer, hauled many loads of boards for packing boxes from Sherwood's to the Bristol Glass Factory.[12]

A sawmill need not keep busy for many years to use up the supply of good trees within easy hauling distance. After that every log coming to the mill cost more and so lowered profits. Sawmills tended to move to where the trees were rather than the other way round. That is why they were usually inexpensive and temporary structures which might be abandoned without much loss. Mills like these were powered by water turning the simplest and least efficient wheels then known, undershot wheels, commonly called flutterwheels. A flutterwheel could function on a small stream. When the water dried up or ran low in midsummer the mill simply ceased to work. Many small mills operated for only three or four months of the year.

The first Livingston mill had an advantage. It was located (according to the earliest maps) on a part of the Sawkill which could make a millwheel turn, except in a very dry season, throughout the year. Old Woodstock sawmills were what are still referred to as "up and down sawmills." A straight saw fixed in a wooden frame moved up and down, doing its work on the down stroke only.

When the flow of settlement into Woodstock's back country grew strong it brought a demand for sawmills close enough to tenant farmers to make it worthwhile for them to have their logs sawed and used at home or sold, rather than simply burned to clear the ground for planting. In 1806 Daniel Lumberd and John Eldridge leased five acres on the Little Beaverkill just below the stream's source in Yankeetown Pond. They agreed to build a sawmill there (with the Chancellor contributing $280 toward its cost) and give the Chancellor "a full one half part in quantity and quality" of everything they sawed "except logs sawed for tenants [for their own use]." The mill stood on the new Ulster and Delaware Turnpike and so might send its products to Kingston as well as through Woodstock to Saugerties.

While Lumberd and Eldridge were negotiating with the Chancellor, so too was Henry Bogardus on behalf of his neighbors in Little Shandaken, where the Beaverkill ran through the Livingston Great Lot 8. Bogardus pointed out in a letter to the Chancellor that he had already discussed with him the possibility of a mill to be built and operated on the same terms as those given to Lumberd and Eldridge. The two hadn't been able to agree on terms. Apparently Sherwood's mill was not then in business.

Bogardus had hoped that "of the logs that we git out of your commons we would agree to let you have half of the boards but of the logs that the people should bring from off the land which is under possession [that is, occupied with or without benefit of lease] one fourth for it is allways customary that the people that bring the logs from their own land has half the boards and the sawyer one fourth and the Mill has one fourth . . ."

Then Bogardus spoke bluntly about the consequences to the Chancellor of not having a mill at Little Shandaken. "If you will not build a mill nor let us have on any other conditions but such as you told me when we was at your house I think you cannot with any digree of propriety lay blame to your Tenants if they bring logs from off the land which they hold under improvement to Mr. Rouw's Mill which he is about to build on Mr. Desbrosses' land for you know we are under the greatest necessity of having a sawmill in our neighborhood for our country is new and we must clear our land and burn our logs if we cannot have a mill . . ."[13]

Here Bogardus was touching a sore spot for the Livingston landlords of Woodstock. Ever since Robert of Clermont back in the early 1760s had formed a scheme for deriving great profits from his Woodstock forests and its sawmill, the same possibility had tantalized his successors. There was timber there in vast quantities and often in excellent quality. Transportation to market was not difficult. The tenants formed a corps of potential workers who would cut trees, get the logs to the sawmill and finally to the Hudson River.

Yet somehow this plan had never worked to the profit of the landlord. In the absence of the close supervision, which no Livingston of Clermont felt inclined or able to give to the plan, holes developed through which the expected profits drained away. The Livingston commons on which tenants were permitted to cut timber for their own use alone were raided for choice white pines, cherry trees and naturally-bent pieces of oak, which were in lively demand as knees for ships, or of ash used for "sley runners."

Sawmills sprang up on adjoining tracts, on Great Lots 25 and 26 and in Hurley. Logs stolen from the Livingston commons were sawed there and sent to market with very little attempt at concealment. The men who ran Livingston sawmills often sent their landlord as his share of the production inferior boards, selling the better ones for themselves. In 1822 Christian Happy told Robert L. Livingston by letter that this was just what was happening at a mill in Yankeetown then run by Solomon Shours or Showers. "I was at Woodstock yesterday," Happy began, "and I think it my duty to tel you of what I was informed concerning the conduct of Mr. Shours with the new Sawmill which was built last Summer he will not saw hemlock for the tenants nor no other wood but whitewood they tel me he has carried between twenty and forty loads of the Choyest lumber to market for himself and has lef 3 or 4 loads of the infearrier quality for Mr. Levingston, my brotherinlaw wanted him to saw the lumber to build his house with, near my father, but he would not do it . . ."

Livingston found it necessary to pay a man and a boy to visit sawmills like this each week to sort lumber and divide it into the landlord's and the sawyer's shares and to arrange to have the landlord's pine, whitewood, hemlock and oak boards, planks and joists sent off to Clermont before they could vanish. This was only one of the many ways in which the Woodstock sawmills piled up costs and diminished profits.[14]

In 1806 the Chancellor and Bogardus had failed to reach agreement on the terms under which a sawmill might come to Little Shandaken. Rouw or Rowe went ahead and set up his mill in Mink Hollow across Livingston's Great Lot 8 line. By 1822 Rouw's mill was no longer active. Nor was Sherwood's. That year fifteen Little Shandaken settlers petitioned Robert L. Livingston, as Bogardus had done earlier, to allow a sawmill in their neighborhood. They warned that "In case we Should be with out a mill we would be under the necessity to burn the timber on our follows . . ."[15]

This would mean a loss to both landlord and tenants. "Follow" in 1822 had a meaning it has since lost. It meant a tract of land covered with felled trees which had to be removed in one way or another before planting could take place.

The petition of 1822 was granted, but with an important additional proviso. No timber was to be cut on the Livingston commons and sawed at the mill. It was probably this that prevented the mill from being built, for the question of the cutting of timber growing on the commons was becoming more and more important and more and more vexatious with every year. Trespassing on the Livingston commons and removing trees was becoming ever more frequent. Deputy sheriffs were sent to Woodstock to discourage it. Though legal actions piled up, the trespassing went right on, becoming part of the Woodstock way of life.

Letters denouncing neighbors as trespassers, lawyers' bills, and legal papers having to do with proceedings against trespassers accumulated in Robert L. Livingston's library at Clermont. A. D. Ladew, who ran a tannery and sawmill at what is now Mount Tremper and was once known as Ladew's Corner or The Corner, and who had "bark rights" on Livingston land, kept an eye on the Beaverkill Valley between his establishment and Cooper Lake.

In 1833, for example, Ladew, who was an agent for Livingston, wrote that he had "detected William M. Cooper, Isaac Elting Sr., Elias Short and Jonas Wisple (usually spelled Whispell) trespassing in our oak bark." He insisted that the men be prosecuted. Col. Cooper, who ran a tavern in the house with a two-story verandah—the house still stands at the top of the Lake Hill—responded to the accusation by telling Robert L. that Elias Short had stolen some pine logs and that Ladew had stopped him, taken possession of the logs and kept them for himself. John F. Winne, who operated a sawmill at the outlet of Cooper Lake, admitted that he sometimes bought pine logs from Livingston tenants for 12 to 14 shillings apiece. Cooper and Elting, Ladew informed Robert L., "are a couple of old foxes and must be narrowly watched . . ." [16]

Although Robert L. Livingston's lawyers and land agents assured him that it would not always be profitable to take legal action against trespassers, those who had saleable possessions could not hope to escape paying for the timber they stole. In 1830, for one example, George Shultis, Jr. (a frequent offender) and William Short had to pay, in addition to damages, five dollars apiece in legal expenses to Cockburn and Sickles of Kingston, who were acting for Livingston.

When William Cusick of Lake Hill was seen by witnesses Abraham Van Gaasbeck and David Miller cutting timber on Great Lot 24, which was then owned jointly by Edward P. and Robert L. Livingston, lawyer William Wigram took successful action against Cusick and Seth Hoyt, who worked for Cusick. Now and then surveyor and land agent John W. Kiersted spent three or four days prowling the Livingston commons in search of trespassers—it was he who had found Cusick to be at work on Lot 24.[17]

In many, perhaps in most cases, prosecution of trespassers simply could not pay because the trespassers were what Livingston agents called "beggars" who had little source of income apart from what they could derive from stealing Livingston timber. Often these "rascals" converted the trees, as their fathers had done, into shingles or staves which were easily carried out of the forest in secret. As Ladew's tannery reached up the valley of the Beaverkill for tanbark, many peeled hemlock trees were left lying on the ground. These too were seized by timber thieves.

Tanbark and timber was often stolen by Woodstock men from landlords other than the Livingstons. In 1832 Jonathan Hasbrouck of Kingston wrote to Richard M. Hasbrouck to get his help in tracking down tanbark thieves. Hasbrouck had received "authentic information" that "very extensive depredations have been committed in the lots in Yankeetown Clove, especially in pealing bark." The bark, Hasbrouck said, was carried away by night. He urged Richard M. Hasbrouck to find the thieves' bark piles and if he couldn't haul them away to burn them.[18]

It is easy enough to understand the attraction of trespassing for many Woodstock men. They lived on very small incomes, surrounded by a wealth of Livingston commons' trees which needed only a little effort and daring to produce cash for them. For half a century the Livingston landlords had been lax in enforcing their exclusive right to cut and sell timber growing on their commons. When after 1804 the Livingstons tried to prevent the cutting of their timber by their tenants, the tenants were indignant at the denial of what they had come to regard as their old rights in the commons.

Resentment against the system of leases for three lives under which most Woodstock people lived gained strength through the 1820s. It expressed itself by ever-increasing acts of trespassing. It was around trespassing that the Woodstock phase of the Anti-Rent War would make itself felt in the mid-1840s.

Faced with the problem of educating and launching into the world his nine motherless children, Robert L. was irritated by the depredations of trespassers and aware of the growing demand for the kind of forest products his lands across the Hudson from Clermont might send to market. He conceived an elaborate system for harvesting and transporting his trees, employing the forests of his commons, the streams flowing through his lands, and the muscle of his reluctant tenants. He named this scheme the Esopus Creek Navigation Company.

18

THE ESOPUS CREEK NAVIGATION COMPANY

For some thirty years after he began managing his lands in Woodstock, Shandaken and Olive, Robert L. Livingston tried to do three things: to persuade or compel his tenants to pay their back and current rents, to derive an income from his forests, and to find and exploit mineral wealth. After hopes of mineral finds died away, Robert L. devised a plan to combine rent collecting with harvesting timber. This plan bore the name of the Esopus Creek Navigation Company.

Because Woodstock's Beaverkill and Little Beaverkill passed through much still untouched forest into the Esopus Creek, Woodstock qualified as a significant field of operations of the Navigation Company. Robert L.'s plan matured slowly while his tenants paid rent reluctantly if at all. They continued to thumb their noses at their landlord, cutting trees on Livingston's lands in open violation of the law. It was these tenants whom Robert L. proposed to persuade to furnish the labor to turn the Esopus and the Beaverkill into channels for carrying logs and timber to market.

During the 1820s Robert L. talked with lumber people and asked them questions. The big problem, he realized, was not the scarcity on his lands of the kinds of timber trees which were in demand but the obstacles to getting them delivered to consumers over bad or non-existent roads.[1]

Elsewhere—and notably on the Delaware and Hudson Rivers—softwoods such as pine and hemlock were being floated to New York fastened together to form rafts. Hardwoods, which would not float, were often piled up on the larger softwood rafts and so sent down the rivers. No streams flowing through Robert L.'s lands were suitable for rafting. The Esopus Creek and its branches would have been usable at times of freshets or "freshes," as they were often called, had it not been for the many places in which rocks and waterfalls impeded its flow.

But this did not discourage Livingston. He knew that with financial help from the state the Neversink River in Sullivan County had been cleared of similar obstructions in 1811 in order to make it suitable for rafting. Livingston also knew that the project had not worked. A number of men had been killed while trying to raft on the turbulent river after it was thought to be safe. But by the 1820s time had dimmed the memory of the Neversink tragedy in Livingston's mind.

Might it not be possible to clear the Esopus and the Beaverkill of obstructions and use them to send his logs rushing to market? It would be necessary to build booms to protect the mills along the upper reaches of the Esopus and its tributaries against damage which might result from bombardment by logs. Another boom at Kingston would stop all logs and keep them from damaging the thriving mills on the lower Esopus. From this point the logs would be hauled overland to Columbus Point (now Kingston Point), where planing, turning and other shops would process some of the timber. The rest could be floated down the Hudson to New York. And finally, as Livingston saw it, a plentiful supply of labor was available to do the dangerous work of rafting. Tenants who were in arrears in their rents might be given the choice of taking to the rafts or having Livingston use the armory of legal weapons available to him to evict them.

Livingston was aware that his tenants would not greet his scheme with pleasure. Yet the theoretical beauty of the plan, which tied together his forests, his water and his recalcitrant tenants, was such that tenant disapproval seemed a very minor matter indeed.[2]

The world was not standing still as Robert L. Livingston made his rosy plans. A period of overspeculation in land and industry was nearing its end in a sharp recession. At the same time enthusiasm over railroads was crossing the Atlantic and making itself felt among the Catskills as a means of checking the slump.

No group of men showed more enthusiasm for railroads than the tanners then at work in the Catskills. They were finding it was not worth the effort to haul out the logs which resulted once they had stripped the tanbark from the hemlock trees. A railroad, they thought, would make it economically feasible for them to saw their hemlock and hardwood logs and to have them moved quickly and inexpensively by rail to the landings on the Hudson and then to market.

One group of tanners proposed a railroad running from the Hudson at Malden above Saugerties through the hamlet of Woodstock, up the Sawkill Valley to the foot of Lake Hill, up the Hill, across the Little Shandaken flats and then down the valley of the Beaverkill to The Corner. Kingston people proposed a road to follow the Ulster and Delaware Turnpike, through Wittenberg and on into Delaware County. This road was chartered in April 1835, the Malden Road two years later. But neither was ever built.[3]

Robert L. was an enthusiast for railroads. He proposed a railroad to link the Esopus Creek at his boom to Columbus Point. This line did not become a reality. But the Esopus Creek Navigation Company did.

In the petition which led to the granting of the Company's charter Robert L. stated that, "the Esopus Creek, ramified into numerous branches, rises in and flows through a country heavily timbered with Hemlock and many other kinds of timber; that from the numerous Tanneries which have been and are about to be established in said region of the country, a great destruction of said timber must necessarily follow . . . the bad state of the roads rendering it unprofitable to transport said timber to market . . ." The Beaverkill in Woodstock was included in the plan. It turned out to be very important for Robert L.'s purposes.

"The E.C. Navigation Company was chartered by the Legislature April 22 1833—The Books were opened by the Commissioners and no persons being desirous of subscribing Mr. R. L. Livingston took the whole stock—On the 26 August the Company commenced blasting a channel of from 30 to 50 feet wide and by unremitted exertions, partially accomplished about twenty-three miles before the 1 of November, In June next the Company will be prepared to continue their operations to the headwaters of their streams . . ." So Robert L. wrote in what was apparently intended as a publicity release.

While waiting for June Robert L. kept busy with the affairs of his company. He was not discouraged by the failure of the public to subscribe to his stock issue, "I still persevere with my great and difficult project on the Esopus Creek," he wrote a little later, "with an universal opinion unfavorable to my success. . . ." Robert L. had thoroughly—even obsessively—committed himself to the Esopus Creek Navigation Company. The criticisms of his friends and the lukewarm participation of his skeptical employees could not deter him.[4]

An important part of the Esopus Creek operation was the

persuasion of Woodstock tenants to work off their back rents by hauling logs and working as raftsmen. In the summer of 1833 two Livingston agents had gone from tenant to tenant under orders to "get money or labour" and to "tell tenants that this was the last call." The tenants were well aware that rafting on such difficult streams as the Esopus and the Beaverkill was cold and dangerous work. Many rescued themselves from the terrors of the Esopus by scraping together a little rent money. A few chose the adventurous life of a raftsman, but a good many of these never showed up for duty.

In the spring of 1834 Robert L. made an inspection trip up the Esopus in what he described as "my New York barge with four oars." It was the first time such a craft had ever appeared on the creek, he wrote one of his sons. By May he had completed planning many details of the company's work. Its corporate seal would show "a Beaver—with a hemlock branch in his mouth sitting on a Log." The flags to be flown on the company buildings and boats would be "white—E.C. Navigation Company in blue." The raftsmen would wear uniforms consisting of blue jackets and white pantaloons.

During the winter of 1833-1834 *my tenants* who *owe rent*," as Robert L. put it, were being urged by Henry P. Shultis, Livingston's Woodstock agent, to cut and haul hemlock logs to the banks of the Beaverkill, where they were to wait until a freshet came along to carry them downstream. "If any rocks on the Beaverkill require blasting . . . let them be drilled by my tenants who owe rent," Robert L. instructed an agent, E. Miner.[5]

Booms of logs and chains were to be constructed to protect mills on the Esopus and the Beaverkill. Each of the existing and planned sawmills would have a basin in which logs for its use might be impounded. Many other details fill Robert L.'s letters of instruction to his agents. He required each of them to keep a journal to enter exactly what work was done each day. Through all the letters the theme of exacting labor from tenants who owed back rents never ceases. "Will any of the tenants come to Kingston and work at the Canal—pay half or a third cash," he wrote in a mood of concession. The canal was being dug as part of the basin for logs at Columbus Point.[6]

On April 15, 1834 Robert L. wrote from Clermont to his son Robert, then travelling in Europe. A heavy rain had been falling for several days and "the streams rose suddenly and very high—some trifling works were destroyed last Saturday and repaired on Monday." At this point in Robert L.'s letter a messenger arrived with cheering news. "The Beaverkill running through Woodstock has risen to an unusual height—that all the Logs, say 4,000—have gently floated into the Esopus Creek and are on the way to my Basin at Esopus i.e. Kingston—accompanied by fifteen hands and several boats. . . . I go tomorrow to visit the Creek."

Robert L.'s imagination often colored events with a look of greater glory than the cold facts warranted—it was so with the news brought by the messenger. William Faulkner, an experienced lumber dealer, visited the Esopus and reported the freshet had not rushed the Esopus Creek Navigation Company and its owner into success. "I was much gratified to find, beyond my expectations, the stream in so fine a situation. But was much disapointed in not finding more Logs floating or that had come down the stream. There seems to a want of management somewhere." In Faulkner's opinion five thousand logs might be brought from Winchell's Falls in Shandaken to Kingston "in the short space of six hours. But they must be attended to at the time the water is in a proper hight." And attended to was what the logs were not.[7]

Faulkner learned a good part of the reason when he met "Mr. Shulters, as I think they call him." This was Henry P. Shultis, who now had added to his duties of harrying Woodstock tenants into paying their rents or working them off for the Company the post of "Superintendent of the Woods or Forests," with responsibility for seeing to the cutting of trees and the hauling of the logs that resulted to the bank of the Beaverkill. Shultis was frank in expressing his views. When the freshet came the tenant-raftsmen had not been willing to "go on the Creek with boats; the men were afraid as the water seemed to high."

"Now, Sir," Faulkner explained in his report to Robert L., "there was much Less danger if any danger exists in high water than in low because you escape all the Rocks if there is any. I did not consider *myself* in danger when left entirely alone in the Boat." Faulkner then offered to buy five thousand logs "during this year." He went on to offer advice. An experienced man should head up the Company, "one man who has been in this business would do more than 50 who do not know any of the movements of the water."

Robert L. did not take Faulkner's advice. He had become obsessed with his position as sole owner and manager of the Company, with its power over the entire watershed of the Esopus, with its ingenious rent-collecting system and with its output of a great variety of wood products (chestnut posts, turnings such as maple bedposts, both French and Field, planks of whitewood, pine, oak and hemlock; ash and maple "joists" for makers of oars and furniture, and many others).[8]

Very promising for a while was the making of hexagonal paving blocks of hemlock, which were used on a trial basis for paving a part of Broadway in New York City. The blocks were set with their end grain up and down and their bases in a waterproof compound. Hemlock lasts well when either always wet or always dry but soon decays when these extremes alternate. It was hoped that the waterproof base would keep the blocks forever wet and enduring. The plan did not work well and the making of the blocks was discontinued.[9]

Eventually the Sullivan County lands which Robert L. owned were brought into the area of operation of the Navigation Company. Products from some of their mills were hauled, usually at ruinous expense, to the Hudson. Cooper Lake in Woodstock was never far from Robert L.'s thoughts. He proposed cutting a channel from the stream which drains Mink Hollow to the lake so that the stream's waters might be sent into the Beaverkill or the lake as desired. Several sawmills on the Beaverkill between the flats at Willow and the Shandaken line turned out planks and boards to be floated or hauled to the headquarters at Columbus Point.

Sometimes Robert L. thought of raising Cooper Lake and changing its original outlet into the Sawkill so it would discharge into the Beaverkill. He planned on using the lake as a storage basin for logs. The old outlet belonged to John Winne and was part of the Desbrossess-Hunter Great Lot 25. In 1837 Robert L. bought water rights from Winne and hoped to set up a turning mill, a cotton mill or a cooperage beside Winne's sawmill. It was at the same time that the Malden Railroad, planned to venture at first to the Smith Bushkill in the town of Shandaken, was chartered. Its promoters hoped their line would eventually link up with a railroad from Kingston to the hamlet of Woodstock.[10]

The Esopus Creek Navigation Company had not paid off. Robert L. Livingston had invested $20,000 in it. With a railroad now promising to add greatly to the value of his lands and to work in cooperation with the Navigation Company, however, he had some reason to hope that his losses might be wiped out. Agent Henry P. Shultis was confident a railroad would work wonders. "This Lake Hill will be a great market place for lumber of all kinds," Shultis wrote, "in case the contemplated Rail Road from Mr. Isham's [Bristol Landing] to the Bushkill in Big Shandaken [would be built] this will be handy for to get Chordwood down from little Shandaken." Being hardwood in nearly all cases, cordwood couldn't be floated down, but had to be hauled by oxen. A railroad would be a great advantage in transporting firewood.[11]

For a time things looked hopeful. But trouble was on the way. The 1830s was a decade of disturbing economic fluctuations. A depression of extreme depth in 1837 brought American business and industry as close to a standstill as it has ever been.

A few years earlier Col. Wm. Edwards and his brother-in-law, Captain Tyler, had agreed to use the hemlock bark from Great Lot 24, then owned jointly by Robert L. and Edward P. Livingston. The tanning industry was hit by hard times in 1833, and the bark contract which Robert L. had expected to bring him an income of $1200 annually for ten years became the subject of a lawsuit. The market for lumber almost vanished and the Esopus Creek Navigation Company died.[12]

When Robert L. founded the Company in 1833 he was fifty-eight years old and in good health. By 1835 he wrote that his "nervous system was much debilitated" and that he'd had rheumatic attacks which left him quite lame. From time to time after that he had spells of fairly good health. He even gave up drinking in the evening and took "only a little wine and cider at dinner." His wine bills had amounted to about $300 per year a bit earlier when the annual expenses of running his household had come to $8000.[13]

Still, Robert L. did not become embittered. His New Year's resolution for 1836 has no reference to health or personal advantages to be gained in 1836. Instead it reflects Robert L.'s image of himself as a Hudson Valley Livingston and the devoted head of a family. It goes, "Let the New Year commence with all the kind feelings of my nature—Let every duty be cheerfully performed—I have no enemies to forgive—many duties to perform—Do all the good you can—strive to render *all* who may depend on you—happy."[14]

By 1838 the Livingstons' family physician, Dr. Knickerbocker, diagnosed Robert L.'s ailment as gout. Soon after Robert L. ordered a sedan chair from a New York City carriagemaker. The chair was duly sent up the river to Clermont with an apology for its shortcomings. "It is an article that few have seen in this country and with which we were almost totally unacquainted," the maker wrote.[15]

Whether Robert L. was ever carried about his estate by a pair of tenants grasping the chair's handles has not been recorded. The following year Livingston was shaken by the news that his eldest son, Robert, had died in Rome. From that time on he had periods of mental confusion. The rumor spread around Dutchess and Ulster Counties that he had "lost his mind."

His oldest surviving son, Eugene Augustus, tried to manage Robert L.'s affairs. In 1840 the son received a promise in writing from his father that upon the old man's death he was to receive the object which more than anything else stood for the greatest moment in the history of the Livingstons of Clermont, the snuffbox given to the Chancellor as a mark of esteem by Napoleon Bonaparte. It showed on its cover the emperor's portrait set in a circle of diamonds (the snuffbox now belongs to the New-York Historical Society).

Soon testimony as to his irrationality was being heard before a lunacy commission (from Henry P. Shultis of Woodstock among others), and then on January 7, 1843 Robert L. Livingston died. He passed away just in time to avoid having to deal with the final chapter of the Livingston dominance over the sixty-six thousand acres he owned in Woodstock and parts of adjoining Shandaken and Olive. He left an estate valued at close to a quarter of a million dollars, most of which went to his sons Eugene Augustus and Montgomery, who also inherited the task of presiding over the dissolution of the Woodstock estate after struggling with their tenants in the rebellion against absentee landlords known as the Anti-Rent War.[16]

TENANTS AND LANDLORDS BECOME UNEASY

T he Anti-Rent War of the 1840s had been a long time coming. Although some tenants found the old leasehold system bearable and a few found it profitable, many had chafed under the restrictions of an Old World system of land tenure established in parts of New York far back in colonial days. Most Americans wanted to banish from their land the ancient inequities of Europe and to enjoy greater freedom and opportunity. From time to time, notably in 1752 and 1766, Hudson Valley tenants had tried to force change through physical violence. Their efforts, however, had no effect on a system that was heartily supported by the rich and the powerful. It was not until the late 1840s that the burden of the old leases for three lives, the payment of fines on alienation, and the other survivals of old European ways were lifted from the backs of the tenants.

The death in 1839 of Robert L.'s son Robert marked the beginning of the plunge of the father into a fog from which he never entirely emerged. This was the year, too, when Stephen Van Rensselaer of the Manor of Rensselaerwyck died, and the year in which his sons tried to collect every cent of the huge back rents owed their father's estate. It was this decision which led to the first explosion of tenant resentment which culminated in the Anti-Rent War.

Eugene A. and Montgomery Livingston were both badly in need of cash when they took over their father's property in 1843. Though Robert L.'s estate was substantial, it was encumbered by debts, the result of a combination of Robert L.'s generosity to members of his family and his poor relations, the losses of the Esopus Creek Navigation Company, and a lifelong habit of living beyond his income.

In order to raise cash quickly the two brothers took the advice of their lawyer and cousin, John Cochran, and sold some of their Woodstock farms and New York City buildings even though the prices they received were low. Also on Cochran's advice, they then decided to sell their entire Woodstock estate, or at least as much of it as they could. They arrived at this decision a few months before their father died and while the Anti-Rent War was gathering momentum on Van Rensselaer lands among the Helderbergs to the north of the Catskills.

Neither Eugene Augustus nor Montgomery had ever given any evidence of a desire to lead the life of an absentee landlord. Their childhood conditioning had given them none of the drive for acquiring wealth and power and land which formed so large a part of American life. Their father had taken an unusual interest in shaping the sons into "accomplished and learned" gentlemen who would feel at ease in what Robert L. liked to call "the best society."

Robert L. gave both sons and daughters every possible opportunity to learn to sing and to play musical instruments, to draw and to paint. They lived at Clermont surrounded by the Chancellor's collection of paintings and antiques. In 1817 Robert L. met the gifted and eccentric botanist C. F. Rafinesque, who was destitute after a shipwreck. He bore Rafinesque off to Clermont to serve as teacher of drawing, botany and Italian to his daughters.

As his children grew older Robert L. took them to New York by winter to expose them to a more sophisticated world than that of Clermont and to widen their acquaintance with the upper class of their state. When his children were away at school he wrote them affectionate letters in which he displayed very definite ideas about the sort of men and women he expected them to become. He once wrote to son Montgomery to urge him to "learn while young, that much happiness consists in the strict performance of every duty—however painful and disagreeable that duty may be—one is always pleased afterwards." [1]

The duty of his young sons, as Robert L. saw it, was to model themselves on the kind of elegant and accomplished people whom Robert L. remembered associating with during his magical years in Paris. As he grew older these people became ever more glamorous and more worthy of imitation. In none of his surviving letters does Robert L. urge his children to practice thrift, to develop sharpness in business, or to add to their wealth.

180

Montgomery and Eugene A. studied at the Red Hook Academy and were sent off at the proper time to Rev. Mr. Smith's White Plains, New York Academy. From there in 1831, as Eugene became seventeen and Montgomery fourteen, the two settled down to study in Geneva, Switzerland, a city about which Robert L. cherished the happiest of memories. The boys paid their own bills from a generous allowance deposited to their credit with the Paris banking house of Baron Hottinguer.

From time to time their older brother Robert visited them. Robert was enjoying the two years of travel which his father planned after each son completed his studies and could speak three or four languages. Eugene and Montgomery boarded at the school maintained by a once-well-known Swiss painter named Toppfer and took additional courses at the Geneva Academy. They were taken by Toppfer on tours of the surrounding countryside. They were visited by the many relatives who were travelling in Europe or living there for a year or two.

It may well have been the influence of M. Toppfer that caused Montgomery to decide to become a painter. His father was all enthusiasm when told of the decision. As he had made clear in his letters, his children were to follow their own inclinations in their choice of careers. He would back them up in whatever might please them. He had already provided them with letters of introduction to upper-class Europeans whom he had known in his Paris days. Now he managed to get his son introductions to Cardinals Wild and Fesch in Rome, where he expected Montgomery would study art "under the best masters." Fesch was a notable collector of paintings, a patron of the arts and, Robert L. assured his son it was being said that Cardinal Fesch was an uncle of Napoleon.[2]

During the 1830s Robert L. had written Montgomery an occasional cheerful bit of news about his Esopus Creek Navigation Company. He once predicted as he was moved up the Esopus on his barge that Montgomery would some day find much to paint on that picturesque stream. The collapse of the Navigation Company in the panic of 1837 made it necessary for Montgomery to cut short his studies in Dresden and Dusseldorf, places which were then becoming popular among young American students and which he preferred to Rome. His brother Robert wrote from New York that "people who were worth $500,000 six months ago are now selling their furniture." Sister Matilda told of the starving poor in the flour riots in New York breaking open warehouses and compelling dealers to sell flour at far less than their inflated prices.

Montgomery returned home in time to set up his "painting room" in the Chancellor's former house and to play his part in the sad final phase of his father's life. He was beginning with his brother Eugene to share responsibility for the management of Woodstock, making occasional trips there to deal with tenants. He was conscious of the rumblings of resentment against absentee landlords which were taking form on the Van Rensselaer estate.[3]

Montgomery continued to paint landscapes. In 1843 he was elected an Associate of the National Academy of Design. In 1844 one of his landscapes was a choice of the American Art Union, a membership organization which distributed works of art among those who joined. He experimented with lithographs of Hudson Valley scenes. Montgomery had gone from gallery to gallery in Europe, absorbed in studying the work of the Old Masters; his brother Robert, who also painted, wrote to him that he could see nothing in Europe equal to the paintings of the American, Thomas Cole. Montgomery's work shows a little of the influence of the Hudson River School which crystallized around Cole.[4]

Eugene increased his wealth by two marriages. He led an active social life, travelling from one fashionable resort in Euope and the United States to another to the end of his long life. His papers relating to Woodstock matters were usually notarized by the American consuls in a variety of European cities.

Montgomery followed a different path. Art was his primary interest, he had a narrow social life, and he often didn't answer urgent business letters. He travelled only to places like the Catskills and the White Mountains, favorite painting grounds for the Hudson River School. Unlike his brother he often dressed in the careless manner of the Bohemian students of his days in Dusseldorf. He wore a beard and long hair.

His wife, the daughter of Samuel Swarthwout, a popular New York official who had been ruined by charges that he had helped himself to public money, was far from an heiress. The verb "Swarthwouting" went into the language for a time as a synonym for embezzling. Mary Swarthout was lovely and charming. She was also very religious. In this she differed from her husband, who shared the skepticism common among young artists of his day. On this point they quarreled.

Neither Eugene nor Montgomery had the character or training needed to deal with the difficulties developing at Clermont and on their lands across the Hudson. Montgomery had hardly set up the painting room which was the envy of less fortunate artists when his father began to be observed to suffer from occasional lapses of memory and an unwillingness to tend to the business of managing his lands. Eugene, who made efforts to help, could do little to bring order to the chaos that was rapidly evolving.

During lucid intervals Robert L. urged his agents with all his old energy to harry trespassers in Woodstock. His tenants may, however, have been encouraged in resisting their landlord by reports of Robert L.'s condition. Between 1838 (the year of the sedan chair) and the death of Robert L. in 1843 tenant resistance stiffened markedly and refusal to pay rents increased.

A notable Woodstock resister in 1838 was John Reynolds. When Livingston agent J. Gale asked for his rent Reynolds said he would not pay, explaining that the Livingstons had no clear title to the land. Gale said he could compel Reynolds to pay, and he returned the next day to try again. Reynolds was not at home, but he had left with his wife $45 of what Gale described to Robert L. as "un current money of different states." It is likely that Reynolds in offering worthless paper money was implying that the Livingston title was worth as much and no more than the bills he offered. Gale refused to accept the money.[5]

That same year tenants in the Beaverkill Valley, Little Shandaken and across the line in Shandaken and Olive were resisting their landlord as a group. They were headed by the Longyear family. Gale believed John Reynolds had come under Longyear influence. One result of this movement toward united action was a lawsuit brought by the Longyears and a tenant named Swarthout against one of the Devalls, a Winne and a Short. The plaintiffs claimed that the Livingston title to lands along the border of Woodstock and Olive was invalid.

In an unusually light-hearted moment tanner and Livingston agent Abraham D. Ladew told Robert L. Livingston that the Longyear side had described the boundaries of the piece of land in question as going from one heap of stones to another on the side "of a Small Mountain called Torneshook bergh [now Tonshi Mountain] hence 600 chains Nly. to stones, thence another course 400 ch. to stones, thence such a course to the Blue Mountains thence as they wind and turn some where else, the devil may know where to the place of beginning, I believe going one and a half [times] round nothing at all." [6]

Several trespassers on Livingston holdings were nabbed in Woodstock in 1839. Livingston lawyer H. M. Romeyn of Kingston demanded high bail for those in custody. When brought before a justice, Romeyn reported, they "pleaded title."

This was Robert L.'s last go at prosecuting trespassers, although the subject remained on his mind. His coachman, Edmund Kelly, testified before the lunacy commission in 1842 that sometimes his employer would demand "Who is stealing my wood?" as he was being driven about.[7]

The two brothers who in 1843 inherited the 66,000 acres of what was usually called the Woodstock tract set about selling in earnest. Though they had originally assumed that Woodstock might be kept and the $2000 per year income from it increased, John Cochran persuaded them that the sooner they sold the better. By 1843 the Anti-Rent War was becoming so serious there was widespread fear among the landlords that they might lose everything if they hung on. This and the interest-bearing debts which burdened Robert L.'s estate were decisive in Cochran's mind.

A draft of an advertisement among Montgomery's papers shows that the brothers first hoped to sell in large parcels rather than to individual tenants. The advertisement offers for sale fifteen thousand acres "in the town of Woodstock." It says in part:

> Heavily timbered and a considerable part lies on or near the Esopus Creek which is raftable to Kingston—on the premises an extensive Leather Manufactory in full business requires large amounts of bark affording a good market for the article . . . a large part of the land good for farming purposes and very valuable to lumbermen . . . also 5000 acres of improved lands in the Valley of Woodstock having the Saugerties Turnpike on one side and the Kingston on the other divided into farms of from 60 to 150 acres each with good Farm buildings—a part of the farms are leased for one life with a rent of from 15 to 20 bushels of wheat per hundred acres—a part rented from year to year and a part let on shares—many of them are well cultivated and valuable farms and from their convenience to Market an object to farmers.[8]

The timbered tract offered was actually partly in the towns of Shandaken and Olive. The leather factory was the tannery of A. D. Ladew at The Corner. The leases for three lives, some of which were still in force in Woodstock, were not mentioned.

In July 1843 a response came from across the Atlantic. A group of English investors expressed willingness to pay cash for the Livingstons' 20,000 acres, on which they intended to "place large improvements by sending out respectable families from England." Anthony Barclay, the British consul in New York and a brother of Henry Barclay, an important man of Saugerties, was handling the proposal. He hinted at a price of five dollars per acre, but said he would have to inspect the land before he could make a definite offer.

The deal, which might have had a decided impact on Woodstock, was not completed. No other offer that seemed acceptable appeared, so Eugene and Montgomery agreed that they would divide the land instead of selling Woodstock and sharing the money received. After that each might go his own way in disposing of his share.[9]

Dividing the land was no simple operation. Surveys from the beginning of Livingston ownership had been piecemeal and often inaccurate. The entire 66,000 acres would have to be resurveyed, and each farm or tract of wild land would have a value placed on it. Here there were some unusual difficulties. Many of the leases for lives had been made years earlier. In some cases the lease had been sold and no one knew where the three people mentioned in the lease had gone.

Each leasehold had a value depending on the number of years it might normally be expected to run—that is, until the death of the last person named in the original lease regardless of who might be living there in 1843. Some "tenants at will" had no leases at all and lived on a farm on a year-to-year basis. Others whose leases were close to running out had paid their landlords in cash to insert another and younger name in their leases and so to extend their likely term. A few had perpetual or "durable" leases.

Eugene Augustus and Montgomery Livingston had limited abilities in dealing with the situation that confronted them in 1843. They were glad to turn over all details to Cochran and his partner Rathbun and to restrict their comments to shocked protests over the size of their lawyers' bills. The surveying project got under way immediately after the Woodstock town election of 1844 and did not reach its conclusion until 1846.

During that time the services of the Livingstons' resident agent, Henry P. Shultis, were of the first importance. Shultis was an outstanding man in his town, of great practical ability, "of exemplary Christian character," and a leader of local Methodism. After the Stilwells had left and before the Woodstock Methodist Church was built Methodist meetings were held at Shultis's house.

As the survey was being organized Shultis, who had already been town supervisor between 1830 and 1837, became a candidate for supervisor of Woodstock on the Locofoco ticket. The Lofococos, the radical, anti-capitalist wing of the Democratic party, flourished among the urban poor. In upstate New York they had strength among a growing number of Anti-Rent tenant farmers. It was a tribute to Shultis's political skill that he could get the votes of his absentee landlord's opponents while he was the agent of that landlord.

Shultis was elected. He put all his energy and the power of his office behind the survey. He acted as its paymaster, using the rent money he collected minus his own fee of five per cent. He soothed the opposition by recommending the hiring of local tenants as surveyors' assistants, boarding the surveyors and their horses locally, and rounding up oldtimers who were glad to earn a little money by pointing out the marked trees and heaps of stones left by surveyors of the past.[10]

Surveyors Henry Ramsay of Schenectady and John B. Davis of Olive were also asked to make an appraisal of each farm and tract of wild land. In spite of Henry P. Shultis's efforts at persuasion many Woodstock people greeted the surveyors with suspicion and hostility. The fact was that the time was not at all favorable for a landlord to set in motion any sort of project on his leased lands without raising tenant uneasiness.

Sheriffs being sent on the Van Rensselaer lands to the north to collect back rents were being tarred and feathered. Their papers were being burned by men disguised as Indians and shouting "Down with the rent." Anti-Rent associations with elaborate attempts at secrecy had been formed. Men known as lecturers were presenting the case against the absentee landlords wherever they could get a group of tenant farmers to listen. With statewide elections due in the fall, politicians of all parties were keenly aware of the strength of Anti-Rent feeling and were making plans to ride into office on a wave of tenant votes.

Although no attempt had yet been made to organize Woodstock tenants into an Anti-Rent association, the time for this was coming. The sounds of quarreling between the brothers in the Livingston mansion at Clermont had been heard in Woodstock, and rumors that Montgomery and Eugene were planning to sell were finding their way into every Woodstock hollow. Were Woodstock farmers about to trade American for absentee British landlords? Or were the Livingstons making their survey the better to squeeze their tenants or in preparation for selling to any stranger who would meet their price?

It was even being whispered around that plans were being hatched by tenants to throw the surveyors out. Cochran and the surveyors realized that the cooperation of Woodstock tenants was needed if they were to complete their task. With Shultis's help they were able to persuade some that their work would make it possible for tenants to buy their own farms.

Some tenants then overwhelmed the surveyors and Cochran with help in order to expand the bounds of their farms at the expense of their neighbors. Some depreciated their lands in order to be able to buy it at bargain prices. One man who seemed to be satisfied with things as they were tried to raise the value of his farm so that no one would buy it. "I think I never knew a more mendacious race of depredators and rascals," John Cochran wrote to Montgomery. "I soon discovered that no one of these could be relied upon." Here Cochran was expressing the contemptuous feeling toward Woodstock tenants which was shared by the Livingston brothers and their adherents.[11]

With Cochran keeping a close eye on the surveying parties, the work went ahead in the spring, summer and fall of 1844. It was suspended for the winter. Henry Ramsay's surviving field notes show that he sometimes enjoyed his labor, especially when it involved working in the woods and among the lonely mountains where he was less accessible to suspicious and wily local farmers.

In May, for example, he wrote in a lyrical manner of a night and day spent along the Woodstock-Shandaken line. He and his helpers had re-crossed the Grogkill and after a walk of almost two miles reached ". . . a delightful place lying in a cove or angle of the mountain S [south] aspect, very fine tall timber. We dined beside a Lympid gurgling spring, canopied with luxuriant maples. We gathered in this little paradise an abundant supply of wild leeks and pepper root which grew in rich profusion about us." As night approached on May 3 Ramsay "Stopped, knocked off, quit, kindled fire, felled trees, built hut or shanty, ate raw pork, pepper grass, prayed, laid down on a piece of hemlock bark and slept in the Woods first-rate." [12]

As Ramsay was describing this idyllic scene, Woodstock farmers were begining to join in the Anti-Rent movement. Within a few weeks they were organizing into an association with tenants of Shandaken and Olive. After that the surveyors and Cochran would feel less secure and the tenants would become far bolder.

THE
ANTI-RENT WAR

Between 1839 and 1844 the Anti-Rent War, as it was coming to be called, was moving ever closer to Woodstock. The War's leaders were succeeding in their aim of bringing most New York State tenant farmers into their movement. Woodstock tenants were easily confirmed in their old suspicion that the Livingstons' title to Woodstock lands was invalid and might be ignored, as John Reynolds had ignored it in 1838. The fraud and chicanery involved in the granting of the Hardenbergh Patent back in Queen Anne's time, the argument that all titles to land granted by the Crown had been nullified by the success of the Revolution, the Beekman claim—these encouraged tenants to test the validity of absentee landlords' titles.

Horace Greeley's influential New York *Tribune* urged speedy court action to test the validity of absentee landlords' titles. Greeley wrote, "We say let all disputed land titles be litigated . . . let whoever claims the land which another has redeemed from barrenness and now lives by cultivating show that it is his . . ." [1]

Woodstock farmers reacted to this encouragement by witholding rents and stepping up trespassing on their landlords' commons. This became especially important to them in the stagnating national economy and hard times of the late 1830s. Until 1844, however, Woodstock's part in the Anti-Rent War remained passive. Then a change came.

It was on July 4, 1844 that Woodstock tenants began swinging into active involvement in the War. On that day a meeting of five thousand people was said to have been held at Pine Hill on the Delaware County border for the avowed purpose of stimulating the formation of an underground Anti-Rent organization in Woodstock, Shandaken and Olive. The *Democratic Journal* of Kingston, edited by Livingston lawyer W. H. Romeyn, took notice of the meeting and said, "Tenants who favor the opposition to the payment of rent dress in Indian fashion, and, as far as possible, in an uniform style wearing mostly frock coats, either of red or some other bright color, with a belt around the waist containing a scalping knife, pistol etc., a false face cut out of leather, and cape ornamented in various ways." The *Journal* ended its account with advice to the Anti-Renters—they had better remain calm and take no rash action.[2]

Woodstock Anti-Renters ignored the *Journal's* advice. Their women got to work cutting and sewing disguises and the tenants strengthened their organization. By this time dinner horns had ceased blowing to summon farm workers to meals. The sound was being reserved to warn of the approach of a landlord's agent or a sheriff. Anti-Renters on meeting whispered or shouted their password of "Down with the Rent," and so became known as Downrenters. Landlord adherents were Uprenters or Tories.

Most Anti-Rent Indians were young. Many joined from serious motives, but many others, as the *Democratic Journal* pointed out, joined "for fun." And indeed the costumes, the music, the disguises, and the sense of brotherhood within a select group provided fun and excitement enough for anybody.

Many years after the Anti-Rent stir was over and half-forgotten Abram W. Hoffman, editor of the Kingston *Freeman*, brought to life once again the fever that gripped Woodstock in 1844 and 1845 by recollecting details handed down to him from Woodstock ancestors or related by veterans of those stirring days. Their organization, Hoffman wrote, "was patterned after the Irish patriotic societies of '98 . . . Each band of ten was known to their leader but not to the members of other bands. The leaders were known to the chief of the organization but not to each other. Thus was the danger of treachery discounted to the utmost. The meetings were in secluded forest glades to which they repaired secretly, only appearing to each other when fully disguised. The chiefs of the bands were disguised as squaws. The chief would hide a bag containing the disguises for his men in a thicket." The men would arrive one by one, don their disguises and would then be led out of the thicket by their squaw-disguised chief. In a lost ballad this process was presented as the giving birth by the chief to ten full-grown Indians.

Hoffman told of the sound of tin dinner horns being heard for miles around at the approach of a sheriff. He remembered a verse of a ballad commemorating one such event:

> The horns will toot from door to door
> While old tin pans they clatter;
> There's Indians scalping all around—
> For Lord's sake what's the matter[3]

As the statewide elections of the fall of 1844 approached, Downrent fever rose in Woodstock. Local people had seen Henry P. Shultis achieve political victory that spring by placing a firm foot in the camp of both landlords and tenants. Now candidates for the governorship and the State Assembly were trying to turn the same trick. Both Whig and Democratic candidates for state office angled for the Anti-Rent vote. In Columbia County, Montgomery Livingston was implored to run for the Assembly on the Whig ticket. He declined the honor. During this time of stress Henry P. Shultis sympathized with the Anti-Renters he met and denounced them to the Livingstons, though in cautious terms. When John Cochran wrote to ask him to supply the names of Woodstock Anti-Rent leaders, Shultis did not answer. Nor did he reply to a second request.[4]

On election day Democrat Silas Wright and a substantial number of Anti-Rent-sympathizing members of the Assembly were elected. A showdown seemed inevitable. The new State Legislature would meet in January.

Much of the fun had gone out of Downrent involvement by December 1844. It was becoming a more serious business. Woodstock people were following reports of upstate incidents in which violence had been used against landlords' agents and could not help feeling that similar happenings might come to their town. In December they listened soberly to reports of the arrest of Dr. Boughton, a prominent upstate Anti-Rent leader, on a charge of murder. After Columbia County Anti-Renters threatened to storm the Hudson jail to release Dr. Boughton, Governor William Bouck ordered militia to the scene.

A few days after Christmas Woodstock people learned that the adjutant-general of the state militia, Archibald Niven (a Sullivan

County lawyer who had been active on behalf of the landlords), had ordered General Joseph S. Smith of Kingston to "hold the military companies under his command in readiness for prompt and energetic action." With this order the possibility of a violent confrontation between landlords and tenants moved closer.

General Smith called up the Rondout Guards, the Ulster Grays, the Hurley Riflemen and other militia units. All paraded in Kingston on December 29. The armed and uniformed men gave Kingston quite "a military air," the *Democratic Journal* reported with evident delight.[5]

Early in January the new governor, Silas Wright, recommended changes in state law to meet some of the Anti-Renters' criticisms and grievances. Landlords quickly stepped up their efforts to fight any change. A landlords' "Freeholders' Committee of Safety" asked the Livingston brothers for a contribution to help keep existing laws untouched. When a trespasser named Short was arrested, local sympathizers helped him escape. Rearrested, he again escaped. Three Woodstock men headed by Issac Reynolds became delegates to an important Anti-Rent Convention in New Bern in the Van Rensselaer country.[6]

Late in that month of January 1845 the Legislature delivered a telling blow to the Anti-Rent cause by passing a law which made it a felony punishable by hanging to be present in disguise at any event at which someone was killed—this even if the disguised persons had nothing to do with the killing. The new law, when added to the military display of December 29, was clearly meant to intimidate Anti-Renters. But it did not succeed. Rents continued to be withheld, Indian disguises to be worn, and, parrticularly in Woodstock, trespassing on the landlords' woods increased.

Henry P. Shultis became bolder in apprehending trespassers. As March drew near Shultis kept an eye on the commons where Woodstock people were making maple sugar in the high-spirited mood that always accompanied this first outdoor work of the spring. Making sugar on the landlord's commons was allowed but cutting timber for sale, of course, was not. While in the woods, however, some tenants took advantage of their opportunity and cut timber.

John Cochran chose this period to come to Woodstock to organize his spring campaign of surveying and appraising. He wrote his employers that he had discovered that trespassers had cut timber not far from Cooper Lake. He notified Henry P. Shultis, who at once sent his neighbor John B. Lasher "to restore the logs to possession," that is, to seize them on behalf of the Livingstons. As Lasher, helped by a yoke of oxen and two Woodstock men named Peter Bonesteel and Ploss (whose first name has missed recording), went about his work, there occurred a struggle which briefly put Woodstock into the news as the liveliest spot of the moment in the Anti-Rent War.[7]

The incident has gone down in Woodstock folklore embellished and embroidered. Around it so many other bits of Anti-Rent lore have gathered that the actual story has become confused. A fairly reliable contemporary account is that given by Major General Joseph S. Smith in his report to Adjutant-General A. C. Niven. Dated March 7, a week after the incident, it was published in the Albany *Argus* on March 10. "Sir," the general wrote, "there has been an outbreak among the tenants of Robert L. Livingston's estate . . . which is likely to lead to serious difficulties. On Friday of last week, they employed a Mr. John B. Lasher to remove a quantity of timber that had been felled by some trespassers on the patent. While engaged in that duty he was suddenly surrounded and taken by a gang of 15 or 16 armed men, disguised as Indians, who required him to desist and be off at once.

"On his refusal he was seized by the Indians, and a severe scuffle ensued, Mr. Lasher resisting to the extent of his powers, and using a handspike to good advantage until it was finally wrested from him. He was, however, overpowered, and, as usual, received a coat of tar and feathers. They then made the effort to throw him from a rock about ten feet in height, in which they soon succeeded, but not without precipitating two of their men, to whom Lasher made good hold during the affray—their masks were displaced during the fall, by which he was enabled to recognize the two. He finally escaped, badly bruised and hurt. Warrants were immediately got and the two he recognized were arrested, but by some unaccountable negligence of the officers, made their escape.

"The proprietors of the land," the general reported, "are determined not only to arrest the offenders, but to collect every cent of [back] rent now due, by legal proceedings. Several writs are now out for the trespass. The under sheriff of this county left here this morning, in company with a constable, for the infected district. . . . Reports are in circulation of Indians from Delaware County cooperating with the tenants of Woodstock. . . ."

Though General Smith's report gives a good chronological account of what had happened in Woodstock between February 28 and March 7, it gives no hint of the doubt and hesitation into which Ulster officials were thrown by the assault on Lasher. The county was under conservative Whig control. Yet sympathy for the Downrenters was widespread among the voters, and if strong action against the Woodstock "Indians" were taken the political results might be unpleasant. Following the escape of the two Indians (no attempt to arrest them or their companions is known to have been made immediately) it is likely that Ulster officials hoped that the incident would be quickly forgotten and that emotions would cool off. They did not count on John Cochran's vigilance on behalf of the Livingston brothers.

In early March 1845 Eugene A. Livingston was in Philadelphia, the home town of his wife. Montgomery was busy in his painting room at Clermont, enjoying what turned out to be the high point of his career as a painter. Cochran, recovering from a damaged arm sustained in falling through the ice while on his way to Woodstock, formed a plan to make the most of the Lasher incident. He urged Montgomery to leave his painting room for Kingston, where he could bring his influence to bear on Ulster officials. Montgomery did his best—it is likely that General Smith's letter of March 7 was a result of his efforts.[8]

On March 8, before General Smith could have an answer to his letter, Sheriff John Schryver of Ulster despatched undersheriff Hiram Schoonmaker and a constable to what Smith called "the infected district." The undersheriff "as was expected . . . was resisted in his attempt to arrest the persons engaged in the outrage upon Lasher. As he was entering the neighborhood where the persons he was in quest of resided, near Cooper's tavern, the horns were sounded, and a general concert was the consequence through the whole settlement. . . ." Disguised Downrenters quickly gathered, seized the legal papers carried by the undersheriff and burned them. Schoonmaker and his constable were allowed to make their way back to Kingston without being tarred and feathered.

Adjutant-general Niven, a holdover from the previous Bouck administration and still on the new governor's staff, answered General Smith's letter promptly after first conferring with Governor Wright. The governor was unwilling to take the responsibility for calling up the Ulster militia as General Smith had apparently hoped. He made it plain that Sheriff Schryver had the responsibility for taking care of the Downrenters. The state could supply ammunition but the sheriff would have to do the rest. On receiving Niven's letter General Smith was at once off to the state arsenal at Albany. He returned to Kingston with "250 muskets and bayonets, 250 cartouche boxes and belts, and 1500 rounds of ball cartridge." [9]

By the time the arms and ammunition arrived Sheriff Schryver had already called up a sheriff's posse formed for the most part of men from the militia units alerted in December but also including others from Kingston, Saugerties, Hurley and Rosendale. Some were Woodstock men.

On the morning of March 10 a company of fifty men drawn from Kingston and Hurley and commanded by undersheriff Schoonmaker left the Ulster County courthouse "in a pelting snow" and headed for Woodstock. There they joined fifty Saugerties men under Sheriff Schryver. The roads "were of the worst possible description," reported the Albany *Argus*. The men were said to be cheerful in spite of their many difficulties, and "high and low, rich and poor could be seen shouldering their muskets."[10]

Cochran kept in close touch with events. Once the posse was formed he took legal actions which he described in a letter to Eugene Livingston, "Our plan is now that the posse is out to commence suits for the collection of *all* rents due and to proceed with a steel hand against the insurgents. About twelve suits in trespass have been commenced, and as many will be for the rent as there is a prospect of collecting—of course no suit should be brought against a well disposed tenant or one of whom nothing can be collected. . . ."

As the slushy snow fell and the wind continued to blow on the night of March 11 a hired carriage struggled along the road to Woodstock carrying a law clerk of Marius Schoonmaker and a large bundle of legal papers to be delivered to the posse's commander and served upon Woodstock tenants. The members of the posse had made camp that miserable night amid the slush and mud of Henry P. Shultis's farm, which lay on the first hillside to be met today on the road leading from Bearsville to Wittenberg. Most of the men belonged to loosely organized and sparsely equipped militia units known as "Joe Bunker" companies. These men wore their everyday clothes.

One unit, the Hurley Greens, had apparently mistaken the nature of the duty they were being called upon to perform and appeared, according to Woodstock tradition, in the splendid dress uniforms in which they may have paraded in Kingston in December to the admiration of the ladies and the envy of the men. "A dark green frock coat with large brass buttons and yellow epaulets for the privates, and gold embroidered epaulets for the officers" was the basis of the Greens' uniform, the historian of the unit recalled. "At the bottom of the coat was a row of black fringe. White duck trousers were worn and a felt hat with two black ostrich plumes. . . ." The Greens, floundering in their finery through the mud and snow, became figures of comedy to their fellow possemen. And so deeply was their pride wounded that once the Woodstock campaign was over they quietly disbanded.[11]

The posse men had come to Woodstock believing that their mere presence in the town would be enough to quiet the Indians. That first night in camp some of the men found that much more than their mere presence was expected. Undersheriff Schoonmaker picked twenty "of the most resolute men" to proceed at midnight "with a proper person as a guide" to arrest the leader of the Woodstock Indians, Asa Bishop, whose assumed Indian name was Blackhawk. After many delays the detachment left their shivering fellow possemen at two in the morning and advanced in Indian file with Schoonmaker in command.

"The night was very severe in the mountains, the hair and clothing of the men were covered with frost, and the ground to the depth of ten inches with snow, and being soft under, made walking almost impossible to men armed as they were. Still they pursued on with determination." So the *Argus* informed its readers on March 17. The men took a roundabout route in the hope of remaining undiscovered, "wading through swamps and morasses." As day dawned they reached Blackhawk's house and knocked confidently on the door.

Mrs. Bishop cheerfully told Schoonmaker that the Downrenters had been expecting the sheriff for some time but that they weren't at home at the moment. The possemen then followed footprints leading in the new snow to the barn and from there to a swamp, where they found a box containing Indian disguises and masks. They recognized one as having been worn by Blackhawk when he had been one of the gang which had stopped Schoonmaker near Cooper's tavern on March 8.

Encouraged by their find, the posse moved forward. Before long five of its members became separated from the rest. While in this predicament they were fired upon by men concealed behind a stone wall on the top of a hill. At this point Sheriff Schryver came up leading the entire Saugerties contingent of fifty men. He ordered the men not to try to storm the hill and deal with their attackers. But some of the men disobeyed, "enraged at being fired upon . . . they raced up the hill and found only marks in the snow" which showed where the snipers had lain.

Through much of the rest of the day the posse with steadily diminishing confidence continued the search for Blackhawk and his men. At one point they saw the men they were after high above them on a mountainside out of gunshot and beyond any chance of capture. "From the nature of this country," the *Argus* declared, "those accustomed to it can defy pursuit and can only be arrested by strategem." Lowlanders accustomed to the valleys of Ulster, the members of the posse now realized that the men of Woodstock formed a more agile breed than they, with an astonishing ability at getting about in rough country.

Despite their difficulties the possemen had some success. Divided into groups determined by the towns from which they came, they overran the Downrent parts of Woodstock, served many of Cochran and Rathbun's papers upon tenants, and arrested a total of nine men. One of these made quite a splash in the newspapers of the time. Nineteen-year-old Elisha Staples of Lake Hill was seized on March 16, as the *Democratic Journal* put it, while "in bed, in a sitting posture, with a loaded rifle and a pair of loaded pistols beside him . . . he made no resistance." Staples was "believed to be one of those who fired upon the posse during Wednesday" and was "implicated in the outrage upon Lasher." Among those arrested was one of the Eighmeys of Willow and "William Cooper, a tavern keeper at Lake Hill, implicated with the Anti-Rent disturbances and resistance to the authorities."

Cooper was often described as an Anti-Rent ringleader. It is certain that his tavern was a center of Anti-Rent fraternizing and discussion. Though the tavern still stands at the brow of the Lake Hill on Route 212, the tollgate which once stood beside it and its noble barns have been gone for many years.[12]

The nine men were a considerable catch for the posse. But nothing could disguise the fact that their principal quarry had eluded them. The possemen learned that Blackhawk had spent a night at Jesse Lockwood's place near the mouth of the Beaverkill and another at Whispel's tavern on Route 28 in Shandaken. On the morning of March 13 Blackhawk "and his comrades . . . went over into Delaware County to raise their allies in that region." That same day,

Sheriff Schryver left for Kingston, taking with him half the Kingston and Hurley men.

That very night Downrenters staged a spectacular demonstration which still echoes in Woodstock folklore. It is sometimes said to have been made to frighten away Livingston surveyor Henry Ramsay. Its larger motivation, however, was the desire to impress Ulster authorities with the power of the Anti-Rent movement.

The demonstration began with the arrival of sixty Delaware County Indians summoned by Blackhawk. The Indians, on horseback and wearing masks and calico gowns, moved swiftly in single file, carrying torches of pine wood. The sixty were the advance guard of a body which reached the number of three hundred. The horsemen every now and then performed what was known as a "snake around," in which they went through intricate maneuvers designed to imitate the writhing of an immense snake.

"The hills resounded with their whoops, . . . hard cider offered by farmers in great quantities" was given the snake arounders at Willow, Lake Hill and Bearsville. The horsemen paused to tar and feather a roadside stone which marked the boundary of Henry P. Shultis's Bearsville farm as a warning of what might happen to Tories. For many years the "Tory stone" was given an annual coat of tar and feathers as an expression of lasting Anti-Rent feeling.[13]

The demonstration marked the summit of open Anti-Rent enthusiasm in Woodstock. The chilling implications of the laws of January 25, which state and county officials seemed to be intent on enforcing, with its possibilities of imprisonment and death, was ever more deeply felt. Some Anti-Rent enthusiasts quieted down. Others, many deeply implicated in violent activities, took off for refuges in other states. Some hiding in the woods or in rock shelters among the mountains were fed and protected by friends and relatives while women and children stayed home and did the necessary farm work.[14]

Early in March military measures directed against Woodstock Anti-Renters were being organized in Kingston. Woodstock Uprenters were timing their activities to coincide with those of the militia. On March 14 Uprenters and a few chastened Anti-Renters met at the house of Elias Van Gaasbeeck in Little Shandaken. One sponsor of the meeting was Barent Eighmey, who leased a Livingston sawmill. Another was prosperous William H. De Forest, owner of the tannery on the Tannery Brook and the nearby general store. Still another was the new minister of the Reformed Dutch church, William

T. Van Doren, recently returned from a year of missionary effort in Java.[15]

Others who supported the meeting were "respectable citizens" of Woodstock, few of them of the class to which the Downrenters belonged. John Reynolds, who had offered the worthless money in payment of rent, however, was among Downrenters who signed the call for the meeting. Resolutions were passed condemning "all acts of violence committed by certain individuals disguised as Indians . . ."

Such meetings were usual in towns in which Anti-Rent outbursts had occurred. It was chilling to hear the news that on March 15 and 16 eight Woodstock men who had up to that point eluded the sheriff and his men were arrested and lodged in the Kingston jail to await trial.

On March 21 Judge Charles Ruggles of the Circuit Court gave his charge to the grand jury. The judge admitted that the Livingston tenantry had some grounds for complaint but advised them to have patience because time would work on their side and that possibly, not in their own lifetimes but at some time in the future, their grievances would be corrected. "It is indisputably necessary that these disturbances should be speedily checked and terminated . . . ," Judge Ruggles told the jury. "They are bringing poverty, misery and disgrace on those who are engaged in them."[16]

Eugene Livingston had again gone to Kingston to exert what influence he could. He soon found it wise to leave. John Cochran explained why in a letter urging Montgomery to keep away from Kingston. "Your presence here, now, would be inexpedient, as the tenants would ply you with petitions for mercy which it might be difficult for you to resist and imprudent to grant—Eugene left on that account." It was clear the tenants were demoralized. Many were willing to submit to their landlords on any terms that would allow them to go on living on their farms as before.[17]

A strong factor in their demoralization was the distribution among them by Cochran of a hundred and fifty copies of Judge Ruggles' charge to the jury, a document which left a tenant not a shred of hope for the betterment of his way of life. Tenants not only begged and petitioned, they scraped together what money they could and made payments on their rents. By March 21, while the grand jury was still sitting, John Cochran collected $300. On April 2 Henry P. Shultis informed Montgomery that tenants who a few weeks before had been refusing to pay rent now pressed money upon Cochran and himself. "I am receiving some money daily in small sums," Shultis reported on

April 2. "The *Indians* have disappeared there is not one at present that will own they have ever had anything to do with it . . ." (that is, with the Downrent agitation).[18]

On March 22 the grand jury, of which Henry P. Shultis was a member, handed up seventeen indictments against Downrenters and a few days later nine more. Most of those indicted were either in successful hiding or had fled the jurisdiction of the court. All but two of those in custody were released on bail. Trial was set for the term of the court the following October. In August public attention had faded almost altogether from Woodstock when Sheriff Osmun Steele was shot and killed as he tried to enforce collection of the rent by selling the cattle on a farm owned by Moses Earle on the Dingle Hill Road in the town of Andes in Delaware County. Delaware Anti-Renters were rounded up and tried. Some were sentenced to death under the law of Janary 25, 1845. In September Blackhawk, wearied of the life of a wandering exile, returned home and was promptly arrested. His trial and that of the other Woodstock Downrenters arrested earlier was held over until the spring session of the court.

But before the spring of 1846 arrived things happened thick and fast to favor Anti-Renters. Revision of the new state constitution outlawed leases of agricultural lands for more than twelve years and did away with important details of the old system of land tenure. That fall John Young, running for governor on the Whig ticket but pledged to carrying out reforms, was elected with strong Anti-Rent support. In January the new governor pardoned all Anti-Renters under sentence or indictment. That included Blackhawk and the other Woodstock Downrenters who had never come to trial.[19]

By early May Ramsay and Davis were surveying again, this time without interruption from tenants; Cochran and Rathbun were supervising the appraisal process. The fact that much of the land to be appraised and then evenly divided between the brothers was under lease for lives produced many complications. In order to determine the value of a leased farm the number of years the persons mentioned in the lease could be expected to live had to be determined. This was done by the use of the Northampton Mortality Tables devised in England about 1780 and already none too reliable. Eventually elaborate schedules listing each Woodstock farm in detail were drawn up. On this basis plus visual examination by the surveyors and discussion with occupants a value in cash was given to each one.

While all this was going on tenants were besieging the

Livingston brothers and their agents with applications to buy their farms. A kind of land rush was in progress. Between 1846 and the mid-1850s Shorts, Shultises, Hasbroucks, DeWalls, Riseleys, Rickses, Happys, Lashers, Winnes, Duboises, Hogans, Eltings, Van de Bogarts, Lewises and other former tenants bought farms. Yet by no means all the Livingston farms were sold. Many tenants could not afford to buy. In 1861 and 1862 agent Henry P. Shultis collected rents from more than twenty Woodstock farmers. The rent money paid those two years amounted to $1174.49. As late as the mid-1880s Eugene Livingston still owned land in Woodstock.[20]

The story of one farm gives a good outline of how the process of transference from lease to ownership in fee simple worked. The farm of Isaac Elting was located to the west and south of the intersection of the Cold Brook Road and the Wittenberg Road. In 1795 Madame Livingston leased a farm of about 107 acres to James Laribe, his twenty-year-old son Asa, and his eighteen-year-old granddaughter, Betsy Brown. Laribe before long sold his lease to Michael Smith. Smith swapped his leasehold to Isaac Elting for a piece of land on what had been Tiebout property close to the hamlet of Woodstock—this at a time when the building of the Ulster and Delaware Turnpike was giving a boost to land speculation along the Wittenberg part of its route. The one-sixth payment due the Livingston landlord upon each of these conveyances was not paid, but Isaac Elting lived on the land and kept a once well-known tavern there while paying rent on the same basis as proper tenants.

By 1830 something happened—possibly Asa Laribe and Betsy Brown died and so terminated the lease for three lives of 1795. Isaac Elting then signed a lease for an adjoining seventy-acre farm. In June 1845 the appraisers called and put a "net value" of $605.39 on his place after deducting the interest which Elting had in the farm by reason of his 1830 lease. Isaac was then seventy-three, his wife Catherine (a granddaughter of old Peter Short) was about the same age. Isaac, Jr. was forty-four. The Eltings could not pay the back rent which they, like many other Woodstock tenants, had withheld during the Downrent times. The Livingstons usually required all back rents to be paid up before they would sell.

At this point Christian Happy wrote to Eugene Livingston and proposed buying the Elting farm. By then old Isaac had died and, as Happy put it, the farm "has his [Isaac, Jr.'s] life and his mothers life on it, I do not want to superced elting . . . pleas send me the lowest price you will take for the elting farm, Soil, so that I shall know how I can deal with elting, I dont want to take any advantage of elting but he tells me there is back rent on his farm and he cannot pay it without selling, and I will not buy without I buy the Soil . . ."

By "buying the soil," Happy meant buying the farm in fee simple and not merely entering into a lease contract. His expression of unwillingness to supersede Elting was surely genuine. Anyone who tried to buy a farm from under the occupant would have been ostracized in the closely-knit community of Woodstock. Eugene Livingston was willing to sell, he noted on Happy's letter, but only if Happy could satisfy him that Elting was indeed "willing he should buy." His price of $9 per acre was very close to that set by the appraisers "provided no lives have died" since the appraisal was made; Old Isaac had died and this would have raised the price a bit because his death diminished the value of the Elting leasehold.

For some unrecorded reason the sale to Happy did not take place and the Eltings remained on the farm as tenants until 1872; that year Elwin L. Elting, believed to have been a son of Isaac, Jr., bought the farm for $1550. The deed was drawn up on behalf of Eugene by his cousin, New York lawyer Lewis Livingston Delafield, noted in his day for both his knowledge of the law of real estate and his devotion to protecting children against maltreatment. Livingston and his wife signed the deed in the office of the American consul in Geneva, Switzerland, where they were pausing in their almost endless travels.

In this deed Delafield included the statement that the farm was sold subject to the lease of May 1830. The sale put an end to the lease (which would otherwise have continued in force because it was executed before the new state constitution of 1846) until the last of the three persons mentioned in the 1830 lease was dead. And so one old Woodstock family after many difficulties at last came into ownership of the land it had long tilled.[21]

While the Livingston brothers were eager to sell their lands in Great Lot 8, John Hunter, owner of Great Lot 25, sold grudgingly and in an embittered spirit. He demanded every cent of back rent in every case (the Livingstons sometimes were willing to compromise on back rents). Hunter sold each farm for an amount which when invested at five per cent would produce the former rent. He instructed his agents never to deviate from this rule.

In the summer of 1845 many large landlords of New York State had been fearful that the Anti-Rent War might cause them to lose their land entirely. They advertised that they were willing to sell on terms similar to those of Hunter. At once Mink Hollow tenants of

Hunter applied to buy. Isaac Mosher, who had been a tenant on the tract ever since 1794, was among the first. Hunter, living in splendor in a mansion on Hunter's Island off New Rochelle, was old, irritable and struggling with physical ailments. Perhaps that was why he did not quickly convey farms to his Mink Hollow applicants. When he died in September 1852, his will provided that any agreements he had made to sell to his tenants should be carried out. In March 1854 Isaac Mosher became the owner of his 154-acre farm on paying $1200 to Hunter's son and executor, Elias Desbrosses Hunter.[22]

With the peak of the land rush over by 1855, most Woodstock farmers owned their own land. This year marked the end of an era in Woodstock. It was that year that William M. Cooper took office as supervisor. He was the same Lake Hill innkeeper who had been so important in the Downrent movement and who had been thrown in the county jail ten years earlier. Before 1855 most Woodstock supervisors had either been close to the Livingstons or to the glassmaking industrialists. Now for the first time as far as is known the voters chose a man who made his appeal to the people rather than to the wealth of the town. Cooper was later reelected (he ran as a Democrat). After him his son, William F. Cooper, who shared his political views, was supervisor for several terms.

Ever since its beginnings Woodstock and its sister settlement of Shandaken had stood aside from lowland Ulster County. Lowlanders regarded Woodstock people living on their leased farms among the Catskills with a feeling not far from contempt. The depth of this feeling had been most sharply revealed when Hurley rejected Woodstock in 1781. Now the way lay open for a better relationship with the rest of Ulster County. The old system of land tenure which had shaped Woodstock life for so long was now removed forever.

The Livingston brothers did not find the sale of their Woodstock lands to be as beneficial as they had hoped. The bill of Cochran and Rathbun for their services in supervising the appraising, surveying and dividing of the lands and their work during the Anti-Rent War amounted to about five thousand dollars. There were additional payments to surveyors and others involved. All this plus the debts of old Robert L. cut deeply into the brothers' inheritance.[23]

Montgomery, with his poor wife, felt the pinch most acutely. He lived on in the Chancellor's mansion at Clermont, finding it hard to economize, especially in such matters as madeira, brandy, oysters and other pleasures of life. His wife annoyed him by constantly urging him to pray. His health soon caused Dr. Knickerbocker to visit him often.

He ceased to work in his painting room. After a trip to Cuba in an attempt to recover his health, he died in 1855 at the age of thirty-nine. He left no children.

Montgomery Livingston did not live long enough to develop the talent he had for painting. He was not a great success as a Livingston. He had few friends, he had many quarrels, he lacked the typical Livingston self-confidence. Yet with his long hair and beard and Bohemian tastes he became long after his death a success as a forerunner of the painters who would one day gather in Woodstock.

With the death of Eugene Livingston in Nice, France in 1893 the last of the old absentee landlords of Woodstock vanished. By that time Woodstock was within nine years of the founding of its art colony at Byrdcliffe—a development of which both Montgomery and Eugene Livingston would surely have approved.

Henry P. Shultis died in his ninety-second year in November 1883. He left five children, twenty-two grandchildren, forty great-grandchildren and one great-great-grandchild. "Father Shultis," as he was known to his neighbors, had retained a clear intellect and a well-preserved body until close to the end. His shrewdness in juggling both sides in the Anti-Rent War and his long life enabled him to become a prosperous and respected patriarch.[24]

Looking back at the days of the Anti-Rent War, Abram W. Hoffman concluded in 1897 that it had resulted in benefits to both sides. The success of the Anti-Renters, he wrote, "changed the whole future of that portion of the state in which they operated. From dragging along half a century behind the age, devoid of ambition and progress . . ." the people of the region emerged into "the front of independence and progress." Hoffman may have overstated the case. Yet it was true that when the Anti-Rent War ended and the old system of land tenure began to be abolished Woodstock and other towns once dominated by absentee landlords showed the effects of their new freedom in many ways—in building better houses and barns, in taking better care of their fields and woodlots, in improving the breed of their livestock, and in gaining the respect of lowland Ulster people who had for so long had viewed them with scorn.[25]

Yet changes came unevenly. Belief in witchcraft, for example, lingered in more isolated parts of the town through the second half of the nineteenth century. Old customs gave way to new ones gradually. And the city people who came to Woodstock by summer and boarded in farmhouses and hotels found the old-fashioned ways added to the appeal of the town's fine scenery and sparkling trout brooks.

WITCHES
AND LEGENDS

In the first blush of pride of
ownership most former Woodstock tenants of the Livingston brothers
were by 1855 making plans for improvements. The population of the
town that year, according to the New York State census, was 1806
persons. The average family consisted of a bit more than five persons.
Thirty-one inhabitants were black, 74 were first-generation
immigrants, and 218 owned land. Only 50 people over the age of 21
could not read or write. Another 16 could read but could not write.

These 1806 people came from a great variety of backgrounds. As
in 1790 some were of German or Dutch extraction, descended from
early settlers in the Hudson Valley. Others had grandparents who had
come to Woodstock from New England. Of the foreign-born most
were Irish. Because of the shrinking in size of Woodstock after 1789 it
isn't easy to be exact about the changes in the number of the
townspeople. Population rose or fell in response to many factors: the
fortunes of the glassmakers, the opening of highways to the outside
world, changes in means of transportation, and other reasons.[1]

Epidemics, common during the nineteenth century, sometimes
reduced the population suddenly. In 1849 and 1850, for example, what
was diagnosed as "a sort of typhus fever, often aggravated or preceded
by a diaorrea" is said to have carried sixty Woodstock people to their
graves. John Reynolds, apparently the same man who had offered the
Livingston agent bad money in payment of his rent, lost several

children. He felt their deaths deeply and became irrational and obsessed by a notion that although he was "in comfortable even opulent circumstances" he was on the verge of "beggary." Reynolds hanged himself in July 1851. The yellow fever and cholera epidemics which ravaged Hudson Valley towns sometimes left Woodstock untouched and brought significant numbers of refugees, some of whom remained in the town.[2]

At times Woodstock was briefly without a resident doctor and at other times it had several. During the 1820s Dr. Ebenezer Hall, superintendent of the Bristol Glass Factory, practiced medicine, and so too did Dr. Larry Gilbert Hall, who lived in the house later torn down to make room for the present Woodstock Library. The old addition to this house, which is still standing, was built in 1812 as an office by Dr. Hall. Its walls are ornamented with pilasters supporting a frieze pierced with stars representing, it is said, the eighteen states then in the union. Though Dr. Hall, confident that the nation would grow, saved room for another six or eight stars, these never appeared on the frieze and the blank space left for them remains blank.[3]

Dr. Ebenezer Hall had no formal training in medicine but learned what he knew as an assistant to a Connecticut physician. Dr. Larry Gilbert Hall had good academic training and a good medical library. He subscribed to medical journals and was the owner of Woodstock's first recorded bathtub, described in the inventory of his estate (he died in 1836) as a "bathing trough." [4]

The next resident doctor in Woodstock was Dr. John Fiero, son-in-law of Ebenezer Hall and descended from a Palatine family of Saugerties. Fiero died in 1841 at the age of thirty-six. He was followed by Dr. Stephen L. Heath, whose house is still standing a hundred feet or so to the east of the brick post office on Tinker Street. Dr. Heath was active in politics, as had been Ebenezer Hall, and was also commissioner of schools. It used to be said by old people that the doctor would ride horseback to the end of Mink Hollow, spend half a day delivering a baby and return home, all for a fee of five dollars. Dr. Heath was at the height of his practice in 1855.[5]

There was no hospital available to Woodstock people at this time, but there were always women with skill in nursing and midwifery to care for the ill in their own homes. There were no drug stores. Each general store kept a small stock of those remedies most in demand. In Dr. Ebenezer Hall's almost twenty years of managing the glass factory in Bristol the enterprise supplied not only a substantial number of drugs but also gave first aid. The storekeeper sometimes pulled teeth, bled a sufferer or lanced a boil.

The glass company owned a copy of the *The New American Dispensatory*, by Dr. James Thacher, Boston, 1817, and probably used this book in making up prescriptions. Among the many drugs and other medicines sold at the glass company store were opodeldoc, a soap-based liniment used to soothe aching backs and sprains, Lee's pills (popular for liver ailments), camphor, spirits of hartshorn, castor oil, quassia, epsom salts, burgundy pitch, balsam copaiba, gum guaicum, syrup of squills, snake root, "volatile liniment." A steady seller was opium in its various forms of laudanum, paregoric (the old soothing syrup for babies) and pure opium.

The quantity of these soothers and painkillers used by some individuals suggest that the town may have had its addicts. Opium was an ingredient in compounds. A surviving note from Dr. Ebenezer Hall to Daniel Elliot, the glass house superintendent, reads, "Dr. Elliot pleas to prepare the following Mixture, for the Complaint called Rum- itis . . . R/Camph,/i/s oz. Rub with ½ oz. spts. terbinth, when dissolved add 2 oz. sweet oil, I oz. Laud, volatile spts. 2 oz., Water, mix all together and bottle."

A number of "doctor books" which have turned up in Woodstock attics show that some people of long ago tried to take care of their ailments themselves by use of book learning. Among these books was an American edition of 1821 of the *Domestic Medicine* of Dr. Buchan of Edinburgh, a book with excellent advice on hygiene as well as many less admirable suggestions for the treatment of disease. An occasional inventory of an estate listed a medical book. When Esquire Daniel Sherwood died he left behind a copy of *Hamelton's Midwifery*.[6]

No "Indian doctor" books are known to have been in use in Woodstock. Yet books like these may well have given guidance to Woodstock healers; they reflected the interest of the time in the virtues of plants, especially those known to have been used by the Indians. Some also recommended such materials as "dog fat," which was produced by roasting a plump puppy on a spit and catching the drip. "Botanical physicians" like New Hampshire's Samuel Thompson were giving rise to many followers. This movement stimulated a revival in Indian doctoring; one Indian doctor, William H. Lake, was practicing in Higginstown on the edge of Kingston as late as the 1870s and had Woodstock patients. And as we shall see there was Woodstock's Indian doctor on Tinker Street.[7]

Until a generation ago Woodstock women gathered plants and converted them into remedies for many ailments. Some became well known in the town for one or two herbal remedies. Aunt Phoebe of Mink Hollow, probably Phoebe Perry Mosher (1795-1882), made a much-valued poultice. Another woman used sheep sorrel in a "cure" for cancer. Among the plants used in "cures" by local women which Anita M. Smith listed in her delightful *True as the Barnacle Tree* (Maverick Press, 1939) are scouring rush (also known as horsetails) for kidney troubles, puff balls for stopping bleeding from wounds, yarrow and mullein leaves for the blood, boneset for stomach disorders, trailing arbutus for kidney ailments, and catnip tea for soothing babies.

When Neva Shultis, long a devoted nurse in Woodstock, wrote her *From Sunset to Cock's Crow* in 1957 she added to Anita Smith's list princess pine for kidney problems, wintergreen for rheumatism, silver leaf (also called touch-me-not and jewelweed) for poison ivy, plaintain leaves for corns and bunions, the leaves of mountain laurel for itch, and mountain ash berries as ingredients of a cough mixture.[8]

Back in the 1830s Dr. Larry G. Hall jotted down in his day book some local herbal remedies which he used or intended to try. They included "take equal parts of bloodroot and sweet flag—dry and pulverize—used as snuff 5 or 6 times a day—is said to relieve deafness." For "dissolving gravel in the bladder" the doctor used "the bark of red thorn berry [probably a blackberry] and high blackberry made into a tea with plenty of flaxseed tea to prevent acrimony in the urine. Tried it on Matthew—it works."

The women of communities like Woodstock were usually responsible for learning and handing on traditional herbal remedies. Yet in some parts of the country men bought a copy of an Indian-doctor book and on the strength of this investment in medical education set up in practice. Woodstock, however, had the real thing in its Indian doctor. And this doctor (his name isn't known) handed on his art to a remarkable white woman named Betsy Booth MacDaniel.

In 1960 Betsy Booth's grandson, Martin MacDaniel, told me that his grandmother's skill as a healer had been learned from the local Indian doctor who taught her to recognize a great variety of plants and to prepare their leaves, bark, roots and other parts in treating human ailments. He remembered that the attic of the MacDaniel house in his boyhood was still filled with dried plants hanging from the rafters. He remembered being told that the Indian doctor had given Betsy Booth one of his most treasured secrets, a "cure for consumption" by herbal means. The Indian gave the secret to his pupil only after she promised never to reveal it lest it lose its efficacy. And so, Martin told me, "the secret died with her."

As Betsy Booth began her practice as an herb doctor, nurse and midwife a bit before 1850 she was breaking out of the narrow role in society usually assigned to women in her time and earning a place as a Woodstock heroine. She was said to have been tireless in her devotion to those she helped. Once, Martin MacDaniel remembered, Betsy was in Platte Clove some seven miles away when she learned that George Dibble, who lived at the head of the Clove, was in bed with pneumonia. She dashed home, ran up a batch of a herbal remedy and carried it back to the Dibble house. She sat up all night caring for Dibble and at dawn walked home to take up the duties of a wife and mother again.

She was sometimes seen wearing pants as she helped out in the fields. She often walked to Kingston and returned carrying a heavy load of purchases. She was a woman of strong good sense.

Late in her life she came into the parlor of the MacDaniel farmhouse and saw some of the summer boarders for whom she was cooking and cleaning seated round a table engaged in the popular sport of "spirit rapping," in which a spirit was thought to answer questions by raps of the table legs on the floor.

"Is your spirit a good one or a bad one?" Betsy Booth asked. Before any one could reply a ball of fire came down the stairs (there was no thunderstorm in progress at the time) and smashed the table to pieces. "I thought as much," said Betsy Booth.

Indian doctoring often involved "powing-wowing," the use of incantations claimed to be the very ones spoken by ancient Indian medicine men. Even though there is no evidence that Betsy Booth ever pow-wowed, others may have done so. Bits of local tradition hint at belief in the practice. As late as the 1930s a man belonging to an old Woodstock family who was working in Lewis Hollow had an ugly growth on his face. When his employer asked what he was doing for it the man said, "I'm having this fellow come in and talk it away." He would give no further explanation. A few weeks later the growth was almost gone.[9]

Allied to pow-wowing was a belief that since illnesses were often caused by spells woven by witches they might be cured by benevolent or white witches, often called witch doctors. Ever since the first white settlement of the Hudson Valley, as in Indian days witchcraft and other supernatural manifestations had been a significant part of daily life.

Strongest of the opponents of the folk belief in witchcraft and magic were the valley clergy. One clergyman, Frederick H. Quitman, founder of Woodstock's Lutheran church and pastor of two churches in Rhinebeck and another in West Camp, was sufficiently stirred up against the belief of the members of his congregations in supernatural doings to write a book called *A Treatise on Magic, or, on the Intercourse between Spirits and Men, with Annotations.* The book was published in Albany, N.Y. in 1810. In a preface the author explains the incidents which caused him to write his thoughts on the history of belief in magic and to give arguments against its existence.

"In the month of October of the year 1808," Quitman wrote, "the house of a respectable farmer, of that district of the town of Rhinebeck, which is called Wertemberg, was believed to be haunted by evil spirits. Stones were continually thrown in every direction, and part of the winter store was either destroyed or carried away . . . the mischief was ascribed by the inhabitants, to some supernatural cause . . . ." Rather than making a "careful examination," people "took the shortest and easiest way and attributed it to witchcraft. In this persuasion, they sent to a famous conjurer from the west side of the [Hudson] river; but the demons, equally superstitious, and fearing the magical staff of the conjurer, departed before his arrival."

The conjurer with the magical staff was Dr. Jacob Brink, the white witch who had served as a minor official of Woodstock not long before. Soon the stones began to fly again, and, Quitman wrote, "I went there, accompanied by a well informed elder of my church in Rhinebeck. But the rumours of my expected arrival having been spread abroad, the house was so much crowded with people, that I could not proceed in the investigation of the matter, in the manner I had wished. However I addressed the incarnate demons and declared to them my suspicions of their wickedness, which at least put a stop to their proceedings, whilst I was there. I am sorry that the delicacy of my situation, would not permit me to bring the offenders to confession, and to deliver them up to well deserved punishment . . . ."

Quitman is saying here that he had discovered the people who were throwing the stones, but because of his position as minister did not feel that he could expose them. Soon, in other parts of Rhinebeck, similar instances of the activities of what are known today as poltergeists came to Quitman's attention. He expressed the fear that "during this dull winter, all the corners of Rhinebeck, for want of other employment, will be infested with demons."

Mr. Quitman had written his book on magic, he stated, "chiefly for the better information of my congregations and as a memento of the instructions, which I have often imparted to them." Yet there is no evidence that Quitman's Woodstock congregation, at any rate, paid attention to his spoken or written denunciations of a belief in witchcraft.[10]

By the 1820s another clerical battler against Woodstock's faith in witchcraft had arrived on the scene. He was eccentric William Boyse, minister of the Dutch Reformed Church and a shrewd observer of local witches and their works. The pamphlets Boyse wrote and sold during his years as a wandering preacher reported many instances of what were taken to be activity by witches in Woodstock. He told of people and cows being bewitched, of witches preventing butter from forming in the churns of their neighbors, of a man being tossed into the town millpond in order to find out whether he was a witch (a witch couldn't sink entirely beneath the surface of the water).

Boyse told of the exploits of the witch doctor Jacob Brink in thwarting the machinations of witches and in performing wondrous feats of healing, especially when uncontrolled bleeding was in question. He met Dr. Brink and interrogated him, but without becoming convinced of his possession of any power against witches. Boyse was a believer in some witches. He wrote "that there have been witches, no one can doubt, who believes the sacred writings." "The best witch," Boyse wrote, "was the Biblical witch of Endor." Yet Boyse did not believe in the witches of Woodstock.[11]

During the first half of the nineteenth century the people of lowland Ulster County abandoned a good many features of the Dutch culture of their parents and grandparents. Among other things, they came to believe less and less in the existence of witches and their power to harm. In Woodstock back country, however, changes came more slowly. Witches formed a threat to peaceful existence until close to the beginning of the twentieth century. Because lowland Ulsterites had long viewed the people of Woodstock and other settlements in the Hardenbergh Patent with amusement as Old World vestiges or relics of a simpler past, Woodstock people were reluctant to talk to strangers about their persistent belief in witches. If they admitted belief they would lie open to ridicule.

Every now and then during the second half of the nineteenth century Kingston newspapers printed stories of the prevalence of a continuing faith in witchcraft "in certain parts of Woodstock"—the Yerry Hill Road-Montoma section, Mink Hollow, upper Sawkill Valley and the black neighborhood adjoining the hamlet of Woodstock.

"The town of Woodstock in certain places has been noted for witches," stated a writer in the Kingston *Weekly Freeman* of April 30, 1880. The writer told of a black witch known as Aunt Zantee (her name is probably a corruption of the Dutch for Susan which is Zanneke). Zantee was believed to have "great powers as a sorceress." A member of a white family in her neighborhood once made a slighting remark about Zantee and Zantee was heard to say that she would punish them. A woman of that family was soon churning, but found that no matter how long or how vigorously she moved the handle of the churn up and down butter refused to come. A friend dropping in said she knew the reason, "Old Zantee has been in the churn."

Old Aunt Zantee was then seen to "be in the highest glee, singing, 'Lord alive! No had churning dar—and if they don't ax my pardon the debbil will be in that house in a little while.' " Sure enough, when the cows were driven home and the milkers went out with their pails not a drop of milk would come. A flock of sheep belonging to the white family became bewitched and ran back and forth at a headlong gait, finally dashing over the fence and running at full speed toward the Overlook. The farmer and his wife went over to Aunt Zantee's and not only begged her pardon but paid her well besides. "At once the cows and sheep returned to normal and butter quickly formed in the churn." After that the white farmer and his wife treated Aunt Zantee with the greatest respect. The old black witch's reputation expanded far beyond the bounds of Woodstock.[12]

Woodstock people were not pleased at reading about Aunt Zantee in the newspaper to which some of them subscribed. Neither were they happy when as late as 1917 an event took place which led to a lively outpouring of tales of witchcraft in Woodstock and adjoining parts of Hurley. Several people then admitted having known witches and having been the victim of their spells.

One day in the summer of 1915 several men were busy tearing

down a small, timeworn farmhouse on the Hurley Patentee Woods just across the Woodstock border. The building had belonged to a member of the Van Etten family formerly of Vandale. Van Etten, becoming prosperous as a manager and owner of bluestone quarries, built a fine two-story house close to his old one, intending to tear the old one down before long. Tearing the old building down did not seem urgent and Van Etten kept putting it off from year to year. Finally another owner came on the scene and attacked the shabby structure with all the vigor of a new proprietor.

By that time the neighborhood of the old house had changed from farming and quarrying country to an art colony whose people knew nothing of local traditions and ways of life. The men engaged in tearing down the building paused in wonder as they began tackling the chimney. Enormous and well-built, it resisted their efforts with what seemed like determination. Finally the chimney began to yield. As its upper half lay on the earth it revealed a fresh cause for surprise. Built into the chimney just above the throat were two ancient scythe blades forming a cross in the chimney opening and firmly fixed into its sides, their sharp edges uppermost.

A novelist member of the colony named Allan Updegraff reported what happened for an art colony publication called *The Plowshare.* "A by-passer suggested that they (the scythe blades) were probably intended to brace the chimney; but they weren't arranged to do any effective bracing . . . ." Then "an old inhabitant" came along and explained that it was a witch-trap. "He pointed out the up-turned edges of the old scythes, and opined that any witch dropping down on them either would have stuck fast or retreated as soon as possible. Since there is no record of any witch actually caught, the probability is that all those who entered went away at once." The oldtimer did not mention the belief that a cross such as that formed by scythe blades was a first-rate witch repellent because it suggested the power of Christ. "There used to be a good many witches around, remarked the ancient inhabitant; in fact as late as twenty-five years ago one lived over Glenford way, near the top of Ohio Mountain."

These words triggered a witchlore hunt. Very soon a formidable body of local witchlore was being assembled, leaving no doubt that belief in witches had once been widespread and still existed in a milder form.

The local people who had once been reluctant to speak of witches to outsiders were morth forthcoming after the people of the art colony proved delighted listeners to tales of witchcraft and regarded the tellers with admiring if condescending interest. To have the spot they had chosen for their colony turn out to be a center of so romantic an activity as witchcraft was pleasant indeed. Local oldtimers reacted by letting loose a flood of witchlore.

Updegraff found memories in his own neighborhood to center around a woman on the top of Ohayo Mountian named Mrs. Grimm (he disguised her name in his published references by calling her Mrs. Dour). None of Mrs. Grimm's exploits as reported by Updegraff resulted in more than minor harm to anyone, yet they gave unmistakable indications that she was indeed a witch. She bewitched the pigs of a nearby farmer and they burst out of their pen, "rushed about with unporcine vigor and tried to root the barn down," Updegraff wrote. The farmer cut a switch of witch hazel, "famed for its efficiency against witches." The pigs, seeing the switch, became "as lambs for meekness" and returned to their pens. As this happened, the farmer looked up. There on the hilltop stood Mrs. Grimm.

As the nineteenth century neared its end, Mrs. Grimm and a "white partridge" (a ruffed grouse) became linked in a mysterious incident. The partridge appeared on Ohayo Mountain and was often shot at by hunters but never touched. One young man became determined to shoot the bird, but a series of unexplained accidents and obstacles appeared. His gun went off unexpectedly, he fell into old quarry holes, he tumbled into pools of water "where he did not remember having ever seen water before."

Suspecting the nature of the white partridge, an oldtimer advised the young man to try substituting a piece of silver for his leaden bullet. He did. He knew his bullet had struck its mark because on the spot where the white bird had stood he found two white feathers and a single drop of blood. The next day he learned that Mrs. Grimm had taken to bed. Obviously she had assumed the form of the white partridge. No witch even in the form of a white partridge is proof against a silver bullet, or at least so many Woodstock people believed.

Mrs. Grimm's neighborhood on Ohayo Mountain at the end of the century was a place of many mysterious happenings all related somehow to her occupation as a witch. Sometimes people travelling the mountain road at midnight saw an indescribable white shape blocking the road ahead of them. One witness struggling for a comparison said the shape resembled a "white-washed stone." People tempted to try shooting at the object were held back by the thought that their bullet might ricochet. When a man named Gray did shoot, the thing vanished.

A good witness to the existence of Mrs. Grimm was Philip Bonesteel, member of an old Woodstock family. Bonesteel told Updegraff that he'd known Mrs. Grimm well, "and trouble enough she's caused me." Bonesteel wanted to take a girl to a party on the same night that Mrs. Grimm was giving a party. "If you don't come to my party you'll wish you had before you get home," said the witch. And that night as Bonesteel and his girl walked through the dark toward the house of their party-giver they heard an ominous chuckle behind them.

Turning around, they saw an immense yellow-eyed black cat sitting on the road. When Bonesteel ordered the cat to go away it remained there with a sort of smile on its face. Bonesteel kicked the cat and his foot went right through it. He threw rocks at it but the rocks went through the cat. The cat sat there grinning. All through the party the cat waited outside. When the fun was over it followed Bonesteel and his girl as they walked home.

Bonesteel knew by this time that the cat was Mrs. Grimm. As the two passed an old deserted house the cat left the road and jumped inside through a broken window. At that moment it gave a shrill and screamy laugh, Mrs. Grimm's laugh. The next day Bonesteel called on Mrs. Grimm. He told her that "there was such things as silver bullets and I wasn't going to stand being made nervous like I had been the night before."

Eventually Bonesteel managed to get even with Mrs. Grimm and, he suspected, put an end to her career as a witch. The old woman had come to his mother's house to borrow some butter but Mrs. Bonesteel had refused to let her have any (it as an old belief that if you lend anything to a witch you put yourself in her power). Mrs. Grimm left laughing, predicting that the Bonesteels would be sorry.

The next day the Bonesteel cow "began to bawl like she was in mortal agony," Philip told Updegraff, but when he came near her the cow behaved as if in the best of health. This was the way cows acted "when a witch gets into them. I'd known of cows being took that way before and I knew what to do. I cut off a little piece of her ear, and burned it in the kitchen stove. If a witch had got into a cow, that'll fix her. . . ." And sure enough it did. A few minutes later Mrs. Grimm's son came running down the hill to say that his mother had burned herself.

The bits of witchlore which were pulled into the open by the power of the witch-trap on the Maverick Road were usually of the mild sort which mark the ending of a period of vigorous belief in witches. One story Updegraff published in 1916 is different. It is a stark little tragedy which strongly suggests the place in Woodstock life held by witchcraft at the height of its importance during the years when Robert L. Livingston was the town's major landlord.

A baby had been taken very ill and the opinion of family and neighbors was that "a witch was into the baby." That being the case, it was agreed that a doctor was needed to expel the witch. When the father started off to fetch witch doctor Streeter from Kingston, "he knew it was a witch because he began to have all sorts of accidents. . . . The witch didn't want them to bring the doctor to drive her out, I guess. . . ." Bonesteel said to Allan Updegraff.

It was midnight before the worried father reached Kingston, and got the doctor out of bed and into his buggy. He told the doctor of the trouble he'd had getting to Kingston and the doctor replied, "We won't have any trouble getting back . . . I'll see to that." And they made a fast, eventless trip to the house where the baby lay.

The doctor assured the parents that he ". . . could cure the baby, if they'd leave him alone with it, and do everything just exactly as he told them to. Two women begged to be allowed to remain in the room. Doctor Streeter finally said they could if they'd not say a word no matter what happened; if they spoke, the doctor said, the baby would surely die. The doctor then removed the baby's shirt. He began cutting the shirt with a knife he'd brought with him. At every cut the baby threw up his arms and groaned. The doctor continued to cut and the baby continued to groan until one of the women could stand the baby's obvious misery no longer. "Oh, doctor," she exclaimed, "I don't see how you can do it!" At this Dr. Streeter threw down his knife and the shirt, "You've killed the baby," he said.

"And he was right," Philip Bonesteel assured Updegraff. "The baby died."[13]

After the breakthrough of 1915 more Woodstock witchlore surfaced. Neva Shultis and Anita M. Smith wrote down incidents in the life of Becky Demilt (sometimes Demill), a Mink Hollow witch. "People even remembered what she looked like," Neva wrote. "She was tall and thin with coal-black hair and eyes, and her skin was white as snow. She had a club foot on which she always wore three stockings, but in spite of this handicap, on moonlight nights she could be seen riding wildly over the mountains on her big black stallion . . . She was mean and vindictive."

Once Becky put a spell on the child of a neighbor who had offended her. The girl ". . . thought she was a horse, she reared and snorted and stamped through the night and in the morning there was the print of a bit in her mouth. Witch doctor Brink was summoned— he covered the girl with a shawl on which he had marked her initials with pins [the witch was supposed to feel scratched unbearably by the pins]."

Then Brink left after warning the parents that soon Becky would arrive and would ask to borrow three things. If they lent her only one, their daughter would never recover. Becky called as predicted and asked for a cup of sugar, which was refused. Then she asked for a needle and thread, which was also refused. Finally she asked for a riding whip which she saw lying on a table. The father gave it to her, but in the form of a smart blow across her face. Becky ran screaming from the house and presumably the girl recovered.

Many other bits of witchlore have come to light in Mink Hollow, Willow, Shady and Lake Hill. They tell of bewitched pigs dancing on their noses, of bewitched churns restored to profitable use when a red-hot horseshoe was dropped into them, of silver bullets demonstrating their effectiveness in wounding witches disguised as deer or other wild creatures, and of a witch known as Aunt Abby being burned when the diaper of a baby upon whom she had cast a spell was put on the hot coals in a fireplace.

Sometimes Woodstock witches combined the usual casting of spells with an ability to look into the future. One of these was described in the Saugerties *Evening Post* of January 20, 1879, ". . . a remarkable witch resided for many years in Woodstock, sixty years since. Independent of her powers in withcraft she had the power of 'vision', or in more explicit language, the power to foresee a death in the family. Many wonderful stories have been told and believed regarding the extraordinary powers of this woman. Dr. Brink finally pushed her from her throne and her charm was broken. . . ." Other soothsayers of old Woodstock were not practicing witches. Among these were several members of the glassmaking and blacksmithing Peets of Shady, known also as men of unusual physical strength.

In spite of so much competition Dr. Brink remained the central figure in Woodstock witchlore. Many tales of witches' work ended up with a victory for the Old Doctor, as he was called to distinguish him from later members of the same family who also practiced as witch doctors. The Old Doctor had lived in the town of Woodstock during the 1790s. Later he moved back to Saugerties, where he had been born. Brink had been the subject of Kingston newspaper articles from time to time especially in the 1870s and '80s.

One such account of the beliefs about Brink recounts the legends about him which had long been told in Woodstock. "Dr. Brink sixty years ago [that is about 1820] was the famous physician in this county who had the power of casting out devils and foiling the arts and wiles of the lawless witches. Brink was the seventh son of a seventh son and whether his gift and power was derived from Heaven or the Devil has never been revealed. None of his cures are recorded in the medical works of the day, but the stories told of the miraculous cures made by his charmed finger would fill a volume. Persons who had been bewitched visited him from far and near. Devils were hurled from their bodies and they [i.e. the patients] went on their way rejoicing— Brink was the only man in the county the witches feared."

After the Old Doctor died, "it is said the witches of Ulster county had a 'witches dance' on the event. . . ." for now their most hated enemy was gone. "To his wonderful power alone can be ascribed the decline of witches and witchcraft among us."[14]

Side by side with a belief in witchcraft went faith in a simple sort of astrology which found its most conspicuous expression in a system of planting and harvesting according to "the signs." Readily available were almanacs which gave the phases of the moon and other relevant information. Often found in Woodstock attics fifty years ago were bundles of worn copies of the *Farmer's Almanac* of Andrew Beers, published annually for many years in Kingston. This almanac also contained a weather forecast for the year and miscellaneous information.

Much lore relating to planting and to weather was handed on orally from generation to generation. A good deal of it was learned indirectly from printed sources. As far back as 1729 Philip Whitaker of the Brabant copied information of an astrological nature from what was probably an English almanac—descendants of Philip lived in Woodstock and one named Peter operated a sawmill on the upper Sawkill. "Sow all seeds after the new moon but round seeds after the opposition; gather fruits the moon Decreasing and before the last quarter, graft in March at the Moon's Increase, fell hard timber from the full to the change . . . geld cattle, the moon in Aries, Sagittarius or Capricorn, kill fatt Swine the better to keep their fatt in boyling about the full moon."

All these and many more bits of information, all consistent with old Woodstock beliefs, were copied by Philip Whitaker. A generation ago old Woodstock people were still guided by the phases of the moon in planting. Potatoes, carrots and other plants producing edible parts below the surface of the ground were planted as the moon waxed. Beans, lettuce and other above-ground crops were best planted as the moon waned. And Woodstock herb gatherers were governed by the signs in gathering leaves, bark, roots and seeds of plants. Each plant had traditional ties to the movements of the planets and the phases of the moon. Today, as astrology has become of interest to many young people in Woodstock, some plant and harvest in accordance with these old beliefs.

Little evidence has been found in Woodstock of medical treatment being given in accordance with astrological wisdom. Yet here as elsewhere it had its practitioners. Philip Whitaker's notes contain a good deal of information about treating ailing people "according to the signs." He wrote that it was "good to let the sanguine blood when the moon is in Pisces, the choleric blood the moon in Cancer, the melancholy blood the moon in Libra, Aquarius or Pisces, the phlegmatic blood when the moon is in Sagittarius or Aquarius. . . ." Choleric, melancholy and the rest refer to the four fluids once believed to make up the human body. Their proportions determined temperament and health. Whitaker set down the good and bad signs for purging, vomiting and sneezing along with a great deal of other advice on health and farming and other matters. "The Secrets thereof are full wondrous," he wrote.

As the people of Woodstock moved through the half-century between 1805 and 1855, they were accumulating a great many of the beliefs, legends and lore that are still alive in Woodstock and help give the town its character. The early pioneers were dying out, having turned over to their children many tales of the hardships of frontier life. Veterans of the Revolution too were fading away.

The last of them is thought to have been John George Happy. Happy was the oldest Ulster County veteran to sit down in 1831 to a dinner in Kingston commemorating the fiftieth anniversary of the surrender of Cornwallis. Before the dinner he marched with his fellow veterans to the sound of "bands of music and cannons booming." According to his tombstone in the Woodstock Cemetery Happy died at the age of ninety-seven years, eight months and twenty-three days on February 14, 1833. His death brought to an end the personal link of Woodstock people to the Revolution.

The celebration of the fiftieth anniversary of American independence on July 4, 1826 stirred memories and imaginations in Woodstock and elsewhere in the United States. Just how the day was marked in Woodstock isn't known, but it is likely that a bonfire was built on top of Overlook, for such fires were lit in many other high places. An inscription on a rock giving the date in lettering consistent with the period may still be seen near the top of the mountain. It was probably cut to commemorate the celebration.[15]

At the same time old people recalled memories and traditions of Revolutionary days and during that year of proud celebration gave Woodstock's tales and lore of the Revolution forms which they have kept to this day. The capture and escape of Peter Short and Peter Miller, the deeds of the Indian Runnip, buried treasure, the maintenance of "picket forts," and especially the activities of the town's Tories were told and retold.

The feeling against Tories was sometimes strong and this is reflected in much of the town's Revolutionary lore. The tale of an Indian refusing to kill a Whig baby at its parents' house in Mink Hollow and the bayoneting of the baby by a local Tory named Newkirk has continued in the tradition to our own times. There is no hint of any such incident in the letters and reports of the time, yet in 1974 the story was reprinted as historically true in a guidebook to the Catskills.[16]

Memories of the days of early settlement were handed on to young people who wondered at hearing of a time when the acres they tilled had been covered with forests of beech and hemlock. Young Shultises were told of the arrival in the town of the first of their name in 1788, Philip Shultis, who reached Woodstock with no possessions beyond the axe and rifle he was carrying and a few belongings tied up in a handkerchief. The young people were shown the very gun Philip had carried; it is said to still remain in the proud possession of Philip's descendants.[17]

This kind of preservation of the legends and traditions of Woodstock's past helped give the town's people a sense of belonging to a community unlike any other and in which all who lived in the town shared. The telling and retelling of the hazards of settlement deepened this sense of a common past. The dread with which the pioneers heard the nightly howling of wolves on their mountainside or the screaming of panthers, the injury or death of grandfathers or uncles beneath a falling tree, drownings of people trying to cross the swollen Sawkill before there were bridges—all these helped make the Woodstock past seem a time of trial from which the town's people had emerged with their plowed fields, their green meadows and their flocks of sheep and other domestic animals to show how well they had triumphed over the hard conditions of settlement days.

It was to this period of a new consciousness of Woodstock as a community with a character of its own that the town's best-known legend owes its beginnings. Solid evidence of the legend can still be found in the Woodstock Cemetery in the form of the gravestone of Catherine Van Debogart, who died on August 2, 1820.

The legend was given its classic form in 1897 in R. Lionel De Lisser's *Picturesque Ulster*. De Lisser wrote, "Woodstock has a fine cemetery . . . from the centre of one grave, near the eastern side of the yard, is a large elm tree, the growth of which has pushed the head and foot stones apart. To this grave is attached a great deal of interest, on account of the story or legend that is connected or goes with it. The story runs that away back in the early history of the town there lived near the village a middle-aged man [John Van Debogart], who had married a beautiful girl [Catherine] much his junior. His jealousy and suspicions, which had been awakened without just cause, made his own life and that of the unhappy wife, most miserable, the neighbors being often called in to arbitrate between them, in the quarrels and bickerings that increased and grew more violent from day to day.

"The well-intended interference by outsiders in favor of the weaker party, adding fuel to the flame, and arousing the passions of the man's naturally rough nature. From bad to worse they went until finally coming home one night from work, he found his wife absent, his evening meal unprepared, and his house in darkness. Failing to find her about the place, his anger got the better of him, and, going out, he sought and cut from a nearby elm tree a stout stick. With this weapon he lay in wait for the return of his child-wife who was soon to become a mother.

"She, hastening back from the bedside of a neighbor who had been taken suddenly ill, was met at the entrance of her home by her infuriated husband, who beat her with the elm stick, regardless of her cries, until she fell insensible at his feet. The inanimate form of the unhappy woman was lifted from the ground by the villagers and placed upon a bed. Upon returning to consciousness the faithful wife, although believing herself about to die, refused to make a complaint against, or implicate her husband in the matter, but asked that the elm stick might be buried in the coffin with her, and prayed that it might take root in her heart and grow into a tree, to serve as a reminder to her husband, and a warning to others. She died that night in giving birth to a lifeless infant, and, with her dead baby lying in her arms, and the stick held tightly in her clasped hands against her heart, she was buried under the shadow of Overlook.

"Then came the wonder, the miracle it was called by the simple country folks, who came in from the surrounding farms to gaze in open-mouthed astonishment at it, for out from the centre of the grave sprang a tiny sapling that grew from day to day and flourished until it became in time a stately elm, until now the great vine clad tree forces the stones that mark the grave apart. . . . The story given above is vouched for by an elderly lady living in the village who had it from her mother. We can only vouch for the tree, the grave and the inscription."

In his Picturesque books De Lisser supplied his public with the kind of sad, gory and sentimental "legends" popular during the 1890s. His books told of "beautiful Indian maidens" like Lotowana and Taw-a-sen-ta enduring cruel and violent treatment with patience even to death. The story of the Elm Tree Grave applies a similar formula to a white woman with much success.

Certainly elements of the legends were in tradition when De Lisser came to Woodstock with his notebook and camera in 1897 or a bit earlier. How much De Lisser actually heard from local people and how much he added are uncertain. Yet the main elements of the story seem to have some traditional basis. Many Woodstock people once believed that John Van Debogart had been the kind of alcoholic who gets mean when drunk and that it was this that impelled him to the fatal beating of his wife. He had once been found, it used to be said, up to his waist in the Woodstock millpond singing away in Dutch, "a language of which he knew not a word when sober." Drinking to excess was a feature of male society in Woodstock in his time, but in Van Debogart it led to irritability, suspiciousness and violent acts.

During the 1930s Woodstock's Jim Twaddell, who combined great inventiveness as a teller of tall stories with the ability to hand on bits of perfectly factual bits of local lore, said that Vandebogart had come home drunk and upset the churn in which his wife was trying to make butter. He ordered her to dance in the cream spilled on the floor. When she proved unwilling he gave her the fatal beating with the elm stick or gad he used to guide his oxen. It was also said that Vandebogart had tried over and over again to cut down the young elm tree on his wife's grave. The tree shot up again each time. More recently the Vandebogarts of a generation ago succeeded in "chopping down" the tree in an effort at stifling the embarrassing legend.[18]

No tale or legend of early Woodstock is more touching or has been more enduring than that of the Elm Tree Grave. It helped give Woodstock the kind of romantic charm the members of the art colony arriving after 1902 valued. And it summed up a number of features of early Woodstock life: the dominance of men over women, the prevalence of heavy drinking, and the willingness to accept the kind of miracle which sent an elm tree growing upward from the coffin of Catherine Van Debogart and her infant.

During the 1930s painter Lucile Blanch made a drawing in illustration of the legend for a postcard. An anonymous art-colony poet put the sad legend in condescending and mock primitive verse:

> This elm burst through an ancient grave
> Of fair young wife and babe
> Beaten by elm switch in the hand
> Of madly jealous young husband.
> When her late return from mercy deed
> Made him to wait upon his feed.
> Labour joined the awful fray
> She grasped the switch and passed away

Belief in witchcraft, the survival of old traditions of healing, the bringing together of those happenings in the past of Woodstock which appeared to have value in nourishing a community spirit, and the putting together of such a legend as that of the Elm Tree Grave with all the light it sheds on life and emotion in its town—all these formed an important part of Woodstock life between 1805 and 1855.

In addition, of course, there were other sides to life in the growing town. This side included activity in politics and government, in religion, in social services and in education, and in all the many other ways in which the people of the town acted together to do things which no one might do alone. Perhaps most important of these activities were those of the teachers, with their power both to enlarge areas of observing and thinking and to train minds into accepted channels, and the churches, which helped to give meaning to life and to provide a social center for the townspeople.

22

SCHOOLS, CHURCHES AND POLITICS

I t was not until the sessions of 1812 and 1813 that the State Legislature got round to creating an effective statewide system of "common schools" financed by state and local governments. Woodstock took prompt action after that. In December of 1814 its voters elected commissioners and inspectors of schools, as required by the new laws. Among those chosen were men known for their intelligence and education such as Stephen Stilwell, John W. Wigram and Dr. Larry Gilbert Hall, as well as others better known for their political skills.

Meeting on January 6, 1815, the commissioners divided Woodstock into seven school districts. This was not a simple matter because of the nature of the town's hill-and-mountain-divided topography. Lewis Hollow parents objecting to the bounds of their district as first proposed were "sot off" and added to the Kingston district. That is why until the 1950s the Hollow children attended the Daisy school across the Woodstock border.

Very soon a trustee was elected for each school district. Schoolhouses were built, teachers hired and the work of educating the town's boys and girls begun. By 1812, the reports made by six of Woodstock's seven school districts tell us, the schools were open for eight months of the year, with 256 children taught of the 311 children between 5 and 15 years of age reported to be living in Woodstock. And when these children grew up most were able to read and write.

The quality of education in each district depended upon the character and ability of its teacher. The teachers were not always as good as they should have been, although some were very good indeed. We know little of Woodstock's early teachers. Now and then the name of one has survived. James D. Hering, for example, who taught around 1816, also wove linen and flannel for the townspeople.[1]

Customs such as an annual "barring out" of the teachers soon became established. On one day of the school year the pupils locked their teacher out of the schoolhouse, and the teacher tried, often in vain, to regain his place inside. Recollections of old people years ago told of brawny older boys trying to make things hard for their teacher as he strove, often by the use of his fists, to obtain mastery over them. Women too taught, but seldom in the districts known for the toughness of their pupils. In spite of all obstacles more and more Woodstock children became able to read and write.

Woodstock's churches had been organized at a time when religious activity was awakening following the long period of neglect caused by the Revolution. The year 1800 had brought a wave of revival meetings to Kentucky and Tennessee. Rolling eastward, this wave had some effect on even such formal denominations as the Dutch Reformed and the Lutheran. By 1805 a modest Dutch Reformed Church was being built in Woodstock on what is now called the Village Green, and a Lutheran Church appeared at about the same time.

With their openly emotional approach to religion, the Methodists were very much in tune with the revivalist spirit. Though they did not organize a "class" until 1828 and did not build a church until 1832 or 1833, circuit riders held services for them in private houses, probably in that of Stephen Stilwell in what is now Shady and a bit later in the farmhouse of Henry P. Shultis, the Livingston agent in Bearsville. They may well have held early outdoor "camp meetings," but of this we have no record.

The Dutch Reformed and the Lutheran churches drew much of their support from the descendants of the early Dutch and Palatine German settlers of the Hudson Valley. The Dutch Reformed denomination was the strongest church in Ulster County, attracting the largest number of prosperous and well-placed people. In Woodstock it was the first to have a resident minister, Mr. Peter A. Overbagh.

Mr. Overbagh was described as "a faithful and useful" man. Apparently he laid stress on love rather than a fear of hellfire.

224

Evidence of this may be found on the gravestone of his son Titus, who died in 1828 at the age of fifteen. The stone still tells us that Titus' "parting words were Father Mother Brother & Sisters I love you all. Love one another. Oh! Love the Lord. He knows that I love Him." Peter Overbagh had studied theology with the eminent Dr. John Livingston, a cousin of the Livingstons of Clermont, but his teacher's dramatic pulpit manner and aristocratic airs were not imitated by Overbagh, who remained throughout his life simple and modest.

Yet with all his good qualities Mr. Overbagh did not succeed in giving his church a solid base for growth and prosperity. One reason may have been that after three years as minister at Woodstock he added to his duties the ministry of a larger congregation at Flatbush in Saugerties. He could only give part of his time to each congregation. In 1817 he gave up his Woodstock duties altogether and took care of the Flatbush congregation alone.[2]

In or about 1806 the Woodstock Lutheran Church made a beginning that has left visible traces. The Reverend Frederick Henry Quitman of Rhinebeck (he became a D.D. in 1814) brought about the organization of Woodstock Lutherans into a church. Very different in personality from Overbagh, Quitman was a huge man who weighed close to three hundred pounds. He was outgoing and had a knack for quick if somewhat coarse repartee. Born in the Duchy of Cleves in the northwestern part of Germany known as Westphalia, he became pastor of the Lutheran congregation at Rhinebeck in 1798. He remained there until he died in 1832.

Quitman preached in English and German on alternate Sundays, wrote several books, and headed the Lutheran Ministerium of the state. In 1809 he sent the Reverend Joseph Prentice to Woodstock as pastor. Prentice also preached in German as well as English and served the Woodstock church until 1814. For several years after 1816 the church was probably inactive; for part of this time the church building on a high outcrop of rock in the midst of a grove of magnificent old white pine trees, with the Sawkill below and Overlook Mountain above it, was used by the local Methodists.

It was probably during this period that John Crawford of Asbury, the first Methodist preacher to serve west of the Hudson under Freeborn Garrettson, preached in Woodstock. The difficulties of the Woodstock churches during this period reflect the economic dislocation which followed the ending of the Napoleonic Wars and the panic year of 1819.

The Dutch Reformed Church experienced no less severe times

than did the Lutheran Church. In 1817 Peter A. Overbagh took leave of his Woodstock congregation. In December 1819 the church was advertised for sale by Sheriff Abram Cantine "at public vendue at the Court-House in the village of Kingston on the seventeenth day of January next." Members of the church took action and the sale did not take place. No new minister arrived, however, and the church became a concern of the Reformed Church Missionary Society, which set up new churches and saved weak ones. In 1826 the Society sent the Rev. William Boyse to Woodstock and Ashokan as missionary for a trial period of three months. The trial must have been successful, for Boyse continued as missionary until he became full minister of the Woodstock church in 1829.

William Boyse must have given something of a shock to the members of the Dutch Reformed Church when he arrived in Woodstock. He could not speak or understand Dutch. He had been born in faraway South Carolina and had graduated from Transylvania College in Kentucky. Until a few months before he reached Woodstock he had been a Presbyterian. The vigorous colloquial words and expressions he used in his sermons contrasted strongly with the more formal expressions of Hudson Valley Dutch clergymen. And Boyse was a decided eccentric in manner, with abrupt and often puzzling changes of mood.[3]

For a few years Boyse reported with wonder to the Missionary Society about the situation in which he found himself. The members of his flock seemed apathetic about religion. They believed in witches. When he called prayer meetings they didn't pray, lacking what Boyse called "praying language." Most of the men and women in his congregation couldn't read or write. Their everyday language, a mixture of Dutch and English, made it hard for him to communicate with them.

Yet in 1831 and 1832 a change came. Woodstock Methodists built their first church and gained many members. The early 1830s climaxed a period when religious revivals multiplied all over the United States. In Woodstock the Methodists, the most hospitable of the denominations to revivalism, seemed to be sweeping all before them. The inactive Lutheran Church offered no opposition.

Watching the Methodists gaining ground in a nationwide rush toward revivalism, William Boyse decided to adopt some of their methods. At the time an epidemic of Asiatic cholera was moving downward from Canada and into New York State. The Dutch Reformed Church had urged all its member churches to observe a day of fasting to avert the misery and death the epidemic threatened to bring. As the epidemic drew nearer, the air became charged with emotion. In this atmosphere Woodstock people were ready to listen to the kind of vigorous preaching and praying which marked revivalism.

In his report to the Missionary Society Boyse told what was happening in Woodstock: "The Methodists had met with us at first, and helped us not a little; but just as we got pretty well a going, they were off—set all their machinery to work, hired the Lutheran church, about a quarter of a mile off [this was a bit before they built their own church], set all their runners a going, called for meetings, sung, prayed, preached, called and dragged to get men, women, boys and children to come to the altar; called for earthquakes, kept their wagons flying like the gangway of a populous city, predicted the sudden downfall of Calvinism, declared they saw it tottering like the temple of Dagon when Sampson [sic] put his hand to the pillar. But all would not do. The whole village joined the Dutch. . . ."

Boyse's extravagance of expression in this account is in keeping with the revivalist exuberance of the time. Though it may have been an exaggeration to write that "the whole village joined the Dutch," yet the Dutch Reformed Church records show that on December 22, 1832 more than thirty people became members of Boyse's church. It is characteristic of Boyse that after the name of one of these new members he wrote, "an odd fish—afterwards joined the Methodists."

The 1830s and the 1840s in Woodstock as elsewhere were decades of lessened public interest in revivalism and a time of consolidations of gains in church membership. William Boyse played only a small part in all this. After conflict with some members of his church he left Woodstock in 1837. His own explanation of why he left hints at the causes without making them entirely clear.

Boyse wrote, "I associated with the young, attended their wedding amusements; heard all their songs; saw all their sports and heard all their stories, their wine and passions, and there was nothing in them that was concealed from me. Our hearts were as one heart. But O what an uproar some of the elders made when they heard of all that. It soon resounded far enough, and all was made of it that could be made. But such a shower of lay preaching as came upon me few men have been blessed with. They could hardly keep their hands off me. They could not hinder their children from these amusements, but they imagined they could hinder me from seeing them . . . after a while they got me away. . . ."

Boyse never held another pastorate, but after 1837 he lived the life of a wandering preacher. He published and sold little booklets of sermons, prayers, reminiscences, autobiography and folklore, with details of his life in Woodstock scattered here and there.[4]

While Boyse wandered Woodstock people entered a period of calm, building up their churches in the wake of the revival excitement which had turned their thoughts and feelings to religion. In 1840 the Lutherans built a new and larger church on the site of their old one. The church was much admired. About half a century ago it was converted into a large house. The congregation had moved in the 1890s to a new building on Mill Hill Road, where it still meets.

Baptists had been active in Woodstock since the 1820s. In 1844 they organized and soon built a church near the junction of the Mink Hollow Road and Route 212 in Lake Hill. The church was known as the Second Baptist Church because it was an offshoot of the First Baptist Church of Kingston. In 1872 the church building was taken down and moved piece by piece to Mount Tremper, or The Corner, as it was then known.

As Willow grew in population its own Methodist church was built in 1853. A group of members of the congregation seceded (it is said there was a dispute about the ownership of a dog). The seceders built Willow's Wesleyan Church, which is still in use. It stands in dignity surrounded by its graveyard at a turn in the road.

By the 1850s Irish immigrants who were Roman Catholics had begun to settle in Woodstock and adjoining towns. To meet their needs St. John's Church was organized in West Hurley.[5]

The religious activities of Woodstock people before they built their churches had been few and formal, with attention paid most of all to baptisms and marriages and occasional attendance at a restrained sermon often preached in Dutch at the Katsbaan or Kingston churches. Difficulties of transportation restricted religious activity. So too did the fact that few Woodstock people could read their Bibles and hymn books.

By the time William Boyse came to Woodstock a new generation of young people who could read and write was beginning to emerge. It was this generation with which Boyse felt so much at home, to the anger of the older non-literate generation. By the mid-1850s the new generation, with its new churches, its broader outlook on life and the release of feeling brought about by revivalist influence on the sermons they heard and the songs they sang in church, was beginning a long new period in Woodstock life in which the churches would play a central part. Ministers during this period, which lasted well into the twentieth century, were the best-educated men in the community and leaders in many phases of Woodstock life.

Many were unusual and interesting men, T. H. Vandoren came to Woodstock in the 1840s after a few years as a missionary in Java. W. H. Emerick, whose career as an evangelistic preacher, including his years at Woodstock's Lutheran Church, inspired his childhood friend Henry Backus, known as the Saugerties Bard, to write and print a long set of verses. They go in part:

V

Who is this servant of the Lord
Sent forth to preach his sacred word?
A rural swain who left his all
God to obey; the Gospel call.

VI

At Woodstock first the Trumpet sounds
The hardened sinner much astound
Like those inspired in days of old
Proclaim's God's truth in language bold.

VII

The gospel seed in Woodstock sown
Now into stately trees have grown,
Sinners believed the sacred word,
And have trusted in the Lord.

VIII

Some scores of souls were here set free
To enjoy sweet Gospel liberty,
Salvation did the Lord reveal,
And at his throne they humbly kneel.[6]

This glimpse into Woodstock religious activities and emotions of the 1840s gives a clear picture of the Biblical imagery and surging religious feelings of the time. For many decades after Mr. Emerick left Woodstock evangelical fervor rose to occasional peaks and then subsided. During these same years the churches as social centers grew stronger. Their Sunday schools, their church picnics at Riseley's pine grove beside the Sawkill, their church-related societies and their social gatherings all brought people together, adding variety and interest to their lives. "Donation visits" became parties to which members of a congregation brought gifts to supplement the income their minister derived from his salary, his kitchen garden, his cow and chickens, and often a bit of farming.

Camp meetings now and then brought peaks of religious excitement to mid-century Woodstock. One of them took place in September 1855 on "the land of B. Eighmey 4 miles east of Shandaken corner" (in Willow). No "hucksters were allowed on the grounds" and "all provisions of the legislative act to protect meetings of this kind from disturbances and annoyances, will be strictly enforced." This was a reference to attempts at curbing by law the unruliness which often marked camp meetings.

So far as is known William Boyse had been the first Woodstock clergyman to see social reform as part of the church's work. In a long sermon on temperance printed in 1838 (and probably originally delivered in Woodstock) Boyse advocated legislation to "save ourselves from the catastrophe into which a continuance of drinking wine and strong drink, has threatened to hurl this country." He saw a marked increase in drunkenness in his own time, "Instead of the sober and steady habits of our parents, their children have seen drunkenness pass over the face of the earth like a flood." Church people worked hard at prohibiting the sale of liquor in Woodstock. Eventually, in 1879, they were to be successful.[7]

Churches and schools were not the only centers of social contact in old Woodstock. Family was of the first importance. Marriages were almost always for life. Unmarried people usually joined a family to which they were related and lived and worked as members. Children were highly valued. They would begin working at eight years of age, and so make a contribution to the family economy. When the huckleberries and wild strawberries which grew on burned or cut-over land were ripe, men, women and children went out in a holiday spirit to pick them. Old members of the family cared for babies or helped out in the hay and harvest fields to the extent that they could; old women spun yarn, peeled apples or vegetables or gave an experienced hand in preparing meat at slaughtering and pickling time. Families were held together not only by affection but by working together as a group in a common economic effort. Orphans were quickly adopted.

When a family became paupers its members were taken into other families. The town would hold an auction and the persons making the lowest bid would be paid for caring for a pauper or his children. The work most of the paupers could be expected to do helped determine the amount of bids. Sometimes the system worked fairly well, and the people obtained at auction became almost members of a family by right of birth.

This, however, was not always the case. In several cases in which the town apprenticed teenaged young people instead of auctioning them in order that they might have a place to live and at the same time learn a trade, difficulties developed. One apprentice's master "misused and evil treated him the said Apprentice in an unlawful manner by Knocking him down with his fist and kicking him after laying on the ground . . . and . . . not giving the said Apprentice sufficient victuals etc. . . ." In another case reported like the previous one by Louise Hasbrouck Zimm from the Woodstock town records, a young girl was apprenticed to a farmer who "misused and evil treated her . . .and corrupted the Morals Destroyed the virtue and injured the character of sd. apprentice." The accused farmer left town rather than face charges.

During the early nineteenth century Woodtock's ill and elderly poor were given help in food, shelter and medical care by the town. When Lewis Edson, Jr., the composer and singing school teacher, became impoverished the town records show that he was given help. When he died he was buried at town expense. When anyone was being buried the bell of the Reformed Church was tolled. In at least one recorded case the tolling was done at the the burial of a pauper at the town's expense.

The method of caring for the poor used in old Woodstock had many drawbacks. Yet it gave local people a sense of belonging to a kind of extended family in which each one, no matter how lowly, had some right to a share in the community's property. About 1817 a change began to approach. It was proposed that a county "House of Industry" be set up and the poor of the county's town be sent there. This proposal was modelled on the recent changes in the British Poor Laws.

Ulster County people did not like the new system. Said the Ulster *Plebeian* on February 1, 1817, "Many poor are actuated by as nice sensations of sensibility as their rich benefactors. Such would, unquestionably rather receive bounty from a neighbor, than from a stranger, and from a townsman, than one of another town or the county at large. . . ." The poor, the *Plebeian* added, "also have their predeliction for the place of their birth, or that which a long residence has rendered dear." These arguments shared by most Woodstock

231

people did not prevail. A county House of Industry required by a state law of 1820 was built.[8]

But what we call "home relief" did not end. The House of Industry, as the county poorhouse was euphemistically called, was not accepted by Woodstock people. Only when a rush of immigrants came into their town, bringing different customs and a different form of Christianity, did they become less strongly wedded to the older concept, a concept which could flourish only in a community whose people had a common background.

People sometimes worked alone in old Woodstock, but more commonly they worked in groups. They lightened their labor with conversation and secular songs and hymns. Men worked in company with others, felling and hauling timber to the glass factories or the sawmills. Teamsters driving back and forth alone to the Hudson landings with wagonloads of glass, sand, foodstuffs and manufactured articles stopped at every tavern along their route "to rest the horses" and to stand at the bar, drinking and swapping stories and jokes with friends and strangers.

Woodstock people worked together at numerous "bees," at which neighbors came together to raise barns and houses, mow and harvest, make maple sugar, cut apples for drying (these bees were called "apple-cuts"), clear away brush or patches of forest, husk corn or butcher hogs. No one was paid for working at these bees, but everyone who benefitted from a bee was expected to return the favor when called upon. Plenty of liquor was served at bees, helping to give these occasions a festive air. Young people sometimes turned a bee called for other purposes into what was called a "kissing bee."

Once in a while a bee became rowdy and ended in a fist fight. At one of these bees as late as 1869 David Short killed Ira Purdy at W. Brower's stone bee held for clearing fields and building stone walls. Both men became irritable from drinking too much rum. Incidents like this tended to diminish the popularity of bees as the nineteenth century moved along.

A favorite bee among Woodstock women was the quilting bee. Patchwork quilts were not only a necessity of life but also a means by which a creative urge was given forms which had decided esthetic interest. Quiltmaking has been carried on from the earliest days of Woodstock settlement to the present. In Shady the hall of the King's Daughters of the Methodist Church was built with the proceeds of quilts made by the women of the church at quilting parties or bees.

In 1937 an exhibition of patchwork quilts and other woven objects was held as part of the celebration of the 150th anniversary of the organization of the town and to give recognition to the place which quiltmaking had long held in Woodstock. The patchwork quilts and examples of woven ones brought out of old Woodstock cupboards and trunks for the occasion were listed and described at the time. They give us a good notion of the interest and quality of these fine crafts.

Among the woven bed covers and blankets listed were a blue-and-white bed cover woven by a Mrs. Risely, born a Short of Wittenberg; a blue-and-white striped wool blanket made by Mrs. Lewis Simpkins; a bedspread "wreath design" woven by Andrew P. Newkerk, a prosperous farmer, weaver and tailor, marked with Newkerk's name and the year 1836; "a butternut-dyed checked blanket, cinnamon and dark brown" woven by Mrs. Hannah Cooper Eldridge. Among the patchwork quilts were a ". . . nine block quilt in browns and red done in a cross pattern, and made by Mrs. Larry Gilbert Hall, wife of the doctor; another quilt by Mrs. Hall had a white ground and a pattern of large and small diamonds cut from calicoes; a Rose of Sharon quilt made by Mrs. Andrew Risely, another of the same pattern done in white, red and green by Mrs. George Risely; a quilt in blue, green and dark blue made by an aunt of Mrs. Peter Ricks in a pattern of hearts and rosettes; a brown, yellow and white quilt in the fox and geese pattern the work of Mrs. Allen Smith of the hamlet of Woodstock." [9]

Political activity was one side of Woodstock life which tended to join people and also to set them apart in two groups. In general political leaders were either connected with the two centers of local power, the land-owning Livingstons or the managers of the glass factories. But pressure was exerted on Woodstock voters by county political operators; it was an old saying that a few gallons of rum could "control the vote of Woodstock and Shandaken." On election day county leaders often sent agents to Woodstock to hand out rum and food to voters before herding them to the meeting at which the voting was done.

In the spring of 1809 an incident took place which shows how far from simple Woodstock politics could be. President Thomas Jefferson, in his efforts to protect American interests during the war between Britain and Napoleon Bonaparte's France, had persuaded Congress to pass the Embargo Act, under which trading by sea with Europe was cut off. The act had so many adverse economic effects that widespread protests harried the federal government. As Jefferson was about to leave office and James Madison to follow him in the White House, many town meetings in New England passed resolutions denouncing the Embargo Act. Jefferson became violently unpopular and the target of much abuse.

But in Woodstock, contrary to the national trend, a meeting was called at Philip Bonesteel's tavern to proclaim enthusiastic faith in the Act. Those who attended the meeting were Republicans (this was the party of Jefferson and Madison). The chairman was blacksmith James Bogardus of Willow, the secretary was farmer and tavernkeeper Isaac Elting of Wittenberg. Their resolution began, "Resolved . . . this meeting reposes full confidence in the wisdom and patriotism of the government of the United States . . . whatever plans and conspiracies may be set on foot for its subversion or destruction . . . they will support it with their lives and fortunes. . . ." The resolution went on to endorse the Embargo Act and to declare opposition to the Federalist party which opposed it.

What lay behind the resolution is still murky. It was certainly not a spontaneous expression of feeling on the part of local Republicans. The *Ulster Gazette*, Kingston's Federalist newspaper, denounced Bogardus as "Doctor Bevier's man of Straw" and accused him of "gross and palpable insults." The Republican *Ulster Plebeian* defended the resolution. An election of members of the State Legislature was approaching and the campaign was soon in full swing. Dr. Ben Bevier (who had practiced in Woodstock a few years before), candidate for the Assembly on the Federalist ticket, was in violent opposition to the Embargo Act. On his election committee for Woodstock that spring was the same Isaac Elting who had helped write the pro-Embargo Act Resolution a few weeks earlier.

By the time Elting had switched to the Federalist party the Embargo Act was repealed by Congress out of a mistaken notion of British intentions. It was replaced by the much less sweeping Non-Intercourse Act. The election that spring was hard-fought. John Suydam, Federalist boss of Ulster, sent a Captain Black to Woodstock, "his pockets full of federal handbills." The *Plebeian* reported that the captain was not even an American citizen but "a loyal subject of his majesty George III" and "and advocate of British taxation as in duty bound. . . ." Though the American Revolution had ended a quarter of a century before, it was still being used to arouse emotion at election time. Dr. Ben Bevier carried Woodstock by a single vote in the election, but the Republicans carried the county.

The elections of 1828 and 1830 also roused great excitement in

Woodstock. By that time the new state constitution of 1821 had given the vote to every white male twenty-one years old and over. Black men could not vote or be taxed unless they possessed an unencumbered freehold to the value of $250. Only one Woodstock black man is known to have so qualified. The more liberal conditions for voting when added to greater literacy increased Woodstock interest in elections and heightened party conflicts.

At issue in 1826, 1828 and 1830 was what was known as Anti-Masonism. A man named William Morgan, who lived in western New York, had threatened to publish a book revealing the innermost secrets of the Masonic order. He vanished after this and was said to have been murdered by Masons. On this bizarre foundation the Anti-Masonic party arose and expanded; it had a strong appeal in Woodstock. Governor Dewitt Clinton was a very exalted Mason, and many of his Woodstock supporters now deserted him. Dr. Ebenezer Hall of the Bristol Glass Factory led the Anti-Masonic forces. When Richard M. Hasbrouck, son of old Elias, ran for the Assembly in 1830, he was characterized in the Ulster *Palladium*, an Anti-Masonic newspaper of Kingston, as "a substantial and intelligent farmer." Dr. Hall carried on lengthy newspaper battles over the Anti-Masonic issue. Hasbrouck was not elected, but his party carried Woodstock by a very narrow margin.

The voters of Woodstock by the time the Anti-Rent troubles arrived had received a considerable education in the ways of the political processes upon which their government rested. They used the ballot effectively. After that for many years they tended to favor the Democratic party, which was the successor of the old Republican or Anti-Federalist party, in state and national elections. But Woodstock preferred men of "substance" for local offices. The men of the town became divided into groups according to their political connections and beliefs. These divisions affected social and working relationships.[10]

Much as Woodstock people were brought together and given a sense of being members of a community and at the same time divided into groups by the way their schools, churches, ways of working and voting impelled them, there were some details of Woodstock life on which all agreed. One of these was the name of a kind of apple originated in the town. Apple people outside of Woodstock called this apple the Jonathan. But those who lived in Woodstock insisted that its only correct name was the Rickey, a name which honored the apple's first grower, Philip Rick, who leased a Livingston farm on the Bearsville Flats.

23

PHILIP RICK'S
REMARKABLE APPLE

Here and there beside Woodstock highways and lanes, in the midst of fields now turned to patches of forest, old apple trees stand singly or in the geometric relationships to a few other apple trees that show the group to be survivors of an orchard. Many survivors of the orchards of the past have been slaughtered by bulldozers preparing the way for housing developments or new roads. A few fortunate old apple trees have been kept alive on the grounds of modern dwellings. There they are treated as pets, tenderly protected against insect and fungus enemies. In the fall young enthusiasts for old ways of life brave poison ivy and blackberry thorns to gather up the apples from under neglected trees and convert them into cider, which becomes the mainstay of a party mingling nostalgia and music.

Apple trees were once a valued part of the economic base of Woodstock. Now they have become symbols of a vanished way of life. In the Woodstock of the 1760s, they were an important part of the kind of farming Robert Livingston of Clermont wished to institute. That type of farming ran its course for a century and a half before giving way to other land uses better adapted to the needs and desires of the time.

These old trees remind us also of a fellow apple tree of theirs which died about a century ago. The most illustrious of all Woodstock apple trees, it was known as the Rickey, the King Philip, the Philip Rick or the Jonathan.

The way of putting the Woodstock landscape to human use planned by old Robert Livingston before the Revolution was carried out even after Livingston was gone. Grain and other field crops occupied the more fertile valley bottoms. In the upper parts of the Sawkill and Beaverkill a string of long, narrow fields, some less than a hundred feet wide, followed the flood plain.

Above, hill or mountain slopes rose abruptly. The lower slopes, where they were not too steep, were plowed and planted with corn or buckwheat until erosion robbed the soil of its fertility and left only the deposits of glacial gravel, stones and clay. Higher on the slopes were cow pastures dotted with chestnut and hickory trees saved for the sake of their valuable nuts, and maple trees tapped each spring for their sugary sap. Higher yet, terraced sheep pastures stretched upward among rocky ledges toward wooded summits. Stands of timber trees stood in many higher and less accessible places. Year after year the trees were cut and hauled by winter to the sawmills which continued to work beside the Sawkill, the Beaverkill, the Little Beaverkill and some smaller streams.

A man looking down from a hill or mountain during this period would surely have noticed that here and there in the valleys below amid the checkerboard of fields and meadows were areas in which trees stood like soldiers in regular formation. These were apple orchards. From the beginning of settlement orchards like these had been planned as useful features of Woodstock farms.

Livingston leases spelled out the way orchards were to be planted and cared for. The lease which Madame Livingston gave to Peter Short, Jr. on May 1, 1794 for a farm near that of the elder Peter Short contains a typical clause dealing with the orchard young Short was required to plant. During the first year of his lease Short was obliged to "strew Apple Seed or Pomace, upon a Patch of Land on said Farm, for a Nursery well prepared for that Purpose, of at least FIFTY foot square, to the intent that within Six Years be planted a regular Orchard of ONE HUNDRED Apple-trees at least, at THIRTY-SIX foot asunder; and as many of them as may happen to die, others in their Stead to be replaced, so that the number of ONE HUNDRED like trees at least, be complete and planted out, and inclosed within a good Fence for their safety. . . . "

The pomace mentioned was the wasted apple pulp, skins and seeds of cider-making. In Ulster County much of the pomace and therefore the seeds came from a variety called the Esopus Spitzenberg, a locally originated red apple "unexcelled in flavor and quality," so desirable as to have been taken across the Atlantic for growing in Europe. It was from a seed of the Esopus Spitzenberg that the first Rickey or Jonathan apple seedling is thought to have grown during the 1790s on Philip Rick's farm on the Bearsville Flats. It was for Rick that the apple was first named.[1]

When the Rickey seedling arrived at bearing age it produced apples not only with many of the fine qualities of the Spitzenberg but also with other desirable ones. It was a sport, the result of the kind of innovative genetic reshuffling which occasionally occurs in the plant and animal worlds, causing changes of many kinds.

The new apple appeared at a favorable time for survival. For some years there had been a good deal of talk about a supposed deterioration of the Esopus Spitzenberg. It was then mistakenly believed that all varieties of plants had a limited life span and that following a period of maturity they grew old and weak and at length vanished. The original Esopus Spitzenberg was thought to be showing signs of senility. Hudson Valley people were on the lookout for a new and vigorous variety to take its place. It was for this reason that the quality of the new tree was quickly noticed and talked about once it had borne a few apples.

In order to be sure of getting an apple tree of a specific variety it will not do to plant seeds of the variety, for these rarely breed true to the qualities of their parents. Instead the process known as grafting or cloning must be used. A scion of the wanted variety must be joined to part of another tree in such a way that the inner bark of the two will grow together. Or a bud of the wanted variety may be joined to another tree. The part of the new tree growing from the scion or bud—and it is usually the entire top—actually grows by a division of cells from the wood of the original tree. It will have the same genetic makeup. All the wood, leaves and fruit of the new tree will be part of the body of the original tree from which scions had been taken. As the original tree—in this case the original Esopus Spitzenberg—grows old and weak and dies, so it was once thought will all its clones.

Slowly at first, the lusty young descendant of the Esopus Spitzenberg increased in reputation in Woodstock. But the apple was too good a thing to remain within the bounds of one small town. A rich man who owned land in Woodstock became the means of sending the Rickey out from Woodstock—but under a new name. This man was Jonathan Hasbrouck, cousin of Woodstock's Elias Hasbrouck, first county judge of Ulster after the Revolution and sometimes described as the richest man in all the county. He had come to own a five-hundred-acre tract in Woodstock (the piece of land bought from Cornelis Tiebout by James Farquharson back in 1776). On this land Hasbrouck built a fine stone house, possibly for use as a summer refuge from the epidemics which swept the Hudson Valley by summer, often sparing elevated back country like Woodstock.[2]

Judge Hasbrouck did his best to turn his Woodstock lands to account. He kept a year-round tenant in part of his big house. He came to an agreement with the Livingstons about the long-disputed eastern boundary dividing his land from the Livingston piece known as the "twelve-hundred-acre lot." He planned a sawmill on the Sawkill at Sully's Bridge at which the trees on the upper part of his land could be turned into boards and timbers.

It is said that the Judge learned about Philip Rick's remarkable apple and passed on word of the apple to a friend much involved in publishing, horticulture, the law and politics. Here the story of the apple clambers onto very firm ground. The friend was Jesse Buel, once editor of the *Plebeian* and like Hasbrouck a judge of Ulster's county court. In 1813 Buel had moved on to Albany, where he edited the *Argus*, a paper of statewide influence. He got himself elected to the Legislature and obtained the profitable monopoly of public printing. By this and through land speculation Buel became a rich man. He was then able to devote himself to the cause of improved farming and to the establishment of a nursery devoted largely to promoting new and improved varieties of fruit trees.

At his nursery Buel tried out new varieties of many plants. He wrote to a customer of the Woodstock apple, "The new Spitzenberg I have found on trial to be a very superior apple." In 1826, thanks to Buel, the apple made its first appearance in print in the Report of the State Board of Agriculture. Buel, a believer in the theory of the degeneration of varieties of plants and especially of the Esopus Spitzenberg, stated in the board's Report that no variety "should be propagated unless the parent tree is known to exist in a healthy condition." And this the Rickey or Jonathan parent did, for "varieties of apples, at least, have their growth, their maturity and their old age," and the tree on the Rick farm was young. In the same report General John Armstrong of Dutchess County laments that "some recent facts warrant us in the belief that our own Spitzenberg is fast hastening to its end."

All this made Buel's efforts at establishing the apple he called the

Esopus Spitzenberg (New) or the Ulster Seedling very promising indeed as a replacement for the Spitzenberg.

Great confusion existed as to names of varieties of fruit trees in the 1820s. Buel, who fought to standardize names, noted that some varieties were known by the same name in only two states, giving many an opportunity to unscrupulous nurserymen. On October 10, 1828 the Rick-Hasbrouck-Buel apple was first put in print as the "Jonathan" in *The New England Farmer*. Buel's publicity release told of scions of the apple being sent to John Claudius Loudon, founder and editor of the British *Gardener's Magazine* and a great authority on horticulture and farming. The old Esopus Spitzenberg was already known and grown in Europe, where American apples were held in high favor.

Within a few years the Jonathan was being grown as far from Woodstock as the island of Jersey in Britain and Hamburg in Germany. Buel took good care to make this fact known to the American public.[3]

To many Europeans Jonathan or Brother Jonathan was the United States personified. This name had been a favorite New England Christian name. There had been Jonathans on the stage and in poetry. A popular New England dessert known elsewhere as apple dumpling or slump was sometimes called Apple Jonathan. The original bawdy version of "Yankee Doodle" printed in London in 1775 had used Jonathan as a familiar American name.

Because the name was so well known until Uncle Sam displaced it and had so much patriotic appeal, it was an excellent one to be borne by an American apple beginning to make its way in the world. With the vigorous help of Jesse Buel, make its way it did. By 1850 it was being recommended in most of the fruit growers' manuals. The *Fruits and Fruit Trees of America, 1845* of A. J. Downing, the eminent landscape designer and horticulturist, gave the background of the apple. "The original tree of this new sort," wrote Downing, "is growing on the farm of Mr. Philip Rick, of Kingston, New York, a neighborhood unsurpassed in the world for its great natural congeniality to the apple. It was first described by the late Judge Buel, and named by him, in compliment to Jonathan Hasbrouck Esq., of the same place, who made known the fruit to him." Downing gave as names by which the apple was sometimes also known King Philip and Philip Rick.[4]

By mid-nineteenth century the Jonathan had made its way to

Michigan, Illinois and other states to the west of its birthplace. Yet in the Hudson Valley and Catskills region it was still slow in becoming established. In 1857 a Woodstock man wrote to the editor of the respected magazine, *The Horticulturist*, giving a boost to the Jonathan apple and at the same time asserting its right to be known by the name of Philip Rick. The writer, H. H. Reynolds, said the Jonathan was "cultivated a little in this vicinity," and that "it ripens about Christmas and deserves a more extended reputation and cultivation." Reynolds told the editor that "this variety has been much esteemed wherever known. . . ." He accompanied his letter with several Jonathan apples, apologizing for the imperfections caused by a bad apple season. It is likely that the H. H. Reynolds who displayed so much local pride was Herman Reynolds, supervisor of Woodstock and a longtime justice of the peace.[5]

While the progress of the Jonathan during its first half century may have been slow, the apple more than made up for this during the century that followed. It reached the Pacific Coast and became a leading apple there. The Jonathan leaped the Pacific Ocean and settled down in Japan, Australia and New Zealand. It found its way to northern Italy and France and to many other parts of Europe. An American missionary took it to Korea, where it became one of the two leading apple varieties in that country's large orchards. And every Jonathan tree anywhere in the world had been grown from the wood of the tree Philip Rick had tended in his lease orchard on a low ridge on the Bearsville Flats in Woodstock.

By 1928 there were more than six million Jonathan trees in the United States and millions more in the rest of the world. The Jonathan turned out to be among the most promising of all apples as a parent for new varieties. Jonathan trees were crossed with other varieties to produce apples with improved flavor and keeping qualities. Gourmets discovered the Jonathan was one of the very best of all cooking apples and made this known in cookbooks and newpaper articles.

In 1927 the importance of the Jonathan was officially recognized when with much ceremony a boulder monument marking the birthplace of the apple was placed on the side of Route 212 on the Bearsville Flats. The bronze tablet fastened to the boulder tells the passerby that the Jonathan has been "long known locally as THE RICKEY or Philip Rick apple from the Discoverer." [6]

This tribute to Philip Rick appeared on the monument because of the never-failing persistence of Woodstock in giving credit for the Jonathan to their neighbor. Old people of Woodstock remember when the apple was never called anything else but the Rickey in their town, regardless of what name it might have been given in the books and in the outside world. They were pleased and proud of honors being given what they thought of as their own Rickey. It may be known by that name now to no more than a half-dozen white-haired Woodstock people who are aware that they have lost the battle of the names. Elsewhere Jonathan Hasbrouck is gaining credit year by year as the man who grew the first Jonathan or at least discovered it.

Jesse Buel and Philip Rick are not often mentioned in the story of the beginnings of the apple as presented to a wide public. But Judge Hasbrouck is. The third edition of the unabridged Webster's Dictionary tells us under the word "jonathan" that the apple is named for "Jonathan Hasbrouck (Am. jurist)." A history of American agriculture published in 1945 states that "Jonathan Hasbrouck living in the Rip Van Winkle country near Woodstock N.Y. tinkered with a sport variety in his orchard and finally marketed it under his given name of Jonathan."

Who rightfully deserved the credit for the discovery of the Jonathan apple? The question has often been debated in Woodstock long after it was settled by authorities on apple-growing in the world outside. Woodstock people remained loyal to Philip Rick. Judge Hasbrouck's prestige was substantial. Though he had no important achievements to his credit, he was rich and belonged to a large family which had many prosperous members and does much prideful delving into its own genealogy. It is not surprising that the apple bore the judge's first name. But was it his first name and his alone that was given to the apple?

The baptism records of the Dutch Reformed Church of Kingston for February 28, 1795 tell of the birth of a son to Philip Rick and his wife, Anna Maria Laun. Witnesses at the baptism were "Jonathan Haasbroek" and his wife Catharina Wynkoop. And the child was named "Jonathan Haasbroek Rick." Years before the first apple appeared on Rick's seedling on the Bearsville Flats a second Jonathan Hasbrouck had come upon the scene, a godson and namesake of the Judge.

Just why the Judge and his wife played this role is not known. Certainly the Ricks (said in family tradition then to have been recently arrived in Ulster County from Dutchess across the Hudson) were not social equals of the Hasbroucks. Perhaps Philip or Anna Maria, or Ami, as she was familiarly called, had been employees of the Judge— employers were often godparents to the children of employees with whom they were on good terms.[7]

So the possibility remains that it was Philip and Ami Rick's son Jonathan and not their patron who gave his name to the apple. We may, if we wish, theorize that it was young Jonathan who made the actual discovery in his father's lease orchard and that the apple was known for a while after that as Jonathan's apple, becoming the Rickey as Jonathan became a man. There are all sorts of theories as to the naming of the apple with which Woodstock people may play. It is unlikely that any one of them can ever be proven. It may even be that the standard one given by A. J. Downing in 1845 may be correct.

Philip Rick and his family deserve to be remembered for their part in Woodstock history not only for their discovery of the Jonathan apple but because without intending to they left us an excellent picture of life in Woodstock in the late 1820s. The couple had eight children, four boys and four girls. Philip's farm, leased on May 1, 1792 from Madame Livingston, had 86 acres on the Bearsville Flats just a bit west of the hamlet of Woodstock, including part of what later became the Eames and then the Comeau place. It was largely fine level land described by the Woodstock assessors as "good" (only about twelve per cent of Woodstock farm land was so described in 1827).

By way of rent Rick paid 11¼ bushels of wheat, 2 fowls and a day's riding. He was not permitted to cut the pine trees on his land, a right reserved to his landlord. When Rick added a woodlot to his farm in 1807 his rent was raised a bit. Like most Woodstock tenants he paid his rents irregularly, sometimes not as required in his lease but in the form of maple and whitewood timber cut on his farm.

Most of the Ricks' children as they grew older and married settled down on farms they leased or which were leased by their husbands. Young Philip moved to Hurley. Jonathan Hasbrouck Rick, however, remained on his parents' farm. As his father grew older and less able to do hard work, Jonathan took over half the farm and helped his father with his own farm work.

Old Rick, among the more prosperous Woodstock tenant farmers, paid a tax in 1827 of $3.71. Jonathan paid an equal tax for his half of the old farm. Rick's tax included personal property assessed at $125. Few Woodstock men of the period had enough personal property to oblige them to pay any tax at all on it. (Old John Wigram, with personal property assessed at $1100, led the entire town, paying an annual tax on real and personal property of a bit over nineteen dollars.) Rick's farm was well equipped for its time and place, with plows, harrows, a cider mill, a loom and tackling, baskets, chains, a "whiting pot," hatchets, hogsheads and "meat casks," hogs, sleighs, oxen, cows and calves, a sleigh, a "dyer pot," an ox yoke, a "cider funnel," sheep shears, gimblets, "wooden box with four legs," and so on. Within the Rick house were looking glasses, chairs, a cupboard, some Dutch books, earthen pots and plates, a "bunk Bettstead," churn, a brass kettle, feather beds, bellows, and so on.

Philip Rick and Ami died early in 1828. A disagreement among their heirs resulted in much legal action, in the course of which a good deal of detail about the two and their possessions was written down. The tattered and fragile paper still exists in the Ulster surrogate's office. Witnesses testified that Rick was believed to have had "a considerable estate." One witness stated that "the old man worked as long as he could" another that "the old gentleman" had said Jonathan was to have a part of his farm and the tools and implements on it. Another witness testified that "old Rick said that he calculated Jonathan would work the farm different from what he had done, he was old and could no longer work, that he need not work as he had enough to live of[f]." Here old Philip was seen as about to turn over his leasehold to Jonathan, who had always seemed the closest to him of all his children and who had continued to live with him and Ami on the farm.

Drs. Larry Gilbert Hall and John G. Fiero took care of Philip and Ami during the last winter of their lives and rendered a bill for $8.75. John M. Lewis, Woodstock carpenter and undertaker, was paid $12 for making coffins for the old couple. Jeremiah Simmons received one dollar for "tolling the Bell for Mr. Reek and his wife." Two auctions were held at "Newkerk's and De Forest's house" (i.e., inn), and there much of the Ricks' moveable property was sold. The clothing of the two was divided into eight piles, one for each of their children. Old Mr. Rick left behind a greatcoat worth ten dollars, a new hat for which he had paid twenty-eight shillings, "an entire new suit, coat, jacket and pantaloons" and "good clothes for common wear." [8]

Jonathan Hasbrouck Rick continued to live on and work the old farm. In 1848 he bought it from his landlords. He lived there until his death in 1872. By then the original Jonathan tree was no longer young or vigorous. It had been weakened, it was said, because so many scions had been cut from it. By 1890 only a dead stump was being shown to visitors. Yet the clones of the tree all over the world were doing well. The old belief that when the original tree of a variety weakens and dies all its clones will weaken and die with it had been disproved, thanks in part to the example of the Jonathan. The original, dead for almost a century, still lives on in the millions of Jonathan trees now scattered around the world.

It would be hard to place a value in dollars on the apple which Woodstock gave to the world. Many millions of people have enjoyed it. Many thousands have profited from growing and selling it. Because of the Jonathan's present role as parent of many new varieties (such as the Ida Red) millions of people of the future will benefit from the genetic quirk which took place in Philip Rick's lease orchard in the 1790s. No event in Woodstock's history has affected the people of the world more than the apple they know as the Jonathan.

Yet the Jonathan has never been much grown in its home town. It requires rich soil, and because of its marked susceptibility to many insect and fungus enemies it does not thrive in Woodstock unless given unusual care and attention. The only Jonathans Woodstock people usually see are those brought from far away and sold at local fruit stands.

24

OLD-TIME CLIMBERS
OF OVERLOOK

Human beings tend to respond with emotion to mountains, deserts and seas, the parts of the earth most recalcitrant to efforts to turn them to practical account. Early in human history mountains were viewed with awe. They were seen as places where earth and sky met, where sacred beings dwelt; the ancient Hebrews "lifted up their eyes" to the mountains and felt the presence of God. In many of the cultures of our world attitudes toward mountains were ambivalent. Mountains were sometimes felt as sublime and sometimes as sources of fear.

To the Indians who were the first humans to see Woodstock's Overlook Mountain, the mountain had a mixed emotional meaning. It formed part of a hunting ground where useful game and plants abounded. And it was probably (for we have no direct evidence on this point) a home of spirits and an entrance to the sky.

Mountains like Overlook were appealing to the emotions of the earliest European explorers who sailed up the Hudson River in two ways. They were symbols of God's wrath against mankind roused by the disobedience of Eve in the Garden of Eden: God as a sign of his displeasure had created mountains on what had formerly been a smooth and perfect earth. Yet at the same time mountains were valued as sources of metals such as gold, silver and copper.

Overlook came to have another practical value—as a landmark. Sailors moving up or down the Hudson knew that they were about one hundred miles above the mouth of the river when they came abreast of Overlook. Because the mountain jutted out from the rest of the Catskills it seemed to assert its presence. And because as seen from the upper Hudson it seemed to bring the eastern wall of the Catskills to a bold and abrupt end on the south, it was called the Short-off or South Peak.[1]

During the early 1700s a fresh way of seeing Overlook began to emerge, part of a growing movement often called Romanticism. Mountains like Overlook became romantic objects, giving human beings a heightened sense of their closeness to the world of earth, rock, sky and living things. Imaginations were freed from commitment to the practical and rational side of life.

Just when Overlook began to be a romantic object we do not know. A view of the Catskills from a sketch by Governor Thomas Pownall appeared in 1766 in the form of an engraving by British topographical artist Paul Sandby. It included a very romanticized Overlook. And we know that on April 9, 1793 Overlook was climbed by Peter DeLabigarre, who wrote about the mountain and its surroundings in a spirit that was at the same time romantic, scientific in a not very professional way, and businesslike. DeLabigarre, an agent of the revolutionary government of France and a friend of Chancellor Robert R. Livingston, was an enthusiastic promoter of such projects as silkmaking and viniculture in America. He saw Overlook's southeastern slopes becoming a wine-producing vineyard. Overlook had a special interest to the Frenchman because it was one of the scenic assets of the Chateau de Tivoli, which he was building across the Hudson with the mountain in full view.

DeLabigarre set down in words his emotions as he looked out from the summit of Overlook. "Elevated and noble ideas" rushed into his mind. He was filled with awe and wonder at seeing the world below reduced in scale until the Hudson, which had taken him half an hour to cross that morning, became a mere rivulet and the sloops on its surface dwindled to the size of canoes. The busy people whom he knew to be at work in the valley were invisible, the sounds of their work and play inaudible.

However excited DeLabigarre was by the world as seen from the top of Overlook, he was not too bemused to observe the trees growing around him. He listed them—pitch and white pines, hemlock, spruce and "large silver fir" trees (these last were the balsam firs of our day, now nearly vanished from Overlook). On his way up the mountainside

247

DeLabigarre had taken note of the mountain's construction in terrace-like layers and of the deciduous trees growing on the terraces—sugar maple, beech, birch, ash, oak and elm. The underwood contained many berry-bearing bushes, wild currants and raspberries among them.

He had made a point of the presence in shady places "of a kind of liquorice very much ressembling that of Italy, as to the taste of the root." This plant, the aralia we usually call false sarsaparilla, still grows in profusion on damp parts of Overlook. Like ginseng, it was once gathered on the mountainside for use as a drug.

DeLabigarre described what is probably the earliest recorded climb up the mountain. He struggled upward in the strong April morning sun over the ledges which make up the northern flank of the Minister's Face. There, he related, he came upon a bank of snow, some of which mixed with the brandy in his flask gave him "delicious drinking tenfold better than any ice cream."

Looking to the south and west of Overlook DeLabigarre saw two lakes, Shandaken Lake, not yet known as Cooper Lake, and Schue's Pond, which is known to us as Echo Lake. He made his way down the mountainside and spent the night of April 9 camping at Shue's Pond. While local folklore even in our day holds the pond to be "bottomless," DeLabigarre was a close enough observer to realize that the lake was shallow. He also found it to be "of an exact circular form." Since 1793 the lake's shape and size have changed, due both to natural and artificial causes.

That night DeLabigarre and his companions (he did not give their numbers or names) slept on the kind of beds of hemlock boughs which were already traditional among Catskill Mountain hunters and woodsmen. They were roused at times by what they believed to be "the howlings of wolves, wild cats and bears." One of the party clutched a hatchet even as he slept "to defend himself against our surrounding musicians." The following morning the party made its way across the present Woodstock-Hunter line to the head of the Plattekill Clove and so down the precipitous clove and on across the Hudson to the Chateau de Tivoli.

Though DeLabigarre's hopes for the Chateau with its surrounding village faded and he went off to die of yellow fever in New Orleans, other imaginative people followed him to Overlook in search of romantic thrills and sources of profitable raw materials. One of these was James Pierce, president of the Catskill N.Y. Lyceum of Natural History, whose account appeared in the *American Journal of Science* in 1823.[2]

Pierce saw the crumbling rocks of the Minister's Face as a possible source of alum. He made much of attempts at coal mining on the mountain. Cornelius Tiebout, Stephen Stilwell and Isaac Roosevelt had once had high hopes of Overlook coal. Pierce described what may have been a relic of their efforts in the form of "a coal excavation" above Lewis Hollow in a ledge still known to Woodstock oldtimers as The Coal Mine Ledge.

The same year that his account was published as "Mr. Pierce Upon the Catskill Mountains," another event caused Woodstock people to look at their mountain with a fresh kind of interest. That year the House on the Pine Orchard, soon to become world-famous as the Catskill Mountain House, opened as a summer resort. Those with time and money could gather there to enjoy the romantic attractions of the place—the panoramic view, the two lakes, the waterfalls and the aura of romance given the neighborhood by Irving's Rip Van Winkle and Cooper's Leatherstocking. Painters and poets, statesmen and businessmen, theater people and many others came to the House, their presence intensifying its appeal to others.

Woodstock people were quick to realize their own mountaintop might become a possible rival to the site of the Catskill Mountain House. From their summit, and from the Overlook Cliff, which soon gave its name to the entire mountain, the view was far more varied than from the Pine Orchard and reached just as far into infinity, with seventy miles of the Hudson River and parts of five states visible. Not too far away was lovely Shue's Pond. Nearby Plattekill Clove had waterfalls rivalling in beauty those of the Kaaterskill Clove near the Catskill Mountain House. At the base of Overlook lay Woodstock, a settlement large enough to supply a mountain house on Overlook with all the human help it might need in its building and operation.

Ten years after the opening of the Catskill Mountain House, James Booth, who lived in the upper Sawkill Valley, made plans for what he called the Woodstock Blue Mountain House. It was to be built on a plateau with an excellent spring only a bit more than one hundred feet below the summit of Overlook and at an elevation (in a day when elevations were of the first importance to romantic projects) of almost a thousand feet higher than the Catskill Mountain House. On July 4, 1833 Booth called together a group of possible backers of his proposed hotel and served them a dinner in a "temporary Mountain House" he had built on the plateau. It was reached by a path which took off from the road connecting Woodstock and the upper glass factory and passed through the "Magic Meadow" a little below what is now known as Mead's. It roughly paralleled the present road from Mead's to the summit.

The Ulster *Republican* of July 10 carried an account of the occasion in which the word "romantic" occurred three times. Its author was either James Booth himself or one of his Woodstock friends. The writer made much of the appeal of the plateau to artists, businessmen, poets and philosophers. Booth had apparently thinned the dense growth of evergreen and deciduous trees in order to reveal the view from the plateau. The path upward took its users through wooded "obscurity."

When the plateau and the Overlook Cliff were reached, "the fancy is instantly regaled in this bright expansion appearing between heaven and earth: and if there is anything between heaven and earth that can regale the romantic imagination, it is here whether we speak of beauty or of sublimity in unbounded variety. Beneath we beheld a cloud suspended and tinged with all the colours of the rainbow. In full sight were the North [Hudson] River and her sloops and steam and ferry boats and small craft, Albany, Greenbush, Schodack, Coeymans, Kinderhook, Athens, Hudson . . . the Livingstons. . . ." and many more localities, with "at the foot of the mountain Woodstock and Marbletown with all the varieties of farms and woodlands interspersing openings with delightful prospects on the beautiful expanse. . . ." Looking out from the top of Overlook, the writer concluded, meant "tracing Nature up to Nature's God."[3]

The day chosen by Booth for his sales meeting may have been fortunate in the excellence of the weather, but it was unfortunate in its economic climate. A long period of stagnation was creeping over the nation. The Catskill Mountain House was losing money at a brisk rate, and for the time any thought of a rival on Overlook became absurd. Though the Woodstock Blue Mountain House never came into being, the dream of such a structure did not die out.

At the same time, people who saw the mountain less as a romantic object and more as a source of profit rummaged all over Overlook. The Bristol glassmakers stripped the mountainsides of deciduous trees. Tanners felled oaks and hemlocks for their bark. Fires made merry in the tangles of dead branches on the ground. The hopes for coal and iron which had surged in Cornelius Tiebout were handed on to new generations.

By the late 1830s the explosion of interest in romantic and picturesque landscape which had done so much to popularize the

Catskill Mountain House and the works of painters working in the hotel's vicinity had sent painters, poets and lovers of the romantic exploring many other parts of the Catskills. The attractions of the Mountain House were no longer novelties. Fresh romantic sensations were in demand.

In 1839 four young men found sensations like these in Plattekill Clove, Overlook Mountain and Shue's Pond. They lived by summer in the picturesque old farmhouse of Levi Myer close to the foot of Plattekill Clove. There they formed what they sometimes called a "brotherhood." They climbed the Clove, they bathed in many pools, they fished for trout in both the Clove and Shue's Pond.

They often climbed to the top of Overlook and spent nights there. And because two of the young men were clergymen-poets (John Steinfurt Kidney and Louis L. Noble) their nights on Overlook took on religious overtones. "We lift our voices in the beautiful liturgy of the Church, at morn and eve on the cloud-envelopped summit." So Noble wrote to painter and writer Charles Lanman, who was one of the brotherhood.

The members of the brotherhood tried to persuade Thomas Cole, whom they all revered as the aesthetic apostle of the Catskills, to visit them and join in their mountain adventures and rituals. Though for a while Cole did not find it possible to respond, his interest was aroused. In late June 1840 he took William Cullen Bryant on a tour of the Plattekill Clove and other nearby scenic treasures of the Catskills. But it was not until 1846 that Cole climbed Overlook.[4]

By then Charles Lanman had enthusiastically described the wonders of Overlook and Shue's Pond in a number of magazine articles written in the kind of feverish prose which appealed to readers of the day. He wrote of Overlook under its older name of South Peak as "the most beloved" of all the Catskills. "Like most of its brethren it is a perfectly wild and uncultivated wilderness, abounding in lofty cliffs and waterfalls, and its solitude is seldom broken by the footsteps of man. Like a corner-stone it stands at the junction of the northern and western ranges of the Catskills, and as its huge form looms up against the evening sky, it inspires one with awe, as if it was the ruler of the world, and yet I have learned to love it as a friend. Its name, its image, and every tree and shrub and vine that springs from its rocky bosom can never be forgotten. I have reflected upon it when reposing in the noontide sunshine, or enveloped in clouds, when holding communion with the most holy night, or trembling under the influence of a

251

thunder-storm. It has filled my soul with images of beauty and sublimity and made me feel the omnipotence of God."

Overlook Mountain as seen from the neighborhood best known to the members of the brotherhood based on Levi Myer's farm is an extraordinarily imposing sight. Around 1840, with the ravages of the great slide of 1833 not yet healed, the mountain had a far more vigorous and wild profile than the one we know. Washington Irving once referred to Lanman as the "picturesque explorer of America." The phrase was apt.

Lanman put his talent and energy to use in exploring and promoting Overlook and its surroundings. He made much of the rattlesnake den on the top of the Minister's Face, and there set an Indian legend which he probably invented. On a ledge of the Face "called the Eagle's Nest," Lanman wrote, "it was said that an Indian child had once been carried there," and cruelly destroyed, ". . . the frantic mother with the mangled body of her babe in her arms leaped into the terrible abyss below."

Nearby, Lanman wrote, he came upon Rattlesnake Ledge. "Here the rocks were literally covered with the white bones of those reptiles slaughtered by the hunter in bygone years, and we happened to see a pair of them that were alive. One was about four feet long, and the other, which was only half as large, seemed to be the offspring of the old one, for, when discovered, they were playing together like an affectionate mother with her tender child. Soon as we appeared in their presence, the serpents immediately ceased their sport, and in the twinkling of an eye, coiled themselves in the attitude of battle. The conflict was of short duration, and to know the result you need only look into my cabinet of curiosities." This earliest known tale of an encounter with rattlesnakes on Overlook seems reliable enough except for the assumption that the rattlers Lanman saw were mother and child playing together, which is not in accord with what is known of rattlesnake behavior.

Though many writers in later years gave us descriptions of moonlight and sunrise as observed from the top of Overlook, none ever surpassed Lanman's rich and indigestible prose on the subject. Here Lanman describes the moonlit mountaintop. "But how can I describe the scene that burst upon our enraptured vision? It was unlike anything I had ever seen before, creating a lone, lost feeling, which I supposed could only be realized by a wanderer in an uninhabited wilderness, or on the ocean a thousand leagues from home. Above, around and beneath us, ay, far *beneath* us were the cold bright stars, and to the eastward the 'young moon with the old moon in her arms.' In the west were floating a little band of pearly clouds, which I almost fancied to be winged chariots, and that they were crowded with children, the absent and loved of other years, who, in a frolic of blissful joy, were out upon the fields of heaven. . . ."

The coming of the dawn gave Lanman another chance to show what he could do to the English language. "The dawn! And now for a sunrise picture among the mountains, with all the illusive performances of the mists and clouds! He comes! He comes! The king of the bright days! . . . Now the crimson and gold clouds are parting, and he bursts on the bewildered sight! One moment more, and the whole earth rejoices in his beams, falling alike as they do upon the prince and peasant of every land. And now on either side and beneath the sun an array of new-born clouds are forming—like a band of cavaliers, preparing to acccompany their leader on a journey. Out of the Atlantic have they just risen; at noon they will pitch their tents on the cerulean plains of heaven. . . ."

Inclined though he was toward the purplest kind of writing, Lanman could also tell tales of hunting and fishing in a jolly spirit that carried conviction even when he indulged in the kind of exaggeration to which he was always prone. His account of a night spent at Shue's Pond, probably about 1840, brought Lanman charges of outright tall-talking. Lanman had set out on a fishing trip to the lake with two companions, Peter Hummel [Hommel], born at the foot of Overlook, and a man known as White Yankee, who had "three blankets lashed up on his back, a slouched white hat upon his head, and nearly half a pound of tabacco in his mouth." Lanman himself had a gun on his shoulder, a powder-horn and shot-pouch at his side, cowhide boots on his feet, and a cap on his head, his beard half an inch long, and his flowing hair streaming in the wind. . . ."

Before dark, Lanman wrote, he and his companions cut eighty fishing poles ". . . to which we fastened our lines. The old canoe in the lake was then bailed out, and having baited our hooks with the minnows we had brought with us, we planted our poles in about seven feet of water all around the lake shore. . . ." At nine that night "forty-one trout, weighing from one to two pounds a-piece" were taken from the party's lines. The next morning's catch brought the total to almost one hundred. As word of Lanman's story of his fishing exploit got around a rush of fishermen descended upon the lake, and when they caught hardly any fish at all they denounced Lanman as a liar.

Yet Lanman's night at Echo Lake or Shue's Pond is a useful document in Woodstock's history, for it has much old local lore and bits of reliable information. Lanman wrote that he had ". . . learned from Peter the following particulars concerning the lake. It was originally discovered by a hunter named Shew. It is estimated to cover about fifty acres, and in the centre to be more than two hundred feet in depth. For my part, however, I do not believe it contains over five acres, though the mountains which tower on every side but one, are calculated to deceive the eye; but, as to its depth, I could easily fancy it to be bottomless, for the water is remarkably dark. To the number of trout in this lake there seems to be no end. It is supposed they reach it, when small, through Sweetwater Brook [the Sawkill], when they increase in size and multiply."

Peter Hommel told Lanman tales of hunting in the vicinity that night as they lay on hemlock beds beside the lake. "In one day he shot three deer; at another time a dozen turkeys; at another twenty ducks; one night an old bear; and again half-a-dozen coons; and on one occasion annihilated a den of thirty-seven rattlesnakes." If these hunting statistics as told by Lanman and Hommel are not entirely accurate, they at least reflect the kind of talk that went on during hunting expeditions in old Woodstock.

In still another way Charles Lanman added to our knowledge of local history in an area which would some day become of great importance to Woodstock. He recorded the first attempt as far as is now known to sketch a landscape from life in the town. While White Yankee and Peter Hommel were tending to their fishing Lanman wrote, "I remained on shore to attempt a drawing, by moonlight, of the lake before me. The opposite side of the mountain, with its dark tangled forests, was perfectly mirrored in the waters below, the whole seeming as solid and variegated as a tablet of Egyptian marble." [5]

Another and much greater painter who was also a writer came to Woodstock and made a sketch a few years after Lanman. English-born Thomas Cole had become an innovator in American landscape painting and the founder of what is usually known as the Hudson River School. He had a fine house and studio in Catskill, and there he reigned as the aesthetic king of the Catskills. Until 1846 Cole had painted only in the parts of the mountains west and northwest of his studio. It is likely that it was Lanman who awakened him to the interest of the central and southern Catskills which stretched away for miles to the southwest.

On August 12, 1846 Cole and a lively and sophisticated exploring party of about a dozen left Catskill in two horse-drawn wagons, bent on climbing and exploring Overlook and then spending the night on its summit. The members of the party had seen Overlook's profile and had speculated about the mountain for many years. Now for the first time Cole and his friends were about to experience it at first hand.

The party of twelve men and women set out from the village of Catskill as soon after dawn as a series of mishaps with their horses' shoes would allow. They followed the base of the Catskills, where, Cole wrote in his journal, the view ". . . was delightful and afforded ever changing views—in the foreground & middle ground rich farms & beautiful trees (chestnuts particularly fine) the mountains distant only a few miles raised their vast verdurous walls here & there broken into gray terraces of rock, but the southeastern aspect of the South Peak, here called the Short Off & and which I had never before approached so near was the grandest feature of the landscape. Here the great range of the Catskills seemed suddenly to terminate in a shattered precipice the Minister's Face whose ragged brow is thrust & whose base sinks abruptly down a jagged slope where the green forests struggle to hide the nakedness of the frantic rocks."

Here Cole was seeing the northeastern aspect of Overlook still showing the effect of the slide of 1833 in the human terms which made so strong an appeal to his generation when writing of landscape and green living things.

The two wagonloads of people with food and baggage sufficient for a two days' trip rounded the base of Overlook and began the ascent of "a toilsome and sun-stricken road which led through a high pass in the mountains." The pass was the Wide Clove, now known as Mead's. It was customary in the early days of climbing Overlook for people to set out by wagon, pass through the Wide Clove, and form a base camp at the abandoned glassmakers' settlement in what is now Keefe Hollow. There they might leave their horses to be cared for and fed, obtain a guide, and often find a meal ready when they came down from the mountain.

Cole's party followed much of this procedure. Cole wrote of it with a delight that seems to carry us back in almost full intensity to that August 12, 1846. After telling of his surprise at seeing the ruins of the glassmakers' village of the upper Sawkill, Cole wrote that "W.

McDaniel & his sons & wife were making hay in the meadow below but she quickly came to us bare footed but of sprightly countenance."

The bare-footed haymaker was the same Betsy Booth MacDaniel who would later earn local fame as an herb doctor. Continued Cole, "She [Mrs. MacDaniel] satisfied us as to having our horses taken care of for the night, went for her husband, and gave us all necessary information respecting the ascent of the South Peak by her called the Overlook (a capital name with some meaning in it)."

Cole took an enthusiastic interest in the place-names of of the Catskills, usually disapproving of most as dull and repetitious. Up to the day of Cole's visit and for many years afterwards a distinction had been made between "the Overlook Cliff," also known as "the Overlook," and the mountain itself. Cole, as far as is now known, was the first person to set down in writing "the Overlook" as the name of the entire mountain. Later "Overlook Mountain" came into use. Yet to this day old Woodstock people usually do not use that name and call their mountain "the Overlook."

Louis L. Noble, clergyman, poet and later professor at St. Stephen's (now Bard) College, was a member of Cole's party; he is cited in the Oxford English Dictionary as the earliest known user of the noun "overlook" in the sense of a high place with a view. It is likely that from the meeting with Betsy Booth on August 11, 1846 the long list of American Overlook Drives, Roads and so on developed, all stemming from the Woodstock mountain.

Cole's journal of his climb of Overlook is a valuable document to anyone interested in the Woodstock of long ago. He conveys with humor and keen observation an unforgettable picture of a night spent on Overlook. He ends in a burst of surrealist fantasy.

As members of the party unpacked their wagons they realized, as have members of many another similar expedition, that they had brought along far too much gear. Cole itemizes a part of it: blankets, shawls, coats, bread, crackers, butter, cheese, cream, coffee, puddings, tin pails, jugs, cups and saucers, hatchets. Laden with their belongings the six men and six women eventually began climbing "MacDaniel's sunny field toward the woody heights like a band of Pilgrim Peddlars—the bare footed lady good-naturedly volunteered to be our guide & headed the procession 'to the Overlook.' "

There was "a path all the way and then only a few very difficult places, but with our heavy packs, we found it sufficiently laborious. . . ." Upward the twelve climbers struggled, sorted out into a long irregular line, with the men at the head and the women trailing far below. They followed the earliest known trail up Overlook, which led directly up the mountainside from a beginning at the upper glass factory to the plateau where Booth had planned his hotel. When they were at last about half a mile from the summit they reached a spring later named the Minnehaha Spring. From there the party climbed up to its goal—the plateau on which the Overlook Mountain House would stand some thirty years later. Its water, Cole wrote, "was delicious and very, very cold." Soon the men set to work to make camp. By this time Betsy Booth had returned home, probably to do her farm chores and get dinner for her family.

Cole wrote:

We commenced the construction of a Wigwam; Mr. Noble who was dextrous with the axe & skilled in camping out was the chief director—The place chosen for the Camp was a pretty level spot about 50 feet from the precipice. We soon cleared a space of brush wood and stones & in an hour and a half our Wigwam was complete even to the floor which was laid with branches of the Balsam fir laid with care. The floor thus made formed an elastic sufficiently smooth couch. The roof, of course, was of the brush wood we had cut & foliage of various kinds mingled picturesquely together. Our fire was kindled about 15 feet from the entrance of the Wigwam, regard having been paid to the direction of the wind in the erection of our leafy dwelling. Dry wood was dragged in from every side & piled up for the night's use. When the Wigwam was finished & the fire kindled the Ladies who had since then arrived at the height and had been enjoying the prospect from the precipice came in to attend to the domestic duties of making coffee & spreading on the mossy ground in front of the Camp a table cloth on which were placed the viands in tempting order. We sat down with rare appetites and the fare seemed to us more sumptuous than an Emperor's.

Once the sun had set, as Cole recalled, the campers built up their fire by adding large logs "& numerous branches & the gummy foliage of the Balsam crackled in a brilliant flame & the smoke rolled over the tree tops swayed hither & thither by a fitful breeze. . . ." Cole went on to describe the scene in minute detail as if, as was probably the case, he had thoughts of using the camp on the Overlook by night as the theme of a painting:

Illuminated by the fire the scene assumed a strange character. The Wigwam of motley foliage glittered all but in its dark recess in which some indistinct forms were perceived reclining, in front of it were figures in various costumes some with blankets, & some with shawls thrown around them, in every position, standing, sitting and reclining. They caught the glowing light on their faces, hands & vestments according to their dispositions. Every light was clear but the shadows mingled with the shadows of the surrounding forest giving a unity of effect which by daylight did not exist. Every figure united thus with the great night-shadow of the forest was a part of the great Mountain top as the rocks or trees. The trunks of the trees that encircled us in close contiguity stood out in strong relief while those more remote gleamed with a fainter & fainter light as they seemed to retreat into the broad gloom of the great Mountain Forest. The foliage overhead shone in a pale green light & the wayward breezes and the heavens above our magic circle seemed immeasurably deep.

The mountain breezes, Cole wrote, carried the "Music of Human Voices" as the men and women gathered around their fire, sang and "gave performances of various kinds." They prayed (there were three clergymen present) and sang "Gloria in Excelsis," which seemed appropriate enough, for it means glory in the highest. Then "one by one we retired under the cover of the Wigwam and stretched ourselves on its fragrant couch . . . the Ladies took one side and the Gentlemen the other. . . ."

Cole alone among the campers had brought no blanket or shawl to shield him from the chilly mountaintop air, but he had taken along the brown hooded monk's robe which he had brought with him from a visit to Italy. Dressed in the robe Cole continued to observe and listen as the voices of his campmates grew lower and less frequent. A few lingered before the fire, their voices sinking lower and lower. "At length no voice was heard among that merry band which a short time ago had made the mountain ring. . . ."

But Cole was too intent upon absorbing the little world around him to sleep. "I did not sleep, I could not sleep & I had little desire to sleep. I gazed from time to time through the leafy roof at the sky and saw the moon . . . I heard from time to time the heavy breathing of a sleeper & then the restless breeze would rush over the forest with fitful melancholy sound rising & sinking, now afar off like the surges on a distant shore, now making the branches swing about in the dim light of our smouldering fire. . . ."

During the night two of the men rose to replenish the fire. One of them (Mr. Noble) "commenced an Indian song & dance, a death song in tones sometimes low, sometimes higher—then breaking into a wilder cry. Mr. N. in his youth was much among the Indians. . . ." Soon Noble "pretended he saw a Ghost in the shape of an immense leg and foot which came stalking over the mountain & left at each step a drift of snow & yet when he came to look at it it was the impression of an infant's foot & for every toe mark there was left a gem which the winds shaping themselves to invisible hands conveyed away. . . ."

The next morning after breakfast Cole continued in a vein of

258

fantasy like that displayed by Louis Noble during the night. From a point close to the top of Overlook he looked down. This is how he described what he saw and how his imagination interpreted the sight, "The vast valley of the Hudson lies like a Sea before and beneath you while the base of the mountain on which you stand rises abrupt & definitely from its misty bosom & seems like the prow of a stupendous vessel ploughing the great deep. . . ."

After his return home Cole made a rough sketch to give substance to his vision of Overlook as a ship. Cole sometimes painted fantastic landscapes (one called The Titan's Goblet is in the Metropolitan Museum in New York) involving strange juxtapositions of objects and a bizarre playing with scale. It is likely he intended to paint Overlook as a ship sailing into the Hudson Valley, but as far as we know he never carried out any such plan.[6]

His trip to Overlook made Cole an Overlook enthusiast. He had known the Catskills since 1825 and had shared in the belief current in the village of Catskill, where he lived, that the view from the Pine Orchard on which the great Catskill Mountain House stood was the finest in the northeastern United States and perhaps in the world. The success of the Mountain House and the prosperity of Catskill was largely founded on the fame of its view.

But by 1846 Cole changed his mind about that view. He wrote in his journal of Overlook, "With respect to the view from this Mountain peak may say that it appears to me to be far finer than the Pine Orchard, High Peak [now Roundtop] or any other that I have seen . . . the view is sublime."

Cole's opinion was rank heresy. He was regarded by Americans as an authority on the charms of landscape and especially on distant views. Had he made public his opinion of the relative merits of the views from the Pine Orchard and the Overlook Cliff, it would surely have aroused a rush to the Overlook and away from the Pine Orchard. But Cole in 1846 was slipping into a phase of depression with religious overtones. His strength soon ebbed and in February 1848 he died without having made public his thoughts on the view from Overlook.

Louis L. Noble quickly set about preparing a biography and critical study of Cole. The book was planned to include some of Cole's own poetry and prose. It was not published until 1853. In *The Literary World* of January 13, 1849 Noble had hastily published an extract from Cole's journals under the title of "A Visit To South Peak: by the late Thomas Cole." This was a very much edited version of Cole's account of his trip to Overlook in August 1846. Noble omits much of Cole's account, and does nothing to identify South Peak. But he does write of "a continuous precipice called by the mountaineers 'the Overlook,' " and so became the earliest known user of the name in print. An even further abbreviated and more extensively edited version was included in Noble's *Life and Works of Thomas Cole*, again without identifying South Peak.

In October 1847, according to Noble, Cole chose the cliff on Overlook as the culminating point of what he seemed aware would be his last ramble among the Catskills. Cole by that time had ceased keeping a journal and as far as is known left no account of this second visit to the top of Woodstock's Overlook.[7]

By 1847, however, the extent, variety and beauty of the view from the Overlook Cliff was becoming known, in part, it seems likely, because of the inevitable talk about it of the dozen people in the Cole party of 1846. A year or two later William Scobie, manager of the Catskill Mountain House, leased the summit of Overlook for the purpose of building a summer hotel there. Climbers greatly increased. More and more accounts of adventures on Overlook were printed in Hudson Valley newspapers. All used every resource of the English language known to them to extol the view from the Overlook Cliff and the summit.

By the late 1840s climbing Overlook had aquired a certain amount of organization. People reached Woodstock from Kingston and Saugerties by wagon (the trip from Kingston took about two hours) and paused at the old inn in the center of Woodstock to rest and brace themselves with a drink. The inn's owner and manager was George William Snyder, son of the William Snyder who had been Ben Snyder's brother and who had worked on the canoe-making project of 1776. George's brother Frederick had a farm high on the road to what is now known as Mead's and was then the Wide Clove. Occasionally Frederick entertained climbers on their way to the summit.

Most people, however, went as steadily as their horses would permit up the mountain road, through the Wide Clove, and down a bit to what was called in 1850 "a few shattered buildings of a glass factory." These buildings were the base for the attack on Overlook; the present road leading upward from Mead's had not yet been built and the path improved by James Booth led from near the factory up the west side of the mountain. Later climbers followed the course of the present road.

One climber of 1849 tells of having a supper of "the entire luxuries of the house, brown bread, butter and milk." This traveller and his companions slept in a single room, some in beds and some on the floor. The room had a "Dutch fireplace" which was probably one without jambs, consisting of a hearth against the wall with an opening to the chimney directly above. The climbers were up at three in the morning and set off under the guidance of a twelve-year-old boy named Nat, the son of the host of the "Mountain House."

Each climber was equipped with a long stick with which to fend off the rattlesnakes which thrived on Overlook. The guide led the way up the path, carrying a dim lantern of pierced tin with a single candle inside. The reason for so early a start was the hope of watching the sun rising. For years watching the sunrise had been one of the amusements of guests at the Catskill Mountain House. Earlier, Europeans had climbed Swiss peaks for the same purpose.[8]

It is likely that about this time Woodstock boys climbed the mountain on their own and returned with a sense of achievement at having overcome the exciting challenge their town's topography offered. Lovers too probably began climbing the mountain together, unaware of the sexual symbolism which such a climb was later found to have.

Every climber who told in print of his climb ended with the same hope—that a summer hotel would soon appear on Overlook. Scobie's plans failed, but others were always ready to try and to fail, too. It was not until 1871 that the "Summer Mansion" of which James Booth had dreamed was finally opened as the Overlook Mountain House.

25

CIVIL WAR TIMES
AND AFTER

Every inhabited place has one look
and meaning to those who live there and quite another to occasional
visitors. Visitors to Woodstock after the middle of the nineteenth
century often saw the town as a romantic old-fashioned place a good
deal like the Hudson Valley towns to which Washington Irving had
given an Old-World glamor.

In 1878 a reporter for the New York *Herald* wrote of travelling
by stage from the railroad station at West Hurley to Woodstock on his
way to the hotel which by that time had been built on Overlook
Mountain, "The view from West Hurley is very pretty . . . on the
way to the hotel you pass Woodstock, a sleepy little village, and the
road meanders through pleasant farms, abounding with corn, beans
and potatoes on every side. You pass old weather-stained farmhouses
and rugged, ancient and horny-handed farmers as gnarled as their
trees, and little brown children, with great straw hats completely
encasing their heads, picking beans and good-naturedly offering you an
apple as you pass by. The driver stops occasionally to leave an express
package of groceries or other necessaries at a farmhouse and when the
homespun farmer's wife asks him how much she owes him 'for his
trouble' he slyly chucks her under her chin and stealthily squeezes her
hand but does not decline the quarter or half dollar which emerges,
after much slow and hesitating fumbling from her capacious
pocket. . . ." [1]

Other outsiders wrote of the Overlook Cliff and its view in

religious, esthetic and mystical terms. Erastus O. Haven, Methodist Episcopal bishop and Chancellor of Syracuse University, recalled in his *Autobiography* published in 1883 what he had seen and felt on top of Overlook more than thirty years earlier. "Overlook," Haven wrote, "furnishes a view unsurpassed in the world for beauty. . . . I stood there once when a light mist hovered over the land. Before me and beneath me, except just where I stood, was invisibility—one step forward and I should have been with the angels. All at once a slight whisper of wind arose in the forest behind us; the mists broke into forms which contended with each other in an aerial ocean. They rapidly spread and lifted themselves into a canvas stretching from the sky down into interminable depths below me; and from horizon to horizon appeared, in lights and shades superior to those of Raphael, that stupendous panorama. Now it was lost; now it re-appeared, and thus it vanished and came into being again and again, and trembled and moved as if quivering with life. I stood entranced and speechless with my friends, till I ventured to inquire: 'Does that seem to you like a picture or a fact?' 'Like a picture,' they all answered, and I knew the scene was not a dream, but a transparency, exhibited by the great Artist on the clouds." [2]

The quaintness and physical beauty, which so forcibly struck summer visitors to Woodstock, formed only a small part of the town as it appeared to those who lived there the year around. These people had their livings to make, their political lives to manage, their religious and social relationships to maintain, and all the other aspects of the society of their time and town to follow in order to give shape and purpose to their lives.

In 1861 the flow of Woodstock life was interrupted by the beginning of the Civil War. The war's effects colored the town's life until long after the end of the century. Like the people of other Ulster County towns, Woodstock people had felt little enthusiasm for the Civil War. The seceding states were far away and had few perceptible economic or social ties with Ulster. Ulster had been a slave-holding county until 1827, and sympathy for emancipation was not great.

Once the war effort began to be organized recruiters got busy. Agents in Woodstock in 1862 and 1863 were Samuel McDaniel and John Burkitt. The two coaxed and reasoned with young men, especially those known to be chafing under the burden of farm chores and an unexciting existence. Many enlisted in Company H of the 20th Regiment known as the Ulster Guards.

Among those enlisting in the hope of finding a more stirring life was sixteen-year-old "Barney" Hoyt, who lied about his age and became a drummer boy, serving for three years. Black Solomon Peters enlisted and became the cook in a white artillery company. A white Woodstock man became sutler (he ran the shop at which soldiers bought necessities and luxuries) in a black regiment. Soldiers were paid very little and were often unable to buy their basic necessities. Some had families back home who had to rely on charity or even go to the poorhouse.[3]

The war as wars always do brought problems to those who stayed at home. The prices of food and clothing doubled. "Crust coffee," made from darkened crusts of bread, became common. The poor lit their homes with a lamp consisting of a saucer of fat with a bit of rag by way of a wick. With so many men gone off to war there was a labor shortage. Wearing pants like their men, some Woodstock women took over plowing and harvesting.

The Woodstock tannery, which had burned down in the late 1840s, was rebuilt, becoming a source of considerable profit to its owner, Orson Vandevoort, as the demand for leather for war purposes soared. When the nation's first income tax was imposed Vandervoort paid more than anyone else in town (only five Woodstock men had sufficient incomes to be obliged to pay any tax at all); his income with exemptions deducted was $1150 and his tax was three per cent.[4]

The war created increased demand for the gunpowder made over the Woodstock line in High Woods and Sawkill and sent Woodstock boys gathering and barking alder stems, used in making powder. Woodstock coopers made powder kegs. A shortage of cash caused the issue of vast quantities of "shinplasters" (fractional paper money with face values of less than a dollar and actual values, often enough, of nothing at all).

In Woodstock as in other towns people organized to give what help they could to their soldiers and their families. A Ladies Relief Society and an Auxiliary came into being and sponsored drives aimed at sending warm clothing, food and other necessities to the men in the army. Women knitted sweaters and mittens. Children too knitted as soon as they were able to manage knitting needles.

The children also gathered wild strawberries and blackberries, which their mothers dried or used in making syrups thought useful in treating the digestive ailments so prevalent in army camps. Betsy Booth MacDaniel up on her mountain farm kept busy making cholera syrup and other remedies and shipping them to her sons at the front.

A successful "Sanitary Fair" was held at the Dutch Reformed Church.

Ever-higher casualties and a widening of the scope of the war caused President Lincoln to resort to conscription early in 1863. Woodstock's quota of men to be drafted was set at 187; by way of comparison Kingston, with its much larger population, had a quota of 1703. Under the new system a drafted man might pay for a substitute. "Substitute brokers" made their livings supplying the demand, usually with poor immigrants recently arrived in New York. Units of government paid increased bounties to men who enlisted voluntarily. The bounties varied. In Woodstock they were three hundred to three hundred fifty dollars in 1863. A man might apply his bounty rights against the cost of a substitute.

The war years were a time of anxiety in Woodstock. No one knew when he might learn of the death or injury of a son, a brother or a neighbor. Some families were worse off in this way than others, for the draft and enlistment sometimes took three or four men from one family and left another untouched. Toward the end of the war a wave of sympathy was touched off for Jonas and Margaret Whispell of Woodstock after it was reported that with seven sons in the service two more had been taken by the final draft early in 1865. The report was exaggerated—the total of the sons of Jonas and Margaret as far as official records' go came to six. One, Abram, died of disease while in the army. His name is inscribed on the war memorial on the Woodstock Village Green.[5]

Aaron Longyear, who like Abram Whispell succumbed to the fevers which were so much a plague of Civil War camps, is not named on the memorial. Two of the lively letters which Aaron wrote to his sister, Mrs. Peter William Risely of Bearsville, were published by the Woodstock Historical Society in the 1930s. Aaron told of the battles in which he had taken part. He told of meeting Woodstock friends and gave many details of army life.

On September 18, 1862 he wrote, "We are again under marching orders ready to start at a moments notice for the battle front in Maryland. We may be called on at any moment perhaps now while I am writing the message is coming. I say let it come and we will do all we can to protect the stars and stripes and if we fall we have the consolation of doing our duty, and all we ask for those at Home is their prayers for our success, and I think God will crown us with success and our enemies fly before us in confusion. . . ." The simple patriotic and religious feeling reflected in Aaron's phrases are touching. They are very different from anything written home by Woodstock soldiers of more recent times.[6]

Once the Civil War was over and Woodstock soldiers had returned home life went on much as before, though with a few more significant changes. The war had stimulated inventiveness and made available labor-saving devices in the home and on the farm. Apple-peelers and dog- or sheep-operated churns began slowly to appear in Woodstock. Farmers turned to using the new horse-drawn harvesting and threshing machines. The war had also given an incentive to preserving foods in tin cans. After a period of hesitation canned foods began to form a part of the Woodstock diet.

Returned soldiers were encouraged at first to talk by the hour about their battles and adventures. Many told stirring tales. Aaron Newkirk Risely, for example, had seen service at the battles of Fredericksburg, Chancellorsville and Gettysburg. He had spent months in Libby and Belle Isle prisons after capture near James City; he had been shifted to several other prisons, including that at Andersonville. When released at war's end Risely weighed but 90 pounds. He recovered his health and strength and lived an unusually active life until his death in 1910.

Egbert Lewis had taken part in an even longer list of battles— those of Fredericksburg, Chancellorsville, Gettysburg, Wapping Heights, Spottsylvania, Wilderness and many others. But he did not return to his home town. He died around the time General Robert E. Lee surrendered.

Civil War veterans played an important role in politics on many levels. Their Grand Army of the Republic (a precursor of the American Legion) was predominantly Republican and helped elect candidates in Woodstock as in many other places. Ill and injured veterans remained for a long time to remind their neighbors of the horrors of war. Peter L. Shultis of "Bears Ville" enlisted in the army when he was twenty-two; a year and a half later he was discharged because of illness he had contracted in camp. Shultis was never well again and for the three years of his life before his death in 1884 "he could not as much as get himself a drink only as it was handed to him. . . . No person can describe his terrible sufferings toward the last."

John Schoonmaker turned his Civil War service to account. Aboard a large and fancy wagon which he had painted himself he toured mountain resorts presenting programs about the Civil War as well as a version of *Uncle Tom's Cabin*. He used a Phantasmagoria, a magic lantern which could give an effect of motion to the glass-slide images projected on the screen. Invented many years earlier, the Phantasmagoria was enjoying a revival in the United States as Schoonmaker set out on his tour in the 1880s.

Until the 1930s a few more fortunate Civil War veterans were picturesque features of Woodstock life. One was John Whitbeck Davis, member of a well-known family of blacksmiths. Like Aaron Newkirk Risely, Davis had taken part in many battles and had been imprisoned in Andersonville, Georgia. Barney Hoyt was still active as a carpenter in the 1920s.[7]

Thanks to a member of the Snyder family, which had played so memorable a past in early Woodstock life, many details of the town and its people between 1850 and 1880 have been preserved. Bide or Byron Snyder is described by those who still remember him as "thoughtful" or "scholarly." He lived behind what had been the Krack house. As Woodstock's art colony arrived and grew he made carved mottoes and picture frames in his woodworking shop and later typed manuscripts. In 1924 he set down many keen observations of the traditions and life in his childhood and youth (he was born as the Civil War neared its end) for the Woodstock *Weekly*, the town's first newspaper.

When the store of his father, Edgar, became a telegraph office with a line running to the railroad station at West Hurley and up the mountain to the Overlook Mountain House, Bide learned the Morse code and became the Western Union operator at Woodstock. Later he helped manage the store. Later he became the caretaker of the Woodstock Artists Association's gallery after it was built in 1923.

Snyder's recollections stress the sides of local life of the past which were of interest to the *Weekly's* editor, and so they omitted a good deal. Yet when Snyder's powers of observation and recollection were at their keenest, he contributed an invaluable picture of the many sides of life in Woodstock. With some rearrangement and editing, his views are worth quoting in detail:

> The store, the tavern and the blacksmith shop were the social centers of the town. The country store at Woodstock would be a curiosity. . . . There were two hotels or taverns as they were called. . . . In the winter the town 'holed up.' The so-called roads were blocked with snow for months. In the spring they were merely seas of mud.
> There was an old legend of a tin peddler, an extinct race who attempted to come to Woodstock in the spring. He had just crossed the little bridge below

the schoolhouse [on the site of the present Grand Union] when man, horse, wagon and tinsmith sank out of sight in the mud. I have heard some of the oldtimers solemnly swear that on certain days one could distinctly hear the rattle of tinware every time a horse and wagon passed over the spot. Be that true or not there were days and days when the frost was going out in the spring that no one could get to Kingston on account of the hub-deep mud.

There were no places of amusement and the store was a sort of club room and general meeting place (for that matter it is yet) for the men who had to stay at home or go to the store. They seldom stayed home. People did not go to the store to do their trading and then go right back. They 'sot around' and visited. The store keeper would go to New York every fall and lay in a stock of goods to last until navigation on the Hudson opened up in the spring. There were no railroads and it took three or four days to make the trip by boat and buy the goods.

During the winter . . . they had a mail once a week, if it could get through. If it didn't come one week it probably would the next and no one was worried. The stores did not carry any canned goods like vegetables, fish, fruit etc. You couldn't take your pick of a dozen kinds of breakfast foods. There was only one breakfast food and that was buckwheat cakes. No packages of fancy cakes or crackers. Soda crackers came in barrels and toward spring they might become a trifle stale but nobody noticed it. When you wanted crackers the clerk would shoo the cat out of the barrel and dig out all you wanted at five cents a pound. . . . Codfish came in big bales of about 100 pounds. They were not the little things that masquerade under the name of cod that we buy now, but great lusty fish that must have weighed from ten to twenty pounds each. The bales were tied with tarred rope and piled in heaps on the floor. That didn't make any difference as there were no germs in those days, at least we never heard of them. Smoked halibut was cheap, good and in great demand. Bread was not sold. You baked it at home.

Tomatoes were not thought fit to eat, they were considered 'pizen.' Every farmer raised his own stuff and the 'women folks' did it up. They had plenty of honey, maple sugar and apple butter . . . they would boil down a barrel or two of cider and cook certain kinds of apples in it. The art of making it has been lost. . . . Granulated sugar was not used much. They had what was known as soft white, almost as white as granulated but soft, and two or three grades of brown sugar. When you asked for sugar the clerk did not put it in a bag. He weighed it out and slid it on a sheet of coarse, brown, straw paper and deftly did it up in a neat package. If you happened to be hungry while shopping you simply sliced off a piece of cheese or took a couple of red herring and never thought of paying for it. If you wanted a smoke, why a box of clay pipes and another of tobacco always stood on the counter. Matches were not free, as they were expensive. Three cents for a box of about fifty.

Molasses . . . was bought by the hogshead. There were generally three of these big hogsheads barrels holding sixty-three gallons or more. One of Porto Rico, one of black strap and one of real New Orleans. The best New Orleans molasses you can get now bears only a faint resemblance to the delicious, golden sugary nectar once known as extra fancy N. O. . . . pure maple sugar was worth from eight to twelve cents a pound.

Oysters were plentiful and cheap, everybody ate them. Clams cost from thirty to forty cents a hundred. After the opening of the shad season everybody lived on fish. You could buy a big roe shad, the very biggest full of eggs, for twenty-five cents. . . . Herring were so cheap and plentiful that the farmers would go to the Hudson river and when the nets were drawn buy a wagon load for two dollars . . . they would drop a fish in each hill of corn. . . . Sturgeon meat . . . was sold by the chunk. As big a chunk as you wanted for ten cents.

The stores carried other staple, everyday articles, such as shoe pegs [wooden pegs used in making shoes], hoop skirts, boot jacks, bed cords [these ropes, criss-crossed, took the place of bed springs], and many other things that are now forgotten. In the fall they would stock up with heavy, stiff, shapeless cowhide boots. Nearly every man and boy wore them. You could not get them off without a boot jack. The women's shoes were just about as heavy and shapeless but not quite so stiff. . . . When women first wore rubbers they were a sight. They looked as though they had two rubber bags tied around their feet. Snuff was another best seller and came in big stone jars. A storekeeper might let the stock of tea or coffee run low but woe betide him if he got out of snuff. The women would get after him.

The old tavern was a long, low, rambling building or rather a collection of buildings, all of different shapes and heights, connected with an immense old barn and cider mill. [This was the tavern torn down by William Brinkerhoff in 1869]. . . . The big bar room took up all the west end of the building and was a general meeting place for the whole town. My memory is rather hazy but I can recall the long tables made of heavy planks, the great wood stove that stood in the center with a copper boiler for hot water on top. On the north side of the outside of the building was a blank wall and this was covered with large circus posters, highly colored. . . . I can only recall two of them. One was a picture of the most terrible and ferocious hippopotamus the world had ever seen. His great yawning mouth could easily hold a piano . . . the other was a rhinocerous. . . .

The tavern did a good business as there were always transients. Teams coming down from Delaware County with butter, bark for the tanneries, cord wood. . . . A night's lodging with a hearty supper and breakfast and a couple of drinks cost four shillings [50 cents]. . . . Rye, Bourbon and apple jack cost three cents a glass holding a little over half a teacup. Gin, Santa Cruz and Jamaica Rum . . . cost six cents a drink. Brandy was a rich man's drink costing from six to ten cents a glass. . . . Lager beer was not in use, at least not in the country. There was a strong, heavy ale, rich and wholesome. You could see the hop leaves floating in the glass. . . .

Every election time things would liven up at the tavern. The candidates would come in. . . . They had a novel way of drawing a crowd. When a candidate would appear, the landlord would go out and ring a big farm bell that hung in front. In a very short time the entire male population would be lined up in front of the bar, the men were treated to free drinks by the candidate as a reward for listening to his pitch.

Election day was an exciting day. There was only one poll and the entire town voted at one or the other of the two hotels. About two o'clock in the afternoon a good share of the voters would be pie-eyed, and by night there would be one grand glorious free for all fight. We had, as did every other town in Ulster, several champions. And every election day they would fight it out. If a man got licked one election day he would nurse his grudge until the next one and try again. Votes were bought openly and the poll worker who got hold of a floater [a man who was entitled by law to vote] would never let go his arm until the ballot was safely in the box. I have seen a worker give a man a ticket and hold him tightly by the wrist until he handed it in. Sometimes two rival workers would grab the same man, then there would be a struggle until one or the other landed him. Often the men from back in the mountains would stay two or three days after election until they got over their sprees. . . .

As a boy in the "village" of Woodstock (properly it was a mere hamlet, as it still is) Bide Snyder met the odd characters who hung around the taverns or lounged in the spring sunshine against the sunny sides of buildings. These people often carried down from an earlier day a good deal of folklore which Bide and his friends could not decide whether to believe. Witchcraft was sometimes the subject of reminiscing by the idle oldtimers. Bide wrote of this:

> Spooks and witches were very prevalent when I was a boy. I never saw any myself, but many a time I have listened open mouthed to the blood curdling yarns of a certain old fellow who had personal encounters with dozens of them. At least he said so and we boys implicitly believed him. He had a deep scar on his shoulder that he said had been inflicted by an ugly old witch who had changed herself into a wild cat and jumped on him as he was on his way home. Of course we believed it, for there was the scar to prove it. The only way you could shoot a witch was by shooting the animal she had turned herself into with a silver bullet. He said he had almost enough silver to make one, and if he had only three silver dimes more, he could melt it up and make a bullet and feel safe. We saved up our pennies until we had thirty cents which we exchanged for three dimes and gave them to him. I never heard if he killed the witch or not, but several hours after we left he was pretty well stewed. Thirty cents would do it in those days.

Snyder recalled for the Woodstock *Weekly* many details of former occupations, of schools and the life of children, of oldtime foods and other aspects of Woodstock life during his boyhood:

> Forty or fifty years ago the town had almost as many people as it has now [1924], except in summer. There were not so many houses but the families were much larger. In Lewis Hollow alone there were about seventy people. Two families alone had thirty-four members. Now there are less than a dozen there and they are all artists. When the old tannery was running there were between thirty and forty men employed in the plant and as many more in the bark woods. They nearly all had big families. The blue stone quarries gave work to between seventy-five and a hundred men. Nearly every day in the winter when the roads were open long strings of teams would daily pass through the village drawing cord wood to the brick yards [of the Hudson Valley].
> There were almost, if not quite, as many children in the old stone school house [at the corner of Route 212 and Pine Grove Avenue]. During the winter months we had men teachers. In those days discipline had to be maintained by brute force and the main qualification of a teacher was his ability to lick the big boys. It often required several fights before his supremacy was established. Sometimes the physical prowess of the teacher was not equal to that of the older scholars and he had to retire. It was useless to try to rule by moral force. We had no morals. [In the summer when the big boys were required for farm work women taught the school.] There was only one room and about sixty pupils. It was heated by an antiquated, big box stove. This stove would be kept nearly red hot and if you sat near it one side of you would be roasted. If away

270

from it you would freeze. On cold days the teacher would keep changing our seats, sort of stirring us around so that we would only half freeze or half roast. . . .

Skating was a great sport. We had places to skate then. Our skates were nothing like the modern ones. They were made of wood with a steel runner. In the heel of each skate was a screw. You bored a hole in the heel of your boot (we only wore shoes Sundays) with a gimlet and then turned the skate around several times until it was screwed up. Then it was fastened more or less securely with straps. Your boots would get wet and freeze stiff. The straps would be coated thickly with ice and you couldn't get your skates off and you would have to hobble home and thaw them out.

There were two fine ponds. They are gone now. Just back of Herrick's [the mansard-roofed building later the Tannery Brook Motel] was Delameter's pond and sawmill. The old dam is all gone and the pond is only a brooklet. The water reached to the upper end of the old tannery. The tannery is gone but the ruins are still there [below the waterfall near the bridge which takes Tinker Street over the Tannery Brook]. The other pond began at a dam near Larry Elwyn's [just above the waterfall]. . . . It reached up back of the Art Gallery [of the Woodstock Art Association]. There was another just back of Sandwich Inn [the Inn stood on the Rock City Road opposite the cemetery]. . . .

The days when Dutch was still spoken in Woodstock and when Dutch recipes were followed by housewives were recalled by Snyder, and he drew a whimsically exaggerated picture of the event known as a "donation supper."

Nearly everybody spoke more or less Dutch when the town was first settled. I have heard often that services were held once a month in that language in the Reformed Church. Now the tongue of the great grand parents of most of us is forgotten. The names of some of the good things they had to eat are still in use. 'Oley Keuks,' I know that is not spelled right but who the devil can spell Dutch anyhow. They were a kind of big fat doughnut, about the size of a base ball, full of raisins and spices and covered with powdered sugar. Another great dish that deserves honorable mention was made of beef cut in small pieces and sewed up in tripe. They looked like small foot balls. After cooking, the balls were put in a big jar and vinegar poured over them and pressed down with a heavy stone until they were partly flattened. No one would take the trouble to clean a tripe and make them now. So they too have passed into oblivion. They had an unpronouncable and unspellable name. Sounded something like 'rolejos,' but that's not it [the name in New York State Dutch was 'rolletjes'].

Every housewife prided herself in 'putting up stuff,' her cellar was full of cans, jars and tubs of preserves and pickles. Indeed a woman's social standing was measured in some degree by the number of different kinds of 'sass' she had on the table when company came.

The church donation was an important social event. Theoretically the members of the church were to meet at the parsonage, donate food etc. and hold a public supper. The money taken in from the supper, to be presented to the minister. The way it worked out was something like this: the hungry crowd would eat up all the stuff they brought and everything else in the house. Then the young folks would romp and play games in every room, leaving the house, furniture, beds etc. a tangled mess of wreckage that took days to straighten out. What little money was taken in for the supper would not pay for the damage.

Finally Bide Snyder mentioned what was probably the last stand of the primeval Woodstock forest to remain close to the social and business center of the town. "Just back of the cemetery was [the] Judge's woods. The giant pines and oaks grew so thickly that it seemed like twilight. Not a trace of those dark, solemn grand old woods is left." [8]

The Judge's woods, named for their owner, Judge Jonathan Hasbrouck, stood on the edge of his five-hundred-acre tract. Just when these woods were lumbered is not known but it was probably in the 1870s. And as this last bit of easily accessible original forest fell, so ended the period when frontier ways still lingered on as part of life in Woodstock.

26

THE OVERLOOK MOUNTAIN HOUSE IS BUILT

By the 1850s something of a boom began to strike places in America to which the richer classes were going to escape summer heat, enjoy a change of scene and feel the excitement of being in the midst of romantic and picturesque views of nature. Along the Atlantic Coast and among the mountains new resorts were joining older ones such as Newport and the Catskill Mountain House. Spas like Saratoga were expanding enormously. After Charles L. Beach bought the Catskill Mountain House in 1846 the place entered three decades of prosperity.

It was inevitable that thoughts of establishing competitive establishments entered many heads. And it was inevitable that the top of Overlook Mountain, with its immense view, its nearby lake and its elevation of a thousand feet above the Pine Orchard on which Charles L. Beach was doing business should become the logical spot to set a rival summer hotel. And it was equally logical that the town of Woodstock at the foot of Overlook should draw summer boarders to its farmhouses and roadside inns.

The town had much to offer. It was now showing the result of the care for buildings, fields and the roadside which followed the end of the Livingston domination. It had excellent trout streams, brooks, waterfalls and lakes. And above all it had Overlook Mountain. Boarders saw the mountain as a central fact of Woodstock. Climbing it was the favorite goal of their excursions. The Overlook Cliff with its view and its fine spring not too far away became the scene of innumerable picnics.

The expectation that before long an elegant hotel would rise close to Overlook's summit gave the whole town of Woodstock the cheerful air that comes with the feeling that prosperity lies just ahead. With a hotel on the mountain at which the rich, the famous and the socially prominent might gather as they did at the Catskill Mountain House, people with less money would be sure to patronize the farm boarding houses and inns down below. With a hotel on the mountain Woodstock's future as a thriving summer resort would be assured. Without it the town would never achieve the first rank of summer resorts.

It was not only in Woodstock that people looked with hope toward Overlook Mountain. In Kingston there was much cheerful talk of "Kingston as a summer retreat." There was talk of building a fine Kingston hotel to cooperate with one on Overlook. Other places on the Hudson River were sharing in the glamor which had hung over the valley ever since Washington Irving back in 1819 had touched the river and the Catskills with magic. Now Kingston businessmen saw no good reason why they might not capture Overlook Mountain as a Kingston attraction and build the kind of mutually profitable relationship which Charles L. Beach had established with the village of Catskill.

Woodstock and Kingston people were pleased when English-born painter and travel writer T. A. Richards praised Overlook Mountain (under its old name of South Peak) in 1854 in the respected pages of the new monthly *Harper's Magazine*. "A monarch among these hills," Richards wrote, "is South Peak, with its crown lifted four thousand feet toward Heaven. It is full of remarkable localities, each enwrapt in legendary lore. Not the least lovely of its possessions is a gentle lake, perched in solitude on its summit. . . ."

Richards exaggerated the height of Overlook. He lifted Schue's Pond about a thousand feet in the air in order to put it on the mountaintop. Yet the mention of the mountain in so widely read a publication as *Harper's* stirred Kingston and Woodstock to new heights of hopefulness. And it encouraged more and more people to climb the mountain and see for themselves its "remarkable localities."[1]

One climber wrote, "We ventured to the edge of a huge rock weighing more than a thousand tons, and yet resting upon one not a thousandth part as large, as a giant would rest upon the bosom of a babe, and looked down into the abyss below. It was but for a moment, as our head reeled, and we staggered back . . . we next visited the Cave letting our bodies down between rocks weighing millions of pounds each, looking as if some terrible convulsion of Nature had parted them, and we peered into the cavern for a moment, and then hurried back as the cold air sent a chill through our whole frame. We next visited a rock known as the 'King of the Overlook'; a fine old gentleman, projecting many feet over the precipice, and thus he has slumbered for many generations, defying the elements, and with none to dispute his title." So wrote the climber in the Kingston *Democratic Journal* of August 16, 1865.

The view from the summit rock and the Overlook Cliff continued to be praised. It was declared the finest in the Catskills, in the state, in the nation and perhaps even in the world. One climber of the 1850s compared the view from the Overlook Cliff to that from Mount Nebo in the Holy Land—it was from Mount Nebo that Moses had first looked down over the Promised Land. The Hudson as seen from Overlook seemed to this observer to suggest the Holy Land even more strongly by the way it appeared to divide in the manner of the Jordan.[2]

The Fourth of July was a favorite day for making a pilgrimage to Overlook's summit and looking out, as one man wrote in the Saugerties *Telegraph*, at "the land of the free and the home of the brave; this writer had climbed the mountain on July 4, 1849 to celebrate the seventy-third anniversary of independence . . . from this natural observatory. . . ." To an American awakened to the glories of his native landscape by the painters and poets of his time, the view from the summit of Overlook at the panorama of settlements, villages, forests, farms, lakes, rivers and mountains produced a mighty swell of patriotic emotion. Bonfires by night and years later fireworks on Overlook helped the mountain share in the great annual patriotic celebration of July 4.[3]

Rumors that a hotel was about to crown the mountain never ceased. This man or that, a corporation of New York City men or of Kingston or Woodstock men was about to begin construction at any moment. Sometimes there was truth in these tales. Kingston steamboat man Nicholas Elmendorf was the hero in 1855. He was negotiating to buy the top of Overlook and planning to build a magnificent hotel there. Unfortunately the mid-1850s were a time of nationwide economic travail and Elmendorf developed money troubles. The praise which had been lavished upon him turned to ridicule as the Ulster sheriff got on his trail.

The Rondout *Courier's* tongue-in-cheek commentary on the

Overlook hotel mania led up to the announcement that at long last a man who was the real thing had taken hold of Overlook and was on the verge of making a hotel materialize in a splendid form on the mountaintop. He was Robert Livingston Pell, descendant of upper-class colonial families, art lover, graduate of Harvard, owner of Pelham Farm on the Hudson River—a farm superior to any other gentleman's farm in the entire state. Pell proposed, the *Courier* stated, to build his hotel "on the best spot of the whole mountain range, commanding the finest view and attainable by a pleasant route. . . ."

Pell had no intention, said the *Courier*, of trying to put Charles L. Beach's Catskill Mountain House out of business. Yet it told a whimsical anecdote purporting to demonstrate that Overlook had been Beach's first choice for a mountain hotel because it offered a far better site than the Pine Orchard. He had built on the Pine Orchard, it was reported, out of pity for the people of the village of Catskill. Nicholas Elmendorf, the *Courier* said, would have built his hotel on Overlook but for the fact that he couldn't widen and dredge the Sawkill in order to make it possible for his steamboat, the *Alida*, to discharge passengers at the base of Overlook. This typical newspaper humor of the day reveals a healthy reaction of at least some disappointed Overlook Hotel buffs.[4]

As talk of a hotel on the mountain went on, settlement moved up Overlook and the ridges which buttress it. By 1855 Henry Fuller had bought land within the Wide Clove. He cleared a few acres and built a small and rough dwelling. Up to this point the MacDaniels and Snyders had a virtual monopoly of caring for the horses of climbers and giving the climbers themselves meals and a place to sleep. Now Fuller, whose place at the beginning of the present road up the mountain from Mead's, began also to take care of climbers' horses and occasionally give climbers sleeping space on his floor. He did not act as a guide, however. When climbers asked him to help them keep to the rough trail up Overlook, Fuller would point in the general direction of the trail's beginning and say, "Follow the plainest path." [5]

While existing American summer hotels did very well indeed when the Civil War came, interest rates were too high and the demand for capital for war purposes was too strong to allow the building of new hotels. Parties from Kingston, Saugerties and Woodstock climbed Overlook in greater numbers than ever as the Civil War raged. One party of seventeen Kingstonians made the climb in 1861 with a Woodstock minister who was something of an expert on the sights of Overlook as guide. When the war ended in 1865 it at once again became possible to think seriously of a hotel on Overlook.

Something else gave added vigor to the hopes of Woodstock people. Surveys were being made that year for a railroad planned at first to connect Rondout and Oswego. One survey sent the line right through Woodstock and up the Esopus Valley at The Corner or Mount Tremper. A "Railroad meeting" chaired by Justice of the Peace Jacob Happy was held. Resolutions were passed recommending the Woodstock route as the easiest and cheapest to build and calling upon members of the State Legislature to help because those Woodstock people "who are to be benefitted by this road must rely upon themselves and not upon foreign capital for its construction."

Woodstock farmers and shopkeepers could certainly expect to benefit from the proposed railroad. But it was felt the greatest beneficiary would surely be an Overlook Mountain House. A station at the base of the mountain would be built to handle building materials, guests, food and all the many other supplies needed to run the project. It is no wonder, then, that talk of a hotel on Overlook took on a more realistic quality and that definite plans began to be made.[6]

In 1863 the MacDaniel family, so long associated with Overlook, opened their new farmhouse not far to the southwest of the Wide Clove to summer boarders. Perhaps stirred by the visions of local prosperity brought on by the possibility of a railroad, George Mead of Kingston bought the Fuller place in 1865 and decided to build a "new and commodius" boardinghouse on his land in the Clove. Until a hotel could be built on the mountaintop, Mead's place could function as a base for those who wanted to climb or explore Overlook and visit Shue's Pond. Mead, a native of Hartford, Connecticut, had been in the business of silverplating metal parts of horse harnesses in Kingston.

On August 8, 1865 Mead opened his "Red House," as people called it from its color, and promised to furnish "refreshments of all kinds and stables for horses" and to leave "nothing undone by the proprietor to render the stay of his guests pleasant and agreable." Mead made an especial appeal to fishermen whom he assured "would find plenty of sport with the speckled finny tribe in the vicinity of this house."

The Rondout and Oswego Railroad, later to become the Ulster and Delaware, bypassed Woodstock after all. The town had to make do with a station at West Hurley from which nine miles of road would lead to the site of the proposed Overlook Mountain House.

Boardinghouses in Lake Hill and Wittenberg were able to use the station at Mount Pleasant. Though this was not what prospective Overlook Mountain House developers had dreamed of, it still gave them an advantage over the Catskill Mountain House, which had no railroad so close. And there was encouraging talk of a branch line shooting out from West Hurley to Woodstock and Overlook.

In 1869 New York capitalists led by Isaac N. Secor were definitely planning a hotel on Overlook. Down in the hamlet of Woodstock preparations for a new life as a fashionable summer resort got under way. William Brinkerhoff, who had followed G. W. Snyder as owner and host of the old Woodstock Inn, in May 1869 tore down the picturesque group of buildings which had stood on the hamlet's most conspicuous corner since before the Revolution and built a fine new hotel, thirty-six by seventy-six feet in size, three stories high and with rooms to accommodate in comfort seventy-five to one hundred guests. A broad two-story verandah faced the street.

A road began to be built from the Wide Clove to a spot next to the copious spring on the plateau on Overlook. There the excavations for the hotel foundations were made. Woodstock people spruced up their houses, repaired fences and roads, planted roadside trees and added rooms to accommodate boarders in their houses. Farmers added to their flocks of chickens and pigs in order to be ready to cope with a notable increase in business. Edgar Snyder talked of an addition to his store and stocked goods most likely to be in demand by summer people.

Then what appeared to some to be the bad luck which had haunted Overlook Mountain ever since it had first been dreamed of as the site of a hotel struck another blow. Isaac N. Secor unexpectedly died in the prime of life. His executors were unwilling to proceed with Secor's plans for Overlook.

By this time there was no drawing back. Though there was a period of shock in Woodstock it soon became apparent that nothing could stop the placing of a hotel on Overlook. Many previous attempts, notably those of Scobie, Pell, Elmendorf and Secor, had been powered by outside people and capital. Now Woodstock people with a few from outside took over Secor's three hundred acres on top of Overlook. They took over the plans for a hotel building and the right of way for a road to the public highway at "The Halfway House," as Mead's was called for a while.

The Woodstock Overlook Mountain House Company was formed

in February 1870 "to build and conduct a hotel on the Woodstock Mountain at or near a place called The Overlook." Woodstock people took the lead in buying the stock issue of 400 shares totalling $40,000. The town had come a long way since its days of domination by leases for three lives and now had an upper class of prosperous people.

William W. Brinkerhoff bought $2500 worth of hotel stock. Andrew Risely, farmer on the Bearsville Flats, bought $1000 worth. Local butcher Cornelius Hogan put in $500, farmer Henry Happy $100. Captain Charles H. Krack, a legal resident of Woodstock and the assemblyman of the district, invested $1000. His career had been picturesque and extraordinary, including army service in Germany in his youth, managing a Georgia plantation, operating a New York hotel, exploring in the West, and making a fortune running an elaborate floating bathhouse anchored in the East River off Grand Street.

A. Bruyn Hasbrouck, the son of Judge Jonathan Hasbrouck, who had played an influential part in Woodstock affairs for many years although living in Kingston with occasional visits to Woodstock, invested $500. Bruyn Hasbrouck had been president of Rutgers College in New Jersey through the 1840s and owned his father's former land in Woodstock. Also among Kingston shareholders were the Van Deusen brothers, who stipulated that the $200 they invested was to be "payable in paints and oils used on the building."

Edgar Snyder, a Woodstock shareholder and trustee of the corporation, ran a big general store in Woodstock and was the local telegraph agent. When the Democrats captured the White House, he became Woodstock's postmaster. The Woodstock investors apparently expected the Overlook House to stimulate business and return good profits in trade to those who invested.

Lewis B. Van Wagonen, architect-builder of Kingston, had drawn the plans for a hotel for Secor and had cut trees and prepared lumber. Van Wagonen now used the plans and materials prepared for Secor. The mansard-roofed building, about 36 by 100 feet, two and a half stories high, amply verandahed and with wings 30 by 60 feet each, began to rise. The building was planned to take care of 150 guests in gas-lighted, steam-heated, wall-to-wall-carpeted comfort.[7]

John E. Lasher, manager of Rondout's favorably-known Mansion House, leased the hotel and began planning to furnish and operate it. Lasher, who had been brought up in Woodstock, was a grandson of Philip Bonesteel, a pioneer Woodstock innkeeper. His presence added to the conviction that the new hotel would be almost entirely a Woodstock show.

As work on the hotel proceeded Lasher saw to it that publicity stories about the place flooded the Hudson Valley. Charles L. Beach of the Catskill Mountain House, one story went, was in an agony of apprehension lest the new and more glorious hotel lure away his guests. He had offered the Overlook stockholders double the amount of their investment if they would only order work on the building stopped. The stockholders had curtly refused. They believed they knew a good thing when they had one.

Lasher's publicity campaign was all too successful. It attracted hordes of "curiosity seekers" who benefitted Woodstock tavernkeepers and innkeepers but gave Lasher endless trouble. It was all very well for Woodstock people to stare in wonder at the wagonloads of black walnut sofas, marble-topped tables and flowered carpeting as these creaked their way up Mill Hill Road, past the Brinkerhoff House and so on up the Rock City Road to the top of Overlook. But it as quite another thing when visitors to Overlook carved their initials on hotel woodwork, stepped on freshly varnished floors, and made a general nuisance of themselves.

Three thousand of these people were said to have swarmed up Overlook in the summer of 1870. Lasher turned the invasion to what account he could by selling the trippers food at a stand improvised in the barn and by converting one of the stalls in the barn into a bar. He even put some of them up for the night in the unfinished hotel. The MacDaniels' Cold Spring House and Mead's in the Wide Clove overflowed with boarders that summer. New York City people and a number of artists were among the guests.

William Brinkerhoff spruced up his inn to enable it to serve as a kind of annex to the hotel above. Guests bound for the big hotel might pause for a drink, a rest or a meal before proceeding up the mountain. Some who could not afford the rates of the Overlook Mountain House might settle down for a week or two. Brinkerhoff commissioned Lewis B. Van Wagonen to build him an imposing mansion beside his hotel echoing the design of the hotel on the mountain so closely as to appear a kind of entrance lodge to the hotel's domain. The house could serve not only as Brinkerhoff's residence but as a place to receive distinguished guests.

It was the handsomest dwelling in all the hamlet. Edgar Snyder planned a similar residence beside the Dutch Reformed church. Van

Wagonen, as was his custom, "got out and dressed the timber " for the Snyder house, which was not completed until 1875.

As the hotel on Overlook took shape many changes appeared in Woodstock. The old Lutheran church was renovated, a new Methodist church was built in Bristol, not yet known as Shady. About this time Captain Krack built a large cube-shaped structure across the Rock City Road from the Brinkerhoff House. There was a cupola on top and verandahs upstairs and down on two sides. Krack planned the building to be used as a hotel, taking in summer boarders and transients alike. With the appearance of these new buildings in the heart of Woodstock and the remodelling of others, Woodstock seemed transformed from a center for farm life to an ambitious summer resort.[8]

The Overlook Mountain House (Woodstock had been dropped from the name) opened officially on June 15, 1871. It was a great day for Woodstock. But nature refused to cooperate. Fog hung low on the mountain, and moisture dripped from the hotel. Much of the public stayed away. The electric telegraph refused to work, the acetylene gas did likewise.

But there were many innovations for visitors to wonder at. Instead of the traditional long dining tables at which guests were seated as they chose and served themselves from platters placed on the tables by waiters, there were small round tables to which guests were assigned. The waiters were young black men, veterans of the Civil War and students at Lincoln University in Pennsylvania. Each table had a menu (the first in any hotel in the Catskills) and each guest's waiter courteously helped him make his choice and served him individually.

All this many Woodstock people took on trust, for all they saw as they looked up at their mountain on the great day was an impenetrable gray mass of cloud. They soon heard that few rich and fashionable members of the upper classes had come to Overlook on the opening day or came in the weeks that followed. Most guests were from Kingston, Saugerties and other parts of the surrounding country. Every day that damp summer thrifty folks from Rosendale, Kerhonkson, Saugerties, Kingston and New Paltz cut their way through the thick air as they climbed Overlook for a day's outing with bags of hard-boiled eggs and ham sandwiches clutched in their hands. Where, Woodstock people had some right to ask, were the fashionable ladies and the gentlemen famed in the worlds of business and finance, government and the arts whom they had been led to believe were panting with eagerness to run to the Overlook Mountain House? [9]

Manager John E. Lasher was a resourceful man. He took action to raise the drooping spirits of the hotel's well-wishers and investors. He announced with a flourish the engagement of Professor A. Lee Van Buren as the hotel pianist. The Professor would do much more than merely play the parlor piano; he would give absolutely free music lessons to all who desired them—free music lessons three thousand eight hundred feet above the Hudson (this was the advertised elevation of the Overlook Mountain House at the time). And by way of good measure Professor Van Buren created an original composition, "The Overlook Hotel Waltz."

By the Fourth of July the weather had improved slightly, and the ranks of the guests had been a bit strengthened. On that day the noted eccentric Boots Van Steenbergh provided a part of the entertainment. Boots delighted his audience with his famous political speech, in which he parodied the kind of bombast in which the usual Fourth of July orators indulged. In spite of the efforts of Boots and Lasher, however, the Overlook Mountain House continued to do poorly.

The stockholders decided upon a kind of imitative or homeopathic magic by which a desired event is imitated in the belief that this will cause the event (in this case the filling up of the hotel with boarders) actually to happen. On the morning of July 12 the Kingston stockholders, accompanied by aunts and uncles, grandparents and little girls in bonnets and sashes, assembled at the Kingston station of the Ulster and Delaware Railroad under "lowering clouds indicative of a storm," and bought tickets for West Hurley, the station for Overlook Mountain. There a long cavalcade of carriages met the travellers and took them through a wide-eyed Woodstock (with rest stops at the Brinkerhoff House and Mead's) to the doors of the Overlook Mountain House. And then, according to one of the pilgrims, sober Kingston lawyer Frederick Westbrook, a kind of miracle took place, "the morning clouds dispersed and the brilliant orb of day shone in unusual splendor."

The Kingston stockholders and their friends and relations now joined the Woodstock investors. All were dressed in their very best as they lounged on the verandahs or looked with what sophistication they could muster at the oil paintings of local scenes hung in the spacious parlor. Professor Edward Lewis had brought his photographic apparatus from Kingston. Lewis, who was related to the Lewises who farmed at the foot of Overlook some two thousand feet below, coated his wet plates. With his head under his black focussing cloth he composed and took an excellent series of stereographic pictures showing the dining room and parlor, the verandahs crowded with stockholders, the Overlook Cliff, and groups of stockholders and their friends posed against backgrounds of thick growths of balsam fir trees and lichen-encrusted boulders.

That evening there was entertainment in the parlor. Professor Van Buren was joined by Professor Pierce, a violinist, and the entire Kingston Cornet Band, whose music, one listener reported, "was sweet and jubilant upon the mountain air." Cornmeal was sprinkled on the parlor carpet to facilitate dancing and save wear on the carpet, and the guests danced. Even Judge Augustus Schoonmaker of Kingston was persuaded to take part in a Virginia Reel. Afterwards Professor Pierce entertained with variations on "The Mocking Bird," in which he deftly imitated the call of the bird to the delight of his listeners.

Stockholders' Day seems to have worked a reasonable degree of magic. Business at the hotel picked up (some said because of an improvement in the weather). New Yorkers fleeing from the unusual heat of their city that late summer found the new hotel to be a cool and pleasant place to stay. And toward the end of July John E. Lasher made an announcement that caused a powerful kind of magic to get to work on Overlook.[10]

That month President Ulysses S. Grant was visiting his very rich friend William Dinsmore at Dinsmore's elaborate summer home at Staatsburgh on the east bank of the Hudson. (Like most of our presidents Grant enjoyed the hospitality of the very rich.) With Grant was his friend General George H. Sharpe of Kingston, who had been the head of Grant's Secret Service during the Civil War and was now a big man in Republican politics in the Hudson Valley. Grant noticed a white patch on Overlook and asked what it was. Sharpe was glad to explain that it was the Overlook Mountain House. Grant's expressed wish to go there was promptly reported in the newspapers.

As Grant and Sharpe sat on the ornate verandah of the Dinsmore house, Grant was running for a second term. His first term had been marred by many scandals and by Grant's failure to show the kind of ability and industry required of a President. Yet his backers believed that he was certain to be reelected because of his great popularity as a Civil War hero. His opponent, Horace Greeley, able editor and politician, was campaigning furiously. But Grant's friends and advisors kept their candidate as quiet as possible in the belief that Greeley's many eccentricities could defeat him unless Grant would make some foolish mistake that might cost him the election. That may be the reason why Grant's wish to visit Overlook was publicized at once but not carried out until after he was safely elected.

Once it was known that the President intended to visit the Overlook Mountain House, business there picked up mightily. It would be hard to exaggerate the delight which the announcement of the President's future visit brought to Woodstock. And the announcement was all the more welcome because the great Catskill Mountain House, which had been in business for half a century, had never had a President as a guest. A cheerful air prevailed among both the staff and the guests. The President had not set a date for his visit. It might come at any moment. Grant was known for making sudden decisions in matters like this. Then Overlook guests might come face to face with the President and forever afterward be able to tell of the "time I had a talk with President Grant at the Overlook Mountain House."

By August 1872 all sorts of people came to the Overlook, including a Quaker family from Philadelphia, New York City doctors and lawyers, and Americans to whom travel had become an accepted part of a pleasant life. Cyrus W. Field, promoter of the the first telegraph cable across the Atlantic, was a visitor. So too were various Roosevelts, De Peysters, Livingstons. Clarence King, famed geologist and friend of the mighty who would soon secretly marry a black woman, was there. So were a few Jewish families, beautiful "daughters of Rebekah," one guest called their women.[11]

For years painters of the second wave of Hudson River Schoolers had been sketching with Mead's and other Woodstock boardinghouses as bases. Charles Herbert Moore, painter, teacher, museum head and medievalist, made a sketch for an etching for a projected Hudson River series from the top of the Minister's Face in 1869—it has been called the finest American etching of its century. Jervis ("Jeddy") McEntee of Rondout was a frequent visitor who first stayed at Mead's and after the big hotel was built stayed there. McEntee was a well-known painter, a member of the National Academy of Design with a wide acquaintance among the most eminent workers in the arts of his time. He sometimes brought his friends to the Overlook Mountain House or Mead's. In 1869, for example, he arrived at Mead's with Raphael Pumpelly, geologist, teacher and bearded mystic. McEntee liked theater people and painted their portraits. These people sometimes came to Woodstock and its mountain house with him.

Little has been done to track down McEntee's Woodstock landscapes. Their character is clearly outlined in a statement he made, "I look upon landscape as I do upon a human being—its thoughts, its feelings, its moods, are what interest me; and to these I try to give expression. What it says and thinks and experiences, this is the matter that concerns the landscape painter. . . ." [12]

The final month of the Overlook Mountain House's first season was a lively one. Hiking over the trail that led along Plattekill Mountain and beyond as far as the Catskill Mountain House was added to target shooting, tableaux vivants and other familiar summer-resort amusements. Guests complained that there were no mountaintop roads suited to pleasure driving. Later on, roads like these were laid out and maintained.

Another cause for dissatisfaction on the part of some was the extreme isolation of the hotel. One reporter wrote, in 1873, "The Overlook Mountain House is a whole town all alone by itself. The people there lead lives as much apart from the lives of those about them in the valleys as it is possible to fancy. They do not bother to bestir themselves early in the morning, but let the sun come up as it may, and without any admiration, as far as they are concerned. When it rains and our mountain is wrapped about with mist, the pleasure-seekers pass their time in yawning over novels, playing cards, dancing etc." [13]

The occasional chilliness of Overlook, especially by night, disturbed most keenly one class of visitors which seemed to be growing larger and larger. People with pulmonary tuberculosis or "consumption" hoped that the high air of Overlook might cure or at least improve their ailments. One of these lung sufferers has left a sharp vignette of life on Overlook in a series of letters which has managed to survive. The writer was Fannie Lawton, wife of an aspiring Kingston lawyer and the mother of two sons.

Mrs. Lawton tells of the kindness of other guests and the management. One day she had nine callers in her room, to which a cough and sore throat confined her. Mrs. Bright, the housekeeper, too was kind; she made a green shade for Mrs. Lawton's window. Mrs. Bright also urged her to drink claret, which she found to be like "inky water." It soon became apparent to Mrs. Lawton as she sat on the verandah wrapped in shawls that many other guests had brought their diseased lungs to the new hotel on Overlook in the hope of a cure.

These people compared symptoms, traded remedies, and praised or criticized their doctors. A doctor who was also a lung patient was there. He had tried the high mountain resorts of Switzerland without benefit, and now he was giving Overlook a chance.

Because the Overlook Mountain House was located at so high an elevation, rival hotelkeepers at lower elevations (Overlook was then said to be the highest resort hotel in all the country) claimed it was in a zone of unusual dampness. Clammy clouds, they said, loved to linger there. But this did not keep the lungers away. On bad days they retreated to the comfort of their own rooms and piled on shawls and blankets. Writing to her son Mrs. Lawton tells of many little details of life on Overlook in the summer of 1871 and 1872.

"My dear little Georgie," she wrote one morning, "there is a beautiful pussy here that loves to be petted . . . and there are two young bears who love to climb trees, walk on their hind legs, and growl sometimes too, they love sugar and candy . . . an eagle too has a nest amongst the mountains and flies over and around the hotel. . . . There is music every evening, and the ladies and gentlemen dance. . . ."

To her husband Mrs. Lawton reported incidents unfit for the eyes of her children. There was a young lady at the hotel, a protegee of Miss Leroy of Vassar College. The girl was "preparing for the stage . . . her dress was cut shamefully low in front. . . ." A "bad woman" was also a guest; the previous winter she had scandalized Kingston by her pursuit of manager John E. Lasher. Now she was up to the same game on top of the mountain.

Mrs. Lawton also discovered that she was expected to tip her waiter and the other help. When she gave the waiter a dollar he brought her an especially tender piece of steak, "Isn't it astonishing how the Almighty dollar smooths the way—I find this feeing is a regular organized system. I think that it is all wrong, but it cant be helped."

The only fruits served at the hotel were apples and huckleberries. Mrs. Lawton asked her husband on the next of his weekend visits to bring some peaches and pears "and a lemon or two." Mrs. Lawton and her husband tried to arrange a method by which they could catch a glimpse of each other during the week, he standing in the cupola of their Kingston house and she on the hotel verandah, each armed with a telescope. The attempt failed.

When strangers come together and are thrown upon each other a great deal, someone often emerges as the outstanding bore of the group. In this case it was an elderly man who "talked incessantly," as Mrs. Lawton several times reported. But one night the old man died and Mrs. Lawton became all remorse and sympathy. She was much touched by the funeral ceremonies held in the hotel parlor. "Everyone here loved" the man, she wrote.

One day a carriage got out of control on the steep road from Mead's to the hotel and a young woman was fearfully injured—for a while this dampened the joy of life at the Overlook Mountain House. Evenings in August grew ever cooler on the mountaintop. The lung people left, some for southern mountain resorts or the seashore. Eventually the hotel closed for the season. Though President Grant had not arrived, Mr. Lasher was firm in his confidence that at the right time he would.[14]

The season of 1872 proved little better than the first one as far as profits and number of guests were concerned. Though the hotel had room for about 300, half the rooms were empty except at the very height of the hot summer. The fact that President Grant was engaged in a campaign for a second term against Horace Greeley made politics of unusual interest on Overlook that summer.

Late in August, with Assemblyman Charles H. Krack of Woodstock as chairman, a mock presidential election was held. The result was close: Greeley 64, Grant 60. When the results were announced by Krack the ladies present at once protested. They had not been allowed to vote, they claimed, and therefore the result was invalid. A heated debate on the subject of women's suffrage, the earliest known incident when a public discussion of votes for women took place in the town of Woodstock, followed.

The next summer the hotel opened again in June. A few weeks later Mr. Lasher electrified his guests with the announcement that President Grant would be at the hotel before the month was over. At once the Overlook Mountain House began to fill up.[15]

PRESIDENT GRANT
COMES
TO WOODSTOCK

Late in July 1873 the management
of the Overlook Mountain House received the telegram announcing
President Grant's impending arrival. By that time the hotel had made
long strides toward providing its guests with the kind of romantic
surroundings and points of interest which had come to be expected of
an American summer resort, especially one set among mountains. In
Rome and in eighteenth-century Europe miniature temples and
resting places on elaborate private estates had been given names
which commemorated real or mythical events and persons. Or they
were simply idealistic shrines, as at England's Stowe. There, for
example, "Ancient Virtue" was commemorated.

Hermitages too helped give a romantic air to a rich man's
ground. In Germany one nobleman put together an imitation Tartar
village and a hamlet inhabited by dwarfs. Another converted a hill into
an imitation volcano which emitted flames when observers
approached.

Between 1871 and 1873 the surroundings of the Overlook
Mountain House acquired a remarkable collection of points of
romantic interest, discovered and named at a rate of speed probably
unparalleled anywhere. Most of these depended upon the resemblance
of rock formations to rooms, benches or walls which seemed capable
of adaptation to human uses. They were given names which suggested
supernatural or historic relationships or commemorated fancied use of

areas on the mountaintop by Indians of the distant past. The Poet's Rock, The Sybil's Cave (the sybil was an Indian), Arthur's Seat (Arthur was an English prince), Glen Evans (named for an imaginary Indian ancestor of a guest at the hotel), The Pilgrim's Pass, and the Witches' Glen were among them.

Early guests at the hotel had cooperated, hunting out interesting spots, naming them and cutting paths to them. One guest who devoted much effort to building up the Overlook Mountain House's collection of these objectives for strollers was J. H. Hopper of Jersey City, N.J., a man of means who had recently arrived in the United States after an ineffectual effort at improving his health in Europe. While other guests played cards, staged "shadow pantomimes," or listened to the music of the hotel orchestra, Hopper devoted himself to clearing underbrush and trees from around a boulder close to the very summit of Overlook.

He made rustic benches from which the view of the Indian Head range, sunsets and the upper Schoharie Valley might be enjoyed in comfort. He and others made two paths, one leading from the hotel to the flat rock at Overlook's summit and the other moving along the Overlook Cliff to the point at which it projected far enough to the east to give the broadest and most impressive view. The paths were made wide and smooth enough to make it easy to spot any rattlesnake determined to cling to its ancient possession of the mountain. With much destruction at their dens, the snakes had been, however, substantially reduced in number.[1]

Ceremonies attended by two hundred jolly people "aged from seven to seventy-seven" took place in August 1872 to "christen" various points of interest. Champagne was drunk and toasts were offered. A poem written by Miss LaVarre of New York in honor of Mr. Hopper had been set to music and was sung by a chorus of young people. It began:

> My gentle hearers please attend,
> As long as you think proper,
> While I relate the deeds of a certain Mr. Hopper
> He came from Europe not long since
> And sought Health's favorite fountain,
> Upon the top of Overlook
> The Catskills' highest mountain.

Many Overlook enthusiasts of the 1870s believed that Overlook

289

was actually the highest of all the Catskills, and that this fact was artfully kept from the public by Charles L. Beach of the Catskill Mountain House.

Following the ceremonies Dexter A. Hawkins, an eminent educator and active enemy of political corruption, read the long paper which explained in whimsical fashion the various names that day officially conferred upon Overlook sights. In the course of Hawkins' talk he offered a great deal of made-up-for-the-occasion Indian lore concerning Overlook.[2]

In the short space of time between the day Grant looked up from the Dinsmore house and the day he arrived on Overlook the hotel's surroundings had been transformed from a partly forested partly cut-over mountaintop to a romantic and mystical park with ancient and at the same time ready-made traditions created after the features of the Overlook mountaintop were hunted out, named and given mock romantic and historical associations. Woodstock people climbed the mountain and inspected them. From the beginning of settlement the mountain had been free for everyone to roam. Now that it was the property of a hotel corporation this was not changed. As at the Catskill Mountain House ever since its beginning, the public was permitted to enter the hotel, feel the depth of the carpets under their feet, admire the furniture, and have a drink or meal at the same tables as the regular guests.

On Sundays religious services were held in the parlor. The ministers, often well-known and occasionally controversial, were usually guests who paid their bills for board and room by preaching. When men like these were scheduled to preach, people from Woodstock climbed their mountain to hear them and often discussed what they heard with praise or shock for weeks.

A religious service that was widely commented upon took place on the evening of Sunday, July 20, 1873 and was described in a long article in the New York *Tribune* of July 26. Said the *Tribune*, "The shades of night had hardly gathered over the ancient mountains when the little group of worshippers assembled, with no smoke of incense, no sound of harp or organ, no groined cathedral arches, no pomp of sacred litanies . . . to open their hearts to the inspiration of their better natures. The preacher was known far and wide for the broad liberality of his religious faith. He represented no sect, was the exponent of no creed. He was without the prestige of any ecclesiastical communion. . . . As this man of gracious gifts and saintly life" spoke,

290

"rarely has a deeper spirit of loving harmony brooded over the congregation in the house of worship. . . ."

The preacher's text was "I will lift up my eyes unto the hills from whence cometh my strength. . . ." The preacher began by alluding "in a fine glow of poetical description to the influence of mountain scenery. He portrayed with the pencil of a consummate artist the solemn majesty and exquisite loveliness that nature's own hand had so curiously blended in our daily spectacle of enchantment. . . ." He urged his listeners to set for themselves high goals in life. "We all worship what is above us," said the preacher. "Our strength comes from the everlasting hills. . . . It is reverence for the highest in humanity that calls forth the highest in ourselves. . . ."

The preacher was Octavius B. Frothingham, who had been characterized by the Kingston *Daily Freeman* a few days before his sermon on the mountain as a "radical." And he was indeed radical in his approach to religion. Frothingham had been shaped by the same New England transcendentalism which had produced Ralph Waldo Emerson and Henry David Thoreau. In New York he preached brilliant and daring sermons to an audience of intellectuals, artists, writers and musicians, not in a proper church but in a public hall on Sixth Avenue. Though some conservative church people regarded Frothingham as little better than a first cousin of the Devil, even they could not resist the integrity and sincerity he radiated.

We don't know what the Woodstock people who climbed Overlook that faraway July evening made of Frothingham, but we may guess that a few admired him but most did not. The fact that the New York radical preacher was also the art critic of the New York *Tribune* made some listen with added interest. Woodstock people of 1873 were newspaper readers, and the weekly edition of the *Tribune* was their favorite. Its former editor, Horace Greeley, had supported the Anti-Rent cause in the 1840s and had always taken the side of farmers and upstate New Yorkers.

There were extra attractions for Woodstock people on the Sunday Frothingham made "the profoundest impression on the deeply interested audience" on Overlook. George Ripley, literary editor of the *Tribune*, and his German-born wife had accompanied Frothingham to the Overlook Mountain House. Ripley, who had been the founder of utopian Brook Farm at Concord, Massachusetts, was an important figure in New York's intellectual society. Present also on Overlook that Sunday were at least half a dozen clergymen of fashionable churches who may have been taking this opportunity to hear a much-talked-of preacher whose public hall they would not have liked being seen entering.[3]

Few Woodstock people of 1873 had travelled far afield; none are known to have visited Europe. On Frothingham's Sunday as on many other occasions the Overlook Mountain House brought the world to them. For those interested in new things, ideas and people, the hotel on the mountain had more than an economic value.

The day President Grant at last came to the hotel aroused far more local interest than any event in all the history of the Overlook Mountain House. A radical preacher is a very minor figure in society compared with a President of the United States and a military hero.

In July 1873 Grant was at a critical moment in his career. In the early summer of 1873 it had become apparent that the President, now just beginning his second term in the White House, was hankering for a third. Those newspapers which usually opposed him were in full cry at his heels, urging readers in the strongest terms to demand that Grant reject unequivocally and in public any notion of another term.

Because an important development might come at any moment, leading metropolitan newspapers sent seasoned reporters to Overlook. Reporters of the New York *Times*, the *Tribune* and the *Evening Post* were among them. Papers like the New York *Sun*, which strongly disapproved of Grant and a third term, contented themselves with giving their readers terse items about Grant's whereabouts and column after column about incipient scandals in his administration and fulminations against a third term.

The newspaper which covered Grant's trip to Overlook the most fully and sympathetically was the pro-Grant, conservative Republican New York *Times*. The *Times* seemed to be already active in a third-term campaign by presenting Grant as a kindly, friendly man fond of nature and children. Its account of Grant's stay on Overlook is the most detailed of any. When checked against anti-Grant reports, it appears to be factual in most respects.

The *Times* and the other papers reported that the President left his summer home at Long Branch, N.J. on July 28, accompanied by his secretary, Gen. Babcock, and Postmaster-General Cresswell. The presence of Cresswell suggested that this was to be a political trip, since the Postmaster-General was a presidential dispenser of patronage and a political aide. That night Cresswell was reported to have been taken ill. When Grant and Babcock left the Fifth Avenue Hotel the next morning Cresswell was not with them.

"The sole attendant" of Grant and Babcock from this point on was "an attache of General George H. Sharpe, whose guests they were to be during the pleasure trip to Overlook Mountain." Sharpe was an old wartime friend of Grant. A Kingston lawyer, he enjoyed the lucrative post of Surveyor of Customs of the Port of New York. The presence of Sharpe's aide beside Grant that morning strengthened rumors that Sharpe was being considered for a high post in the political structure of his party and state.

Until July 26 the press had not been told of Grant's proposed expedition to Overlook. When news of it got round a flurry of speculation linked Sharpe to a possible shakeup in the state political machine which might be a preliminary step toward a third-term push by Grant.

As Grant steamed up the Hudson on the richly-appointed steamer *Chauncey Vibbard*, the telegraph wires between New York and the Overlook Mountain House were kept busy carrying messages arranging for reporters to be present on the mountaintop. Ambitious politicians alerted to a chance of getting the ear of the President began converging upon Overlook from all parts of the Hudson Valley. The *Vibbard* steamed up the Hudson, her bands playing, her passengers shaking the President's hand or merely staring at him.

At landings along the river local bands played and local dignitaries came aboard for a handshake. At Rhinecliff opposite Kingston the Rhinebeck Band was waiting to blow the President ashore. Local political workers were waiting for a handshake. Here General Sharpe joined the President.

As Grant crossed the Hudson on board the tug *Sandy*, all the steam vessels within hearing saluted him with their whistles. At the Rondout Landing the Rondout Cornet Band was lying in wait for him. So were many people intent on shaking the presidential hand. Preceded by the band, the presidential barouche proceeded to General Sharpe's residence through streets enlivened, said the *Times*, with flags and streamers and cheering throngs (anti-Grant papers were considerably less specific on this point).

After lunch, amid even greater enthusiasm than before, according to the *Times*, the President was driven to the Kingston and Syracuse Railway Depot, where he boarded a special train. "Amid the hurrahs and demonstrations of the multitude" at the depot the President's train went off. It was met at the West Hurley station by "a full band wearing new uniforms and playing national airs; flags and evergreens decorated the depot, people from twenty miles around were assembled. Handkerchief waving and showers of flowers welcomed the visitors."

Again Grant shook hands with all who wished. Two barouches each drawn by four of the fastest horses obtainable rushed the presidential party to Woodstock, making the fastest time ever recorded, it was said, between the two points.

Woodstock was ready to greet the President. "The verandahs of the Inn were occupied by ladies and children in holiday dress, who showered down bouquets of choice flowers and evergreens upon him as he passed beneath the porch into the parlor, where dozens of the more established residents were watiting to be introduced. The handshaking was once more repeated and two pretty children handed the President a couple of elegant nosegays." So said the *Times*.

The way to the hotel on the mountain was steep and slow. The two barouches moved through a thick fog. At last the hotel building emerged from the fog. The verandahs were crowded with about two hundred and fifty people, all cheering and waving handkerchiefs. The manager stepped forward and spoke a few words of welcome. The President's response was inaudible. Several rockets were set off and fizzled in the fog. The hotel band directed by the Wagner brothers of New York struck up and the President entered the hotel under an archway on which the word "WELCOME" had been worked in montain laurel leaves. As the President moved ahead "showers of flowers and favors" fell upon him.[4]

While the President found only boredom in music and art, Americans of 1873 knew, he took extreme pleasure in flowers and especially in the elaborate arrangements of flowers and foliage put together in those days to ornament buildings in which festive events took place. The lady guests of the Overlook Mountain House had been busy since early in the morning of that July 30. By the time the President arrived at about seven p.m., they had decorated the public rooms of the hotel with an elaborateness never before or since approached in Woodstock. Laurel twined round pillars and draped chandeliers. Bouquets of flowers occupied every conceivable perch. Over the mantel in the big parlor the ladies had worked a floral masterpiece featuring the President's initials U.S.G. plus a sword, a gun and a shield.

Grant was summoned to the verandah soon after he entered the hotel. A startling break had occurred in Overlook's wrappings of cloud and fog. The famous view in which the hotel owners took such pride had become partly visible. Said the New York *Tribune*, ". . . The clouds which had so closely besieged Overlook for several days were being slowly pressed by a northwest wind, and began to rise, at first slowly, and then gradually faster, until they were fairly flying with extraordinary speed over the mountains, and every moment they gave a new feature to the landscape. . . . Sometimes they were overhead, sometimes at our feet, and so they kept their wonderful play while the beaming rays of a gorgeous sunset gave a wonderful effect to the whole. . . . It appeared to your correspondent, however, that the President had little time to enjoy the beauties of nature as many of the inmates of the house were desirous to go through the constitutional hand-shaking, and it must be said he was extremely affable. . . ."

After "a sumptuous repast" the members of the Wagner Band took up their instruments. The shining black walnut parlor furniture was set against the walls, cornmeal was sprinkled on the scrolled and flowered carpet, and a ball in Grant's honor brought all the adult guests and temporary visitors to the parlor. Grant, as was his unvarying custom, did not dance but spent his time admiring the floral trophies, shaking hands (he is said to have shaken three hundred hands that night), and chatting with the ladies. At one point that evening Mr. Eisner, the band's violinist, played a solo—Yankee Doodle with variations. As the music ended Grant is said to have remarked, "That's good."

Once Wagner's Band had reached the end of its evening's work, a new musical group took over. The waiters and kitchen help, the young black Civil War veterans and students at Lincoln University, stood on the back verandah and gave a program of Civil War songs. They had the benefit of coaching from several members of the once-famous Hutchinson Family Singers who were guests at the hotel. The Hutchinsons had sung abolitionist songs, freedom for women songs, temperance songs and during the Civil War they had sung to cheer Union soldiers. The Hutchinsons, in their concern with social improvements, foreshadowed singers of a century later, singers like Pete Seeger, Joan Baez and Bob Dylan, who sang to support causes in their own time.[5]

After breakfast, said the *Times*, "The ladies and gentlemen at the hotel put on fatigue suits, took large staves [locally known as mountain sticks, these were useful among other things in despatching rattlesnakes], and escorted the presidential party up the mountainside to its highest point, whence the finest views were obtained. During the ascent led by General Grant and two little girls [described by another newpaper as wearing white dresses, blue ribbons and flaxen hair], the guests sang war choruses and patriotic songs. As each level spot was reached the procession halted to note the increasingly beautiful view and to take breath. When Hopper's Rock near the summit was attained, the President sat with a few ladies and children under the shade of some spruce trees. At that moment, nearly 4000 feet above the sea, a hundred voices broke forth in the glorious old anthem, 'America'."

This singing of the national anthem was taken up by other newpapers as the climax of the President's morning. The Newburgh *Daily Journal* headlined its account, "America at a High Altitude." Following the singing of America, said the New York *Times*, came "several excellent melodies, sung by Mr. and Mrs. Patton (formerly Miss Hutchinson) and a member of the famous family of singers."

Continuing upward the procession came to a halt at the very summit of Overlook where the fire tower now stands. "Here," said the *Times*, "the children, having culled wild flowers and beautiful shrubs, insisted upon decorating the President, who, seated on a rocky projection, gravely submitted." After this the President and his followers made their way back to the hotel by the Overlook Cliff with many pauses and much music.

In later years General Sharpe recalled that he and Grant had climbed to the top of a huge boulder which crossed a chasm (then known as the Devil's Kitchen) and ended at the cliff's edge. The two sat on the boulder smoking their cigars. As Sharpe remembered, it was he who suggested naming the rock Grant's Rock, a name it bears to this day. According to one whimsical story which found its way as far abroad as the *Times* of London, John E. Lasher, hearing Grant express admiration of the Rock, gave it to him, suggesting that it might make a good "Parlour ornament" and could be shipped to the White House by William Dinsmore's Adams Express Company.

Pro-Grant newpapers pictured the President as enjoying the excursion to the top of Overlook very much indeed. Anti-Grant papers like the *Tribune* detected on Grant's face the glum, tired expression he often wore when listening to music or taking part in ceremonies which bored him.

That afternoon at 3:45 the presidential party left Overlook Mountain by carriage and "were driven rapidly down the steep mountain road amid the hearty cheers and farewells. . . . People all the way to the depot were waiting for the carriages and demonstrated their delight in various ways. At the West Hurley station crowds were assembled . . . a special train of the Kingston and Syracuse Railroad, decorated with flags, was waiting."

Shaking hands until the last minute Grant boarded the train and moved toward Kingston accompanied by waving flags and booming guns along the way. That evening he shook hands for more than two hours at General Sharpe's house in Kingston and at midnight appeared at a balcony to tell the "multitude waiting outside with unshaken hands that he had found his two days in Kingston and on Overlook Mountain 'most enjoyable' but that he was very tired and was going to get to bed." The next day he took the early morning boat down the Hudson to New York.[6]

The New York *Times* had described Grant's excursion to Overlook and Kingston as a mere "pleasure trip," and the *Times* may well have been right. There was no promotion of General Sharpe, who remained Surveyor of Customs for another three years. There was no Declaration of Overlook Mountain in which Grant either rejected or openly asked for a third term. By lending his prestige to the Overlook Mountain House in which General Sharpe was said to have an interest, he had done a favor to Sharpe and his powerful Hudson Valley friends, a favor which might be returned in the form of backing for a third term. Before long, however, Grant's third-term ambitions subsided, only to rise again in 1880, when they were forever thwarted.

The President's less than twenty-four hours in Woodstock left no mark in history. Yet they greatly enriched Woodstock folklore. A large area of that folklore was triggered by an item published in the savagely anti-Grant Rhinebeck *Gazette* as Grant was shaking hands and acknowledging cheers in Kingston on July 31. It read, in part, "The peripatetic head of this great and glorious republic, redolent with the stench of the back pay swindle and cheap whiskey . . . arrived in Rhinebeck. . . . He was, as usual, drunk."

The report at once raced up and down the Hudson Valley. It was reprinted and widely embellished. General Sharpe had been seen trying to take a whiskey bottle away from the President. A drover passing Grant's barouche near Woodstock had distinctly seen Grant to be drunk. The pro-Grant Kingston *Daily Freeman*, which had had reporters close to Grant throughout his excursion, denied that the President had given even the slightest hint of tipsiness.[7]

THE UPS AND DOWNS
OF THE OVERLOOK
MOUNTAIN HOUSE

Eighteen seventy-three was a bad year for U.S. Grant to come to the Overlook House. During the campaign of the previous year the heavy drinking of his earlier years had become part of his legend. It was used effectively by his opponents. Democratic and Liberal Republican candidate Horace Greeley did not drink or smoke. He was a vegetarian. At various times he had advocated almost every one of the many social reforms, many of them very bizarre indeed, which marked the mid-ninteenth century. To many people Greeley represented virture while cigar-smoking, fast-horse-loving, materialistic Grant represented evil.

Ulster County was anti-Grant territory (many of its people had strongly opposed fighting the Civil War in which Grant played so important a part). As Grant came to Ulster many had been on the alert for signs of the perpetual drunkenness of which so much had been made during the campaign of 1872. The issue was being revived now that a third term was being promoted. Once he became President in 1869 Grant had given up heavy drinking; he was not known to have been drunk while in office. Yet the legend of his earlier drinking bouts clung to him to the end of his days.

The temperance movement had made great advances in Woodstock by the 1870s. The movement had begun nationally about 1800. The Reverend William Boyse had strongly denounced drinking during the 1820s and 1830s (heavy drinking was one of his own failings). The Ulster Temperance Society could report in 1843 that "In the town of Woodstock, where, until recently, there have been four taverns and as many groceries [these were places where liquor was sold by the glass to be drunk on the premises], but two taverns and no grocery licenses have been granted this spring." [1]

Yet liquor continued to be sold without benefit of license. Even the state law forbidding the sale on Sundays was flouted. In August 1864 George William Snyder of the old Inn was called upon by a committee of his church, the Dutch Reformed, because he sold liquor even while services were being held on Sundays. Mr. Snyder received the members of the committee with the most elaborate courtesy. He did not for a moment question their right to protest, he explained, yet it was his intention to continue to sell liquor on Sundays; the committee might take whatever action it deemed appropriate, but his barroom would remain open seven days a week. And it did.[2]

In Woodstock as elsewhere in the United States temperance was being promoted most assiduously with the help of the clergymen. Most men, however, clung to the taverns which served as their clubs and often their centers of business life—where horses were sold and bargains for crops were made. Travelling shows continued as in earlier days to be given there, and there women of unconventional morals might be met.

Some of the more prosperous Woodstock men sided with their women and the clergy. The opening of bluestone quarries in town had brought in many Irishmen, most of them young and single, who found the taverns attractive and who also set up "shebeens" or drinking places of their own. With their new customers the taverns lost some of their charm for the more prosperous Woodstock men, who then became less reluctant to back the temperance movement and help close the taverns.

By July 1873 there were only two places in Woodstock where liquor was being sold legally—and President Grant visited both of them. They were the Overlook Mountain House and the old inn then run by H. S. Van Etten. No wonder that temperance-minded Woodstock people hearing of the report in the Rhinebeck *Gazette* drew dreadful conclusions. Quickly Woodstock tongues whispered into shape a Grant legend.

Though that happened more than a century ago, the legend is still alive and well. The De Forest house, now the home of the Woodstock Guild of Craftsmen, is still pointed out as the place where

President Grant "slept it off" when his friend General Sharpe wouldn't let him go up Overlook "because he wasn't fit; he went up the next day he was half-fit by then." To this day Woodstock men quote the driver of Grant's barouche as saying, "Grant was drunk when they got him off the train at West Hurley. It took a pint of whiskey to get him to Woodstock and another to get him up the mountain to Mead's. There he had a third pint to refuel him for the trip to the top. By the time he got to the Mountain House they had to pour him in bed through a funnel."

In fact, the President had made one sober trip to Overlook Mountain. Yet before long this was magnified into half a dozen rip-snorting binges. A Woodstock man used to claim that he'd held Grant's horse while the President tanked up at a tavern on the Kingston-Woodstock road. After that whenever the man shook hands with anyone he'd say, "You're shaking the hand that held General Grant's horse while the General was having a quick one inside." [3]

Mead's register shows Grant's name twice in 1878. Neither signature is in Grant's handwriting. On both occasions he was hundreds of miles away. "He was in no shape to hold a pen, his secretary signed for him" is the way some Woodstock people explain it.[4]

In Lewis Hollow, some two thousand feet below the Overlook Mountain House, they used to say that President Grant was the innocent means of depriving a quarryman's wife of the solace of an alcoholic-laden tonic known as Pee-runa to which she turned for daily support. Mrs. Spenser's son Bill had heard that Grant was expected on the mountain. He begged his mother to take him to see Grant. Mrs. Spenser hesitated. After all the Spensers were Democrats. But at last she yielded, took a good swig of Pee-runa, and soared up Overlook with Bill.

The expedition was a failure. Bill burst into tears at the sight of Grant, for the President looked no more impressive than the men Bill saw in the Hollow every day. That evening Spenser came home from the quarry to no wife, no son and especially to no dinner. When at last Mrs. Spenser arrived, he exclaimed, "Do you mean to tell me you climbed all the way to the top of Overlook just to take a look at General Grant? Alright then, me girl! No more Pee-runa for you, you don't need it." [5]

A non-alcoholic legend of Grant on Overlook is a tall tale usually attributed to a horseman, drover and hotelkeeper of bygone days named Jim Twaddell. Twaddell's versions varied considerably. One saw print in a Woodstock magazine named *The Overlook* on July 30, 1932. Here is a much-embroided version which was told around Woodstock during the 1950s.

On the morning of July 31, 1873 Twaddell was busy in the stable of the Overlook Mountain House. Grant walked in. He said he'd admired Twaddell's horse Scott the day before when Twaddell and the horse had escorted his carriage up Overlook. Now he'd come to take a better look at the horse. Twaddell offered to saddle Scott for Grant, and a few minutes later Grant was riding the Overlook trails with Twaddell beside him mounted on a mare.

Soon Twaddell saw with amazement that the combination of riding so fine a horse and breathing the rejuvenating air of Overlook (one writer on the subject had proposed bottling the air and selling it under the name of Overlook Oxy-gin) was having a remarkable effect on the President. The careworn lines were leaving his face. He was growing younger and younger by the minute. He became fifty years old . . . forty . . . thirty-nine. . . .

Suddenly Grant brought Scott to a halt. "Twaddell," he said, "I'll be in trouble if I get any younger. The Constitution says that the President must be above thirty-five. I'm having trouble with Congress. They'll impeach me and throw me out of the White House."

"Make for the stables, Mr. President," shouted Twaddell, "and give Scott his head. If any horse on this earth can get you back in time, it's Scott."

Never had Overlook Mountain known so fine a display of horsemanship as it saw that day. Scott left the trail and headed straight for the stable, down cliffs, over boulders, and through tangles of balsam firs. The President guided Scott with superb skill while the faithful Twaddell and his mare followed after.

As Grant leaped from his horse at the stable door his proper age—he was fifty-one—came back with a rush that staggered him.

When Scott died Twaddell buried him at the exact place along the Overlook Road where he and his master had first caught a glimpse of the President. As Twaddell reached this point in his story, he'd say, "Ever wonder why that long steep grade above Mead's is called Scott Hill? Well, now ye know." [6]

President Grant had reached the Overlook Mountain House at about seven p.m. and left at 3:45 the following day. Though his stay was brief, it had, for a time at least, a substantial effect on the fortunes of the hotel. During the rest of the season of 1873, people thronged to the hotel to inhabit, if only for a few days, the little world in which the President had briefly lived. A cheerful mood prevailed among Overlook guests. Their hotel had acquired the status that would inevitably result in success and fame.

Down in Woodstock many people looked toward Overlook with dour faces. They were determined to deprive it and Van Etten's hotel of the liquor license which made them attractive to people like Grant.

That August a coastal storm swept up the Hudson Valley. It demonstrated that while Overlook Mountain was a good place to escape the heat of cities its coolness might sometimes be overdone, as was surely the case that second week of August. "During the recent storm," the *Freeman* announced, "the thermometer was down to fifty-four; fires were lighted in the stoves; shawls and overcoats came into use, and there was generally a pinched and chilled look to the nose of every guest. But after the sun came and Overlook took off his overcoat, the spirits of those on the mountain-top rose with the mercury. . . ."

A correspondent of the Springfield (Mass.) *Republican* who travelled to the Overlook Mountain House at this period admired the location but expressed doubt. A guest taking the train at Kingston, heading into Woodstock's "queer medley of old Dutch sleepiness, Irish briskness and genuine New York culture" had to take to one of the Overlook "wagons" at West Hurley and then endure "a slow, toilsome jolt over nine miles of meadow and mountain" to the summit.

"The rates at the hotel were equal to those in New York," wrote this writer. "We might be tempted by social considerations to stay at the Overlook for, this year it is visited by some of the best people in the country; but a mountaintop 3,000 feet above tidewater, has, at best, a rough summer climate and the violent changes try even a vigorous constitution." Other writers complained of arriving at the top of Overlook with aching bones, and deplored the strain to which the horses were subjected.[7]

Occasionally an accident on the rough road cooled enthusiasm, although the trip down at high speed gave something of the excitement of a roller coaster. In August 1873 "Cornell" Winne drove a surrey-load of his boarders from Shokan to Overlook, where they ate, drank and admired the view from the verandahs. Winne drove his people down to Mead's in exactly fifteen minutes "without causing a scream from the most timid passenger." From Mead's to Van Etten's hotel in Woodstock took another thirty minutes. This trip may have established a record.[8]

But for the completion of the railroad to West Hurley, the Overlook Mountain House would not have been built. It quickly became apparent, however, that the station was too far away. The obvious answer was a railroad spur from West Hurley to the foot of Overlook. This was endlessly discussed, planned and prayed for, but every time a railroad spur seemed about to be realized a downward turn in the economy or the death of one of the promoters put an end to the possibility. Yet the stockholders continued to hope, and business was good enough following Grant's visit to be encouraging if not exactly profitable.

The season of 1873 had many very hot periods. The coolness of Overlook was attractive to New Yorkers who saw horses drop dead from the heat in the city streets and heard about children dying in the crowded slums. But 1874 brought a damp, cool and rainy summer.

During sunny intervals guests arrived and sat on the chairs used by President Grant, walked over the carpet he had stood upon, admired Grant's Rock, Glen Evans, the Witches' Cave and the other attractions. That spring the paths radiating from the hotel were greatly extended. There was much talk of building a road to replace the bridle path linking the Overlook Mountain House and the vicinity of the Catskill Mountain House. That road would also make Echo Lake, "set like a gem in the mountain," accessible by carriage. The road would also bring the wonders of Plattekill Clove, its waterfalls and pools, its sheer lichened cliffs and dense hemlock woods, within easy reach of summer people.

A "legend" of Echo Lake was devised and set afloat in a skeptical manner in the New York *Times* of July 19, 1874. "It seems an Indian girl, once upon a time a few centuries ago, was in the habit of meeting her lover along its shores. She was the daughter of a chief of unpronounceable name, who frowned upon their love-makings, and one night, so the story goes, killed the youth. The maiden then threw herself from one of the cliffs, and, of course, was found a cold corpse. It is said her spirit haunts the lake each night, near the hour of 12, which is extremely interesting to those ladies who have no fear of rheumatism and have lovers to help them watch for the phantom form." [9]

At the same period "a remarkable echo" was discovered at the lake. Parties "of ladies and gentlemen who had been told of its wonderful repeating capacity" rowed out on the lake and shouted "Hello!" with varying degrees of success. Echo Lake had been earlier called Shoe's Pond, Schew's Lake, Schrew's Lake, Horse Shoe Pond,

Shen's Lake (due to a misreading of a surveyor's handwriting). Shen's Lake sometimes became Athen's Lake. A newspaper of the 1850s mentions it as Balsam Lake. Although there are many Echo Lakes scattered across the United States, that name became accepted in Woodstock and is still in use.

Overlook Mountain was at its best that summer of 1874. As the *Times* put it, "The unusual amount of wet weather has forced vegetation, so they [the Catskills] have become covered with a rank, luxuriant growth of the richest green." The rains of early summer had "so purified the atmosphere that at times objects are plainly visible to the eye which can usually be distinguished only with a glass."

The air at Overlook seemed to many to have acquired, thanks to being washed by the rains, a purity that intoxicated more than ever. "To live here must give a hardy healthful constitution," said the *Times*, "for the air exhilarates like wine, the water from the mountaintop spring is pure, and the perfume of mountain shrubs just blossoming pervades the atmosphere. . . ."

As the hotel closed for the season at the end of that summer its backers felt reasonably cheerful. It was true they were continuing to lose money. Yet there was reason for hope. The visit of the President had gotten Overlook much talked about. The enthusiasm with which newspaper writers were writing about the extraordinary quality of Overlook's air would be sure to have its effect.[10]

April Fool's Day, 1875 dawned clear and warm. The sun began to gnaw at the snow which lay deep on top of Overlook. John E. Lasher left the mountaintop on which he and his family had spent the winter. Lasher was heading for Kingston to have a talk with John W. Kerr, former sheriff and a member of the posse which had come to Woodstock to quell the Down-Rent agitation of 1845.

The subject of the talk was to be money. Lasher had put all he had into furnishing the hotel on Overlook. He claimed he had spent $25,000. He was without the capital to open the hotel for the coming season. He was so broke he had even allowed the insurance on the hotel furnishings to lapse. Kerr had expressed interest in supplying the cash Lasher needed in return for a half-interest in Lasher's lease. Or so they were saying in Kingston.

Lasher left two workmen repairing some of the damage caused on Overlook Mountain by the wind and ice of the previous winter. Mrs. Lasher was busy with housework in the Lasher apartment. Her children were playing. Little Rena Lasher ran out on the hotel verandah where one of the two men was at work. "Come quickly, Mr. Rowe," she urged. "There's a funny noise inside."

Rowe laughed and told Rena to try to fool someone else. She wasn't going to make an April fool of him. Rena then called her mother. Mrs. Lasher found that a chimney was ablaze. With quick action it might be kept from spreading to the rest of the building on this windless morning. Mrs. Lasher sent Rena on the run to the second man working on the mountaintop. This man laughed, too.

By this time one of the Lasher boys had saddled a horse and was on his way to Mead's through the waist-deep snow. The boy came back with George Mead and a half-dozen other men. It was too late to save the insured hotel building. Mrs. Lasher directed the men to save what they could of the uninsured furnishings. The parlor piano, the flowery carpet over which President Grant had walked, the marble-topped tables and the oil paintings were scattered on the snow.

In Saugerties, Kingston and Catskill, in the City of Hudson, on Poughkeepsie porches, on the estates of Livingstons and Astors, people gathered to watch the column of smoke rising from Overlook and drifting across the Hudson Valley. They smiled. By now an April Fool's Day fire on Overlook (usually of tar barrels) had been set to burning so often that it had become a dependable part of the day's observance. The first time people had been taken in. Woodstock men had dropped their work and toiled up the mountain, only to be met by laughter. On this April Fool's Day of 1873 they knew better than to take the fire seriously.

Someone in Kingston was watching the fire through a telescope. "It's the real thing this time," he announced. Quickly the news spread. When John E. Lasher heard, "he wept like a child." He hired the fastest horse and the best driver he could and sped toward smoking Overlook Mountain.

By then Woodstock men and boys were racing upward on foot and on horseback to help. A Kingston editor authorized Edgar Snyder to wire a blow-by-blow account of the blaze. Snyder tapped away on the telegraph instrument in his store as volunteers brought him bits of news and rumor about the fire. That afternoon Snyder sent his final message: What had been a hotel on Overlook that morning was now a heap of charred timber.

The burning of the hotel was a blow to Woodstock in more ways than one. The New York *Times* published a long editorial denouncing April Fool's Day pranks, singling out the extinction by fire of the

Overlook Mountain House as an example of what pranks might lead to. Because there had been false fires on Overlook in previous Aprils, said the *Times* "when the alarm was given at a distance of a few miles no movement was made to render assistance."

Other papers made harsh judgments about how Woodstock people had behaved that April 1. The Kingston *Daily Freeman* said on May 19 that ". . . the farmers in Woodstock are much troubled because the Overlook House is not going to be rebuilt. When the house was in operation they had an excellent market for all their poultry and vegetables, but now there is no sale for these things, and the people are actually forced to live on a chicken diet, much to their disgust, for farmers consider eating chicken to be rather expensive business. They don't go half so far as pork. No one feels very sorry for them, however, for these Woodstockers never did anything to help the house along unless they could make some money out of the operation to put in their own pockets."

The *Freeman* held their failure to respond to the fire on the mountain against Woodstock people, even though they could have done litttle to check the flames if they had dashed up Overlook at once. The economic distress which the *Freeman* referred to, however, was real enough.[11]

Woodstock had done a great deal to adapt to its new role as a popular and even fashionable summer resort. The elegant Brinkerhoff and Snyder houses still stood as reminders of Woodstock hopes; so too did the Brinkerhoff Inn and Krack's Hotel. Throughout the town farmers with a few extra bedrooms "took" summer boarders. This practice continued even after the big hotel burned. Some farmhouses eventually developed into sizeable boarding houses holding twenty to seventy people.

In the meanwhile the site of the fire proved to be irresistibly attractive to great numbers of people. Many hired horses and wagons in Woodstock and made the ascent in groups. Once on the mountaintop they turned scavengers, loading themselves down with lumps of melted window glass, bottles twisted in the fire and fire-stained hotel china. All these were soon on display on parlor what-nots labelled "Relics of the Overlook Mountain Hotel Fire, April, 1875."

The fire had not touched several minor buildings on Overlook—the laundry, the "gas house" (where the acetylene gas was made), and the stable or barn. In this last Henry Happy of Woodstock set up a "dining saloon" and restaurant for relic hunters. Happy supplied cooling drinks, stabling for horses, and hay and oats.

The hotel property was advertised for sale at an auction to be held May 4. The sale was postponed because insurance disagreements remained unsettled. On October 1 a large crowd gathered at the Kingston Court House and heard the property sold to Captain Jacob H. Tremper for $7400.

Economic conditions had been discouraging through the early and mid-1870s. But by 1877 things were improving. Captain Tremper was able to sell his speculation to the Kiersted Brothers, John and James of Saugerties. The brothers belonged to an old local family which had acquired money through surveying, land speculation and tanning. They announced that they would build a new hotel on the old site, that it would be a temperance hotel (the brothers were teetotallers), and that an architect named Wood (probably J. A. Wood of 240 Broadway, New York) was at work on plans for the building. The management would place a Bible and perhaps also a hymn book in every room.[12]

The ashes of the old hotel had hardly cooled when John E. Lasher took over the lease of the Brinkerhoff House in the hamlet of Woodstock. He proposed running it primarily as a summer hotel. He sodded the hotel's surrounding land, planted flowers and gave the building a more elegant interior. Lasher had built up a following during his years as manager of the Mansion House in Rondout and then of the Overlook Mountain House. He was confident that he could attract many of his former guests to his new hotel. There horses and carriages would be waiting to take guests up Overlook to spend a day relic hunting or enjoying the view.

Though Lasher's food and beds were excellent, and his manner as genial as ever, he realized when the Kiersted Brothers got to work in earnest building the second Overlook Mountain House in 1877 that he could not hope to compete. He left to manage a succession of large urban and resort hotels.

There was another reason why Lasher moved on. Woodstock opinion was moving rapidly toward forbidding the sale of alcoholic liquors in town. By 1875 public pressure had reduced the places selling liquor to a single one, Lasher's new hotel. Lasher had little faith in the ability of a hotel like his to run at a profit without a bar. Prohibitionist sentiment was reaching a new peak. At a "Temperance meeting" in Woodstock that April one hundred and fifty people were reported to have signed a pledge to refrain forever from alcohol. The crop of untrue tales of President Grant's drunkenness helped greatly in moving Woodstock toward the refusal of all licenses to sell liquor. That came in 1879.

By December 1877 the Kiersted Brothers had signed contracts for building their hotel on the foundations of the old one. Wagons pulled by four powerful horses were drawing building materials to the site from Saugerties. The weather was good until the end of the month. Then work ceased. A Saugerties man named Tom Bradley was installed on the mountain as caretaker of the great accumulations of timber and other materials piled up there. Much was made of Bradley's lonely life as a "hermit" on Overlook. He passed the winter there without difficulty.

The Kiersted Brothers were determined to have their hotel ready to open in June 1878. The weather cooperated. In intervals of good weather throughout the winter building materials were hauled up Overlook. By the third week of February the snow in the valley was nearly gone. Heavily-laden wagons again began climbing Overlook in force, meeting deep snow only between Mead's and the hotel site. Tom Bradley returned to Saugerties.

The Kiersteds let it be known that they would quickly build a good road to "Shoe's" or Echo Lake and would stock the lake with "game fish." By March 1 work began on the building. The Kiersteds promised that daily newspapers would be delivered at their hotel. They announced that Colonel James Smith of Poughkeepsie's renowned Smith Brothers' Cough Drop family had leased the place and would manage it personally. The new Overlook Mountain House would be run as "a first-class hotel." Smith at once began furnishing the building. "The material is to be of the very best," said the Saugerties *Daily Post*.

By the middle of April the hotel was being painted. On April 10 the steamboat *Ansonia* delivered at Saugerties Long Dock "80 black walnut suites for bedroom furniture" for the new hotel.

As the hotel was being rushed to completion by Saugerties labor and capital, the businessmen of Catskill and Kingston were unhappy and asked if Saugerties was about to become the "Gateway to the Catskills" and put Catskill and Kingston in the shade. "Saugerties is destined to become the great thoroughfare from the Hudson to the Catskills," the Saugerties *Daily Post* had predicted in the summer of 1877.

The Catskill *Recorder* responded that "grass was growing on

Saugerties' Long Dock built in anticipation of vastly increased traffic on the Hudson at Saugerties." Saugerties, the paper said, was "the dullest, sleepiest, town along the Hudson, inhabited by descendants of Rip Van Winkle. . . ."

In Kingston agitation for building a narrow-gauge railroad connecting the Ulster and Delaware station at West Hurley with a point as high as possible on Overlook once again made a good deal of noise. Such a railroad would make Kingston and not Saugerties the base for the Overlook Mountain House. Samuel J. Coykendall, son-in-law of the Ulster and Delaware's president, Thomas Cornell, was quoted as saying that he was in favor of the railroad and that it would cost $150,000 to build. Woodstock boardinghouse keepers, owners of small farm boardinghouses and local shopkeepers began dreaming again of a railroad.

In the spring of 1878 it looked as though the Overlook Mountain House might have an unexpected problem before its second season came. It was reported that Christian Baehr, for whom the hamlet of Bearsville is named, was planning to build a rival to the Kiersteds' hotel on a level area a little below, a location mentioned in newspapers as "Bear's Whortleberry Flat" (the word huckleberry was regarded at the time as inelegant). The hotel was never built.[13]

The new Overlook Mountain House had been scheduled to open on June 25. Through immense effort the Kiersted Brothers managed to meet this commitment and the hotel opened. As on the date its predecessor began life (June 15, 1871), it had to contend on the day of its opening with rain, fog and wind. But more than two hundred people were on hand for the ceremonies. In Saugerties fireworks and cheers greeted the event. The first stage to leave the village for Overlook set off amidst the firing of guns and the waving of damp flags.

The food and service that first day were very bad indeed. The band of Colonel Smith's 21st Regiment couldn't make it and another—Burger's Band—was hastily substituted; Mr. Burger was a violinist, a cornet player and on most days a hairdresser in Kingston. Very soon the food and service greatly improved. But for weeks the weather remained uncomfortably cool. When the people of Hudson Valley cities suffered from summer heat, many fled to mountain hotels like the one on Overlook. In cool weather they stayed at home.

Having learned from the experience of their predecessors, the Kiersteds had installed a steam heating system which they put into use that July. Soon the weather changed and the hotel quickly filled up. Cots were placed in the halls and in the parlor. Some people were sent down to Woodstock and advised to find accommodations there. Every hotel and boardinghouse in Woodstock that August was filled with summer people, every farmhouse had at its full quota of "city people."

The new Overlook Mountain House rates were $3 to $3.50 per day and $15 to $20 per week. The waitresses were "buxom, rosy and amiable farmers' daughters and school teachers." The absence of a bar was more than made up for by guests being permitted to bring their own liquor or buy privately what they wanted from members of the hotel staff. Colonel Smith, it was being said, "aimed at a high moral tone" in his hotel, and Woodstock people applauded this objective.

The building of a carriage road to what was still often called Shrew's Lake (in the belief caused by a surveyor's error that it was rich in those ferocious little mammals) was pushed to completion. Four new rowboats were set afloat on the lake. Paths leading to bizarrely-shaped rocks and points with extensive views were multiplied. Romantic names were freely given to many new points on the hotel property.

Entertainments were often presented in the hotel parlor. One evening there were songs by New York's excellent Mendelssohn Society. Another evening featured a "literary festival" of which no description has survived. On Sunday there was the usual religious service. A sermon that summer of 1878 by Dr. Thwing of Brooklyn's Church of the Covenant on the text of "He took them up into a mountain apart" made an excellent impression. Dr. Thwing, it was said, was at work on a history of the Catskills.

Chester Alan Arthur, just fired from his post as Collector of the Port of New York in a political shakeup billed as a reform move, was a guest at the hotel that summer. Arthur, an elegantly dressed, urbane man with flowing side whiskers, was a lawyer who had made his mark back in 1855 by winning a court decision giving blacks of New York the right to the same accommodations as whites on public vehicles. A bigwig in New York State politics, Arthur had been dismissed from his job when his faction lost ground. With the courtesy that distinguished him, Arthur ordered a bottle of wine and drank to the new collector's success. After that he hastened to Overlook to think things over and to plan for the future with a gathering on the mountain of upstate Republican politicians. When he returned to Overlook in 1884 it was as President of the United States.[13]

310

There were other distinguished visitors that summer. They included W. E. Griffis, ambassador to Japan and former professor at Japan's Imperial College.

Colonel Smith seized every advantage to promote the prosperity of his hotel. He named the spring on the plateau beside the hotel the Minnehaha Spring after the heroine of Longfellow's *Hiawatha*. He published the claim that the spring water was "the best in the world." He arranged for reporters to come to the mountain and write glowing accounts of the place. The Colonel proclaimed far and wide that the Overlook Mountain House, thanks to the purity of its air, was also a sure cure for malaria and hay fever.

The Kiersted brothers, impressed by Colonel Smith's success in literally packing the hotel with people, contracted to build an addition increasing capacity to over three hundred. It was expected that the Colonel and the Kiersteds would lose money their first year, everyone said. The future, however, seemed bound to become profitable.

Winter arrived early that year, and by mid-December ice seven inches thick was being cut on Cooper Lake and stored in large quantities for use at the hotel the next summer. Shares in the Overlook Turnpike Company, which would operate the road from Mead's via the Overlook Mountain House and Echo Lake to Platte Clove, found ready buyers when they went on sale.

The season of 1879 opened with a French chef hard at work, the road to Echo Lake functioning and moving on to Platte Clove, and a boat house and refreshment saloon on the lake shore. An artist named Hart made a page of sketches of the hotel and its attractions for the New York *Daily Graphic*. Colonel Smith paid $150 to have this done, agreeing to buy a large number of copies of the paper for free distribution.

That same year a handsomely designed and printed booklet, *A Catskill Souvenir*, backed by the Ulster and Delaware Railroad, contained an impressive two-page view of Overlook giving a sense of almost Alpine grandeur, with the hotel perched close to the mountain's summit. The upturn in the nation's economy which had begun in 1878 after some years of depression continued and helped the fortunes of the Overlook Mountain House.

By mid-summer every room at the hotel on the mountain was taken. In the valley below Aaron Riseley's Mountain View House, Howland's, Snyder's and Disch's were all full. So too were Mead's and the MacDaniels' Cold Spring House. City people reaching West

Hurley without reservations were warned not to go on to Woodstock unless they intended "to sleep out of doors." Many did camp out, some on Overlook and others elsewhere in Woodstock.[14]

From the opening of the first Overlook Mountain House the presence of timber rattlesnakes on the mountain had caused nervous people to stay away. Each spring men continued as in earlier years to kill emerging snakes at their great den on top of the Minister's Face. But the rattlers persisted, and tales of the snakes being discovered close to the hotel, on its verandahs and even within were whispered. The management of course did all it could to discourage such talk. But with business so good by 1879 stories of Overlook rattlers were more often printed in regional newspapers with a kind of pride.

In 1879 the Honorable John Ferris, member of the State Assembly from northern Delaware County, saw a rattler "preparing to spring" at his horse's leg. Ferris killed the snake with his whip. Moses Becker of West Saugerties killed a four-foot rattler close to the hotel and also killed "thirteen young ones about six inches long."

What looked like a rise in the rattlesnake population did nothing to check the popularity of the hotel. It was gaining in 1879 in reputation as a health resort. Gustavus A. Kahnweiser, a Washington, D. C. engineer who believed that his daughter had been greatly benefitted by a stay on Overlook, proposed dividing the mountaintop into small lots on which cottages for the ailing might be built. As many others had suggested earlier, a narrow-gauge railroad was again planned to run as far up the mountain as possible.

Many had predicted that a "temperance hotel" like the one on Overlook could not succeed. When it appeared to be doing so in 1879 there were some sneers and unpleasant rumors. Someone signing himself "R" wrote to the Saugerties *Telegraph* to charge that Colonel Smith had been seen drunk at his hotel. The Colonel's reply was a model of brevity and forcefulness. He wrote, "Editor Evening Post, Dear Sir—publish the following to 'R' of Saugerties *Telegraph*; You are a liar. James Smith, Proprietor, Overlook Mountain House." [15]

In the spring of 1879 after Woodstock had gone dry many Woodstock people resented Colonel Smith's policy of allowing drinking on the sly at his hotel. "R" may have been one of these.

Until 1883 the hotel on Overlook drew substantial numbers of guests. Hudson Valley people, New Yorkers, Germans and Englishmen, distinguished painters and writers, well-known politicians—all came to the Overlook Mountain House. Woodstock people and their summer boarders continued to climb the mountain for excursions and picnics.

The next year a non-alcoholic drought struck Overlook. Rainfall became too slight to replenish the Overlook spring and fill its huge stone-walled reservoir. Water had to be hauled up the mountain by straining horses and cursing teamsters—this even though the hotel did not have flush toilets and other thirsty features of modern plumbing.

Yet the hotel owners showed resolution in improving the place for the expected future flood of guests. They began building a bowling alley on the very edge of the clifftop just below the level of the hotel. The alley was completed in the summer of 1881 as an addition to the caretaker's lodge. Attached to it were some rooms in which day visitors to the mountaintop might take refuge from showers. Nearby a picnic ground was marked out and maintained for the visitors. Higher on the mountain a children's playground appeared.

That same season of 1881 saw the building of a frame three-story tower on Overlook's very summit. The building was topped by an observation platform seven hundred feet higher than the highest tower of George Harding's rival Kaaterskill Hotel then being built some twelve miles to the north. A telescope fixed on the platform was much used by guests. Strong iron cables held the tower fast to its rocky base. It was not until the spring of 1901 that a fierce storm uprooted the structure and scattered its clapboards far and wide.[16]

By 1882 the road linking Plattekill Clove, Echo Lake, the Catskill Mountain and Overlook Mountain Houses was in good condition. C.W. Squires, the Overlook's new manager, succeeding Colonel Smith, made much of the convenience and scenic charm of the new road and gave his hotel historic glamor by stating that the Plattekill Clove had long ago been used "by the French and Indians."

Starting in the spring of 1881 Echo Lake, which had been stocked with trout, for a few years roused the interest of fishermen guests at the Overlook hotel. An earlier attempt at stocking the lake with black bass had not turned out well.

Eighteen eighty-three saw the completion of the Kaaterskill Branch of the Ulster and Delaware Railroad. This gave the hotels along its line a decided advantage over the one on Overlook. At the same time the efforts of mid-Hudson capitalist Thomas Cornell and his son-in-law Samuel Coykendall brought railroad service up the west bank of the Hudson to Kingston, Saugerties and eventually to Albany.

All this gave little encouragement to holders of stock in the Kiersted Brothers' hotel. Stockholders complained that Cornell was deliberately manipulating train schedules to favor other hotels in the Catskills in which he had financial stakes. Steamboat companies also were said to be joining in a conspiracy directed against the Overlook Mountain House by refusing to stop at Saugerties' Long Dock, from which access to the Overlook was shorter and easier by stage than via Kingston Point, which was under the thumb of the Cornell forces.

The rush of economic euphoria which began in 1878 had run its course by 1883. The managers of many summer hotels built during those cheerful years began to count their empty rooms and try to cut operating expenses.

Though in 1884 the Overlook Mountain House had plenty of empty rooms it continued to operate much as before. Distinguished people arrived now and then; one was President Chester A. Arthur, who drove over the fine new Plattekill Road from the huge Hotel Kaaterskill, where he was staying. Arthur was accompanied by Chief Justice Morrison Remick Waite, Miss Freylinghusen of The Secretary of State's family, and three carriage loads of other important people. All had lunch at the Overlook Hotel and inspected the sights. On their way groups of women stopped the carriages and presented the occupants with bouquets and wreaths of flowers until at last the members of the party were almost smothered in what one newspaper called "floral blooms."

That same summer New York playwright and producer Steele MacKaye spent a long time on half-deserted Overlook, struggling in vain to put together a play that might rival his *Hazel Kirk*, one of the most successful melodramas of its century.

MacKaye may have been disheartened, but the Kiersted brothers tried hard to keep up an appearance of hope and confidence. During the playwright's stay a relative of the secretary of the Overlook Mountain Hotel Company, Mrs. A.E.P. Searing of Saugerties, published a splendid book called *The Land of Rip Van Winkle*, in which she strove valiantly to draw attention to the beauties of the Overlook Mountain House. With its fine wood engravings and its lively text, the book was much admired. It did little, however, to send guests rushing to the hotel it celebrated.[17]

As the Eighties moved along and the Nineties began the hotel was being called Kiersteds' Folly. The brothers saw with growing unhappiness the fortune brought together by years of Kiersted effort feeding the endless appetite for money of their hotel.

From time to time during the Eighties fresh rumors of an impending railroad spur from the line of the Ulster and Delaware at West Hurley brought bits of hope which quickly faded. Woodstock farmers and businessmen who hoped for good profits from a successful mountain house on Overlook came to believe that they could expect nothing from the railroad as long as it was dominated by Cornell and Coykendall. A proposed "air-line" from Saugerties was talked about for a few months and then forgotten.

By the 1890s the "electric road" or trolley car was rousing the imaginations of American speculators all over the country. The Kingston *Argus* pointed out that such lines would soon convert isolated farmers into suburbanites, rid the country of provincialism, make urban education possible for rural children and confer many other benefits. Woodstock and especially Overlook Mountain became the targets of several proposed trolley lines beginning in Saugerties or Kingston and running to the base of Overlook, where a cable car was planned to haul guests and supplies up the mountain. A cable line (the Otis Elevating Railway) was already being sent from Palenville to the old Catskill Mountain House.

By 1891 both Kiersted brothers had died. James' son Egbert J. became president of the hotel company which he and his wife Jennie at times managed personally and at other times turned over to a rapidly changing succession of lessees. Most were experienced hotel men with Saratoga, New York or Southern resort experience. None proved able to solve the old problems which had for so long haunted Overlook. In 1892 one lessee closed the place in mid-season.

After that the fortunes of the hotel promised to become more dismal than ever. Egbert Kiersted was an unusual man with talents in mathematics, gardening and civil engineering. Yet the hotel baffled and frustrated him. In 1897 he committed suicide. That summer the Overlook Mountain House operated as a restaurant only. Many of its none-too-numerous patrons came over the Overlook Mountain Turnpike from hotels in the Haines Falls-Tannersville area. By this time an occasional visitor to Overlook was arriving by carriage from the railroad station at Haines Falls.

In 1898 a surge of hope came once again to Woodstock people and Overlook Mountain House stockholders. It was made known that an energetic and apparently well-heeled manager was making extensive improvements to the hotel and the road leading to it. He was B. F. Bruce, secretary to Grover Cleveland. Ex-President Cleveland was expected to lend the power of his presence to the place that summer. Bruce undertook an ambitious program of landscaping the hotel's surroundings in the taste of the times. But he reckoned without Overlook's capricious frosts and winds. His bedding-out plants were nipped by cold and their remains blown into the valley.

The next year the hotel stood empty. Its windows were shuttered. A caretaker did what he could to protect the place. A series of bad winter storms damaged buildings and unusually heavy accumulations of ice broke down the balsam fir trees which until then had been a valued feature of the mountaintop. It looked for a while as if Overlook's career as the site of a summer hotel was over. Stock in the hotel company and in the turnpike company sank almost to the point of invisibility.[18]

But the charm of the site remained. People who had yielded to that charm had been beggared and driven to illness and even suicide as they struggled to make their dreams for the mountaintop emerge into reality. As the twentieth century arrived the charm of Overlook remained, and before long new hotel dreamers would succumb to that charm.

The largest of the Indian rock shelters on Overlook Mountain, 1917. Photo by Max Schrabisch. *(Courtesy of New York State Museum.)*

A fragment of Indian pottery found in an Overlook rock shelter, drawn by an artist named Schneble, 1917. The original is in the collection of the Woodstock Historical Society. (*Drawing courtesy of the New York State Museum.*)

The Lake Hill Stone, found at the bottom of Cooper Lake in the 1890s and once believed to be an Indian artifact. Photo by Harry Siemsen. (*Author's collection.*)

The Newkerk house on Old Route 212 in Zena was built in many stages, probably beginning around 1720. During the Revolutionary War it was the scene of Tory activities. Photo by Roger Vandemark, 1957. *(Author's collection.)*

Below, detail from a map drawn by William Cockburn in 1773 showing a part of the Hardenbergh Patent. The new settlement of Woodstock is drawn with considerable accuracy, as are Cooper Lake, Kingston, Saugerties, the Katsbaan Church (at which most Woodstock settlers worshipped), and the Hudson River mansion of Judge Robert R. Livingston, Woodstock's absentee landlord. *(Courtesy of Ulster County Historical Society.)*

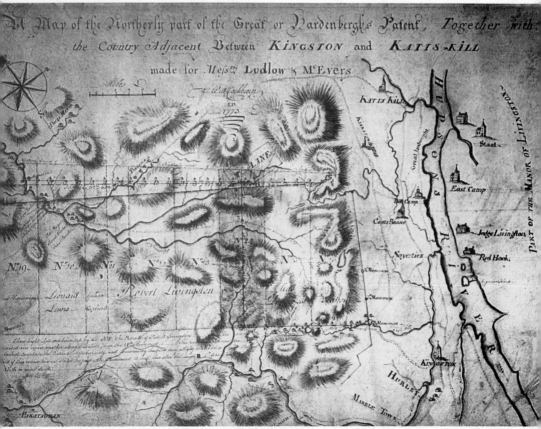

A Revolutionary War bayonet found beneath the cellar floor of the Newkerk house. *(Bayonet courtesy of Ludwig Baumgarten, photo by author.)*

A portrait of Madame Margaret Beekman Livingston by Gilbert Stuart. Most Woodstock farmers paid their rents to Madame Livingston during the final decade of the 18th century. *(Courtesy of New York State Office of Parks Recreation and Historic Preservation; Clermont Historical Site.)*

At a Town meeting held the first Tuesday In June 1787 at the House of Elias Hasbrouck In the Townships of Woodstock In the County of Ulster, by Virtue of an act of the Ligislature of the State of New York, passed the 11th Day of Aprile 1787. for Erecting the Settlements of Woodstock and Grate an Little Shandaken into a Siparate Township; The following Parsons ware by Pluralyty of Voyces Chosen Town Officers for Said Town

Viz   Elias Hasbrouck   Supervisor
         John Row ——— . Town Clerk

         Petrus Short —
         Samuel Mowers   } Assessors
         William Snyder —
         Zachery Short — . Collector

         Samuel Mowers }
         Petrus Row — } Constables

         Andries Riselar } Overseers of the Poor
         Dament Lewis   }

         Petrus Short —
         William Snyder } Commissioners of Highways
         Hendrick B Krom

         Aurey New herk }
         John Karl —   } overseers of the Highways
         Hendrick B Krom }
         John Longyyard —

First page of the Woodstock Town Clerk's Minute Book, 1787-1804. It records the meeting at which Woodstock people began existence under their own town government. This happened on June 5, 1787. Photo by Mary Hunt. *(Courtesy of Woodstock Town Clerk's office. The original minute book in the possession of the Town of Shandaken.)*

A now-vanished log house which stood on MacDaniel Road. Known as the Tompkins house, it was built early in the 19th century with methods similar to those of many earlier ones. *(Author's photo, c. 1955.)*

Jonathan Hasbrouck, first county judge of Ulster, was said to have been the richest man in Ulster County. Portrait by John Vanderlyn. *(Courtesy of New York State, Office of Parks, Recreation and Historic Preservation; Senate House State Historic Site, Palidades Interstate Park Region.)*

Interior of the Riseley house on the Bearsville Flats, built about 1790. Photo by longtime owner Conrad Kramer, 1930s. (Author's collection.)

Interior of the lower glass factory main building, long used as a barn. *(Author's photo.)*

Portrait of Mrs. John Maritje Schoonmaker Wigram by Ammi Philips, about 1820. *(Courtesy of Henry Scott, Charleston, S.C.)*

Portrait of John Wigram by Ammi Philips, about 1820. *(Courtesy of Henry Scott, Charleston, S.C.)*

The Reynolds sawmill in Shady, typical of Woodstock's many small sawmills, about 1905. Here a long wooden flume carries the water to the millwheel. *(Author's photo of post card, courtesy of Elizabeth MacDaniel, Shady.)*

Making maple sugar, about 1910. Photo by Sam Wiley. *(Author's collection.)*

Henry P. Shultis, Livingston land agent. *(Photo courtesy of William Kiessel, Woodstock.)*

A wagon makes its way through flood waters of about 1905, near Riseley's Bridge on the present Route 375 near the Woodstock Playhouse. *(Courtesy of Mrs. Robert C. Bradley, Woodstock.)*

Mural by Mary Earley of Anti-Rent War scene, in the Delhi, New York post office. *(Author's collection.)*

Frieze of the office of Dr. Larry Gilbert Hall, now forming part of the Woodstock Library, showing the stars which stand for the number of states in The Union when it was built. *(Author's photo.)*

The elm tree grave in the Woodstock Cemetery. *(Photo by Andrea Barrist Stern.)*

Below, parlor of the first Overlook Mountain House, 1872. Photo from a stereograph by Edward Lewis, Kingston. *(Author's collection.)*

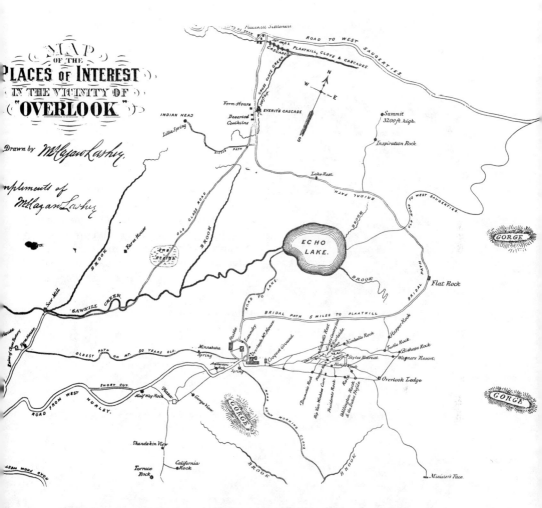

Map drawn by M. Hazzard Lasher around 1874 intended to point out to visitors the various features close to the Overlook Mountain House, then under lease to the mapmaker's father, John E. Lasher. (*Courtesy of Robert Lasher, New Paltz.*)

A post card of Boots Van Steenberg, the local eccentric who liked to entertain Overlook Mountain House guests. *(Author's collection.)*

Below, the laundry building and reservoir on Overlook. Once plumbing was installed at the hotel, water supply problems were frequent. The octogonal kiosk in the middle foreground protected the spring at which guests drank the water in the belief that it had medicinal properties. *(Photo courtesy of Eugene Dauner.)*

The bluestone wall of a quarry forge where tools were sharpened and repaired. (*Author's photo, c. 1960.*)

Coon Lasher about to shoe a horse at his Bearsville blacksmith shop, August 15, 1919. (*Author's collection, courtesy of Jean Gaede.*)

°TOWN OF WOODSTOCK

Scale 10 Rods to the inch

Map showing the hamlet of Woodstock, 1875. *(Beers' Atlas of Ulster County, 1875.)*

Panoramic view of Overlook Mountain from the Wide Clove to the Minister's Face with A.N. Riseley's Mountain View House and Riseley's Bridge and grist mill dam in Woodstock. *(Advertisement in Walton Van Loan's Guide to the Catskills, 1883).*

OVERLOOK MOUNTAIN, FROM NEAR WOODSTOCK.

ALEXANDER LONGYEAR,

WOODSTOCK, Ulster County, N. Y.

NEW THREE-STORY FRENCH-ROOF HOUSE, in the village of Woodstock, five miles from Railroad Station of West Hurley and four miles from the OVERLOOK MOUNTAIN HOUSE.

WELL-FURNISHED AND WELL-VENTILATED ROOMS,

WITH HIGH CEILINGS.

TERMS—$6 to $8 PER WEEK.

FULL VIEW OF THE OVERLOOK MOUNTAIN,

AND OTHERS SEEN FROM THE HOUSE.

ACCOMMODATIONS FOR TWENTY.

IN THE MIDST OF THE CATSKILLS.

WOODSTOCK HOUSE,

WOODSTOCK, ULSTER COUNTY, N. Y.

A. E. WINNE, Proprietor.

Situated in the beautiful village of Woodstock, four miles from the OVERLOOK MOUNTAIN HOUSE, the highest mountain hotel in the Catskill Range. The House is surrounded by romantic scenery and stands amidst an abundance of shade.

The Grounds have been Improved and the House Enlarged

during the past season. Livery attached. Telegraph and Post Office opposite house. **TERMS, $7 to $10 PER WEEK.** Stages meet all trains at West Hurley Station of the Ulster and Delaware Railroad.

REFERENCE: Alexander Thain, 8 and 10 Wall Street, New York; J. Bently Squires, 21 East Seventy-ninth Street, New York; Dr. Geo. R. Fowler, 457 Marcy Avenue, Brooklyn.

See picture of House and surroundings.

A. N. RISELEY'S

MOUNTAIN VIEW HOUSE,

Woodstock, Ulster County, N. Y.

Large farm residence of 160 acres, pleasantly and conveniently located, a large stream of water running through it, and two stage roads passing the door.

The House is situated on high ground, from which a beautiful view of the surrounding country can be had in all directions. In full view are OVERLOOK MOUNTAIN HOUSE, four miles distant; WOODSTOCK village, half a mile distant, where there are three churches, post-office and telegraph station.

The House is four miles from West Hurley Station on the Ulster and Delaware Railroad.

ACCOMMODATIONS FOR TWENTY-FIVE.

Tony Denier, clown and pantomimist, was Mrs. Dan Sully's second husband. Author's photo. *(Poster in Lincoln Center Theatre Collection.)*

The Episcopalian Chapel at Mead's, later the Church of Christ on the Mount, 1920. Photo by Louis E. Jones. *(Author's collection.)*

A group of Byrdcliffe people pose before the new fireplace at the Lark's Nest, 1904. Ned Thatcher, Isabella Moore, Lucy Brown, Carl Eric Lindin, Ethel Canby, head cabinetmaker Erlenson, an unidentified woman, and Olaf Westerling, a woodcarver. *(Photo courtesy of Woodstock Historical Society.)*

Byrdcliffe chest, Byrdcliffe pottery and a hanging by Marie Little. Photo by Harry Siemsen. *(Author's collection.)*

The deck at Mullersruh, later Eastover, with grapevines. Photo by Jessie Tarbox Beals, c. 1908. (*Courtesy of Mark Willcox.*)

Students at Art Students League starting a climb up Overlook Mountain, 1909. Second from right is Aime Titus. Photo by Sam Wiley. *(Author's collection.)*

Art students going sketching on Tinker Street, c. 1910. Photo by Sam Wiley. (Author's collection.)

"Tearoom at the sign of the hearse." An art students' conversion in the former Hiram Bovee livery and undertaking establishing on Tinker Street. Photo from the Aime Titus album. *(Courtesy of Woodstock Library.)*

"Mrs. Riseley" poses for art students wearing the sunbonnet and voluminous skirt which women of her generation sometimes wore when this photograph was taken, c. 1910. From the Aime Titus album. *(Courtesy of Woodstock Library.)*

Mrs. Stoehr and daughter in the garden of their East Riding house Hi-Lo-Ha, c. 1912. Photo by Mary L. Webster. *(Author's collection, courtesy of Aileen Payne.)*

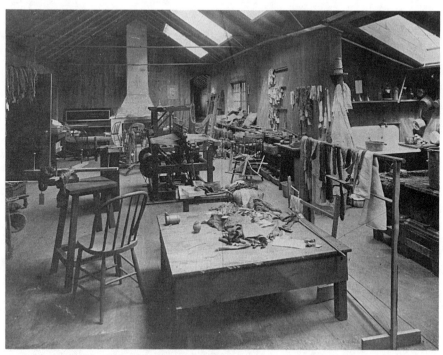

The interior of the Loom Room attached to White Pines. Photo by Jessie Tarbox Beals, around 1908. *(Courtesy of Howard Greenberg.)*

Woodstock women vote for the first time in a state election, November 1918. (*Author's collection.*)

Selling walking sticks at a Maverick Festival. Photo by Stowall Studios. (*Courtesy of Woodstock Library.*)

Building the Maverick ship, the Ark Royal, for the Festival. *(Courtesy of Woodstock Library.)*

The audience being seated in the outdoor theater for a Maverick Festival performance. Photo by Stowall Studios. *(Author's collection.)*

Unity Club members folk dancing in front of the Overlook Mountain House, around 1920. *(Photo courtesy of the International Ladies Garment Workers' Union.)*

The Knife and Fork, Woodstock's first sidewalk eating place, 1920s. *(Author's collection.)*

Looking from the Village Green toward the former post office, 1920s. *(Author's collection.)*

Maverick Festival celebrants: Hippolyte Havel, Pierre Henrotte and others. *(Courtesy of Woodstock Library.)*

The newly built Maverick Concert Hall with the "flying buttresses" used as temporary supports, 1916. Hervey White is seated in the left foreground. Photo by Louis E. Jones. *(Author's collection.)*

Salammbo rehearsal scene, Maverick Festival, Hervey White, directing, is at lower left with back to camera. *(Courtesy of Woodstock Library.)*

Sculptor John Flannagan, Linda Lilly Sweeney and the Maverick Horse, 1920s. *(Courtesy of Linda Sweeney.)*

Painter Charles Rosen dresses as Cupid for a Maverick Festival of the late 1920s. *(Author's collection.)*

The logo of the first issues of *The Hue and Cry*, summer, 1923. *(Author's collection.)*

The Cheats and Swings square dancing group rehearsing in 1938. From left to right, callers Dyrus Cook and Percy Hill, musicians Walter Shultis, Dick Gray and Willard Allen, dancers Frances Woisceske, Alfred Van Etten, Rose Petrucelli and Irwin Arlt. *(Courtesy of Woodstock Library.)*

Bolton C. Brown working on a lithographic stone. Photo by Alfred Cohn, 1925. *(Courtesy of John Ludwig.)*

Eleanor Roosevelt (on left holding trowel) lays the cornerstone of the National Youth Center building on Route 212 near Easton Road. The building was occupied later by the Art Student's League school and then by the Woodstock School of Art. *(Photo courtesy of D.J. Stern.)*

"Primitive Life in Woodstock—Going to Cider Mill," reads the legend on this post card. Photo by Louis E. Jones, around 1915. *(Author's collection.)*

Volunteers help repair the Family building on Rock City Road, late 1970s. *(Courtesy of Woodstock Library.)*

29

BLUESTONE

During the years that passed between the end of the Civil War and the beginning of the twentieth century Woodstock changed, sometimes slowly and at other times in sudden spurts. The size and shape of the town changed. The last survivors of the days of settlement died. A new industry grew to fill the gap left by the passing of glassmaking. The daily lives of people became more sophisticated. The increase in the number of summer boarders had effects on the town which, in 1902, would make it attractive to the founders of an art colony.

Before a boundary agreement with Hurley in 1853 put Yankeetown Pond and its surroundings inside Woodstock, most people seemed to believe that the shape and size of Woodstock had been fixed forever. Yet this was not the case. And in 1879 some eight thousand acres were added to the town as a result of a chain of events emanating from the growth of the bluestone industry in Woodstock and surrounding towns.[1]

Early in Woodstock's history Livingston leases forbade the "carrying away" and selling of the town's bedrock. This bedrock was a stratified Upper Devonian sandstone, hard and easily quarried in the large smooth slabs favored for sidewalks, steps, cellar floors and many other uses. By the 1840s Livingston tenants were quarrying bluestone to be sent down the Hudson to New York. They were paying their landlords a royalty of $2.50 per thousand square feet for all stone quarried. By the 1850s the royalty had risen to $3.00.[2]

Before the 1840s the stone had been put to a variety of home uses as gravestones, as pavements around wells and in front of doorways, and as material for cellar floors, hearthstones, chimneys and hitching posts. It was skillfully worked into troughs and bowls for holding salt, food and water for domestic animals. In the 1840s Woodstock quarries joined those worked here and there all the way along the bluestone ledges beginning a bit below Albany and extending across the Pennsylvania line.

The stone began to count more and more not only as a substance useful in crafts but as a source of income from outside the town. The earliest commercial quarries known were worked by the Lewises of Lewis Hollow. For sidewalk flagging in New York and other Hudson Valley towns and cities new quarries were opened along the lower slopes of Overlook all the way from Shady to West Saugerties, at Snake Rocks (so called because of the prevalence there of rattlesnakes), up Hutchin Hill, in Wittenberg and Willow.

These quarries were often worked by one to three men and usually during the warmer months. Their stone was hauled to where stone dealers and finishers had their "docks" in Saugerties or Kingston. Teamsters receipts of the 1840s and 1850s show that flag and curb stone, gutter, sill and bridge stone, coping and the large thick stones called platforms were all in production.

Often enough the quarrymen finished their stones roughly, leaving final smoothing and squaring up to the stonecutters who worked for the dealers at the stone docks. Bluestone quarrying was much affected by the ups and downs of the economic system. After a vigorous spurt during the early 1850s the number of local quarries dwindled according to the New York State census of 1855 to a single one turning out $2400 worth of stone per year and employing nine men. By 1860 quarrying was expanding again. Through the Civil War and for a few years after it enjoyed a period of boom, and outside capitalists gained a large measure of control. Then the uncertainties of the mid-1870s closed many Woodstock quarries.[3]

By that time much of the rough, often hazardous quarry labor was being done by Irish refugees from social injustice and famine. The large families in Lewis Hollow which Bide Snyder remembered were Irish and the Hollow was known by a new name—the Irish Village. The men of the Village worked the enormous California quarry, Keegan's, Elliott's, Magee's, Murray's and other quarries strung along the long ledge on the lower slopes of Overlook known as the Quarrybank.

These lively, often boisterous people lived intensely, danced on a wooden platform in the woods, drank heavily at their shebeens and produced their large families. Some single men lived in large and ill-built boardinghouses. One of these stood a little below and to the east of the California quarry, where its sketchy foundations may still be seen. On Election Day the Irish of Lewis Hollow, as did so many other voters, got drunk and went down to the polls to vote in a body late in the day. As they reached the center of the hamlet men and boys who had been awaiting their arrival set upon them and a fist fight would follow on the Village Green.[4]

Woodstock's Irish Village resembled other Irish quarry settlements located not far from the Woodstock boundary line in the valley below. Stony Hollow, Jockey Hill and Hallihan's Hill, all in the old Town of Kingston, were among them. These settlements acquired political importance when the City of Kingston was formed from the villages of Kingston and Rondout in 1872. The new city after that was almost completely surrounded by the remains of the old Town of Kingston in which Stony Hollow, Jockey Hill and Hallinan's Hill were important centers of Irish population.

Democratic politicians of Palatine and Dutch ancestry dominated the oddly-shaped town through Irish lieutenants who took care of the quarry workers in times of need and in return expected their support on Election Day. Because the bosses had no effective opposition within the town they were able to wring remarkable profits from the place through every device known to the corrupt politicians of the time. On Election Day gangs of Irishmen marched in and surrounded the polls and prevented the voters of the opposition political machine from voting. There was violence and bloodshed. The bosses of the Republican machine which had had things pretty much its own way since Civil War days took action. They planned to carve up of the Town of Kingston in a way that would give them assurance of control.

At the politicians' instigation Republican voters first signed a petition calling for the annexation of the Town of Kingston's School District Number One to Woodstock. The petition charged that during the past few years the voters of District Number One had been "robbed of their elective franchise by a lawless gang of perjurers, ballot-box stuffers, jawbreakers, thieves and able-bodied paupers. . . ." The Ulster County Board of Supervisors, to whom the petition was addressed, with state legislative approval broke the Town of Kingston up into three pieces. One became the Town of Ulster. The part then known as Vandale and later as Zena was added to

Woodstock. What was left, the part which surrounded the City of Kingston like a dragon on all but one side, remained the Town of Kingston. In this way Democratic strength was diluted and the threat of a revived Democratic domination of Ulster County was averted.[5]

Woodstock people had hardly become used to the new size and shape of their town when local bluestone gave them another jolt in the form of a spectacular accident followed by a hard-fought lawsuit, Lucius Lawson vs. The Town of Woodstock. The accident was a result, in part, of the local obsession with the gigantic slabs of bluestone known as "platforms" in the trade and as "big stones" to most people.

Up to the late 1860s Woodstock quarrymen sent few very large slabs of bluestone out into the world. Most of the flagstones produced in the town's quarries were of the size still in use on the sidewalks of many village and city side streets up and down the Atlantic Coast. But the time came when there was a demand for big stones, perhaps twelve by fourteen feet and five inches thick. Urban millionaires used these stones as sidewalks in front of their mansions. These status symbols testified by their size and smoothness and five to ten tons of weight to the power and wealth of the men who had paid to have them quarried, transported and laid in place.

Woodstock quarries tried to outdo each other in the size of the stones they quarried. The Snake Rock quarries (there the Stoutenbergh quarry was sometimes called the Giant quarry because of the size of its stones), the Lawson and Ingram quarry in Shady, the Vandebogart quarry and the California quarry all produced big stones. As the big-stone fever mounted, the departure of a big stone from its quarry became a matter of public rejoicing.

The late Ben Snyder remembered the day when a big stone left the California quarry with its stonecutters riding on the huge slab, smiling and waving at the men and women, children and dogs who walked alongside singing, barking and cheering. Arriving at the old hotel, once the Brinkerhoff House, the stonecutters and teamsters entered the barroom and were treated like heroes. They could barely stagger out to their horses again.

County newspapers proudly printed the dimensions of especially big stones. They reported early in 1881 that William H. Vanderbilt had offered his agent $10,000 for a single "flagstone twenty-five feet long and fifteen feet wide" for the sidewalk in front of the block-long and graceless mansion he was building on New York's Fifth Avenue. The stone had to be "without flaw."

It was said that a stone weighing twenty tons hauled from

Woodstock to the Bigelow dock at Malden by seventeen horses broke down every bridge on the route. On July 1, 1881 the New York *Times* reported that a stone twenty-five by sixteen feet weighing twenty tons had been hauled to the Fitch Brothers dock at Wilbur, destined for William H. Vanderbilt's sidewalk. Another stone thirty-seven by fifteen feet had been quarried "but was broken while being trimmed." The origin of these stones was not given. They could well have come from Woodstock.[6]

An unhappy climax to Woodstock's big-stone fever came on August 8, 1881. Just before dusk on that day a moderately big stone which had left the Lawson and Ingram quarry in Shady at eight a.m. crashed through Riseley's Bridge above Hugo Disch's grist mill, killing one horse and injuring another, shaking up two teamsters, damaging the stone and resulting in a lawsuit which became the talk of Woodstock for many years.

Woodstock's narrow valleys and numerous streams make it a town of many bridges. In the early days of the town, bridges were sometimes put in places where they might easily wash out in times of flood. But as the habits of Woodstock streams became better known bridges were better located. Washouts became less frequent.

Bluestone quarrying, especially after the big-stone fever came to town, put a new strain on bridges. The bridges were required to carry weights far beyond those for which they had been designed. The biggest were only twelve feet between their braces and most were narrower. Many big stones could not get through without resort to prying or gouging the side braces or canting stones by raising one side in order to work a fourteen-foot-wide stone across a twelve-foot-wide bridge.

Taxpayers of the 1870s and 1880s were no more eager then taxpayers of today to spend more money than was strictly necessary on bridges able to take heavy loads. The Woodstock Commissioners of Highways seldom replaced a bridge until after it had given obvious signs of weakness.

With Charles DeForest driving the lead horses and Charles Eldredge taking care of the wheel horses, the big stone left the quarry at eight a.m. on August 8, 1881. The men knew that their stone, about fifteen feet long and almost eleven feet wide and five inches thick, would have to cross four fairly large "gallows frame" wooden bridges and four smaller ones before they would reach the Woodstock line and enter the Town of Hurley.

The road down from the quarry was so steep that the teamsters thought their brake would not hold the push of the six-ton stone. They chained their wagon wheels and added another two horses to the two they began with. They later added a fifth. The roadbed was so loose and gravelly that the chains had to be taken off to keep the wheels from sinking too deep into the roadbed.

About eleven o'clock the teamsters reached the bridge over the Sawkill beside the Reynolds and Elting grist and cider mill at Shady. Though the stone was able to pass between the braces on each side of the bridge, it struck one of them. The brace had to be pried back with an iron bar before the stone could be pulled across. By this time the hub of one of the huge wheels had cracked. An hour and a half went by as the wheel was replaced with one of Andrew Elting's. While this was being done the teamsters solaced themselves with some of the hard cider which had been gathering strength in Elting's cellar since the previous fall.

Encouraged by the cider and the sound new wheel DeForest and Eldredge took off from Elting's. When they came to the next bridge across the Sawkill (the one midway between Shady and Bearsville, then known as the Hollow Bridge), they found that their stone was a tight fit. They had to gouge wood from the braces to get it through. From that point all went well for a while. Even the Tannery Bridge over the Tannery Brook gave no trouble, although as usual it trembled considerably.

A few minutes after that the stone wagon drew up in front of Winne's Hotel (formerly the Brinkerhoff House). There a crowd of men and boys were waiting to see the big stone of which they had been hearing for weeks. One man noticed that the stone was so heavy that it caused the wagon wheels to sink some eight inches into the road's surface. A number of people expressed doubt that the stone could ever get across the bridge at Disch's mill.

One testified later that Harrison "Bub" Elwyn, the blacksmith, had warned, "If you go on this bridge, it will go down with you, it never will hold." Says DeForest, "If she goes down I will go with it. We run fast in the Hollow Bridge and cut our way through and we will go over this."

With the eyes of a good number of Woodstockers upon it, the big stone rumbled down Mill Hill Road, turned right and crossed the underground raceway which supplied water to Disch's mill. One witness at the trial of Lucius Lawson vs. The Town of Woodstock was well placed to see what happened; nineteen-year-old Walter Cottrell was an employee of a New York broker in coffee, tea, sugar and spices. From the porch of Aaron Riseley's boardinghouse (now Deanie's Restaurant) at which he was spending his vacation he watched for the stone's arrival while talking with three or four young lady boarders. He saw the horses start across the bridge at a good clip. Then he noticed that a corner of the stone they were pulling had struck one of the side braces of the bridge.

At this the teamsters "whipped up their horses and yelled to them to get over and they started up again, and went over and struck the other brace." The braces were responsible for much of the support of the bridge. As they fell the entire bridge collapsed. Three of the horses had crossed the bridge. The other two, the wheel horses, fell down with the bridge in a tangle of harness, timbers and splintered planks. One horse was drowned. DeForest and Eldredge, who had been sitting on the front end of the big stone, were shaken up but not badly injured. So large a piece of the big stone was broken off that it was no longer a true "big stone" and its value was substantially reduced.

A stream of Woodstockers came to see the broken bridge during the next few days. While the bridge had seemed sound before the accident its timbers had now been revealed to be rotten in a number of critical places. Very promptly the town replaced the wrecked bridge with an iron one believed to be the first of its kind to come to Woodstock.

When Lawson vs. Woodstock came to trial in Kingston in 1883 before Judge Ingalls the lawyers for Lawson subpoenaed many witnesses in order to prove that the bridge was old and weak and that while the Woodstock Commissioners of Highways were able to obtain public funds to repair or replace it they had not done so. These witnesses swore too that the big stone had been driven across the bridge in a "proper manner" and that the braces had not been struck.

The witnesses for Woodstock gave testimony to show that the bridge was structurally sound and that the braces had indeed been struck because of the carelessness of the two teamsters in entering on the bridge. A model of the bridge was made and was used in the courtroom. In his charge to the jury Judge Ingalls said that if it had been proved to the satisfaction of the jurymen that DeForest and Eldredge had been in the least negligent in driving across the bridge, Lawson could not win his case under existing law.

The jury found that Woodstock had been negligent in caring for the bridge. They awarded Lawson $510 plus five per cent of that sum. By that time Lawson had suffered so much from a slump in the bluestone industry that he was bankrupt.[7]

Quarrying continued a part of Woodstock life for many years after the case of the falling bridge had been settled. When the demand for the stone slackened, quarries closed. When demand revived they reopened. In order to make even a meager living the quarry workers had to be ready at short notice to leave town and look for work elsewhere, perhaps as harvest hands in Delaware County, perhaps in other quarries at a considerable distance; wages fluctuated. In 1888 the quarry operators cut pay for "top men" to one dollar per day, giving as their reason a fall in the price of stone.

Quarrying was an unsettling factor in Woodstock. It brought profits to some but only problems to many others. Strikes were frequent among quarrymen. The men were not always able to work together to counter the close cooperation of the quarry operators and big riverside dealers in stone. At one point the quarrymen in Sawkill in the Town of Kingston sent a deputation to Woodstock to forbid Woodstock stone to be hauled through their town on its way to the docks at Wilbur.

The development of cheaper ways of making Portland cement brought ruinous competition to the sale of bluestone for use in sidewalks. The entire bluestone industry tottered on the edge of total collapse. In 1902 Samuel Coykendall, a power in the nearby Rosendale cement industry, announced that he was setting one hundred men to work in Woodstock quarries with the aid of the most modern machinery. The hope was to quarry only the very best quality of stone and so revive the industry and give its product a reputation for quality. The project began and then faded away in the face of hard economic facts. After that until the 1920s a Woodstock quarry was occasionally opened to fill a special order.[8]

When the great engineering feat of the building of the Ashokan Reservoir began in 1903 many Irish Village workers became stone cutters for the City of New York on the site. After the reservoir was completed about 1915 some of these people, already employees of the City, were able to get work as city policemen and firemen. Others, their lungs wrecked by silicosis or tuberculosis (occupational diseases for bluestone workers), drifted to the New York South Bronx Irish colony and there spent their days gathering in taverns and reminiscing about the great days of bluestone quarrying, which they sadly admitted would never return.[9]

Descendants of the quarry people merged into the population of Woodstock, and the prejudice once held against them died away.

30

FARM AND FAMILY LIFE, 1870-1900

A good deal still remains to remind Woodstock people of life during the years when memories of the Civil War were still vivid. There are the old houses in which large families worked at farm-related tasks and enjoyed a pleasant social life, and the bluestone cellars, their walls and ceilings bearing remnants of the whitewash once regularly applied to keep them fit for dairy purposes. The shelves which once hung from the beams and held the pans of milk as the cream rose have vanished to make way for heating and hot-water devices. Upstairs, the parlor organ once stood, perhaps in the room where the television set now reigns, and around it family and friends gathered to sing hymns and openly sentimental secular songs.

Bits of paper remain, not only mortgages and deeds but pages of verses, invitations to parties, clippings from county newspapers and letters, and reminiscences like Bide Snyder's. All can put us in touch with life in Woodstock during the decades when farming seemed a stable way of life that would never end. Modern houses often contain rush-bottomed chairs with stencilled decoration and cherry drop-leaf tables, walnut-framed sofas and parlor chairs, and old farm tools now retired and hung on the wall by way of ornament. All these items, often bought at local auctions or from Woodstock antique dealers, act as pleasant recorders of the town's past.

During the early decades of the present century Woodstock people looked back on their late nineteenth-century past as at a kind of golden age. Bruce Herrick, Woodstock's hometown poet, expressed this feeling about his "pastoral haven" in the words of an innocent song called "Woodstock, The Town of Our Dreams." It goes in part:

> How well we remember this town long ago
> With its little old stone village school,
> And the old fashioned stage coach that carried the mail,
> As it rocked on its way to and fro.
> The old tannery ruin; the Overlook house,
> Are all in the realm of the past. . . .

In his book *The Vanishing Village*, Will Rose conveys the same sense of the passing of the old farm and summer boarder centered life as the town was invaded by the twentieth century—and by an art colony.[1]

Statistics of the period make it clear enough that quarrying and caring for summer boarders had economic and social importance. But farming was dominant. The statistics show that local farms varied a good deal in quality and productiveness.

Most prosperous of all the farms were those with ample acreage of lowland along the Sawkill and Beaverkill. Here the descendants of early settlers were in possession of the best farmland. The most valuable farms belonged to Lashers, Van Ettens, Vandebogarts, Riseleys, Shorts and a very few others. The farm given the highest assessed value in 1896, belonging to Alvah Lasher (along Route 212 below the present Country Club), was given a value of $5000. Other Lasher farms were assessed at $3000, $4600 and so on.

Along the road between Bearsville and Yankeetown an almost unbroken series of Shultis farms had values of up to $2000. Peter Keegan's fifty-acre farm in the Irish Village had an assessed valuation of $650, high for a mountainside farm.

The number of Woodstock farms in 1875 was 148. Most consisted of from 50 to 100 acres, and many had woodlots sometimes of about the same size, often high on hill and mountainsides. The total number of acres under cultivation in 1845 had been 7757. By 1875 that total had grown to 12,248. By 1875, however, the increase of pests and the deterioration of the overworked soil had caused the cultivation of wheat to come almost to an end. Instead rye became a major crop, with buckwheat, corn and oats widely grown.[2]

Apples were a feature of all farms. Hard cider production amounted to close to one thousand barrels per year. Apples packed in barrels were shipped to New York. One fall a Wittenberg farmer claimed to have sent 500 barrels of apples to New York via the *Ansonia*, which took the apples on board at Saugerties' Long Dock. A late spring frost might kill apple blossoms and reduce the yield of Woodstock's more than 14,000 apple trees to almost nothing. In years like that temperance people, who saw the frost as a blow directed against hard-cider drinkers by the Lord, rejoiced.

Apples and grapes were grown to be sold to the Overlook Mountain House and the Tremper House in Phoenicia. Chickens and eggs, honey and maple sugar, ham and bacon also found a market at local summer hotels and boardinghouses, to Kingston and Saugerties people, or were consumed by the farmer's own boarders. The Overlook Mountain House during its best days bought three thousand pounds of butter each season. Much of this was churned and worked by Woodstock farm wives, sometimes with the help of a treadmill operated by a dog or a docile sheep.

According to the New York State census of 1875, 275 working oxen and steers labored on Woodstock farms and roads as against 311 horses two years old or older. Horses and oxen held a place in the life of old Woodstock similar to that held today by the family car, except that they probably aroused greater feelings of affection because they were living creatures. This was especially true of the horses, to whom their drivers often talked. And the horses listened, if without understanding.[3]

In a society in which the horse supplied so much of the energy that made things move, horse-related activities were many. Harnessmaker William Ploss kept busy in his shop between the Rose and Beekman store and the Dutch Reformed Church. The many local blacksmith shops made and attached horseshoes. Some also had ox stocks, a device for holding oxen quiet as they were having two iron shoes attached to each of their four feet. The blacksmiths also "ironed" wagons, sleighs and carriages. Beside each blacksmith shop was a large square piece of bluestone used in replacing the iron tire of a wagon wheel. Oats for horses' food were grown often in small fields high on the hillsides.

A family's social status was usually given visible form by its possession of an especially fine horse. The Woodstock doctor was likely to have the fastest horse or horses in town. The undertaker's horses had to be black and impressive. The bluestone quarries were work places for many strong horses whose drivers had to be skillful in persuading the horses to move heavy weights over difficult terrain. Oldtime quarry teamsters like John Herrick and Sanford Magee were heroes to the town's boys. As the quarry horses went to work in the early morning the boys would tumble out of bed to watch them going by.[4]

It was every boy's ambition to own and drive a fine horse when he grew up. Many boys began learning about horses by feeding them, cleaning the rye straw bedding from their stalls, and currycombing their coats in the morning. It was a big moment when a boy was allowed to help put the harness on the horses and a much bigger one when he first held the "lines" and guided a horse while sitting beside a grown man behind the dashboard of a buggy.

When snow covered the land the work of oxen and horses took a new turn. The oxen hauled logs out of the deep woods from places which the snow and frost had made accessible. On highways and lanes snow was not pushed aside as it is today. It was packed down whenever possible to form a smooth and sleek surface over which the runners of sleighs and farm bobsleds might move almost effortlessly. Horses which had spent the milder months at mundane farm tasks seemed to take delight in pulling a light cutter over the smooth surface of a well-packed winter road, or, sleigh bells jingling, in hauling a box sleigh full of Woodstockers to a party or to Cooper Lake for skating.

Disputes about the relative usefulness of oxen and horses were carried on with enthusiasm year after year around the stove in Snyder's store and in Woodstock taverns. Outstanding as an authority on oxen and their lore was Cambridge "Came" Lasher. Came had been brought up surrounded by oxen. His father had been "bound out" to Henry P. Shultis, the Livingston agent, but had run away and ended up with a good farm of his own, with five or six pair of oxen to help work it.

Between 1888 and 1910 Came was a dealer in oxen. He travelled incesssantly over half a dozen counties from his Woodstock base. The oxen Came bought and sold usually had traditional names, Buck and Bright and Duke and Dine the most usual. As the Irish population grew Pat and Mike became oxen names.

Came liked to maintain that oxen were just as intelligent as horses and a lot easier to train. He had an almost uncanny ability to judge the weight of an ox. When a farmer wondered how much his oxen weighed (a team weighed from 2000 to 4000 pounds), someone would remind him, "Wait till Came comes along. He'll tell you."

Came would look at an ox and tell whether, as he reminisced in the 1930s, "he'd be slow or whether he was a bird and so fast he'd make a driver's shirttails fan." Came often said, "It's a good pair of oxen that'll run away." It was his job to provide a pair that could run and then see to it that they didn't.

Oxen, Came believed, were capable of just as much sustained speed as horses. One year his father's oxen drew twenty-five loads of cider and apples to Kingston. The drivers peddled their products and returned to Woodstock all in the same day with their oxen moving, as Came put it, "down on a walk and back on a walk." Once Came remembered a team of oxen drawing a load of lumber to Rondout following another load drawn by horses. The oxen kept up with the horses all the way. Reported Came, "Some has a lively step and some a lazy step, and those with the lively step never dropped behind the horses." [5]

Oxen gave rise to much folk talk, and so too did horses. Best-remembered of all the Woodstock tales about horses was the one about the day George Washington came to Woodstock—not the George Washington who was father of his country but a Sullivan County man of the same (probably assumed) name who claimed to be skilled as a farrier or horse doctor. Washington had come to Woodstock in the early 1870s peddling a patented lamp burner. He returned in the late summer of 1875 and let it be known that he was able and ready to treat ailing horses.

An epidemic of what was called black mouth broke out among Woodstock horses, and Washington treated case after case with success. Then one day the men talking the time away at the bar of Winne's Hotel compared notes. They found that in every case of black mouth Washington had been seen close to the horse before the symptoms developed. Someone remembered that the horse doctor had been seen by a little girl pouring something from a can into the mouth of a horse standing under the Reformed Church shed (which stood behind the church) just before the horse first got a sore mouth.

The Kingston *Daily Freeman* of September 23, 1875 told with gusto what happened next. "A public meeting was accordingly called at the Brinkerhoff [or Winne] House on Saturday night to take some action in regard to the matter. The gathering was a very large one and after a general comparison of notes it was judged best to arrest Washington on a charge of poisoning the horses." Justice Ploss (who was the harnessmaker in private life) issued a warrant and Washington was brought before him at the Brinkerhoff House. Soon a hearing was under way with the room packed with aroused people.

Methodist minister J. E. Gorse was testifying when a most extraordinary event cut off his words. As the *Freeman* put it, "no warning whatever was given, but with the suddenness of thought the whole floor sank in, and chairs, tables and ink bottles, law books, clients, witnesses, the court, and all the paraphernalia of law were dumped into a heap on the cellar bottom. Everyone yelled, thinking the house was falling in and [Derrick W.] Sparling [the lawyer for Washington] says the room was so completely changed he couldn't think first where he was. For a time there was a complete pandemonium, but though a great many persons were scratched and bruised, luckily no one was seriously injured, though the chairs and tables were broken into pieces. Nearly two hundred people were in the room at the time, and it seems the beams broke off by the great weight."

One of the greatest 'sufferers' by the accident was a Mr. Lasher "who lost his tall white hat." After he was "hoisted out of the cellar, and saw the condition that hat was in," said the *Freeman*, "they say it was fearful to hear the blessing he gave the man that built that house. It would not have been suitable at a camp meeting." According to the folk version of the incident, the prisoner, Washington, took advantage of the collapse of the room to make his escape and was never seen again in Woodstock. However, what little evidence has survived suggests that he was eventually tried, though whether he was convicted isn't known.[6]

A variety of domestic animals was very much part of daily life in the Woodstock of post-Civil War years. Many animals besides oxen and horses lived with Woodstock families.

Fewer sheep than in earlier days grazed on Woodstock's high pastures. There were about 700 in 1875 as compared to more than a thousand in 1865, according to census figures. While women and girls still spun and wove they did it on a lesser scale than in earlier times. Yet in 1868 16-year-old Ophelia Stone of what is now Wittenberg wove 100 yards of woolen cloth. She was rewarded by the editor of the New Paltz *Times* with a year's free subscription to his paper.

Hogs grunted behind almost every house and supplied the pork which was standard fare through the winter in the form of bacon, ham, sausage, head cheese and plain salt pork. Ducks and geese swam on farm ponds. Almost everyone kept chickens. People competed in the productiveness of their chickens; in 1884 Isaiah Short of Bearsville boasted that his flock of 54 hens had presented him with 7000 eggs between February and October.

Milk cows were numerous. The townspeople owned more than 700 of them in 1875. A kitchen garden lay close to every house, and people like to compare notes on the size of the vegetables they grew. In 1884, for example, Philip Shultis announced that he'd grown a beet which weighed twelve pounds and a winter radish of sixteen pounds, while Luther Shultis was proud of the fact that from a single kernel of corn he'd planted that summer he harvested 1530 kernels.[7]

As during the first half of the nineteenth century, the cutting down and processing of the trees of Woodstock's forests gave work and income to many people working full- or part-time. Sawmills continued to do business on the Sawkill, the Beaverkill, the Tannery Brook and other secondary streams. Small dams like one high on the Fountainkill in Lewis Hollow have survived. They indicate sites of small sawmills which must have operated only during those few months of each year when the water was high enough.

Other water-operated mills made turnings. The Vosburgh mill in Shady produced porch pillars, balusters, parts for chairs, tables and cradles to be assembled elsewhere, and souvenirs for summer boarders, including bowls, lazy Susans, mountain sticks, pin holders and many other objects. In Mink Hollow the Wilber turning mill did a similar business and also made furniture. Toward the end of the century Oscar Mosher turned souvenirs there which he peddled over the adjoining counties from his wagon. In Wittenberg, then known as South Woodstock, several sawmills were in operation along the Little Beaverkill. There the Shultis brothers made headings for the cement barrels used by the makers of Rosendale cement, Isaiah Short made headings near Bearsville. So did others on the lower Sawkill.

Railroad ties were cut especially in Mink Hollow and might be seen ninety years ago stacked up along the Mink Hollow road waiting to be drawn to the Ulster and Delaware Railroad during good sleighing weather. Hardwoods were cut and taken to the great chair factory at Chichester, whose owners also owned tracts of hardwood forest in Woodstock. Oak and pine were cut for the shipyards of Rondout. Woodstock lumbermen were proud of the immense white pine masts they sent to Rondout every now and then. Alder was gathered to be made into charcoal and used in the gunpowder mills at Fish Creek.

Once the Ulster and Delaware Railroad was functioning after

1871, wood products from the upper part of the town were hauled to the Mount Pleasant railroad station for shipment. Shinglemaking machines were set up in several parts of the town (while some oldtimers continued to turn out shingles by hand). By the 1880s steam engines were beginning to take the place of water power. Ulysses Boice used steam to make shingles on Mill Hill Road, and steam sawmills were operating high on Boggs Hill and elsewhere in the town. On the Glasco Turnpike close to the Rock City crossroads Luke Lewis had a little turning shop powered by the waters of the Wide Clove Brook. Some of Lewis' chairs which have come down to our day have a rose carved on the upper rail and a cane seat.

Back among the mountains in Shandaken large chair factories were in operation. From time to time a huge wagon laden with the frames of chair seats and bundles of cane would come to Wittenberg and Willow to leave seats and pick up others Woodstock women and girls had caned. Five cents apiece was paid for the work. It was possible for a fast worker to finish ten in a day. Children as young as five or six were able to do the work and add materially to the family income by this form of child labor.[8]

A few small wintergreen distilleries were once at work in Woodstock. The owners sent their children out to gather the wintergreen plants which grew plentifully on mountainsides beneath the branches of oak trees. One of the little operations run by an Irishman named Balfe occupied a cellar (now a mere cellar hole) high in Lewis Hollow.

In a few odd corners of the town people who were usually at the bottom of the economic and social scale made baskets in the intervals of picking and selling huckleberries and cranberries from door to door. Some of them lived as squatters along the Hurley line from Yankeetown Pond eastward through The Vly, which lies beneath the Snake Rock quarries.

Probably descended from the migrant people known in Ulster County as "the Schoharies," these people moved seasonally from the Schoharie Valley to the Hudson Valley at Kingston selling brooms, baskets and woodenware of their own making and wild berries of their own gathering. In them Indian, white and black strains were mingled. They lived beside lakes and ponds such as the Ulster Binnewaters once the forests there had been felled. Later their descendants settled permanently along these shores.

The Vly is a New York state corruption of "vallei," which is the

Dutch word for a valley, and the people who lived there in Woodstock were called the Vly Yonders. Proper Woodstockers living on good farms viewed the Vly Yonders with a little suspicion, and liked to suggest that their morals were not of the best. And some were indeed the kind of offbeat characters around whom bizarre tales crystallize. One was Sebastian Rhinehart, who on his return from the Civil War took to living in a dugout on an island in Yankeetown Pond. Unable to bear living underground, his wife went off and found another mate. Rhinehart was said to have murdered their daughter but was never formally charged with the crime. He lies buried on his island, his gravestone long ago tumbled down.

Another Vly Yonder was Mrs Steward. Some said she was black, but she maintained that she was a Seneca Indian. Her "fancy baskets" were much admired. Mrs. Steward had many friends, and when she died her funeral was "largely attended." In DeVall Hollow near the Shandaken line a man named Philips made and dealt in baskets on a larger scale than the Vly Yonders.[9]

By the mid-1880s some Woodstock carpenters and masons worked at their trades at the "parks" which were being built at Tannersville and Haines Falls, coming and going over the Mink Hollow Road.

Travelling photographers had visited Woodstock in the daguerreotype days before the Civil War and had recorded the faces of townspeople. By the 1870s, with the wet plate in use, photographers continued to arrive. They now also photographed houses and an occasional barn for their customers. In the late 1870s Thomas Herrick moved to Woodstock, where he worked as resident photographer, taking tintypes in Woodstock and in the surrounding summer boarding region as well as at the Overlook Mountain House. He made some fine wet-plate negatives of local buildings.

In Wittenberg in the 1890s Lorenzo Short set up as a photographer. He left town from time to work as an itinerant and opened a studio in Rondout. Short took photographs of school children posed against their schoolhouse each June and Herrick did the same. Such photographs by the 1890s were an indispensable part of the annual school ritual. Crayon enlargements of family photographs hung in most Woodstock parlors.[10]

Life in Woodstock in the years between the end of the Civil War and the arrival of the twentieth century demanded hard work, especially from the hillside farmers who were called by valley people "buckwheat farmers" because their thin soil was not up to growing anything better. Woodstock women, with their traditional devotion to keeping their houses neat and clean and sewing, mending and carrying on butter-making, preserving, caring for children and helpless old people, seldom had an idle moment. The strain of this relentless existence sometimes made itself visible.

In 1888 Mrs. Albert Rose of Hutchin Hill smashed all the furniture in her home and then left her husband. That same year Mrs. Alphonso Carl left her husband and departed with their baby for her mother's home. A few years earlier Mrs. Hosea Happy of Wittenberg had persuaded her husband to deed his farm to her; neighbors said Mrs. Happy scolded her husband constantly and seemed determined to force him to leave. In this attempt the Happy's twenty-year-old son joined. Hosea was said to have responded by becoming a heavy drinker, or perhaps the drinking came first.

One cold February night Happy had spent a day in drinking his way to Kingston and back again. When he reached home he found the door locked but he got in through a window, armed himself with a scratch awl, put on his nightshirt and got in bed beside his wife. The son, who was married and lived upstairs in the same house, came down armed with a poker and with the help of his mother put nightshirted Happy out of the house in the midwinter cold.

Happy proceeded to rouse the vicinity with yells and shouts. Mrs. Happy and the son tried to quiet him and a scuffle followed. The son's chest was pierced by the scratch awl. Dr. Montgomery was sent for. Old Happy expressed contrition and made no attempt to flee. The doctor took a serious view of the son's wound, but nevertheless the young man recovered. Happy was not arrested. It was thought at the time that Woodstock sympathies were strongly on his side.

In 1876 Mrs. Albert Lane, who was caring for her own baby and three children of her widower father, took "an ounce of very strong laudanum" in an attempt at suicide. Her father gave her a cup of strong coffee and sent for Dr. Lyman B. Smith of Woodstock, who arrived as fast as his pair of fine horses could get him there. Mrs. Lane recovered. After the doctor left, her baby, whom she had been nursing, showed signs of laudanum poisoning. Dr. Smith returned and the baby's life was saved. Mrs. Lane "expressed dissatisfaction at the timely arrival of the doctor and says she will repeat the act the first opportunity she has," wrote the Woodstock correspondent of the Kingston *Argus*.

Men as well as women sometimes sought escape from life by suicide. Sixty-year-old Uriah Lane of DeVall Hollow took an overdose of opium in 1875. Opium was still easy to buy, and a number of Woodstock people had acquired the habit.[11]

Fistfighting continued to be frequent. The fighters were usually tipsy and sensitive to insulting words or gestures. The Election-Day brawls of which Bide Snyder wrote occasionally had fatal results. On January 3, 1881 Jacob Clapper, a poor, basket-making Vly Yonder, died from the results of injuries sustained the previous Election Day.

Bees were often the scene of fights because liquor was drunk freely as men worked. In 1869 a "stone bee" (stones were being hauled from a field) held by William Brown resulted in the death of Ira Purdy. Purdy had been teasing David Shultis and struck him with an ox goad. Shultis grabbed a stout stake and fractured Purdy's skull. Ten years later another bee led to the death of Peter Bill Shultis at the hands of his brother Charlie. Charlie was found guilty of homicide and given a sentence of three months.

Bees sometimes stirred up local excitement because of the sexual activities which marked them. In the early fall of 1879 schoolteacher S. A. Mosher was widely criticized because he attended an "apple-cut followed by a bussing bee" (here the peeling and slicing of apples for drying was followed by a period of kissing games). "Professor Mosher was said to have kissed the girls present with remarkable assiduity." Some of them were his own pupils.[12]

Sexual activities not sanctioned by the mores of the time sometimes took place. In 1876 Sarah E. Bonesteel brought suit against Ephraim Lasher, charging breach of promise of marriage and seduction. Miss Bonesteel stated, "I have known the defendant from childhood. He came to see me first in June 1872; he asked me to marry him; after he promised to marry me I had connection with him; a child was born; it was born blind. . . . He [Lasher] frequently promised to marry me, and the day was fixed but he refused to marry me." Miss Bonesteel won her case and a jury awarded her $10,000.

Printed pornography was not unknown in Woodstock of the post-Civil War days. A federal agent made his way to the home of twenty-year-old Chauncey DeVall, who lived close to the Woodstock-Shandaken line in DeVall's Hollow, in 1874 and arrested him on a charge of "sending immoral publications" through the U.S. Mail. DeVall had advertised in the *School Day Journal*, offering for sale "crystal visiting cards with your name beautifully engraved" and two chromos thrown in free, all for only fifty cents. DeVall sent purchasers exactly what they had paid for, but his free chromos were not the pretty scenes or figure pictures his customers expected but contained "indecent acrostics." It was a matter for added local horror that some of the acrostics had been sent to women and children.[13]

Violence, suicide and departures from the norm of sexual activity were all part of Woodstock life, but side by side with all this the quiet sort of life admired by visitors from the outside like the *Herald* man of 1878 flowed gently along. Sustaining many Woodstock people amid the ups and downs of life was a strong religious faith with an attendant belief in personal survival after death.

During the diptheria epidemic of 1880 twelve-year-old Sara Sagendorf lay dying. Her brother Madison had died three days before. The father asked Sarah if she knew that she was dying and Sarah answered, "Yes, father, and I wish to go." Sarah's willingness to die probably was a result of the beliefs she acquired through attendance at church and Sunday school. In Woodstock Sunday schools of the last quarter of the nineteenth century children learned to see Jesus as a loving and compassionate figure who would welcome the souls of children to the joys of Heaven.[14]

Attendance and the number of communicants at Woodstock churches increased through the decades following the end of the Civil War. The Methodist Church usually led in popularity, with the Dutch Reformed and the Lutheran churches following. The Baptist Church building of Lake Hill was taken down in 1872 and reassembled in Mount Tremper. In 1876 Shady Methodists, who had been meeting in the homes of their members for many years, erected a church building of their own; four years later Wittenberg Methodists did the same. In the 1890s the members of Woodstock's Lutheran congregation left their old church building on its rocky knoll overlooking the Sawkill near the juncture of the Chestnut Hill Road and Route 212 and built a new church of Gothic inspiration on Mill Hill Road closer to the center of the hamlet.

As the nineteenth century neared its end there were six active Protestant churches in Woodstock. The predominantly Irish-born quarry workers attended St. John's in West Hurley after its organization in 1857. This church was said to have had a membership of about 600 by 1870. More numerous than churches were Woodstock's Sunday schools, of which there were twelve in the 1890s.

Although many of the Sunday schools were closed in the winter, when access to them was apt to be difficult, they were centers of community life. Their combined libraries amounted to almost 1300 volumes by 1878. That same year their scholars numbered 550.

Social life in Woodstock centered largely around the church and Sunday schools. The church fairs—the Dutch Reformed Church held its big annual fair on the Fourth of July—were great events each year. Examples of quilts and other needlework achievements were sold along with many other objects. The Woodstock band was in attendance. Sometimes joint Sunday school picinics—Union Picnics— were held in Riseley's Grove beside the Sawkill. There Woodstock Sunday schools and others from outside the town came together in a grand outdoor celebration involving many hundreds of people and featuring food and non-alcoholic drinks, sermons, prayers, music recitations and games.[15]

A splendid stand of tall white pine trees formed the grove; the trees grew upward from a soft floor of brown pine needles. In the center of the grove was a wooden platform used on secular occasions for dancing but now serving as a stage on which speakers and singers took their places. Around the edges of the ground were parked carriages, wagons and horses. Other groves, one in Bearsville and others surrounding other churches, were also the sites for summer picnics. In 1879 the members of the Methodist Church at Wittenberg planted maple trees around their church in order that they might eventually have a shady grove of their own.

A popular social event was the surprise party. No specific cause for celebration was necessary. Someone was selected as a host, often with the connivance of a member of his or her family, and a laughing group of young people carrying food, drink and musical instruments would knock on the host's door at night and burst into the house, hopefully to the complete surprise of the man or woman being honored. It happened sometimes that the host wanted no party. Then he or she would repulse the merrymakers, who would then select another host and proceed to that front door. Though a birthday was often the occasion for a surprise party, no specific cause for celebration was necessary.

Another event to supply light-hearted enjoyment to Woodstock people until the 1950s was the skimelton, a mock serenade or "shivaree" staged outside a house in which a newly-married couple had just gone to bed. Tin pans, cowbells, horse rattles and other noisemakers roused the couple and did not cease until the bridegroom had emerged from the house and distributed cigars among the performers. Occasionally the skimelton party would be invited inside and treated to food and drinks by a couple who expected the serenade and good-naturedly made the best of it.

A good deal of social activity surrounded the singing schools which flourished in Woodstock as in many other American towns. A teacher would come to town and announce that he would conduct a school for a period of weeks. When the school came to an end a concert would be given. During the first half of the nineteenth century the songs sung were likely to be the ones which followed the traditions of Billings and Woodstock's Lewis Edson the elder. By post-Civil War days they had become very different.

A review of one such concert, possibly the first review of a musical event taking place in Woodstock, was published on the front page of the Kingston *Press* of January 19, 1871. It begins, "The concert given by the members of the Woodstock singing school on the evening of Jan. 12 was the finest ever given in our village. The pieces were excellent in tone, of a high moral character, and many of them appealed to our finer sensibilities with a force that left lasting impressions. . . . 'Sweet Spirit Hear My Prayer,' 'Moon Behind the Mill' and 'The Little Brown Church' carried us far back in the shadowy past and filled our eyes as we thought of the dear ones at home or of those who lie by the Little Brown Church in the dell. The 'Laughing Song' caused us to grin immensely . . . the 'Bashful Girl' who was so 'nin-niny nervous that she could hardly sing . . .' and a Temperance song could hardly be beat. . . ."

Instrumental performers too did their best. The reviewer singled out for praise Franz Kotzwara's once-popular composition, the "Battle of Prague." The concert, said the *Press* reviewer, was under the direction of Mr. G. N. Hermance. Today the performance may seem naive. Yet it clearly reflected the tastes, musical and otherwise, which prevailed more than a century ago in American towns and cities.

While singing schools and Sunday schools played their parts in Woodstock life, the town's six or seven elementary or district schools formed the backbone of education. These schools belonged to the third of the three school districts into which Ulster County was divided. With Woodstock in District Three were Denning, Hardenburgh and Shandaken. All these were "mountain towns" where incomes were lower and educational advantages less than in the county's other two districts.

Each year the commissioner who presided over a district visited the schools, made recommendations and tried to enforce them. The commissioner of the Third, however found the going hard. Voters were reluctant to spend money on schools; until the 1890s the amount of "public money" supplied by the state was larger than that raised from local taxation. In 1878, for example, $1,087.13 was furnished by the state while $839.12 came from local taxes.

That year eight teachers were at work teaching 309 children in buildings valued at about $350 apiece. Textbooks were not uniform. Schools seldom had such aids as blackboards, maps, dictionaries or globes. Schoolhouse grounds were bleak and usually without a single tree.[16]

But all this had begun to change during the late 1870s. Then the Wittenberg school, according to the Kingston *Daily Freeman*, acquired ". . . a fine large blackboard. This is a very important step. In many of our schools the blackboard is almost excluded. . . ." Fifteen years later blackboards, dictionaries and globes were to be found in all local schoolhouses. Teachers, thanks to attendance at Teacher's Institutes and the founding of the New Paltz Normal School, showed greater professionalism.

Attendance at school became compulsory by state law and truant officers were appointed. At first these officers were slow in rounding up the large number of children who did not attend school. But eventually attendance at school became almost universal. Few Woodstock children went on to secondary schools. Those of the prosperous valley farmers occasionally were sent to Kingston to attend its excellent academy.

Public libraries did not exist. The high hopes once felt for the district school libraries were not fulfilled and the libraries stagnated. The Sunday school libraries were helpful to children with intellectual curiosity, but their quality and breadth of subject matter were narrow. In the parlors of the more prosperous Woodstock families a glass-doored bookcase might be seen. It usually contained a few novels by Dickens, James Fenimore Cooper and the Rev. E. P. Roe, who lived along the Hudson at Cornwall. Also likely to be found in the bookcase were Hamilton Child's *Gazetteer of Ulster County*, French's *Gazetteer of New York State* and Sylvester's *History of Ulster County*, which included a portrait of Woodstock's Herman Reynolds, its insertion paid for by the Reynolds family.

On the marble-topped center table would lie the huge family

Bible, with its entries of births, marriages and deaths. No other book was ever placed on top of the Bible, for if this were done bad luck would be sure to follow. Stored away in a trunk would be the Dutch or German Bible brought to Woodstock by grandparents—no one in the family could read it now, but it was brought out now and then for the sake of its lively pictures.[17]

From the late 1870s until the twentieth century young people, especially girls, often carried an autograph album to the parties they attended. The book was passed around, with friends, relatives and acquaintances writing verses or prose sentiments and signing their names. The surviving albums of this period say a good deal about the life of the time. Although the verses and sentiments were selected from among the hundreds that were popular among all Americans, the writers chose from among the many ideas afloat in American minds, adapting them to local circumstances.

Even the handwriting was revealing. Old people, for example, wrote with obvious labor because their education had been limited and their hands stiffened by hard manual work. Young people with many more months of education usually wrote in the flowing script of their time, often trying to do ornamental lettering.[18]

The older people tended to write religious or moralistic sentiments. In 1883 Wilson Mosher wrote in Zella Wolven's album, "Remember now thy Creator in the days of thy youth."

"May you and I in glory meet, and cast our crowns at Jesus' feet,' wrote Lillie Miller. "By faith we are saved," admonished "Grandma." "Be a good girl and mind your mar," wrote Peter Wolven in 1883.

Girls usually chose album verses dealing seriously with friendship and with the brevity of life. They often expressed wishes for a happy marriage. Wrote Effie Eighmey in Zella Wolven's album on October 5, 1883, "May your life be a long and a happy one, your husband, a tall and a handsome one."

"Friendship is a golden knot tied by an angel's hand," Rachel L. Sagendorf assured Zella. Here is the sentiment of Eva Devall:

> Remember me and bear in mind
> A kind true friend is hard to
> find but when you find one kind
> and true change not the old one for the new.

Sometimes girls like to write verse which treated marriage in a light-hearted way. Wrote Anna E. Hasbrouck of Lake Hill:

FARM AND FAMILY LIFE, 1870-1900

> Long may you live
> Happy may you be
> And when you get married
> Come and see me.

Men and boys shied away from the sentimental approach the girls seemed to prefer. On October 29 in the early 1880s Erving Lasher wrote this very rational yet poetic observation in Zella's album:

> The autumn days are passing by
> And Winter comes so swift and sly.

Here is the request in 1885 of Henry L. Dunegan:

> When filling memory's wood box
> Throw in a stick for me.

Seventeen years later Dunegan added, "Still alive but badly battered."

Wrote "your cousin S.W.":

> When you are old and can not
> See put on your specks
> And think of me.

Wrote Willie Miller in April 1883:

> Poor ink poor pen
> poor writer amen.

Here is the sentiment of Nelson Hoyt, written in 1885:

> How sweet to court but
> O how bitter to court
> A girl and then not gitter.

When handed an album and asked to write in it, some people felt an urge to do something novel. There was a good choice of sentiments expressed in offbeat ways for these people. Zella's cousin, Alice M. Schutt of Rondout, wrote in Lake Hill in 1883 a two-line verse which began in the lower left corner of a page and slanted upward toward the right-hand corner:

> In coming days and come they will
> Think of her who wrote up hill.

373

Woodstock children, before they had reached the proper age for writing in their friends' albums, got into practice by writing verses in their schoolbooks. Favorites among such verses were those which warned schoolmates not to steal their book. Evelyn Cooper of Lake Hill wrote in her copy of Goold Brown's *Institutes of English Grammar*:

> Steal not this book my honest friend
> for fear the gallows will be your end
> And when you die the Lord will say
> "Where is that book you stole away."

As if not satisfied with the deterrent power of this verse which many previous generations of students had used, Evelyn added:

> Steal not this book for fear of life
> The owner carries a big jacknife.

And then she went on to play a little game which involved the use of a verse. On page 235 of her Thomson's *Practical Arithmetic* Evelyn wrote, "If my name you wish to find look on page 109." Turning to that page a fellow student would read, "If my name you cannot find, close the book and never mind."

The writing of verses in albums and in the margins of schoolbooks owed much to the literacy which had become almost the rule in Woodstock. So too did the interest in fancy penmanship which found its way into albums. John E. Hasbrouck and John Sickler were especially good practitioners of fancy penmanship.

Woodstock tastes of the decades following the end of the Civil War were formed less by books and more by the newpapers which many local people read regularly. Among them were such weeklies as Bonner's New York *Ledger*, which featured serialized novels, a poem or two, and short stories. All were filled with violence, romance and sentimentality. This material had something of the quality of the soap operas of a later day. Kingston papers which were read in Woodstock carried similar, if shorter, stories along with a poem and the news. During the 1870s these papers began to print local items collected by correspondents living in the various towns of the county and this increased their circulation in towns like Woodstock.[19]

Important to the forming of Woodstock tastes was the closeness of Kingston, Saugerties and Rondout. These villages, located convenient to transportation by water and by rail from New York, were able to attract theater troupes, lecturers and musicians who could be heard in winter by Woodstock people willing to drive by sleigh an hour and a half over well-packed winter roads; the snowless parts of the year took longer until roads were improved late in the century. Representative of what Kingston and Rondout had to offer Woodstock people were lecturers like Wendell Phillips and Frederick Douglass (the great black orator); plays like *East Lynne*; Joseph Jefferson's performances of *Rip Van Winkle, Don Cesar de Bazan, The Four Sisters or How He Loved Them All*; baseball games and roller-skating virtuosos; the survivors of the Greely Lady Franklin Bay Expedition in a Great Arctic Rescue Scene; and the reformed drunkard John Gough. Those who could afford this kind of entertainment generally lived on the prosperous valley farms or owned the bigger stores. Hillside farmers, farmhands, teamsters and woodcutters were less likely to take advantage of the cultural attractions of Kingston. They lived in an older world in which witchcraft, traditional songs and crafts survived. All these continued to be part of the life of even the more sophisticated local households.[20]

In 1931 Mrs. Hannah Catherine Cooper Vosburgh recalled "Life Fifty Years Ago in a Farm House" for the members of the Woodstock Historical Society. Mrs. Vosburgh, the daughter of William Cooper, was brought up in the big house still standing on the crest of the Lake Hill. Her grandfather, Jacob Cooper, had bought John Winne's tavern and farm close to what came to be called Cooper Lake. The farm was stony. The Coopers "dabbled in politics, were Supervisors of their town, operated the toll-gate of the Saugerties—Woodstock Turnpike which ran past their house, served as postmasters for Lake Hill, ran a sawmill at the outlet of the Lake and kept a general store." They did all this while operating their tavern.

The Coopers became a prosperous family leading an ample, patriarchal existence. They preserved many features of the life of an earlier day. Mrs. Vosburgh recalled the humming of the spinning wheels of her girlhood, the baa-ing of the sheep being washed before clipping in the pool just beneath the outlet of the Lake. She remembered shoes being made at home, yeast being made from hops and cornmeal, cooking buckwheat cakes, plucking goose feathers for pillows and featherbeds, butchering time and the making of the rolletzes of which Bide Snyder had told. She spoke of the activities centering around the Lake, of fishing sometimes for pickerel by the light of torches made of pine knots, of boating on the Lake by summer and of skating in the winter when horse races were also held on the thick ice—turning mill owner James Vosburgh of Shady owned a French-Canadian horse with a record of trotting a mile over the ice in two minutes and fifty seconds.

"In the summer before the hay was harvested, the barns were swept clean, lanterns of tin with sockets for candles were hung on the rafters," recalled Hannah Vosburgh, "and we would have a good old-fashioned barn dance, with 'Kit' Lindsley or some other good fiddler to furnish the music. One of the favorite tunes played and sometime sung by the fiddler was 'and she danced all night with a hole in her stocking, and her heel kept a-rocking, and her heel kept a-rocking.'" Others reminiscing of the same period could tell of Irish fiddlers playing Irish music for dancers on an outdoor floor in the quarry settlement in Lewis Hollow or of dances in Aaron Riseley's Grove, with local and summer people both taking part. This may help suggest the variety and richness of Woodstock life of a century ago.[21]

31

RAILROAD DREAMS, BOARDINGHOUSES AND DAN SULLY

During the last thirty years of the nineteenth century Woodstock people had good reason to look to their past with pride and to their future with hope. The national celebration of the hundredth anniversary of American independence in 1876 and the centennial of George Washington's inauguration as President in 1889 helped stimulate interest in the Woodstock past.

A few men and women who had come to Woodstock as youngsters in the settlement years following the end of the Revolution were still living. One of them, 93-year-old Mrs. Sally Goodrich, was in 1875 the oldest person in Woodstock. Mrs. Goodrich was regarded with a kind of awe because she had seen George Washington riding through her native New Haven while he was making a tour of the New England states when she was a girl. Still active in Woodstock at 83 was Henry P. Shultis, who had been the Livingston land agent in the far-off days when leases for three lives were a hard fact of Woodstock life. When 86-year-old Elizabeth Cutler died in 1880, the Kingston *Daily Freeman* reported that Mrs. Cutler "and her husband came here [to Wittenberg] when it was one vast forest. They moved here [from Dutchess County] with an ox-team, into a small log house with only half an acre of clear land."

In 1884 the death of Jonas Whispell of Hutchin Hill (he was the man who'd had six sons in the Civil War armies) aroused wide interest. Whispell claimed to be a few months short of 108 years old.

He had been active until a few years before his death until he wounded himself with an axe while cutting firewood; when he was 100 or so Whispell had walked down Hutchin Hill over a slippery January snow to pay his taxes. The rugged old man had been notably devoted to hard liquor and tobacco.[1]

By the 1870s Woodstock people were thinking of their town as an old and mellow one. In 1871 a writer in the Kingston *Press* (probably W. H. Dymond, a Baptist preacher and house painter who lived in the house with the octagonal tower next to the Colony Inn on the Rock City Road) deplored the spirit of "Away with antiquity" and wrote of the ". . . beautiful and ancient village of Woodstock. It contains many families who have lived in the old homesteads from generation to generation and who are imbued with the same ideas and principals [sic] as their forefathers." The writer was shocked by the tearing down of the old Woodstock Inn by William Brinkerhoff a few years earlier and its replacement by a "mansion." [2]

During these years the descendants of Peter Short and Peter Miller told a Kingston newspaper reporter the tale of their ancestors' captivity by Indians. Other oldtimers with Revolutionary incidents in their stock of traditions were eagerly listened to and asked to point out local sites of Revolutionary interest.

Toward the end of the Centennial year of 1876 the Reverend William Sharts, pastor of Christ's Evangelical Lutheran Church, wrote an almost three-page history of his church divided into three sections: *A Historical Sketch, Historical Items and Untoward Events.* Mr. Sharts' excellent history was reprinted with a few changes in N. B. Sylvester's massive *History of Ulster County*, published in 1880. It was Woodstock's most enduring contribution to the Centennial celebration, and more than that the first substantial effort at recording a phase of local history by a Woodstock person.[3]

When Woodstock people turned their thoughts from the past to the future they persisted in seeing prosperity and a growth in population arriving by rail. They knew that many other American towns had experienced booms when they acquired a strip of railroad and a station. They knew that other towns lacking access by rail had stagnated. Ever since tanners and large absentee landlords had urged the building of a railroad from the Hudson River above Saugerties through Woodstock and on to the Esopus Valley back in the 1830s, hopes for a railroad had never died out.

There had been many disappointments. When the Rondout and

Oswego was built, it failed to go through Woodstock. Proposals to build a branch line from West Hurley and later from Saugerties rose up and withered. Surveys were made and meetings were called to demonstrate Woodstock support. But all this effort came to nothing.

In 1874 a railroad map even included a branch of the Ulster and Delaware ending in Woodstock. In 1889, when the summer colonies called parks were being established in the upper Schoharie Valley, surveys were made for a line to begin at West Hurley and proceed by way of Mink Hollow to the Town of Hunter.

The same year rival railroad enthusiasts made surveys for a narrow-gauge line which would reach Woodstock's Lewis Hollow via Rock City. A funicular railroad was planned to take guests from the Hollow up to the Overlook Mountain House. An extension of the line would reach the foot of Plattekill Clove, and from there another "air borne" line would rise to the head of the Clove. Passengers on this line could be whisked from Kingston to the top of Overlook, it was promised, in forty minutes. If the line were built, local people speculated, it would result in a string of mountain houses along the tops of Overlook and Plattekill Mountains, bringing unimaginable wealth to the vicinity. Mead's and MacDaniel's would enlarge and flourish and the long-rumored hotel of Christian Baehr might at last come into being.

But this railroad, like so many of its predecessors, never got beyond the dreaming stage. In September 1891 a bold new railroad scheme was unveiled to a meeting at the old Brinkerhoff House (then operated by Vernon Lake). President J. H. Ramsey of the Canadian Pacific Railway outlined plans for a railroad reaching southward from Canada to New York, in part along the eastern base of the Catskills. Woodstock would have a station on this line.

A committee formed "to solicit subscriptions" included "Messers Krack, Snyder, Rose, Longyear and Lake of Woodstock, Vactor Shultis of Bearsville and William Cooper of Lake Hill." These were all moderately moneyed Woodstock men who hoped the proposed railroad would make them more monied. It would stimulate a rise in land values and an increase in business activity. It would rescue the ailing Overlook Mountain House and step up the annual flow of summer boarders to valley boarding and farm houses.

Almost at once, as so often before, Woodstock's railroad hopes collapsed. The promoters of the new scheme made a deal with the West Shore Railroad, agreeing to scrap their plan in return for advantages which did nothing for Woodstock. Though Woodstock people were discouraged, they did not lose all hope.

In 1902 a group of German capitalists were said to be on the verge of taking over the top of Overlook and connecting it with Kingston by a line which would convey crowds to Overlook in cars suspended from a cable. Woodstock people did not care for the scheme, for it promised nothing for them. It was described as a proposal to turn the top of their mountain into a "German beer garden," and Woodstock was glad when the scheme was dropped.[4]

With the beginning of construction of the great Ashokan Reservoir in 1905 many Woodstock people hoped that a chance to rectify what they saw as an injustice done when the Ulster and Delaware bypassed their town might now be at hand. The railroad would have to be rerouted, in part to accommodate the needs of the reservoir, and what could be more logical than sending its tracks right over the route petitioned for back in 1866? A committee formed to urge their hope was unsuccessful.

By then a bit over a mile of the U&D's tracks passed through the southeastern corner of the territory annexed to Woodtock in 1879. The tracks barely touched the town. Woodstock people had wanted tracks to charge right up the Sawkill Valley and over Lake Hill. To placate them the new station was given the name of Woodstock. Irate West Hurleyans protested against what seemed to them an act of highhanded theft of name. Woodstock people fought back only feebly and in 1915 the station was officially named West Hurley again.[5]

Morris Newgold, a New York real estate manipulator and hotel man who bought the Overlook Mountain House in 1917, made Woodstock's final attempt to get a railroad. The Otis Elevating Railroad, the cable line which connected the Catskill Mountain House to the lowlands, had been abandoned thanks to the conquering onrush of travel by automobile and bus. Newgold proposed buying the line, taking it down and reassembling it to carry guests and freight upward from high in Lewis Hollow to his hotel. A path running up the mountain was cleared of trees and brush in preparation. But that was as far as Newgold's proposal went. The path can still be traced after a light snow.

Finally, after passenger service on the Ulster and Delaware ended in 1954, Woodstock's Victor Basil bought one of its stations, had it hauled over the highways to Woodstock and set it down next to the post office on Tinker Street. And there it stood, serving as a hairdressing salon. Woodstock's dream of a railroad, which had dazzled local people for more than a century and a quarter, had reached the point at which the people were willing to settle for a railroad station but no railroad.[6]

Although the frequent railroad disappointments of the second half of the 1800s seemed to emphasize that Woodtock was destined to remain a very small town, a good deal was happening which showed that some of the town's people were in step with what was going on in other American towns and cities and that the more prosperous ones were growing more sophisticated. One indication of this was the planting of modest flower gardens and a passion for exotic house plants.

In 1881 Woodstock people were admiring the fragrant sweet jasmine grown indoors by the wife of Dr. Thomas E. Montgomery. Reverend I. Short of Bearsville was becoming known for having "the finest show for flowers of any other place in the town, so many varieties and such profusion of blooms." By this time bay windows were appearing on the houses of the more prosperous farmers. To have one of these filled with exotic plants was a symbol of elevated status. Collections of plants like these were being written about and illustrated in magazines like *Peterson's* and *Godey's*, to which a few Woodstock women subscribed.[7]

Woodstock women lost none of their old enthusiasm for making patchwork quilts, often at bees which served as social occasions and opportunities for trading designs and skills. In 1879 Huldah A. Shultis was proud of having completed on her own a quilt of 3,312 pieces. That same year "a lady of three score years pieced a basket quilt of two hundred and ten blocks, without glasses. . . ."

While quilting along the old lines continued unabated, novelties in needlework were being made in accordance with instructions printed in magazines. Mrs. Thomas E. Montgomery finished her third knit spread in 1881. Each had over 700,000 stitches. The annual fair of the Reformed Church featured a knit afghan in a calla lily design— calla lilies were a popular motif of the period.[8]

Among the men of Woodstock hunting was far from dying out. Bears were shot, notably by Mink Hollow hunting families like the Howlands, and the meat was sold at fifteen cents per pound. Bounties on mammals and birds considered harmful to farmers stimulated hunters. In 1874 the town paid Grenville Quick $2 for bounties on four hawks. Charles Short received $3 for bounties on foxes and James

McDaniel $5 for wild cat bounties. Even though upland farmers still hunted to obtain food and furs, the trend toward hunting largely as an expression of manhood and as a traditional American rite had set in.[9]

An occasional tramp arriving in Woodstock gave rise to folk tales which survived in local memories. One tramp came to Lewis Hollow and asked for work. The farmer to whom he spoke asked if the tramp had ever laid a stone wall. The tramp hadn't but said he was willing to learn. The farmer instructed him and set him to work building a wall up a steep hillside.

By that evening the tramp had built a beautifully-laid wall, said to be the longest wall ever known to have been laid in one day in Woodstock from the earliest days of settlement. That night the farmer paid the tramp for his day's work and told him to come back. He had lots of work for a man as good as he was. But the tramp took his money and left. He was never seen again in Woodstock. The wall he built still makes its way up the hillside under the branches of a row of twisted old apple trees. It is sound except in one place where a woodchuck with no respect for good craftsmanship has burrowed under it and caused its collapse.[10]

Another group of outsiders coming to Woodstock found a far warmer welcome than the tramps. These were the summer boarders. They increased steadily in numbers during the last quarter of the 1800s. "The superb combination of the grand and beautiful among the mountains and valleys of Woodstock renders it a famous resort for summer visitors . . . a large number of people are employed in caring for the wants of mountain visitors, and there is considerable capital invested in hotels and boarding houses. . . ." So wrote the author of an account of Woodstock which appeared in 1880 in N. B. Sylvester's *History of Ulster County N.Y.*

Even lacking a railroad, the Overlook Mountain House by 1880 was usually a very busy place. Although it continued to lose money, many rich and famous people spent summer days on the mountain and took special delight in the cool nights which prevailed in July and August. Sometimes the nights were so very cool as to annoy guests who shivered even with the steam heat functioning in the public rooms (although not in the guests' bedrooms).[11]

In 1880 George Mead built an addition to his house 80 by 30 feet in size. Mead soon installed a cook stove weighing 975 pounds and taking 39-inch sticks of wood (length was an important consideration in the days when firewood was sawed by hand). Among guests at

Mead's was architect Stanford White and his in-laws, the Smiths of Smithville, L.I. White's friend, architect George Fletcher Babb of New York, sometimes accompanied him. Jervis McEntee, Frederick E. Church and S. R. Gifford were painters who stayed at Mead's. Because it was open the year round Mead's appealed to hunters and fishermen. In the 1890s an Episcopalian chapel was built near Mead's and was used by summer people.

With room for eighty boarders (Mead's capacity was fifty) the old Brinkerhoff House was second only to the Overlook House in size. A. N. Riseley's Woodstock Mountain View House, or Riseley's, as it was usually called, was greatly enlarged in 1879 and after that was one of the town's important boardinghouses. Each Decoration Day for many years Woodstock's Civil War veterans, local clergymen and friends of Mr. Riseley met for dinner at his house following services in the Dutch Reformed Church and the decoration of veterans' graves in the Woodstock Cemetery.

Riseley's offered guests the milk produced by twenty cows grazing on what later became the golf course of the Woodstock Country Club, and vegetables grown on the farm. In the fall (Riseley's was open until late in the year) guests were allowed to gather without charge all the chestnuts, hickory nuts and butternuts they wanted. On fall evenings "chestnut boils" were a feature of life at Riseley's. Riseley's stated in print its policy of "No Hebrews Taken."

Smaller than Riseley's were several dozen boardinghouses with weekly rates of $6 to $8 for room and board. This was a bit less than the rates of larger places like MacDaniel's high above Shady. Well-known boardinghouses in and close to the hamlet of Woodstock included James Beekman's, Dr. T. E. Montgomery's, Alexander Longyear's (in what has long been known as the Longyear House). Others belonged to grocer Edgar Snyder, butcher Orville Snyder, Benjamin DeGroff and Peter B. Elwyn. Boarders travelled to these places via Hudson River steamers to Kingston and from there to the West Hurley station of the Ulster and Delaware Railroad. A few took the river boats to Saugerties, where they were met by their hosts and driven by wagon to Woodstock.

In the upper part of the town were many boardinghouses whose owners met boarders at the Mount Pleasant station. These owners were DeValls, Howlands, Wilbers, Eighmeys, Moshers and other long-settled people of Willow, Mink Hollow and Lake Hill. Each could take care of from five to twenty people. Cooper Lake was one of the scenic attractions of the vicinity. In 1888 "two parties, one of them seven times a millionaire" inspected the lake and stirred local hopes that it would become a resort center.[12]

There was good reason for hope. The Catskills were becoming an immensely popular summer boarding area. One of the most profitable centers of the industry was Tannersville, only a few miles from Lake Hill by way of Mink Hollow. Lake Hill people saw no reason why Tannersville's popularity might not spill over to Cooper Lake. Lakes, rare in the Catskills, were of great interest to summer people. The old Mink Hollow road was repaired in order to bring Tannersville even closer to the lake, but the Cooper Lake resort center was never born.

Yet even without it the summer boarder capacity of Woodstock, as given by a list in Kirk Monroe's *Summer in the Catskills* of 1883, came to somewhere between five and six hundred, even without counting the many smaller places which did not make the Monroe list. Although Woodstock was only rarely filled to its boarder capacity, this meant a substantial increase in the town's summer population and income.

Most Woodstock summer boarders were respectable and genteel people. New York teachers, lawyers, doctors and men who owned their own businesses came to Woodstock by summer. Mead's attracted artists and intellectuals. The wife and children of a "well known New York banker" named Edmund Cortelyou boarded in Woodstock one summer. Missionaries returned from the Far East and "The Reverend Charles Harris, well known as the converted Jew" (he had turned from Judiasm to preaching Christianity) spent summer vacations at boardinghouses in the valleys of Woodstock.

When it was in business the Overlook Mountain House attracted people famous in society, the arts and other fields. It remained the favorite goal of valley boarders when they took excursions, Woodstock residents accompanied visiting aunts, uncles and cousins up Overlook as the high point of a visit to Woodstock. Even the burning of the hotel in 1875 only increased the popularity of a trip to the top of Overlook. The mountaintop, said the Kingston *Daily Freeman* in 1877, "is quite a favorite resort for summer boarders for miles around and wagons bring loads from Palenville, Boiceville, Mount Pleasant and even the Catskill Mountain House." Here the attractive power of a ruined building was clearly demonstrated.[13]

As summer neared its end Woodstock boarders, like those in other parts of the resort area, found the kind of barn dance described by Hannah Cooper Vosburgh to be seductive. In Woodstock the traditional barn dance had survived in special strength. Callers, fiddlers and players of the accordian were numerous and much admired.

When Norman Wolven died in 1931, the Woodstock *Press* put in words the feelings of many year-round and summer people. It said Wolven would be missed "by every person who ever chanced to attend one of the genuine country dances where 'Norm' crouched lovingly over his accordeon, drew from it marvellous strains, at the same time calling out the numbers for lancers or quadrilles, and, when necessary, setting confused dancers to rights by stepping out on the floor himself and showing them how it should be done. Norm was the real thing; he knew all about sashays, a la main lefts and a la main rights, balancing to the partner and all the rest. . . . His bent and rustic appearance was combined with a courtly manner, winning smile, and air of modest but confident authority. . . . Norm made but one stipulation, a jug of [hard] cider had to be especially provided for him, and the quality had to be right—and St. Peter will know where to find a good accordeon player, if his harpists should go on strike."

Relations between summer people and year round residents were usually fairly formal, though occasionally warm friendships developed and love affairs and marriages occurred. Sometimes Woodstock keepers of farm boardinghouses packed apples, potatoes and butternuts in barrels by prearrangement for shipment by Hudson River steamboats to boarders living in New York or Brooklyn. And so the relationship continued through the year.[14]

By the 1880s city people were associating in clubs which operated the "parks" of the Catskills. Here people had summer homes of their own often grouped around an inn at which they might take their meals and hold social events. Here and there city people who wanted a different kind of summer than the parks provided were setting up summer homes among the mountain people. In Woodstock the most glamorous of these were Dan and Louise Sully, who lived in Mink Hollow and later in the building in Woodstock known as Mill Stream Lodge.

Dan Sully was a figure of considerable importance in the American theater. As a boy he had run away from his home in Rhode Island, and had become a circus acrobat, a black-faced comedian and then an actor. When he revised a successful English play which he named *The Corner Grocery* Sully struck it rich. The play had a long

New York run and then very profitably toured the country.

Soon Sully wrote and staged a long succession of plays in which he acted as "the natural Irish comedian." This meant that, as Sully put it, he acted Irish roles without the Connemara whiskers and caricatured language and mannerisms popular among the stage Irishmen of the day. Among the plays which he wrote or commissioned were *O'Brien the Contractor, The Millionaire, Daddy Nolan, Con Conroy, The Tailor,* and *The Parish Priest.* Though none of them were great plays, all were filled with human warmth and presented Irish people with sympathy. Sully was at his best playing his favorite role of an Irish priest.

In 1886 Sully married Louise Dulany Fox, an actress whose mother had been born in Mink Hollow and had married as her second husband George Fox, a clown in the famous Humpty Dumpty Pantomime Company which toured the United States with great success. His marriage brought Sully and his bride to Mink Hollow, where a little colony of theater people had become established just after the ending of the Civil War.[15]

There Sully took to farming with enthusiasm and there he brought his acting companies to spend the summer rehearsing. Each player, Sully liked to say in his publicity releases, was given a chore on the farm at the same time that he or she received a new part.

Dan Sully was an enormously likeable man, full of laughter and wit. He became captivated by Woodstock, and Woodstock people responded by giving Sully a special place in their affections. Although Sully was a Roman Catholic and often suspended acting during Lent, Woodstock Methodists were glad to have him use their church hall built in 1886 to rehearse his plays. Sully contributed to all local appeals for help. When the wife of the Lutheran minister was in a New York hospital awaiting a serious operation he staged one of his plays in the Methodist Church Hall as a benefit.

Sully plunged into all sorts of Woodstock activities. He managed a sawmill first in Mink Hollow and later on at what has been known ever since as Sully's Bridge. His farmhands carried out teaming contracts. Sully bought and sold horses and kept the finest pair in town for his own use.

Mrs. Sully—Louise Arzula Dulaney Fox Sully, to give her all her names—aroused much interest in Woodstock, especially among the town's men, who found her manners sexually stimulating. She often rode through the town on her horse wearing a broad-brimmed hat and "fringed mittens." Sometimes she drew up at the Brinkerhoff House (by them known as the Irvington Hotel) and ordered drinks for everyone standing at the bar. Men sometimes skulked in the shrubbery around the Sully house to catch a glimpse of its mistress and on one occasion Mrs. Sully fired on a Peeping Tom.

Woodstock people were welcome observers at the Sully rehearsals, first in the Mink Hollow barn (at one point a huge cutout of a railroad train crowned the barn roof) and later in Woodstock. In 1888 Sully tried to bring Woodstock people into "an extravaganza" he hoped to take to Broadway. Sully had given a large square dance party in Mink Hollow "at which local talent furnished the music, called the figures, and mastered the ceremonies." Sully and his Woodstock performers "have it down fine and will make a ten strike in the amusement world," predicted the Kingston *Weekly Leader*. But the dance act never made it to the big time.[16]

A Sully play with a local setting, *The Old Mill Stream*, did get to Broadway, however, and had a moderate success. Sully had commissioned an actor named Fitzgerald Murphy, who happened to be hiking one summer day through Mink Hollow, to put together some of Sully's own ideas into the form of a play. When the play came to Kingston in 1902 Woodstock people were delighted with this "simple story of life in the Catskills" and recognized the Lake Hill Post Office, Sully's Mill and Tom Hubbard, the old stage driver.

The play, set in Mink Hollow, belonged to the class known as "sawmill plays," although it did not actually have a scene in which the heroine was threatened with death at the teeth of a circular saw. The plot hinged on conflicts between a Mink Hollow sawmill owner-storekeeper and his neighbors. Such local names as Howland, Lasher and Winne were bestowed on the play's characters, to the amusement of Woodstock people. The play's title many years later gave rise to an erroneous belief that the once-popular song 'Down by the Old Mill Stream' had been written at the sawmill which Sully later ran at Sully's Bridge in the hamlet of Woodstock.

After they moved to Woodstock Dan and Louise Sully set up at their new mill the "Catskills Mission Art Works" and began making a variety of "Mission novelties" with "everything made from native Oak—bringing out and not concealing the natural beauty of the wood—wax finished in Weathered Oak—Flemish Oak—and Golden Oak." The Sullys were responding to the Mission furniture wave which was sweeping the country. One of their proposed items was a

"Combination hall clock, hat rack and umbrella stand." Another was their "Rip Van Winkle Clock."

In 1910 Dan Sully died at fifty-five after a fall from a wagon drawn by runaway horses. His widow continued to live at Mill Stream Lodge. Her Dulaney relatives operated the sawmill and woodworking venture at the Bridge. Eventually Mrs. Sully married Tony Denier, who had been script writer and a clown of the Humpty Dumpty Pantomine Company. Some regarded Denier as one of the greatest clowns of his time.

After Mrs. Sully and Denier died following a troubled marriage, there were still a few people left in Mink Hollow who were related to them and had been connected with the theater or circus. Mrs. George S. Wilber, Mrs. Sully's niece, had once appeared as a babe in arms in a Sully play in California. An illness terminated her stage career and she led a long and useful life as the wife of Mr. Wilber, who was a skilled wood turner. Crane Wilber, another relative, went from the Hollow to a career as a director and film writer. Someone in the same family married the actor Tyrone Power. . . . Today Mink Hollow's glamorous days of associations with the theater and the circus are over, and the Hollow is largely reverting to forest.[17]

388

CAVES, TROUT
AND WATER

Among many Woodstock efforts
at providing points of interest for summer visitors was one aimed at
discovering a romantic cave. By the time the Overlook Mountain
House began its long struggle to remain alive, mountain summer
resorts were finding caves to be of great interest to their customers
and were making the most of whatever caves or near-caves they had.
Caves were then popular features of romantic novels and paintings. By
the last half of the nineteenth century they had reached a peak of
appeal to a wide public.

From far back in history human beings have viewed caves with
keen interest, in part because they symbolize two dramatic enclosures
at the opposite ends of life, the womb and the tomb. During the early
years of the Overlook Mountain House local people were hearing
much of Jager's or Yawger's Cave ("jager" is Dutch for hunter).
Hunters and woodsmen had heard of the cave long before, and a few
had found and explored it. They knew that it lay in the wildest and
least accessible part of Woodstock to the northeast of the summit of
Overlook Mountain and close to the town line. They repeated lore
about the cave. This lore began to find its way into print as far back as
the 1840s, when Charles Lanman visited the cave and presented it in
romantic terms. As far as we know no one in Woodstock read
Lanman's account and the cave had to be rediscovered thirty years
later.

In his narrative of a climb of Overlook Mountain from the foot of Platte Clove Lanman wrote:

> Our first halt was made at a singular spot called 'Hunter's Hole,' which is a spacious cavern or pit, forty feet deep and twenty wide, and approached only by a crack in the mountain sufficiently large to admit a man. There is a story connected with it worth recording. Many years ago a farmer, residing at the foot of the mountain, having missed a favorite dog, and being anxious for his safety, called together his neighbors, and offered a reward for the safe return of his canine friend.
>
> Always ready to do a kind deed, a number of his neighbors immediately started in different directions for the hunt. A barking sound having issued from this cavern, it was discovered, and at the bottom of it, the lost dog which had probably fallen in while chasing a fox. "But how is he to be extricated from this hole?" was the general inquiry of the assembled hunters. Not one of all the group would venture to descend, under any circumstances; so the poor animal remained a prisoner for another night.
>
> But the next morning he was released, and by none other than a brave boy, the son of the farmer, and playmate of the dog. A large number of men were present on the occasion. A strong rope was tied around the body of the boy, and he was gently lowered down. Having reached the bottom, and by the aid of his lamp discovered that he was in a "real nice place," the little rogue thought he would have some sport; so he continued to pull down more rope, until he had made a coil of two hundred feet, which was bewildering enough to the crowd above; but nothing happened to him and the dog was raised. The young hero having played his trick so well, it was generally supposed, for a long time after, that this cavern was two hundred feet in depth, and none were sufficiently bold to venture in. The bravery of the boy, however, was eventually the cause of his death, for he was cut down by a cannon ball in the war of 1812." [1]

Soon after the opening of the Overlook Mountain House in 1871 Jager's Cave was rediscovered. For a very good reason it was not usually listed among the hotel's attractions. The cave was not for everyone. It could be entered only through a passage sloping downward at an angle of about forty-five degrees and only eighteen inches in height and width. Thin people might descend with the aid of a rope, and then find themselves in the cave proper. But even the slender found the climb back into the sunlight not at all easy. It is hard to wriggle upward in a confined space over a steeply sloping floor. Now and then an adventurous person was stuck in the long entrance passage and endured a harrowing hour or two before managing to escape. Among these was a seventeen-year-old girl named Ruth Reynolds, who suffered the ordeal about 1912.[2]

Explorers of the cave after the Overlook Mountain House came into being sometimes wrote reports of their findings for newspapers. One of these was printed by the Kingston *Daily Freeman* on October 15, 1875 under a headline that read "GREAT DISCOVERY ON THE

OVERLOOK." Since the discovery ". . . many people have been on the mountain to see the curiosity and the Woodstockers greatly marvel at Nature's workmanship in the clean carving of this place in the rocks. Some think it must have been the dwelling of a mountain hermit, and tell stories in relation to a man with long hair and beard having been seen on this peak before the house [the Overlook Mountain House] was built. These tales, however, we think have originated from the brain of some romancer of the village . . . the entrance is very narrow so that a fat man by no means whatever, except by blasting away a portion of the rock, could crowd himself into it. . . ."

"YAWGER'S CAVE/THE WORLD BENEATH THE CATSKILLS" was the headline under which the *Daily Freeman* in 1879 reprinted an account of a visit to the cave first published in the Saugerties *Telegraph*. It was here that a reference to the use of the space during the Revolution occurred.

The discovery of the cave is presented like this: A hunter loses both the bear he's pursuing and his dog in the cave and returns a day later to rescue the dog. A description of the cave in the account makes the ceiling of the principal chamber to be twenty feet above a man's head and "appears arched, something like the inside of a building." The length and breath of the chamber are not given but a second and much smaller chamber is described as reachable by crawling through a six-foot-long passage. This chamber is "four feet high and about six feet square, its top is composed of different sized rocks all wedged together . . . every one of our party thought it a little dangerous for us to remain."

The climb upward when leaving the cave is described as "the most fatiguing part of the expedition." Said the writer, "A man of square build with good capacity for the expansion of the lungs will get his powers of endurance sorely tried before he can call himself safe above mother earth. He will advance only inch by inch and will find himself besmeared with dirt; in fact looking very forlorn."

The guide of the 1879 explorers was Herman Dubois, believed to be a Woodstock man. It may have been from Dubois that the writer got the bits of cave lore he used. "Old settlers," he wrote, "had often told boys not to go into this cave. They had dropped stones into it but they could not hear them strike the bottom. Others said there was a large lake of water which could only be reached by going down a perpendicular many hundred feet. Another old legend said there was a large chimney from the roof of this cave leading off nobody knew where. This chimney caused such a current of air that no torchlight or lantern could be kept burning and persons who went in were in danger of being forever lost."

The *Freeman's* reporter wrote that ever since the summer of 1871 Jager's Cave "has been visited by many people (especially during boarding season) from all parts of the country." This was the period when the first and (after 1878) the second Overlook Mountain Houses were at the height of their popularity. And so too was the cave.[3]

Ladies in their walking dresses, very bulky by modern standards, and gentlemen in light-colored trousers and norfolk jackets took a look at the forbidding entrance, which seemed like a chute leading to the dark entrails of the underworld, and turned away. They were satisfied with listening to their guide relate the legends and lore about the cave.

Woodstock boys, their feet bare and their heads protected by battered straw hats, set up as guides to the cave and the other wonders of their town which might while away the hours of summer boarders. Additional wonders were the twin coal-mine caves above Lewis Hollow and the great Indian rock shelter not far off the road leading to Mead's. A rediscovery of 1879 was said to have been a cave on the farm of Henry Winne near what is now known as Wittenberg. In this cave "a man can walk erect for seventy feet; at the mouth of the cave is a beautiful spring." [4]

The 1870s saw fascination with caves in the Catskills going wild. In 1874 G. W. Owen published his *Leech Club; or the Mysteries of the Catskills*. Here an Indian chief came back to the home of his ancestors and foiled the machinations of evil politicians by popping up from caves beneath the mountains at critical moments. The Catskill Mountain House, lacking proper caves, made do with large overhangs and broad fissures in the rocks roofed over with slabs of rock placed there as the last ice sheet vanished. The Overlook Mountain House did its best to promote the grottoes, rocky overhangs and clefts in the rocks within an easy walk of the hotel.

Today Jager's Cave is talked about by boys in the exploring and camping stage of life, and plans are often made to find it. But this doesn't happen. By summer the cave is guarded by what seems to be a very determined concentration of rattlesnakes. In the winter its surrounding ledges are apt to be slippery with ice. The cave remains a good deal of a mystery. Is it a natural cave once used by Indians and early white hunters or is it a relic of the days when prospectors were digging into the Catskills' bedrock for precious metals or coal? The question after a century and a half of speculation still remains unanswered.

Far more important in its impact on Woodstock than its caves were its streams and ponds. As outside urbanization grew, Woodstock water seemed to be in danger. This water had value not only because it was used daily by local people but also because it was among the chief delights of summer people.

Beneath the surface of the Sawkill, Beaverkill, Yankeetown Pond, Echo Lake and lesser streams and ponds swim and wriggle a host of living things ranging from single-celled organisms to the mammalian complexities of amphibious beaver and muskrat. Of greatest appeal to summer people were the fish—the pickerel, bullheads and sunfish of warmer water and expecially the "noble trout" of the swift-moving and cold Sawkill and Beaverkill and their tributaries.

Old published accounts of Woodstock mention the town's trout with gusto. James Pierce's *Memoir On the Catskill Mountains* of 1823 tells us that "Shues Lake contains trout of large size" and that a beautiful circular basin of water four miles in circumference called Shandago [Shandaken, now Cooper Lake] ". . . is deep, containing pickerel, Trout, Perch and other fish. Several streams which have their source in the mountains to the westward of this lake [Mink Hollow and Silver Hollow] and pass through romantic ravines, are uncommonly well stored with trout. Five hundred of these fish have been caught by an angler in a day."

As mentions in print of trout fishing in Woodstock increased, more and more fishermen came to the town. For a while Woodstock people welcomed these outsiders, for they brought profit to inns and local stores. By the 1840s many fishermen stayed for a few days at the well-known inn of Mr. and Mrs. Milo Barber along the Esopus close to the point at which Woodstock's Beaverkill joins the creek. After having read in newspapers of the excellence of the fishing and the charm of the scenery in this upper part of Woodstock, the fishermen hired a horse and wagon and fished their way up the Beaverkill into Mink Hollow.

Charles Lanman's writings praising the trout fishing of Shue's (Echo) Lake and the upper Sawkill (which he named Sweetwater Brook) brought many fishermen to these localities. The completion of the Ulster and Delaware Railroad put emphasis on the Woodstock Beaverkill, which the New York *Times* described in 1874 as closest to the City of New York of any important trout stream. It could be reached easily in two hours by train from New York, said the *Times*. The result of this ease of access was soon apparent.[5]

Woodstock farmers who had been pleased when they saw city fishermen along the Beaverkill and Sawkill now began to feel uneasy. Ever since the time of the earliest settlement of their town they had enjoyed and benefitted from excellent fishing. Now their streams, lakes and ponds were showing the effects of overenthusiastic fishing by New Yorkers and other outsiders.

Not that fishing had become altogether unrewarding to local people. In 1879 Fred Happy, a Woodstock fishermen, could boast of having caught 195 trout in a single day. In 1884 George Mead mounted a remarkable trout caught "near his hotel" by a boy. Mead boasted that this was "the largest trout ever caught on top of the mountain." In 1894 Marshall Roosa took a 24-inch trout from the Sawkill a bit below the hamlet of Woodstock by the now-illegal method known as "guddling," the art of stroking a fish for a prolonged period until it can be caught with the bare hands. Roosa said he spent nearly half a day catching his trout.[6]

It was plain by the mid-1870s that trout were decreasing in number in Woodstock streams as tourists and summer boarders were increasing. By 1875 farmers who lived along the Beaverkill and Sawkill were putting up what were then called "boards" warning fishermen to stay out unless they had permission to fish. That year the Kingston *Daily Freeman* as an aid to Woodstock farmers printed the proper legal form for such signs.[7]

A writer for the *Daily Freeman* by 1879 offered a lyrical lament for the good old days when outside fishermen had wandered freely along the banks of the Beaverkill and raised a song of praise for Woodstock scenery. The Beaverkill, he wrote, after leaving the shady woods of Mink Hollow "emerges in the valley, through which it runs a few miles, a fine brook bounded by rich meadow land, and then rushes down DeVall's Hollow, making a great deal of bustle and noise until it empties in the Esopus Creek at Mount Pleasant, on the railroad twenty-four miles from the city [Kingston]. The route from Mount Pleasant is by the side of the creek and it has so many beauties of its own that a ride on it with a buck-board wagon ought to be enjoyment for any man or woman who has sufficient taste to know what is beautiful in nature. About five miles is the distance to the valley of Little Shandaken, which lies almost like an amphitheater among the hills. In the spring of the year it is one of those sunny spots where the birds love to congregate and fill the air with their songs, where the clover blossoms early and violets and buttercups line the banks of the stream—in fact such a place as Washington Irving would have loved to see and describe with his pen. The writer of this article was there not many seasons ago, and he caught a fine mess of fish almost without stirring from his tracks; and while he was fishing the bobolinks danced in the air, sending forth the most delicious of rollicking songs, the blue-birds made love in the clumps of alder nearby, the sun shone from a clear sky. . . . There were no dogs there with sharp teeth (as there are now) to enforce obedience to the warning against trespassing, and the land owners did not have to be looked up and their consent given before fishing. . . ." [8]

Stocking Woodstock streams with trout, begun during the 1870s, did something to stem the deterioration of fishing. But at the same time a fresh complication in the relationship of Woodstock people and their streams began to become apparent. As far back as 1861 the trustees of the Village of Kingston had begun to look thoughtfully at the water which poured down the town's mountain and hillsides after every rain and when every winter's coat of snow melted.

As it grew larger Kingston needed a good water supply, and Woodstock seemed a logical place to find it. Though convenient to Kingston the Esopus Creek was polluted by the wastes of many tanneries. The Sawkill above the hamlet of Woodstock was pure. Its water flowing down from the mountains above could easily be collected in reservoirs and piped to Kingston.

As the Kingston trustees took their time in coming to a decision, a New York businessman named Samuel P. Low brought together a group of Kingston backers and organized the Kingston Water Works Company, which offered its stock to the public in August 1873. Ten years later Kingston was being supplied with water from a reservoir on the Sawkill in Zena at the place where the old Wynkoop's snuff mill had once stood. In dry seasons the water supply ran low and there began to be a good deal of talk of bringing Echo and Cooper Lakes into the system and so monopolizing the water resources of Woodstock.[9]

Water rates to users being higher than those in municipally owned systems led to agitation for Kingston to take over the water company. Eventually this was done and the original stockholders were paid off with interest. The City of Kingston now began to make extensive improvements, creating a second reservoir on the lower Sawkill and in 1893 leasing water rights on Cooper Lake from William P. Cooper, who owned much but not all of the lake's shoreline. The lake was to be used as a place to store water, including that piped in from Mink Hollow for use when the water impounded on the lower Sawkill should prove inadequate.

The summer of 1894 was almost rainless. Draining and cleaning Cooper Lake got under way. The drought continued until "the center of attraction in the town of Woodstock both for its scenery and fishing . . . has been drained by the Kingston Water Company until it is a mere pond of scarcely one acre of water. . . . The shores are literally covered with fish dead for want of sufficient water. . . ." So wrote the Woodstock correspondent of the Kingston *Argus*. For the first time Woodstock people began to realize that they had lost control over the waters of their town to Kingston. And that was not all.[10]

In 1893 Kingston turned serious attention to the possibility of building a reservoir in the Esopus at the point where the Ashokan Reservoir would some day be built—by then the polluting tanneries upstream were gone. At the same time a scramble for water by others was under way. A corporation called the Ramapo Water Company was trying to monopolize possible sources of water for the City of New York. They had surveyors at work and lawyers drawing up options in New Jersey, Connecticut and New York.

In 1894 rumors were sent dashing through Woodstock set off by the presence of surveyors in Willow, Lake Hill and Wittenberg. The Ramapo Water Company was planning to convert the entire valley at Willow into a lake covering over one thousand acres supplying not only water but electric power as well to the City of New York. A similar lake of close to nine hundred acres was projected for the upper Little Beaverkill in Wittenberg. This lake was planned to swallow up Yankeetown Pond.

The lakes never came into being. The Ramapo Water Company and the City of New York locked horns as the City awakened to its need for a water supply derived from the Catskills. Eventually the City won the right to construct and operate a publicly owned and managed source of water. Because the Woodstock Beaverkill and Little Beaverkill flowed into the Esopus Creek, which flowed into the City's Ashokan Reservoir, the City of New York has the right to inspect the watersheds of these streams and to enforce sanitary restrictions.

Kingston acquired rights over Woodstock lakes and streams by contract with private landowners. There had been no public discussion or consultation with Woodstock people as a whole. That helped explain why a good many people resented the taking over of rights in their water by their bigger and stronger neighbor. Kingston inspectors tried to enforce their sanitary code on people living along the Sawkill and Mink Hollow parts of the Beaverkill, but they met with considerable resistance. Had not Cooper Lake come into the possession of Kingston, some pointed out, it might have become the site of a large summer boarding development of great economic value to all Woodstock.

The Johnstown, Pennsylvania flood of 1889 had made a great impression on the entire country when it caused the death of over two thousand people who lived below a dam which burst during a flood. As the Cooper Lake dam was raised from time to time to care for Kingston's growing use of water, some Woodstock people predicted consequences similar to those following the breaking of the Johnstown dam. The raising of the dam caused Cooper Lake water to overflow at times onto the Lake Hill Flats and to make marshes of formerly dry land. A dike was built in an effort to correct this.[11]

Fishing, picnicking and boating were permitted for many years on and around Cooper Lake. Fishing in the Sawkill and Beaverkill went on as usual. This helped mollify Woodstock critics. But in the twentieth century hostilities would rise again and a number of harsh confrontations would stir Kingston and Woodstock people.

Kingston's takeover of many of Woodstock's water resources had its beneficial aspects. It preserved Cooper Lake as a lovely body of water unsullied by commercialism and a scenic treasure of the town. Improvements in water-use technology may some day even make it possible for the lake to be used for recreation.

The beauty of Cooper Lake was one of the features of the Woodstock landscape which in the spring of 1902 would draw the approval of a man named Bolton C. Brown. Brown, hunting for a site for an art colony, set the town and its people on a new and unexpected course.

33

AN ART COLONY APPROACHES

By the year 1902 Woodstock was giving some signs to suggest that it was bent on becoming as much as possible like any other American small town bypassed by a railroad. This evidence was strongest in the hamlet of Woodtock and on the prosperous farms bordering the Sawkill. There some men and women followed New York fashions in dress and in amusements. They played the popular game of Parcheesi and tried their skill on the puzzle called Pigs in Clover. They greeted each other with the newly coined advertising slogan, "Good morning, have you used Pear's Soap?" They rode their bicycles on the bicycle path which ran from the center of Woodstock to Bearsville, and the young riders ended their evening trips by circling the Village Green even after darkness fell, their acetylene bicycle lamps aglow.

In the outlying parts of the town, on Hutchin Hill, in Yankeetown renamed Wittenberg, in Shady (since 1892 no longer called Bristol), and among the farms on top of Ohayo Mountain the pursuit of modern ways was carried on spottily. Vly Yonders coming down to peddle berries and baskets in Woodstock looked with amusement and wonder at the bicyclists and expressed contempt for the young dudes among the local men and summer boarders whom they saw smoking "paper cigarettes" or wearing striped blazers and tight cycling pants.

Though still alive, memories of the older Woodstock, with its awe of Madame Livingston, its leases for three lives, its glass blowers and its frontier days, were growing dim. In Woodstock the changes taking place in American life were making themselves felt even though grandmothers still sang babies to sleep with Dutch lullabies, farmers in moments of strong emotion swore at their horses in Dutch, and old ladies wore bonnets.[1]

The Woodstock of 1902 was among the few towns in the Catskills that had not become a crowded summer resort for low- and middle-income people. It had remained determined to keep out Jewish residents, summer boarders and businessmen. In contrast with nearby Tannersville, Woodstock had clung to much of its nineteenth-century appearance and ways of life.

Yet this resistance to contemporary forces had its price. With upland farming becoming less profitable, with bluestone quarrying and the Overlook Mountain House declining and with hopes of a railroad fading, the town had little power to retain its ambitious young people. The young people often left Woodstock for greater opportunities elsewhere.

The loss of the young may have been among the reasons why Woodstock was known as a town full of old people. Dr. Downer, who settled in Woodstock in the late 1890s, liked to say that his studies of vital statistics had convinced him that Woodstock was the healthiest town in all the state of New York. The Woodstock correspondents of Kingston newspapers now and then collected items such as one about an eighty-nine-year-old woman with an active ninety-nine-year-old husband trading butter of her own making for groceries at Rose's general store.

In 1907 a Kingston paper printed an article headlined "WOODSTOCK WHERE PEOPLE SELDOM DIE." Of Woodstock's about 1700 people one in sixteen was between seventy and eighty, one in thirty-two was an octogenarian, and Margaret Burkin at ninety-five headed a half-dozen nonagenarians. Andrew Cole of Zena, who was ninety-four, lived to the age of one hundred four.[2]

Its retention of old ways, its absence of commercial, industrial and big resort-town bustle, and the presence in it of so many spry old people as well as lovely mountains, fields and streams all worked together to prepare Woodstock for the role of art colony. The town had a sense of conservatism that caused sophisticated outsiders to call it "unspoiled."

Rural art colonies are thought to have originated in France as a byproduct of the great development of interest in landscape painting which began early in the nineteenth century. Some young French painters, Corot, Millet, Daubigny, Diaz and Harpignies among them, left their Paris studios to paint landscape from nature and settled down at Barbizon on the edge of the Forest of Fontainbleau. Most took rooms at a local inn and ate and talked at their host's table d'hote. Between 1830 and 1870 the Barbizon group flourished.

By the late 1860s another group, the Impressionists, were painting in the fields and by the streams of France. Eventually they established themselves at Giverny, with Claude Monet at their head and young Theodore Robinson leading the American students who would soon carry Impressionism across the Atlantic. French art colonies multiplied. One arose at Grez in the department of Seine et Marne southeast of Paris. There an American student named Birge Harrison spent summers. Later on Harrison would help shape the art colony of Woodstock.

Robert Henri, who was also to have a strong influence on Woodstock, became in 1890 a member of the summer art colony at Concarneau close to Pont Aven on the Brittany coast, where Paul Gauguin and his friends had lived. These colonies were favorites of American, English and Canadian art students.

As French art colonies were established, a similar process was taking place in the United States. In 1825 English-born Thomas Cole began sketching in the Catskills and in the Hudson and Mohawk Valleys. He soon settled down in the Town of Catskill. He and the painters who followed him formed what was later called the Hudson River School. They radiated not only to every isolated part of the Catskills but also to the White and Green Mountains, the Adirondacks and even farther afield.

In the Catskills painters often boarded in valley settlements while sketching. A few boarding houses such as Lane's in Lanesville and Brockett's in the Kaaterskill Clove took on a bit of the character of the French art-colony inns. In the 1870s Easthampton and neighboring towns on Long Island were beginning to attract painters who boarded at an establishment they called "Rowdy Hall." A decade later landscape painter Thomas Moran built the first studio to rise in the colony. Soon leading American Impressionist Childe Hassam was working in Easthampton.

By the mid-1880s Arkville was emerging as a little Catskills art colony. Many earlier painters had sketched there, Worthington

Whittredge and Jervis McEntee among them. J. Francis Murphy took to staying at the Hoffman boardinghouse, later the Pacatacan Inn. Before long Murphy, Alexander H. Wyant and half a dozen other painters had set up summer studios of their own beside Arkville's Bushkill. George Inness and J. G. Brown were painter visitors at the Arkville colony.

In Tannersville rich grocery magnate Francis Thurber and his sister Candace Wheeler established Onteora Park and welcomed painters, musicians and writers to the place. Mrs. Thurber was a notable patroness of music in New York. Candace Wheeler worked in a number of crafts and was a founding member of the Society of Decorative Arts.

During the last two decades of the nineteenth century art colonies were being founded in many other parts of the United States. In 1900 landscape painter Henry W. Ranger moved from the colony at Mystic, Connecticut to Old Lyme, where he boarded with Miss Florence Griswold. Other painters joined Ranger. Miss Florence, as their hostess was affectionately known, presided over the physical well-being of the colony's painters as French women similarly placed had done at Barbizon and Grez.[3]

When the Woodstock colony was founded in 1902 it did not follow the pattern usual among most French and American art colonies. It did not grow from a haunt of painters on sketching forays who favored a local inn and set up summer studios in its neighborhood. It began less spontaneously—as a deliberately planned project paid for by one man and intended to be a center for dedicated handicrafts workers with a school for students of painting, decoration and the crafts attached. Only some years later did this lead to what might properly be called an art colony.

The arts and crafts movement, by 1902 several generations old, had begun as an act of protest against some of the evil effects of the Industrial Revolution. The big thinkers of the movement, men like Thomas Carlyle, John Ruskin and William Morris, pointed out that workers were deprived of the wholesome satisfaction of carrying the making of products from beginning to end when objects were made in factories by the use of steam or water power and with a division of labor in effect. These workers were no more than machine tenders laboring for wages rather than for the joy of creative effort. The crowding of workers into factory slums and the heartless organization of child labor for industrial profit might be swept away if only men and women might return to the old system of handicrafts.

Carried along by ideas like these, a growing number of people in Europe and then in the United States organized in arts and crafts groups in order to work at handicrafts and live quieter and happier lives than were possible in the tense and shallow environment of industrial society. Some of these groups looked forward to the development of a socialist society. Others aimed at no more than a chance to work with their hands in some quiet corner of the world.

The Centennial year of 1876 had aroused Americans to the appeal of what was not yet known as the arts and crafts movement. Exhibitions of handicrafts sent from England to the Centennial Exposition at Philadelphia played a large part in this awakening. The arrival in the country on a lecture tour in 1882 of well-known apostle of aesthetic enthusiasm Oscar Wilde, the founding of the Society of Decorative Arts, and the formation of arts and crafts societies in many parts of the country all demonstrated the strength of the movement transplanted to American soil.[4]

As Americans celebrated their centennial of independence a tall, sandy-haired and reserved young Yorkshireman was studying at Oxford's Balliol College. A bit more than a quarter of a century later Ralph Radcliffe Whitehead would become the founder of Woodstock's art colony. At Oxford Whitehead came under the influence of John Ruskin, the Slade Professor of Art. Ruskin was a hero to young men with an urge to reform their society, to clean up the English landscape from industrial pollution, and to dedicate themselves to work in the handicrafts.

Whitehead's family had long been mill owners who had played a part in polluting the valley of the Tame in which their woolen and felt mills lay. They had become rich in the process. Now, under Ruskin's influence, Whitehead resolved that when the time came for him to inherit the family felt mills at his native Saddleworth in Yorkshire he would convert them into idealistic cooperatives turning out beautiful cloth made by happy handicraft workers. A quarrel with his father followed. Whitehead left Oxford and went to Paris, where he worked for a year as a carpenter's helper. It was, Whitehead said long afterwards, the happiest year of his life.

The quarrel was patched up. Whitehead returned to Oxford, which he left in 1880 with the degree of M.A. On coming into part of his inheritance not long after, he led a life in which variety and contradictions were blended. He acted as a justice of the peace in the

West Riding of Yorkshire. He lived at Borden Wood in Sussex, travelled extensively on the continent of Europe. He lived in a Styrian castle, in a Venetian palace and in Avignon.

Whitehead at times led an active social life of the sort possible to the rich of his time and class. But he also continued to study in an effort at arriving at an understanding of the place of the arts in life. For a time he plunged into philosophy, with concentration on Plato, Kant and others. Then he took to painstaking analysis of significant works of art which he sought out in many parts of Europe. He aspired to develop a canon by which all painting and sculpture might be judged.

In his studies of literature he was excited by Dante, whom he had learned to revere from the English painters who were leading a return to what they believed to be the honesty and directness of the Italian painters who preceded Raphael. To them Dante's poetry had the pre-Raphaelite quality they were trying to revive. Whitehead began bringing together an extraordinary library of books relating to Dante. This library eventually was brought to Woodstock. At the same time Whitehead assembled a collection of books and prints relating to painting, architecture and craft work. This collection too came to Woodstock and was not dispersed until 1976.

Whitehead's interests led him in 1892 to editing and publishing Dante's *Vita Nuova* in a way that would make it, as he put it, "accessible to readers of modern Italian." During this period Whitehead's self-image was of a successor to John Ruskin, both to the young Ruskin who had become an innovative authority on aesthetics with his *Modern Painters* and the older Ruskin who had made eloquent pleas for social reform as outlined in such works as *Fors Clavigera.*[5]

About 1890 a fresh and decisive influence came into Whitehead's life and helped turn his thoughts to the United States. His old master, John Ruskin, had disliked the United States and had only a very few American friends. But Whitehead, led on perhaps by an enthusiasm for the poetry of Walt Whitman, saw the New World as at once romantic and a promising seedbed for his ideas of social reform. About 1890 he met a young American woman, Jane Byrd McCall of Philadelphia, who shared many of his views.

By this time Whitehead had matured into a man with a reserved, hesitant—almost apologetic—manner. Though he was not handsome he gave the impression of thoughtfulness and a shy kind of intensity.

The few Woodstock people who still remember Jane McCall think of her as a small and frail woman of about ninety, eccentric to the point of requiring occasional periods of seclusion in sanitariums. Yet this same woman, when Ralph Whitehead first met and fell in love with her, had all the charm that marks the heroine of a Henry James novel.

In the 1880s many rich Americans, especially those with an interest in the arts, were drawn to Europe, which they saw as enveloped in a lovely haze compounded of images of cathedrals, castles, titled persons, elegant manners and the works of the Old Masters. To penetrate this haze, and better yet to live within its embrace, was the dream of many Americans.

To Mrs. Peter McCall and her two daughters, soon known in Europe as "the lovely Misses McCall," the appeal of Europe was strong. They answered it with eagerness. They visited Italy, Germany, France, Wales and Scotland. But it was in England, where the two young ladies were a social success, that they found their hopes come closest to realization. They were presented at court and so became eligible to associate with upper-class Britons, peers and peeresses, archbishops and the owners of great country houses. Jane McCall sketched well and assiduously; she painted in watercolor a long series of excellent studies of British wildflowers.

If Mrs. McCall was like other mothers of her time and station in life she aspired to have her daughters marry titled Englishmen. But this was not to be. As Jane and Ralph Whitehead became seriously interested in each other Mrs. McCall must have felt some disappointment. Yet the arts and literature were rapidly rising in social favor, and Ralph was showing promise of becoming the literary man and reformer he hoped to be.

There was one very discouraging obstacle to the marriage. Ralph Whitehead had already made an unsuitable marriage and had been divorced. Because both the prospective bride and groom were Episcopalians, a church which frowned upon the remarriage of divorced persons, a proper marriage seemed out of the question. However, neither of the parties was more than superficially attached to their church. They set about overcoming their scruples. An Episcopalian clergyman in Portsmouth, New Hampshire, near a summer residence of the McCalls, agreed to perform the marriage rites even in the teeth of his superiors' disapproval. Jane McCall became Mrs. Ralph Radcliffe Whitehead in Portsmouth in 1892.

A bit of Whitehead lore still being repeated in Woodstock helps illuminate the romantic aura which the young couple saw surrounding them and their future. They spent their honeymoon on a small boat off the coast of Maine. When the honeymoon ended they beached the boat and burned it in order that it might never be put to a less glorious use.[6]

Yet in spite of all this as long as she lived Mrs. Whitehead felt doubts about her wedding day because she questioned the validity of her marriage. She became upset by any reference to her husband's first wife and his divorce. She removed all mention of details of Ralph's life between his Balliol days and 1892 from his trunks of papers, photographs and other memorabilia. She handed on her obsession to her son Peter, who always denied that there had been a first marriage or a divorce. But there was no hint of the secretive and eccentric Mrs. Whitehead around whom legends would pile up in the Woodstock of the 1930s and 1940s in the charming and happy American girl whom Ralph Whitehead assiduously courted in 1891.

During their period of courtship Jane and Ralph wrote each other every day. Ralph Whitehead's letters had a double purpose. Not only were they expressions of his feelings toward Miss McCall, but they also put into words his ideas about art and social reform in a way which he hoped would prove suitable for publication. Here he followed John Ruskin, who framed his *Fors* as a series of letters. Whitehead's letters, however, were without the arresting torrent of verbal imagination or the vivid phrasing of sympathy toward the poor which made Ruskin's writings at their best so appealing. Instead Whitehead expressed Ruskin shaped ideas in a quiet, correct and rational manner devoid of verbal fireworks.

It is not surprising, then, that when some of Whitehead's letters to Jane McCall appeared in his book entitled *Grass of the Desert* in 1893 they drew little attention. Yet to anyone interested in the story of the Woodstock arts and crafts colony the book has great value. Whitehead lays out the design of his colony to be and gives a clue to his conclusions about the relationship of art and life. These conclusions were among Whitehead's influences when in 1902 he founded his colony at Byrdcliffe.

In a letter titled "Work," dated Florence, April 1891 and included in *Grass*, Whitehead refers to a previous attempt or perhaps merely a discussion of a colony. "One thing I know," he writes, "that you and I, before many years are past, shall start some rational life of our own, and through that life we shall form around us a community, it may be only of two or three, and those not under the same roof, whose lives shall be happy and reasonable because of the reason and happiness of our own. The idea of doing something useful, and living a life healthy in body and thought and emotion, is no new one. . . ." [7]

Whitehead's detailed outline of his proposed community made it clear that he wanted to establish a group somewhere in the country, probably, he wrote, in the New World, in which the arts and a close relationship to nature would combine to bring about the happy and reasonable life which was his goal. The production of works of art was not to be the purpose of the community. This would have a minor place. Like Ruskin's St. George's Guild, given to the public in *Fors*, Whitehead's community was to be an experiment showing the path to a better life through the turning away from the mechanization of society and the pollution of air, land and water brought about by the Industrial Revolution.

Unlike Ruskin he did not lay stress on farming. Nor did he relegate the women of his community, as Ruskin did, to the kitchen and the nursery. Ruskin had sketched the St. George's Guild with passion and a strange mixture of conservatism and socialism. Whitehead's community was outlined in an orderly, coolly intellectual manner.

Of one aspect of the place in which he and his wife would begin their "rational life" Whitehead was sure. He had a clear image of its landscape setting. Ruskin had described in *Modern Painters* what he regarded as the best possible kind of place in which "good work" might be done and a good life might be led. William Morris had written that beautiful work could be done only in beautiful places, and with this Whitehead agreed. With his community so carefully planned only one thing remained. That was to find a suitable place, to bring his colony dream to earth and persuade it to send down roots. [8]

34

BYRDCLIFFE
IS BORN

As Ralph Whitehead adapted to
life in the United States he seemed in no hurry to put into execution
his long-cherished plans for a community dedicated by means of the
arts and crafts to a better life. Yet he kept his hopes alive. He thought
about them, changed them in the light of fresh information and
understanding, and talked about them with his wife and many others.
He was a thinking man rather than a doer and required a strong
stimulus to be roused to action. And that stimulus was slow in coming.

After a period of hesitation the Whiteheads settled down in a
neighborhood of Santa Barbara, California called Montecito. Santa
Barbara had its charm. A Spanish-American air emanated from its
plants, its topography and the adobe houses in which descendants of
the old Spaniards lived in picturesque poverty. The Pacific (whose
color strongly reminded Whitehead of the Aegean) lay on one side,
and on the others were mountains. The human stratum in Santa
Barbara in which the Whiteheads felt most at home was largely
composed of new arrivals who had the leisure that comes with good
incomes. These people rode a great deal, picnicked and with the help
of their Chinese servants gave well-planned dinner parties.

Travelling Englishmen had praised Santa Barbara. A few years
before the Whiteheads fixed their affections on the place, Walter
Crane, Pre-Raphaelite artist and designer and the director of the
Chiswick Press when it published Whitehead's *Grass of the Desert*,

had been delighted by Santa Barbara. Very soon the Whiteheads bought a tract of some two hundred acres and built a house unlike anything known to Santa Barbarans. It was of Latin inspiration, elegantly fitted with furniture and draperies made by William Morris and Company, and with Mediterranean and other antiques.

Ralph Whitehead once wrote that of all the arts that of living was the greatest. At Arcady (for so they named the place) the Whiteheads practiced this art with success. The gardens which surrounded the house blended classic Italian elements with naturalistic California simplicity. Gardening provided a pleasant outlet for Whitehead's creative urges. He spent two hours each day working with his hands at gardening, making endless changes to try to carry out his vision of perfection. Those two hours had a double purpose. They also afforded the amount of daily manual work Whitehead believed necessary if life were to be good.[1]

Many Arcady activities joined to make the Whitehead art of living visible to Santa Barbarans. The dinner parties served by a butler displayed elegance in food, china and silver. The stairway, the wall hangings, the furniture and the tiles gave full room for the aestheticism of the Ruskin-Morris movement to appear at its best. And there was the library, where shelf after shelf of rare, learned and beautiful books of poetry, art and aesthetics, architecture, and work in the crafts reflected the taste of the two people who had brought the books together—he a tall, tweedy Englishman, she a little copper-haired American, around whom filmy veils floated and whose friends called her Bird, The Bird or Birdie.

The art of living as the Whiteheads saw it involved much more than an elegant background and the entertaining of friends. It involved a California version of the kind of effort at raising standards of taste among the people to which Ruskin and Morris had given so much energy. A low building of mixed English and Californian elements rose at Arcady. It was the Arcady Sloyd School. Under the direction of an arts-and-crafts expert brought from Philadelphia, children—some of Spanish and others of Anglo-American backgrounds—were taught weaving, wood carving, modelling and other crafts.

The Whiteheads took a personal interest in their school and its students. Once when a boy proved awkward with his hands, and Whitehead detected a musical bent in him, he offered him a workbench if he would learn to play the harmonica. The boy received as fine a bench as any boy could wish.

A number of cottages and studios built on the Arcady estate were used by young painters, sculptors and musicians whom the Whiteheads felt were worth helping. A group of musicians was formed and performed classical chamber music for the Whiteheads and their guests. The musicians were sent out at Whitehead expense to play in the schools of Santa Barbara.

In 1901 the Whitehead desire to awaken children to the wonders of the arts took the form of an exhibition of their collection of large photographs of masterpieces of European art. Santa Barbara teachers were offered their choice of photographs to hang in their classrooms. In 1902 a selection of these photographs featuring angels was published for the Whiteheads as *Birds of God*.[2]

During his Arcady years Ralph Whitehead wrote a good deal in an effort at following Ruskin in reforming society and education. His *The Lesson of Hellas* booklet argued for the wisdom of following examples set by the ancient Greeks. *The Unemployed* suggested a Ruskinian and socialistic solution to the unemployment which plagued the 1890s. Whitehead contributed advice to an educational publication advising teachers on methods of arousing students interest in art.

And all this time visitors were coming and going at Arcady for stays of varying lengths. Some were arts and crafts people, socialists, members of the local gentry and young painters and poets. These people did not drop in. They were properly invited and were expected to follow carefully planned schedules (like those prevailing at English country houses). The Whiteheads' place was thought of by some Santa Barbarans as an outpost of what they called "the William Morris cult." And there was truth in this. Arcady did much to turn Santa Barbara toward a strong interest in the crafts. By the time the Whiteheads sold Arcady in 1911, some excellent craftspeople of whom Morris would have approved were hard at work in the town in the Whitehead wake.[3]

Outstanding among the guests at Arcady was a bearded young social worker, poet and novelist named Hervey White, introduced to Whitehead by the leading feminist of the time, Charlotte Perkins Gilman. White was remarkable in his combination of simplicity and sophistication, of idealism and a down-to-earth practicality. He was gay and buoyant, deeply interested in others and eager to help those in trouble. It is no wonder that Ralph Radcliffe Whitehead found White charming when he first met him in Chicago during the late 1890s.

A native of a small town in Iowa, Hervey White went from there as a boy to a sod house on the Kansas prairies where he learned to fiddle at dances besides working on his father's farm. He took off for the University of Kansas and to an exploring and scientific expedition in the mountains of Mexico. He left Kansas for Harvard and after graduation made a walking tour of Italy.

White's warmth toward his fellow humans made him an enthusiastic believer in the social and aesthetic reforms capturing the emotions of many of the young people of his time. Giving dignity to manual labor, turning back the tide of industrialization in favor of handicrafts, working toward the freeing of women from their bonds, tearing down the structure of laissez-faire capitalism and substituting socialism—all became goals which White worked toward realizing. He took up residence at Jane Addams' Hull House in Chicago, a pioneer American settlement house inspired by London's Toynbee House, set up to help the poor and named in honor of a Balliol graduate of a few years before Whitehead.

While earning his living as a reference librarian and organizing dramatic, musical and craft projects at Hull House, White wrote his first novel. Based on White's Chicago experiences, *Differences* was well received. It helped its author become a friend of many people who were in the forefront of the reform movement: sociologist Thorstein Veblen, psychologist and educational reformer John Dewey, lawyer Clarence Darrow, Charlotte Perkins Gilman and Oscar Lovell Triggs, the arts and crafts authority and teacher.

By 1900 White was working at his second novel. It appeared the next year as *Quicksand*. At once the book aroused enthusiasm, causing some to predict that White would take his place among America's greatest writers. Theodore Dreiser called *Quicksand* one of the six "great novels of the world." While the book moves slowly by contemporary standards, it is filled with acutely observed detail and excellent, unpretentious writing. It begins in the New Hampshire upland farm country where White had spent summers while he was studying at Harvard, working on the farm of Harvard secretary and writer of nature essays Frank Bolles. It then continues in the Midwest of White's boyhood.

Its characters, drawn with great sympathy and with under-standing of the problems faced by simple rural people, has a special feeling for the effect on the character of women of a society making impossible demands on them while denying them the rewards given to men. This last aspect of *Quicksand* led White's friend Charlotte Perkins Gilman to urge its publication by the respected Boston firm of Small, Maynard and Co.[4]

410

Whitehead, impressed by the young novelist and social worker with whom he shared so many dreams and goals, invited White to Arcady. There White became pleasantly immersed in the Whitehead atmosphere of enjoyment of the arts, luxurious daily living, riding, gardening and intellectual challenge. Before many months Whitehead asked White to join his effort toward establishing the kind of colony he had sketched in "Work." White accepted the generous salary offered.

Whitehead was aroused to renewed enthusiasm for his colony dream when June Reed, pianist in his little chamber group, told him in 1899 of the existence of an idyllic clearing owned by her brother at Alsea in west central Oregon. A pure brook ran through the grassy clearing. All around stood ancient forests dominated by an occasional Douglas fir almost four hundred feet in height, one of which had been felled and lay across one side of the clearing—twelve feet in diameter at its butt and eight feet where it disappeared into the rich encircling forest. A fire had attacked the tree some three years before and was making its leisurely way along the immense trunk at the rate of eight feet per year.

A gateway had been hacked through the trunk to make possible entrance to the enchanted clearing. Whitehead decided that here was a promising site for his colony. The forests around would supply timber from which he and his colonists could make and sell furniture to support the venture; the brook would supply the needed water power.

For months Whitehead, as was his way, planned the colony in every detail. He ordered buildings, a large central common building and cottages of logs for the colonists. He planned to open the colony in a most auspicious manner—with a program of Beethoven trios played by his musicians, Mrs. Reed, a shy cellist named Opid, who was a nephew of the great Polish actress Madame Modjeska, and violinist Louise Tolles. The three were sent ahead to rehearse in order to have the program ready when Whitehead, White and a few other friends would arrive.

When that time came it was apparent that Whitehead's careful plans had gone awry. The musicians had quarrelled. Since they were not on speaking terms they had not rehearsed. There could be no Beethoven trios to inaugurate the colony in the romantic clearing. Whitehead took all this well, with the keen sense of humor he rarely lost. An appreciative connoisseur of the whimsicalities of human behavior, he found his Oregon adventure rewarding.[5]

With the Oregon project forever buried, Whitehead, back at

Arcady, was soon forced into a more serious attempt at founding a colony. By then the charm of his courtship and marriage with Jane McCall had somewhat dimmed. By the time the couple's first child was born in 1900 Whitehead had slipped into a sexual adventure with a member of the group of outsiders who were making Santa Barbara into something of a resort. A rich Mrs. Hart from Cleveland had built a house in Santa Barbara, where her rebellious daughter Louise lived and astonished her neighbors by dancing in the moonlight barefoot and draped in trailing veils. She wrote poetry and, after her mother's death, smoked opium supplied to her, it was said, by an old Chinese servant.

Separated briefly, the Whiteheads became reunited upon a pledge by Ralph Whitehead that he would give up Miss Hart and, after a trip to Europe, buckle down in earnest to establishing the arts and crafts colony which the two had been discussing almost daily from the moment they first met.[6]

Although Hervey White had come to take the Whitehead plans for a colony with considerable skepticism, he realized in the spring of 1902 that this time his employer meant business. Whitehead summoned him to the house of Dr. Fletcher of Indianapolis, a man of whom White had never heard. There Whitehead presented to him the doctor's son-in-law, Bolton Coit Brown. Whitehead explained that he had hired Brown to design furniture to be made at his proposed colony.[7]

Brown, an able and talented man, had a knack of antagonizing people who should have liked him. That he had earned the degree of Master of Painting from Syracuse University in a day when few practicing artists had degrees, plus, as Carl Lindin put it, his belief that he "was always right" made him unpopular. At Syracuse he had been a track star and had organized athletic events. Brown's passion for physical fitness led him to take cold baths the year round and to climb mountains by winter, to the envy and derision of softer acquaintances.

While heading the art department of Leland Stanford University he had become a charter member of the Sierra Club. He wrote accounts of rugged climbs for the club's *Bulletin*. He was the agnostic son of a conservative upstate New York minister. His teaching background when he met Whitehead was considerable—he had taught at Toronto and Cornell after leaving Syracuse. Rising interest in Japanese prints had induced him to study the subject and to become a dealer in the prints, and it was as a print salesman that he had first called upon Whitehead at Arcady. Perhaps upset at the introduction of a fellow worker in Whitehead's arts and crafts colony hopes, White took a dislike to Brown—a dislike which softened with the years but never entirely left him.[8]

At the Indianapolis meeting Whitehead and his assistants studied maps and gazetteers. And after much debate and some compromise they agreed on a program. Bolton Brown would make for the Catskills and explore that region, while Whitehead and White would examine the mountains of Virginia and the Carolinas.

Whitehead was far from enthusiastic about the Catskills. He was anti-Semitic and felt repelled by the large Jewish summer population of the mountains where he had once spent a few days in a large hotel. Yet he could not deny that a location amid the Catskills might meet the conditions which John Ruskin had laid down in *Modern Painters* as best suited to good work in the arts. Ruskin believed that elevations in the temperate zones of above fifteen hundred feet provided too harsh an environment and that lower elevations were too enervating. At fifteen hundred feet and a bit lower conditions were admirable. Whitehead believed with Ruskin that the surroundings of a place adapted to good work should consist of land where grain and grapes could be grown, and that the place should be within a reasonable distance of centers of population.

In his usual spirit of energy and thoroughness Bolton Brown began his exploration of the Catskills for a place which could meet Ruskin's conditions. Equipped with the official contour maps of the region, he followed the fifteen-hundred-foot line. He made his beginning at Windham and for three weeks, usually on foot but now and then in a hired buggy, he left no promising nook of the Catskill unvisited. "Afoot and alone," Brown recalled toward the end of his life, he ". . . scrambled over summits so wild it seemed no man or even animal could ever have been there. Some were flat table rock, covered everywhere with dry grey moss a foot thick, the same grey moss hanging in sad festoons from all the branches of the few stunted spruce trees that barely survived. I am an old hand at mountain work, having served my apprenticeship in the wildest of the California Sierra, but for sheer savage impenetrability and utter laboriousness some of these Catskill trips really capped my experience. I tore and ripped my clothes, on one occasion, to an extent that forced me, on regaining the region of farms, to borrow a threaded needle and sew myself up before I could meet people. . . ."

Finally, one May morning Brown "walked up the back side of Overlook" and stood in the notch at Mead's Hotel. "Exactly here," Brown wrote, "the story of modern Woodstock really begins for it was at just this moment and from this place that I, like Balboa from his 'peak in Darien,' first saw my South Sea. South indeed it was and wide and almost as blue as the sea, that extraordinarily beautiful view, amazing in extent, the silver Hudson losing itself in remote haze, those furthest and faintest humps along the horizon being the Shawangunk Mountains. . . ."

Brown walked toward a white-bearded man he glimpsed at work in a blossoming apple orchard beside the road leading eastward from the Wide Clove. He pointed to the cluster of buildings far below and asked the name of the place. The old man, George Mead, replied that it was Woodstock.[9] ·

Bolton Brown was not a man to rely too much on the delighted feeling which had seized him as he first looked down from the Wide Clove. He walked down the slope examined the farms strung out along the mountainside and then made his way to Woodstock. He observed the place with his usual sharpness. He asked pertinent questions. And only then did Brown make up his mind.

He entered Snyder's store and asked Bide Snyder to tap out a message to Ralph Whitehead. The exact words of the message haven't been preserved and it is unlikely that Bide caught their significance. Brown had been secretive about the reasons which had brought him to Woodstock. Word of his intentions might have caused a rise in the price of the farm or farms which would have to be bought for the colony's purposes. But Whitehead and White got the message and the three soon met in Washington. Whitehead reluctantly agreed to consider the Woodstock site.

On May 31, 1902 Whitehead, White and Brown met at Mead's and walked down the mountainside as Brown had done a few weeks before. Whitehead had arrived in Woodstock clinging to his prejudice against the Catskills. But now the beauty of the landscape and its conformity to John Ruskin's standards conquered him. He was impressed by the absence of Jews in the town. He gave White and Brown authority to act for him in buying not one farm as they had expected but seven farms lying along the slope beneath and to the west of Mead's. Then he returned to Santa Barbara.

How Brown and White went about buying the farms without giving a clue to the use to which they were to be put is part of

Woodstock legend. The tricks and strategems Brown used in getting some of the unwilling farmers to sell do not make pleasant reading even in Brown's own account. Once the farms were bought the need for secrecy came to an end. Soon garbled versions of what was going on began circulating.[10]

Two friends of Hervey White arrived to help give a physical shape to the colony. One was Swedish-born Carl Eric Lindin, painter and charmer of women. The other was Captain Frits van der Loo, who had fought in the Boer War with De Wets' raiders. Americans sympathized with the Boer side in the war, and van der Loo, wearing the remains of his Boer uniform, was a hero to them. Whitehead and White had first met van der Loo on board a trans-Atlantic liner the previous year.

Bolton Brown was never a man for holding back when credit for any achievement might be claimed. In his account of the beginnings of the colony he wrote:

> We rented one of Cal Short's barns, up at Rock City, boxed off a section, put in a window, a stovepipe hole and a stove and there we had the first "studio" in Woodstock. Installed at a draughtsman's table I, jack of all trades, was transformed from a go-getter [here Brown is proudly referring to his energy in buying the seven farms] to an architect. I planned Whitehead a house and one for me. When built he called his White Pines and mine is now Carniola. We decided other building sites—that of the library and dance hall, the eating house, a studio or two, a barn and so on—and, vaguely, the layout of roads to serve them. Whitehead [who had briefly returned to Woodstock] put more money in the Kingston bank to my credit and disappeared into California for the winter. I got out and hired every able-bodied man I could see. One gang with teams and lumber wagons I sent out over the fields to gather up stones and haul them to where the pick and shovel men were sinking cellars and foundation trenches. Others ran pipes from springs up on the mountainside, in ditches three feet deep, sometimes through solid rock. A box-like shelter for the time keeper was the first new building. A cold rain threatened and the men were for knocking off. My nimble riding pony carried me swiftly to Ed Harder's store, and before the rain had time to get a going I was distributing to my workers free, oil cloth suits. Winter was coming: I could not afford to waste an hour.
>
> Volunteers to lay up cellar walls were called for and promptly stepped up . . . and while they laid walls and the wagons brought stones to them I peeked through a little instrument and staked out the exact line of the roads—none have a grade greater than three degrees. And the road gang began to build roads. Lumber we would need and I roamed widely, searching out all the little local sawmills and buying in more than one case, their entire stock. Some of the buildings called for unusually large beams. The mill man and I would go into the woods to hunt out and mark, one by one, the chestnut and oak trees that would yield the beams we wanted. Frits and Hervey, all this time, were also building themselves a house, over to the west, with their own gangs. They lived in it when it was done.

415

Bolton Brown was a romantic when it came to his own actions. In the account of the building of Byrdcliffe which he wrote in the early 1930s he told in detail of the building of Carniola, his own large house. The front door "was eight feet wide and commanded all creation"; a "catamount got into the cellar and I saw its round head, back beyond a beam, its two eyes glaring from the light I held."

Brown laid the stones of his fireplace with his own hands and told about it with gusto. It was in the middle of a very cold winter, so to prevent the mortar from freezing he had to keep a fire going. Each morning he rode up to the house on his saddle horse Billy from Rock City, where he boarded with Mrs. Ella Riseley. He led Billy inside one very cold day "and stood him in a corner head outward, where he could see me. I replenished the little fire, then stretched myself on a carpenter's bench and lay so all night, rising at intervals to put on more wood. And the pony's eyes would shine from the firelight. At early dawn I rode back—the air so cold you could hardly breathe it—to eat for breakfast Mrs. Riseley's buckwheat cakes. Thus for a week I beat Jack Frost."

The brisk and jaunty style in which Brown wrote carries conviction. Yet there is evidence that the designing and building of Byrdcliffe was not the nearly one-man job Brown makes it. Peter Whitehead, son of Ralph and Jane Whitehead, insisted that the basic design of the buildings and their siting were largely his father's work, although carried out and elaborated by Brown. Hervey White remembered that when Whitehead returned to Byrdcliffe in the fall of 1902 he vetoed Brown's intention of building his own house of stone and gave a large share in the building and road-building to White, Lindin and van der Loo.

By this time Whitehead was beginning to feel dissatisfaction with Brown's way of plunging ahead on his own without paying sufficient attention to his employer. Yet, in spite of everything, Brown threw his energy into what he was doing and carried his share of the project ahead. The buildings and the roads under Hervey White's direction also pushed ahead. As winter neared its end the major buildings at Byrdcliffe and some of the minor ones visibly materialized. Work on them went on for a few years, with studios being built up to about 1912.[11]

All the buildings were given names which reflected the Whiteheads' interests. The boardinghouse for students, with its cluster of outbuildings, became The Villetta, from the Italian for little village.

White Pines was named for the trees that stood beside it as well as for Whitehead. Casa Carniola, in which the Bolton Browns lived, got its name from a part of Central Europe where Whitehead had once lived. Mullersruh (later Eastover) was named for an early occupant, Yggdrasil for the tree of life in the Norse mythology so well loved by William Morris. Angelus, Morning Star, The Looms, and The Hermitage were other names.

By March 1903 the Whiteheads' White Pines was ready, and the Whiteheads with their two little sons moved in. Horses, vehicles, books, works of art and crafts and household goods then made the move to Byrdcliffe. Whitehead at once took firm charge. All the winter he had been planning. Now he got to work buying and installing the equipment needed for the craftsmen he expected to arrive before summer. He set about recruiting workers for the colony in ways he hoped would attract the sort he wanted and would weed out others. The Whiteheads named the place Byrdcliffe, from syllables of their middle names.

Most urgent at this point, as Whitehead saw it, was letting the world of arts-and-crafts enthusiasts know what was happening at Byrdcliffe and inviting their cooperation. For this purpose he wrote a manifesto which he titled "A Plea for Manual Work." In it he re-used much of what had appeared in 1893 in *Grass of the Desert* as modified by the deeper understanding which had come to him from studying the ideas of American sociologists and psychologists.

He submitted the "Plea" to the editor of the new and ambitious organ of the American arts and crafts movement, *Handicraft*, and in June, 1903 it was published. In the "Plea" Whitehead explored the shortcomings he found in American life and character. He expressed the conviction that "living in peaceful country places" while working at crafts and enjoying music, literature and painting might help turn Americans away from the rush and hurry of their cities. It would bring the "repose" he saw them as so conspicuously lacking. He concluded the "Plea" with these hopeful words:

> It is too early to speak of our work at Byrdcliffe. When we have organized some small industries here; when we have proved that it is possible to combine with a simple country life many and varied forms of manual and intellectual activity; when we have made some furniture and woven some handmade textiles which can hold their own, the writer hopes to be permitted to give an account of our doings. Meantime it is sufficient to say that we have acquired a tract of land in Woodstock, Ulster County, New York, situated on the southern slope of the Catskills, twelve miles south [sic] of Kingston-on-the-Hudson; that

our locality was chosen, after a search made from the Adirondacks to the mountains of Carolina for three things: its beauty, its healthfulness, and its accessibility; that we have arranged for a summer school of painting and decorative design; that we are prepared to take pupils in cabinet-making and in wood-carving; that it is our intention to make furniture of a simple kind, which shall be good in proportion, and to which distinction may be given by the application of color and carving by artists' hands; that we intend to make a specialty of frames for pictures, which painters find so difficult and so costly to procure; that we hope to make a beginning of the truly democratic art of color-printing, by which work in colors of really artistic worth may be made accessible to those who cannot afford easel-pictures; and finally that we will give a welcome to any true craftsmen who are in sympathy with our ideas and who will help us to realize them.

At the same time Whitehead distributed a prospectus for the Byrdcliffe Summer School of Art, at which painting, decoration and handicrafts would be taught. He emphasized that the Byrdcliffe "art village" of which the school formed a part was not a "community" but an association of independent artists and craftsmen. This marked a change from his earlier plans for founding a "community."

He described his school as "unique," as indeed it was in at least one important respect. It was placed on a tract of twelve hundred acres "in order to guard against the destruction or vulgarization of the landscape" in its vicinity by land speculators, a breed whom Whitehead, following Ruskin, held in contempt as polluters of the earth. And while it supplied boarding and rooms in the Villetta next door to the school and recommended Woodstock farmhouses for those unable to afford the Villetta's rate of six dollars per week, it also told students that "there are delightful camping places" available to them in the vicinity.[12]

To those in sympathy with Byrdcliffe's objectives and with the money to afford it, the prospectus offered land on which to build. A little later this land was named the East Riding. The workshops, studios, White Pines and the other buildings which formed the heart of the colony of 1903 lay in the West Riding.

From their arrival in the late spring of 1902 the strangers who had come to Woodstock proclaimed their difference from other Woodstock people: Whitehead by his wealth and his aloof intellectuality, slight Jane Whitehead by her unmistakeable air of superiority, Bolton Brown by his conviction that he was always right, and Hervey White by his manner and dress—he wore no hat, his hair was long, he favored short tight bicycle pants and was seldom without a flowing red Windsor necktie to assert his belief in socialism. Captain

418

van der Loo and Carl Eric Lindin further emphasized the difference of the new people, van der Loo with his bits of Boer War uniform and Lindin with his polished manners and Swedish accent. When the two with White took to living in the discarded Lutheran Church, using the pews for beds and the pulpit for an easel at which Lindin worked, Woodstock felt uneasier then ever.[13]

Though ministers of the Woodstock churches calling at White Pines were received with politeness, it was made apparent that the Byrdcliffe people would not attend their churches. Nor, it developed, would they regard the local schools as "rational" enough for their own children. They would contribute moderately to local community projects but without giving them personal support.

Earlier in Woodstock's history outsiders had caused old inhabitants to regard them with doubt. In the decades following the end of the Revolution the Yankees had arrived, the glass workers had come, and later the Irish quarry workers. Summer boarders had made their appearance and brought with them their urban ways. In each case the outsiders had proved an economic boon to the town. In a few cases there had been intermarriages and a gradual merging of cultures into acceptable form.

Byrdcliffe people, however, were unlike any who had come to Woodstock. They puzzled local people and set many old and accepted ideas at defiance. But as Byrdcliffe craftspeople, students, and artists began work in June 1903 Woodstock people could not help realizing that they were giving the town a very welcome economic boost. For that they might be forgiven a great deal.

35

WHITEHEAD'S REALM

Byrdcliffe deserves a place in the long list of ideal communities, beginning long before Plato's *Republic*. In our own day, this list takes varied forms based on religious, occupational, dietetic, or sexual and family restructurings, or on a combination of all these. Every ideal community originates in a rebellion against accepted ways of living and proposes to set an example of a better way for others to follow.

Because breaking away from the customary structure of society requires great energy and a strong faith, those communities which make the jump from paper or spoken words to a material existence are begun in an outburst of bouyant optimism. Byrdcliffe belongs to the select group of ideal communities which made this jump.

At his colony's beginning, Ralph Whitehead remarked to Hervey White that he would be willing to go away, leaving the affairs of the place "in the hands of strangers" in full confidence that Byrdcliffe would succeed because of the sheer rightness of its purpose. Although his manifesto of June 1903 is characteristically restrained in its phrasing, it radiated this confidence.[1]

The roles of Ralph and Jane Whitehead in the founding of Byrdcliffe were suggested by a characterization of the couple given in her old age by a woman who had known them in Santa Barbara about 1900. Jane Whitehead, this woman said, had "her head in the clouds . . . not the Gibson girl type . . . very articulate in her poetic way, but not at all realistic." However, she did have "the perception and the ability to criticize."

Ralph Whitehead, the woman thought, "had the real gift, and was the dreamer and the planner and the worker." Until his death in 1929, Ralph Whitehead remained firmly in control. As was the way of most women of her day, his wife remained in the shadows, emerging now and then into the light with acts that strangers often regarded as eccentric, but sharing her husband's faith in the rightness of Byrdcliffe.

Not all the little group of Byrdcliffe founders had confidence in Ralph Whitehead's ability to guide the project to success. The mood of the Byrdcliffe colonists during their first summer—and their second one, too—has been preserved in the reminiscences of survivors set down some thirty years later. Then Bolton Brown, his wife Lucy Fletcher Brown, Carl Eric Lindin, Hervey White and craftswoman Bertha Thompson all gave their own versions of life during those first two seasons at Byrdcliffe.

Accounts like these are valuable. Yet none by itself can hope to give a factual picture. They are colored by the teller's inevitable compulsion in old age to justify his or her existence and to see his or her own share in events in a comforting light. When put together and balanced with the aid of scraps of newspaper and magazine information as well as by bits of traditional Byrdcliffe craft objects, paintings and buildings, however, these accounts speak out clearly.

While they admired Whitehead for his kindness, generosity and intelligence, Hervey White and Carl Eric Lindin continued to regard him as a dilettante. They predicted he would soon tire of his Byrdcliffe toy and then drop it in favor of a new plaything. When that happened White and his friends were prepared to step up, buy the place, and carry it forward in a more dedicated and rational way.

Bolton Brown also had his doubts, and these doubts grew as he came to be less and less in favor with Whitehead. He had expected to be head of the Byrdcliffe School of Art, which he planned to make into the best school of its kind in the country. But hardly had the school opened when he was demoted to the post of drawing teacher. Whitehead was heard to say that "Bolton would be a fine fellow if he weren't so cute." By cuteness Whitehead meant Brown's compulsion to assert his superior command of every subject that came up, from the handling of a horse or dog to running an arts and crafts colony.[2]

By June 1903 Brown felt that he was being squeezed out of his expected place at Byrdcliffe. By then White and Lindin had recognized that their dream of buying Byrdcliffe could never be.

The sheer size and scope of the place and the huge amount of capital invested—including that for its costly plumbing—made it impossible. Like other Englishmen of his time and class Whitehead was a believer in what he called "the use of the tub." He believed that frequent bathing and brisk outdoor exercise helped account for the superiority of upper-class Britons. So every habitable structure at Byrdcliffe, however humble, had its bathroom, complete with an amply proportioned tub. The tubs were supplied by what White described as miles of water pipes running interminably under the soil of Byrdcliffe and in trenches cut through rocky ledges.

Hervey White, on the other hand, did not regard bathtubs as of the first importance to a good life. He saw the Byrdcliffe plumbing chiefly as a blow to his hopes of ever taking over.[3]

With the Whiteheads rejoicing and White, Lindin and Brown doing their duty in a mood of restrained hope Byrdcliffe swung into action. The young students of painting, drawing and of woodworking, carving, weaving and metalwork felt the Byrdcliffe experiment as a forerunner of a future similar to the one they had read of in William Morris' *News From Nowhere*, in which pollution of air and water had ended, money had become a mere curiosity, and all shared in a life of creative fulfillment.

The setting for the venture into a new world was inspiring. Behind the buildings which formed the heart of the colony a steep, wooded mountainside gave the experimenters a sense of being in touch with the savage side of the power of nature. In the opposite direction the landscape formed a strong contrast. Made up of cultivated fields separated by mellow stone walls or hedges, patches of woodland, winding roads, farmhouses and barns, church steeples and brooks, it all melted away into the sky far across the Hudson River. The buildings themselves were as new as the world which they were hoped to foreshadow—the Studio, the Villetta, White Pines, Casa Carniola, the metal- and woodworking shops, the Double Barn and a few smaller buildings. All were covered with brown stained flush siding, window frames painted a uniform blue and roofs made of fresh wood shingles. The structures were tied together by roads and paths which helped emphasize Byrdcliffe's aim of the association of independent workers in a cooperative effort.

The new buildings stood together on the upper edge of a great sweep of hillside pastureland, in places smooth as a well-kept lawn, in others dotted with clumps of trees or with boulders placed in position during the retreat of the last ice sheet. Behind the buildings, farm woodlots rose to meet the ledges of Huckleberry Mountain and Sawkill Head and pushed forward to furnish a few trees which gave shade to the new buildings.

Beneath the pasturelands and the plowed fields which bordered the Glasco Turnpike were ranged the houses and barns of some of the farms which had been swallowed down in the making of Byrdcliffe. A group of these buildings had been converted from the farmstead of former Woodstock town supervisor Mark C. Riseley to arts and crafts colony uses. It was named the Lark's Nest. The old farmhouse, little changed outwardly, had been enlarged by the addition of one of its barns, opened to the fine valley view by large windows, and given an Italianate fireplace. Other farm buildings became dwellings or studios linked to the farmhouse by paths shaded eventually by a growth of grapevines. These vines, as if to emphasize John Ruskin's belief that good work could be done only on land suited to the culture of grapes, appeared beside most Byrdcliffe buildings.

The group of buildings on the turnpike formed one of the two centers of gravity of the West Riding of Byrdcliffe. The upper center was tied to the lower one by a lane. It differed to the eye in its newness and in its overhanging eaves and balconied gable ends and its flush siding stained dark brown. It had an alien and even aggressive look in the wild countryside behind it.

The Riseley buildings, on the other hand, retained much of their nineteenth-century rural American air, with new features added as if to symbolize a merging of two cultures—a merging which in fact did not exist. Byrdcliffe in its entirety behaved like an enclave in the older Woodstock to which it related economically but not culturally.[4]

It is not surprising that work got going slowly at Byrdcliffe. Much of the equipment for crafts which Whitehead had lavishly provided had still to be installed. Work on some of the buildings was not completed. Workmen came and went. As the weeks passed, however, the colony began to emerge out of an aimless if cheerful bustle into orderly movement toward its goal.

Photograper Eva Watson (her darkroom was in the long, low structure known as Skylights) began recording Byrdcliffe people with her camera. Jewelry, and iron, door latches and other useful objects began to be made in the metalworking shop later called The Forge; work in brass and copper was also begun. So too was weaving and furniture-making under a Norwegian cabinetmaker named Erlenson, Swedish woodcarver Olaf Westerling and shop foreman Fordyce Herrick (who had been boss carpenter of some of the Byrdcliffe buildings). The design and the painting of panels on furniture were the work of Whitehead's painters, craftspeople and advanced students.

The Byrdcliffe Summer School of Painting began departing at once from the plans Bolton Brown had formed. Tempted by the scholarships offered by Whitehead, the students conformed in their attitudes to Whitehead's own. Though all may have had a love of art, few had been subjected to the kind of discipline Brown, who expected students to begin by learning correct drawing, thought essential. The school permitted them to paint or draw as they pleased, under whatever master they might prefer. It was when most painting students chose tall Herman Dudley Murphy of Boston, that Brown sank to the post of drawing teacher.[5]

Even in the midst of the bustle of Byrdcliffe's first season a zany threat to its existence arrived. It involved the setting up of a kind of comic-opera colony on top of Overlook Mountain. The new colony was to be run by Hervey White with the help of van der Loo.

When he looked back on the episode years later, the scheme seemed to Hervey more fit for an adventure yarn than for real life. Yet for a time that summer it was real enough to dazzle him because it offered a substitute for the loss of his hopes of taking over Byrdcliffe. Hervey wrote in the *Maverick Hoot* in 1927 that the site of his project was ". . . no less than the old Overlook Mountain House. . . . The entire property, house of two hundred rooms, furniture in good condition, gas plant, water system, heating, laundry, bakery—everything was offered to us for nine thousand dollars and not a cent to pay down . . . . The owners were tired of [paying] the insurance. Our idea was to run it piecemeal as trade demanded . . . no gas plant, no laundry, no hordes of servants . . . to advertise for actors and musicians by means of friends, guests who would be capable of amusing themselves on an isolated mountain top. . . . We would capture the old derelict with a bunch of pirates, fly the Jolly Roger from the flag-pole and take each adventure as it came. . . ."

It may have been only van der Loo's marriage that summer to a charming woman rumored among Byrdcliffe people to be the heiress to a vast Central American coffee fortune that kept Overlook from being captured by the pirates. Deprived of van der Loo's support,

Hervey quickly cooled toward the scheme and put his energies into making hay and caring for cows and chickens while working on a novel. The Overlook Mountain House went on offering hope and disappointment to an almost-endless succession of prospects.[6]

Color printing and framemaking were among Whitehead's major interests during Byrdcliffe's first summer. Herman Murphy was a recognized master of designing and making frames. With the help of a student named Edwin Slater he set up a framemaking project which immediately did well. It may have been the only one of the Byrdcliffe crafts to show a profit.

The color printing venture had a different fate. Scottish painter and lithographer John Duncan, a personable man who shared most of Whitehead's views, came from Chicago to organize printmaking. Duncan had worked at Hull House, where a lithographic press had been set up about 1895. He urged Whitehead to get a similar press for Byrdcliffe. Whitehead refused even after Hervey White and Carl Eric Lindin, both of whom had seen the Hull House press in operation, had backed Duncan.

It is likely Whitehead's prejudice against lithography had grown out of its association in his mind with its many commercial applications. He must have known that the Hull House press had been intended for use by students of illustration and commercial art. White and Lindin, however, believed his opposition to lithography was an example of Whitehead's determination to boss the colony even if that meant thwarting worthwhile proposals of others. Color printing hopes faltered after that not to revive until the following summer.[7]

While the Hull House lead had not been followed in Duncan's case, a good deal of its influence was visible elsewhere in Byrdcliffe, especially among the people sheltered in the former farmstead of Mark Riseley. The Lark's Nest was managed by White and Lindin. It was planned as a kind of sorting-out place for people who might, if they passed inspection, be invited to join Byrdcliffe. Residence was by invitation only. Invitations were sent to people involved in the arts and crafts and in social reform—many with connections to Hull House.

One of these was Ellen Gates Starr, who was close to Jane Addams in the founding and operation of Hull House. Largely responsible for giving Hull House its craft program, she herself was a fine bookbinder who had learned the craft from London barrister

Richard Cobden-Sanderson. Miss Starr moved up the hill to Skylights, where she worked and taught. Charlotte Perkins Gilman was an important Lark's Nester who attracted followers to the feminist movement. The plan of the Lark's Nest probably owed much to one of Ms. Gilman's ideas, a central building used for cooking, eating and social gatherings surrounded by cabins and cottages for members of a colony to live in. The purpose of the scheme was to minimize housework.

While arts and crafts advocates like Oscar Lovell Triggs showed up at the Lark's Nest social reformers predominated. Their arguments over their sometimes-conflicting theories led the place to be nicknamed The Wasp's Nest.[8]

As the fall of 1903 approached Whitehead asked Bolton Brown to leave. He gave as his reason "You have mistaken your place." Whitehead was generous in his final payment to Brown and expressed pleasure at the thought that Brown intended to "settle in the neighborhood." Brown bought some thirty acres on the Mead's Mountain Road and there built a little studio and then a house. This marked an important milestone in the history of the art colony. For Brown became the first person to break out of the enchanted *News From Nowhere* boundaries of Byrdcliffe and take to living among the people of Woodstock. Others would follow. The influence of Byrdcliffe would roll down the mountainside, invade Woodstock Valley and even cross the town line into Hurley's Patentee Woods.[9]

A fair number of students and craftspeople did not return to Byrdcliffe for the summer of 1904. Some of them felt that too little freedom was permitted to colonists under the rule of the Whiteheads. A kind of hierarchy had been set up in which everyone from the Whiteheads down had his or her fixed place. Though John Ruskin had favored this kind of social stratification in his St. George's Guild, it was hard for most Americans to accept.[10]

While some people left, new recruits arrived and set to work with enthusiasm. Outstanding among the new people was Whitehead's old friend Birge Harrison, who now headed and gave new life to the disorganized art school. Hervey White liked to say that it was Harrison who "saved Byrdcliffe," and there was truth in this. For Harrison was not only an outstanding landscape painter of his time, but he also combined personal charm and warmth with the ability to inspire confidence. Harrison more than anyone else led the transformation from the Ruskin-Morris goals of Byrdcliffe to the lusty, uninhibited art colony of Woodstock.

426

Harrison was a slender man in tweeds and metal-rimmed glasses; he usually wore a watermelon-pink necktie. A skillful teacher, he tried to guide students toward their own objectives rather than insisting that they follow him. His own paintings dealt with meadows, brooks, harbors and city streets seen under a variety of lightings. He favored moody, foggy skies and was a master at conveying atmospheric effects. He liked to say that a landscape had both a body and a soul—the body was the natural material, the soul the feeling given by the painter on his canvas.

As Ralph Whitehead was studying at Balliol College, Harrison had been an art student in Paris, where he formed part of a group of American painters who later won wide approval both in France and the United States. It was at a summer art colony in France that Harrison became a friend of writer Robert Louis Stevenson.

Harrison himself became a writer-illustrator and produced sketches of his travels in the 1880s and 1890s to the South Seas, the Indian country of America's Southwest and other places. These appeared in *Scribner's*, a respected monthly magazine. Although modern readers may find Harrison's style at times over-precious, the sketches are still worth reading for the keen observation they convey and the sympathy and warmth with which people of differing cultures are portrayed.

Carniola, vacated by the Bolton Browns, became the Harrisons' home. And the building served Byrdcliffe as more than that. It became a refuge to which students with problems might come to find help and comfort from two warm and sympathetic people.

The Whiteheads realized that their colony needed more to hold it together than shining idealism, instruction in the arts and crafts, and the best available tools and studios for workers. To take care of social needs they provided frequent dances in the Studio, some in costume. Mrs. Whitehead, who wanted to encourage a revival of old English dances (this was also part of arts and crafts aims elsewhere), required students to appear on the terrace in front of White Pines late in the afternoon to dance. The necessary human warmth was often lacking on these occasions. It was not until the Harrisons' arrival in the second summer that Byrdcliffe acquired a kind of pleasant social cement which gave the colony a suggestion of community.

The second summer was distinguished by a number of changes. For one thing, important new craftspeople arrived. The first summer a slender teenager named Edward Thatcher had been sent to Byrdcliffe by Arthur W. Dow, his teacher at Brooklyn's Pratt Institute, which then specialized in engineering and the applied arts. Dow disapproved of Whitehead's master, John Ruskin, yet liked the objectives of Byrdcliffe. He was a gifted teacher who left his mark on the teaching of the arts, especially in the public schools.

After a study of Japanese wood-block printing Dow had evolved his own distinctive Ipswich prints. Young Thatcher had gone in for metalworking at Pratt and had become one of Dow's most promising students. At Byrdcliffe he plunged into metalworking. He made hardware for furniture, and a long range of other metal craft pieces, including jewelry.

Thatcher was the forerunner of other Pratt students. Notable arrivals the second season were Zulma Steele and Edna Walker, both painters and talented designers and craftspeople who contributed designs for furniture, cottages, lamp shades and many other objects. Because it was Ralph Whitehead's conviction that Byrdcliffe design should relate to its natural surroundings, Steele and Walker and a few other people made careful drawings of chestnut blossoms and fruits, grapevines, tulip tree and lily flowers, woodbine fruits and autumn foliage, and so on. These were conventionalized in the Dow manner and then applied to chests and cupboards either as carvings in low relief or as paintings.[11]

Furniture was sent to craft exhibitions and to James McCreery's department store in New York. This store was a leading channel for putting arts and crafts work before the public. It was a time when the movement was reaching a crest in public interest, with articles on the subject appearing in such widely circulated publications as *The Ladies Home Journal*, which also offered plans for arts and crafts houses, including some by young Frank Lloyd Wright and designs for furniture by Will Bradley and others.

Byrdcliffe furniture reflected the influence of many designers from William Morris on. The large pieces—and they were sometimes very large—had a monumental quality lightened by panels painted with moody local scenes or vegetation. The finish was light, with gray or other colored paint rubbed into the grain. Pieces like these had great distinction.

Smaller tables, lampstands and dining chairs had considerable variety in design. Chairs shared in a restrained way in the simplicity of what was coming to be called the Mission style. Other smaller pieces suggested the innovative approach of such European designers as C.T.A. Voysey—the hinges used on the drop fronts of small desks also had a touch of the Voysey influence.

The furniture was well made, nearly always of local woods, and was finished with craftsmanlike care. Yet it did not sell in the competitive marketplace where machine-made furniture of related design was being offered at lower prices. At the same time the new look known as art nouveau was becoming fashionable among those arts and crafts enthusiasts who could afford to keep up with changes in taste. It became apparent as the summer of 1903 moved along that furniture-making could not become the source of income for his colony for which Whitehead had hoped.

Metalworking was second only to furniture-making as a Byrdcliffe craft. Laurin F. Martin came from Boston with the highest recommendation of the Handicraft Society to teach in the metalworking shop. In the eastern end of the shop Bertha Thompson began her long and productive career as a maker of fine jewelry and silver tableware. The western end continued to be Edward (Ned) Thatcher's domain, shared with several other workers in brass and iron—one was a New Zealander named Chapman.

Weaving was actively carried on, with Marie Little, a tall Virginian who appeared to have stepped out of a pre-Raphaelite painting, doing very individual work. She dyed muslin, tore it into strips, and wove hangings, cushion covers and so on in her favorite colors of yellow, orange and brown. Whitehead built a cottage known as The Looms for her. It stood near White Pines for years, only to vanish at last in fire.

After its unpromising start of the previous summer printmaking made a fresh beginning. Vivian Bevans, who had studied the art in Chicago with B.J.O. Nordfelt and John Duncan, worked in the printmaking studio in Skylights. Zulma Steele made some prints of lilies that showed the Dow and Whitehead influence. Birge Harrison, Bertha Thompson recalled in 1933, did the only work of distinction. His prints using pastels and rice paste had a delicate quality.[12]

During the summer of 1903 Hervey, to his own astonishment, had fallen in love with pretty printmaker Vivian Bevans. That winter the two were married in New York. Lindin, who was the first prize in Byrdcliffe's mating market, married Louise Hastings, who had studied bookbinding with Ellen Gates Starr. Hervey and his wife remained in New York for the winter. Hervey had a job with the city's Fine Arts Commission, headed by his Midwestern friend John Quincy Adams.

In the summer of 1902 White and Lindin had rented the former Lutheran Church in Woodstock. After their marriage the Lindins converted the church into an imposing residence described, after much local doubt, as in the "Swedish Tudor style." The little group which had started Byrdcliffe threatened to fall apart after only a year of work in the arts and crafts. And in the midst of the second summer as he was falling in love with Vivian Bevans it was Hervey White's turn to leave.

Ralph Whitehead must have been aware of Hervey's lack of confidence in Byrdcliffe's future under Whitehead rule. He liked Hervey. He nicknamed him "Niccolo" and sometimes let Hervey melt his reserve to a point at which he could tell him the kind of details about his past which he was unwilling to share with others.

Yet little by little incidents piled up which put a barrier between the two. When the Byrdcliffe farm under Hervey's management failed to produce enough milk for the Whitehead family during the summer drought of 1904 Whitehead exploded. He asked Hervey to leave at the end of the summer. And while he kept on friendly terms with others who left Byrdcliffe he drifted into being unwilling to speak to Hervey. He kept up good relations with Birge Harrison even after Harrison left the Byrdcliffe School of Art as the season of 1905 ended—the Harrisons built a house for themselves not far from Byrdcliffe's western boundary.[13]

While Bolton Brown, Hervey White, Birge Harrison and Carl Eric Lindin eventually left Byrdcliffe they did not leave Woodstock. Each one of the four in his own way contributed to the birth and growth of the art colony which evolved from the Byrdcliffe experiment.

The defection or discharge of some of the original founders and the failure of many students and craftspeople to come back after an initial sampling of life at Byrdcliffe had not been able to bring the colony to a halt. That Byrdcliffe went on was to due to the character of Ralph Whitehead. When Hervey White was an old man he summed up that character by writing that Whitehead ". . . was one who enjoyed life to the full. It was his weakness that he always craved enjoyment. Nothing of ugliness, nothing of drudgery in his religion. Enthusiasm and aesthetic appreciation all the time. But it was loyalty to his ideals that made his life significant. He never wavered, he never deviated from their narrow way. . . ."[14]

The Byrdcliffe oldtimers of the 1930s and 1940s remembered that in the early days at Byrdcliffe they had felt confident that they would paint pictures, model craft objects and write poems that would arouse the world to admiration. Their example of a life devoted to creative work and simple living would contribute to leading Americans away from their concentration on making money and competing savagely with one another toward a peaceful, cooperative way of life. Bertha Thompson recalled that ". . . Whitehead had dreamed of a community of workers in the arts and handicrafts, associated but independent, living a simple and satisfying life amid beautiful surroundings. Perhaps his dream came as near to being realized that summer (1904) as it ever could." [15]

As an old man, Hervey White saw his Byrdcliffe days in a less romantic and more practical light. He had enjoyed his work at the Lark's Nest not only because he had a genuine liking for people but also because he used it as a kind of laboratory in which he might observe varied eccentrics and pit them one against the other, persuading them to yield up nuances of behavior which might be useful to him as a novelist. He had watched with keen interest the people who came to Byrdcliffe to be instructed, to work or to observe the utopian attempt. He worked many of these characters into the novels he wrote.

He remembered an Anglo-Italian named Rogers, an almost middle-aged remittance man (his family paid him to remain at a safe distance from them, it was said). Rogers flitted from interest in one craft to another and never settled on anything for long. Well-bred young American girls at Byrdcliffe regarded Rogers as sinister and nicknamed him Satan. At night they barred their doors against him because they sensed a threat in the man's formal, Continental gallantry.

Another Byrdcliffe resident was even more interesting a character to White. C. H. Hinton had taught mathematics in Tokyo and at Princeton. He had become obsessed with the then-novel concept of space-time relationships called the fourth dimension. He brought to Byrdcliffe a little machine he had made to demonstrate his theories and to teach fourth-dimension thinking. He would take time off from working on the Byrdcliffe farm to put his machine through its paces for the benefit of anyone willing to pay attention.

Following Hinton's instructions the interested person would move the red, blue and yellow cubes at the heart of the machine. Soon, as Hervey White phrased it, "by his wizardry he had annihilated space." Hinton would then exclaim with satisfaction, "Ah, you have it. That will do for your lesson for today." Byrdcliffe students seldom came back for a second lesson, they doubted Hinton's sanity. Hinton urged Hervey to write a poem about the fourth dimension. Hervey obliged with one he called "A Ship of Souls."

Because Byrdcliffe was a society put together for a purpose in a single year, its population had certain things in common. It lacked the usual quota of everyday Americans with the usual interests of their society. For one thing, it was heavily populated by women, who took a leading part in the colony's activities.

Writer Mary Manning was one whom Lucy Brown remembered in later years. Annette Butler had taught Sloyd at the Whitehead's Arcady school. Lou Wall Moore and her daughter were both professional dancers, and Mrs. Moore was also a sculptor. Edith Wherrey, who haunted "moonlit meadows and streams on the lookout for a pixie or two," was a novelist had been born in China. She could entertain Byrdcliffers by reciting the Lord's Prayer in Chinese. The students in the art school formed a contrast to other Byrdcliffe groups—they were mostly male.[16]

From time to time relatives of Mrs. Whitehead descended from the upper levels of Philadelphia society to inspect Byrdcliffe. At the time eccentric Englishmen as portrayed on the stage and in novels aimed at American audiences were much admired. In Ralph Radcliffe Whitehead the McCalls had a superb example right in their own family.

Mrs. Whitehead's older sister sometimes visited Byrdcliffe. She had never married, it was said, because of a passion for Owen Wister, who had managed to surmount social eminence sufficiently to write a popular novel of 1902 called *The Virginian*. In this book Wister had given literary birth to that memorable command, "When you call me that, *smile*."

In 1905 as in the previous year many members of the little Byrdcliffe society were dispersing to other parts of the world while new ones were arriving. In all this movement the most significant current for the future of Woodstock was the one which flowed down into Woodstock Valley led by Birge Harrison and Hervey White. That year Hervey bought a farm across the Woodstock line in what had once been called the Hurley Patentee Woods. Harrison agreed to teach painting at the summer landscape school of the Art Students League of New York, to be opened the next summer not in an isolated spot like Byrdcliffe but in the very heart of the hamlet of Woodstock.

A number of deserters from Byrdcliffe were soon settling down at Rock City where the Glasco Turnpike crosses the Rock City Road. Some were students. Others were more mature people who painted or wrote poems. They formed a conspicuous part of the tide of art-colony people who would eventually spread out over nearly all of Woodstock.

36

THE ART COLONY GROWS UP

t the Art Students League of New York, founded in 1875, students set policy. There were no entrance requirements, no diplomas. Fees were only large enough to cover expenses. The school had a strong appeal to young people with unconventional ideas. When the Summer School of Painting opened at Byrdcliffe in June 1903 several scholarship students came from the League. And this began a relationship between the League and Woodstock which was to lead to Woodstock becoming a true art colony centered around landscape painting.

By 1903 American interest in landscape painting was booming. The older kind of landscape painting of the Hudson River School and followers of the Barbizon School in France had come to seem somber and overly polished. Under the influence of hints from the French Impressionists some American landscapists like Birge Harrison were dealing with atmospheric effects and what they called "the moods of nature." Others like John Twachtman, who taught at the League school in New York, were following closely behind the Impressionists.

In 1898 the League set up a summer landscape school at the Norwich (Connecticut) Academy, with Twachtman and Bryson Burroughs in charge. The school moved about and changed. During the same year the Byrdcliffe school opened, the League Summer School was located in Lyme, Connecticut, which was already something of an art colony. Lyme proved to be not entirely satisfactory a location (especially after Byrdcliffe was discovered).

A committee of League students headed by John F. Carlson, who had studied at Byrdcliffe one summer, was asked to find a new location. Woodstock was quickly chosen and Birge Harrison persuaded to head the school. In this way the Byrdcliffe School began giving way to that of the League. The Byrdcliffe School lived on in a modest fashion for several years after the Art Students League school opened in 1906 in a former livery stable on Tinker Street.[1]

Byrdcliffe's impact on the older Woodstock was limited by its distance from the center of Woodstock activity. It caused few outward changes in the look of the town. The Art Students League Summer School and its students, however, could not help shocking and upsetting the townspeople into whose midst they had been dropped.

It is true that much had happened to help prepare Woodstock for the student invasion—the old glassworkers, the summer boarders, the urban fishermen and the travellers headed to and from the market towns of the Hudson Valley. There had been the rise of nearby summer colonies with emphasis on the arts as at Arkville and Onteora Park. The town was no longer as insulated from the rest of the world as it had been in the days of leases for three lives and the slow dying out of a dialect of Dutch.

The reputation of the League as spread by metropolitan newspapers was disquieting to Woodstock people. Anthony Comstock of the Society for the Suppression of Vice regarded the League's use of nude models with horror and battled the practice with vigor. As the League came to Woodstock Comstock was arranging the confiscation of its catalogue. He charged that the examples of students' work shown there were no less than pornographic. The students derided Comstock and made him a butt of their jokes and caricatures. And in this way they spread the reputation of the League for being, to say the least, an unconventional place in which Comstock's charges might very well have some foundation.[2]

Woodstock people were prepared to be astonished as the League school opened. Yet in one way the impact of the students was positively pleasant, for few people can resist the appeal of young, high-spirited men and women, especially when they have the liveliness and imagination which so often mark art students.

In Woodstock as in other American and French art colonies a few local women showed such good will and helpfulness toward students that they became enshrined as heroines in local memories. These women usually came into close personal contact with the students as keepers of boardinghouses or inns.

Outstanding among such women was Woodstock's Mrs. Sanford Magee, better known as Rosie. Her husband, once a farmer and skillful bluestone-quarry teamster, had never adjusted to the decline in quarrying. He spent much of his time sitting on the porch of the Magee house at the Rock City crossroads while his wife ran the place as a students' boarding and eating house.

In 1923 English literary man Richard LeGallienne wrote that Rosie was known to all the young artists as Mother Magee: "She made it her business to feed many of them in her great kitchen, and the excellence of her dinners is still traditional whenever Woodstockians get together of an evening for talk of the old times. But she was more than an inspired cook, she was over-flowing with human kindliness and hearty humour and no little native intelligence, and while she was too busy feeding her hungry young people grouped about her kitchen table to sit down with them, she was never left out from their mirth and those discussions on art and every subject under the sun which set the table on a roar after the manner of artistic youth in all ages. The kitchen indeed made a sort of artistic centre of the gay 'vie de Boheme' which was a feature of Woodstock then as today [1923]. Her opinion was asked on every question . . . and she even decided an argument though it was generally a compromise which would hurt no one's feelings." [3]

Rosie Magee's place soon became one of the two centers of the social life of Woodstock art students. The people fed and mothered by Mrs. Magee came to be known as the Rock City group. Rock City owes its name to the ribs and shoulders of rock which push out from its thin hillside soil. The name, not an uncommon one, is given to places of which it has been said, "If we had as many people as rocks, we'd have a city." [4]

Young painters, students and poets, many of them refugees from Byrdcliffe, lived in the barns and farm outbuildings which clustered around the intersection of the Glasco Turnpike and the Rock City Road. They sometimes called themselves "the Barnacles." The Barnacles were the most intellectual and the oldest of the members of the art-colony groups outside of Byrdcliffe.[5]

Less intellectual and with much greater visibility to local people were the students whose social center was the boarding and eating house of Mrs. Cooper in the old Dr. Stephen Heath house opposite the Lasher undertaking establishment (funeral homes had not yet come into the world). She was seen as surrounded by an aura of her own, to which her husband modestly contributed. The husband operated the butcher shop next door. There he slaughtered hogs and cattle in the open air to the discomfort of urban students never before exposed to the raw facts of rural life. Cooper had lost a finger (students said by a misjudged swing of his cleaver), and he used to scratch the missing finger while explaining that even though it wasn't there it sometimes itched.

Mrs. Cooper was quick to adapt her establishment to the needs and customs of her students rather than to those of the summer boarders whom she had previously "taken." She allowed the students the use of her verandahs and parlor, her lawn and her octagonal summerhouse for all sorts of social events by day and night. These included wrestling matches, dancing, singing and playing instruments, and as meeting places of young people for romance, conversation and general frolicking. The Barnacles often walked down from their City to join in the fun.

It became Mrs. Cooper's habit to serve her bountiful midday twenty-five-cent dinner in two rooms. In one she placed the older and less lively students (and any of the usual summer boarders who might drop in). In the other she seated the more high-spirited students presided over by one of their instructors, Walter "Pop" Goltz, who was on very good terms with Mrs. Cooper. He was said to "steer" students to her place. As noon approached hungry students headed for Cooper's from their sleeping and working places, from the League studios into which the upper part of the livery stable had been converted (with a little student-run shop for art supplies below), from rented rooms in houses here and there and in the hamlet, and from less pretentious living spaces.

Some lived beneath a piece of oilcloth stretched against a boulder on a hillside with a lovely view making up for the lack of other comforts. Many took up residence in parts of barns and stables, where two cents a day would buy enough milk at milking time to help put down a bowl of cereal by way of breakfast and supper. A number of students lived dormitory-style in the spacious attic of the Sherman Elwyn house—the one built by Judge Jonathan Hasbrouck. These students were remembered as marching Cooperward for dinner at noon, each one placing his hands on the shoulders of the one ahead of him as they sang their way along Elwyn Lane, Mill Hill Road and Tinker Street.

One former student recalled in his old age that he paid twenty-five cents a week for a "half interest in a haymow." Below the haymow more elegant quarters rented for five dollars per month. Close by was a disused stable with a cot taking the place of a horse in each stall. The art students looked at the Byrdcliffe people with scorn. Edward L. Chase, later to become a well-known painter of both humans and horses, remembered being invited with other students to a performance by "a male toe dancer" at Byrdcliffe. "We thought of the Byrdcliffe people as fairies and old maids in burlap skirts," Chase said.

And indeed the difference between the ways of living of the Art Students League people in the valley and the Byrdcliffers on the mountainside were marked enough to rouse emotion even while having some features in common. One Byrdcliffe woman who had been brought to the colony by John Dewey remembered in the 1950s that "we wore corduroy and denim but we always had a butler and ate by candlelight." Though the valley students got along without butlers, some of them, the ones who slept beneath a bit of oilcloth, did use candles. Barn, stable, chickenhouse and corncrib dwellers used kerosene lamps. By day they worked by the light of windows cut into the north sides of their dwellings.[6]

Inevitably, occasional conflicts between students and people of the older Woodstock developed. One fertile source of trouble was student carelessness in disposing of paint rags, which were sometimes left on the grass beside easels. Cows which came along and found the paints rags appetizing ate them with sometimes fatal results. Farmers in whose fields and meadows students worked in classes of up to fifty or alone were naturally indignant. They demanded payment for the value of the cow, which usually turned out to be of prodigious milk-producing power.

Acts of vandalism which happened then as now were sometimes impulsively blamed on the students. One such act involved the overturning and damaging of gravestones in the Woodstock Cemetery. Students were said to have held a "ghost dance" amid the graves. It was true that students had danced that night but in an abandoned bluestone quarry at a distance from any graves.[7]

Because of the association of artists with nudity so powerfully publicized by Anthony Comstock it was to be expected that Woodstock people would be on the lookout for artists cavorting in the nude. Some claimed to have seen such behavior, and a few reported it to town or county officials. But these reports rested for the most part on misunderstandings.

An instance of conflict between students and townspeople which aroused much feeling was the case of the girl art student and the expressman. The girl had the reputation of behaving with condescension toward local people. The expressman, Stanley Longyear (a descendant of the Jacob Longyear who had come from Germany), lived in a big mansard-roofed house on the Rock City Road and profited greatly from the presence of the growing art colony. While relations between most local people and the art students were usually outwardly pleasant and even warm Longyear formed an exception. As one student put it, "Longyear hated us and we hated him." [8]

Among Longyear's activities was a stage service carrying both passengers and packages between the West Hurley railroad station and Woodstock. The girl art student accused Longyear of charging her five cents too much for carrying a package. She tried to make off with the package from the Longyear porch after offering what she regarded as the correct fee. Longyear tried to prevent her, and in the process, the girl charged, she injured her knee. The girl hired a Kingston lawyer. Longyear was ordered to appear before Woodstock's justice of the peace, Washington Shultis.

An audience of almost two hundred people assembled in the Methodist church hall to watch the trial before a half jury (of six men). The girl offered to drop charges if Longyear would contribute five dollars to the Woodstock Club, which, organized by Byrdcliffe and art colony people, among other services had provided the town with a library. There was a barb hidden in the girl's olive branch—Longyear was well-known for his reluctance to contribute to local causes, especially when they seemed likely to benefit the "new people." He refused the offer and the trial proceeded.

When the testimony had been given the judge explained that the lawyers for both sides had come from Kingston to argue for their clients, who had paid them for the job. They had "no special desire to get at the truth." Shultis warned the jurors, who were all local men, that because the verdicts of Woodstock justice's juries in recent years had been reversed when the members showed a bias in favor of their friends and against strangers they should avoid being influenced by the fact that they knew one party and not the other. The jury quickly decided in favor of Longyear, whom they all knew.

Relations between the two groups went on as before. Each group profited from the existing arrangement, the townspeople in cash income and the artists because of the value to them of Woodstock as a place in which to live and work.[9]

The students became of even greater value to the economy of Woodstock when they began remaining in town and painting through the winter. In 1909 the New York *Herald* published a long article on winter painters of Woodstock. Birge Harrison wrote in *Arts and Decoration* of May 1912 in praise of the Woodstock landscape for a painter's purpose at all seasons of the year. The quality of this landscape, he believed, had helped make the League's summer school "the most important and successful institution of its kind in the world."

It was a pioneer school, Harrison wrote, because:

> . . . Here, for the first time in the history of art, instruction in landscape painting is given the same serious attention which has from time immemorial been accorded to the teaching of figure painting. Here at last it is recognized that landscape has taken a leading part in the art production of the world, and that in America, at least, it promises to outrank figure painting in the near future . . . it was early seen that the valley of Woodstock was peculiarly rich in picture motives and that these subjects lay within half a mile of the white steeple of the old Dutch Reformed Church, which marks the center of the village community.
>
> First, there is the winding Sawkill, with its mills, its falls and its long reaches of quiet water, overhung with branching trees; then the gleaming white houses of the little village itself, seen from the flat meadows, which are intersected everywhere with gently flowing streams and still pools; then the farms, the fields, the forests and the eternal soaring mountains. . . . Woodstock Valley is a valley only in name; for while to the west the view is hedged in by the twin peaks of Tonshe and Tystoneyck, and north and south rise the heights of Overlook and Ohio Mountains, to the east the horizon lies far and open as the plains of Holland, and the view stretches away across fifteen miles of wood and meadow to the valley of the Hudson River, whose vapors rise roseate in the early morning sunlight or shroud in pale mystery the rising moon. . . .
>
> The close juxtaposition of the mountains and the plains make possible many beautiful picture motives which could have existed under no other conditions, for the low-lying country to the east, with its long level horizon, furnishes just the ideal landscape over which to paint the clouds which had been tossed into racks of magnificent and dramatic beauty by the towering mountain peaks to the west.[10]

Great as are all these advantages to a landscape painter, Harrison wrote, "There is yet another known only to those who remain in Woodstock the year round." Then the landscape is seen "under a mantle of snow, when the hills, seen through the golden winter haze, are like mountains in fairyland, when the mornings are all mother-of-pearl, the noondays sparkling diamonds, and the evenings amber and turquoise—for the exquisite color scheme of Woodstock in winter can only be described in the language of jewels."

Harrison went on to describe the appearance of a Woodstock hill, "At sunrise its summit receives the first rosy kiss of the morning sun while all else sleeps in amethystine shadow. At noonday it rises pale and beautiful through the sunny winter haze—a symphony in mother-of-pearl. At twilight it looms a mass of ultramarine and turquoise against a sky of palest amber; and under the ghostly light of a December moon it floats a dream mountain of faintest blue against the deeper blue of the midnight sky."

The landscape which Harrison praised still speaks to us from the works of early art-colony painters and photographers. Much of the charm and variety that drew Ralph Whitehead to found Byrdcliffe and its art school still remains, although lessened by the efforts of speculators and by the pressure of an increasing population. Aggressive houses are appearing to break the integrity of the town's high mountainsides. Once neatly cultivated valleys are vanishing in housing developments, commercial ventures and brush lots. Streams once acclaimed for their purity are polluted. The vast view from Byrdcliffe of 1902 is masked behind tall trees. It was in large part the love of art-colony people for their landscape that indirectly impelled its partial destruction.[11]

The Art Students League's summer school flourished under Birge Harrison. John F. Carlson, who became Harrison's assistant in 1907, moved away from his master into a vigorously brushed handling of landscape related to the French Impressionists, and many students followed him. After Harrison resigned because of lessened physical vigor in 1911, Carlson took his place, with Frank Swift Chase and Walter Goltz as assistants. These instructors, both former Harrison students, gave up their master's manner for one featuring the blue shadows on snow, the broken color and the loose and vigorous brushwork of the American Impressionism which was then coming into public favor. At the same time among the Barnacles of Rock City Impressionism was already being rejected in favor of newer European models.

In the 1920s a writer in the *International Studio* recalled that in Harrison's day as a Woodstock teacher certain "prescribed conventions" had been followed at the League's school. Landscapes painted there had "definite relations between foreground, middle distance and horizon [with] a low horizon line, big skies and wooly clouds. . . . "[12]

Harrison landscapes, popular though they were with art dealers, American collectors and the general public, were finding it ever-harder to prevail in the minds of young students against the new ideas stirring in Europe in the wake of Impressionism. These ideas had been talked of in Woodstock ever since the group headed by Henri Matisse and nicknamed the Fauves, or wild beasts, had aroused the European public by their Paris exhibition of 1905.

Earlier Americans who had studied art in Rome, Dusseldorf, Munich and Paris had come home to work in ways strongly marked by their European models. During the last quarter of the nineteenth century French Impressionism had given birth to work by a group of Americans including Childe Hassam, John Twachtman, Theodore Robinson and others. As the nineteenth century ended a few Americans who had gone to Paris to study painting were first amazed and then conquered by the work of such painters as Matisse, Gauguin and Cezanne.

One of these was a Paris-born Woodstock student named Andrew Michel Dasburg. Dasburg returned to Woodstock to spread the new gospel. Of Dasburg his friend Carl Eric Lindin wrote, "Dasburg was always the discoverer, the experimenter, the worker and the fighter. I believe he loved fighting for its own sake, but in the main he was right, for he fought for a new and perhaps better way of seeing and creating. . . ."

Dasburg had stirred Rock City painters before 1911 when he persuaded them to join with him in what came to be known as the Sunflower Club, dedicated to an anti-Harrison way of seeing and painting. The Sunflower people "wanted to see a picture made of clear color, undisturbed by the color of a mood. They preferred to paint on clear sunny days when the motif stood clearly revealed. . . ." So one observer recalled in later years. The sunflower turns so as to keep its face ever toward the sun—hence the club's name.[13]

One member—the tallest, lankiest painter in Rock City—was Daniel Putnam Brinley, later a successful painter of decorative murals but in his Rock City days a rebel who liked to deal with the visible part of the world in terms of light, color and pattern.

The oldest painter of the group, James H. Wardwell, was not only kind and generous to his younger friends but had the advantage, rare for the place, of an assured income. Wardwell liked to say that he had come to Woodstock to live and paint "before there was an art colony" and this gave him a claim to respect as a painter-pioneer of the place. In her eighties his sister Alice told of letters she received from her brother in the late 1890s. He wrote of boarding on Tinker Street and being awakened at dawn by the sound of horses and oxen drawing loads of farm and forest products through Woodstock to the railroad station at West Hurley or to Kingston or Saugerties.

By 1911 the Sunflower Club began losing much of its value as the spearhead of the latest and most advanced movement in Rock City painting. That year Dasburg returned from a long visit to Paris where he had met Matisse, Picasso and other French painters of advanced ideas. Dasburg was filled with a missionary enthusiasm for converting Woodstock painters to the new approach to art. Very soon Dasburg's enthusiasm coupled with similar influences from other sources was showing results.

Much soul-searching and balancing of possibilities occupied the minds of Woodstock painters. Some resolved on as complete a break as they could with the past. Henry Lee McFee, Hervey White recalled, "burned all his lovely landscapes and began to see barrels and funnels. The hills were all moulded into cylinders; the valleys became various inverted cones. . . . " McFee's wife Aileen, Bolton Brown's sister, was asked if she liked her husband's new paintings. She replied, "I mean to like 'em if it kills me." [14]

Many members of the art colony were not so impartial. They made up their minds to have nothing to do with the revolution in art. One man who had been doing well as a painter in the Sunflower manner felt strongly attracted by the new revelations. Yet he wanted to get married, and that, it was being said, was making him choose to follow the safe and sure path on which he was launched. He followed that path to the end of his days.

Dasburg was not alone in turning ideas about painting topsy-turvy. In 1911 and 1912 Konrad Cramer was brought to Woodstock by his bride, Florence Ballin, who had studied at the Summer School before going to Europe, where she had met her husband in Munich. There Cramer had come into excited contact with the Blau Reiter schoool. He carried to Woodstock the new way of painting being represented by Kandinsky and Marc. Cramer and Dasburg became close friends. By their example they stimulated discussion of the art gospel according to the new European heroes.

By the time the Armory Show opened in 1913 and showed Americans what avant-garde European pianters were doing Woodstock was giving promise of becoming a vital center of the kind of art which was spreading out from Paris and Munich. Rock City painters were contributors to the Armory Show. Daniel Putnam Brinley was a very active member of the committee which organized the section of the show devoted to contemporary American painting.

Dasburg sent three paintings and a piece of sculpture. Brinley sent seven paintings and sketches. Bolton Brown, conservative as he remained, also contributed. For the show's American painters represented many aspects of American art. Four of Brinley's "color notes" were sold to the same West Coast dealer who also bought the star of the show, Marcel Duchamp's "Nude Descending a Staircase."

When the show ended Brinley drew much public attention for his part in the final celebration in the Armory, which was used as the exhibition hall. Then "an impromptu snake dance" led by the regimental fife-and-drum corps got under way "with Putnam Brinley, his lanky height topped by a bearskin hat, acting as drum major. . . ." Hervey White commented favorably on the Armory Show and wrote of the "wonderful sense of uplift" a visitor felt on entering the Armory. He asked incredulously, "Can this be New York?"

Following the boost given to the fresh waves in art which followed the Armory Show every new European movement roused both interest and opposition in Woodstock. When the anti-art, anti-tradition movement known as Dada rose during the First World War, Rock City painters staged a Dadaistic ceremony. They dug a grave in front of a studio, and into it painter after painter threw a canvas with the cry, "Art is dead! Let us bury him!" A tombstone was set up and inscribed "Here lies Art." [15]

During the years prior to the First World War the Whiteheads could still look down over fields and meadows from the windows of White Pines to Woodstock Valley. There was little change visible, but the Whiteheads knew it was there. And they were not happy about it. What was coming to be called "modern art" seemed decadent to them. Their response was to go their own way, confident that eventually the art madness that was seizing young people in the valley would run its course and fade away.

BYRDCLIFFE CARRIES ON

hough the Byrdcliffe of 1907 to 1914 moved along on the path laid out in 1902 and 1903, it did show evidence that the Whiteheads were yielding to the increasingly mechanized society in which their colony was set. The metal-working shop acquired an enamelling kiln with baths for plating by means of a small dynamo. A gasoline engine supplied power for this and other machines as well as for machinery in the woodworking shop.

These were innovations of which John Ruskin would never have approved, for they made use of what he saw as "unnatural" sources of energy. For a time Whitehead battled against the automobile as Ruskin would have done and posted signs at the entrances to Byrdcliffe forbidding motor vehicles to enter. But eventually he gave in. He bought himself a Winton touring car in which he took great pleasure.[1]

Ralph Whitehead and a few craftspeople remained at Byrdcliffe from February 1903 to February 1904 before Whitehead returned to the warmth of Arcady. After that he usually left Byrdcliffe as winter approached, and the colony suffered from this failure to function year-round. In a 1907 booklet meant to attract new colonists, Whitehead gave an account of progress at Byrdcliffe. "Since its foundation Byrdcliffe has grown steadily," Whitehead wrote. ". . . It is still growing and no summer passes that does not see the completion of some new cottage, shop or studio. . . . In the coming spring a tennis court will be laid out and probably a small swimming pond will be made."

The plans for a tennis court and a swimming pond gave evidence that Byrdcliffe emphasis was shifting by 1907 toward summer life more like that prevailing in the Catskill Mountain "parks," especially at Onteora and Twilight. Though still valued, painting and the arts and crafts were sharing the field with the pleasures of summer life to those who could afford them.[2]

Land in the East Riding was being sold to people who had interests in the arts but had money accumulated in other fields. Between 1907 and 1914 Whitehead made about ten sales of land in the East Riding, all subject to lengthy restrictions on their use.[3]

For a time the Whiteheads' two sons were intensifying their parents' interest in education. Whitehead had modified the ideas he had inherited from John Ruskin on the subject after becoming exposed to the thinking of John Dewey and other American educational reformers. In 1907 he wrote of his plans for a Byrdcliffe school to operate the year round.

"In this school," he wrote, "the newer methods of education which have been worked out by Dr. John Dewey, Mr. Hanford Henderson and others, will be applied. Children should be taught to do things. They should not learn from books alone. Books have their place, of course, in any rational system of education, but the age at which they are useful and the extent of their use should differ considerably from the practice of the best schools of thirty years ago. It is proposed at Byrdcliffe to combine the best features of the ordinary class-room with the practice of various simple handicrafts and with instruction in art and music. . . ." There would also be classes in clay-modelling and Swedish gymnastics. The school as envisioned by Whitehead never came into being.

While teaching at the University of Chicago in the 1890s Dewey had conducted classes at Hull House and had been part of the Hull House-centered group of reformers which Hervey White had joined. Dewey had become very much interested in the Byrdcliffe experiment. After Dewey began teaching at Columbia University in 1904 he encouraged fellow-teachers to settle by summer in Byrdcliffe's East Riding. Historian James Shotwell, Norman Towar Boggs and later Harold Rugg were among these.

One summer the Deweys, who had five children, rented Carniola. In accordance with Dewey's and Whitehead's belief that children may learn by doing, his five built a playhouse with a brick fireplace and chimney. The little structure, sadly worn by time and neglect, still stands, although overwhelmed by brush and rampant wisteria vines.[4]

In 1909 writer Poultney Bigelow, a frequent visitor to Byrdcliffe and an admirer of Whitehead, wrote in his sometimes extravagant manner that ". . . Byrdcliffe is frankly a benevolent despotism. Whitehead is the absolute monarch, and no one is tolerated who is not in sympathy with his rule. No idlers or mere pleasure-seekers are allowed to cumber these classic shades. . . . Absolute monarchy saves the colony from a vast amount of wrangling and wasted time which has usually wrecked other efforts in this direction. . . ."

Of Byrdcliffe's arts and crafts programs, Bigelow said that Whitehead devoted ". . . much of his fortune . . . to paying the salaries of instructors in different branches of handicrafts. . . . Whitehead is virtually the president of a high-grade art university equipped with admirable faculty, laboratory, library, gymnasium, recreation grounds, and a course of work superior to anything of its kind in the Western World." All this supplies a good clue to Whitehead's self-image and, liberally discounted, describes the aims and achievements of the Byrdcliffe of 1909.[5]

The Whiteheads continued to invite people of distinction in the arts to Byrdcliffe. In August 1908 Mr. and Mrs. Arnold Dolmetsch arrived. They were English makers and players of replicas of old and almost forgotten musical instruments. At Byrdcliffe they gave a series of performances of baroque music. A clavichord and a viola da gamba made under the Dolmetschs' direction by Chickering of Boston remained at White Pines.[6]

Among writers to visit the Whiteheads was John Burroughs, who celebrated the Catskills in his popular essays and encouraged birdwatching among Americans. He listened to music played by Byrdcliffe's resident pianist, J. Aldo Randegger, and others. He watched with interest young Byrdcliffe people dancing on the terrace at White Pines. And Burroughs studied a family of albino squirrels which had taken up residence in a Byrdcliffe tree. The Whiteheads sometimes visited Burroughs at his summer home at Roxbury or at West Park where Burroughs had a little fruit farm.

An important writer at Byrdcliffe was Ralph Ashbee, a leading British arts and crafts authority whose colony at Chipping Camden was making history.[7]

Weaving took on fresh importance at Byrdcliffe after 1904. The Whiteheads added a structure they called the Loom Room to White

Pines and connected it to the main building by a labyrinthine passage which crossed a covered bridge. There workers set up looms, spinning wheels and dye pots. Ralph Whitehead himself worked at weaving in this large room, with its air of a William Morris workshop and with furniture made at Byrdcliffe. Whitehead's silk scarves were sold in craft shops such as the one of the Handicraft Society in Boston. For his work as a weaver he was listed by the Society as a master craftsman.

One of the best-known Byrdcliffe weavers was Marie Little, who found it uncongenial to work with others in the Loom Room. In her own shop Miss Little lived and worked in the kind of aesthetic atmosphere beloved of the pre-Raphaelites and arts and crafts enthusiasts. Her life, her works and her environment were as thoroughly arts and crafts as anything in Woodstock. Miss Little left Byrdcliffe about 1915 for Woodstock Valley and eventually settled in a brown-stained house on Plochmann Lane in Woodstock. There she recreated the austere and lovely living and working rooms which had been so much admired at "Looms." [8]

The making of pottery had not been mentioned as among Whitehead's objectives in either his essay on "Work" or in the "Plea" of June 1903. It was not until the end of furniture-making that pottery came into its own as a major effort at Byrdcliffe. By 1907 examples shown at an exhibition of the New York Society of Ceramic Arts were meeting approval. In his *Art Pottery of the United States* Paul Evans tells of the beginnings of the Byrdcliffe Pottery. Charles Volkmar, eminent landscape painter, teacher and potter, came to Byrdcliffe and fired the first pieces.

Byrdcliffe pottery, says Evans, "was produced and characterized by pure handicraft." No wheel was used and later work was fired in open-air kilns. Color was an important concern of Byrdcliffe work, with the principal glazes designated "Byrdcliffe blue," "apple green" and "withered rose." Edith Penman, born in England, and Elizabeth R. Hardenbergh, one of the descendants of Major Johannis Hardenbergh (with Mabel Davidson a bit later), operated the Byrdcliffe pottery in a building below the carpenter shop.

There, as Bertha Thompson remembered, the potter's kiln was often ". . . the rallying point for gay spirits bent on pleasure. I could tell you of many a merry midnight hour spent with them as we watched the pots glow to a white heat. The work from their kilns was shown in many exhibitions throughout the country." [9]

Courses in painting drew a fair number of students. Whitehead described the Studio as having a main room with 1200 square feet of floor space. There "on rainy days, with a cheerful blaze in the fireplace, a costume model is posed. . . ." In good weather the students worked in the open at landscape painting. Twice a week they could attend dances in the Studio and hear "good music there on Sunday evenings."

When Birge Harrison ceased teaching at Byrdcliffe in 1904 Whitehead chose as a successor another moods-of-nature man. Leonard Ochtman was a native of Zonnemaire in Holland and a tireless winner of medals and prizes for his landscapes. He painted "with subtletey and delicacy" in an Impressionist-influenced manner. With Ochtman's association with Woodstock, writers on the place could give it a hint of a connection with the great Dutch tradition in landscape painting. Woodstock was called a Dutch village, and the Dutch church was invariably referred to. Some writers were so carried away with Dutch fever that they referred to the town's grist and saw mills as "Dutch mills."

Harrison had written of the resemblance of the country to the east of Woodstock to parts of Holland. This helped build up an image of the town as being more Dutch than it had ever really been.[10]

For several years longer some of the best craftspeople of the first two years remained loyal to Whitehead. One was Edward (Ned) Thatcher. Another metalworker to remain was London-born Bertha Thompson. Miss Thompson wrote of Thatcher, "The metal shop in those days [that is, 1904] meant Edward Thatcher. It was a long sunny workroom with forge and bellows, and every conceivable kind of equipment that a metal worker could want for Mr. Whitehead's generosity knew no bounds in providing tools and materials for the craftsmen in these shops. The sound of the anvil could be heard at all hours of the day and night as Thatcher forged red-hot iron and steel into hinges, lock-plates and drawer pulls for the furniture being made in the carpenter shop, or fashioned candle-sticks, lanterns, and many other things beautiful in design and workmanship. . . ." Thatcher continued to work at Byrdcliffe and later on in his Striebel Road studio making jewelry as well as the objects Bertha Thompson mentioned.

Ralph Whitehead sometimes said that it was possible to hate someone for no more than ten years. And he may have meant that seriously, for in the fall of 1914 he wrote to Hervey White in a spirit of reconciliation. He invited White to the "at homes" he and Jane Whitehead were beginning to hold. Those present at this at-home, according to the Kingston *Freeman*, included not only Byrdcliffe people but many who had left Byrdcliffe. Birge Harrison, Mr. and Mrs. Neilson Parker (she had been Zulma Steele, who had left Byrdcliffe after 1907), Mrs. Bertha Poole Weyl, wife of economist and writer Walter Weyl, social worker Paul Kennaday, painter Eugene Speicher, Mr. and Mrs. Henry Lee MacFee, Woodstockers Dr. and Mrs. Mortimer Downer, Jane Whitehead's sister Miss McCall, and others.[11]

Not present although invited was Hervey White. In answer to his invitation White wrote, "I am not, nor do I wish to be, a conventional gentleman. . . . At all such social functions I am only playing a part. . . . The older I get the more distasteful the part becomes to me. . . . I find I am getting back to the customs more and more of my childhood . . . that I am more brusque, more impatient and more boorish than ever . . . and a new alliance between us on such lines would surely come to grief.

"There are, however, I am sure, many ways in which we might work in sympathy, things that we may be doing in the community for the arts and for the people. Can we not meet naturally and fraternally in these, and recognize that our early associations as well as our temperaments would make social exchanges disastrous?" [12]

Behind the exchange of letters between Whitehead and White lay a decided change in relations between Byrdcliffe and Woodstock. Before 1913 the Whiteheads had stood aside from Woodstock. That year they made evident a desire to cooperate with the townspeople for the common good. Ralph Whitehead took the initiative in forming the Woodstock Club, whose members were divided between art colony and local people. Its purpose at first was to supply a number of services seen as needed by the community, a nursing service and a library among them. The library soon began many years of activity and growth. The first showings of motion pictures in town were sponsored by the Club.[13]

Hervey White was not among those asked to join in the Woodstock Club. His farm lay outside the town limits, so perhaps that was why. But the Whitehead invitation of 1914 recognized not only that the bitterness between the two men had ended but that Hervey White was no longer a solitary refugee from Byrdcliffe. By 1914 he had established himself as head of a colony set outside Woodstock's borders. Yet, while legally part of the town of Hurley, it was an important element of the growing Woodstock art colony.

THE BLUE DOME, HERVEY WHITE AND THE MAVERICK

Between the time of Bolton Brown's expulsion from Byrdcliffe in 1903 and the beginning of the First World War people involved in the arts settled in most parts of Woodstock. A few of these people lived in isolation. Most were concentrated in Rock City, in the hamlet of Woodstock, where the Art Students League flourished, and in Hervey White's Maverick across the town line in the Hurley Patentee Woods.

Another small concentration lay just to the west of Byrdcliffe, where Birge Harrison had built his house on the Glasco Turnpike. Near there craftspeople Bertha Thompson and Zulma Steele set up their studios. And so too, about 1907, did a pair of women named Dewing Woodward and Louise Johnson, who built an imposing house known from the tiles which covered its roof as Red Roofs. Miss Woodward was rich; Cornelius Vanderbilt was said to have been a cousin of her father's. Miss Johnson was Miss Woodward's longtime close friend and associate.

Red Roofs had a large square living room which took up the first floor. The room was paved with local bluestone and had a fireplace at each end. Dewing and Johnson filled their house with fine antiques collected during years of living in France. They lived in a manner that suggested a kind of Continental ease and elegance unknown in Woodstock.

The two women brought a good deal more than an extension of

the growing art colony to the west of Byrdcliffe and well within the
sound of the bell of the little Methodist church of Shady. What was
significant about their presence was that they emphasized painting the
nude in the Woodstock landscape. Her Blue Dome Frat or Fraternity
or Fellowship, as Woodward variously named it, was novel in that it
was directed by women and taught the painting of nude female models
in the open air.

A piece of blue-tinted gauze was sometimes stretched above to
modify the light, following a French innovation. The group's name
refers to the blue dome of the sky. The students who worked under
Dewing and Johnson's direction in the fields and beside the streams of
Shady were mostly women. When the Blue Dome students exhibited
in New York the work of men who had been Blue Dome students was
included. Their work was not of nudes "painted under the open sky"
but landscapes. Among the men were Jonas Lie, a new associate of the
conservative National Academy of Design, and Alfred Hutty, who
later on achieved success as an etcher. Edmund Rolfe, the former
Byrdcliffe metalworker who lived close by, also contributed
landscapes.[1]

The predilection of Woodward and Johnson for their own sex did
not prevent them from being on friendly terms with men. Hervey
White for a while avoided Red Roofs and its mistresses because, as he
put it, "the place smelt of wealth."

Yet he soon detected "a deeper, wider fragrance" there. He
discovered that the kind of wide-ranging conversation familiar to
Continental intellectuals with literary and artistic interests flourished
at Red Roofs in complete freedom from the petty conventions dear to
the hearts of American hostesses. There White enjoyed meeting
people who were not shackled by the arts and crafts limitations which
sometimes made Byrdcliffe seem a dreamy little island cut off from the
rest of the world.

Poultney Bigelow often drove over from his Hudson River place
at Malden in his tandem (two horses hitched one in front of the
other), with two greyhounds running beside the vehicle like
"outriders," as Hervey White remembered it. Bigelow had a volatile
and eccentric appeal which brought him the friendship of many
notable people. He had been on intimate terms, for instance, with
Kaiser Wilhelm II of Germany. The two had first met as boys in
Berlin, where Bigelow's father served as American ambassador.

While Red Roofs had an undeniable charm to men like White

and Bigelow, the place was viewed with suspicion by many of the older people of Woodstock, who glanced quickly at Red Roofs as they passed by on the turnpike and then averted their eyes. These people had been shocked when the Art Students League Summer School had arrived amid a little storm of rumors about the League's interest in nude human beings. Now at Red Roofs nudity was being brought out of doors, and by a woman at that.

Yet there was reassurance in learning of the approbation of Woodward and Johnson shown by the press. In 1916, for example, the New York *Tribune* (then the preferred New York City paper of Woodstock people) devoted a whole page to Miss Woodward and her work. The head of the Blue Dome Fellowship was shown standing beside her easel in the Shady woods surrounded by a group of her works.

One of these showed a band of skittish nudes engaged in a harvest dance in southern France. Another showed half a dozen nudes, each with a shapely back against a Shady pine tree whose spirit she seemed to symbolize. Pictures of seated nudes and standing nudes were all painted in the open air of the Fellowship, located to discourage voyeurs, the *Tribune* stated, in a remote part of the Catskills which could be reached only "on foot or by stage." [2]

The connection of the Blue Dome project to the expanding Woodstock art colony was real enough. It had a measurable effect on the larger colony. By 1920, as John F. Carlson, head of the League Summer School put it, the League "became possessed with a desire to operate a "figure-out-of-doors-class" similar to Miss Woodward's. Carlson was doubtful. He was willing to allow the class only if its students were first required to pass an examination as to their competence in figure painting. This was contrary to the League's usual policy of requiring no entrance requirements at all to any of its classes. So Carlson resigned and after a few years of struggle the League closed its Woodstock Summer School. [3]

While Miss Woodward was trying without much success to make Red Roofs into the center of a little art colony of European flavor, Hervey White was beginning, after much hesitation and delay, to give his farm on the Maverick Road (bought in 1905 in partnership with Fritz van der Loo) a new birth as an American colony in which many old restrictions on individual freedom might be scrapped and where men and women might live in accordance with the rule of Rabelais' Thelemite monks, "Fais ce que voudra," or, as Hervey like to put it,

"Do what you what want to (as long as you don't harm others)."

The Maverick's birth pangs were severe. White and his new wife had spent the winter of 1904 in New York. There White fell back on teaching. Two sons were soon born to the Whites. Struggles with childhood illness and the problems of trying to live adequately in New York on a teacher's salary proved discouraging.

In order to increase his income White worked at free-lance writing. A childhood friend named Ned Slosson, the editor of a liberal and long-established magazine *The Independent* (Slosson once said that Hervey White had "a genius for friendship"), accepted a number of pieces which showed White's abilities as a writer. His articles had a good deal of warmth and at the same time took a critical view of American society of his time. He did other writing, including even a script for a vaudeville act.

The kind of life White had been living became less and less appealing to him. In 1908 he decided to give up New York and settle year round on his farm. Vivian White was less eager to leave the city; she wanted a career of her own in some sort of craft work. The color printing venture which had brought her to Byrdcliffe had failed. She had then turned to pottery. Ralph Whitehead had promised her a scholarship to study at Alfred University, where important potter Charles F. Binns was teaching. After her marriage Whitehead's scholarship became a check for one hundred fifty dollars. Mrs. White spent the money on a fur coat.

On the farm Hervey built a simple structure to serve as Vivian's pottery studio. That same summer he built a cabin for cellist Paul Kefer, who had first come to Woodstock to play at Byrdcliffe. With these two buildings, simple though they were, he may have caused Ralph Whitehead to view him as a rival bent on drawing supporters from Byrdcliffe. White and Whitehead had remained on fairly friendly terms, but now the Whiteheads, as White put it, "ostracized" him and his wife. This ostracism showed no sign of ending until Whitehead sent White the letter of the fall of 1914.

During the first three or four years after the break with Byrdcliffe in 1904, personal problems arose to change the direction of the lives of Hervey and Vivian White. A few years after the birth of their two sons the couple began to drift apart. White's genius for friendship, he found out, had a homosexual element which became stronger as he grew older. Not long after a temporary separation Vivian and the two boys left Hervey for good and moved to the Middle West. They lived there with her mother until a divorce made her free to remarry. From this time on Vivian's mother took care of the support of the boys. Hervey was freed from the family burdens which had weighed heavily upon him since his marriage.[4]

While the boys were still with him and his wife in New York Hervey worked his farm in an irregular way. He continued to write novels and poetry and for two seasons taught school, most of the time at a little schoolhouse which stood near the point at which the Maverick Road joins what is now Route 28. He returned to New York for the winter, and out of his school experiences teaching in West Hurley grew an article for *The Independent* called "Our Rural Slums," in which White analyzed the local society of which the school formed a part.

In a manner recalling the ideas of Jane Addams, he told of the difficulties of teaching children whose poverty-dominated backgrounds made learning hard. With the human sympathy which was always with him, White also wrote of the willingness of his pupils to help one another and of the eager hospitality of their parents when strangers called at their small and overcrowded houses. These people were largely bluestone quarry workers who made up the poorest layer of local society. When White later taught at another nearby school, he found the more favorable home background of the children of the prosperous classes made them far more receptive to learning.

During these years White did another kind of occasional work which gave him an outlet for the desire to help his fellow mortals, a desire which had been with him ever since his Harvard days. He came to know and admire the local family doctor, Mortimer Downer. Whenever Dr. Downer needed a male nurse to help one of his patients he called on White, who worked at the task with great skill and understanding.

White valued his experience at nursing because it gave him a chance to get close to the local people and to give them evidence of his sense of sharing with them a common humanity. Unlike Ralph Whitehead, who conducted Byrdcliffe as an enclave of enlightenment set amid what he saw as a dull and backward population, White hoped that his own farm might become a thing of value to local people as well as to outsiders. He sometimes saw its future as what he called a kind of "rural Hull House." [5]

Throughout his adult life White remained committed to the principles of socialism. This commitment was most evident in the early years of his colony on the Maverick. Later in his life it became less obvious. His early guests, and he had many, were seldom people involved in the arts and crafts movement or in painting. They were social critics and reformers like Clarence Darrow, the atheist lawyer, and Thorstein Veblen, the unorthodox economist who was then antagonizing classic economists with his theory of conspicuous consumption.

From the past of the old farmhouse on the Maverick Road in which the two were sitting, White once delighted Veblen with an example of conspicuous consumption even among the poor. "The woman who lived here before I came used to scrub the dirt floor of this cellar every Saturday afternoon, whitewash the stones and wash potato bags for carpets and spread them down to have the place neat for Sunday," White said. Veblen in turn told White of the woman he'd known who washed the blacking from her kitchen stove with soap and water, blackened it all over again and scrubbed the inside of the firebox with brick dust and a rag.[6]

Veblen's theories made a strong appeal to White. They strengthened his determination to keep his colony from becoming a place where conventional ways of display might hamper people in their attempts at living freely and well.

Each summer, especially before 1914, White's farm became a meeting place not only for theorists like Veblen, Charlotte Perkins Gilman and similar intellectuals but also for people who were active on the practical level of social work in New York and Chicago. Some were taking part in organizing labor unions and conducting strikes. People like these had been visitors and boarders at the Lark's Nest; now many of them followed Hervey White to his farm.

To accommodate these people White built cabins of rough local materials and the simplest construction. Yet his structures had a decided visual appeal to those freed from slavery to the usual kind of outward show. The names he gave his cabins were unlike the romantic ones used for Byrdcliffe buildings. One was called Birdseye, a name suggested by that of the author of a series of library reports White had read during his teaching winters in New York. Another, the summer place of Frank Bolles, was called Bearcamp. It was there Bolles wrote several books of charming nature essays.[7]

The name Maverick came to be used for the colony little by little over a period of years. The word had haunted White ever since he heard it in the 1890s in Colorado while visiting his sister on a farming commune in which he owned shares. There, as White remembered many years later, he had been told of a wild white stallion known locally as the Maverick Horse which lived alone and in freedom in a canyon.

Two groups of folk motifs came together. One deals with the White Steed of the Prairies, the Ghost Horse of the Plains, the Pacing White Stallion or the Phantom Wild Horse, all of them fast and free and belonging to no one. The other group of motifs is that of the Texas Maverick, an unbranded animal, usually a steer, which belongs to whoever can catch him. If he ever had a place of his own, Hervey resolved on that Colorado visit, he would call it The Maverick to symbolize his passion for free, unfettered living.[8]

In 1911 the Maverick Horse appeared as the hero of a long and vigorously phrased Byronic poem Hervey composed as he walked back and forth between his farm and Woodstock. The poem got good reviews. Harriet Monroe, founder in 1912 of the influential magazine *Poetry*, wrote of *The Adventures of Young Maverick*, "The spirit of the West is in this poem, its freedom, spaciousness, strong sunshine; also its careless good humor and half sardonic fun. . . ."

The poem was printed and published by Hervey White himself at his Maverick Press, which had begun serious operation in 1910. After a fire in his Boston publisher's warehouse destroyed stocks of his previously published books, Hervey lost faith in trade publishers. He then revived a long-felt wish to do his own printing and publishing.[9]

The Maverick Press soon became the clattering heart of the Maverick colony. Maverick tenants and their children were put to use collating, sewing and pasting the paper-covered Maverick Press imprints. Earlier Jane Addams had refused White's request to allow him a printing press at Hull House. Later at Byrdcliffe he made the same request of Ralph Whitehead, who also refused. But when White became committed to the Maverick colony the desire to own a printing and lithographic press and publish his own and other people's writings and graphics came to the surface again. With the help of Carl Eric Lindin, then as always friendly, helpful and understanding toward the many disparate elements which made up Woodstock society, he bought a printing press.

With money saved from a New York City job with the Fine Arts Commission he bought type. George Daulton, a writer friend who spent much time on Hervey's farm, taught him the art of printing. By 1910 three little books containing poems by Hervey came from what was now named the Maverick Press. One of these books, *In An Old Man's Garden*, was attractively designed with rough paper covers, green ink and type ornaments in orange. The poems in all three books are short and lyrical and bear signs of hasty composition. Although some have a singing charm they are not well suited to the taste of our own day. Like some oldtime newspaper printers Hervey often set type without the help of a manuscript.

The following year saw the publication not only of *Young Maverick* but also of a play, *The Assassins*, a tragedy set in South America, and a broadside, *The Passing Year*, a calendar with appropriate quotations from the English poets for each month, printed with a good deal of visual charm. That same year the Press published a volume of poems by Harriet Howe, the feminist who had come to the Lark's Nest in the train of Charlotte Perkins Gilman.

Nineteen thirteen saw the publication of *The House in the Road*, a novel which tells of how its hero, Mortimer Lackland, finds freedom and happiness by living a simple life only to lose both after he marries. Each chapter is prefaced by an often moving poem or fable by Lackland. The book reflects an aspect of Hervey's own life after his marriage and separation. From 1913 until the 1930s the Maverick Press under White's management printed not only books of plays, poems and novels by Hervey himself but material by others in addition. The Press was useful, as Hervey's colony grew in ambition and size, in producing publicity materials for projects of "The Maverick." Job printing provided Hervey with a small source of income. As no record was kept of this sort of printed material, little is known of its quality or volume. [10]

Much more is known about a monthly periodical *The Wild Hawk*, which began publication in November of 1911 and did not cease until October 1916. When it died it was quickly reborn as *The Plowshare*. The first number of *The Wild Hawk* offered an essay inspired by a robin singing in late fall, a poem on the changing seasons by Edward Yeomans of Chicago and Woodstock, a whimsical appeal for subscribers by mythical editor Algernon Applebloom, essays on a mountain and a valley by Yeomans, and two translations, one by cellist Paul Kefer from the French of Octave Mirbeau and the other by Carl Eric Lindin from the Swedish of Bo Bergman.

The major contribution to this initial number was the beginning of a serial story by Hervey White, "A Hornless Dilemma." In a jumpy series of scenes, the story deals with the relations of a rebellious banker's daughter and a poor musician who communicates through a hole in the wall which separates their rooms in a boardinghouse. The story proved unpopular with *Wild Hawk* readers and was discontinued. Yet it had its importance. Changes were taking place in Woodstock writers' minds as well as in painters' minds. Hervey had been impressed by the talk of the revolutionary changes taking place in painting and music in Europe and wondered whether something similar to "Futurist or Cubist" painting, as he put it, might not be done with writing.

In 1911 poets and prose writers in Europe and America were feeling a rising surge of the spirit that would before too many years make the names of Ezra Pound, James Joyce, T.S. Eliot and Carl Sandburg respected. In a Woodstock in which avant-garde theories in the arts were everywhere being discussed, White no longer wanted to write in the realistic manner which had brought him praise from such judges as Dreiser. Hervey was aware "A Hornless Dilemma" was by no means an artistic success. Of the story he wrote, "Whatever we may seem in our struggle for modernity, we are not willing to give up the ancients who have taught us the principles of unity and variety." [11]

The Wild Hawk through the years preceding the outbreak of the World War gives convincing evidence of Hervey's struggle to free himself from bondage to the ways of writing he had learned in his youth and to become what he called "modern." His poetry lost much of the careless jingling quality that had previously marked it. His untitled poem about Chicago published in the *Hawk* of January 1912 represents a new and arresting departure. It presents the big, brash energetic city as a struggling organism:

> panting breathlessly,
> Till what was lake and marsh and prairie-grove
> Is now a heated plain of brick and iron
> Ten story-strata deep, and in and out
> Among the heated chambers run the men
> Gone method-mad with countless things to do,
> And iron chain-like trains with snorting steam
> Glide in from every point the compass round.
> And ships from on the bosom of the lake
> Unload to trains, and trains unload to ships,
> CLANG! Beats relentlessly the falling hammer.

The poem had power and drive, yet like so much of Hervey's verse it made too much use of worn poetic diction and imagery. Hervey liked to write impulsively without revising. This helped make his poem ignored while Carl Sandburg's "Chicago, hog butcher to the world," which appeared a few years later and had some similarities in theme and treatment, rose by reason of its strong fresh colloquial phrasing to the stature of an American classic.[12]

It might be convenient if not entirely accurate to accept the beginning of the First World War as marking a milestone in the growth of the Woodstock art colony. For one thing Byrdcliffe by then had fallen into a way of life different in many features from that with which it had begun in 1902. Whitehead's attempts to modify the Ruskinian commitments which had motivated him ever since his Balliol days by trying to merge them with others learned from American shapers of a new society had not succeeded. Try as he might, Whitehead could never escape from remnants of the conservatism in which he had been steeped at Saddleworth. Though he might talk in terms of progressive reforms, his actions stifled every try at putting them into being.

39

THE FIRST
WORLD WAR

Americans have always been slow to unite in enthusiasm for war. Their Revolution had its confusion of Whigs and Tories. The Mexican War roused widespread skepticism and disapproval. The Civil War saw Copperheads in Ulster County and elsewhere in the North rising to prominence and demanding an end to hostilities. The World War began with a marked division of Americans into camps which favored one or the other side or denounced both.

People of the older Woodstock followed the progress of the war as it was described and pictured in great detail on the front page of the Kingston *Freeman*, which had a large circulation in the town. Most Woodstock people were Republicans in politics. The *Freeman*, a Republican paper, was close to the well-organized political machine which ruled Ulster County. The paper's role in forming opinions was decisive. At the beginning of the war the shooting seemed very far away, and the *Freeman*'s war news was presented as thrilling and entertaining drama. Only when the war grew in size and cruelty later on and began to take on the look of a threat to their safety did Woodstock people take clearcut sides. They relied, to a great extent, on whether they approved of the policies of President Wilson.

Wilson, a Democrat, was not highly regarded by the *Freeman* and the Ulster County political hierarchy. After the Germans invaded Belgium in July 1914 and Britain declared war, Woodstock people of

460

Irish descent tended to favor Germany against their traditional British enemy. Some Woodstockers took the Allied side. Among the members of the art colony a similar division took place. At Byrdcliffe the Whiteheads were very much on the British-French-Belgian side. But some of the prosperous summer people at Byrdcliffe were of German origin.

Martin Schutze, with his deep involvement in German literature and his German university training, found it hard to accept the divisions of opinion that he saw harming Byrdcliffe, for which he had long felt a deep affection. Looking backward as a new World War was brewing in 1938, Schutze wrote that "under the stress of altered conditions, especially since the beginning of the First World War [Byrdcliffe] gradually lost its original feeling of easy fellowship and creative leisure." [1]

Anti-German feeling among the painters, writers and musicians on the Maverick, at Rock City and elsewhere in the valley grew as news of the destruction of great cathedrals and other Continental landmarks arrived. Though the art-colony people had a great variety of ethnic backgrounds, most had either studied in France or come to respect French innovations in the arts. They felt dismay at the destruction of cultural monuments. Many people in the fall of 1914, however, were taking a neutral position, declaring all war evil and barbaric.

Anti-German feeling was especially intense on the Maverick, where the Belgian-born musicians who had followed Paul Kefer there were loud in their anger against Germany. That year Belgian-born Pierre Henrotte gave a violin recital at Woodstock's chief meeting place, the Firemen's Hall, and the performance was applauded by all levels of Woodstock society. Soon after, Kefer, Roger Britt, Henri Michaux and Henrotte—all Belgians—performed quartets in the Hall for the benefit of Belgian war relief. These were the first musical events of high quality and open to the public to come to Woodstock. They helped intensify local feelings of sympathy for the Allied side in the war. Other fundraising events followed, notably collections in the churches and a rummage sale in the rooms of the Woodstock Club.[2]

While there was sympathy for all victims of war, opinion as to the rightness of the Allied or the German cause continued to be divided. In Kingston a German Lutheran Church was packed with people of German background for a program aimed at expressing sympathy for the German side and for collecting funds for Germans war victims. There were people in Woodstock who shared these objectives.

As the German war machine crashed across France in the face of stiffening resistance, Hervey White became discouraged and denounced war in all its forms. His *Wild Hawk* for August 1914 carried a poem in which he told how his initial exultation at the resistance to the Germans of the Belgian people had given way to nausea "with this glut of blood." He and others, "fainting, look beyond the smoke,/The wreck and ashes of a war-cursed land . . ." to see "but one great hero for the race,/One man to celebrate in future years. . . ." That man, Hervey wrote, is the one who says "I will not fight." [3]

Hervey's horror of war reached a peak in his poem called "Christmas-1914," which began:

> Cease with your jangling Christmas chimes,
> Your recitation of dead creed,
> When youths are sacrificed for greed
> Throughout the land in million crimes;
>
> When kings parade their cruel God
> To hide their lust for private gain,
> And deluge with their iron rain
> The nauseated shuddering sod
>
> Where spattered filth and splattered brains
> And shreds of entrails bits of bone
> Still wait the endless coming on
> Of fresh-cheeked boys in armored trains . . .

Hervey wrote a one-act pacifist play called *Fire and Water* dealing with the meeting on the battlefield of two French and two German soldiers who discovered that although their duty was to kill each other they were very much alike and could quickly slip into friendship. Staged by New York's Washington Square Players at their Bandbox Theater on 57th Street near Third Avenue, the play got a good review from The New York *Times*.[4]

Hervey White's pacifism did not survive the entry into the war of the United States. He tried to become a YMCA worker with the American troops. In response to a news item in the Kingston *Freeman*, he did his best to enlist for duty on a bomber. In both attempts he was turned down. Later in life he said that people who were not moved by mob hysteria didn't understand that men yearn to go to war. "I have felt the exhilaration of it several times," said Hervey, "and strangely enough I am proud I have responded." [5]

Hervey's shift from pacifism to military enthusiasm was characteristic of many during the war years. Even the Kingston *Freeman* gave up berating President Wilson and became a booster for what it had seen a short time before as his personal war.

As the United States plunged into the war, in the wake of the sinking of the Lusitania in 1914, neither Hervey White nor the German-born Woodstockers could easily shake off the popular feeling that they were dangerous pro-Germans and probably spies. Ralph Whitehead, who never wavered in his pro-Allied stand, took part in Red Cross and Liberty Bond drives. Many years later he confessed with a smile that he had watched from Byrdcliffe with a telescope mysterious lights going on and off along the Maverick. He had feared these might be indications German agents were preparing to dump poisons in the nearby Ashokan Reservoir and wipe out the population of New York City. The lights Whitehead had seen, Hervey explained to him, were those of his own tenants putting their children and chickens to bed.

With the declaration of war against Germany of April 6, 1917 and the enactment of a conscription act on May 16, enthusiasm for the war became widespread. Suspicions like those Ralph Whitehead had felt toward the Maverick bubbled up in many minds. People of German descent were watched with uneasiness. A display of aurora borealis sent a body of Woodstock men tramping up Overlook Mountain. They were afraid that the spears of light they saw apparently emanating from the mountain might be signals to German submarine commanders lying in wait off the Atlantic Coast.[6]

The Overlook Mountain House had been bought in 1917 by Morris Newgold. His German name alone was enough to make Overlook Mountain something to be watched. When archeologist Max Schrabisch began excavating in Indian rock shelters on the mountainside, he was seized and hauled off to Kingston on suspicion of planning machine-gun emplacements to menace Woodstock. A guest at the battered hotel on Overlook came under suspicion because his hobby was the radio, or wireless, as it was called, and he kept some equipment in his room. Rising high above Woodstock, Overlook became the focal point of German-spy hysteria. Until the war was over no one with a German name felt easy about climbing the mountain.[7]

There was acceptance of if not always enthusiasm for Red Cross and Liberty Bond drives. Meetings were addressed by county and Woodstock political leaders, who often visited the homes of local people to make personal appeals. A wooden thermometer was set up on the Village Green to record the progress of Woodstock contributions. These were substantial. On Saturday mornings women, mainly wives of painters or other members of the art colony, set up booths and sold a great variety of foodstuffs, plants and cut flowers, craft objects, bric-a-brac, clothing and much more for the benefit of the Red Cross. The women's imaginative and picturesque costumes helped make the Market Fair a success and to keep it alive as a Woodstock institution until the 1970s.

Even the draft caused little criticism. Hervey White remembered one Woodstock farmer who told him that he was proud that his sons were going into the army. Yet should a rumored draft of capital arrive, the farmer said in an anxious voice, he would not be pleased because it didn't seem right that the government should take away what a man had saved. This same man, Hervey said, would gladly have spent every cent he had to help his sons if their lives were threatened by illness; he had been conditioned to respect property so much that he was easily drawn into his ambivalent position.[8]

The war brought prosperity to many local people who found well-paying jobs in Rondout shipyards or in war industries far from home. Members of the art colony also joined in the war effort, and to some it seemed that the drain would mean the end of the colony. Many painters and other creative workers managed to hang on to their chosen way of life while doing their share in the war effort. Edward (Ned) Thatcher put his great craft skills to work devising means of helping toward recovery those wounded in the war. He taught them to make toys from discarded tin cans, and in 1919 he wrote *Making Tin Cans Toys*. When a shortage of rubber developed Bolton Brown made tires of steel springs and wood for his car. The loud clattering of these substitutes as Brown drove was long remembered in Woodstock.[9]

In 1918 the great epidemic of influenza which ended the lives of over half a million Americans hit Woodstock hard. Hervey White often took time from his effort at building up the Maverick to serve with great devotion and energy as Dr. Downer's assistant. Though nursing was important in treating influenza, most people hesitated to help for fear of contagion. Dr. Downer asked Hervey how he felt "about taking a chance at death." Replied Hervey, "Life is not so sweet that I can't do my duty."

464

"That's the way I feel about it," the doctor said.

When Will Peper, son of blacksmith Henry Peper, fell ill with influenza, Hervey nursed him. Will had been deferred in the draft because his brother was serving in the army and he was needed to help take care of the family blacksmith shop. When Will died his brother was permitted to come home from France to take his place. Another young victim of the epidemic—and many were young—imagined in his delirium that he was in a hospital in France and that his mother and Hervey were nurses there. Hervey asked if he recognized him and the boy replied, "Maybe you might be an angel." And both laughed.[10]

The war came to an end to the sound of wild rejoicing. Florence Ballin Cramer told in her diary of getting the news by telephone from New York. "The Armistice has been signed," she wrote, "it means Peace! The dreadful constant sense of oppression that five years of War has caused was lifted instantly—It was like seeing sunshine after having spent years in a cave, we became dazed. . . . Konrad and I rushed out doors and danced around madly in sheer joy. . . ."

The two got in their Model-T Ford and drove to the houses of friends to spread the news. With painters Andrew Dasburg, Caroline Speare and Paul Rohland aboard, they drove through the center of Woodstock leaning out and shouting "Peace!" to everyone they passed, friend or stranger. They headed toward Saugerties to buy some wine for celebrating but found the place they knew had burned down. They drove on and found another and returned home with wine and food and reveled until far into the night.

Two young men of Woodstock, Louis Harrison and Sheldon B. Elwyn, did not rejoice that November day. They had died during the war while in the armed forces. Their names are on the war memorial on the Village Green.[11]

The years between the beginning of the war in 1914 and the return to what presidential candidate Warren G. Harding would soon refer to as "normalcy" did not bear out fears that the Woodstock art colony would prove to be a casualty of the war. There certainly were changes on all levels of Woodstock life, however. The upheaval of the war years had caused a lessening of old moral standards. Woodstock painters and intellectuals had begun to read and discuss Freud, Krafft-Ebbing and other writers who were opening new ways of relating to sex. The writings of Dostoevsky and revolutionist Maxim Gorki were being widely read in the art colony.[12]

In 1917 New York State women won the right to vote. The state had long been a leader in "votes for women" agitation, and in 1920 Woodstock women voted in their first presidential election. Prohibition, on the wings of war enthusiasm and hostility to the big brewers, with their German antecedents, became law in 1919 and went into effect the following year. Military training for high school students had been a war measure which lingered on after peace had come.[13]

The Russian Revolution of the spring of 1917 was regarded with a good deal of sympathy on all levels of Woodstock society. The harsh and repressive rule of the Czars had long been criticized by Americans. Intellectual and artistic Europeans and Americans made something of a cult of Russians. Many Russian artists, dancers and musicians were sent from their homeland by their government to earn hard currency and to improve relations with Western peoples whose governments were committed to attitudes of hostility toward the November or Bolshevik Revolution of 1917.

Like most wars, the World War had stimulated inventiveness, the making of labor-saving devices and the substitution of other sources of energy for human muscle. In spite of the wartime shortage of materials, the automobile, flush toilets and central heating strengthened their place in Woodstock life.

By 1917 the number of telephones in town had grown from the two installed in 1879 to over eighty. The first phones had connected the Overlook Mountain House with Snyder's store in Woodstock and the store with the West Hurley R.R. station. By 1903 a few small private systems were in use. One of these was that of William Short of Wittenberg, who had linked his steam-powered saw, shingle, barrel heading and feed mill with several houses in a little system which used wet batteries. Most of the telephones of the war period were concentrated in the hamlet of Woodstock. In outlying places there were few. In Shady, for example, there were only two, one in Burhans' general store and post office and the other in the Vosburgh and Stone turning mill.[14]

There was more and more talk of the possibility of supplying Woodstock people with electric current. Some discussed forming a cooperative system using the power of the Sawkill, but centrally-produced electric power did not reach Woodstock until 1924.

Byrdcliffe under Ralph and Jane Whitehead still clung tenaciously to much of the way of life set up on the mountainside in 1902. Down in the valley the Rock City painters and the Maverick people liked to say that Byrdcliffe was through as a creative place and had become little more than a summer resort for rich families. Yet this was far from true. Side by side with the summer people craftsmen, painters, musicians and writers formed part of the little world of Byrdcliffe. Louella Stewart wrote in May 1915 that "Byrdcliffians make pottery, jewelry and metal work, baskets, hand woven rugs, draperies and hangings. In August they hold their annual exhibition, to which the resident artists contribute etchings, small oil paintings, and water-color sketches." [15]

The two Whiteheads had become active craft workers themselves. A well-built pottery building rose close to the house, and there the White Pines Pottery was set up for Whitehead use. White Pines pots were based in design on old Chinese and Persian models. Some of those of Chinese inspiration were said in 1917 to be hard to tell from the ancient ones. Examples of White Pines pots were exhibited here and there. They were shown in 1918 and 1920 in Santa Barbara, where a lively pottery center had developed. A reviewer of the exhibitions mentioned "turquoise blues, both in bright matte and glazes and . . . light sea-green pots in matte glaze . . . among the pots of all colors . . . there are some very good ones in red and orange, some of the reds being like the autumn coloring of the sumac, in the east. . . . A few are in 'tea leaf' color . . . and there is a group of little pots decorated with eucalyptus leaves and seed pods. . . ." The painted decorations were usually the work of Mrs. Whitehead—the eucalyptus tree imported from Australia was rapidly making itself at home in Santa Barbara.[16]

The social isolation of Byrdcliffe from the hamlet of Woodstock was modified to a small extent by the events of the First World War. Joint fundraising drives for wartime charity and the perception of a threat from the German spies supposedly operating from the old hotel on Overlook had done something to bring Byrdcliffe people and those of the Woodstock valley closer together. And Byrdcliffe people during the war years began to attend the cultural and social events taking place in the art colony centered in the hamlet of Woodstock and across the town line in the part of the old Hurley Patentee Woods now becoming widely known as The Maverick.

THE MAVERICK GROWS

From his days as a student at Harvard Hervey White had never relaxed—at least for long—his determination to live in accordance with the socialist ideals in which he had come to believe. He saw human life as best motivated more by cooperation than by competition. His four years at Hull House had given concrete expression to his beliefs. He felt that no man or woman had a right to profit by the advantages given by position on the social scale or by any special talents. Those fortunately situated in life owed it to the less fortunate to share what they had with them.

In accordance with this belief Hervey had tried to give the royalties he received from his first novel to an impoverished artist friend. Ralph Whitehead had strongly disapproved of this action, socialist though he was.[1]

Hervey's connection with the Byrdcliffe experiment had given him hope that he could realize his dreams of a socialistic community. When Byrdcliffe proved a disappointment White's hopes came to be centered on the farm he bought in the Hurley Patentee Woods. There he worked toward making the place into his rural Hull House. But it was not until the First World War that his farm could become firmly established as "The Maverick." [2]

Changes in American life brought into the open by the shock of war helped make the Maverick's growth possible. Then widespread questioning of old values and repudiation of old ways of living had taken a grip on many young Americans, especially those with an interest in the arts and social reform. A class of people like these had begun to become clearly visible following the French Revolution. By the end of the nineteenth century they formed little enclaves in a number of American cities. Chicago's colony of innovative and rebellious people, with which Hervey White had been connected, was among the most vital in the country. It supplied recruits to Byrdcliffe and to Hervey's farm in its earliest years.

By 1914 New York's Greenwich Village was growing and thriving as it drew unconventional young people from all parts of the United States. The Village, as it was called, was close geographically to Woodstock. As word of Hervey's ambitions for the Maverick spread, Villagers arrived to join the musicians, social reformers and assorted intellectuals who were finding the Maverick atmosphere agreeable.

The arts, with music and especially chamber music the most highly valued, came more and more to dominate the Maverick. And strangers detected a kind of Maverick snobbishness which looked down as from a superior position on business and profit-motivated Americans. A businessman venturing on the Maverick felt it necessary to explain himself to old hands.

On his first morning on the Maverick, George Plochmann met Hervey White as both approached the communal well with buckets in their hands. The two introduced themselves. Hervey asked what Plochmann did. "I'm afraid its pretty bad," Plochmann said, "I'm a banker." And then he added in self-defense, "But I also play viola." Plochmann remained to marry pianist Elizabeth Kimball and become a useful member of the Maverick's musical set. The banking side of his personality was ignored.[3]

With its scorn for conventional values, the bohemian attitude toward life had been felt in Woodstock ever since the foundation of Byrdcliffe. The arrival of the Art Students League had intensified it. And when Greenwich Villagers sought out the Maverick the hedonism which formed a part of their style began modifying the more serious air of the early Maverick, where what came to be called "do-gooders" had often set the pace.

Hervey White was unusually sensitive to the thoughts and feelings of those about him. As life there became more playful and a bit less socially conscious, he took steps at the Maverick to provide centers for the kind of activities which both old and new Maverick people valued. One of these—musical performances—became an institution which has continued strong to this day in the Maverick Concerts of chamber music.

The concerts had their beginnings in the private performances at Arcady and Byrdcliffe to which Ralph Whitehead had carried the devotion to music he had acquired at Oxford. Visitors to Byrdcliffe as to Onteora Park and other similar oases among the Catskills found classical chamber music a highly valued part of summer life. On the Maverick this kind of music became a central aspect of the colony. Contemporary music, which might have seemed more in tune with the emphasis of Maverick people on struggle against the restrictions imposed by the past, was little played. Hervey, unconventional in many other ways, remained within the bounds laid down by his musical conditioning.

Hervey White's youthful musical involvement had been restricted to playing the fiddle at dances in Kansas, and later managing musical performances at Hull House. On visits to Ralph Whitehead's Arcady he became exposed to chamber music as one of the pleasures for those who could afford it in the days before the phonograph made it more widely accessible. Once he was established on the Maverick, Hervey was surrounded by musicians, some of whom had previously played at Byrdcliffe. Private musical afternoons and evenings, often "under the pines," drew Maverick people and soon their friends from Woodstock and even from Byrdcliffe. After the performances at the Fireman's Hall in the early phase of the First World War the drawing power of well-played classical chamber music became apparent.[4]

Hervey White was convinced that regularly-scheduled chamber music concerts open to the public at a small charge might be possible. To find a suitable concert hall would involve spending money—and Hervey had no money. However, the problem was solved with the help of an extraordinary series of events once widely acclaimed as the Maverick Festivals.

The first Festival owed its birth to the need for a good well for the increasing number of summer residents on the Maverick. The original shallow dug well was never very productive because the water table under Hervey's farm was far beneath the surface. Several unusually dry years had pushed the water table even lower than normal. The drilling of a well was begun by a man with the memorable name of Rockafeller. Payment was to be made over a period of years. By the spring of 1915 drilling ceased at a depth—unprecedented for the vicinity—of five hundred and fifty feet.

Hervey was faced with paying Rockafeller fifteen hundred dollars for the well, far more than he had expected. In this fix he wondered whether the kind of lively, imaginative parties which were part of Maverick life and had long been a tradition among artists and students might not be turned into money-raising events. After discussion with many friends the first Maverick Festival was roughed out. It would bring together as its audience not only Maverick and Woodstock people but also those of Kingston and Saugerties, and of the summer resorts and parks of the Catskills. Hervey had the almost-obsessive hope of uniting by means of a Festival the entire community on all levels in understanding and enjoyment of the arts.

Hervey wanted a Festival that would make use of music, dancing, pageantry, picnicking around campfires, dressing up in fantastic costumes, selling craft objects and food at booths as in Old-World fairs, and the display of artists' skills and imagination in banners hung from trees and buildings. He wanted the design of the pageants and the kind of games and athletic contests all to contain the features of communal celebrations from the days of the ancient Greeks and before.

Because the Maverick had moved into a position of leadership of the Woodstock art colony and because of the force of Hervey's charm and friendliness toward almost everybody, hundreds of people quickly rallied to the cause of sharing in lifting the debt owed to Rockafeller.[5]

First there was the question of a suitable place for the festival. "Spying around on the mountainside" above the Maverick, writer Ivan Narodny found an abandoned bluestone quarry which was a splendid site for the pageant. Hervey and several helpers plunged into three months' of hard labor converting the quarry into a roofless theater with walls of natural stone. Hervey recalled years later that "people scoffed and said that I was crazy" because the hillside leading to the quarry was felt to be too steep for most people. Hervey replied that "people like to take a climb and then brag of it."

As the quarry-theater reached completion, with seats and stage and orchestra pit ingeniously improvised, confidence in Hervey's Festival project rose high. Local farmers who had become friends of Hervey worked with teams and axes to prepare the picnic ground near the present Maverick Concert Hall and agreed to serve during the Festival itself in a great variety of capacities. Artists got to work painting posters to be displayed in Woodstock, Kingston and elsewhere and to make spectacular banners (one was twelve by

471

eighteen feet in size) for use in enlivening the grounds; Andrew Dasburg, Henry L. McFee, Frank Chase, Ilonka Karasz, John F. Carlson and Konrad Cramer were among the artists to contribute their skills.

Edward Thatcher, who was teaching a craft program at Columbia University's Teachers' College as well as keeping up his own workshop, put together a system of electric lights for the theater from odds and ends. Artists' wives sewed costumes and banners. Aileen McFee "treadled miles on her sewing machine." Woodstock shopkeepers sold the materials for booths, banners and the theater on Hervey's credit. Confidence in the Festival grew from day to day as the work went forward. And as August 26 approached the grounds, the theater, the musicians and the performers were ready.

Hervey was proud of the booths, at which a great range of objects to eat, to wear, to amuse and to display were to be sold. The booths, he wrote, ". . . were arranged in semicircle, built of poles and covered with muslin stretched smooth. Their colors were mainly blue and yellow, and two towers at the ends were topped with black. The booths were let out to other artists for fake shows or gaming tables or fortune telling. All profits from everything went to me except food booths set up by my farmer neighbors who gave me ten per cent of what they sold."

In his print shop Hervey put together a flyer and an attractive little booklet covered in butcher's paper, both of which were sent out over the countryside and up and down the Hudson Valley. In them Hervey turned promoter, making his upcoming Festival seductive to a broad range of humans. The flyer hinted at "wild sports going on," and told that the Maverick people had "set up a real theater in a stone-quarry and great musicians are coming up from New York . . . and great singers . . . will sing and famous dancers. . . ."

The principal dancer, Lada, "illumines beautiful music like poems, and makes you feel its religion . . . you cry, it is so exquisite to see. . . . All this in the wild stone-quarry theater, in the moonlight, with the orchestra wailing in rapture, and the jealous torches flaring in the wind!"

And this was by no means all. "In the afternoon there is also a concert, with a pageant, and strange doings on the stage . . . they talk of having a machine up from New York to take our moving picture, when a French horn has made us drunk with wildness and a flute and harp have charmed us back to peace. . . . But the funny part will be a fair and picnic below, before the great concerts begin. For there will be a village that will stand for but a day, which mad artists have hung with glorious banners, and blazoned in the entrance through the woods. And in the village will be booths of things to sell, and you and I will take things to sell in baskets. I am taking vegetables but you can take anything you like, fruits or flowers or fancy work or goodies . . . if you are clever you can make enough money to pay your way into the concerts . . . the price is fifty cents for each one. . . ."

The little booklet made a less emotional pitch than the flyer and emphasized Hervey's plan for his Maverick's future. "Building on its past reputation the colony is now coming forth with a long cherished plan, namely to establish an open air theater with a permanent orchestra, and a company of actors and dancers, that will give its own entertainments and serve as a nucleus to attract other musicians, artists and composers who will come here to try out their new productions, or repeat those adapted to the open air." [6]

In another flyer (whether of 1915 or 1916 is uncertain) Hervey urged "taxpayers and property owners" to cooperate in making the Festival a success, for "It is my plan to make this theatre a permanent affair, and this festival an annual celebration. The fame and excellence of our artists . . . will advertise our community . . . clear across the continent . . . you must stand with us . . . it will be money in your pocket in the end. . . ." Relying on a favorable but inaccurate weather forecast by astrologer Evangeline Adams, the festival was twice postponed. But when it did finally come into being it was with a huge crowd of eager participants and with unbounded enthusiasm.[7]

Festivalgoers had been urged to come in costume and this they did with such imagination, daring and in some cases painstaking adherence to respectable tradition that the initial response of all comers was one of delight. Pirates, Puritans, French eighteenth-century courtiers, medieval ladies and knights, Parisian gamins, Indians, Africans, Polynesians, hoboes and others all stared at one another with the broadest of smiles under the great banners swinging overhead near the entrance to the grounds. Singly or in groups, art-colony people circulated among the crowd putting on what Hervey called "stunts" of juggling, singing, dancing or playing a variety of musical instruments. Among the stunt people were some of the liberated young women who were playing an important part in art-colony life. Frances Rogers, illustrator and writer, feminist writer

Frances Maule and writer Alice Beard were all notable performers of Maverick stunts.

When Captain Jenkinson, Rock City's metalworker and professional super-patriot who had seen service in the Philippines, expressed disapproval of the absence of an American flag from the collection of some thirty banners Hervey appointed him Grand Marshal of the Games and authorized him to put up a flagpole and run an American flag to its top just before the games began. This the Captain did with gusto, and as the flag waved on its pole he gave a smart military salute. The Maverick had acquired a local reputation for pro-Germanism in that August of 1915, and Hervey had realized that a display of the flag might quiet the rumor. He went on to arrange for a young woman, a Miss Tiffany, to sing the "Star Spangled Banner" that evening as the festivities at the quarry theater were about to begin.

The games proved a great success. Even some in the flowing robes of Arabs or Turks joined in high-jumping and foot-racing. Climbing a slippery pole to win the five-dollar bill pinned to its top, capturing a greased pig, competing in the sack and three-legged race all found eager contestants, as the audience cheered and laughed. Hervey himself, with vine leaves wreathed about his head in his character of the Pan of the Catskills, joined in the three-legged race.

Though the games had been criticized in advance as likely to sound too vulgar a note as part of a Maverick Festival, they proved their value in attracting people who might otherwise have stayed at home. The games were free, as was entrance to the picnic grounds. Hervey relied on the sales at the booths and on those carrying baskets of this and that for sale to make a profit. Sales, however, were not brisk. Viola player Gabriel Peyre and his wife, who had painted Maverick scenes on bits of native chestnut board, sold only a single one.

Admission to the afternoon and evening performances in the quarry cost fifty cents each, and while the paid events were by no means up to the standard of attendance set by the free ones they were excellent. Those who paid their way in felt they got more than their money's worth as fifteen fine musicians of the Metropolitan Opera orchestra played under the direction of Leon Barzin.[8]

Throughout the afternoon and evening, copies of *The Wild Hawk* and the Maverick Press books were on sale. Sales on this one day are said to have surpassed those through the rest of the year.

474

After the bustle of the picnic down below, that night Thatcher's ingenious gadgets helped the moon light up the stage of the theater, where there was more music, songs by Wagnerian Madame Narodny and dances by Lada. When it was all over no one could doubt that the Maverick Festival had been a smashing success both as entertainment and as a way of paying for a well. Then and there Hervey White announced that the next year would see the beginning of a series of chamber music performances in a hall to be built for the purpose— these of course became the Maverick Sunday Concerts. Soon he let it be known that the Maverick Festival would be repeated annually and that it and the concerts would become part of a larger plan which he outlined in *The Wild Hawk*.

Now at last his Maverick farm seemed about to realize a new dream of Hervey's with a lessened color of Hull House. He would have a permanent orchestra and even a school for orchestra players. Composers and managers and producers of plays would be drawn to the Maverick quarry-theater. Dancers would use the musical skills gathered there. A dining club and a dormitory would be built to accommodate festivalgoers and concertgoers. Exhibitions of paintings and crafts would accompany each concert and Festival.

Wrote Hervey, "And if a criticism comes as to our continuing athletic games and races at our festival, can we not answer that these have always been connected with the arts. In themselves they are the development of the body beautiful and they are a constant source of inspiration to the sculptor. As to the costuming and mummery of the pageantry it will furnish many a motive to the neighboring schools of painting. . . ."

Hervey's hopes were rising high in 1915 and 1916. He wrote, "Things are but beginning in the Catskills. Rip Van Winkle is slowly rousing from his slumbers." And Hervey's hopes were justified. Woodstock artists of all sorts had joined in creating material for his Festival without any payment. Other workers had been paid the day after the Festival, and the local storekeepers who had furnished much material on credit were also paid. The entire community seemed united in wanting the events which Hervey had started on the Maverick to go on into the future. All this encouraged Hervey to renewed effort in his plans for a fresh try at bringing the artists and non-artists closer together.[9]

In *The Wild Hawk* for March 1916, Hervey analyzed the relationship of artists and Woodstock townspeople and concluded that while "artists live in a highly specialized world of ideas" and "find aesthetic companionship with each other" rather than with the townspeople, yet "there are motives that bring opposites together" and one of these might well lead to a better and closer relationship between the two groups, which, as Hervey phrased it, "are not building the sociological structure together."

Hervey's remedy was to arrange for the artists to begin "the decoration of local public buidings . . . the schoolhouses first, the village hall, if there is one; in case some are diplomatic enough they might even secure a church . . . a church would be a sociological victory worthy of a jubilee." When Hervey discussed his plan with W. H. Hook, manager of the Ulster County Farm Bureau, Mr. Hook "offered to act as envoy to our rural districts, so that the artists will have a definite mediator. . . ." [10]

In spite of Mr. Hook's help, the plan for bridging the gap between artists and others by the decorating of public buildings was a complete failure. Not a single commission resulted. It was quite otherwise with the Festivals and soon with the Maverick Concerts. Rooted as both were in the fertile soil of economic advantage to the people of Woodstock, they rested on a solid base.

And besides, 1915 was a year when certain outside conditions favored Hervey's plans. The staging of pageants had come to the United States in 1907 under the direction of Percy MacKaye. The first one, honoring sculptor Augustus St. Gaudens, was held in Cornish, N.H. Soon many others followed, often with great artistic and popular success. These pageants involved people from all levels of a community.

Chamber music too was finding an ever-larger niche in American life. Symphony orchestras were multiplying in the larger cities. Their musicians, like those in opera-house orchestras, had their summers free. Many like those who came to the Maverick were eager to exercise their skill and taste in the satisfying work of playing the chamber-music classics and some of the newer works. Though the audience for chamber music was still not large, Hervey and his musicians realized that it was growing.

Linking together music, pageantry, art, athletic contests and revelry to form an annual festival under the light of the August moon was a new variant of a very old event. Harvest festivals have been held for thousands of years in many parts of the world. And of course the Maverick Festival owed much to the artists' balls which were a feature of bohemian life in France and the United States. But the Maverick Festivals were seen by many people as pagan revels unrelated to solemn Christian harvest feasts like our Thanksgiving Day.

Hervey White realized that some people would not accept the pagan side of his Festivals, of which he was well aware. For that reason he tried to balance the joyous paganism of the Festivals with the religious feeling which he wove about the Maverick Concerts. The way the building itself was put together (by Dayton Shultis and a group of his relatives) largely of timbers and boards covered with bark had been inspired by the communal houses of the Fiji Islands. To this was added doorways which suggested by their peaked arches a Gothic religious structure. The windows formed of stock six-light barn-sash set diagonally in great clusters also had a Gothic air.[11]

As Hervey and his helpers built the Concert Hall during the spring and early summer of 1916, a promotional booklet went out from the Maverick Press, telling of the background of the concerts and encouraging a broad public to support them. There Hervey made it clear that the concerts to be held on Sunday afternoons would have nothing about them that might conflict with the strictest "Sunday observance." And then and to the end of his life he stressed his belief that the concerts came close to forming religious events.

Many years after the beginning of the Maverick Sunday Concerts Leonard D. Abbot, the conservative-radical editor and reformer, wrote that on attending one of the concerts he felt as though he ". . . were witnessing a religious rite. For the moment Hervey White suggested an officiating priest. I know, of course that he is a pagan and not at all a priest but I also know that the motive which has kept these impressive functions going for seventeen consecutive summers must have had in it something that for want of a better name, we call religion. Perhaps . . . there is a point at which the best kind of art and the best kind of religion fuse." [12]

The Festival of 1916 featured Russian dancer Tharma Swiskaya, an expensive attraction who required that she and her retinue be well paid and cared for. She, her companion Baroness Seidlitz, a young man named Portapovich who was her dancing companion, and a male admirer who was observed taking off the dancer's shoes from time to time and massaging her feet were all put up at Byrdcliffe's Villetta. Four days of rain caused the Festival to be postponed four times, with an unhappy effect on attendance and a quadrupling of Swiskaya's expenses. When the Festival at last opened. Madame Swiskaya's butterfly dance, in which she emerged from a gorgeously-colored caterpillar which had crawled on the stage and then spread her wings and danced, earned frantic applause from the small audience.

The Festival that year lost a good deal of money, yet not enough to discourage plans for a third. For the 1917 Festival Lada returned in a loosely put together version of *Rip Van Winkle* with local overtones. Rip Van Winkle, played by young painter Jack Bentley, appeared as the play began fast asleep, with a wood nymph in the person of Lada trying in vain to rouse him. At Lada's summons representatives of the various schools of painting then active in Woodstock tried in turn to rouse the old man.

The Byrdcliffe painters bored him. The Blue Dome group represented by nude models (with painters in smocks dancing around them) gave Rip pleasant dreams from which he refused to awaken. John Carlson and his followers had no effect at all. Nor did the teachers at the Reiss School of Advertising Art. When the "Cezanne moderns," with Dasburg and Henry MacFee leading them, burst upon the stage Rip stared in horror and fled into the woods.

This performance was notable in that for the first time Hervey White relied on local art-colony people as performers, with only Lada representing professionalism. The art-colony people acted and danced and sang with zest. And in succeeding Festivals they played major parts on the stage. Painter George Bellows, William L. McFee, Andrew Dasburg, Robert Winthrop Chanler and others not only designed stage sets but also acted. Sculptor Raoul Hague danced. Often a spectator in the theater would be startled by a costumed artist sitting near him jumping up and exclaiming, "There's my cue," and a moment later acting on stage.[13]

In this way the community participation which Hervey wanted so much moved forward. Non-artists like old Jim Twaddell and Luther Russell, who drove a taxi, were among local peole who took part. Children of local families were sometimes forbidden by their parents to attend the festivals. Some "spent the night with friends" at whose houses they put on their costumes.

The Festival of 1918 continued the precedent set the year before. Robert Edeson, much respected since he had created the role of the Little Minister in J. M. Barrie's famous play, was the only professional. Because the country was at war with Germany Hervey offered a farce which ridiculed the Kaiser. The Kaiser was sent a gift of lobster by his old friend Poulteney Bigelow. The lobster was spoiled and made the

Kaiser ill. Poultney Bigelow played himself, Byrdcliffe's mystical painter William E. Schumaker played the lobster, and Edeson was the Kaiser. Various parts of Woodstock represented the Allies. Byrdcliffe was Britain, Zena was France, Shady was Poland, Bearsville was Serbia, while the hamlet of Woodstock took the part of Russia.

In an attempt to broaden the appeal of the Festivals during one of the early years two Graeco-Roman wrestlers worked at their trade on the stage. Their names were Lurich and Alberg. Their great European fame could not keep their performance from boring the Maverick audience. Their kind of wrestling, with its slowness and its many restrictions, did not appeal to the American taste for speed and fast action. However, the two powerful men, as they wandered about Woodstock holding hands or sitting under a tree listening to Hervey White reading aloud from his poems, roused an amused interest.[14]

By 1920 the Maverick Festivals were attracting more and more visitors from other art colonies, and some of these remained to join Woodstock. Provincetown, Massachusetts came to have close relations with Woodstock, and especially with the Maverick. In 1920 the much-talked-about Provincetown Players planned a play for that year's Festival. Hervey liked the play very much. Like his *Fire and Water*, it was an anti-war play which had been given its first performance by the Washington Square Players.

Unlike Hervey's play Edna St. Vincent Millay's *Aria da capo*, written in the fall of 1919, had already made its author famous. Miss Millay with her sister Norma, Norma's fiance Charles Ellis, and James Light, who had designed the sets for *Aria da capo* in New York, all took up residence in a Maverick cottage. They delighted art-colony people with their singing of the girls' poems set to music, with the rebellious behavior of Light's miniature automobile, and with Edna's brief affair with an Italian tenor who sang at the Festival.

Also performing that year were Maverickers disguised as giant insects. They were headed by "King Bug." When the other Provincetown actors failed to show up the Millays and the two men staged and acted *Aria da capo* themselves.[15]

One big event of the afternoon of the 1920 Festival was the arrival of the Toonerville Trolley, made by Walter Steinhilber, Walt and Al Peters and others. The trolley was built on the base of a hay rigging supplied by the nearby Barnes farm, which also provided the team of horses. In 1921 the same group built the tree houses of an imaginative African village, the houses connected with rope walks. A

479

"totem pole," a cannibal's stew pot and dancing natives entertained during the afternoon.

On another afternoon in the early Twenties a portable stage was wheeled among the celebrators. Anyone who wanted to was urged to get aboard and do an act on the moving stage. Many responded. Many of the skits that resulted were "created on the spot." Hervey White acted as barker for the show.[16]

It was during the performances of the Millay plays that Hervey could not avoid recognizing the inadequacies of his quarry theater. A thousand celebrants had strained the theater's capacity. He put together an open theater closer to the entrance of the Festival grounds. Its stage could hold five hundred actors without crowding. An audience of five thousand might be accommodated. With its hundred-foot proscenium the theater was planned for the kind of large-scale pageantry which was coming more and more to dominate the Festivals.

The new theater had its tryout during the Maverick Festival of 1921, when the most ambitious pageant yet attempted on the Maverick was presented. It used Hervey's adaptation of Flaubert's romantic and richly colored *Temptation of St. Anthony* with music played by Pierre Henrotte and a large group of Metropolitan Opera orchestra players. The pageant's story of how the Devil tempted St. Anthony as he lived in monastic seclusion in a desert by parading before him the most alluring worldly pleasures offered opportunity for playing on the aesthetic and sensuous emotions of an audience. Some five hundred people worked at making the pageant ready. Two hundred appeared on the stage (many without having rehearsed). Painter Alexander Brook was brought in at the last moment to replace writer William Murrell, who was stricken with stage fright. Brook went through his part while drunk.

On one side of the stage stood the Saint's simple cabin. Seated on the roof was the Devil, played by William Schumaker. As Schumaker capered in delight and swished his tail, the pleasures of the earth made their appeals. A curtain of freshly cut green boughs was swept away to reveal Nebuchadnezzar's feast, with the king and his courtiers eating and drinking while the captive kings languished in chains at the king's feet.

Stage designers Andrew Dasburg, Walter Steinhilber and Harry Gottlieb had made a great table with trick-perspective effects which made the table seem to recede far into the background of trees. It was built to narrow rapidly from front to back, and the people seated at it were chosen for size, with the biggest in front and the tiniest in the back. The Queen of Sheba and her girls danced voluptuously before the Saint. The queen offered to kiss him. Great jewels and other treasures were brought on to dazzle the Saint's eyes. From a casket borne on by slaves emerged a dancing girl who moved faster and faster at the urging of the whip of her showman.

Finally the splendor and power of the church had its turn. A great procession of priests telling beads, acolytes and monks swinging censers, nuns and richly dressed high ecclesiastics moved across the stage led by a stately archbishop on whose costumes the utmost elaboration had been lavished. The archbishop was banker-violist George Plochmann. George Bellows, as narrator, could be heard from the most distant seat. The procession, Hervey liked to recall, was the most impressive he had ever seen, far surpassing, he thought, the Christmas procession at St. Peter's in Rome which he had seen during the tour of Europe of his youth.

The Saint watched, greatly tempted by the lure of ecclesiastical grandeur and glory opened to him. But he resisted and withdrew to his cabin. At this moment as the stage darkened and the music changed the audience turned to look at the back of the theater. There a singer dressed as an angel in white sang "Glory to God in the Highest" in token of Anthony's victory over earthly temptation. And so, as Hervey put it, "our greatest pageant ever given" came to its end.[17]

The form which the Maverick Festivals took after the first few years had become predictable, helping give them acceptance almost as if they were ancient folk festivals which had been repeated with never-ending delight for centuries. There was the gathering of the people in costume beginning at three in the afternoon. There were the colorful booths and the banners, the dancing on the grass, and the wandering performers, sometimes with the portable stages which invited spectators to join in impromptu acts. In mid-afternnon there were musical or light dramatic events. All afternoon acrobats, clowns and hawkers of crafts mingled with the crowd.

As dusk approached hundreds of campfires were lit. Beside them family groups and groups of friends (or sometimes strangers who had just met) had picnic suppers. After dark the big spectacle of the Festival came on in the open-air theater. Finally the dance in the Concert Hall brought the celebration to a close at dawn.

In a day or two Hervey would sit in front of his cabin at a table laden with the cash taken in at the Festival and pay all debts incurred in staging the big annual event. Later he would be host at a jolly "pig roast" to which all who had helped put the Festival together would be invited.[18]

In 1922 the great success of H. G. Wells' *Outline of History* suggested to Hervey dramatizing the progress of the human race from its simple beginnings to its twentieth-century complexity and contradictions. In 1923 Russel Wright, a young designer soon to become immensely successful, staged a "Cubist Circus" using huge angular and distorted animals of cloth and paper on armatures of wood and chicken wire, relying for motive power on the muscles and minds of art-colony people hidden in their interiors.

The next Festival, that of 1924, was long remembered both for its extraordinary visual impact and for the months of effort which went into its production. Its dramatic feature involved a story of the capture by pirates of a ship on which a princess was travelling to be married to a king. The ship was eighty feet long and sixty feet high. It had every detail which could add to the romantic look of an old sailing vessel. Walter Steinhilber, painter, illustrator, designer, wrestler and later candidate for state office on the Socialist Labor Party ticket, staged the play. He played the part of the pirate chief. The play ended with the princess giving up the king for the pirate chief. The ship, the *Ark Royal*, was then, to the amazement of the audience, burned.

Less than two months after the burning of the *Ark Royal* another conflagration took place in Woodstock. This time the victim was real enough. It was the old Overlook Mountain House. The chain of events which seems to have led to the burning of the hotel began in the spring of 1921 as art-colony people were beginning to put together the *Temptation of St. Anthony* for their festival.

41

OVERLOOK MOUNTAIN, BLOOMER GIRLS AND COMMUNISTS

Between 1890 and 1921 a whole generation of Woodstock people looked up at Overlook Mountain with conflicting feelings. They were proud of the mountain, but at the same time they were disappointed by the failure of its hotel to live up to expectations.

Old people liked to hand on some traditions of the mountain. They talked about President Grant's visit and about the April Fool's Day fire of 1875. James Booth's 1833 vision of a Woodstock Blue Mountain House had been forgotten. Memories recalled how the struggles to put a summer hotel on the mountain had led to the ruin of a succession of ardent promoters. There were tales of rattlesnakes startling guests strolling near the hotel or even venturing into the billiard room in the basement.

Some oldtimers said they believed that a curse put on the mountain had caused it to bring ill fortune to so many. Most people, however, rejected this gloomy kind of talk. They went on hoping that some day the right man would come along and make a hotel on Overlook an immense success for himself and for the Town of Woodstock. The hope persisted as promoter after promoter vanished in a cloud of legal actions and unpaid bills.

Even when the storm-battered building lapsed into a doze, local people likened it to a sleeping beauty waiting to be brought back to life, gaiety and profit once again. Hunters who passed the hotel as it creaked and groaned in the late autumn winds swore that it was haunted.[1]

When a clergyman became the owner of the Mountain House in 1906 the old visions revived. Henry Allen Tupper was no ordinary clergyman. He was D.D., Litt. D., a writer, lecturer and active participant in countless charitable and religious organizations. In some minds he was viewed with skepticism.

Tupper chose Willam E. Reynolds as manager of the hotel. Reynolds was the operator of a summer boardinghouse on Mead's Mountain Road. To get his venture off to a rousing start Reynolds had printed by May 1906 a little booklet phrased in a low-keyed manner quite different from the inflated prose and extravagant claims usual in such productions. He even added only fifty feet to the altitude of Overlook—this at a time when other hotel proprietors in the Catskills thought nothing of adding a thousand.

The booklet began:

> Doubtless many persons will learn, with pleasure, that the picturesque Overlook Mountain House, located on the top of Overlook Mountain (3200 feet above the sea), the highest point occupied by a building in the Catskills mountain, will be opened on June 15, 1906. The present owner regrets, on account of his recent purchase of the property, that it will be impossible, this season, to make the elaborate improvements he desires; but the main building and out-houses will be repaired and painted, the waterworks and plumbing will be placed in good condition, the furniture and all of the household goods will be renewed, the extensive grounds, covering five hundred acres, will be made attractive, and the manager and his wife assure the public that good, wholesome fare will be served in abundance to satisfy the keen appetite created by the invigorating mountain air . . . for this season the popular prices are $8.00 and $10.00 per week.

The vacationing public, accustomed to sledgehammer advertising, did not respond to Reynolds' mild efforts. In mid-August Tupper made a try at testing the power of his own prose to draw people to Overlook. On August 16 the Kingston *Daily Freeman* published a fervent prose poem by Dr. Tupper under the heading, "Sunrise from the Overlook." The article carried to fresh heights a tradition of ecstatic admiration of sunrises from Catskill summits dating back to even before the birth of the old Catskill Mountain House in 1823. Thomas Cole had written on the subject in the 1820s. Charles Lanman had described a sunrise from Overlook (see Chapter 24) in gold and purple terms.

Tupper steered perilously close to Lanman's kind of prose. As the sun first began to light up the sky to the east, he wrote, "The moon turned pale, the stars one by one faded from view, and the flushed face of the eastern sky beamed with joy as it greeted the king of the new day. His brilliant appearance was heralded by splendidly costumed forerunners who paved the pathway with layers of burnished gold and announced his coming by the flight of arrows of light through the reddening sky. These prophecies of the newborn day were the signals of universal joy. The trees waved their glad salute; the birds sang their morning symphony. . . ."

The *Freeman* commented cautiously that Dr. Tupper's tribute to the sunrise from his hotel was "well worth reading." But no one's prose, however rich, had the power to change the luck of the Overlook Mountain House. When the usual kind of guests failed to come Dr. Tupper filled the place with friends and relatives from his native Virginia. His daughter Katherine, later to marry General George C. Marshall, was there. His son Tristram, who later became a successful Hollywood scriptwriter and during World War II was a brigadier general handling public relations, also helped fill the hotel. So many of Dr. Tupper's friends and relatives gathered at the Overlook House that one guest of that time recalled that the place had more the air of a lively house party than of a summer hotel.

Acting as host of a summer-long house party could not save the day for Dr. Tupper. As the season of 1907 ended he realized that his venture into hotel-keeping had been a failure. He became entangled in legal snarls and lost control of the mountaintop.

During Tupper's period as the chief Overlook dreamer a new means of transportation was coming into use. The automobile was giving reason for hope that even the Overlook Mountain House might become more readily accessible without too great a cost. The first car climbed the steep road to the hotel a little before Dr. Tupper took over. Others soon were making the trip, with much clanking of metal, boiling of radiators and bursting of hard-used tires.[2]

This time of testing seemed to demonstrate that the automobile was not yet ready to become the savior of Overlook. Until 1917 the hotel inched along, sometimes open on a small scale and often closed. In April 1917 a new owner took charge and gave the hotel an unexpected change in character.

By 1917 great changes were taking place in many parts of the Catskills. Following the establishment of the Catskill Mountain House in 1823 the summer hotel and boardinghouse boom which followed had made the Catskills famous as a resort region. Early hotels had been favored by Protestants who expected Sunday to be observed as a day of sermons, prayer, hymns and quiet. They carried with them the ways of life which prevailed among Protestants in American towns and cities, as well as on farms and in villages.[3]

By the end of the nineteenth century some of the older hotels were changing hands and catering to newly-arrived immigrants from Germany and central Europe. Many of these were Jewish. In Tannersville, Hunter and Haines Falls, Jewish boardinghouses and hotels had become dominant, and in Sullivan County a similar development was taking place. Woodstock had determined to remained Protestant, although rumors of the sale of one of the boardinghouses or hotels to Jews ran through the town from time to time. With the sale of the hotel on Overlook to Morris Newgold a rumor of this sort seemed to some Woodstock people to have solidified into fact.

Newgold was an experienced New York hotel man who made something of a specialty of buying (without any payment in cash) hotels which no one had been able to run at a profit. Newgold saw automobiles, buses, a funicular railway running up Overlook from a base station in Lewis Hollow, and even the use of airplanes as possibilities which might play parts in making the hotel on the mountain profitable. In the early summer of 1917 he reopened the hotel with a ceremonial raising of the American flag. The United States had just entered the First World War and Newgold's German name made this a sound move.[4]

Guests that summer were none too plentiful. They were drawn largely from the patrons of Newgold's big Times Square Hotel in New York. Old Overlook observers in Woodstock saw the hotel's new owner as about to join all the previous owners in defeat. But Newgold surprised these people as the summer of 1918 came in sight. He leased the hotel to a membership organization which operated the place— renamed Unity House—for two seasons. The organization was called the Unity Club.

It is likely that the hotel for the first time since the late 1870s made a profit for its owner that year. What is more certain is that the presence of the guests paved the way for an event of May 1921 which eventually made Overlook Mountain the subject of sensational headlines in newspapers and gave it a unique place in the history of radicalism in America.

The Unity Club was a recreational offshoot of the International

Ladies Garment Workers Union. Each summer several hundred of the club's members, all young women, "swarmed," as one observer put it, on Woodstock's Tinker Street dressed in uniform white blouses and dark bloomers. Woodstock people took to calling them "the bloomer girls." Though some local people welcomed the bloomer girls, because most of them were Jewish others saw them as an advance guard of an invasion by Jewish summer boarders similar to those who were thronging to Tannersville, Hunter and Pine Hill.[5]

After its second season on Overlook the Unity Club moved on to Pine Hill and then to other places. It still survives and flourishes. After the bloomer girls left, however, the Overlook Mountain House never managed to get into operation again. But its Unity Club period had drawn the attention of people to a conflict within the club's parent organization, with a surprising result.

As the bloomer girls vacationed on Overlook their union was torn by internal conflicts because of a division of opinion which had resulted from the Russian Revolution of 1917. Many union members working in the needle trades in New York City were of Russian and East European Jewish origins. They had carried with them to America when they fled from oppression and cruel anti-Semitism in their native towns and villages a strong dedication to socialism. And when the Russian Revolution triumphed in the spring of 1917 union members rejoiced at what they accepted as the end of a tyrannical government.

Many returned to Russia in full confidence that the suffering of their people caused by the actions of the Czar's government was over for all time. Those who remained, like other socialists throughout the United States, lined up in opposing camps and divided into splinter groups over the question of support for the new Russian government. The divisions became acute after the moderate Kerensky government of the spring of 1917 gave way to the radical Bolshevik one of the following November.

The government of the United States grew increasingly opposed to that of Russia. The American people, who had at first accepted the new regime in Russia, turned against it. Government agencies made life hard for supporters of the Russian government, and soon official action was taken to suppress the people now identified as Communists.

In 1920 Attorney General A. Mitchell Palmer brought deportation proceedings against hundreds of men and women of foreign birth and Communist sympathies. In an atmosphere of crisis Palmer and his new assistant, J. Edgar Hoover, launched a series of raids on people suspected of Communist beliefs. The Communists, by then virtually outlawed, decided to follow Russian precedents of Czarist times and go underground. Meetings were held in secret, assumed names were used, and strict discipline imposed.[6]

As they went underground the internal conflicts of the Communists grew sharper and further splintering occurred. Meanwhile, the Russian government was planning to hold a World Congress of the newly formed Third International in Moscow in the summer of 1921. It was felt to be of the first importance for a strong American delegation to be present. Yet how could that delegation be chosen with American Communists divided into so many groups each claiming to possess the only true dogma?

Party Secretary Zinoviev sent out a demand that the Americans form a single united party and then choose their delegates. If the Americans remained slashing at each others' throats, Moscow would shove them all aside and set up its own version of a Communist Party for the United States. The two American parties, then known as the Communist Party and the United Communist Party, as well as various splinters would be expelled from the Comintern. Speedy results followed Zinoviev's move. The two major Communist parties formed a Unity Committee whch quickly decided to hold a secret convention at the Overlook Mountain House at which the two parties would unite, form a new Communist Party for the United States, and agree on a slate of delegates for the World Congress.

"On May 15,1921 the Unity Convention was called to order in the open air, the delegates seated in a semi-circle, the U.C.P. delegates on the right and the C. P. delegates on the left, in a natural amphi-theatre with a boulder for the chairman's desk. The session was opened with short introductory remarks by the representative of the Pan-American Agency, introducing the impartial chairman who had been decided upon in advance by the Unity Committee." So *The Communist* of July 1921 reported. Present were thirty delegates apiece from each of the two major warring factions plus six additional "fraternal delegates" representing Moscow. The Pan-American Agency man was one of these.

In keeping with the underground nature of the proceedings delegates addressed each other by assumed names. According to later accounts elaborate precautions were taken to ensure secrecy. Guards were posted at railroad points between New York and West Hurley, where carriages for Woodstock waited. The delegates were not told of their destination in advance. Once on the mountaintop they were searched at intervals and forbidden to make notes on what went on. Down in Woodstock a guard kept an eye on local police, and other guards were placed on mountaintops from which the Overlook Mountain House might be watched.[7]

All this was similar to the way underground left-wing meetings were set up in Russia in Czarist days. While the reports are likely to be exaggerated, they ring true in essentials.

Knotty problems faced the delegates. For one thing many did not speak English. For another they were often far apart in their beliefs as to methods of establishing a Communist state in America. The proceedings were often so deadlocked that they were halted while caucuses of opposing groups, some lasting all night, were held to hammer out bases for compromise. At the end of almost two weeks of strenuous effort the delegates acomplished the business for which they had been brought together. The had organized the Communist Party of America and put together its lengthy constitution. And they had chosen delegates to send to the midsummer congress in Moscow.[8]

The people of Woodstock went about their normal business in complete ignorance of all this. The comings and goings of the Unity Club people had accustomed them to the presence on their mountain of people with ways different from theirs. They were used to hearing these people speaking foreign languages. A few Woodstock people had done business with the Unity Club people on Overlook, supplying them with milk and eggs, for example, but they did their work, received their money, and did not inquire into the doings of their customers.

No one in Woodstock suspected until almost twenty-eight months after the mountaintop convention closed on May 29 that some of the most powerful people in the Communist organization had been their visitors at the hotel where President Grant and so many other notables had once stayed. Among well-known Communists present were Louis Fraina, Charles E. Scott, Jay Lovestone and Sen Katayama, all working under assumed names.[9]

If Woodstock people had known what was happening on the mountaintop, with its predominantly Jewish Communists, they would have been uneasy. Until 1917 few Jews had lived in Woodstock. Important people in the town, including Ralph Whitehead, were determined to exclude Jews especially from the ownership and operation of hotels like those which were rapidly supplanting the older predominantly Protestant ones in other parts of the Catskills. Anti-Semitism, long present in Woodstock, now grew and expanded like a weed in a June garden. The arrival of the Unity Club people seemed to mean to some that the Overlook Mountain House at last was about to become a Jewish resort hotel undistinguishable from those which filled nearby Tannersville.

In 1920 Morris Newgold's stepson Gabriel took over management of the Irvington Hotel in the heart of the hamlet of Woodstock. Anti-Semitic feeling rose high. Newgold ran the hotel quietly, treated his local employees well, and allowed Roman Catholics the use of the hotel for Sunday services. Gabriel Newgold, who had a talent for music, hoped to make his hotel a center for musical performances. Yet Woodstock remained suspicious.[10]

While the Newgolds were trying to establish their hotels in the hamlet and on the mountain they became central figures in an incident which brought much hidden anti-Semitism into the open. By the early 1920s part of the strong patriotic feelings engendered by the World War had been diverted to nativism, anti-Communism, and hostility to minorities.

The Ku Klux Klan had been revived and had added anti-Semitism to its earlier anti-Catholicism. The Klan was being carried to many parts of the nation by aggressive organizers. Many Woodstock people of right-wing convictions, many business people and descendants of early local families who lived in outlying Wittenberg and Shady, sympathized with the Klan. These people continued to be determined to keep Jewish business people and summer boarders out of the town.

An assault on Gabriel Newgold which took place a little after one on the morning of September 4, 1922 aroused Klan sympathizers, who saw the incident as useful in discouraging Jewish penetration of Woodstock. Ever on the alert for sensational material to be discovered in the art colony, Kingston reporters gleefully burst out with front-page stories long on excitement and often short on accuracy.

In its leading story on September 5, the Kingston *Daily Freeman* changed Newgold's last name to Hugo and built up the events which followed the entrance into the sleeping hotel of three young men in search of a telephone—there were then no telephone booths available round the clock in Woodstock.

490

There were plenty of witnesses to what happened, but as is so often the case their versions of events varied. What is clear is that the three men—Ralph Whitehead, Jr. was one—had been drinking Prohibition gin and were in a boisterous mood. They roused the sleeping inmates of the hotel. Mr. and Mrs. Newgold, the cook, the baker and the paying guests all trooped into the lobby. When Newgold ordered the three intruders to leave, they tackled him and inflicted injuries to his head and ribs. The three men were arrested and taken before Justice of the Peace Elwyn, who ordered two of them—both lawyers named Kelley—held for action by the grand jury. The two were released on bail. A few days later young Whitehead was also arrested.

Eventually an out-of-court settlement was reached, but not before Woodstock people had been thoroughly aroused by inflammatory testimony as reported on the *Freeman's* front page. There Mrs. Whitehead was said to have sprung to the defense of her son by testifying, "I hope it is not irrelevant for me to say that the men in my family never lose their heads when they drink and he [young Ralph] wouldn't touch a Jew with a ten foot pole."

The attack on Newgold as reported by the *Freeman* and distorted by gossip had shocked or titillated Woodstock people in accordance with their prejudices and convictions. A year later the same people were startled by a revelation with sinister implications. This time it was not the hotel in the hamlet but the one on Overlook Mountain that was reported as the scene of a surprising happening. It made the front page of the *Freeman*:

COMMUNIST PARTY OF AMERICA FOUNDED IN WOODS ON SUMMIT OF OVERLOOK MOUNTAIN.

And on October 31 the *Freeman* provided its readers with another shock when it announced in front-page headlines:

OVERLOOK MOUNTAIN HOUSE BURNED TO GROUND: HALF COUNTY SAW IT.

What lay behind these headlines was as dramatic a pair of events as has ever startled Woodstock. The first—and some say the second too—was a byproduct of the attempt of the dominant faction within the Mine Workers of America to prevent Communist control of their union. The *Freeman* story, which also appeared in other newspapers throughout the nation, was written by public relations men of the Mine Workers as one of a series of anti-Communist releases.[11]

The Mine Workers' release precisely located the Communist convention of May 1921 on top of Overlook. Otherwise it followed material already published and of varying degrees of accuracy. The *Freeman* story of the fire referred to the 1921 convention and the Overlook spy scare of 1917. It also gave a long history of the Mountain House.

Then, on November 2 the newspaper returned to Overlook Mountain with this headline, again on the front page:

$1000 REWARD FOR CONVICTION
OF OVERLOOK MOUNTAIN FIREBUG

Offer Made by Proprietor Nugold, Who Says Someone Burned Property with $75,000 Loss—Will Promote Bungalow Colony on Top of Overlook

The *Freeman* reporter quoted Newgold as saying that the story of the Communist convention recently published "was false in every particular and thinks it is possible that some misguided patriot having read the story that such a gathering had been held might have had something to do with setting the building afire." Newgold's reward was never claimed.

The revelations of the Mine Workers Union and the fire which came so close upon them left a legacy to Woodstock. Though ever since 1902 the town had been known for its unconventional thinkers, these people had not aroused much official hostility. Once it became known that the American Communist Party had been founded on the very summit of Woodstock's Overlook, things changed. Every period of crusades against opponents of the standard American ways of thinking and behaving brought attention in Washington to bear on Woodstock. The widespread turning leftward of young Americans of the depressed Thirties, the spy scares of the Second World War, the opposition to the rise of movements aimed at securing justice for minorities, the McCarthy hunt for Communists in positions of authority—all these added to federal interest in Woodstock.[12]

J. Edgar Hoover, who had gone on from sharing in the direction of the Palmer raids of 1920 to become head of the Federal Bureau of Investigation, never forgot the May 1921 meeting on Overlook Mountain. In his 1958 book *Masters of Deceit* he summed up his view of what had happened on the mountain and its far-reaching results in these words:

492

"Finally in May 1921, after another year of bickering, the United Communist Party and the remainder of the Communist Party formed the Communist Party of America, Section of the Communist International at a secret two-week convention at Woodstock, N.Y. The group's program among other things provided that the Communist Party would work for violent revolution, preparing the worker for armed insurrection as the only means of overthrowing the capitalist state. The convention officially accepted the twenty-one points for admission to the Comintern. The Communist Party was now a complete prisoner of Moscow." [13]

One puzzling aspect of the Overlook convention was that neither Hoover nor anyone else has ever given the public an explanation of just why the convention managed to be held in such complete secrecy. All other Communist gatherings of the period were infiltrated by federal agents. As far as is known today, the one on Overlook formed a notable exception.

The convention delegates of May 1921 were probably the last paying guests of the Overlook Mountain House. Though Morris Newgold continued trying to put his hotel on a profitable basis, he never succeeded. Kingston architect Gerard Betz made plans for a modernization of the building, and Newgold set men to work at making small improvements to the place. The fire of 1924 put an end to all that.

A year after the fire Woodstock people were roused by an event which took place on the night of August 21, 1924 in the field near the stone house built by Jonathan Hasbrouck and then owned by Sherman Elwyn. The burning of a fiery cross by a local unit of the Ku Klux Klan was "due no doubt," as the Woodstock weekly *Hue and Cry* put it, "to the influx of undesirable aliens to Woodstock."

A few weeks earlier a Klan organizer had come to town and signed up a group including some of the most prominent businessmen in Woodstock as paying members. Its activities were directed, depending on local hostilities, against any of a variety of ethnic, religious and political groups. In Woodstock left-wing thinkers and people of Jewish and Central European backgrounds were prime Klan targets.

The Klan's appearance did not win substantial approval in Woodstock and it soon vanished from public sight. An anonymous printed sheet widely circulated following the cross burning expressed much local thinking when it stated that on August 21 ". . . there occurred a meeting in our town of Woodstock professing to uphold

493

the ideals of Americanism which at the same time spread insidious propoganda contrary to the ideals of our forefathers. We, the people of Woodstock, who live in peace and harmony in a well governed community, resent all such outside interference." [14]

Nineteen twenty-four marked the peak of the religious and racial prejudice which had long existed in Woodstock and had been growing with vigor since the end of the First World War. It did not mark its end. At various times it resurfaced, most notably during the late 1940s and early 1950s in response to the investigations of the House Un-American Affairs Committee and the charges made by Senator Joseph McCarthy.

The economic value to Woodstock business people and land speculators of the arrival in town of increasing numbers of people of Central European origin and Jewish religion or radical political beliefs helped muffle hostile feelings.

42

THE BOOM
OF THE TWENTIES

In August 1923 President Harding died, and Calvin Coolidge moved into the White House. For the next six years a boom spread throughout the country. The period, with its feverish speculation in the stock market, greatly enhanced expectations of future prosperity and eventual collapse, was similar to previous booms. In Woodstock an aggressive spirit of competition reigned over the hamlet even while remnants of the cooperative spirit for which the Whiteheads and Hervey White had hoped remained alive at Byrdcliffe and on the Maverick.

The town reacted to the boom spirit in many ways. According to the federal census Woodstock's population increased during the decade of the Twenties by about eleven per cent, or two hundred persons. The summer population, which was no business of the census-taker and so went unrecorded, was estimated by local boosters to have grown by many times that amount. On a genial summer weekend it was said to have reached eight or ten thousand.[1]

The new people pouring into Woodstock on the wings of the boom and the growing reputation of the art colony were a mixed lot. Many remained only a few hours or a few days. Others settled down and dug in. Some arrived with an eye on the profits to be made in a town where land values were rising, studios and dwellings were multiplying, and new business ventures were being started, sold and resold at progressively higher prices.

Studios, the favored dwellings of artists and non-artists alike, were hastily run up in all sizes and flavors. Novelist and playwright J. P. McEvoy remarked that the demand for studios was so great that within an hour after a man's hat blew off and landed in a field a local entrepreneur would have given it a skylight and a sign reading "Studio for Rent." [2]

Amid protests from old art-colony people newly established shopkeepers created a Chamber of Commerce, which began to do business in 1928. The Chamber published a booklet featuring an essay on Woodstock by Bruce Herrick. It backed a number of improvements made necessary by the thick clustering of shops and people in the hamlet of Woodstock.

Most of the people hastening to Woodstock did not have profit on their minds. Those people arrived to share in the more free and more exciting life they had heard existed in an undiluted form in Woodstock. They were arriving in varied ways: by stage from the railroad station at West Hurley, by steamboats touching shore at Kingston Point and Saugerties, by foot or in their own cars, and a few astride bicycles or motorcycles.

If some were disappointed that life in Woodstock proved less lurid than reported, most were pleased. A few serious art people found the excitement of the place unfavorable to steady work and left. All newcomers received an effusive welcome from real-estate dealers and shopkeepers. And a good many old art colonists welcomed the newcomers because they were flattered that the town with which they were identified had become so attractive to a new generation.

Only at Byrdcliffe was there undiluted displeasure at the boom's effects. There Jane and Ralph Whitehead deplored the arrival in what had been their own personal utopian base of so many people whom they regarded as frivolous, immoral, inept or decadent in the arts and crafts, or worse, as flamboyant Greenwich Villagers. Whitehead had once written that the greatest of the arts was the art of living. But not, in his opinion, as some of the new people practiced that art. [3]

No one gave a more triumphant expression in words to the boomtown spirit of Woodstock of the 1920s than the editor of the *Hue and Cry*. As the boom was reaching its peak in June 1929 before sliding down to doom the editor wrote of "the phenomenal growth of Woodstock" which had brought to the place "a surplussage of fine cars, attractive homes and a constantly increasing leisure. . . ." All these benefits, the editor believed, flowed from "the great unearned increment that is America's, nowhere can that pyramiding increment of wealth be better observed than in our village . . . it's wonderful. . . ."

As the boom had begun to gain speed in 1923 the Woodstock correspondent of the Kingston *Daily Freeman* had made a prophetic comment when she wrote of overflowing boardinghouses and eating places. She had predicted that "Woodstock is the coming town." And indeed it seemed to be, for the town had moved a long way from its earlier simplicity to the sophistication of the 1923-1929 period.

Exultation over the boom was widespread yet not universal. Woodstock has long been known as a town in which unanimity on any subject is rare indeed, and every matter of public importance has found the town's people divided into opposing camps. Anti-boomers expressed the fear that Woodstock was being converted from an art colony to "a fashionable summer resort" or to an overcrowded place like Tannersville.

From time to time these possibilities were being seriously considered by New York newspapers and other periodicals. Woodstock papers carried vigorous expressions of opinion on the subject. Some art-colony people remained calm. Author-educator Hughes Mearns, who wrote, "Summer Resorters, welcome to Woodstock," pointed out that the boom people were bringing profits to local shopkeepers and others. If the colony's "working people" in the arts wanted to avoid the noise and hurly-burly of the "mob," it was a simple matter for them to retreat into the rural parts of Woodstock. Mearns himself had found refuge in Bearsville, and if necessary he proposed to "crawl further back in the woods." [4]

Throughout the boom years ridicule was heaped by art-colony sympathizers on those who were scrambling to profit by the boom at whatever cost to the survival of their colony. On September 8, 1923, for example, *The Hue and Cry* set townspeople chuckling with a story headed "WOODSTOCK SUBWAY SOON." The story told of plans being made by Stanley Longyear to build a subway running beneath Tinker Street and Mill Hill Road, with stations at frequent intervals. The paper piled absurdity upon absurdity as it gave details of the subway's depth and width and of the engineering difficulties which would be met and conquered.

Until the boom ended, this kind of humorous ridicule in print and in conversation served to vent resentment at the way the town was changing. At the same time resentment often took a more serious form, as it did in an anonymous broadside distributed in the mid-Twenties. The broadside was headed, "DON'T HOCK WOODSTOCK. Exploitation is not development. . . . Don't let short-sighted greed and personal rivalry cloud your vision into the future and leave WOODSTOCK unprotected to be reduced to the condition of other towns [here Hunter, Tannersville and similar Jewish resort towns were meant] in the Catskills. . . . Keep the oldtime native in Woodstock, the old-fashioned home, the old trees, the clean brooks, and the old friendships. Keep the artist and the student in Woodstock. They may be penniless in themselves but wherever they establish a colony people of wealth follow them." [5]

In the hamlet of Woodstock the changes being viewed with apprehension by the broadside's author were plain enough. There were new buildings, set more closely together; a multiplication of shops; sewage flowing into the brooks which formed so large a part of the charm of the hamlet. By summer nearly every house in the hamlet was filled with boarders. And while the Woodstock Valley Hotel, now called Woodstock Lodge, was outwardly much the same old-fashioned country inn as it had been for generations many people felt uneasy about its future. Ever since the first inn had appeared on the site in the 1790s and perhaps earlier the place had been one of central value to Woodstock people. There social events were held, travelling shows were presented, town meetings took place. The inn seemed to many to symbolize the older pre-boom Woodstock.

In the spring of 1926 a group of Woodstock people, headed by Ralph Whitehead, Alice Wardwell, William S. Elwyn and Eleanor Rixon Blomshield and including Woodstock's best-known painters, bought the hotel from Gabriel Newgold and announced that it would now be run "on conservative lines." The name of the place was changed from Woodstock Lodge to Woodstock Valley Inn. Renovations were made. William H. Wilber, an experienced hotel man, was installed as manager. The hotel was advertised not as a summer resort but as a center for the Woodstock art colony.

That same spring, on the Saugerties road across the Woodstock line, the Shagbark colony was organized as a "restricted-to-Christians" membership resort, emphasizing sports and the resort's close relation to the Woodstock colony. Both these moves cheered those who agreed with the "Don't Hock Woodstock" broadside that Woodstock was in danger of becoming "the squabbling bargain counter of the ordinary Catskill Mountain town," doomed to be discarded when its resources were used up by exploiters.[6]

The purchase by the Woodstock Valley Inn Corporation of the Woodstock Lodge was followed by two unexpected developments. Gabriel Newgold set about building a large new hotel close to the old inn on the Rock City Road. And high on Overlook his stepfather, Morris, having sold his Times Square Hotel in New York, was pouring his enormous energy into building a new Overlook Mountain House.

Designed by Kingston architect Gerard Betz, Gabriel Newgold's hotel on the Rock City Road was three stories high, of brick with stuccoed front. It was a fine example of the Spanish taste then popular in New York suburbs and in the growing summer resorts in New York's Sullivan County. The hotel was, as its owner openly proclaimed, "pretentious." It was unlike anything that had ever before appeared in Woodstock. Byrdcliffe and Maverick buildings had been ostentatiously simple. The Colony at Woodstock, as the new hotel was named, was not.

As it was being built Woodstock people were being told that the hotel would offer "petite food shops," "morning musicales," a hotel orchestra, the "Miramont Gallery" in which paintings by Woodstock artists would be shown, a "literary lobby" or library open not only to hotel guests but to all Woodstock people. Building materials were often imported from out of town, and so too were many workmen. Local people also worked on the building. Blacksmith Henry Peper, who was one, made ironwork to the designs of the architect. The hotel was not hailed with enthusiasm by art-colony people, some of whom felt that its design made it inappropriate to Woodstock.

Work on the structure proceeded by fits and starts. Local newspapers and magazines usually ignored it, mentioning it only in such terms as "the brick synagogue," demonstrating the wave of anti-Semitism which had made the Newgold hotel a target.[7]

As the Colony Hotel was put together, Morris Newgold was pushing ahead with his new Overlook Mountain House, with designer Frank P. Amato carrying out Newgold's ideas. A massive monolithic concrete structure emerged, with a smaller one known as the Lodge beside it. The Lodge, completed about 1929, served as living quarters on Newgold's visits and had a drafting room for Amato.

Bungalow colonies like the one Newgold had said he planned for Overlook after the fire of 1923 were doing well in Sullivan County resort centers and other resort areas. Yet no such colony came to Overlook. Newgold planned a by-now anachronistic summer hotel that would carry on the earlier Catskill Mountain tradition of large structures commanding extensive views. The old Catskill Mountain House, the Hotel Kaaterskill, the former Overlook House and the Grand Hotel at Pine Hill had been hotels of this kind. Newgold's massive concrete hotel was to be built a few hundred feet to the south of the burned-out ruin but on the same tract of about six hundred acres.

By that time many old-fashioned frame summer hotels in resort sections of the country had been destroyed by fire. Potential guests were becoming wary of trusting themselves to timber buildings, located far from fire-fighting equipment and good supplies of water. In Sullivan County old frame hotels were being coated with stucco to suggest fireproof walls. The new Overlook Mountain House was similar to these in outward appearance, except that its three-story tower of timbers was covered with clapboards and composition shingles. Structural timbers throughout the building were of mixed origins, many being locally cut round timbers not always stripped of their bark.

As the booming Twenties ended the hotel was far from completion. Construction was entering a less energetic phase, with men and materials being marshalled to be put to work at irregular intervals.

The Colony at Woodstock did achieve completion. It was operated sporadically. It never reached its owner's goal of becoming (as its name was intended to suggest) the center of art-colony life. Guests were usually from out of town. The exhibitions by local painters and the "literary lobby" did not materialize. Many practical operational difficulties caused it to fail to open when scheduled and to change direction from time to time, offering for example a cafeteria at which Woodstock artists might obtain the same kind of food available in similar eating places in New York.

The Colony and the Overlook Mountain House were not the only factors to muddy the local hotel waters. It was generally recognized that the art colony needed a good hotel to serve as a social center. With the Colony's owner aiming at supplying this need even in a way not acceptable to any but a few art-colony people the future of the Woodstock Valley Inn became dimmer.

A fresh competitor appeared in the form of the Twaddell House on the Village Green. This building, once the summer home of the Honorable Charles H. Krack, had gone to his daughter Josie, whose husband, former drover and horseman Jim Twaddell, ran it in a relaxed way. Twaddell sold the place to a man new to Woodstock, Stephen B. Ayres.

A former congressman and newspaper man in western New York, Ayres was owner of a fruit-growing farm in Florida, a writer and a resolute foe of all modern art. Before long the Old Woodstock Inn, as Ayres named the place, was renovated and enlarged and was offering formidable competition to the others. It gave space to a gallery in which the paintings of Birge Harrison and other conservatives (by then in retreat from the usual local shows) were exhibited.[8]

The battle of the hotels came to an inconclusive end with none of the dire results which had been predicted. The Overlook Mountain House was unfinished. The Colony never got off the ground. The Woodstock Valley Inn burned in 1930. That left the Old Woodstock Inn as the town's chief place of its kind. The predicted conversion of the town into a fashionable summer colony did not happen.

Nor did the swamping and extinguishing of the art colony by a wave of Jewish summer boarders ever take place. Jews arrived in ever increasing numbers, it is true. But many were gifted people with interests and skills in the arts. They merged into the colony, kept its traditions alive and gave it a strength without which it might have foundered.

The battle of the hotels was one feature of the boom years. Another, which became known as the Battle of the Theaters, grew out of the boom-powered expansion of national activity in the performing arts. By the late Twenties dancing, musical performances and the theater had all become conspicuous parts of the Woodstock scene.

The performing arts of course had played a part in the life of early Byrdcliffe. Chamber music, an occasional performance by a ballet dancer, and the folk and social dances favored by the Whiteheads had enlivened Byrdcliffe existence. With the arrival of the young people of the Art Students League in 1906 social dancing, amateur theatricals and vocal and instrumental music by the students all flourished. Yet it was not until the boom of the Twenties struck that the performing arts became a central fact in art-colony life and a magnet which drew outsiders to visit or settle in the town.

The Maverick Festivals had begun the process in their own way in 1915. During the Twenties there were many performances by interpretive and other dancers on the Maverick. Dancers came to live in Woodstock. Some of Isodora Duncan's dancers performed in

Woodstock; Duncan's friend and biographer Madame Desti built a house on the Maverick. Artists and craftspeople like Ned Thatcher and Konrad Cramer played for social dancing at local parties and art-colony people enjoyed taking part in the barn dances which were an old Woodstock tradition. Much-admired callers and fiddlers like Norman Wolven supplied a tie between art-colony people and those of the older Woodstock.[9]

Conspicuous among professional dancers for many years was Alexis Kosloff of the Maverick, a Moscow-trained former member of the Russian Imperial Ballet. Kosloff took part with his students in Maverick Festivals. During the winters he was active in New York where he designed dances for Broadway musicals and the Metropolitan Opera. In his old age Kosloff was a picturesque part of Woodstock, a spry little man carrying under his arm the kit or small violin which was the badge of a dancing master and surrounded by the children who were the students of his final teaching phase.

During the Twenties a good deal of excellent music came to Woodstock. Singing groups were organized. The Ambrose choir of 1923 sang baroque and Renaissance music. Its members were both art-colony people and those of the older Woodstock. Painter John F. Carlson, Eugene Speicher's brother Charles, and Marion Eames, all excellent singers, took part in musical events. An opera group gave scenes from popular operas at the Fireman's Hall. The Maverick Concerts continued to do well and the Maverick musical colony to grow.[10]

The most spectacular development of the performing arts of the boom years was in theater. A theater is a strong influence economically and artistically in any community and quickly reflects economic pressures. During the boom period Woodstock's theaters played a critical part in keeping the boom in motion. They stimulated the opening of art galleries, tea rooms, restaurants and gift shops, and lent their facilities to performances of music and the dance.

The little theater movement was making great progress in the United States, with theater groups in rebellion against the country's standard commercial theater springing up in towns and cities throughout the country. In 1915 the Provincetown Players had made their beginning. There was much visiting back and forth between Provincetown and Woodstock.

In 1922 painter Harry Gottlieb came to the Maverick proposing to earn a living by painting while making picture frames. Gottlieb, who had designed and painted scenery for the Provincetown Players, had developed a deep interest in the theater. In 1923 he was visited by actor Dudley Digges, a friend connected with the Provincetown Players. Digges had been one of the founders of the Irish National Theater, which had become part of the European little theater movement.

Digges' visit supplied the spark that ignited the theater hopes of Woodstock. When he watched the Maverick Festival and met some of the colony people prominent in the arts and in intellectual life, Digges became convinced that the place offered unusual possibilities for a theater in the little theater tradition. From a total of about fifty in 1915 they had multiplied to about two thousand by the early 1920s. Digges proposed to Hervey that he be allowed to stage a series of plays in the Quarry Theater the next summer. He would supply professional actors and actresses usually unemployed in summer. Theater people would jump at the chance to have what Digges called "a holiday in the woods" while earning their keep and enjoying a release from the commercialism of Broadway.

Though delighted by the proposal, Hervey expressed doubts about the use of his open-air Quarry Theater. Hard experience had taught him that performances postponed because of rain seldom drew good audiences. Yet he was eager to take up Digges' proposal. Ever since the performance of his anti-war play by the Washington Square Players Hervey's interest in the theater had deepened. He dreamed of seeing an experimental theater as part of the Maverick. There his own plays and others too adventurous in subject and technique for the Broadway stage might be performed.

Digges seemed an ideal man to make that beginning. The chance he offered seemed too good to be missed. Hervey made up his mind to build a theater and have it ready for use by the next summer.

Available for Hervey's purpose was an excellent group of carpenters. Dayton Shultis of the well-known old Woodstock family based in Wittenberg and Bearsville headed the carpenters. He was helped by about half a dozen of his brothers and cousins. The Shultises had already built a number of structures for Hervey, including Langner's studio. They had learned to work with Hervey and carry out his ideas, however eccentric these might seem.

The theater that resulted was framed with timbers cut in the Maverick woods. It had an earthen floor sloping toward the stage, which was equipped with a row of kerosene lamps by way of footlights. Above the benches which gave seating space for more than six hundred people hung a ceiling of bark-covered structural timbers joining and intersecting in a manner that gave an irresistible feeling of a dense and rich forest ceiling. Hervey like to say that he and his carpenters had captured the "spirit of the woods," and there is little doubt that they had.

Outside, the building's frame was covered with bark-covered slabs nailed on the diagonal. The numerous doors made necessary by safety regulations followed the precedent of the nearby Concert Hall. They were topped by sharp angles which suggested Gothic arches. Most of the doors were never used.[11]

On the night of July 4, 1924 the theater opened with a performance of *The Dragon* by Lady Gregory, who, like Digges, had helped make the Irish National Theater a success. Advance publicity told the public that *The Dragon* was "expected to please both the intellectual and the tired businessman." The role of the princess would be played by Helen Hayes, one of Broadways outstanding ingenues. The cast would include such men as E. J. Ballantine, who had played Laertes to John Barrymore's famous Hamlet, and Edward G. Robinson, who had recently been acting with the renowned Mrs. Leslie Carter. The capacity first-night audience at the Maverick Theater applauded wildly for the play, the cast, the theater and Hervey White.

Yet as performance followed performance audiences dwindled in numbers and enthusiasm. The fact was that the members of the cast were taking Digges' promise of a vacation in the woods too literally, resulting in ragged performances. The choice of plays proved more to the taste of Woodstock intellectuals than to that of the tired businessman of Kingston and Saugerties who had to be pleased if the theater were to pay its way.

That summer a number of acting companies followed the Digges players to the theater, presenting a variety of plays. The Percival Vivian Players, who had grown out of the once-famous Ben Greet Players, gave Shakespeare's *Comedy of Errors* and a modern comedy in the Open Air Theater, where the preceding summer they had given two Shakespeare performances to large audiences. Hervey experimented with encouraging pre-theater picnic dinners on the Festival grounds and winding up the evening with an after-theater dance in the Concert Hall.[12]

Yet Hervey was forced to admit at the end of the season that the theater which had cost him some seven thousand dollars of borrowed money to build was losing money. Hervey explained that he didn't mind. He would not object if some philanthropist came along and endowed the theater. But on the other hand, he wrote, "money usually damages an institution as much as it helps. . . ." As long as his Festivals could help keep his theater alive, he would be pleased.[13]

As the Maverick Theater was being conceived and born another theater hope was stirring at Byrdcliffe, thanks to the flowering of longtime theatrical dreams of young Ben Webster. It would falter, and be reborn as a lasting part of Woodstock's theatrical activity even to the present day. The theater is now a central part of the National Historic District at Byrdcliffe.

From 1924 to 1928 the Maverick Theater remained active, if in a floundering way. Many theater groups, some experimental and some conventional, used it. One of Hervey's own plays, *The Blizzard*, which had a Mexican background, was presented, but without an encouraging response. Well-known people sang, danced or acted at the Theater, among them Paul Robeson, Ruth St. Denis and the Fiske Jubilee Singers.

Plans for theatrical rivals to the Maverick were drawn up. And when 1929, the final year of the 1920s orgy of irrational hopes, speculation and self-delusion, arrived it brought with it a powerful rival. The Woodstock Playhouse was run by David O. Reasoner, son-in-law and former student of well-known painter Abbot Thayer.

The Playhouse was part of a larger project begun in 1928. Following the death of Civil War veteran Aaron N. Riseley, Riseley's farm and summer boardinghouse were bought by a local group which proposed turning the property into a country club, with golf course and restaurant attached. As the plans were carried out, the fine old Riseley barn became the Playhouse.[14]

News of what was proposed for the old barn faced Hervey White with an unpleasant choice. He knew his theater could not match the new one in equipment and convenience. He realized that his building needed repairs and that its stage needed wings and more backstage space. Hervey hesitated briefly and then made a reluctant choice. He leased the Maverick Theater to three capable people of Broadway background.

The three were E. J. Ballantine, who had directed and acted with the Provincetown Players and was an old Maverick hand; accomplished and attractive actress Gladys Hurlbut; and director Allen

DeLano. To house their company the three leased about a dozen of Hervey's cottages close to the theater. They persuaded Hervey to let them renovate the theater, enlarge its stage space and facilities and bring in electricity to replace the undependable generating plant which had done duty ever since the original oil lamps had been discarded. They also pressured Hervey into allowing the rutted Maverick Road to be repaired.

All this sent Hervey into a spell of doubt. Ever since he had started his colony he had remained steadfast in avoiding any "improvements" which would make life on the Maverick more expensive and complicated. Now he saw his plan threatened by a devotion to gadgetry which he feared might destroy the simplicity and creative atmosphere of the colony and might raise the living expenses of its people.

Never had a more intense display of competitive spirit descended upon Woodstock than in the spring of 1929. With its great hewn beams and well-equipped backstage, the Playhouse had emerged as a theater which had a right to be thought of as among the very finest of its class in all the United States. As renovation and improvements moved along at the Maverick, its supporters could point to the excellent traditions of their theater and of the Festivals and concerts to which it was related. The new leaseholders were careful to retain the undeniable appeal of the theater's splendid ceiling and its earthen floor.[15]

Woodstock people settled back to enjoy what local writers and some on Broadway were calling "The Battle of the Theaters." Local businessmen got set to enjoy an unrivalled summer. Ten restaurants were in operation that summer, and bootleggers and owners of stills tucked away in the back country looked ahead with pleasure.

The Playhouse or "The Golf Club Playhouse," as some called it, presented Eugene O'Neill's *Emperor Jones*, starring Charles Gilpin, who had helped make the play so great a success during its Broadway run. On the Fourth of July the Maverick presented a light comedy, *Wedding Bells*, preceded by a picnic and followed by fireworks. The varied performances at both theaters between dramatic events made it obvious that each was aiming at dominance in the entire body of local performing arts.

Pierre Henrotte, then concert master of the Metropolitan Opera orchestra, left the Maverick for the Playhouse, where he headed a chamber-music group rivalling that of the Maverick. The Playhouse offered movies of quality. Dancers and comedians came to its stage. At one point a festival to rival the Maverick's was considered. On the Maverick a School of Acting was organized. Travelling theater troupes such as the Jitney Players relieved the resident company, which made a profit by giving several performances in the resort center of Fleischmanns some twenty-five miles away. The Maverick Players scored with a performance of *Rain*. Woodstock's own Clemence Randolph was the play's co-author. Gladys Hurlbut gave a fine performance as Sadie Thompson.

Business on Woodstock's Tinker Street had never been better than in the summer of 1929. Important Broadway theater people coming to Woodstock as observers were watched with awe taking refreshment in local eating and drinking establishments. Now Woodstock people began hoping that their town would soon nose out Provincetown as a summer-theater center. It didn't especially matter that neither Woodstock theater was believed to have shown a profit or that audiences were thinner as the summer waned or that the productions were usually humdrum. Nineteen twenty-nine had definitely put Woodstock on the theater map and the future looked good.[16]

Changes in Woodstock were clearly visible on any winter day in the late Twenties after the high tide of summer people had receded. Older buildings in the hamlet had been enlarged and adapted to commercial uses. Streets had been widened at the expense of picket fences, lawns and cottage gardens. Gas pumps were conspicuous in front of Frank B. Happy's general store and Peper's blacksmith shop (now become a garage). The old Woodstock Valley Inn still dominated the hamletscape around the Village Green. The former Krack House had acquired a large portico facing the Green, had lost its cupola and its two-story verandahs, and had gained a large extension on its Rock City side. Most other buildings near the Green and on the sidestreets leading to it remained much as they had been. Although the outlying parts of the town, Wittenberg, Lake Hill, Shady and Zena, had been affected by the increasing ownership of automobiles, most of the colony's studios were concentrated in and close to the hamlet.

Many studios had been improvised in existing farm outbuildings by cutting north windows into walls. Others were now being run up by local builders for rent or sale. Many of these followed Byrdcliffe precedents in design. Smaller ones had no cellars. They had dry-wall foundations, flush siding, and usually a chimney resting on a wooden bracket about five feet above the ground.[17]

Chimneys like these, which had the advantage of resisting

damage as a structure with sketchy foundations responded to the freezing and thawing of the earth on which they rested, were common in the older Woodstock and had been used at Byrdcliffe. More elaborate studios with frost-resistant foundations often followed the example of Byrdcliffe's Yggdrasil, which had a balcony at one end of the high studio room and a fireplace at the other. Though some fireplaces, like the one Bolton Brown made at Carniola, were built of rounded stones from the Sawkill bed, most were of bluestone. Sculptor Bruno Zimm was sometimes called in to build one of these fireplaces.

A bluestone-paved terrace usually provided an outdoor living space to studios. Studios began to appear beside abandoned bluestone quarries. Pools fed by underground springs opened up by quarry operations could be used as swimming or ornamental pools. Surrounded with massive ledges and broken rock, these old quarries had a hint of the look of the grottoes of European landscape designs.

Some artists built homes and studios of marked individuality from local materials. In Zena at the end of the 1920s graphic artist Hanson Booth began building with his own hands a three-story bluestone house with bluestone floors and stairways and handmade wooden shingles. The stone was cut from a hillside quarry beside the house. During the almost ten years the house was being built Booth lived in a shelter within the foundation walls.

Since most studios were intended for summer occupancy and their owners were not rich, carpenters were urged to keep costs down. And so local men who were excellent craftsmen tended to produce shoddy work. In this way the arrival of an arts and crafts colony lowered local standards of craftsmanship. On the Maverick simple cabins were slapped together every year. In 1927 Hughes Mearns wrote of these cabins and their settings with approval, "The Maverick is dream valley. Houses are built while you wait. Rents are paid or not. . . ." [18]

A restaurant named The Intelligencia was built to take care of the people working at or patronizing the Maverick Festivals, the concerts and the theater. The building was shaped like a Greek Cross, with the kitchen and serving area in the center in order to save steps between kitchen and diners and to give the members of the "cliques" into which Maverickers divided themselves a chance to dine separately. The stone floor resulted in many broken dishes. The first cook, Greenwich Village anarchist Hippolyte Havel, sometimes astonished respectable diners come slumming on the Maverick by hissing "capitalist pigs" as he deftly served them. Among managers were painters Arnold and Lucile Blanch, who had returned broke from a year of "Guggenheiming" in Europe and were glad to have the jobs.

The building was better built than most of Hervey's. Its builder, Wallace Gray, had come down from the top of Ohayo Mountain to do the job. Hervey remembered him saying, "We must make it almost perfect." The Intelligencia (a name then popular in a slightly different spelling, among approvers of the Russian Revolution) was ornamented with a "Freudian symbol" painted on its chimney by Konrad Cramer.

Less perfect was one of the Maverick studios built around this time. According to tradition it was built in five days by two men and six quarts of applejack.[19]

Through the Twenties the churches which had played so large a part in the life of the older Woodstock showed few outward changes. Two new churches joined them. In 1923 the Roman Catholic Chapel of St. Joan of Arc appeared on the Rock City Road. Its parishioners were largely descended from the nineteenth-century quarry workers. A Christian Science church was built on Mill Hill Road close to the Woodstock School. It was backed by Mrs. Edgar Eames and her musician daughter Marian. In 1911 the Eameses had built the house now used to hold the offices of the town of Woodstock. Christian Science believers were largely drawn from the ranks of art-colony people.[20]

Many fields, especially those close to the hamlet of Woodstock, ceased being tilled or pastured as their value for building sites rose. Brush was taking the place of rye, oats and corn. By the end of the 1920s some of the well-kept look of Woodstock, which had charmed the early art-colony settlers, was dwindling. Yet there was still enough of it left to lure new people to exclaim over the old-fashioned rural appeal of the place.

As pastures were less carefully maintained, mountain laurel expanded into conspicuous groups on hillside pastures in Wittenberg, Lake Hill and Shady. When the shrubs flowered in late June art-colony people made pilgrimages to see them. Louis E. Jones, who had come to town as an art student and remained to run a gift shop and make photographic postcards, found that cards showing mountain laurel in bloom were as popular as those which celebrated the Sawkill and other Woodstock streams in their various seasonal aspects, or as those which paid nostalgic tribute, as did the work of a good many painters, to the dwindling farm landscape of the more remote parts of the town.[21]

43

ARTISTS AND
CRAFTSPEOPLE
IN THE TWENTIES

W hile theaters, hotels and
boardinghouses, shops and other business enterprises reacted most
conspicuously, the force of the boom spirit was felt in nearly every
avenue of Woodstock activity. Painting and the crafts as well as the
theater were affected in quantity if not always in quality.

Painting had been given only a minor place in Ralph Whitehead's
plans for Byrdcliffe. Work in crafts had predominated in importance.
Yet as the colony in the valley below Byrdcliffe grew stronger painting
gained on crafts as the major art-colony activity. The process had
begun when the Art Students League Summer School held its first
classes in 1906, The draining-away of students by the demands of the
First World War and the lessened appeal to young painters of the
League's emphasis on open-air landscape painting caused enrollment
to dwindle and the school to close just as Woodstock began to boom in
1923. However, private art schools multiplied and, helped along by the
boom, the number of workers in all the arts increased.[1]

The artists of the Woodstock colony of the Twenties represented
almost every approach to art, from the most advanced to the most
conservative. In the public view a few artists stood out, forming the
upper level of a kind of hierarchy. At the topmost peak of the
painters, as far as public respect went, stood aging but active Birge
Harrison. Symbolizing Harrison's position was the annual celebration
of his birthday on October 28, in which even those younger people

who thoroughly disapproved of the Harrison way of painting happily joined. And to conservative painters Harrison remained the living and revered embodiment of their creed.

Just below Harrison in the hierarchy was his former student, John Fabian Carlson. Carlson had been a student first at the Byrdcliffe school and then at that of the Art Students League. As League teacher, Carlson carried on the Harrison tradition in landscape painting. He developed a manner marked by brighter color, excellent composition and a deep devotion to the mountains, the trees and the streams of Woodstock.

After Harrison's death in 1929, Carlson took Harrison's place in the esteem of Woodstock's more conservative painters. His sometimes violent expressions of hostility to the work of the local avant-garde, however, kept him from ever replacing Harrison in the affections of the art colony. Many Carlson students remained to work in Woodstock and painted in personal modifications of the Harrison and Carlson manners. A few painters were still carrying on this tradition as late as the 1980s.

The painters who disapproved of Harrison's and Carlson's work did not form a unified group. They were divided into what some termed "modern" and "ultra-modern" groups. Of the two the "modern" had the highest spot in public estimation and was the more successful in the marketplace. The modern was slightly affected by the then-recent European revelations in art. The ultras showed a great deal of that influence.[2]

Three modern painters stood next below Harrison in the hierarchy of the art colony. The leader of these, Robert Henri, had spent no more than a single summer, that of 1921, in Woodstock. Yet because of his talents as painter and teacher he left a decided mark on Woodstock painting. George Bellows and Eugene Speicher were the two men who shared with Henri an elevated level among local painters. They had met and become friends while members of a Henri class.

After a long period of diligent study, Henri had painted for a time under Impressionist influence in France and America. Then, after studying the work of Franz Hals and Velasquez, he adopted the forceful and direct kind of brushwork which he found to give his work life and immediacy. He took to attacking his canvas rapidly and with intense concentration. Standing aside from the tumult awakened by the Armory Show, he sought instead a scientific basis for painting in the set palette devised by H. G. Marratta, which had an analogy to the musical scale. He became an enthusiast for Jay Hambidge's system of dynamic symmetry. Hambidge had worked out the system after a study of the proportions of ancient Greek vases. Both the Marratta and the Hambidge theories left noticeable marks on Henri's work.

As a teacher Henri was inspiring. He taught his students to value individualism and to lose their fear of adventure in paint. His forceful manner of painting and his occasional choice of such subjects as industrial scenes resulted in his being hailed as a truly American painter. He became a leader of a group which because it liked to paint everyday subjects was named the Ashcan School.[3]

Of all Henri's students none was closer to him than George Bellows, a tall, vigorous man with a very American temperament. Like Henri, Bellows painted figures, portraits, landscapes and subjects of everyday life with vigor, his color and composition influenced by Maratta and Hambidge. After a period of occasional visits Bellows became part of the Woodstock colony.

Bellows at once plunged with characteristic enthusiasm into many phases of Woodstock life. He took a leading part in art-colony activities. At the same time he coached local boys in field sports; he managed the local baseball team. The new French and German innovations in art had little interest for him. He like to think of himself as "an emotional realist" who aimed at translating into paint his own feelings about life.

Others who detected a different motivation saw Bellows as an intensely competitive man who liked above all to paint "smashing" canvasses which would dominate any exhibition in which they might be hung. Bellows' essential conservatism brought him election to the National Academy of Design, which gave him the right to place the letters "N.A." after his name. Henri before him had received the symbol, as did Carlson and Speicher a bit later. Membership in the National Academy in Bellows' day was regarded as a passport to prosperity. Bellows came to be known as the most prosperous N.A. of his time.[4]

Like Henri and Bellows, Speicher combined great natural facility with the ability to study and work energetically and conservatively in the face of revolutionary changes around him. He did not go in for "smash" but was influenced by a manner handed down from the time of Titian and given a fresh turn by Renoir in his later years. The public understood his work and respected it for the dignity and solidity of his portraits and figures.

Speicher won many prizes, was represented in many public and private collections, and won popularity contests sponsored by galleries and art publications. As a portrait painter he became so much in demand that he could afford to turn down commissions which did not appeal to him. He thus found time for the landscapes, drawings and flower paintings which gave him greater freedom.

From his arrival in Woodstock in the summer of 1909 as a student until his death in 1962 Speicher was popular socially in the art colony. As he prospered he lived well in a much-admired house which he had designed himself. His wife was a talented hostess and cook. The dinner parties which the couple gave became Woodstock legends. During the final phase of Speicher's life he filled a position similar to that held by Birge Harrison in the earlier days of the colony.[5]

As Bellows and Speicher were enjoying their prosperity another group of painters who seemed unlikely ever to become N.A.s—unless they changed their ways—was turning the attention of the art world toward Woodstock. These people emerged as a recognizable artistic unit in November of 1923. The Woodstock Artists Association members, after ending the first exhibition in their new gallery, then put together a show at the New Gallery in New York. The show, which opened early in November, made a decided impression. The critic of the New York *Sun and Globe* wrote that "this group of men and women who have made the Catskills their home are developing a school of painting which reveals much serious work in the experimental sphere of modern art."

The critic set aside Bellows, Speicher and Henri, whose work was included in the show. The three, the critic said, belonged "to quite another phase of our present day art." He named Dasburg, Warren Wheelock, McFee, Alexander Altenberg, Henry Schnakenberg, Hermon More, Caroline Speare, Paul Rohland, Peggy Bacon, John Carroll and Ernest Fiene as true members of the new group. The Kingston *Daily Freeman* reprinted the *Sun and Globe's* story under the heading "Woodstock's New Painting School," and so gave local approval to the existence of what was soon being called the Woodstock School.

Just what was the Woodstock School? No one seemed quite sure in 1923 and no one has sharply defined it since. Some claimed that the School's painters, diverse though they were, had in common an addiction to somber, earthy color and to subjects such as the landscape, people and flowers to be found in Woodstock. They were also, it was being said during the mid-Twenties, serious people with a strong desire to create a truly American approach to painting.

Henry Lee McFee conformed to all this in his color, his seriousness and his choice of Woodstock subjects. But Paul Rohland, who sometimes painted tropical landscapes in bright color, did not. Dasburg turned to the American Southwest and favored New Mexican subjects. John Carroll painted nudes with no discernible Woodstock character. And Eugene Speicher, who was not usually regarded as a member of the Woodstock School, often seemed to join them in his landscapes and flower paintings. Frank London painted still life, with his models often Victorian decorative objects found at local auctions.

What gave the Woodstock School artists a common note was probably their attempt at finding a compromise between European innovations and American tradition. All had been impressed by Cezanne, the Cubists, Matisse, Kandinsky and the other pioneers of modern art. The work of McFee and Cramer was strongly marked by the Cubist manner as well as by that of Cezanne. This pair of influences affected many painters of the School.[6]

By the 1920s Woodstock painters in substantial numbers had accepted a new approach to art. No longer did they follow in the footsteps of their predecessors as closely as possible, with only individual talents to give work personal distinction. They became committed instead to the restless change and the constant exploration of life and reality which were hallmarks of the twentieth century.

Most of the artists went through many phases during their lifetimes. Retrospectively their life work might seem to a conservative observer to be self-contradictory or confused, with the work of one group of years appearing to have so little in common with that of another. Yet to an observer more in tune with the times the personality of the painter would clearly survive many outward changes.

Seldom did a painter make a break with one way of working and embrace another in so thorough a manner as to suggest a total rebirth. Leon Kroll, for example, was painting figure subjects with strong Henri and Manet qualities during the early 1920s. When he turned to working under Cezanne-Cubist influence his individuality continued to be obvious. Charles Rosen, who became next to McFee the most respected of the Woodstock School, made an about-face in his work which put an almost unbridgeable gulf between his earlier and later work. Pennsylvania-born Rosen was a successful American Impressionist of the New Hope colony in Pennsylvania.

Rosen's landscapes, especially those of winter scenes, had made him an N.A. Then in 1919 Rosen came to Woodstock to teach at the Art Students League Summer School. From that year on he struggled to leave his successful painting past behind him. By 1920 he had settled permanently in Woodstock and was evolving a new manner in which elements inspired by Cezanne and the Cubists were fused.

Like many painters of the Woodstock School Rosen liked to paint buildings. With their sharp edges and angles, American buildings were excellent models for painters who followed Cezanne in emphasizing planes. McFee had used Woodstock's white houses and red barns during the World War years. By the Twenties he and others, including Rosen, had gone afield to paint industrial and waterfront structures as well as Hudson River tugboats and barges in Rondout, Eddyville and Saugerties. The pictures which resulted struck observers as "smashing" rather than beguiling.

Meanwhile, the Harrison way lived on with such men as Allen Cochran, Walter Goltz, Samuel Wiley, Harry Leith-Ross and other former students, swearing everlasting devotion to their master. Painters who could properly be included in none of the recognized Woodstock categories also worked through the Twenties. One was Robert Winthrop Chanler, a descendant of many well-known early American families.

Chanler had a good income and was able to give generous help to less fortunate painters. He was first known for the screens he designed and for the often huge murals and swimming pools he created for the homes of the rich. During his Woodstock years he turned to lively and penetrating portraits which suggested "a raucous Matisse" to one critic. Tall and genial, Chanler walked with a limp and liked to wear the kind of white overalls more often seen on plasterers and house painters. His parties, which were frequent and elaborate, hold a special place in the lore of the Woodstock of the boom years.

Working apart from the main stream of the Woodstock School were a number of other painters of distinction. Yasuo Kuniyoshi had come to the colony during the 1920s. He developed into one of Woodstock's best-known and most individualistic painters. William E. Schumaker, who had come to Byrdcliffe in 1911 after many years in Paris, painted his Fauvish compositions in which cats and goats figured. Henry Mattson set up his studio among the trees and pastures of Rock City and there painted seascapes which at times had an emotional kinship to such American classics as those of Chauncey Rider and Ralph Blakelock.[7]

Sculptors had lived in Woodstock before the Twenties. Grace

Mott Johnson worked at her animal sculptures. Warren Wheelock turned from sculpture to painting and crafts. Abastenia St. Leger Eberle and Myra Musselman-Carr, who had studied in Paris with Bourdelle and had become innovative teachers, were among the women who formed a significant part of the art colony. Alexander Archipenko, who endlessly experimented with new directions in sculpture and painting, was an innovator in what was later called mixed-media work. Alfeo Faggi, born in Florence, Italy, developed a personal style which owed much to his interest in archaic sculpture. Faggi made bas-relief portraits of many well-known person, as well as religious sculptures.

An exalted place among Woodstock sculptors of the Twenties belongs to John Flannagan, who from time to time joined the growing group of workers in the arts who spent summers on the Maverick. Flannagan's small, rounded animals and sometimes humans are far better appreciated today than they were in his lifetime. He left a decided mark on Woodstock in 1924 when with an axe as his major tool he hewed the Maverick Horse, an enduring symbol of the Maverick, from the trunk of a chestnut tree cut on the hillside above the Concert Hall. Hervey White, who believed that all useful work was of value and that of an artist no more to be rewarded than any other, paid Flannagan the prevailing wage of fifty cents an hour.

The Maverick figure, eighteen feet high, shows the horse emerging from the outstretched hands of a man in turn emerging from the earth. The horse represented to Hervey the kind of freedom which he encouraged among his Maverick tenants—"he belonged to no one and at the same time to whoever could catch him." It now stands in the Maverick Concert Hall. Some see the carving as having religious imagery, with the head of the man on which the horse rests representing Christ.[8]

The Woodstock Artists Association could boast of nearly one hundred fifty exhibiting members in 1921. Other local painters, sculptors and other workers or dabblers in the arts were not members. Bolton C. Brown was a conspicuous non-member. John F. Carlson remained a member for a few years and then stalked out in anger at the radical company in which he found himself.

In 1927 the Association members were divided amongst conservatives, radicals and shilly-shalliers who shifted categories. They were divided too among painters, sculptors and craftspeople. Non-member Brown led Woodstock printmakers with his work in lithography. Conservative members Alfred Hutty and Orville Peets had become etchers, Maverick painters Arnold and Lucile Blanch and Harry Gottlieb, who had joined the Woodstock School, were also members. Craftspeople included the metalworker Captain Jenkinson, tapestry-weaver Mary McQuaid, the Byrdcliffe potters Edith Penman and Elizabeth Hardenbergh, Zulma Steele, silversmith Bertha Thompson and batik man Pieter Mijer. Craftsman Ned Thatcher was not a member but his wife Isabel was. So too was potter Carl Walters.[9]

Painters dominated the Association's list of members. Besides the familiar names already mentioned there were other painters. Pamela Vinton-Brown did miniatures. Van Deering Perrine, who had nothing to do with other Woodstock artists, painted and experimented with color music. Georgina Klitgaard produced panoramic landscape with the charm of American primitives, Otto Bierhals remained true to the standards of nineteenth-century Germany. Peggy Bacon was making a stir with her sharp satirical drawing. Her husband, Alexander Brook, painted landscapes and figures.

Illustrators were also present both as members and as independents. Maud and Miska Petersham were writing and ilustrating children's books with great success. Cushman Parker was drawing magazine covers. E. B. Winslow, John Striebel and Ivan Summers also illustrated. Alfred Cohn and Eva Watson were photographers, although Watson was taking to painting. All this should be enough to suggest the great variety of efforts in the arts which were being made in the Woodstock of the Twenties.

Bolton Brown had emerged as an important force in American printmaking. Before the Twenties he had published a book on the technical side of painting. In 1924 his "Lithography" was published, followed in 1929 by "Lithography for Artists." By 1919 Brown had established his Artists Press in Zena, where he printed lithographs for George Bellows and others. As interest in lithography expanded in the United States Brown taught at his "Woodstock Summer School of Lithography and Etching." A lithographic press was set up on the Maverick. Designer Ilonka Karascz and others made prints there. Artists Association member Paul Johnston did fine printing and binding during the Twenties and published some numbers of his *Book Collectors Packet* in Woodstock.[10]

By the 1920s the back-to-crafts movement given such power by the genius of John Ruskin and William Morris was losing some of its strength. Machine-made objects for daily use were firmly established.

Few people saw the older hand methods as having any chance of surviving except as a means of individual expression. The simplicity of arts-and-crafts design and its stress on adapting design to the character of materials had influenced industrial design. Machine-made objects were losing their slavery to historic styles, owing much to the effect of the arts and crafts movement.

In Woodstock crafts continued to make their contribution to the colony's life. Interest in crafts objects on the part of visitors to Woodstock led to the stocking of local gift and other shops with "peasant" clothing and household objects from Germany, tinware and pottery from Mexico, and pottery from France. The "Woodstock dress" devised by Augusta Allen was based on high-waisted Central European peasant models. For many years it was worn by women members of the art colony and bought by visitors.

The Market Fair had booths at which local crafts (including the Woodstock dress) were sold. But the sale of these crafts dwindled. And the Artists Association, on whose exhibitions many craftspeople hoped for display and sale, proved uncooperative. Although the Association held an occasional small craft exhibition many painter members felt that the presence of crafts detracted from the dignity of their gallery. It is a tribute to the vitality of the craft movement in Woodstock that craftspeople went on working even in the face of much commercial competition and local apathy.

After a short period of teaching at Byrdcliffe, master metal craftsman Edmund Rolfe set up his own shop and school nearby. His devotion to his craft was inspiring to others and praised by Hervey White. He experimented with materials and techniques. When he solved a problem he did not go on to produce objects for the market, but instead turned to another problem he hoped to solve. He and his family slept beside his shop on cots covered by canvas—to Hervey White they seemed to be living in a cluster of prairie schooners.[11]

Having left Byrdcliffe, Ned Thatcher continued to work in a studio he built on what is now Striebel Road. Bertha Thompson and Marie Little left, Miss Thompson to establish her silver-working shop—Hillside Studios—beside Byrdcliffe, Miss Little to build her house close to the hamlet of Woodstock. New craftspeople arrived every year, Neil Reber to make modern furniture, Mary McQuaid to take pupils in her craft. Penman and Hardenbergh left Byrdcliffe and set up their pottery beside the Glasco Turnpike in the vicinity of the Lark's Nest. Until the late 1920s the Whiteheads continued to make their White Pines pottery and exhibit it around the country.

Harry Gottlieb made frames for paintings and mirrors, as did a number of other painters. Painters Paul and Caroline Speare Rohland painted silken fabrics in their Chitra Studio on the Speare Road of today. Arnold and Lucile Blanch painted and wove on the Maverick.

Edward Thatcher was among the earliest Byrdcliffe craftspeople who continued active in a wide variety of fields. He not only published his book on making toys and other objects from tin cans and taught crafts at Teacher's College in New York but also made and wrote about ship models. By so doing launched an enduring activity among hobbyists. And at the same time he continued to make much distinguished metalwork, including jewelry.[12]

Pottery never ceased being made. Zulma Steele, having become by marriage Mrs. Neilson Parker, made tableware which she named Zedware. Bolton Brown turned to pottery. So too did sculptor Alexander Archipenko, who took over the Byrdcliffe Pottery for a while after Hardenbergh and Penman left. Sculptor Hunt Diedrich, born of a Hungarian father and a New England mother, was also a potter. His large plates with their spirited decorations based on archaic Greek animals and humans remain impressive objects. Diedrich was better known for his metal work, including weathervanes in which he used the same kind of flowing rhythms which marked his pottery. Diedrich also made objects of the found materials for which he was ever on the lookout.

On the Maverick Carl Walters was becoming an outstanding craftsman. Walters had been a friend of Harry Gottlieb in Minneapolis. After many adventures in the West and Midwest, Walters turned to making pottery in Greenwich Village. He set himself the goal of discovering the means of making a green-blue glaze similar to the one he had admired on Persian and Egyptian pottery in museums. He was successful. He then followed Gottlieb to the Maverick, where Hervey White built him a kiln and a cottage. There Walters became well-known for his ceramic animals, some finished with his smooth blue-green glaze and others in a variety of colors and textures. All radiated the warm and humorous quality which was a part of Walters' own personality.[13]

In addition to the older weavers like Marie Little new weaver-recruits came to work in Woodstock. Craftspeople of the pre-art-colony Woodstock were stimulated by the approval of the newer people to carry on. Blacksmith Henry Peper, who had converted his blacksmith and wagon-repairing shop into a garage, took to making hinges, latches, andirons and other ironwork of traditional design and excellent quality. The women of Woodstock churches found that the patchwork quilts which they made were admired and bought at church fairs by art-colony members. The church hall of the Methodist church of Shady was paid for by the sale of fine quilts made by members of the King's Daughters of Shady.

In the hamlet of Woodstock Iris Wolven made furniture and clocks. Arthur Stone, partner in the old turning mill in Shady, made superb lazy Susans, lamp bases, sleds and wheelbarrows. He and other local turners were always glad to make wooden objects designed by art-colony people or anyone else. In this way as the Twenties boomed along furniture and architectural elements, rolling pins, baseball bats and potato mashers of local making all were parts of daily Woodstock life.[14]

Woodstock's activity in the arts and crafts was of little interest to many of the curious visitors who began coming to the town from the surrounding country. From the beginnings at Byrdcliffe the people of Ulster and nearby counties had observed the experiment with interest and with amusement.

Nothing about the Byrdcliffe people amused them more than the way they dressed. Ralph Whitehead in his tweed Norfolk jacket was not amusing. But his red-haired wife afloat on pale and filmy veils certainly was. So too were Hervey White, at first in short bicycle pants and red Windsor tie and later in a Russian blouse, and van der Loo in his battered army uniform. The Byrdcliffe rank and file were amusing in their own way. Many dressed in work clothes as if for a hard day in the fields and then sat down at a loom or an easel, rising up at intervals only to pick flowers or dash up Overlook Mountain. So it seemed to outsiders.

By 1915 the effect of the arrival of the Art Students League and immigrants from Greenwich Village had made Woodstock even more amusing. Visitors were arriving in good numbers for no other purpose than "to look at the crazy artists." As seen through conventional eyes the artists were well worth looking at, especially because of the way they dressed.

In 1917 reporter Louella Stewart set down her impressions of Woodstock dress. She realized that the emphasis on work clothes of the kind usually worn by laborers had its logic. She wrote that "it must take bales and bales of khaki to supply the elite of Woodstock for all dress in this artistic, dirt-concealing, barbed-wire-fence-resisting fabric. The men wear baggy trousers of it, low-necked shirts to match, with passionate-hued ties, 'peanut' hats or dashing sombreros, and high tan boots or barefoot sandals." The wide brims of sombreros and floppy peanut hats were popular because they shielded open-air painters' eyes from the glare of the sun.

"The middy blouse, cheap, comfortable and easily washed, is the favorite feminine supplement of a khaki skirt and barefoot sandals. Next in favor comes a man's shirt, worn loose over the skirt and cut off for short sleeves." Women, Stewart noted, also wore peanut hats, brims turned up in this way or that and decorated with roses painted by the wearer or a friend.

In their leisure or playful hours, Stewart reported, Woodstockers threw off all sober restraints. One woman whom she saw, wore "a gray linen Norfolk blouse, very daring in the 'V'; a very short khaki skirt, a bright green headband four inches wide, barbaric gold earrings about three inches long, bright green stockings and white sneakers." A six-foot young man wore "a pink silk shirt, with a white string tie, white linen trousers, red socks, white sneakers, and a cute little Tyrolean hat adorned with a fuzzy feather some eighteen inches long."

Most of the workers in the arts and crafts who came together in Woodstock of the Twenties were serious people who kept busy with their work. Yet the tourists who came in ever-larger droves to the town saw little of these people at work. They saw Tinker Street filled with people not with a passion for the arts but a very strong preference for bizarre clothing and lively behavior. Dilettantes drawn to the town played at being artists. They lived in studios and wore paint-spattered pants local rumor said had been bought already-spattered from young art students.[15]

As the Twenties rolled toward their climax a feverish kind of spirit becoming evident in the town took forms that delighted the tourists. One dancer who had taken up painting held an exhibition of his work in the summer of 1929. The Woodstock *Bulletin* commented that the paintings were "mostly concerned with sexual nightmares . . . of monstrously abnormal creatures." The show was "not for the squeamish or over-sensitive. . . ," said the *Bulletin*. The paper added that the painter's admission fee of twenty-five cents included a cup of tea. He would also give free tango lessons in the gallery "to any woman who asked for it." [16]

During the Twenties the beret came into fashion among the

artists. Soon almost everyone in town wore one, even plumbers and the Woodstock doctor. Tourists soon realized that by wearing a beret they might pass as art-colony people. And so the sale of berets became a source of income to shopkeepers.

The reputation of Woodstock as a place in which it was possible to amuse oneself in ways not available in more conservative communities had brought tourists with ample money to spend. Businesspeople reacted to this situation by devising more and more ways of getting into their own pockets the dollars of the tourists, both the transient ones and those who later settled in Woodstock. Painters too seized the opportunity, turning out little landscape and flower subjects which went on sale to tourists in local shops up and down Tinker Street. These sold well.

The belief that Woodstock was turning from an art colony to a business colony had some evidence to support it. Had it not been for the blows dealt to business by the Great Depression of the 1930s, the art colony might well have wasted away. While the boom continued, its feverish spirit touched all aspects of local life. Even the Maverick Festivals, which had begun as annual celebrations in which art-colony people joined in joyous expression of their way of life, became more commercial as the Twenties moved along.

It could not have been otherwise. The Festivals brought thousands of potential customers to local businesspeople. Though many of these people disapproved of the Festivals on moral grounds, yet as sources of profit they won hearty approval and support. An uneasy alliance between art and business had been formed.

44

THE MAVERICK
FESTIVALS OF
THE LATE TWENTIES

The effects of the boom of the
Twenties on Woodstock were clearly visible as preparations for the
Maverick Festival of 1925 got under way. The idealism which had
been so essential a part of Byrdcliffe was losing some of its grip.
Getting rich was becoming the major goal of life even to many artists.
Speculation in common stocks had come to town. Local and art-colony
people might be seen leaving Leon Carey's News Shop studying the
stock-market quotations in the New York papers, oblivious to old
friends. Clara Park, widow of the Rev. Clearfield Park, once minister
of the Dutch Reformed Church, was heavily engaged in selling Florida
lots—Woodstock artists, eager to get in on what seemed to be a sure
road to millions, were buying with a small down payment and
installments to be paid far into the future.

Yet the big Maverick spectacle that year managed to enlist the
help of a good number of art-colony people, even those deep in
speculation.[1]

Nineteen-twenty-five saw a return to a story by Flaubert as the
base of the spectacle in the Maverick amphitheater. "The beautiful
story of *Salammbo* in pantomime," it was billed. "The sacrifice to
Moloch, the siege of the barbarians, grotesques, solo dances and ballet,
in all some two hundred actors on the stage, many of them from our
most distinguished citizens." Walter Steinhilber designed the
architectural stage set. Arnold Blanch made the colossal black figure of

Moloch. When the Steinhilber baby was passed into Moloch's flaming belly as a sacrifice the audience was at first stunned and then delighted.

The next summer a ballet and a jazz pantomime by composer John Alden Carpenter were the evening features. The ballet was based on comic strip artist George Herriman's *Krazy Kat* and the jazz pantomime on Oscar Wilde's *Birthday of the Infanta*. Local talent was put to work in both. Harry Gottlieb was the stage designer. Woodstock dancer Ruth Schrader led young Woodstock people in gypsy dances. The New York *Times* sang of the Festival of 1926 in such lyrical terms that Woodstock people felt certain that their festivals would go on endlessly, spreading their town's fame, making money for local business, and providing an annual climax to art-colony life.

On the morning of the Maverick Festival day the *Times* proclaimed: "The artists of the East held carnival today. This was the day of the Maverick, the annual costume festival of the Woodstock artists, known to painters, sculptors, musicians, writers, actors and other servants of the seven arts throughout the country. . . ." The events were described with breathless enthusiasm. Famous names were listed as present. "The villagers gathered from miles around," said the *Times*, "looked on and gasped" while "the throng" of festival-goers "wandered . . . laughing, cheering nymphs and dryads running through mountain scenery in search of Pan. . . ."

In an editorial headed ARTISTS IN ARCADY the *Times* of the day following the festival further built up the appeal to the public which its news story of the day before had expressed so strongly. Once a year, the *Times* editorialized, artists heard the call of the Maverick. "From garrets, from cellars, from studios, from shops they come pouring to answer the pastoral piping of Hervey White. In his flutings they hear the promise of music and dancing, eating and drinking and sweetly simple entertainment. . . . It is not merely the unknown, the humble, the jazz performer, the Charleston dancer, the artist's model who so eagerly take part in the rites of Pan. The great, the famous, the learned also come trooping to dance barefoot on the velvet grass. . . ." [2]

As consideration of the Festival of 1927 began, the exhilaration caused by the enthusiastic reception of the previous festival still ran high. By this time the art colony was rapidly expanding to include more glittering people than the art students, craftspeople and social reformers of earlier years.

Among these people was successful novelist and Broadway and Hollywood writer J. P. McEvoy. Though people like McEvoy enjoyed and admired the Maverick Festivals, they regarded them as having a somewhat old-fashioned air. As national attention became turned upon the festivals, McEvoy and others felt the urge to give them a boost by tying them to subjects of wider interest among smart people. In the mid-Twenties New Yorkers who wanted to be in the advance guard of contemporary interest were going to black Harlem and attending black night clubs where they listened to black jazz and watched black theatrical performances. McEvoy used his influence to bring to the Maverick as its major event for 1927 an all-black revue, one of whose actors was Thomas Douglas of a New York show called *Africana*. The performance was not successful enough to encourage further imported presentations.

The next year saw the return of a Festival in the former Maverick spirit. The Maverick's Alexis Kosloff was director of the festival's big show, and talented Takashi Ohta was stage designer. In 1917 Kosloff had choreographed a Broadway musical success called *Chu Chin Chow*, based on the Arabian Nights. His Maverick show owed much to *Chu Chin Chow* transplanted from China to Baghdad.

Under Kosloff's direction the stage of the amphitheater reflected the Western world's image of Oriental voluptuousness—near-nudity, gorgeous costumes, bejewelled properties, impassioned music and dances. Kosloff's students danced. John Striebel, soon to become well-known as the artist of J. P. McEvoy's comic strip, Dixie Dugan, played the "Pshah." Painter Paul Rohland was Chief Eunuch. Farrell Pelley, once of the Irish National Theater, was stage designer. Music was by a twenty-five piece orchestra directed by the Maverick's Pierre Henrotte.[3]

That summer of 1928 also saw the gathering of the opposition which would contribute to the downfall of the Maverick Festivals. A clergyman arrived in Woodstock and registered shock at the goings-on. He was reported to have said that he would "clean up the Maverick Festivals or die in the attempt." It was true enough that the festivals were becoming less an expression of creative community exuberance and more an occasion for people of all sorts from near and far to cast off their inhibitions. Bootleggers in that time of Prohibition set up in business in the woods of the Maverick. Big people in the underworld were said to have attended. More state troopers were needed to curb brawling and violence.

Newspaper reports of the 1928 Festival show a decided change from the approval of a few years earlier. The New York *Herald Tribune* reported that three thousand revellers came to the festival, among them young women who "were happy to gambol with a nameless young man whose hair was curly and whose eyes were dark and piercing. There was wine and song and there were men and women. . . ." The celebrants, according to the *Herald Tribune*, included "press agents, brokers, bankers, bootleggers, interior decorators, photographers, grocers. . . ." [4]

Through the spring and early summer of 1929, Woodstock was a-buzz with rumor and controversy. Plans for new restaurants, shops and hotels were multiplying. The artists-vs.-tourists-and-businessmen controversy was reaching one of its peaks. Preparations for the Maverick Festival scheduled for August 30 were being watched by clergymen and others who were following their lead in regarding the Festivals as hotbeds of sin. Businesspeople who profited by the crowds brought to town were finding it hard to take firm pro- or anti-Maverick stands.

The 1929 Festival was planned to follow familiar lines. There would be the usual "general gathering and stunt throwing" in the afternoon. Games, country dances and a "camp fire supper" would follow. The big event would be the nine o'clock show in the open-air theater. The theme would be the Gay Nineties.

A Grand Parade of Nineties celebrities, with Lillian Russell, Diamond Jim Brady, Sitting Bull, Admiral Dewey and William Jennings Bryan prominent among them, was scheduled. Then would follow a series of acts with a Gay Nineties color marked by a great deal of dancing: Alexis Kosloff offering classic ballet, Ruth Schrader leading a reborn Floradora Sextet, black dances, a can-can number, a bathing beauty number, tap dances and a cake walk. Eminent flutist George Barrere would lead a classical band, and Ernie's Jazz Band would also play. The John L. Sullivan-Jim Corbett heavyweight fight would be reenacted. Ned Thatcher would devise "fountain effects." Director of the whole show would be Walter Steinhilber. [5]

A week before the Festival Day the anti-Festival forces hit hard. The blow was delivered by means of a broadside sent by mail, addressed to the "Citizens of Woodstock," and signed by "The Committee of Fifty." The heart of the message was an appeal to "good thinking people" to report all "wild parties," nude bathing, indecent dress and indecent behavior to "Kingston 489, which is the Sheriff's Office. The office is open day and night. . . . With such cooperation no element in the community will be able to destroy the charm and attraction of Woodstock for all."

The committee's broadside precipitated as vigorous a controversy as Woodstock has ever endured. An investigation disclosed that the anonymous members of the Committee of Fifty were actually only four, including the pastors of the Dutch Reformed and Methodist churches, Harvey Todd and William Peckham. Two days after the letter was sent The New York *Times Sunday Magazine* added to the excitement by publishing a long account of Woodstock under the title, "An Eden of Artists Fights a Serpent." The *Times* serpent was not the committee but Woodstock's threatened change from an art colony to a summer resort.

Though the Maverick Festivals, wrote the *Times'* R. L. Duffus, were "a means of enabling people to get rid of their inhibitions," so many inhibitions had been shed at the 1928 Festival that there had been talk in Woodstock of giving them up. The 1929 Festival was critical, Duffus reported. It was expected "to decide the issue of whether or not to continue the annual celebrations or orgies as they had come more and more to be called." [6]

Hervey White paused in his Festival preparations long enough to do his best to bring peace. Since his early years in Woodstock he had made an effort to become acquainted with the town's ministers. He once wrote that Woodstock ministers were in a difficult position since they had far more conventional education and exposure to the outside world than did the members of their flocks. He respected the clergymen and enjoyed exchanging views with them. He was not being naive or insincere, as some thought, when he let the public know that he thanked "his rural neighbors sponsored as they are by their pastors Mr. Todd and Mr. Peckham for their friendly assistance and advice . . . in their attempt to bring back an old-time Festival."

He got ready for what he was sure would be the biggest festival ever. Trees were cut down in order to enlarge the Maverick parking lot. [7]

Faced with so much argument and conflict some art-colony people withheld their usual help in staging the Festival. An air of worried expectancy pervaded Woodstock. No one was surprised to find that the 1929 Festival drew the largest attendance of any ever held. The New York *Herald Tribune* estimated six thousand paid admissions. Other estimators added gatecrashers to bring the total as high as eight thousand.

The state police tried to keep order and prevent violence, not always with success. Highways were blocked; cars and people clogged the center of Woodstock as it had never been clogged before. Contemporary accounts of the 1929 Festival vary with the prejudices of the reporters. None questioned that unprecedented publicity had made the Festival a crowd-attracting and moneymaking triumph. The character of the entertainment offered and the lessened degree to which art-colony people shared in putting on and enjoying the event provoked disquiet.

One newpaper found the Festival to be "just about as sinful as a Thursday night meeting of the Ladies Aid Society." Another described dancers coming on stage "in succession with a closer and closer approach to complete nudity. . . ." Detecting less gaiety than usual, The New York *World* said "the old Greek spirit has been abased by a squad of state police, a recrudescence of Puritanism, and hordes of fat, goggle-eyed curiosity-seekers. . . ." [8]

Less than a month after the end of the Festival of 1929 the stock market embarked on a series of precipitous declines. The national economy gave indication that all was not well in many aspects of American economic life. In Woodstock as elsewhere in the country few people saw the dismal events as anything but short-term setbacks. President Hoover reassured the nation with cheerful comments.

Throughout the winter there was much discussion in Woodstock as to whether the Festivals should go on. Newpapers usually expressed doubt. But Hervey's friend, Tom Comerford, in his Kingston *Daily Leader*, was confident of the future. He wrote, "The Maverick Festival is and has been receiving so much publicity that it is safe to assert that it will be held again and again and again. . . ." Comerford had helped mightily in building up Festival publicity. He was described when he died in the 1930s as having been the art colony's and the Maverick's best friend.

Comerford, as it turned out, was at least partly right. Preparations for a 1930 Festival went forward against a background of increasing economic dislocation. In Woodstock people were handing round a rumor that the town board was trying hard to find some legal technique by which another Maverick Festival might be headed off. Hervey White stated boldly that the coming Festival would be "the most stupendous event ever held in America." [9]

Somewhat discredited, The Committee of Fifty continued active. Prospects for the 1930 Festival began to dim even in Hervey's mind.

He found many of his old art-colony helpers disinclined to help in what was beginning to seem a doubtful venture. Hervey then turned over the major entertainment feature to professional theater people named Viehman and Beckhard. In the hope of soothing the critics he announced that the costume dance which as usual would bring the Festival to a close would be held not in the Concert Hall, whose dark surrounding woods had been the scene of the rowdy events of recent Festivals, but in the Woodstock Valley Hotel in the very center of the hamlet of Woodstock.

The Festival was held as scheduled in September. During the afternoon the Ithaca Conservatory band under the baton of Ernest Williams played and staged a "colored wedding," with the roles of groom, bride and priest played by clarinet, oboe and bassoon, respectively. Next came a boxing match, and then an exhibition of the Dyrus and Edith Cook camping project, complete with the burros used by the Cooks to take people on guided tours of the Catskills from their Woodstock base. After the usual picnic suppers and the "Grand Promenade of Costumed Revellers," to quote the program, Viehman and Beckhard presented a three-hour vaudeville show of acts brought in from New York.

At nine that evening Felix Kolb, a Rochester, New York dancer who had taken part in previous Festivals and had taught in Woodstock, augmented twenty professional dancers with some of his local students in a dance concert. At eleven the "Festival Ball" began. The 1930 program entirely lacked the spectacular visual features provided for earlier Festivals by art-colony people working long hours for no reward beyond the satisfaction of their creative urge.

Given this and the declining state of the economy, fewer customers than in previous years showed up. Because of its location, the Festival Ball gave less work to the police. But it irritated the townspeople. The comings and goings of dancers and their cars, the shouts, and the laughter and screams mingled with the sound of the orchestra did not allow hamlet people to sleep that night. Some stood in the streets until dawn brought peace staring at the brightly lighted hotel, making derogatory remarks about Hervey's Festivals.[10]

Once again people expressed doubt about whether the Festivals would continue. Once again Hervey decided to hold another celebration the next year. Woodstock people had become increasingly more polarized into pro- and anti-Festivalites. In this state of feelings all sorts of incidents came to be drawn into the continuous controversy, sometimes punctuated by harsh words and displays of prejudice. Yet Hervey remained hopeful.

The next summer an epidemic of infantile paralysis played a part in the tangled cluster of emotions which was affecting the future of the Maverick Festivals. The epidemic had begun in Brooklyn and then slowly swept upstate. By mid-August or so twenty cases were reported in Ulster County. Health officials were urging parents to refrain from doing anything that might bring their children into contact with visitors from the infected areas.

As the warning went out, Hervey White came to an agreement with the Rev. Harvey Todd and the other members of the Four to use a religious theme, the Children's Crusade, for his 1931 Festival. Costumed village children between the ages of six and thirteen would march from the Village Green in front of the Dutch Reformed Church in the afternoon and take part in a pageant based on the crusade of the year 1212. Some saw Hervey's Children's Crusade plan as a craven caving in to the clergy. Many declared the subject inappropriate to the Maverick. But the Woodstock children volunteered with alacrity. Rehearsals were begun in the Athletic Hall on Rock City Road.

A week before the Festival day Hervey announced that because of the danger to the children from the polio epidemic the Children's Crusade theme was being cancelled. Instead the local riding academies which had arisen during the Twenties would stage a riding event in the afternoon. Old Jim Twaddell would drive a coach that would be held up by bandits. During the evening professionals would give a vaudeville show. There would be no dance following the evening performance.[11]

Hervey White then publicly recognized the advent of the Great Depression. He urged those who'd had a bad year to come to the Festival and forget their troubles and those who'd had a good year to come to celebrate.

Newspapers made much of the disorder of previous Festivals. The Kingston *Daily Freeman* reported that bootleggers had been observed scurrying down from the mountains and converging on the Maverick in the days before the event. The papers also told of the Maverick's national fame and of the celebrities a festivalgoer might expect to see.

It was rumored in town and reported in the *Daily Freeman* that the Reverend Harvey Todd of the Committee of Four (or Fifty) had been so pleased with the original intention of the Festival organizers to stage their Children's Crusade spectacular that he had promised to stay away and to persuade the other local clergymen to do likewise. Earlier, the impression had spread in town that the clergy would censor the Festival in person on the spot.

A Woodstock publication called *Art Notes*, subsidized by Woodstock Chamber of Commerce members, was mollified by the apparent success of the Committee of Four. It took a conciliatory attitude, aiming at retaining the profit-making potential of the Festivals now that they appeared to have been bowdlerized. Said *Art Notes*, "For many years the Woodstockers avoided the festival as something not of their own. . . . Now Hervey White wants to make a radical change, and to be successful he needs all of Woodstock behind him. So won't you all, village folks, artists and summer visitors, come and make the Festival this year something you can enjoy?"

The *Daily Freeman* was less concilatory. It stated that "the Left Wingers in the Artists vs. Churchmen fight, that is to say the radicals and free-thinkers, are prophesying . . . that the 'Children's Crusade' will turn out to be a wild party." The almost-last-minute switch from the Children's Crusade theme to vaudeville came too late to be digested and reported in any depth by the newspapers. As the day of the Festival arrived there was general agreement that this year would be critical. If it succeeded, the Festivals would go on. If not they would end.

The Festival of 1931 was not a success. Attendance was a mere six hundred and the event lost money. After the show had ended on the night of September 4, diehard Maverick supporters rushed the Athletic Hall and put on an impromptu dance. But even to the dancers it should have been obvious that the series of sixteen Maverick Festivals had come to an end. Unemployment and bank and business failures were giving signs that what would soon be known as the Great Depression had arrived. Years of wrangling over the claimed immorality of the Festivals, combined with undistinguished productions, dwindling attendance and the withdrawal from participation in staging the event by many art-colony people, had led Hervey to conclude that his Festivals "had run out and become profitless." [12]

The purpose of the Festivals—the paying off of Mr. Rockafeller and the financing of the Maverick as an arts-and-crafts colony—had been achieved. There was no longer any good reason for struggling against the combined forces of the economic depression and the anti-

Festivalites. Though still in vigorous health in his sixties, Hervey felt a lessening of his former drive. In 1931 Hull House was a long way in Hervey's past. The objectives which had seemed so attainable under the influence of the glamor of Hull House had faded. The Maverick had not become the heart of the "social unit" of craftsmen and artists the way Hervey had once hoped. The Maverick Festivals had been distorted by the strength of forces which were leading deeper and deeper into an industrialized and materialistic society. They were offering something not too different from the kind of entertainment available on Broadway and in a thousand Main Streets across the country.

The Committee of Four had won "the battle of the artists vs. churchmen." Yet, as the Great Depression descended on the land, many of the committee's business supporters wondered if they had not in their zeal for "cleaning up" the art colony cut off a vital source of income for themselves.

45

WRITERS, RADIO
AND PHYSICAL FITNESS

During the 1920s the annual
Maverick Festival had come to be accepted as one of the higher points
of the Woodstock year, equal in its power to arouse anticipation and
emotion to the Fourth of July and Christmas. In between these high
points Woodstock people were responding to the varied pressures of
the times. For one thing, they were getting used to the coming and
going of many young writers, whose attention the Woodstock of the
Twenties had caught and who had been tempted to give the place a
try. For another, Woodstock people were adjusting to many changes in
daily life. And they were experiencing one event which demonstrated
that given a strong enough motivation all classes in the community
might cooperate for the common good.

While early Byrdcliffe was best known as an arts-and-crafts
colony, it had been hospitable to writers drawn in some cases by
Hervey White's gift for friendship and by the respect he had earned by
his early novels. These writers also found Ralph Whitehead a
sympathetic presence. They were glad to use the splendid library he
cheerfully offered for their use. Early Byrdcliffe writers tended to be
people who did not stray too far from the accepted literary
conventions of their time. Most were without much originality and did
not foreshadow the future. They have faded to dim shadows in the
cellars of literary history.

Charlotte Perkins Gilman's standing in the women's liberation movement made her summer at the Lark's Nest an event to be remembered. Her *Women and Economics* and her utopian novel *Herland* have recently been reprinted. But Charlotte Gilman's followers Harriet Howe, who wrote poetry, and Edith Wherry, who wrote novels, are unlikely ever to grope their way out of obscurity.[1]

Some Byrdcliffe writers joined the painters who congregated at Rock City. Editor and poet Isabel Moore and poet Grace Fallow Norton (the wife of painter George Macrum) both became members of the Rock City group. Wallace Stevens was one poet of decided stature who spent some time at Byrdcliffe in 1915. Richard LeGallienne first lived close to the hamlet of Woodstock on what is now called Plochmann Lane; later he bought the Birge Harrison house across the western edge of Byrdcliffe.

On Ohayo Mountain across the valley of the Sawkill from Byrdcliffe, Walter Weyl, economist and political idea man, worked on his influential books, of which *The New Democracy* is the best known. There Weyl and his wife Bertha, a Hull House alumna and the sister of social worker and proletarian novelist Ernest Poole, entertained many of the leading figures in the liberal political movements which had centered around Theodore Roosevelt's Progressive Party. Weyl was one of the editors and founders of *The New Republic*. He died in 1921.[2]

Among the writers was Hart Crane, who, although he remained in Woodstock only two months in 1923, yet managed to convey in a series of letters an absorbing picture of the colony's life on the level Crane knew, a level on which writers explored, and, in Crane's case, recorded the Woodstock scene.

In October 1923 Crane left New York and the job as advertising copywriter that he hated. As a poet he had learned much from the French Symbolists, especially Mallarme, Laforgue and Rimbaud. Like these poets he had come to believe that he could write best when in an altered state of consciousness brought on by alcohol or sexual exaltation. But prolonged heavy drinking and a love affair with a sailor had left him only depressed and weakened.

It was in the hope of recovering both his physical strength and his ability to write poetry that he made for Woodstock, a place of which he had been hearing a great deal. With Malcolm Cowley, then known as a Dadaist poet, Crane headed first for the large country house of Eugene O'Neill at Ridgefield, Connecticut. There, Crane wrote, he had "a roisterous time. Cider, belly dances and cake walks . . . and we didn't get to bed until daylight." Then Mrs. O'Neill drove him to Woodstock.

For over two months Crane lived in an old house on Plochmann Lane as the guest of two friends, Slater Brown, the writer who figures so largely in e.e. cummings' *The Enormous Room*, and painter Edward Nagle, who was then contributing drawings to *The Dial*. The house was an interesting one. Starting off as the farmhouse of Livingston tenant Philip Finger on "Livingston's twelve hundred acres" in Great Lot 26, it was eventually bought by George Plochmann, who soon built nearby a house designed with musical performances in mind.

Plochmann sold the old house to an inventor named Enoch Rector, a strong and eccentric character who had worked with Thomas Edison on developing sound recording and motion pictures. Rector's daughter, a painter, was Nagle's wife. Though Crane knew little of the background of the house, he found both it and the kind of life lived there delightful.

The Woodstock landscape impressed Crane. "There isn't any more beautiful country in this continent than right here," he wrote. "The mountains around here are so beautiful in their various aspects and under different skies . . . they are very much an easy and careless part of a natural landscape." Crane found life among the art-colony people as appealing as the landscape in which it was set. Malcolm Cowley too remembered Woodstock of the early Twenties as "a wonderful unspoiled place . . . with serious and intelligent artists about." Crane heartily agreed with this and embarked on what may well have been the happiest part of his tragic life.[3]

It was a time when all the art-colony people (except for the landed gentry among them) religiously cut with axes and hand saws the wood with which they heated their houses. Crane found his own wood-cutting rites exhilarating. He reported to friends that he grew stronger and healthier daily. At the same time he shared with zest in the lively social life of the colony. There was much visiting back and forth, many parties to attend. And there were hikes around town and up Overlook Mountain. All this gave room for a good deal of conversation about art and life.

Thanksgiving Day was a highlight of Crane's time in Woodstock. Among dinner guests that day were novelist John Dos Passos, Stewart Mitchell (who was on the staff of *The Dial*), and sculptor Gaston Lachaise and his wife. The hosts decorated the studio attached to the old farmhouse with pine boughs. Crane stuffed the turkey, which was cooked on a spit in front of the studio fireplace. After dinner Crane made a funeral speech over the turkey's bones and then cremated them in the fire. That night brought dancing and a good deal of drinking of Marsala and local red wine, hard cider and cherry cordial. The party danced until after three a.m. to the music of phonograph records.

William Murrell (Fisher), who lived nearby, was a frequent visitor. When Crane once spent an evening at Murrell's house, Murrell showed him the manuscripts of Samuel Bernhard Greenberg's poems. Crane became so stirred that he sat up late reading them. "No grammar, nor spelling nor scarcely any form, but a quality that is unspeakable eerie and the most convincing gusto. One little poem is as good as any of the consciously conceived 'Pierrots' of Laforgue." [4]

Crane put together a collage of fragments from Greenberg in a poem called "Emblems of Conduct," which appeared in 1926 in Crane's book *White Buildings*, but without credit being given to Greenberg. After Crane's death by suicide in 1932 this resulted in charges of plagiarism. The collage and his letters were the chief products of Crane's Woodstock period. The exhilaration and sense of robust good health which resulted from the out-of-doors fury of wood-cutting and the pleasures of life in the colony did not provide the state of consciousness which Crane found favorable to work. Too many afternoons were taken up with talking with friends, with dancing, at which Crane considered himself an adept, and with drinking.

In Woodstock as in other American places Prohibition, which had been imposed in 1919, was changing American drinking habits. The art-colony people bought hard cider and elderberry wine by the jug or barrel from local makers; some gathered elderberries or elderberry blossoms and made their own. In the cellar of the old Philip Finger farmhouse in which Crane lived was a whole barrel of elderberry wine which was precious in the eyes of its owner, old Enoch Rector.

The presence of the wine was too much of a temptation for Crane and his friends. Little by little they lowered the level of the wine until it approached low tide. At that point Rector arrived to spend a few days. He upset the usual course of life in the house with his sputtering and smelly car, which was equipped with a kerosene-fueled engine of his own invention, and with his descent into the cellar, a small pitcher in hand, to inspect his barrel of wine. As Crane and his friends held their breaths Rector came up the stairs without having detected the unhappy state of his barrel. He poured out a small glass of wine for each guest, and all drank guiltily.

Crane's delight in Woodstock and his enjoyment of art-colony life could not continue for long. He was broke and living as a guest of Brown and Nagle, contributing toward household expenses only the tiny amount sent him by his family back home in Ohio. It was necessary for him to get back to working at a job, even an unpleasant one. And here a chance seemed to turn up of both a job and an indefinitely prolonged stay in Woodstock.

A few days before Crane arrived in Woodstock the second Overlook Mountain House had burned down. A caretaker had been installed in one of the several buildings which remained intact close to the ruins of the hotel. In one of these there lived two horses, a cow, and a flock of chickens, and in another the caretaker. The caretaker was not pleased with his isolated job. When Crane told him he'd like to take it on, the caretaker was agreeable.

Crane at the time imagined himself a hardy country dweller, at home with all the buffetings and endearments of nature. He wrote critic Gorham Munson of his Overlook hopes that "It would be a hard winter, perhaps a terrific experience. . . . I'm strongly tempted and would like to try out loneliness and hurricanes and drifts at the pleasant risk of only monthly or bi-monthly visits to the nether world of common speech," Crane wrote to hotel owner Morris Newgold. For whatever reason, he was rejected. Early in January he left Woodstock forever.[5]

Crane's letters show that the line in art-colony tradition that separated the artists and the local people was still holding firm through the Twenties. The presence of the art colony continued to guarantee prosperity to the people who provided food, fuel, shelter and services. Except for Hervey White, however, the art-colony people seldom showed an acceptance of the older Woodstockers as social equals.

The local people often found the artists' ways irritating. They were especially annoyed at the artists' refusal to join or attend their churches. When local Roman Catholics built St. Joan of Arc's Chapel in 1923 and some art-colony people organized a Christian Science Church, members of the town's earlier churches were not warm in their welcome.

If artists did not attend local church services, they often did attend traditional church suppers. But here awkward incidents sometimes happened which have gone into local folklore. One such story tells of John (Jack) Bentley's attempt to attend a pancake supper at the Dutch Reformed Church. Bentley, an early art student and landscape painter, had heard that the supper was to be held but had not been told that it was to be followed by a lecture with slides on Chinese missionary work. A bit befuddled by hard cider Bentley arrived at the church late, found the basement darkened for the lecture and burst into the room shouting, "Where the hell are those damned pancakes?" [6]

Not long after Bentley's adventure in the church basement the darkness of Woodstock nights began to be modified by electric lights. In March 1922 the Woodstock Electric Light and Power Company, organized by local people, asked the town board to grant it a franchise to furnish the town with electricity from a local plant using the energy of the upper Sawkill. The town board put the request on the table, and soon a competitor, the United Hudson Electric Corporation (a predecessor of the present Central Hudson Corporation), also requested a franchise—and received it.

Before this there had been a few gasoline-powered electric generators in use at Byrdcliffe, in hotels, and in a few other places. In 1924 the lines of the United Hudson Corporation made their way to Woodstock and Bearsville from a plant in Saugerties. Some people had their houses wired with a single bulb hanging from the center of the ceiling of each room. And when the current was turned on they were appalled by the brightness and crudity of the resulting illumination. Every flaw in their household furnishings was shown up. Old people swore that reading or living by so fierce a light was impossible.

Soon, however, people learned about table lamps and shades, and the new kind of light was accepted. The artists centered criticism around the street lights proposed for the center of Woodstock hamlet. They were reluctant to see Woodstock losing the charm which it had exerted over them in the past. A. B. Campbell-Shields, a lecturer for a rival of Christian Science called New Thought, addressed a protest meeting on the Village Green by the light of Japanese lanterns strung on wires overhead. An unexpected windy shower was said to have put out the lanterns as Campbell-Shields was denouncing electric street lights.

What happened the day before Christmas of 1924 made the Campbell-Shields adherents feel a sense of triumph. The electric power failed. Woodstock's first electric Christmas was carried on by candlelight. Kerosene lamps were brought down from attics and used to light shop windows filled with Christmas merchandise. Some church services were postponed and parties cancelled. The townspeople were angry because they felt that the power company showed little concern for them. Many urged that the franchise be taken away and given to Woodstock's own company. But eventually the power went on and the "distant power corporation" retained its franchise. Interruptions of power were frequent for years.[7]

Radio began to be talked about after the World War's end. There was great interest in radio by both artists and local people. Battery-powered sets came into use. Some boys and young men made their own using galena crystals as detectors. Talk of the great possibilities of the new invention bubbled among the art-colony people. The finest music would soon be available to everyone at any time in their own living rooms. Lessons in languages, science, history, painting and sculpture would be sent out over the air waves. The level of popular sensitivity to the arts and of knowledge of the modern world would rise to a point at which society would be revolutionized.

But all this was only a dream. As early as 1917 radio operator David Sarnoff had pushed for a link between radio programming and advertising. By the time Coolidge prosperity was spreading its blessings over the country the advertising business had taken control of radio. For a time some degree of hope persisted that the public interest might yet prevail.

On January 8, 1925 local people drawn from many levels of the community staged a Woodstock Show on Kingston station WDGZ, operated by the Ulster County Boy Scouts and located in Kingston's City Hall. Clara Wullner Chichester played classical pieces on the piano. Her husband Cecil sang comic songs. Jack Roublou, handicapped veteran of the British army, gave English and Scottish ballads. Lighter music including "The Overlook Blues" was played by Clarence Bolton, artist-printer and with his wife onetime proprietors of The Nook (later the Cafe Espresso). Birge Harrison was prevented by a bad cold from talking on "Old Times in Woodstock," but Dr. Downer came through with an instructive discussion of "Our Unseen Foes," these being the causes of infectious diseases. And there was more—the reading of poems by Richard LeGallienne (who was away on a lecture tour), and so on.[8]

Woodstock had hopes the program would be picked up by one of the networks then spreading their grip over the air. But nothing of the sort happened and the programs came to an end. They could never play the part of a cultural missionaries from Woodstock to the rest of the country. Beside being too narrowly local in their makeup, they were hopelessly ill-suited to earn profits. Yet in one way the

Woodstock Show proved a success. With electricity available in the most heavily populated parts of the town it boosted the sale of radio sets in a splendid manner. This was the beginning of a period when radio comedians, sports broadcasters, popular music performers and the stars of serial radio plays became local as well as national heroes.

The ever-increasing improvement and production of power-driven tools and appliances and their skillful advertising in the booming 1920s began to make obsolete the old local custom of cutting ice and storing it for summer use, and brought in electric refrigerators. Once men and boys had gathered to cut ice on Cooper Lake, Jones' Pond, Yankeetown Pond, Mead's Pond and every other sizeable body of water in town. Ice houses were built or dug into banks. Cakes of ice were packed there in sawdust to await use in the hot days of summer.

Electric water pumps made bathrooms possible for more and more people. Wood and coal lost out to oil, bottled gas and later on electricity as a cooking fuel. Life was being made more comfortable, though at a loss of the independence which had once made many a Woodstock household able to get along through the winter on its own, with cellar and barn stocked with food and with the woodlot contributing warmth.[9]

By the Twenties most Woodstock mills had converted to steam or gasoline power. Some conservatives, like the owners of the turning mill in Shady, still clung to waterpower. The artists applauded this kind of conservatism for aesthetic reasons. Local people usually were firmly on the side of what they called progress.

Yet when the interests of the town groups seemed to coincide they could agree to work together. One such instance came along when the Woodstock Athletic Club was organized in 1924. The fashion for physical fitness launched during the World War and given a symbol by Walter Camp's exercises, known as the "daily dozen," was something in which Byrdcliffe, the Maverick and the village people could join.

On the board of directors of the Woodstock Athletic Club were Ralph Whitehead. Alice Wardwell, John F. Carlson, Hervey White, George Bellows, Frank B. Happy, Dr. Downer and George Neher. The club bought what is now the town's main recreational field from farmer Cyrus Russell. It initiated basketball locally, with games in the former Art Students League studio in The Pines, even before the Club was properly put together. Programs were begun for citizens of all ages and both sexes. Plans were made for a tennis court and a building to be used for basketball, billiards and so on. The club sponsored a good baseball team. A holding company was formed and stock was offered to the public.

The Club's achievements were not as great as had been hoped. The stock did not sell well. Yet the recreational field, now called Andy Lee Field, remains to tell of the enthusiasm for physical fitness of the Athletic Club's founders.[10]

Another example of local cooperation followed a bitter collision between Kingston and Woodstock in 1922. Most Woodstock people of all sorts were then brought together into an effective defensive force. At issue was the extent to which Kingston controlled the waters of the Sawkill.

Ever since Kingston had first acquired the right to use the water of the Sawkill, disputes had been frequent. Summer boardinghouses and millowners established on the Beaverkill and Sawkill had protested that their trout fishing or water power was diminished by Kingston's demands. The safety of the dam at Cooper Lake was questioned. Periods of drought forced Kingston to supplement the dwindling water from the Sawkill and Cooper Lake with water from the contaminated Esopus. And at the same time dry summers provoked some Woodstock people to agitate for abrogating the Kingston rights to Woodstock water in order that their own town might use it.

James M. Caird, the chemist of the Kingston water department, reported early in May of 1915 that the Sawkill water supply was "practically sterile and absolutely pure." The water was filtered before entering the pipe leading from the Kingston reservoir in Zena after it had flowed through the open Sawkill as it wound its way through Shady, Bearsville and the hamlet of Woodstock.[11]

With pollution a greater possibility as Woodstock grew, this state of things could not go on. The piecemeal way in which the Kingston water rights had been assembled since their beginnings in the 1870s had not been favorable for the obtaining of riparian rights along the Sawkill. Kingston claimed the right to enforce sanitary regulations all along the Sawkill. But since Kingston had only scattered riparian rights some Woodstock people refused access to their property to the water inspectors.

By the spring of 1922 it became obvious that the question of Kingston's rights to control the use of the Sawkill had reached a point of crisis. By then the Woodstock art colony was growing rapidly. Buildings were crowding the banks of the Sawkill. Restaurants, speakeasies and boardinghouses were threatening to send a flood of sewage toward or even directly into the Sawkill.

Even if the Kingston water supply was still pure and wholesome, now new factors were making Kingston people feel uneasy. The new people crowding into Woodstock each summer no longer had that look of genteel prosperity which had marked many of the Byrdcliffe arts-and-crafters of the colony's beginnngs. More were eccentric in their dress and hair styles. More and more came from Greenwich Village, which was being written about in the newspapers as a lair of unwashed, unsavory people who idled away their lives behind a pretense of being artists. When these people discovered Woodstock they found few aspects of local life more appealing than bathing in the rocky pools which the Sawkill offered between its many falls and rapids.[12]

WATER RIGHTS AND NEWCOMERS

Kingston people who came to Woodstock to visit the art exhibitions or "to look at the artists" carried home tales of having seen strange sights as they crossed Riseley's Bridge. There bizarre-looking people who seemed to conform very closely to the newspaper descriptions of Greenwich Villagers were seen cavorting in the rock-edged pools in such numbers as to leave little room for the respectable summer boarders at the Riseley boardinghouse across the road.

Very soon a tide of apprehension rose in Kingston. Word of what was going on in their water supply spread from street to street. Some frightened Kingstonians set about opening up wells disused since back in their grandparents' time. Others applied pressure on their city officials. The officials responded by placing signs forbidding bathing in the Riseley's Bridge pool and others, and threatening dire legal penalties to Sawkill bathers.

Woodstock bathers were astonished to learn that Kingston had what its officials believed to be a sound legal basis for their signs. They had quietly arranged leases of water rights with the largest propertyowners on the Sawkill as it flowed through the hamlet. Among the owners were people who were close to the life of the art colony, Carl Eric and Louise Lindin, Gabrielle Moncure, Mr. and Mrs. Neilson Parker (Mrs. Parker had been Zulma Steele, the Byrdcliffe craftswoman and designer), and Louise Sully, widow of Dan Sully.

Dr. Downer vigorously urged Woodstock people to bathe in the Sawkill for the benefit of their health. Social worker Paul Kennaday and A. B. Campbell-Shields called a mass meeting held in the Firemen's Hall. Resolutions denouncing Kingston's action were passed. Money was pledged to provide for the bail and defense of any bathers who might be arrested. It was decided to hold a meeting the next morning on the Village Green, and from there to march to the Riseley's Bridge pool and defy Kingston by jumping in.[1]

A marvellously miscellaneous group of about a hundred people met on the Green in the morning and set off for the pool, led by a man on horseback and a fat man with a baby perched on his shoulder. Some who came as mere spectators were said to have been so carried away by the spirit of the occasion that they too dived in, clothes and all.

The *Daily Freeman* of Kingston reported the mass bathing party under a bold headline:

100 Assert "Right to Swim" in City's Drinking Water

Artistic Temperament of Transplanted Greenwich Villagers in Woodstock Breaks out in a New Form of "Self Expression" Which Involves Bathing on City's Property and Polluting City's Water Supply

The headline and the story beneath did more than retell the facts about the swimming party. It exposed the hostility felt by many Kingstonians toward the unconventional people streaming into postwar Woodstock. The story tried to make the point that the bathers were not solid Woodstock citizens but the scorned Greenwich Villagers. Yet this was not altogether the case. While oldtime Woodstockers were not conspicuous in the agitation against Kingston's assertion of riparian rights on the Sawkill, they were strongly behind it. One indication of this came when Woodstock's town board, on which neither Greenwich Villagers nor artists were represented, denounced Kingston's signing of leases deliberately intended to keep local people away from the banks of their stream.

As Woodstock stood firm, Kingston took strong action. It obtained injunctions forbidding Dr. Downer, Paul Kennaday, Campbell-Shields and a number of other from bathing in the Sawkill or inciting other to do so. Woodstock's health officer, Dr. Downer, was Kingston's principal target. When Kingston hesitated to carry out its threat to arrest the bathers Woodstock people continued to bathe, although in smaller numbers. An impasse seemed to have been reached. But Kingston did not give up.[2]

544

In 1927 New York State inspectors were enlisted by Kingston to study the Sawkill and its tributaries. The inspectors found many polluters. Some polluters, including Ralph Whitehead and Rufus Van de Bogart, complied with the inspector's recommendations, but many others held back. Jim Twaddell positively refused to clean up his pigsty. Chauncey Snyder, offered a free new privy if he would demolish his old one, would have none of it.

The Kingston *Daily Freeman* carried a front-page story about fearful sanitary conditions among the pigs at the Cooper barns on Cooper Lake, which were actually the property of their own water department, and urged action. And soon action came. The City of Kingston, faced with so much opposition from Woodstock people, abandoned its program of inspection and insistence on compliance.

By 1929 the city had completed the installation of a cast-iron pipe to carry the water from Cooper Lake and the Upper Sawkill on a six-mile trip beneath the hamlets of Woodstock, Bearsville and Zena. The plea of the new-born Woodstock Chamber of Commerce to grant Woodstock the right to install fire hydrants along the line of the pipe was rejected, but the courts decided that Woodstock might use the water of the Sawkill and the Mink Hollow stream above the Kingston intakes, should it be able to devise a way of getting it where it was wanted.[3]

After that, bathing in the Sawkill was resumed at a livelier clip than ever. A major threat to the booming of the town had been removed. Without a bathing place the art colony might have become less attractive. For the many pools in the Sawkill had been one of the summer charms of Woodstock ever since the beginning of summer boarding in the town.

The Art Students League had made Sawkill pools social centers as well as places which students living without bathtubs might soap and scrub. Natural pools like those of the Sawkill also had great visual charm for the art-colony people. They were aware that pools like these had long been favorite subjects for landscape painters. John F. Kensett had become famous largely because of his devotion to Catskill Mountain pools. His modestly-sized paintings and those of many followers looked out of heavy gold frames in innumerable American parlors.

As the booming Twenties got up steam natural rocky pools lost some of their charisma. Artificial concrete swimming pools, once possessions of the very rich alone, began appearing on the lawns of upward-climbing suburbanites. These pools rapidly became conspicuous symbols of the acquisition of a more than generous share of Coolidge prosperity. In Woodstock artificial-pool-minded people took an ever-larger part in the colony's summer life and brought about many changes.

Most conspicuous among these was Joseph Patrick McEvoy. McEvoy was well rewarded by almost everything he undertook. As a writer at first of very remunerative greeting-card verses, then of novels, plays and the comic strip Dixie Dugan, McEvoy took immense pleasure in his prosperity and his Broadway and Hollywood ties. In 1924 he bought the old James Johnson house and its surrounding farm acreage on the Bearsville-Woodstock road (the place was later known as Woodstock Estates). He remodelled and enlarged the buildings into a splendor which would have dazzled the Johnsons.[4]

This was a period when prosperous Americans, including some with connections with the arts, were taking to making over and greatly expanding old farmhouses in such favored places as Fairfield County, Connecticut, Bucks County, Pennsylvania and similar centers. These little estates impressed the surrounding population with their swimming pools, barbecue pits and farm outbuildings converted into play rooms, all set in the midst of artfully landscaped stone-paved terraces, broad lawns and winding streams. All these soon became features in dwindled form of many surburban dwellings of modest scale throughout the country.

McEvoy, who had come to Woodstock at the urging of novelist and editor Manuel Komroff, in turn urged others to come. His house on its knoll off the Bearsville road was filled weekends with famous Hollywood and Broadway actors, actresses and producers, comic-strip artists, musicians, cartoonists, novelists and others who found work in the arts capable of providing enough income to support this moneyed way of existence.

The McEvoy kind of life was very different from that which Hart Crane had reported among the "serious" artists and writers who were his Woodstock friends. It was very different too from the Byrdcliffe style, or that of the Art Students League people or the colony's successful painters like Bellows and Speicher. But it was much admired by local people, whose prosperity had become so closely linked to the spending of money by the colony people.

Under the urging of the boom spirit and the introduction among them of a more hedonistic style of living, these people altered their own ways. Their lives became less church-centered. Some took to spending winters in Florida as many of the art-colony people did. Their children went on to high school in Kingston and a few even to college.

The McEvoy style was also in great enough contrast to that of the poorer painters, poets, craftsmen, musicians and others who were filling Woodstock's rooming houses, corn cribs, barns and even obsolete chicken houses each summer. It was in greater and very striking contrast to the restrained kind of life which had once filled the old Johnson homestead.[5]

James Johnson, born in 1801, had become a Livingston tenant and had worked his forty-two acres on the long-settled Bearsville Flats. Johnson had married Elizabeth Shultis, the widow of a local Elting. The pair had a large family. Two daughters died young in the 1840s. Two sons enlisted in the Civil War, and only one came back alive. When the Woodstock Methodist Church was founded in 1831 James Johnson was among its promoters. He shared too in the establishment of Woodstock's cemetery (in which the burial of blacks was forbidden) a year later. He is not known to have been active in the Anti-Rent War or in politics. He kept his mind on his farm work, farming to such good effect that he became moderately prosperous, bought his own farm from Montgomery Livingston, and bought and operated another farm in addition to his own.

When he died at eighty-nine he was able to leave his son Thomas lands valued by the assessor at close to four thousand dollars. He left legacies of several hundred dollars in cash to each of many children and grandchildren (in 1876 James had disinherited his son Eugene for what reason we do not know).

It was on the same stage on which James and Elizabeth Johnson had played out their life drama, and where Thomas and Adeline had followed them, to be succeeded by Thomas' son Ransom and his wife, that McEvoy staged the Woodstock part of his own life story to the accompaniment not of hymns sung to the music of the parlor organ but of jazz. The talk was not of crops, cows and hopes of a life to come but of Broadway and Hollywood hits, gossip about theater people, doings of the rich in Paris and on the Riviera. Elsewhere in Woodstock during the Twenties, other old farmhouses were being transformed to new uses by newly arrived possessors.[6]

Conspicuous among these was an old farm lying on fifty flat acres beside a bend in the Sawkill in Zena. With its outbuildings the old stone house ended its long career as a working farm during the boom of the Twenties and was reborn as the country estate of prosperous woolens manufacturer Alfred De Liagre and his wife Frida. The place acquired all the signs of being in the hands of sensitive and rich owner of the time. It had a Colonial quality of an accepted character inside and out. The smokehouse and other farm buildings were adapted to fresh uses. There was a swimming pool. A hedge separated the house from the eyes of passersby on the public road while permitting glimpses of the handsome buildings and landscaping.

Early in 1930 the place was sold to an owner who aroused intense local interest. B. H. Schulte was said to be the proprietor of a lengthy chain of optometric establishments. In the shop window of each was a "hand-painted" oil portrait of a man or a woman on which a pair of genuine Schulte eyeglasses had been fastened in a Dada-like gesture. These portraits became the trademarks in the public mind of Schulte products and services.

Schulte's patronage of art seemed to give his presence in the colony an odd appropriateness. He announced that an increase in the grandeur of his place was to occur. He was having a landing field for planes constructed. He proposed to commute to his office in New York daily. With this announcement a new note of progress seemed to have been struck. Speculative Woodstock minds became busy with thought of the conversion of their town into an opulent suburb of New York, now apparently only an hour away by air.

The air age did not come to Woodstock so easily. As Coolidge prosperity gave way to Hoover optimism the transformation of building after building gave visual notice that the town was on the move. The old gristmill below Riseley's Bridge became the clubhouse of the Woodstock Country Club. What had been Aaron Riseley's fields became a golf course. The old Riseley boardinghouse emerged as a smart restaurant.[7]

Other buildings began new careers as eating places, of which there were said to have been about thirty before the Twenties ended. Next to the art gallery what had once been Justice of the Peace William H. Ploss' harnessmaking shop and then the Mower fruit, vegetable and ice cream establishment became the Knife and Fork Restaurant. Sidewalk tables were shaded by an awning. The Woodstock Valley Inn added a restaurant on its portico overlooking the Village Green.

A trolley car was hauled by Albert Cashdollar to a position beside Mill Hill Road. Established as a diner, it grew step by step into a large two-story building housing Deanie's Restaurant. The old De Forest-Vandevoort-Rose house beside the Tannery Brook was altered after a stint as a crafts studio to become the Jack Horner shop. There Eugene and Minna Haile Schleicher sold German toys, clothing, carvings and American antiques.[8]

These and the other transformations of the time showed that more money than ever was pouring into Woodstock. Builders, plumbers, electricians, cleaning women, gardeners, taxi drivers and others were kept busy coping with the demand for their summer services. The number of men and women with incomes swollen by success in practicing some form of the arts increased. Best-selling authors like Will Durant, whose *Story of Philosophy* did so well in 1927, came to Woodstock for a weekend with J. P. McEvoy and returned as a resident.

Some Woodstock painters already established in the colony prospered. Every year Speicher, John Carroll, MacFee, Judson Smith and others won important prizes at the exhibitions of the National Academy of Design, the Pennsylvania Academy or the Pittsburgh International. As if there were some magic which might be communicated to newcomers, other artists were drawn to the colony. Magazine illustrators who often had painting ambitions settled in Woodstock. Cartoonists and comic-strip and commercial artists added their summer and in some cases year-round presence to the colony.[9]

As more people swelled the colony and more money was spent, the list of old buildings put to new uses lengthened. Irving Riseley's barn beside the Tannery Brook Bridge was converted into a very popular social center with soft drinks, ice cream and sandwiches. The walls were covered with hasty little landscape and flower paintings run up by colony artists for the tourist trade. The Nook, as the place was called, changed hands a number of times. During the boom years it was run by George Neher, a local man known as the builder of many of the colony's early studios and a cheerful landlord to many art-colony people.

A byproduct of the boom was the emergence of Woodstock into political power on a level higher than the town. Earlier Woodstock politicians had occasionally moved on to the larger stage of the county. Glassmaker Daniel Elliot and hotel and bathhouse man Charles Krack had represented their district in the state legislature. Now Senator Arthur Wicks of Kingston would soon run the county's Republican machine, and Woodstock's Kenneth L. Wilson was becoming Wicks' right-hand man. Woodstock would soon become a center of Republican political activity.[10]

Europe and Asia sent representatives to Woodstock to join the American-born workers in all the arts. Some were Chinese, Japanese, Hungarian or Indian by birth. Tourists taking in the sights of Woodstock were sometimes impressed by hearing a half-dozen languages spoken on Tinker Street. They were surprised too to learn that the town had a resident astrologer, Edith Harlan, the niece of a justice of the U.S. Supreme Court (and "a specialist in astro-psycho-analysis and hororary charts").

As the town grew, private schools appeared. In 1915 a Montessori School had been founded by Zoe Bateman, who had studied under Maria Montessori herself. The school still lives. Art schools, especially as that of the Art Students League faltered and vanished in 1923, became numerous. John F. Carlson and Walter Goltz had their own summer schools. Sculptor Alexander Archipenko had his. A group including Judson Smith had still another. Many painters took a few private pupils without having organized a school. Some attributed the closing of the Art Students League's School to the strength of the competition which had developed even before 1923.

Textile designer William Arlt opened a school. Interior designer Winold Reiss had another. A school for advertising artists appeared. Alexis Kosloff was only one among the dancers who attracted pupils to their private schools. Schools of acting were attached to the theaters at the Maverick and Byrdcliffe. Several printing shops were opened.[11]

The creative and educational stir of the Woodstock of the Twenties helped draw people of outstanding eccentricities. Tourists were astonished by a Russian emigre who handed out pamphlets setting forth his own personal version of recent history, by idiosyncratic painters like Jascha Schwamd (who was known as The Playboy), by The Nature Boy (with leaves on his head and a club in his hand), by health-food advocates who delighted in telling strangers of the diet of nuts, fruit and whole grains on which they subsisted, by people with convictions as to needed reforms in the way Americans dressed. These people wore turbans, wigs, veils, or almost nothing at all. There were men dressed like women and women dressed like men, devotees of long hair or of shaved heads. Observers of life as it passed by on Tinker Street likened the scene to a circus—or to a preview of the future.[12]

While Woodstock and the Maverick of the Twenties seethed with what was being hailed as progress, Byrdcliffe presented a look of dignified aloofness. Not that changes did not take place. The Whiteheads passed from middle age to old age and lost much of the drive they had shown in earlier years. In several ways they displayed an inclination to play a part in the larger art colony which was being put together from elements of the three centers of activity in the arts which now formed the colony.

The Whiteheads continued to work in their White Pines Pottery and to encourage and help craftspeople to work around them at Byrdcliffe in weaving, wood working, metal working and other crafts. They rented cottages to a rich assortment of painters, musicians, stage and academic people. Their social life depended much on the prosperous people who had built in the East Riding. And they leased The Villetta to a manager who ran the place as a summer boardinghouse not too different from many others in the thriving Catskill Mountains resort region.

Ralph Whitehead's last summer at Byrdcliffe was in 1928. He spoke regretfully to a guest of the fading-away of the idealistic hopes he had once had for Byrdcliffe. The guest pointed toward the valley where the hamlet of Woodstock and the Maverick lay. What was happening down there, he said, the continuing commitment to work in the arts and crafts, was a result of what had been begun at Byrdcliffe.

And Whitehead, the guest reported, "seemed greatly pleased." He had come during the final phase of his life to look less harshly on the raw vigor of the colony. That November Ralph Whitehead, Jr., with a new degree in engineering, was about to set off for a job in South America. The Whiteheads gave a party for him. Among the many Woodstock guests was Hervey White, who had not visited White Pines since he left in 1904. The *Vestris* on which young Whitehead sailed foundered on the voyage, and Whitehead was among those lost. His father, now seventy-four, never recovered from the shock and soon died. Jane Whitehead did her best to guide Byrdcliffe into the future.[13]

NEWSPAPERS
AND MAGAZINES

As an accompaniment to the boom of the Twenties something new and significant in its effect on the town came to Woodstock. Newspapers and little magazines made their appearance.

As early as August 1912 a single number of *The Pochade*, a proposed weekly paper put together by students of the Art Students League, had marked Woodstock's entry into serial publication. Its editor was art student A. B. Titus, who was making an impression with cartoons. Titus ended up as a California real-estate dealer. Though chatty and slangy, the paper devoted much space to personalities, effectively reflecting the spirit of the concerns of Woodstock summer art students. *The Pochade* (the name is taken from that of a small painting usually made inside the cover of a sketch box) did not have a successor as a Woodstock paper until 1923, and that successor was very different indeed from the usual small-town paper.

Woodstock lacked the potential advertisers that made possible a local newspaper until the boom of the Twenties. Up to that time Woodstock people had relied for most of their news of events in their town on bits of information or speculation passed on from one person to another. This information, much of which could properly be called gossip, was exchanged at social meetings—at the tavern, the quilting party, the general store, after church or at work.

Kingston newspapers began to be published after the end of the

American Revolution. These papers sometimes printed Woodstock stories. The Ulster *Plebeian* gave an account of the proposed glass factory on the Sawkill in 1809. Later stories dealing with ascents of Overlook Mountain and the building of highways through Woodstock made the county's papers. Advertising columns in these papers were sometimes used for selling Woodstock land, for public notices affecting the town, and for letting the public know of such things as missing cows and in one case of the loss of some books on the Ulster-Delaware Turnpike.

By the 1870s Woodstock "items" were being sent to Kingston papers by women who acted as local correspondents. Since the item collectors were very poorly paid, it often happened that no one could be persuaded to undertake the task, and then the flow of items would be cut off for a time. Feature stories about the town's happenings increased after the birth of the art colony and the growing outside interest in what was going on in Woodstock. County newspapers were especially sure to provide complete coverage of any incident of blood or violence.[1]

A heavily-covered crime story of this period was the killing in 1905 of Oscar Harrison, son of the superintendent of the Kingston Water Company's Woodstock operations. Returning from some months spent with an acting troupe, young Harrison had become involved in a dispute over a woman with a black friend named Cornel Van Gasbeek. Van Gasbeek lived in the old house on Route 212 later owned by Robert W. Chanler and still later by Chanler's old friend, playwright Clemence Randolph. The two men fought. Harrison was fatally injured. Van Gasbeek then fled up Overlook Mountain and into Greene County. A Kingston law officer named Everett Rose, described as "a devotee of Sherlock Holmes," tracked Van Gasbeek up and across Overlook Mountain and into Greene County, and eventually found him. At his trial in January 1906 Van Gasbeek was found guilty of manslaughter and sentenced to seventeen years in Dannemora Prison.

Another piece of blood journalism came out of Woodstock in 1915. Luther Lounsbury, the cook at the Woodstock Hotel, became enraged because he thought his wife was unfaithful to him. He murdered Mrs. Lounsbury in their room and then committed suicide in the hotel stable.

A Woodstock story printed late in 1913 and early in 1914 combined several elements needed to titillate readers of Kingston newspapers. On a snowy January night three young Woodstock men, one of them taking his fiddle along, drove by sleigh across their town boundary to visit a resort close to Shultis Corners known as Aunt Nellie's. Aunt Nellie's was already being much whispered about in Woodstock. A tavern like this placed close to a town boundary line might be patronized by men who wanted to attract no attention from their immediate neighbors.

The three young men did some drinking at Nellie's bar. Then the fiddler of the three played while a woman attached to the establishment danced in the nude. At half past three later that night the woman headed for her own home nearby. Confused by alcohol she wandered in the snow and finally fell down and died from exposure not far from her house.

"DISGUSTING ORGIES AT COUNTY HOTEL" was one Kingston *Freeman* headline. Summoning many witnesses, including the three Woodstock men, a grand jury looked into the case. Aunt Nellie was sentenced to a term in the county jail on a charge of running a disorderly house.

The story has become part of the underground folklore of Woodstock. And it has another kind of value. It dragged into the open a side of American small-town life which is usually kept under cover and doesn't often find its way into published local history. There was also an element in the story of Aunt Nellie's unfortunate girl that had more than only local interest.

The girl who died in the snow belonged to a group of sharply differing yet related families which have achieved importance in the study of inherited tendencies toward anti-social behavior. In 1883 they were given the fictitious name of "Jukes." Eighteenth-century squatters in the part of the Shawangunk Mountains known as "The Trapps," some of the Jukes had by the early nineteenth century spread to Woodstock, where they figured in the poormaster's records and in police actions. They shared descent from the great New England theologian and metaphysician Jonathan Edwards with a contrasting group of families whose behavior was exemplary and many of whose members were people of outstanding ability and success both worldly and intellectual.[2]

It was inevitable that the atmosphere of the Woodstock art colony would stimulate magazine publication. Hervey White's *Wild Hawk* had been Woodstock's first serial publication to achieve more than a single number. But by 1916 the *Hawk* seemed to Hervey a bit out of step with his more ambitious goals for the Maverick. It needed a change.

Since its founding in November 1911 the magazine had existed largely to provide Hervey an outlet for his own work. Carl Eric Lindin had contributed translations. Now and then Hervey featured a scattering of work by Maverick writers. The purchase of the magazine by tourists as a souvenir of the art colony helped bolster the modest local circulation. Very rarely was the magazine given notice outside its home place. Once it was mildly praised in the *Mercure de France* in an account of American poetry written by Theodore Stanton, a friend from Hervey's Chicago days and a grandson of famous feminist Elizabeth Cady Stanton.[3]

By 1916 exciting new directions were becoming evident in the literary world. The rise of Cubism, Futurism, and what would soon be Dadaism was being accompanied by radical changes in poetry and fiction. While the *Wild Hawk* followed its own familiar path, rival little magazines elsewhere were publishing work by T. S. Eliot, Ezra Pound and James Joyce. Joyce's *Ulysses* and Eliot's *The Waste Land* were soon to burst upon the world.

Hervey responded not only by loosening some of the bonds that had tied his own writing to the past but also by putting the *Wild Hawk* through a metamorphosis from which it emerged as *The Plowshare*. The magazine shed its sober cover of butcher's paper favored at the height of the arts-and-crafts enthusiasm and appeared in a new and brighter coat. The covers carried wood or linoleum block prints, depicting landscapes and figures, sometimes in three colors.

Much of the character of the former *Wild Hawk* hung on inside. There were serials and poems by Hervey and some other Woodstock people. Lindin furnished cover designs and translations, as well as some of the capital needed to keep the magazine afloat. Editor Allan Updegraff, fresh from Paris, wrote local comment on such matters as the persistence of witchcraft, lore of the anti-Rent days, and the occasion on which Woodstock women voted for the first time.

Some numbers of *The Plowshare* contained stories, poems and sketches from outside the Woodstock colony and often from across the Atlantic. This printed matter sometimes matched the brightness and modernity of the covers. As *The Plowshare* was being born, a fever for emigration to Europe and especially to Paris was infecting young American writers who wanted to break new ground. Pound and Eliot had been pioneers in this wave of self-transplantation to what seemed more fertile cultural soil.

Some American writers during the years of the World War

expressed their loss of faith in American culture and their confidence in Europe by signing up for military service under Britain or France or as ambulance drivers. At the war's end the editorial staff of *The Plowshare* was joined by Gustav Hellstrom, a cosmopolitan Swede who had been the foreign correspondent of a leading Stockholm daily in several of the capitals of Europe. Transferred to New York, he had married Louise Schoonmaker, an American painter with Woodstock connections. Hellstrom was a novelist and playwright with many friends among the literary avant-gardists of Europe. He obtained for *The Plowshare* a striking war sketch by Blaise Cendrars, a Swiss-born Parisian "Cubist poet." This piece was accompanied by drawings by Fernand Leger, the early Cubist artist who had turned to using forms derived from machinery.[4]

Dutch poet H.E.W. Cramer, who had come to live on the Maverick, contributed poems. William Murrell was responsible for the publication in two numbers of *The Plowshare* of the earliest poems of his protege Samuel Bernhard Greenberg, who later so inspired Hart Crane. Greenberg died young in a charity ward of a New York hospital, leaving many poems which broke through the barriers of familiar poetic language to say fresh and arresting things. In *The Plowshare* Murrell compared Greenberg to William Blake and Gerard de Nerval. After Greenberg's death from tuberculosis, contemporary American poets were influenced by his work. It was an indication of the limited circulation of *The Plowshare* that academic commentators on Greenberg's poetry during the 1930s and 1940s overlooked the magazine's part in giving his poems their first public showing.[5]

Most little magazines of the period had short lives. *The Little Review*, founded in Chicago and edited and published by frequent Maverick visitors Margaret Anderson and Jane Heap, folded up after its publication of part of Joyce's *Ulysses* incurred the wrath of postal censors. Others gave up when it became apparent to their editors that they had little new to say. *The Plowshare* came to its end with the summer of 1920 without any official explanation beyond a simple statement of the fact and a brief farewell poem. Hervey explained to friends that he had become overburdened with the details of many other Maverick projects.

Between 1920 and the summer of 1923 Woodstock got along without any serial publications of its own. Then the *Hue and Cry* was born. It was said to have been inspired by a paper its editors, painter Alexander Brook and his wife, satirical writer and artist Peggy Bacon, had seen in London.

The stories carried by the *Hue and Cry* provided the strongest imaginable contrast to the feature stories of Woodstock life occasionally spread on the front pages of Kingston newspapers and the local items modestly tucked away inside. Hervey White once called this weekly summer paper "an artists' joke paper," and so it was. It was a kind of lively prank aimed at Woodstock artists for the purpose of amusing and satirizing them. Painter Henry Billings and a few others helped Brook and Peggy Bacon with the writing. Hervey White gave his approval and acted as publisher. Like the burial of paintings and the proclamation of the death of art at Rock City over a decade earlier, the publication was a manifestation of the irreverent and playful spirit which marked American Dada.

Hervey White accompanied the magazine's editors to Kingston to sell advertising space. He was amazed at the enthusiastic response. His friend Tom Comerford, editor and publisher of the Ulster County *Daily Leader* and the weekly Ulster County *News*, agreed to print the first issue. Most Kingston people saw Woodstock as a decidedly strange place filled with strange people. Yet they recognized that the town was a good market for their plumbing fixtures, automobiles, household goods and other sources of Kingston prosperity.

Once the first issue had been printed, however, doubts overcame both editors and printer. Had they gone too far in satirizing Woodstock? Might they become the targets of lawsuits should their paper be published? It was concluded that the first issue would have to be destroyed and a new and safer one written and printed. But destroying bundles of six-page newspapers is not always easy. The editors' first impulse was to snatch some benefit from their unfortunate fix.

They concocted a scheme. Billings would appear on the Village Green with the entire printing of the paper and pretend to be trying to sell papers. Hervey White would rush up shouting, "How dare you try to sell so scandalous and indecent a sheet?" He would then seize the bundled papers and ignite them. The resulting blaze would bring the whole village together. The fortunes of the future *Hue and Cry* would be assured.

This plan was abandoned. The papers were disposed of with considerable difficulty, some by fire and some by burial. Rumors that a few copies had escaped were once current. It was said that they would reveal astounding secrets of Woodstock life. But as yet none has turned up.[6]

The new issue of *Hue and Cry* soon appeared. It was a success from the start. Brook and Bacon had launched the paper in a burst of satirical energy. They soon became unwilling to go on. Both were at the beginnings of promising careers in art. After its second number they turned the *Hue and Cry* over to Paul Johnston, a printmaker and typographer who took on as an assistant nineteen-year-old Frank Schoonmaker, just emerged from Princeton. Before the summer of 1923 ended Schoonmaker was sole editor and publisher.

Though under Schoonmaker's guidance the *Hue and Cry* lost much of its initial Dadaist quality, it went on delighting the imaginative, baffling the slow-witted, and drawing Woodstock's attention to many problems facing the town. Scorning ordinary newsprint, the paper appeared on yellow, pink, green and blue stock. As the summer of 1923 ended it went into hibernation, reappearing the following June as a biweekly summer magazine featuring reproductions of the work of local artists.

For the next two summers Schoonmaker got the paper out weekly. At the same time he published two annuals, elaborate in style and makeup and intended, as Schoonmaker wrote, to serve as "an expression of the significant side of Woodstock." He explained his understanding of that significance in this way: "Pursuit is, in Woodstock, the universal pursuit. We are all of us baying on the track of something, the good, the true or the beautiful, forming together a sort of *Hue and Cry* in pursuit of the seven arts. . . ."

Right enough, the pursuit was part of Woodstock life. Yet another force also helped the *Hue and Cry*. Ever since Hervey White's *Wild Hawk* arrived in 1911 hopes for their own little literary magazine had remained alive among Woodstock people. The little-magazine wave reached its height around 1924. Nowhere were the magazines more abundant than in Greenwich Village. And among the Village little magazines of the Twenties the most elaborate was Egmont Arens' *Playboy*. *Playboy* was much admired in Woodstock and a good many Woodstock artists contributed to it. When Frank Schoonmaker decided to publish a *Hue and Cry Annual* for 1925 and 1926 he took *Playboy* as his model, modifying it to give it a Woodstock flavor.

The cover of the 1925 Annual was a linoleum cut by Pieter Mijer, the foremost Greenwich Village and Woodstock expert on batik, the Javanese craft then sweeping into popularity in all American art colonies, urban and rural. The cover, representing a characteristic Woodstock scene, the Market Fair, was carried out in a manner that suggested a Cubist influence. Within, both *Annuals* were hospitable to a great range of Woodstock work in the graphic arts and in literature. Half-tones of paintings and sculpture by Rosen, Speicher, Brook, Mattson, Fiene, John Carlson, Birge Harrison, Peggy Bacon, Archipenko, Faggi and others were inside. Original wood and linoleum cuts and drypoint etchings by Louis Bouche, Rohland, Carl Walters and Arnold Blanch gave color and a no-expense-spared look to the publication.

The poems, essays, short stories and critical articles of the *Annuals* were less broad in range than the art work. The older Woodstock poets were heavily represented. Hervey White, Anne Moore, Grace Fallow Norton, Edwin Davies Schoonmaker, father of the *Annual's* editor, and others of the older generation gave a twice-told look to the poetry pages. A very few younger people, like Glenway Westcott, contributed poems of no great distinction. Short-story writer Richard Hughes, later well-known as the author of *High Wind in Jamaica,* contributed an effective short story. Danish sailor Kaj Klitgaard's fantasy of life at sea had an eerie quality of its own. Other stories were less impressive. Among the pieces devoted to Woodstock doings in the theater, Hervey White's statement of the Maverick Theater's purposes and motivations was excellent.[7]

When it became known that the *Hue and Cry's* originators had found advertising space easy to sell, dreamers of other publications awakened. In September 1923 Francis Gardner Clough began publishing the *Woodstock Weekly*, which he intended as a small-town newspaper of the usual kind, but with enough attention to the arts to capture subscribers among members of the art colony. The paper made a promising start, but its editor's goal of five hundred subscribers proved impossible to reach. The paper had been launched at an unpromising time of year. Clough soon lost control. After a few months of squabbling and changes of management the *Weekly* died.[8]

As the *Hue and Cry* entered upon its season of biweekly magazine form in 1924, writer Ernest Brace and painter and advertising artist Rudolf Wetterau published their *Woodstock Almanac 1924* in the hope that it would become the forerunner of a series of comic almanacs. The fifty-two-page booklet had no success either in the amount of advertising it attracted or in its sales. It printed spirited linoleum cuts and woodcuts by many of Woodstock's best-known artists. It included a reprinting of Bide Snyder's reminiscenses, first published in the *Woodstock Weekly*. It had a piece on the bloody but once-popular sport of cock-fighting by sport-loving painter John Carroll, written in the distinctive style used by oldtime writers on cocking.[9]

One feature of both the *Almanac* and the *Hue and Cry* which excited much approval among art-colony people and disapproval among people of the older Woodstock was the humorous verses and prose observations on Woodstock life written by craftsman Edward Thatcher under the pen name Iddie Flitcher. Thatcher broadly parodied the speech and ways of older Woodstock people. The generation of Woodstock art-colony people to which Thatcher belonged often saw local people as the kind of rustics frequently caricatured in humorous magazines of the turn of the century. Here is a typical Iddie Flitcher poem from the *Almanac*:

SUM-IZ—SUM AINT

Sum-mer guests
'n sum-mer boarders
Sum we like will kum agin
'n sum we hope they never kin.

The failure of the *Woodstock Weekly* and of the *Almanac* did not discourage editors of Ulster County newspapers from hoping to imitate the success of the *Hue and Cry* by providing far more space for Woodstock news. Kingston editor Thomas Comerford advertised in 1925 that "Everybody in Woodstock reads the Kingston *Daily Leader*." Soon Comerford started the weekly Ulster County *News*, which he advertised as "Woodstock's newspaper." Meanwhile, the Kingston *Daily* and *Weekly Freeman* paid Francis Gardner Clough to contribute occasional stories on Woodstock exhibitions, concerts, theater and other art-colony events.[10]

In spite of the competition the *Hue and Cry* lived on. Promising Yale undergraduate William Harlan Hale, who also edited Yale's *Harkness Hoot*, was editor. Between 1927 and its death in the early fall of 1929 Hale ran the *Hue and Cry* in a bold and lively fashion and took a strong pro-art colony stand. In 1928 a tough assault against the advertising revenues of the *Hue and Cry* and those county papers with Woodstock ties was launched by Clough with the backing of Chamber of Commerce adherents along Tinker Street. Clough's *Art Bulletin* was a giveaway summer weekly printed like *Hue and Cry* on colored stock. It made its appeal primarily to visitors to the art colony who wanted guidance to what was going on. In this the *Art Bulletin*, like the *Hue and Cry*, did a creditable job.

Clough tried to avoid joining in the polarization which was dividing Woodstock artists and businesspeople. The son of a former local minister and the husband of a woman who belonged to an old Woodstock family, Clough seemed to many to belong to the business stratum of the town. Yet he saw himself as a poet and essayist in the tradition of Henry Thoreau. This bent him toward sympathy with the art colonists.[11]

As the gulf between artists and businesspeople grew in the final months of the boom of the 1920s, Clough took recognition of what was being called the "Woodstock Feud." In one of the pieces he was continuing to write for the Kingston *Daily Freeman* he predicted that the actions of the Committee of Fifty would result in "more open abandon on the part of the summer residents" and that any further work by the Committee "would only expose them to the ridicule of the whole colony for a long time." This disapproval of the Committee caused Clough's business backers to threaten to desert him. At the same time his wife obtained a divorce. The *Hue and Cry* gave up after its Maverick Festival issue of August 20, 1929. Clough too ceased publication and left town for a winter in Greenwich Village. The following summer he revived his *Bulletin*. Due both to weakening local support and to the national business slump, he had little commercial success.

A few other hopeful magazines burst into life and swiftly died in the late Twenties. One was *The Maverick Hoot*, which even some good pieces by Hervey White could not keep alive for more than seven numbers printed at the Maverick Press. *The Saturday Morning*, described by a contemporary as the "house organ" of the hotel-operating Newgold family, is not known to have survived the summer of 1928. In the summer of 1930 R. W. Marchand, a tall eccentric Swiss entomologist, published one number of his sixteen-page *Marchand's Review* in Woodstock. Marchand is remembered as a companion of Joe Gould, artist's model and self-proclaimed compiler of an immense *Oral History of Our Times*.[12]

Woodstock business people were determined to have a local weekly which would serve their interests. They agreed to back a new paper to be edited by Edward Perkins, son-in-law of conservative Stephen B. Ayres. The first number of Perkins' Woodstock *Press* came out in the spring of 1930. The paper brashly boosted Woodstock as a source of business profits and gave ample space only to those art-colony doings which had demonstrated power to affect business favorably. The theater was leader among these.

The boom of the Twenties had enough momentum left to carry over for a time even after the stock market catastrophe of 1929. In the sluggish atmosphere of Woodstock, plans were being made for theatrical, art-gallery and other colony doings. As 1930 came to its end the *Press* was giving the town's businesses artificial respiration via loud booming sounds. Francis Clough was letting it be known that he proposed to publish a Woodstock "art magazine" with well-reproduced illustrations on good paper. In Albany Governor Franklin D. Roosevelt was recommending legislative action to deal with the worsening economic situation. These measures foreshadowed much of what would soon become known on the national scene as the New Deal. And certain programs of the New Deal would have a profound effect on Woodstock workers in the arts, especially painters.[13]

Ever since *The Plowshare* had suspended publication in 1920 Woodstock writers had talked about reviving it or of starting another serious literary periodical. The early 1920s were a time of much literary pioneering and little magazines abounded. The flow of literary and art emigrants from the United States to Europe increased when war-caused inflation made living there even cheaper for Americans. More members of the Woodstock art colony spent their winters in France. Little magazines like *Broom*, begun in 1921, and Gorham B. Munson's *Secession* of 1922 were published and edited by American expatriates who found that they could have an edition of five hundred copies printed in Vienna or Rome for as little as twenty dollars.

Secession was founded and edited in large part by Munson, with the help of Matthew Josephson. Munson moved in and out of the Woodstock colony. He had contributed a short story to the *Plowshare*, but that had not been an altogether pleasing experience. Reading the story in the magazine in 1920, poet Hart Crane wrote Munson to denounce Hervey White's editing and to characterize him as "an ordinary ass." Both *Broom* and *Secession*, like *The Plowshare*, ran into editing conflicts. With Munson in Woodstock and Josephson in Europe, each boiling with his own notions of what the magazine should print, trouble was inevitable. In 1923 both *Broom* and *Secession* became the centers of a furious literary quarrel which echoed noisily in the memoirs of the time, resulting in a much-written-about fist fight on the Maverick between Munson and Josephson.

By the year of the literary fist fight both *Broom* and *Secession* had changed editors and were setting up shop in the United States. A passion for selected aspects of American culture had seized upon the Paris expatriates. Defying even the high cost of living and printing in the United States, they were soon hard at work and play in Greenwich Village, Bucks County in Pennsylvania, rural Connecticut, Woodstock and similar places. Neither *Broom* nor *Secession* found it possible to become acclimated and began stumbling toward extinction. An attempt at cutting costs by having *Broom* printed in Kingston failed. Josephson became infuriated against fellow editor Munson following a bizarre editorial conference in Greenwich Village. He pursued Munson to the old farmhouse on the Maverick where Munson was staying with William Murrell and subjected him to a vigorous verbal attack.

Murrell proposed ending the hostilities in a traditional fist fight. He led Munson and Josephson outside to a field well muddied by the November rain. There both editors took off their coats. With Murrell holding a watch and keeping track of three-minute rounds, the fight began.

Munson had the advantage of being considerably heavier than Josephson, but he was handicapped both by being in a state of convalescence from flu and by having a large waxed mustache in which he took pride. The two swung at each other, clinched, fell down in the mud and panted loudly. They then rose, shook hands and separated. Each claimed the victory.

The fight did not settle the fate of *Broom*. Not long afterward the U.S. Post Office seized what turned out to be the final issue of the magazine in the belief that it contained obscene references. A final half-hearted attempt at keeping the magazine alive was then made by two men, poet Malcolm Cowley and Slater Brown, in a cold Maverick studio with the wind rattling the skylight and a fire of chestnut wood (one of the least efficient fuels obtainable) dying out in the stove. The two drank gin mixed with cider, tried the popular fad of automatic writing, at intervals ate the standard Maverick dish of salt pork and lentils, glanced at the manuscripts proposed for a new number of *Broom*, figured with horror the cost of printing the magazine, and gave up forever.[14]

Broom had failed to rise from the dead in a Maverick studio that winter of 1924 and this stimulated other little magazines to arrive. The magazine format of the *Hue and Cry* of that summer was one, and the *Annual* of the next summer was another. One promising little magazine which was a valid successor to the Atlantic-hopping *Broom* and *Secession* appeared in July and struggled through four numbers before expiring. *1 9 2 4* was edited and published by Edwin Seaver, a newly graduated Harvard man who had already edited left-wing college papers and worked on New York's Socialist dailies, the *Call* and the *Leader*. The magazine demonstrated the excellence of Seaver's judgement. It contained much that still remains of interest today, including a debate between Ezra Pound and Gorham Munson on the meaning of T. S. Eliot's *The Waste Land,* poems by William Carlos Williams, Hart Crane and Yvor Winters, a story by Kenneth Burke, and an account of the work of Woodstock painter Henry Mattson.[15]

Through the 1920s, Woodstock newspapers and little magazines had given the colony's people a self-image of a creative, bustling, money-making, ever-expanding place. To many this accurately reflected the local realities of the time. It was almost inevitable at the climax of the boom in 1929 that some Woodstock people, and especially the older ones, should look backward with wonder and try to bring together past and present to form an explanation of the town which would come closer to their understanding than that offered by LeGallienne, Benignus and others. So in high hopes of forming a link between old pre-art-colony Woodstock and the life of the colony, the Historical Society of Woodstock (usually called the Woodstock Historical Society) was born.[16]

Among those who looked back and tried to assess the character and the history of the town, the leader was Martin Schuetze. Active in the development of the art colony almost ever since it was founded, he had been a close friend of Ralph Whitehead, Bolton Brown, Hervey White and Carl Eric Lindin. Schuetze saw Woodstock as a remarkable place. In Woodstock he saw "the development from the purely agricultural to the most modern stage of social life, which in general history required hundreds and thousands of years . . . telescoped into a period of less than one generation, so that each of us has, day by day, seen the fundamental forces of human history at work." Schuetze proposed that a history of the town and especially of its post-1902 period be written.

Addressing a meeting of the Historical Society of Woodstock in 1930, Schuetze dealt with the philosophy of history, expressing his conviction that Woodstock's place in history was a remarkable one. He said, "I believe that the promise of Woodstock is as great as that of any place in the past which has become the high seat of civilization. I do not believe that there is in this or any other country a village which has achieved in less than one generation a richness and comprehensiveness of culture and cosmopolitan importance as this little village in the Catskills has achieved." Schuetze added that he believed that Woodstock was destined to become "a historic center of a great civilization." [17]

It would be easy enough to dismiss Schuetze's ideas about Woodstock and its history as no more than symptoms of a severe attack of local pride inflated by the boom years. Yet there was some truth in Schuetze's view. Woodstock was indeed a remarkable place. It had changed more in a single generation than most similar towns do in a century. It had pushed ahead into a position of cultural leadership in some fields. The daily ways of life of its art colony did foreshadow the American society of the 1960s and 1970s. Another reason why people in 1929 were stimulated to look backward was that in this single year many people who had played key parts in the town's development had died. Ralph Whitehead, Birge Harrison, Dr. Downer, George Plochmann, Paul Kennaday, Rosie Magee, Will Wolven, Aaron Riseley and others were gone beyond any possibility of telling what they had seen and experienced. Others of their generation would soon join them.

Founded on September 20, 1929 with Schuetze as president, the Historical Society of Woodstock accepted as its goals the publication of a town history, the collection of historical materials and the creation of a museum. It was noteworthy that few of the original members belonged to old local families. They were art-colony people who were enthusiastically adopting the Woodstock background as their own. Only a few local people with close connections to the art colony joined, among them postmaster William S. Elwyn and his wife Bertha.[18]

At once Society members began collecting and putting into publishable form many essays on Woodstock history. Its meetings were very popular. For the next decade the Society played an important part in Woodstock's social and intellectual life. And its influence still persists in local historical writing such as this book.

48

THE GREAT
DEPRESSION
TAKES HOLD

The Great Depression did not come
with a bang. It crept into the American consciousness after a series of
little shocks following the big stock market crash of October 24, 1929.
But by 1931 no one could deny that the Depression had arrived and no
one could guess that it would not relax its grip until the 1930s were
almost over.

The first years of the Depression found Woodstock people
confused and unwilling to accept the reality of the hard times into
which they were sinking. The emotional momentum created by the
boom years was not easily halted. And so new gift shops,
entertainment ventures, restaurants and art galleries opened while
others were closing.

Problems had been caused by the expansion of the heedless boom
years. The private wells on which the expanding hamlet of Woodstock
depended were being polluted by haphazard methods of sewage
disposal. Highways and back roads were proving inadequate to
handling the increased amount of motor travel. Elementary schools
were crowded and out of step with the times; high school education,
twelve miles away, was expensive. Primitive methods of snow removal
kept cars in outlying parts of the town immobilized for weeks or
months after blizzards.

Though Woodstock people talked about these problems, they
realized that in the growing stringency of the times they could see no

easy way of solving them. On December 3, 1929 the town board appropriated additional money for helping the town's poor. Budgeted funds had been exhausted. This was the town's first official action in recognition of the economic storm that was preparing to burst upon Woodstock and the country.[1]

Life went on and things got done as the Depression deepened. By 1931 the pressures exerted by the increase in automobile use caused the town to find the funds to hire its first policeman, whose principal duty was to direct traffic. In 1932 the town bought its first motorized snow plow. While President Herbert Hoover reassuringly urged Americans to solve their economic woes by being kind to one another, in Albany Governor Franklin D. Roosevelt initiated a series of programs intended to give work to the unemployed by using them to build public works. By act of legislature TERA (Temporary Emergency Relief Administration) was set up in 1930. One of its sponsors was Ulster County's Republican boss-to-be, Senator Arthur Wicks.

Under TERA funds were made available to Woodstock for hiring workers on highway and other local projects as well as in home relief. Since overall control of the agency was in the hands of officials of the state's Democratic administration, Woodstock officials, fearing advantage to the opposition party hesitated at first to apply for TERA funds. In July 1932 Supervisor Albert Cashdollar asked the members of the town board to submit plans "to assist in the alleviation of the unemployment situation that the taxpayer may have some material benefit in return for relief so promoted." [2]

In November 1932 Governor Franlin Delano Roosevelt was elected president. The Woodstock Town Board promptly held a special meeting and applied for "$4,000 in State money" to be used "to alleviate unemployment." Soon the former Woodstock-Saugerties Turnpike (Route 212) was being widened and resurfaced. New bridges were being built in Shady and Willow. A proposal to revive the old Schohariekill Road through Mink Hollow in order to route tourists going to and from the upper Catskills through Woodstock was rejected.[3]

By 1933 one-third of the nation's workers (officially sixteen million people) were listed as unemployed. Mortgages on farms and homes were being foreclosed at an unprecedented rate. A third of the railroad mileage of the country was in bankruptcy. Industry was faltering. During the whirlwind early months of his presidency

Roosevelt brought about the creation of federal agencies empowered to spend money to stimulate the economy and to aid distressed people. Among these agencies were several which eventually would have decisive effects on Woodstock and its art colony. But before that could happen Woodstock art-colony people had battled the Depression on their own.

Few local people on both art and non-art levels were unaffected by the national and worldwide malaise. The dividends which had enabled Woodstock's country gentry to live as they did dwindled, forcing them to retrench. On less elevated social levels the dreams of prosperity of a few years earlier had dissipated. Unemployment was causing misery. Most men had been conditioned to believe that a man's first duty was to earn the income needed by his family. The inability of these men to land jobs was a blow to their self-respect. Some never recovered.

Housewives did not swell the unemployment statistics. They went on being housewives, with additional burdens caused by lower family income and by the necessity of devising stratagems to stretch their dollars. Some housewives with unemployed husbands found that they could get jobs while the husband took over running the household. But most women repaired old clothing instead of buying new coats and socks for their children. Men glued patch soles to worn shoes. They recycled razor blades in a gadget sold for the purpose and collected and used all sorts of lore about making things last. Vegetable gardens flourished and grew larger. Women canned and dried and pickled as their mothers had done in the pre-boom days.[4]

The urge to live on a little subsistence farm rolled over the country, including Woodstock, and a book titled *Five Acres and Independence* became a heavy seller. Goats began to munch in brushlots and supply families with milk. Hogs consumed table waste and produced ham and bacon. A vision of cutting loose from the foundering economy and becoming free and self-supporting took possession of many Woodstock minds. Eventually, under the impact of hard work and small returns for the effort, the vision faded.

Cars were coddled to persuade them to last longer. One old car on Tinker Street had a lusty clump of mushrooms sprouting from the decaying wooden supports of its roof, but before an expert could arrive and pronounce on the mushrooms' edibility they had aged and died. Gathering berries and nuts took on a certain amount of urgency.

The town's chestnuts, once a good source of food, had slowly died, victims of the chestnut bark disease first recognized in Woodstock on Thanksgiving Day, 1911. The chestnuts were now almost gone. But hickories remained in many pastures and butternuts flourished in damp woodlands. Black walnuts were to be found here and there in the lowland parts of the town. The Maverick's staple dish of salt pork and lentils was served far more frequently, with frankfurters now often taking the place of pork. In the spring milkweed and pokeberry shoots, dandelion leaves and mustard-bud clusters were gathered and boiled.

By June 1932 the prices of the necessities of life had tumbled in response to slow demand. A Kingston market sold hams at thirteen cents per pound, coffee at twenty-nine cents and ice cream at twenty-five cents per quart. The Maverick Theater lowered its admission charge to fifty cents and one dollar. The Woodstock Historical Society cut its membership fee. The Rev. Harvey Todd, now turning from efforts at regulating morals to helping those hardest hit by economic distress, announced that he would be glad to hear from anyone who might give work to the unemployed. From that time until the end of his life he was active in a great number of useful projects which earned him the affection and respect of art-colony and local people alike.

The Great Depression did not bring about a flight from Woodstock. Instead the population grew by about three hundred during the 1930s. People formerly employed in cities decided to live year-round on their Woodstock summer places. Young people who had gone away to make their fortunes returned and lived with their parents. In that era without building regulations some hasty and ramshackle building was done. Additions were made to older houses and shelters were run up to house returning families. The children of new arrivals added to the crowding of the district schools.

People with imagination took to working in surprising ways in an attempt to scare away the Depression. Dyrus and Edith Cook were examples. He was a salty, outspoken native of Indiana, she a craftswoman in jewelry, greeting cards and textiles. The two had operated "Cook's Tours of the Catskills" during the late Twenties. Mounted on amiable donkeys, their patrons were carried on overnight camping trips through the mountains. When the Depression crippled their tours the Cooks held square dances in the hotel built by Willard Allen and known as Allencrest. This grew into a very popular dancing group named the Cheats and Swings.[5]

In the fall of 1932 the Cooks set out with a donkey named Jack, travelling southward, camping by night when necessary, and giving lectures on their adventures in the Catskills and on their project. They illustrated their lectures with slides. "Donkeying Through Seven States," the account of their trip, was published blow-by-blow in the Catskill Mountain *Star*. The 1933 book version tells of encounters with a wide variety of people: the Virginia hunting set, Depression-battered poor black and white people, and rich winter vacationers in the fashionable resort of Asheville, N.C., where they spent many nights as guests of a wide range of sympathetic humans from a bootlegger to a college professor.

When the Cooks began promoting square dancing they were responding to a national rush of interest in the American past. In painting, in music and in many other ways the Depression was stimulating a return to what seemed the pleasant simplicities of earlier days. The barn dances of old Woodstock which summer boarders and then art colonists had found so charming formed a local base which square dancers might use as a foundation for their efforts. Oldtimers played for the dances with the traditional jugs of hard cider beside them. Art-colony people and members of old Woodstock families could join in dancing and so ignore for a time the barriers that separated them in everyday life.

Regular square dances were held by the Wittenberg Sportsmen's Club, Keefe's Wagon Wheel Inn on the Saugerties Road, and the Irvington Inn. In 1938 a square-dance contest was held at the Maverick Concert Hall. All local dance groups competed, the women wearing Woodstock dresses, the men clothes which suggested the nineteenth century. A visiting team from Cornwall, N.Y. put on a demonstration of their skill. The Cheats and Swings won, making a big impression with their firemen's dance involving twelve couples. The Cheats and Swings were invited to dance for the Franklin D. Roosevelts at Hyde Park. There fiddler and caller Percy Hill made a memorable splash by falling into a pool. Square dancing continues to have its enthusiastic practitioners.[6]

Local businesspeople gave credit to an unprecedented number of people. George Layman, a kindly and gentle man who operated the grocery store once owned by Edgar Snyder, gave credit so freely that he was forced out of business. Farmers who had turned to "peddling milk" during the Twenties turned to other things. Their customers, one said, "couldn't pay their bills."

Neither could many of Woodstock's ill. In 1928 George Lambert had taken over Dr. Downer's practice. He made house calls by day and night in all sorts of weather and in other ways tried to keep up the country-doctor tradition amid difficult economic days. After he left in 1937 because of his own illness Woodstock doctors became less willing to make house calls and were quicker in sending their patients to the Kingston hospitals. A good many local people began using Kingston doctors, turning to Woodstock doctors only late at night or in very bad weather when the Kingston men's fees were higher. Woodstock still had no resident pharmacist. Stowell's store at the corner of Tinker Street and Rock City and Mill Hill Roads sent prescriptions to be filled to Saugerties. Earlier, local doctors had compounded most of their own prescriptions.[7]

The square dancing revival served to boost the spirits of Depression-ridden people. And many sought the lift that comes from starting enterprises that promised them money. Some who had special skills taught riding, music, painting or dancing. Business-oriented people tried a broad range of ventures. One was a midget or Tom Thumb golf course, another a ping-pong parlor above The Nook.

Artists who would have scorned such work during the Twenties prepared samples and made the rounds of New York publishing and advertising offices. People who had long felt that they "had a book in them" got to work at novels or memoirs. Ned Thatcher told friends he was writing his life story, but the manuscript has never turned up. Konrad Cramer, painter-photographer and Jack-of-all-creative-work, offered to hold classes in a "Woodstock School of Miniature Photography" in which he would teach how to work with the 35-millimeter cameras then coming into serious use after a long period of development. In 1937 Cramer became professor of photography at Bard College, the first such position at any American college. One young man peddled walking sticks which he made from ash saplings, carved and colored. Women who had never dreamed of doing such drudgery for pay took to washing, sewing and cleaning for more fortunate neighbors.

In the topsy-turvy world of the Depression an electrical engineer of excellent academic background took to selling Fuller brushes from door to door. A onetime successful salesman of mechanical earth-moving equipment bought a secondhand truck and went into garbage disposal, with a bit of bootlegging on the side. Though some claimed the man made his gin from his garbage, he did fairly well.[8]

People from outside the town finding times hard saw Woodstock as a place where they might do better. The Summer School of the

Clarence H. White School of Photography, with local photographer Alfred Cohn in charge, came to Woodstock. The school offered courses in a wide range of photographic subjects. It gave a course for children, who were taught everything from making a camera to finishing prints. For a while a panel of well-known Woodstock painters criticized the work of White students.[9]

A competitor to the local Chamber of Commerce, the Woodstock Community Association, was organized. All, including art-colony people, were urged to join. Temporary offices were set up on a vacant lot while contributions were sought to buy a permanent site. Under the Association's prompting the old bulletin board which had long stood covered with tattered paper in front of the Twaddell House was removed as unsightly. The Chamber's members talked about issuing scrip as a substitute for money. Due bills (acceptable, when presented, in goods or services) came into use, as did barter. A butcher who had accepted a number of paintings in payment angrily returned them in a wheelbarrow after he found they had no market value. The heavy stream of tourists of the 1920s receded although it did not cease.[10]

The ending of Prohibition in 1933 was expected to prod the national economy. Woodstock businesspeople shared in this expectation. Bars and liquor stores soon reappeared after the long drought. However, many Woodstock people and especially church members saw the return of open consumption of alcohol as an evil. They complained of noise emanating from taverns and of the corruption of young people.

In 1936 a petition with more than three hundred signatures asked that Prohibition return to Woodstock under the local-option provision of state law (forty other New York State communities were taking similar action). The issue divided the town and created much animosity. The validity of some signatures on the petition survived a court challenge. Local liquor dealers claimed that the town would die as a summer resort if liquor selling were forbidden and that the only people who would be happy would be the "illicit apple jack distillers back in the mountains." The question came to a vote and the wets won. The apple-jack distillers went right on working in their hideouts. Their product was cheaper than that sold in the licensed establishments because its makers paid no excise taxes.[11]

The acceptance of the sale of alcoholic liquors had no noticeable effect in returning Woodstock to the prosperity of the Twenties. And by 1937 hopes for giving a boost to the local economy were being pinned on something very different.

A SESQUICENTENNIAL
CELEBRATION AND
AN ARCHBISHOP

It was in the Depression years of 1936 and 1937 that plans were made for an event which it was hoped could result in a greater local awareness of Woodstock's past and at the same time bring paying visitors to town. This was a celebration of the 150th anniversary of Woodstock's beginning as a town. Representatives of the fifty-four organizations of all sorts which existed in the town were summoned to a meeting. The Sesquicentennial Celebration was planned to last a week.

People on all levels of Woodstock society plunged into preparations for the events. Costumes were designed and sewed in the Fireman's Hall. Hundreds of yards of bunting in the Dutch colors of orange, blue and white were used in draping buildings. The surface of Tinker Street was repaired. The post office's pillared front facing the Dutch Reformed Church across the Village Green was freshly painted. A pageant was written largely by Miss Sidney Dyke, who had an antique shop in the brick-and-timber building to the west of the Playhouse. Miss Dyke claimed to be a grandniece of the son who was the issue of an affair between Napoleon I and Countess Walewska.[1]

Each of the hamlets of the town was given an appropriate event. One playlet was set in the days when Dutch influence still survived in Woodstock. An Anti-Rent War episode featured costumed Anti-Rent Indians and their opponents, the sheriffs, all on horseback. A town meeting of 1837 was reconstructed. There was a maypole dance by children on the golf course. In the pageant on the last day of the celebration hundreds of Woodstock people played parts while thousands watched scenes dealing with Woodstock's history.

Local pride was buttressed as photographs and long stories appeared in leading New York newspapers. The celebration, however successful it may have been in arousing interest in Woodstock's past, did not succeed in lifting the town out of the Depression. Yet in a minor way it helped keep the town going. And so did two projects backed by the Chamber of Commerce.[2]

Through their Chamber of Commerce Woodstock businesspeople experimented with promoting a winter sports program as a means of bringing outsiders to town. In 1928 winter sports were bursting into popularity around the country, and there had been talk of organizing a Woodstock project. By 1932, with painters Konrad Cramer and Arnold Wiltz supplying enthusiasm and skill, a beginning had been made. By the mid-Thirties winter sports were promising to become a success. A toboggan slide was built on Ohayo Mountain near the present Riding Club, and an ice skating pond appeared. The New York Central Railroad provided weekend "snow trains" for New Yorkers to travel to skiing centers at Rosendale and Phoenicia as well as Woodstock. Buses carried sports fans from the West Hurley station to Woodstock. Since the plan was dependent on favorable winter weather, it was only moderately successful.

Far more profitable was another Chamber of Commerce project. In cooperation with the Woodstock chapter of the American Legion the Chamber organized and operated a midget automobile racetrack called the Woodstock Legion Speedway amid the rolling country along the Cooper Lake Road. Racing drivers came from many states to compete on Sunday afternoons. Local automobile mechanics quickly became experts in the maintenance of racing cars. For several summers in the 1930s cars roared around the track, with large audiences and much publicity in regional newspapers. It was said that state troopers estimated the crowd drawn to town as high as eight thousand (possibly an inflated estimate). Traffic, it was said, was sometimes "backed up as far as Stony Hollow.'[3]

With the woes of the Depression hovering over them Woodstock people often showed a cheerful side. Early in the Depression the Woodstock *Press* helped keep spirits up by printing an editorial under the heading "Woodstock and the Depression." "We are indeed fortunate to be here," said the *Press*. It went on to urge that "everyone of us do his or her best to help those whom we may chance to know who are in need of any assistance no matter what the nature. This is a period when the milk of human kindness needs to flow as it never did before."

Here the Republican *Press* was following the lead of President Hoover, who saw no need for governmental help for the economically distressed. The Hoover approach proved inadequate to the magnitude of the problem. Yet in Woodstock the milk of kindness did flow. This brought about a strong sense on the part of many of being in a common fix and needing the support of friends and neighbors. Once government assistance programs were in effect after the beginning of the Roosevelt presidency this sense lessened. Then those helped by federal and state agencies sometimes became the objects of hostility by some who did not share in this help.

Woodstock people were indeed fortunate to be where they were as the Depression raged. Mortgage foreclosures in the town were fewer than in similar small towns. Money from earnings outside the town trickled in to artists and writers and to those whose art activities were being financed by patrons or relatives. Tourists still came and left their tributes in money, even if in smaller amounts than in the Twenties.[4]

During a spell of heavy rain a visitor to Woodstock recalled a sardonic saying remembered from her childhood. It went: "When fire, war and famine threaten the good Lord looks down from heaven at his suffering people, rubs his hands and says, 'Now let's have a little flood.'" Old local people used to say that misfortunes come in threes. They said that the 1930s brought fire, unemployment and floods.[5]

Ever since the Woodstock landscape was given its character by geological forces floods had come along at irregular intervals. Some notable twentieth-century floods happened in 1905, 1917, 1924, 1933 and 1935. The flood of 1905 swept away mills and fences and tore out streamside roadbeds. The 1917 flood put Tinker Street in some places almost knee-deep in water. After two days of hard rain in October 1924 both the Sawkill and the Beaverkill did great damage. The Sawkill threatened for a time to burst its banks on the Bearsville Flats and rush through the midst of the hamlet of Woodstock. The streambed above the hamlet was soon afterwards cleared of stones and gravel to avert disaster.

Heavy rains of October 5 and 6, 1932 and of August 23 and 24, 1933 did enough damage to cause the town board to appropriate a total of five thousand extra dollars for highway repair. But it was the storm of July 7, 1935 that gave Woodstock people so great a shock that their worries about the Depression were forgotten at least for a few days.

On July 7 the usual Maverick Concert was in progress. The drumming of the rain on the roof of the hall effectively drowned out the music. As darkness came that day many people were leaving their homes to take refuge with friends living on high ground. Two to three feet of water swirled on Tinker Street and dashed down Mill Hill Road. Great logs, household furniture and parts of buildings piled up at bridges, some of which gave way under the stress. The old de Forest house now owned by the Woodstock Guild of Craftsmen and the "Old Forge House" across the Sawkill had four feet of water on their first floors.

The Ralph Johnson family living beside the Sawkill near Shady fired a shotgun into the black night to summon help when their house was surrounded by six feet of rushing water. They and their dog were rescued with the help of ropes by their neighbors, the Schraders.

Mrs. Charles Cooper with her three children and their nurse tried to flee from their home on Millstream Road. But the Coopers' Packard touring car became pinned by the force of the flood against a railing of Riseley's Bridge. One of the children managed to swim to safety. The rest of the family clung to a six-inch elm tree until rescued by the Kingston Fire Department after the fury of the Sawkill held back the Woodstock Fire Department.

The next day people returning to Zena saw houses near the Sawkill moved from their foundations and carried downstream. Piled up inside the recently renovated old Hardenbergh mill were several feet of mud, stones and household goods from upstream. But by what some saw as a miracle no one was killed. And for the first time in Woodstock history federal money helped repair the damage and gave work to the unemployed.[6]

Woodstock's theater fever survived the three plagues of fire, flood and unemployment. Woodstock did not experience a single Depression summer without some theatrical performance. Byrdcliffe too struggled to hold at least part of its own under the assault of the Depression. It managed to remain alive although its estate income dwindled and repairs to buildings and roads were seldom made. Each summer cottages were rented to painters, poets, craftspeople and to others who merely like to live among artists.

The Villetta, although it had become rather shabby in furnishings, was operated as an inn open to the public and advertised as standing at "The Gateway to the Catskills." Now and then a theatrical venture came to the old art school. None found it profitable to linger for long. Though the prosperous people who had built fine houses in the East Riding grumbled at the decline in the maintenance of Byrdcliffe, they nevertheless returned summer after summer.

Following the death of her oldest son and of her husband in 1928 and 1929 Jane Whitehead turned to faith in mysticism and in Oriental religions. She believed in reincarnation. At the same time she clung to a determination to carry out the plans she and her husband had formed for Byrdcliffe in 1902 and to keep the place as much as possible as it had been in its most promising days. When an old employee came to her after Ralph's death and offered his resignation she said, "No, no. My husband wanted you here. You must stay." From time to time a flurry of dusting off of Byrdcliffe's disused craft shops gave notice that plans for a revival of craft work was being dreamed of with son Peter Whitehead in charge. Peter, however, had not "settled down" and did not long remain interested in a revival.[7]

A growing dissatisfaction with the deterioration of Byrdcliffe to which they were so closely tied led East Riding people to assert themselves in 1933 and to try to take a Byrdcliffe revival into their own hands. Ben Webster, whose theatrical hopes at Byrdcliffe had been dashed by Ralph Whitehead in 1926, drew up a scheme for converting Byrdcliffe into a center for the performing arts, similar, he said, in its scope to that at Salzburg in Austria. The land would be owned by a corporation in which the Whiteheads held fifty percent of the shares. Two theaters, the smaller seating six hundred and the larger twelve hundred, would be built. An open-air Greek theater holding six thousand could accommodate pastoral dramas, pageants and outdoor concerts. A restaurant with terraces overlooking the Woodstock Valley would also serve as a place for "dancing after the play." A hotel with swimming pool and riding ring would appear beside the theater. "Majority control will always rest in persons who own property in Byrdcliffe and who are not of Hebrew extraction," the plan said.

Although the Whiteheads were interested in Webster's proposal, they preferred selling most of Byrdcliffe outright for $140,000. Consulting Francis Smyth of the august law firm of Cadwallader, Wickersham and Taft, who were attorneys for the estate, they received a very discouraging reply. Mr. Smyth viewed the establishment of Byrdcliffe Inc. as of dubious legality and "highly speculative in nature and of doubtful success."

Yet Mr. Smyth conceded that "some such extraordinary proposal is the only method of moving forward the realization upon the investment." In the climate of 1933, with the Depression at its most acute point, Byrdcliffe was in fact virtually unsaleable. At the same time the Whiteheads did not have the income to maintain the buildings and pay taxes. Mrs. Whitehead paid tribute to the beauty of the scheme for an American Salzburg and turned it down.[8]

The dissipation of Ben Webster's dream shocked some East Riding owners into considering another but far less imposing scheme to safeguard their investment in their houses and gardens. In a draft proposal which was probably never submitted to the Whiteheads they stated that the "original idea (of Byrdcliffe) was to establish a community of creative people with kindred interests," and that after East Riding people bought their land the place had "degenerated into a run down summer resort." The draft proposed that the Whiteheads "recognize obligation to buyers," and cooperate in forming a Byrdcliffe Club. Their troubles, they stated, had been caused by "the retention of control in Ralph Whitehead's hands without sharing responsibility with buyers."

The Byrdcliffe Club would better guard against invasion by tourists. It would eject non-paying tenants, destroy all unprofitable buildings, tear down the Villetta and salvage the materials, and enforce a more businesslike method of collecting rents. Like its predecessor this plan came to nothing. It served, however, to point out the difficulties which were besetting Byrdcliffe during the Depression and which were testing its power to endure.[9]

Not long after the failure of the two plans Martin Schuetze of the East Riding, a survivor of the beginnings at Byrdcliffe, was turning over in his mind still another project which might lead to a revival of Byrdcliffe without departing from its original aims. On a summer afternoon in 1937 he outlined his ideas to Jane and Peter Whitehead as they sat in the garden of his place named "Hohenwiesen." Schuetze's proposal involved setting up what at first was called a "School of Thought" at Byrdcliffe. Distinguished scholars would lecture there and students would gather to listen and learn during a month or so each summer.

The Whiteheads were interested. From Byrdcliffe's beginning a school of some sort had been dreamed of. Numerous efforts to start a school had been made and none had succeeded. As Schuetze saw it, the school would involve no great investment. The Villetta could be used for housing scholars and students, and the library-studio for holding the lectures. The project might very well in Schuetze's view lead to a drawing of attention to Byrdcliffe by the kind of people who might settle there and help it survive and perhaps flourish.

Encouraged by the Whiteheads' interest Schuetze went ahead. Two distinguished East Riding summer residents, Columbia University history professor Dr. James T. Shotwell and woolens manufacturer Alfred de Liagre, a man of broad culture although he sometimes described himself to Byrdcliffe people as a "spinner and weaver," joined Schuetze. The more relaxed name of Byrdcliffe Afternoons was given to the lecture series. In the announcement for the sessions to be held in July 1938 its promoters stated that "We address ourselves principally to the minds of cultured laymen—men and women—in an endeavor to develop sound principles of thought as the only means of understanding and judging the ever increasing volume, speed, confusion and force of the environment in which a person of our time has to find his way to a good life." The lectures were planned to be purely intellectual, involving no agitation for social, religious or political action.[10]

Dr. Shotwell opened the series with a lecture on "History and the World today." Dr. Schuetze ended it with "An approach to an Understanding of Art." In between Dr. Waldemar Kaempffert, science editor of the New York *Times*, spoke on "Science and Culture," and Dr. Gerald Walsh of Fordham University spoke on "Dante and Thomas Aquinas." There were lectures on poetry, fiction, African music and opera. L. Moholy-Nagy gave a lecture on "Bauhaus Education," and four Woodstock painters discussed art. Attendance was good and the prospects for a continuation of the series seemed bright.

Yet by the spring of 1939 the path of the Byrdcliffe Afternoons was not altogether smooth. Jane Whitehead at times feared that the Afternoons might lead to a loss of her control over Byrdcliffe. She reacted to the progress of the Afternoons with suspicion. Drs. Schuetze and Shotwell, of very different academic backgrounds, did not always agree. And the rush of events in Europe left scars on the Afternoons.

Following the Munich agreement with Neville Chamberlain, Adolf Hitler had occupied the part of Czechoslovakia known as the Sudetenland in October 1938. World War II seemed inevitable. Drs. Shotwell and Schuetze began planning the Byrdcliffe Afternoons for the next summer in the spring of 1939. The two men were in violent disagreement.

Shotwell was closely in touch with the conflicts then going on between European nations. A leader in the international movement to abolish war, he had worked ever since the First World War to prevent a recurrence of another similar war. He had helped in the establishment of the League of Nations, in what emerged as the Kellogg-Briand Pact to outlaw war as a means of national policy, and had served on countless committees organized to secure peace between nations. Now Shotwell saw all progress toward the abolition of war threatened. He wrote to Schuetze that the world stood on the brink of a dark age similar to that which had engulfed Europe in the fifth century. He proposed bringing to the Byrdcliffe Afternoons representatives of various European cultures who might talk about the reaction of their people to invasion.

Schuetze was aroused to something close to anger. His life had been spent in teaching and analyzing German literature and in theorizing about the arts. He represented much that was best in the German traditions of scholarship, a tradition which valued "disciplined thought" above the kind of participation in events which was so important to Shotwell. Schuetze had seen the Byrdcliffe Afternoons as a bulwark of "disciplined thought" against the emotions of contemporary life. In a letter Schuetze denounced Shotwell for departing from the approach he himself believed in and had imposed on the Afternoons.

In the summer of 1939 there were two series of lectures at Byrdcliffe. Schuetze organized and presided over one and Shotwell over the other. Shotwell's series dealt with Latin-American culture, Schuetze's carried on the series of the previous year. Shotwell's series was published by the Columbia University Press, Schutze's (as the previous year's) by Charles Gradwell and his newspaper, The Overlook.

By the summer of 1940, German troops were attacking and conquering much of Europe. Shotwell was plunged into activities related to the war and attempts to curb it. Schuetze held the Byrdcliffe Afternoons of 1940 before a diminished audience in the studio beside his house. There were no more Byrdcliffe Afternoons. The new war absorbed the world's attention and made even disciplined thought appear frivolous.[11]

While the various attempts at a Byrdcliffe revival of the 1930s had little impact on either Byrdcliffe or the colony below, an incident in Jane Whitehead's life in 1936 did have a long-range effect on the colony and the town. Mrs. Whitehead and Peter usually spent the winter at a hotel in Santa Barbara or elsewhere. At one hotel she met a remarkably charming clergyman, William Henry Francis. Mrs. Whitehead was then much concerned about her thirty-five-year-old son Peter. Peter hadn't done well in school; he showed little promise of applying himself to anything but enjoying life day to day in the ways common to the sons of rich families.

The charming clergyman seemed to have gained Peter's confidence and respect. This promised that Father Francis might help guide Peter into a kind of life more acceptable to his mother. Mrs. Whitehead invited Father Francis to come to Woodstock and keep an eye on Peter. Once there Father Francis remained to become a significant if controversial influence in the town until he died at the age of over ninety. While he was both respected and denounced in Woodstock, his career was a mystery to most local people.

Father Francis had been brought as a boy to the United States from Nottingham, England. He entered the priesthood and soon became a member of a Benedictine Monastery at Waukegan, Illinois. The work of the monastery was largely among the foreign-born poor who formed a good part of the population of the manufacturing and lake port city. The Benedictine community and its missions were taken into the Old Catholic Church in 1907 and in 1913 Father Francis became the community's abbot.

On October 3, 1916 Francis was consecrated as a bishop by Bishop and Prince de Landes and Burghes de la Rache of the house of Lorraine-Brabant, who had come to America to try to unite the separate Old Catholic churches which had arisen there among emigrants from Old Catholic centers in Europe. The following day de Landes also consecrated Carmel Henry Carfora as a bishop, and the two new bishops were soon locked in conflict. Carfora set up the North American Old Roman Catholic Church, and Francis the Old Catholic Church in America. At a meeting of Old Catholic clergy in Chicago in 1917 Father Francis was elected archbishop of his division. Carfora became archbishop of his. From that day on the two struggled for control of the Old Catholic Movement in America, each accusing the other of being a self-made archbishop.

Archbishop Francis's position was not an easy one. Not only was he locking horns with Carfora but the entire Old Catholic Movement in America was also being fiercely attacked by groups within the Roman Catholic and Protestant Episcopal churches. Yet the modern Old Catholic Movement remained alive in the United States, testifying to the strength of the feelings which had led to its birth in the early 1870s, when the Vatican Council had proclaimed the dogma of papal infallibility. Roman Catholics who could not accept the dogma rejected the pope's authority and organized their movement, which they believed marked a return to the purity of the early Christian church. Some Old Catholic churches used the ritual of the Eastern Orthodox Church while others retained the Latin ritual.[12]

As a young priest Father Francis had worked among poor and often exploited industrial workers in and near Chicago. He had gained the respect of these people by his lack of social or racial predjudice, and by his warm and helpful understanding of the problems of the poor. By the time he met Jane Whitehead he was established in the City of New York, where his branch of the Old Catholic Movement had fewer than two thousand members. He functioned from St. Dunstan's House on Stuyvesant Square, close to fashionable St. George's, known as the J. P. Morgan church. There he headed a community of Benedicine monks noted for their work in the arts and crafts. The once-elegant private house was filled with examples of the monks' skill in ecclesiastical art. During this period Father Francis associated with rich and socially prominent New Yorkers as well as with the poor.

During the final decade of his life Francis sometimes said to Woodstock people, "I came here to convert Woodstock but Woodstock has converted me." It was true enough that Woodstock turned the course of his life. There he found that his awareness of social injustice was similar to that which had helped found Byrdcliffe and the Maverick. His skill in crafts—he was a woodcarver—and his willingness to work with his hands formed a passport to Woodstock acceptance.

Once he settled in the town he took up residence in a disused chapel at Mead's high on Overlook Mountain. The chapel had strong roots in local history. It had been built by the Mead family in the 1890s on an acre of land contributed to the Protestant Episcopal Diocese of Albany by Chauncey Snyder, who lived in a nearby farmhouse and was the same man who was evicted from his farm in 1902 in order that the land for Byrdcliffe might be assembled. The Meads were Episcopalians and they planned the chapel for the use of the guests at their thriving summer hotel and for those who were expected to gather at the Overlook Mountain House once the big hotel had overcome its difficulties and become prosperous.

The Overlook Mountain House, which was destroyed by fire in 1924, never reached a point at which it could house fashionable church-going guests. Mead's became somewhat less popular among churchgoers and the chapel languished. By 1931 the Board of Missions of the Episcopal Diocese of New York took it over, but did little to check the growing deterioration of the charming rustic building and its grounds or the dwindling of its congregation.

The Old Catholic Movement was usually on good terms with the Anglican Church and the American Protestant Episcopal Church. Yet problems developed when the chapel became the center of the Old Catholic Church in America. William Manning, bishop of New York and some said a man with a medieval mind, objected to the presence of the Old Catholics on his church's property. Jane Whitehead bought the chapel from the board of the diocese and allowed Father Francis to remain in possession throughout the rest of his life.[13]

The church on the mountain was hard for many parishioners to reach in bad weather and especially in the winter. One of the parishioners gave Francis the use of an old barn she owned on Route 212 a bit to the east of the beginning of the Chestnut Hill Road. Very soon Francis had converted the interior of the barn, with its massive timbers, into a convincing echo of a thirteenth-century English church rich with old and new ecclesiastical art and decoration. Father Francis and his helpers did much of the work with their own hands.

Tourists found St. Dunstan's to be one of Woodstock's prime attractions. Its congregation increased among older art-colony people who found the aesthetic and liturgical aspect of the church appealing. The impact of the war in Europe with its shattering effect on the Polish Old Catholic movement gave Archbishop Francis greater authority. Young aspirants to the Old Catholic Church in America's priesthood came to him to be instructed and ordained from industrial cities where Polish and other workers had settled.

The beginning of the Second World War left marks on the Old Catholic Church's activities in Woodstock. In Poland the Church, administered by the Mariavite Order, was in disarray following the German invasion. Father Francis then served as head of the Mariavites. In 1939 he set up a home for refugee Mariavite sisters in Camelot, the former Snyder farmhouse high up on Mead's Mountain Road. The Mariavite sisters did not remain long in Wodstock, where it had been hoped they could teach and do social work as they had in Poland. As the war grew in intensity Father Francis was well-established in Woodstock, with a good following especially among Byrdcliffe people and the country gentry. The war and its aftermath would lead to a new role for Francis.[14]

THEATER, FIRES
AND FRIENDS
OF ART

As the first signs of the coming economic depression were being treated lightly in the fall of 1929, plans were being made for a resumption of Woodstock's Battle of the Theaters. New York producers planned to lease the Maverick Theater and form a circuit, including Saugerties and Kingston. A special bus would be available to transport theatergoers. Jane Meredith, leading lady at Reasoner's Playhouse, would manage that theater.

By the spring of 1930 Woodstock was informed that Madame Ouspenskaya and the American Laboratory Theater would lease the Byrdcliffe Theater (opposition to its use as a theater had disappeared with the death of Ralph Whitehead). Experimental plays and an acting school would be offered there. Gladys Hurlbut and Allen DeLano, having broken with Hervey White, would move to the Firemen's Hall in the heart of Woodstock and carry on from where they had left off on the Maverick. Other theater ventures were rumored to be in the making. "Nineteen thirty was the Renaissance, the golden age of theater consciousness in Woodstock, with, believe it or not, five theaters operating simultaneously," wrote playwright Anita Phillips in 1933.[1]

The Woodstock show was indeed going on in the summer of 1930. Dismal losses were run up by all five Woodstock theaters, and before the summer ended theatrical wreckage littered the landscape. The Maverick Theater alone survived (after a mid-season change of management). At midnight on March 31, 1931 the Woodstock fire alarm was sounded to tell the town that their Playhouse was ablaze. Soon the beautiful barn theater, with all its expensive fittings and equipment, was destroyed. All insurance had lapsed. Though Dave Reasoner talked of rebuilding, no one paid much attention. Woodstock's theater battle of the boom years was over and everyone concerned had lost.

The Battle of the Hotels also ended in flame and smoke. Early on the morning of October 22, 1930 someone noticed a fire blazing in the basement of the three-story Woodstock Valley Inn. The fire spread with appalling speed through the 61-year-old frame structure. Owner William Wilbur and seven sleeping guests were roused and escaped, with one guest who found the stairway impassable and made his way down a ladder. The Woodstock Fire Department worked hard, though handicapped by a low water supply caused by an almost rainless fall. The heat was so intense, oldtimers recall, that a bunch of bananas in the window of George Layman's grocery store across Mill Hill Road was baked and the paint on the Old Woodstock Inn blistered.

Other fires followed in Zena, Bearsville and Keefe Hollow as well as in the hamlet of Woodstock. Never had the townspeople felt more threatened by fire. A mass meeting called to deal with the problem never took place. Though no public announcement was made as to why, it was rumored around town that a firebug belonging to a well-known local family which wanted no publicity had been responsible. The incident set off a great deal of discussion about ways of getting better protection against fire.[2]

For more than a century every big fire in town had set off a similar explosion of talk. The burning of the first Overlook Mountain House in 1875, the big fire in the center of the hamlet in November 1888, the fire that for a time had threatened the entire hamlet in May 1900, and others stimulated attempts to deal with the danger of fire.

Nearly all the buildings in town were of flammable wooden construction. Ponds and streams to supply water were sometimes low. A bit more than a century ago what was sometime inaccurately called the "village water works" came into being behind the Edgar Snyder house next to the Dutch Reformed Church. A windmill raised water primarily for Snyder use (whether from the northern branch of the Tannery Brook or from a well is not clear) and provided some pressure. Sometimes the system worked well, but at other times it proved inadequate to quench fires.

In August 1906 a barn belonging to the Reformed Church parsonage burned. A meeting was called at Dr. Downer's house for the purpose of working out a better way of dealing with fires than the prevailing bucket-brigade-and-rallying-round-of-the-neighbors method. The Woodstock Fire Company was incorporated and has functioned well ever since. The Firemen's Hall (replaced in 1937 by the present building) was erected in 1911. In 1921 an "American Fire Engine" capable "of throwing a good stream to the top of the highest building in town" was bought. An addition to the Firemen's Hall was built to house it.[3]

Owners of land along the Tannery Brook were encouraged to make dams to impound enough water to douse a big fire. Such dams caused neighboring cellars to be flooded when water was high, and dams were torn away every now and then by a stream swollen by heavy rains.

The epidemic of fires of 1930 and 1931 effectively sent local hotel hopes up in smoke. Though it could not destroy Woodstock's theater fever, it checked it. The summer of 1933 saw the Byrdcliffe theater remain dark while the Villetta and the Maverick Theater joined together with a mixed group of performers, students and managers. Harry Benrimo was director. The students, who paid for board and tuition, lived at the Villetta and were told they could stage plays of their own while helping out the professionals of the Maverick Theater.

In the strained atmosphere of the Depression the venture ran into a remarkable number of difficulties. Advance hints had promised glamorous actors and actresses—Ethel Barrymore was one—but as the project took concrete shape the performers turned out to be unknowns. There were rumors of misappropriated student fees, bad food at the Villetta, and the disappearance of key people at critical moments. Yet the theater venture struggled on.

The company's first offering at the Maverick received a slashing, ill-tempered review in the *Hue and Cry*, revived that summer by Herbert and Deborah Johansen after a dormancy dating back to 1929. At once company manager O'Hanlon cancelled advertising in the paper and refused to provide free tickets to *Hue and Cry* reviewers. It was charged in town that business people were being pressured to refuse to advertise in the paper, which was barely able to hang on to life as it was. The desperate editors of the *Hue and Cry* tried to mend their ways by printing less acid reviews, but the advertising did not return.

THEATER, FIRES AND FRIENDS OF ART

Although the great stars of Broadway never appeared on the Maverick stage that summer, local people were somewhat mollified by the first appearance in Woodstock of two of their own young people. One was Jean Bellows, daughter of George Bellows, for some of whose most notable paintings she had posed. The other was Robert Elwyn, descendant of the Jan Elwyn who had arrived in Woodstock during the 1790s and given rise to a long line of local innkeepers.[4]

An ambitious effort of the theater was an open-air production of *The Willow Tree,* written by Benrimo and Harrison Rhodes some fifteen years earlier and a great success on Broadway. The *Overlook* had just shed its format of a little magazine for that of a weekly newspaper. It was run by Charles E. Gradwell, who edited its theater reviews to eliminate anything that might cause so much offense that O'Hanlon and Benrimo would withdraw further advertising. The *Hue and Cry* published a review in which the play was praised but the performance damned. It followed this with an interview with Woodstock painter and stage designer Takasha Ohta, who pointed out that the play aimed at using the Kabuki tradition of his native Japan and that this required the deliberation and stylized manner for which the actors had been so severely criticized.

The O'Hanlon-Benrimo season left scars in Woodstock. It was notable, however, in that it marked the beginning of Robert Elwyn's emergence not only as an actor but as a manager of local theaters. The next year Elwyn managed and directed the Maverick Theater. He provided plays of proven attractiveness plus some tryouts of new plays aimed at Broadway. His plays and productions, though above average for summer theaters, were rarely adventurous. Hervey White, whose desire for an experimental theater on the Maverick had never died and who would have liked to see some of his own plays produced there, was not very happy even though Elwyn paid his rent promptly.

In 1937 Elwyn decided he needed a theater of his own. He built the Woodstock Playhouse in 1938, using Albert Edward Milliken as architect and Arthur Wolven as builder. Until the gasoline rationing of the Second World War brought the theater to a halt in 1943, Elwyn continued much as he had on the Maverick, but with more elaborate facilities. The Playhouse did well during these years in spite of competition from the Maverick.

A number of producers tried without success to make a go of Hervey's rustic theater. E. J. Ballantine and Cecil Clovelly took over in 1939 and also had a student theater there. By 1942 they succumbed to the wartime gas shortage.[5]

Local artists and encouragers of art reacted very differently from Woodstock theater people to the Great Depression. A year before the town board first applied for federal money to relieve unemployment, the artists had begun demonstrating a strong urge to pull themselves out of the slump by their own efforts. In the fall of 1932 the Friends of Art was organized as an offshoot of the Woodstock Artists Association. It was given muscle by a gift of $500 from Juliana Force, the director of New York's Whitney Museum, a friend and admirer of many Woodstock artists, and a summer resident of the town. Konrad Cramer set the project going, Carl Eric Lindin headed its board. The colony's country gentry contributed money.

According to their director, painter Judson Smith, the purpose of the Friends was "not charitable but protective." Their aim was to enable Woodstock artists to keep on painting by selling their work to the Friends. The Friends would sell the works at auction to help pay the program's costs. Or they might hold some of them to form the nucleus of the long-dreamed-of Woodstock Museum of Art.[6]

Artists were cheered when New York State employed several hundred urban artists at painting murals in settlement houses and elsewhere. They were cheered too by the arrival of one of the peaks of self-congratulation which now and then came to Woodstock's art colony. Nineteen thirty-three marked the thirtieth anniversary of the beginning of Byrdcliffe's working existence in June 1903. The Artists Association planned a series of commemorative exhibitions and an elaborate banquet.

At the opening of the first Association show of work by the colony's pioneer painters, historian James Shotwell stated that art had flourished only in times of prosperity. In the harsh weather of the Depression, Shotwell said, government help could appropriately make up for the shortage of purchasers of art caused by the lack of business and industrial vigor. Among Shotwell's auditors was painter George Biddle, who had written a few weeks earlier to his Harvard classmate President Roosevelt advocating federal help for American art and artists. Biddle suggested hiring painters to ornament public buildings with murals. Roosevelt was favorably impressed. After much debate the federal government launched upon a series of programs which for the first time in American history recognized both the legitimate place of art in life and the right of artists to assistance, in time of need, from public money.

As congressmen and bureaucrats argued the appropriateness of federal involvement in the arts, the Woodstock Friends of Art program got off to a splendid start on its own. Fifteen painters were soon hard at work for the Friends. A dance and two raffles were held to add to the Friends' funds. In September a rollicking Artists' Carnival was held on Judson Smith's farm. Included among the many events was an auction of the Friends' stock of oils, watercolors and prints.

The carnival brought back to life the spirit of the Maverick Festivals. It began in the afternoon with a grand horseback parade through the town. At three o'clock the Friends presented act after act by art-colony people, some humorous, some serious, with a puppet show, a peep show, dance acts, a numerology booth, and so on, all helped along by music and the attractions of a beer garden and a Continental cafe, Prohibition having by that time vanished.

The Friends continued their work the following year. There was another carnival and an auction in the fall. Then they disbanded because federal art projects were promising to employ many Woodstock people. The effort of the Friends did much to hold the art colony together at a time of crisis. It not only kept artists from leaving town in search of work elsewhere but also raised morale and prepared the way for an acceptance of the federal projects. To some the Friends seemed to be bringing into being Hervey White's dream of seeing Woodstock become a "social unit" in which mutual helpfulness and good will would take the place of the harsh competitiveness and striving for worldly success which formed so conspicuous a part of American life.[7]

By the fall of 1933 the Public Works of Art Project (PWAP) was employing many needy Woodstock artists. But the PWAP was not to be surrounded by the happy aura which the Friends had generated.

While the Friends were an organization of art-colony neighbors, the PWAP was managed from afar, subject to political pressures and the unfriendly scrutiny of many congressmen and members of the business world. Painters at work under the Friends had painted in much their usual way and collected their pay with hardly any paperwork at all. Those who came under PWAP were required to fill out forms, to work specified numbers of hours each day, and to estimate in advance the time required for each painting. In addition they were expected to confine themselves to realistic work showing the "American scene" in an approving manner.

The paintings, sculptures and prints produced under PWAP

would become the property of the federal government, to be used in decorating federally-owned buildings. Congressional and business hostility was to be blunted by a combination of help for the needy (PWAP artists had to supply evidence of their neediness), encouragement of the arts, and an essentially conservative and patriotic approach to art.

Because Woodstock was so outstanding in the number and quality of its workers in the arts, it gained a conspicuous place in the national project. Almost fifty Woodstock artists worked on PWAP. When a national exhibition of the project's results was held twenty-five works by Woodstock people were shown. A modest PWAP effort was made to help craftspeople; under it, Ned Thatcher designed and made lighting fixtures.

The ending of PWAP in March 1934 did not halt federal encouragement of Woodstock artists. A succession of other programs took over and lasted until the Second World War brought a return of prosperity to the country. Under these programs Woodstock artists were enabled to continue working provided they conformed to the American-scene formula. Though a few who did not conform managed to remain on the projects, conforming presented few problems to most Woodstock painters, for whom landscapes and figure subjects with a local flavor had long been in high favor.[8]

Painters whose success in the marketplace was assured were of course not eligible for project work. Some helped out by serving as advisers and interceders with the federal bureaucracy on behalf of local artists who felt they had not been fairly treated. Here Carl Eric Lindin was active.

In spite of all this Woodstock artists did not have an entirely pleasant trip through the Depression. Because most painters had to be chosen from many applicants, they were put into competition with one another. Old animosities and feuds between conservatives and moderns revived. With the coming of the Fine Arts Projects (FAP) which followed the PWAP, emphasis was placed on murals and other works for Ulster County public buildings.

As the mood of hopefulness which Franklin Roosevelt had aroused in Congress and the public by his energy and buoyancy settled down into a less optimistic one marked by struggles and name-calling between New Dealers and those whom Roosevelt named "economic royalists," those responsible for federal art projects reacted to the pressures put upon them. They became more fussy about whom they would hire. When their annual appropriations were running out they terminated the employment of many workers.

The interest in social reform which had been a part of Woodstock life ever since the founding of Byrdcliffe caused trouble. In the country as a whole left-wing thinking and commitment had increased under the stress of the Depression. The American Communist Party vigorously sought new adherents among intellectuals and people working in the arts. The Socialist Party too became more aggressive. Yet the combined popular Presidential vote of all left-wing parties of the Depression years never came near the almost 900,000 rolled up by the Socialist Party in 1912. The New Deal measures of Roosevelt had blunted the left wing.

Nevertheless, the opponents of the New Deal liked to portray Roosevelt as an ally of Russia. In Greenwich Village and in Woodstock's art colony a mild sympathy for the kind of changes in society and government advocated by Socialists and Communists was common. Yet on Election Day in 1936 only 44 votes were cast in Woodstock for Socialist Norman Thomas for President, although Thomas had personal friends in town. Roosevelt's opponent, Alf M. Landon, carried Woodstock by an overwhelming majority.[9]

During the hard-fought campaign of 1936 older Woodstock art-colony people were saddened by the death on September 15 of Bolton Brown. Because of the irritating front Brown presented to the colony and his withdrawal from most art-colony activities, few of his neighbors had regarded him with affection. Yet almost all respected him. He had long before moved from the house he had built on the Mead's Mountain Road and settled down in a pleasant old farmhouse in Zena. There he threw himself into making experimental pottery. Far more important to his place in art history he had mastered and was practicing art lithography. After his trip to London in 1915 to learn the craft, he had made fine lithographs using the Woodstock landscape. He made lithographs for George Bellows and others. His school of printmaking trained many artists to become leading practitioners.

Bolton Brown's wife Lucy, whose intelligence and warmth had meant much to the early art colonists, had left Woodstock for a career in teaching. Bolton lived in Zena and worked on. From his school days he had been obsessed with the need of keeping his health at its best. He continued through his last years to begin each day with a cold shower and vigorous exercises. His diet was of the starkest vegetarian simplicity. Finally he was carried to his grave wrapped in his old blue cloak on a bier of white birch poles (these were his favorite tree). With Ralph Whitehead gone in 1929, that left only Hervey White, Jane Whitehead and Carl Eric Lindin of the five who had shared in shaping the colony at Byrdcliffe.[10]

During his Woodstock years Brown had seen the colony undergo many changes. He had seen Byrdcliffe lose much of its original glory, and had seen the rise of the Maverick and the arrival, prosperity, decline and departure of the Art Students League. Yet through all these years he had seen one thing remain constant. That was the division of the townspeople into groups with differing views of life and with misunderstanding and sometimes hostility toward one another.

51

NEW DEAL
PROJECTS
COME AND GO

From the infancy of the art colony
cultural differences between artists and townspeople had inevitably
bred simmering irritations ready to break out whenever some often-
trivial event triggered confrontation. Even the recognition of the
artists' economic value to the townspeople could be overcome at times
like these. Class hostilities were reaching one of their periodic peaks
during the New Deal. The peak this time grew out of the federal help
given to Woodstock artists.

Some townspeople saw federal money as worthwhile in enabling
local artists to live and work. Political leaders on the town and county
levels, however, had denounced New Deal policies. Republican boss
Philip Elting angrily charged that Ulster County's share of the "New
Deal debt" amounted to over four and a half million dollars. This kind
of talk helped Woodstock and Kingston townspeople feel that they
were being taxed heavily in order that Woodstock artists might do
work of less value to the community than honest pick-and-shovel or
clerical labor.[1]

Added to the internal conflicts among the fifty or so artists on the
federal payroll as to who should be hired or fired and who should act
as director, the conflict between artists and non-artists made the
Depression years turbulent. Yet the federal projects under a variety of
acronyms went on and produced an impressive body of work. Painter
Walter Sarff reported in 1937 that in two years Woodstock artists had

completed 1100 pieces of work, including 300 oil paintings, 400 prints, 300 original poster designs (some promoted the Woodstock Winter Sports program and others advertised on behalf of the State Conservation Department and other public agencies), 30 pieces of sculpture, 50 drawings for the Index of American Design (set up to preserve a record of representative examples of the American tradition in crafts and design), 25 completed pieces of metalcraft work, 30 watercolors and 6 mural paintings.

Among recipients of these works of art were state hospitals, the New York Conservation Department, public libraries in Woodstock, Phoenicia and New York, and public buildings in Saugerties and Kingston. Woodstock artists appeared to be making their contribution to the plan of federal agencies aimed at elevating American taste in art and using works of art publicly displayed to intensify American pride in its own land and culture. Yet the works of art were often rejected or bitterly criticized.[2]

Early in 1938 Judson Smith, who had spent two years heading Woodstock projects in the arts, found it necessary to defend the colony's artists in a talk to the Kingston Lions Club. Smith pointed out that some artists had long hair because they couldn't afford haircuts, that some wore flowing neckties to hide their lack of a shirt, and that baggy pants were popular among artists because they were cheaper than the well-cut variety. He reassured his audience that federal subsidies were not intended as a permanent solution to the artists' problems. The artists, he said, had to learn to deal with buyers without the intervention of government or of middlemen.[3]

To expand efforts toward the overall goal of making art visible to a wide public, the Section of Fine Art was created within the Treasury Department in 1934. Its purpose was to hold competitions among non-needy artists, with the winners to paint murals to decorate the walls of public buildings owned by the federal government, all the way from small-town post offices on up to seats of power in Washington. Interest in mural painting had swelled during the boom years of the 1920s. The Art Students League in New York had offered a class in mural painting under Kenneth Hayes Miller, some of whose students became active in Woodstock. It seemed to some that a new era in which art would contribute to emphasizing the majesty of American government was dawning. Eventually Americans would take it for granted that their public buildings would be adorned with murals celebrating the glories of their past and present in a kind of painting easily understood by everyone.

By the time the Section went out of business, murals by Woodstock people had found their way to many parts of the country. Efforts to place a mural in Woodstock's new town hall failed, however. Murals using regional themes were placed in Kingston and Saugerties. Mary Earley's depiction of a high point in the Anti-Rent War is still to be seen in the post office at Delhi, N.Y. In 1935 the Guild of Mural Painters and Sculptors was founded in Woodstock to elevate the level of mural work.[4]

Artists employed by the succession of federal agencies helping to keep Woodstock alive as an art colony were subject to many uncertainties, including the ups and downs of appropriations by Congress and the mobilization of public opinion against left-wing sympathizers on federal projects. This helped lead toward the organization in 1938 of the House Un-American Activities Committee, which viewed most artists with suspicion. The project artists also had their internal conflicts.

Whenever appropriations were cut, some project members would have to be chosen for dismissal. This always produced unhappiness made publicly visible in the form of charges of favoritism, outright dishonesty and inept management. In 1936 artists employed on New York City projects attracted widespread attention with a mass demonstration against cuts in their projects. Woodstock project members soon formed the Ulster County Artists Union and put on an orderly sit-down strike in front of Judson Smith's Woodstock house. For the next two years controversy bubbled within and around the projects.

The turmoil in the artists' working lives was not unrelated to other events taking place in Woodstock. The New York State Department of Education was urging the centralization of rural schools. Federal grants were available to pay one-third of the cost. A hotly-debated proposal to centralize Woodstock's seven school districts with those of Daisy and High Woods in Saugerties was defeated in Woodstock in 1935. The pro-centralizers did not give up. They kept on agitating and maneuvering until the Second World War put a temporary end to their hopes.[5]

It was the fate of the art projects to become conspicuous targets of local anti-Communists, anti-Semites, anti-New Dealers and right-wing politicians eager to hold their restless constituencies together in the face of the liberal administrations in Albany and Washington. In 1937 Judson Smith resigned and Eugene Ludins took over. Ludins had been an active member of the Ulster County Artists Union and had connections with the New York City Union, which in turn had endorsed the League for Peace and Democracy. That group had been denounced on the front pages of the country's newspapers as a Communist front. Phrases like "fellow traveller" and "Communist dupes" were freely tossed about in Woodstock.[6]

The project artists kept on working in spite of an overly-publicized dispute within the ranks of the Artists Union and an occasional blast from the Ulster County enemies of the New Deal. Some artists who were not eligible for other projects set up a project of their own. In the spirit of the times the Sawkill group was put together in the spring of 1935 as an attempt at reaching more members of the public and making more sales than the Artists Association seemed capable of. The Sawkill Gallery was opened in the old De Forest house next to the Artists Association.

Here a group of younger artists, Joseph Pollet, Wendell and Jane Jones, Austin and Marianne Mecklem, Gene Ludins and others, found their work sold well at prices lower than those that were the rule next door. Helped by excellent publicity releases written by ex-advertising copywriter Pollet, the Sawkill Gallery at first did well. The members aspired to branch out into neighboring communities and for a time exhibited and taught in Saugerties. After about three years and declining sales, however, they disbanded and were absorbed into the Artists Association.

Similar in spirit to the Sawkill group's private project was a public one, the WPA's (Work Progress Administration) Federal Art Projects Art Caravan. An old army ambulance was converted into a mobile gallery equipped with moveable devices for displaying paintings and other works of art both indoors and out. It had a slide projector and sixty-six works, all but a few (which were by schoolchildren) by workers in the federal art projects. Active in designing the Caravan was Gene Ludins.

The purpose of the Caravan was to promote interest and involvement in the arts in communities in New York, New Jersey and Pennsylvania where people had enjoyed little chance to come in contact with art as a valuable enhancement of life. People of the communities visited were invited to express their interest in having instruction in art and in the setting up of a local art center. The project was a decided success. It carried forward in a practical way some of the idealistic aims which had motivated Ruskin, Whitehead and Hervey White. In May 1939 the Caravan appeared on

Woodstock's Village Green for the benefit of visiting delegates to a Home Bureau Convention and to give local people a chance to study it. Shortly afterwards appropriations dried up and the Caravan project reached its end.

The Art Caravan and the some other Woodstock federal art projects benefitted the town and American art in spite of the hostility with which they were received by some and in spite of their internal dissensions. It was quite otherwise with another federal project, the Woodstock Resident Craft Center, a National Youth Administration (NYA) project under the Works Progress Administration (WPA). From its beginning in 1935 the Youth Administration was intended to help unemployed young people to find part-time work and to acquire working skills.[7]

The Woodstock Resident Craft Center began taking shape early in 1939. Its primary purpose was to give young men a chance to learn such skills as wool processing, woodworking and metalworking, stonecutting and building. The program in Woodstock, the only one of its kind in New York State, was "based upon the Folk School concept which has furnished a pattern of integral living for such diverse peoples as those of Denmark, Nova Scotia, Sweden, Wisconsin, Georgia or Arkansas." It was to include not only practical instruction in many crafts but also classes in the history of the arts and crafts, public speaking and subsistence farming. There would also be discussions of current events and social problems. The declared purpose was to help students toward "a happy and productive life."

Cooperative methods would be employed in order that students might learn how to organize working cooperatives and credit unions. The Center itself would be run as far as possible by the students working in cooperation with elected group leaders, councilmen and house captains. A constitution echoing the national one was drawn up; it began, "We, the youth of the NYA Resident Youth Center of Woodstock, in order to form a more perfect Center, establish justice, insure domestic tranquility, and promote the general welfare, do ordain and establish this Constitution for the youth of the NYA Resident Youth Center in Woodstock."

Art-colony people and townspeople welcomed the Center with enthusiastic help. A committee of prominent people in the arts, music, social work and literature saw to it that Center students were invited to studios and workshops as well as homes in town, were given free tickets to Maverick concerts and the auto races at Bearsville. To many art-colony people the Center's involvement in the arts and crafts, its interest in cooperation and in subsistence farming seemed an extension of the ideas which had led Ralph Whitehead to found Byrdcliffe. These people hoped that the Center would become a permanent part of Woodstock life.

Land for the Center was acquired in Mink Hollow. Kingston objected on the ground that the Center might pollute its water supply. But in the cooperative spirit which marked the arrival of the Center, Kingston offered the Center a long leasehold at a token rent of a dollar per year of land they owned on Route 212 at Easton Lane. The Center took temporary quarters at the summer resort called Wildwood Farms in Willow while its faculty and students plunged into clearing the site at Easton Lane. Buildings to house shops for the various crafts and for other Center purposes were begun. A sawmill was set up on the property, classes in stonecutting were begun in sculptor Tomas Penning's studio in High Woods, and other classes found space in the Allencrest hotel buildings in the hamlet of Woodstock.

The cornerstone of the main Center building, designed by Albert Graeser, was laid by Eleanor Roosevelt, who had shown great interest in all the federal art projects which came to Woodstock. The Center with its fifty and more students got off to a promising and productive start.[8]

The NYA Resident Craft Center and the federal art projects were only a few among the many signs that the Great Depression had loosened up American thinking. The propriety of government help for people in need and for artists and craftspeople had become widely accepted. At the same time, many individuals and private groups were dedicated to innovations in organizing their lives. Some pursued the simple life through subsistence gardening with goats, chickens and other animals. Ralph Borsodi, apostle of existence on a few acres, came to Woodstock to speak. The Catholic Workers movement had Woodstock followers. Schemes for cooperative shops and other instruments of rebellion against the accepted order were widely discussed.

With the appearance of *Order* in 1936 the town had a publication which faced up to the ferment of the times, albeit in its own unpopular way. *Order*'s editor was Norman Towar Boggs, son of the former clergyman who had come to Woodstock at the urging of John Dewey. His paper showed awareness of the clashing social and political ideas which were assuming varied forms in Germany, France and the United States. *Order* tried to take a middle ground among Fascism, capitalism and Communism while accepting involvement in the arts and crafts, subsistence gardening and farming. In an effort at fairmindedness it published an apology for Fascism by Benito Mussolini and so came to be regarded by some as a Fascist organ. It soon ceased publication. Its editor became educational director of the Resident Craft Center.[9]

The end of the Maverick Festivals in 1931 had marked a turning point in Hervey White's life. With the income produced by the Festivals no longer coming in, new building and other expansion at the Maverick came to an end. In 1934 Hervey made a final try at publishing a little magazine. With writers Henry Morton Robinson and Earnest Brace as co-editors (and co-typesetters, printers and distributors, too) he revived *The Plowshare*.

The new *Plowshare* was ambitious. Offering "one man exhibits" of the work of serious American intellectuals, it made no concessions to the non-intellectual public. New Critic Kenneth Burke wrote the entire first issue. Under the title of "Interpretations" he dealt with the thesis that "our ideas as to how the world is constructed affect our explanations as to why people do as they do" and that "our vocabulary responds to this situation." Alexander Laing devoted the next number to ideas on the life, death and current use of the English language.

The Plowshare went out to several hundred subscribers, only eighteen of whom renewed at the end of the first year. And so the magazine gave up. In 1935 Hervey printed two of his own plays in separate volumes. These were the last of his writings to come from the Maverick Press.[10]

Some artists working on federal projects lived on the Maverick year-round during the Depression, getting along on minimal incomes and diets and gathering and cutting their own firewood. They benefitted from Hervey White's guidance. Yet it was obvious that the place had slowed down.

In 1933 Hervey put into bold words what the Maverick had meant to him for so long. Dancer Alexis Kosloff and his wife had opened a bathing project on their land adjoining the Maverick and called it Maverick Beach. The Beach boasted "a tropical white sand beach," beach umbrellas, beach chairs, a lounging room, a solarium and parking spaces, it was claimed, for 800 cars. Hervey readily agreed to say a few words at the beach's grand opening.

"I have been accused of softness in letting another man use the word 'Maverick' in the name of his amusement park," Hervey said. "Well, this is what I have to say. A Maverick is anyone's property—anyone who can capture it and hold it, can have it. If another man wishes to try it, good luck to him, but I know it would be easier to steal Hercules' club than to attempt the proprietorship of something that is as free as the air, as restless as the wind."

Coming into the world at the lowest point of the Depression, the beach failed. The bluestone quarry pool which had been its heart returned to the custody of its oldest inhabitants, a community of leeches.[11]

As the Thirties moved along Maverick people recognized that Hervey was declining in vigor, though he remained the same generous and alert friend he had always been. Hervey, who had enjoyed caring for the simple daily needs of those around him, took to running what he called a "men's boardinghouse." By this he meant that he cooked for a group of six to eight young Maverick men toward whom he behaved as a surrogate father.

A publisher was persuaded to give him an advance on a proposed autobiography which would make much of the many famous people whom Hervey had known. The book got written in the hasty unrevised manner which had become Hervey's way; the writing habit had come to have so strong a hold on Hervey that he couldn't shake it even when he had little to say. The disappointed publisher rejected the manuscript because it dealt with many unknown people who had aroused Hervey's interest and often dismissed the famous ones in only a few words.

As Maverick winters became harder for him to endure, Hervey began going south each fall to a rundown farm on the southernmost border of Georgia where the St. Mary's River flows into the Atlantic. There his interest in people and places stimulated him to organize an annual performance of an Easter passion play using several hundred of the cooperative local black population as actors and singers. The stage set was a ruined old church of tabby or oyster-shell masonry some ten miles from his farm. Over this venture Hervey's creative energies had their last short revival.[12]

During this final phase of his existence Hervey never ceased being receptive, helpful and encouraging to people who came to the Maverick with ambitions to do any sort of work in the arts or crafts. One man whom Hervey so helped was James Peter Cooney, a rebellious son of conventional Irish immigrants. By the spring of 1938

Cooney had been given the use of the Maverick Press. There he began publication of a little magazine called *The Phoenix*. The new magazine was far more than another literary quarterly. It served as a vehicle for promoting the hopes for a better social order of its editor and the group of friends who surrounded him.

With Hervey's encouragement the *Phoenix* group set up on the Maverick a commune dedicated to putting into practice the social aims of writer D. H. Lawrence, who had died in 1930. The Western world, Cooney believed, tottered on the edge of collapse. Men and women, trapped in a society which exalted technology and business above all else, had "been betrayed and have not the strength and courage" to wriggle out of their traps. And no wonder "for the betrayal begins with the vulnerable, unprotected years of earliest childhood, and is perpetuated by parents, teachers and priests, by church and state and nation." In this situation, Cooney believed, "there is only one man to whom we can turn, only one man whose fiery spirit has blazed a way through to deliverance. And that man is D. H. Lawrence."

In the pages of *The Phoenix* Cooney proclaimed his intention of making a beginning of establishing a Lawrentian colony on the Maverick. But the colony could not remain there. For, in accordance with Lawrence's teachings, it would have to be based not on the European culture which had left so strong a mark on Woodstock but on that of the American Indians who had flourished until the invasion by Europeans of Central and South America.

Pending the removal of the colony to a site at which Indian culture might be revived and carried forward, however, the Maverick would do. There the commune struggled to maintain itself with its members working for outsiders as well as themselves as carpenters and at the old craft of building with bricks of rammed earth. They also hunted, fished, raised vegetables and shared in the job printing done there.[13]

Cooney's excellent editorial judgement made *The Phoenix* the best of all the little magazines born in Woodstock since Seaver's *1924*. Henry Miller was its European editor and a contributor. Anais Nin, Kay Boyle, William Everson and Lawrence (posthumously) also contributed. Lawrence's widow, Frieda, gave the magazine and the commune her blessing from afar. *The Phoenix's* fine design and printing did not suggest the rebellion which was evident in much of its text. Both were in marked contrast to Cooney's ideas and solutions, which were occasionally phrased with a gift for invective seldom matched since William Cobbett ceased harassing the British establishment in 1835.[14]

The chilling expansion of the Second World War could not leave the Maverick's Lawrentian commune untouched. It battled for pacifism, to which two issues published in 1940 were devoted. In the autumn of 1940 *The Phoenix's* editor announced that the magazine was suspending publication due to "our imminent departure from Woodstock and our journies to a neglected old farm on the southern coast of Georgia." Cooney hoped to help restore part of the farm to cultivation and there carry on his plan for a colony inspired by his "Morning Star," D. H. Lawrence. The farm to which Cooney and his fellows went was the place on which Hervey White was to play out several scenes of the last act of his life story.[15]

Through the final years of the 1930s Woodstock people watched helplessly as the world drifted toward war. With the Japanese attack on Pearl Harbor in 1941, their own country became a party to the war. The St. Mary's Easter play and the assembly on its new site of Cooney's colony both came to an end. Throughout Woodstock, taking part in the war became a dominating activity.

52

THE SECOND
WORLD WAR
AND WOODSTOCK

Throughout the Great Depression
Woodstock people were made aware of the many steps which were
bringing war closer. Yet few grasped their significance. The rise of
Hitler and National Socialism in Germany, of Fascism in Italy and of
militarism in Japan, the expansion of German and Italian territory, the
Spanish Civil War, the Munich pact of 1938 and other events were
reported to Woodstock people as similar events had been on the eve
of their involvement in the First World War. Yet people, anticipating
the return of American prosperity which they hoped would be the
result of industrial activity for European war purposes, were more
interested in carrying on as usual.

The European developments of September 1939 shocked
Woodstock people into an uneasy realization that the whole world was
in trouble. When the Germans invaded Poland from the west and the
Russians from the east, it became apparent that the whole structure of
international agreements set up to preserve peace after the First
World War had become unworkable.

By this time Woodstock had acquired residents of many national
and ethnic backgrounds. Some of these people reacted to September
1939 with an apprehension which was shared only to a lesser degree
by most older Woodstock people. Some of German origins celebrated
the fall of Warsaw to the Germans late in September with a party.
American Communists at first denied that the invasion of Poland by

Russia had taken place, showing copies of *The Daily Worker* which said that the story of the Russian invasion was merely a bit of capitalist propaganda. After Germany went on to invade Russia in June 1941 and the Russian cause became one with that of the Allied powers, American Communists turned into enthusiastic supporters of the Allies.[1]

Through the bombardment from the air of Britain in 1940 and the adoption by the United States of the lend-lease program furnishing war supplies to the Allies sympathy for the Allies in Woodstock increased. The sympathy was not lessened by the fact that the Depression drained away and prosperity came back. A hint of a revival of the boom spirit of the 1920s was soon felt.

By 1941 Charles E. Gradwell was giving a voice to this spirit. His booklet titled *Woodstock, N.Y. 1941, Facts and Figures About Our Town*, listed town officials and organizations, sketched the town's early history, and presented a picture of the place as he saw it in the summer of 1941. Ignoring the tensions and disagreements which existed between artists and townspeople and within the art community, Gradwell tried to create an image of a peaceable little enclave set in an idyllic pastoral landscape.

Woodstock, Gradwell wrote, was a place of extremes and of paradoxes. Although it was an art colony, most of its people were not artists. Although it had a country club and a "brick block" like those in Westchester County (the Longyear Building), it was not a suburb. "It is rural in spirit," wrote Gradwell, "a place of farms and farmers, yet it rivals West Fifty Second Street in the number of its night clubs."

Woodstock, Gradwell wrote, "is the most cosmopolitan village in the world. It includes men with beards, ballet dancers, farmers, flute players, business men, actors, poets, restaurateurs, potters, writers, weavers, painters, press agents, politicians, lawyers, historians, illustrators, cartoonists, philosophers, remittance men, educators, theatrical producers, wine merchants. . . . Modern Woodstock," Gradwell concluded, "is everything, it is intensely active, intensively alive. . . ."[2]

Active indeed the town was in 1941. With the rebirth of selective service, the first young Woodstock men were drafted for military service in October. In December Congress declared war on the Central Powers. Less than a year later there were more than 120 Woodstock men in the armed forces and one woman, Dorothy Shultis, a Navy nurse.

Before Pearl Harbor Woodstock people had openly expressed

their sympathy for the Allies. They set up a Red Cross table at their Market Fair and made contributions to Bundles for Britain and other relief organizations. Women knitted scarves and mittens for British soldiers.

Once their own country became a party to the war, Woodstock people plunged into a greater variety of activities, some mandatory, others voluntary and some in between. Strong leaders in home-front war work emerged from the various layers into which the townspeople were divided. Aging Carl Eric Lindin served as a member of Ulster County's Rationing Board. Lawyer Martin Comeau managed the headquarters of the Civil Defense program from an office in the Comeau Building on Tinker Street, opposite the stone gateposts which marked the entrance to the Comeau estate.

Other art-colony, clerical, business and country-gentry people became leaders. Anita M. Smith devoted less attention to her Stonecrop Gardens, where she grew and sold herbs, and headed the Plane Spotters, whose job was to keep track of planes flying overhead, a task they performed from a wooden tower built on Miss Smith's property. Local politicians, realizing the advantages of keeping in the public eye and exerting control over aspects of life affected by the war, joined ordinary citizens on home-front committees.[3]

No member of the town's country gentry held quite as secure a place in home front activities as did Dr. James T. Shotwell. In the summer of 1942 Shotwell resigned his professorship at Columbia University. With more time to devote to Woodstock, he spoke impressively at war rallies and meetings. Eminent leaders of Allied nations who were his friends visited him and his family, often lending their voices to local fundraising events. When an elaborate benefit performance for Chinese relief was held at the Playhouse in 1942, Dr. Shotwell spoke, as did his guest, Huh Shi, the Chinese ambassador. The event cleared $1200.

That same year a scrap drive produced seventy-four tons of metal. The American Legion post founded after the First World War collected old phonograph records for recycling as new records to be sent to the armed forces. The Navy Relief Society, Russian War Relief, France Forever and similar organizations all benefitted from Woodstock events. The art colony had long been known for the liveliness and gaiety of its many parties. Now the same spirit was cheerfully turned to practical use against a background of the horror of war.

The town's churches sponsored more conventional fundraisers. A campaign for selling $100,000 worth of War Bonds was launched. Shortages of many articles of daily use preceded the rationing of sugar, automobile tires, gasoline, coffee and meat. "Victory gardens" were planted on allotments on the Comeau and Byrdcliffe properties and elsewhere.[4]

As war spirit intensified, German and Oriental residents were eyed with suspicion. Woodstock people sent denunciations of their neighbors as enemy agents to the Office of Strategic Services in Washington. "Local Family Servant Unmasked as German Spy" ran a headline in the *Overlook*. The suspected spy was the maid of a member of the De Liagre family, which spent summers in Byrdcliffe.

As during the First World War agitated attention was directed toward Overlook Mountain, from whose summit, it was once again believed, enemy operators might send signals to raiding submarines or spy out the land. The nearby Ashokan Reservoir, so vital to the welfare of the people of New York, was guarded and protected. This did not prevent rumors of sabotage from running around Woodstock.[5]

During the war years with few exceptions Woodstock people worked with a sense of common destiny rare in the divided town. This did not mean that the division of Woodstock into layers of people with differing ways of living and thinking had come to an end. Artist-townsman tensions remained alive if subdued for the duration.

Among art-colony members, as the colony reached its third decade, some were noticing a division into three broad classes: those people who had arrived early or at any rate before the First World War, the new arrivals through the mid-Twenties, and those who had settled in Woodstock later. Each class regarded its own as the true Woodstock, which they often saw as degenerating under the impact of fresh arrivals.[6]

Pacifist convictions bred by the slaughter and destruction of the First World War had not been uncommon in the Woodstock of 1914 to 1940. Once their country was committed to combat, however, not many Woodstock people clung to their committment to pacifism. Yet there were some. In June 1942 Holley R. Cantine, Jr. published the first number of *Retort*, a periodical which he and co-editor Dorothy Paul set, printed and partly wrote themselves. *Retort* did not take sides in the war then in progress but made clear its editors' belief that the chief enemy of human happiness was "the state" in whatever form. By 1947, with poet Dachine Rainier as co-editor, *Retort* was describing itself as "An Anarchist Quarterly." The variety of libertarian thinking represented by *Retort* has had a following in Woodstock up to the present.[7]

Although Woodstock plunged with vigor into war-related work much normal activity continued as in times of peace. Speculators and shopkeepers remained in business in spite of shortages, higher taxes and more forms to fill. A few shops did not. The Jack Horner Shop, which dealt in gift and decorative objects imported from Germany, made it known that it was going out of business "for the duration." Mrs. Grimm's clothing shop folded up forever.

On the surface at least, the town retained its older appearance, with new building and other changes limited by wartime shortages. Occasionally there were even revivals of the bizarre quality which had lightened existence in the zany Twenties. Billy Whiskers, a wandering eccentric notable for his white beard and a costume liberally covered with buttons, came to town and took up residence in the old sheds behind the Lutheran Church. Billy arrived in 1942 and predicted that the war would be over by the end of the year.[8]

Morris Newgold died on the eve of the entrance of the United States into the war. His heirs were soon plunged into fierce litigation over his Overlook Mountain property, estimated in the course of the proceedings to be worth one million dollars. The work on the hotel buildings which had gone on in a spotty way during the depressed Thirties ceased altogether.

The hotel doors and windows were closed with metal lath and wooden shutters. The amount of material stored on Overlook was immense. The hotel rooms were piled high with building materials, cases of telephones and plumbing fixtures, mattresses, rugs, second-hand furniture of the kind used during the first two decades of the century, chinaware, cutlery and so on. Outside a half-dozen New York sightseeing buses which had been used as workshops were lined up. So too were toilets and other objects which it was once thought could be woven into the hotel structure. There was a powerhouse, separate cottages and farm buildings left over from the earlier hotel complex. All were filled with hotel-related objects.

As scarcities of materials developed, the things stored on Overlook took on a value which led thieves to raid the place. Vandals followed. Truckloads of metal left the mountaintop in broad daylight. Furniture and crockery were hurled down the mountainside from windows from which their protective covering had been pried. The never-finished hotel took on the look of a bombed-out result of the war raging in Europe. Porcupines found their way into the old clifftop bowling alley (built in 1879) and gnawed wherever human hands had left a touch of salt. In many houses in the valley below bits of furniture and other objects from the hotel found places. One cold January afternoon two local men were seen carrying an old-fashioned woodburning stove down the snowy side of Overlook.

Hunters camped out in the hotel lobby and kindled fires in its big fireplace. By summer young people spent nights there. Like a great ship lured ashore on a rocky coast the hotel was looted and explored and further wrecked by the nearby inhabitants. For a century isolated summer houses and hotels in the Catskill had been subjected to this kind of treatment, but seldom on the scale that devastated the top of Overlook.[9]

Billy Whiskers was wrong. The war would not reach its end until 1945. By that time over three hundred Woodstock people were away in the armed forces or in such ancillary services as the Red Cross or the Merchant Marine. Others not included in the three hundred were working in war industries away from home.

Painting and writing had gone on even during the most unsettling days of the war. There was a difference, partly the result of the federal art projects. The Woodstock School kind of painting had by 1939 given way to the federally-approved American Scene variety. Yet there were many dissidents. A few clung to the kind of "modern" painting with which Woodstock artists had experimented ever since the days of the Rock City School. Some doggedly applied the lessons learned from Birge Harrison or John F. Carlson, working on snowy landscapes, winding brooks or autumn foliage. Many younger artists, regardless of the categories in which their work might be placed, were restless under the dominance in their colony of the Woodstock Artists Association. They saw the Association as controlled by a clique whose members were reluctant to admit outsiders within the walls of their Gallery, and they made their resentment felt.

By 1940 a little artists' war centering around the Artists Association was brewing. In September 1940 both Carl Eric Lindin and Judson Smith "stunned" the members of the Association by resigning. Both men, long guiding spirits in art-colony affairs, announced that they were through struggling to keep order and peace in the Association. In his speech of resignation Lindin characteristically quoted Horace twice, and Aesop's Fables and Shakespeare once each. He paraphrased Schopenhauer's fable of the porcupines who huddled together for warmth on a cold day only to be repelled when their spines pricked each other. Lindin compared the situation of the Association members to that of the porcupines, who both needed and needled each other.

Ever since the beginning of the art colony Lindin had been an understanding arbiter between conservative and modern artists. Now he sadly relinquished that role. "For my part," he said, "I am too old, and also too old-fashioned to understand or even to care to understand these new developments in art and in life. Everywhere there is suspicion, hatred and violence. How to get out of this state of mind is your task. I know well that under the superficial stream of modern life there are deeper subconscious currents, which will in time, bring back the great humanitarian ideals which have always been the goal of all civilizations worthy of the name. . . ." [10]

A committee was appointed to chart the future course of the storm-battered Association. Serving were seven conservative and Woodstock School painters: Joseph Pollet, whose Sawkill group of younger painters had by then returned to the Association; Eugene Ludins, active in the federal projects; the widely respected Charles Rosen; Norbert Heermann, who aspired to become a fashionable portrait painter; Frank London, who remained devoted to painting elegant still lifes; Julia Searing Leaycraft, a good country-gentlewoman painter; and Wendell Jones, promising mural painter in his own variant of the American Scene manner. These people gave assurance that the Association, while coming into the care of younger people, was far from surrendering control to those whom the *Overlook* called the leftist "malcontents" who had exalted "the soapbox" above "the easel." [11]

A serious cause of trouble was the fact that the WAA Gallery was still owned by the Realty Company whose stock, in spite of early attempts to sell to painters, was controlled by the country gentry. Young artists were restive under what they saw as pressures by conservative forces whose thoughts about art had been shaped in the early years of the twentieth century.

A time of crisis and deadlock arrived. Through the summer of 1941 there were no shows by members of the Association, though the Gallery was rented several times for other exhibitions. At a meeting in September the members decided to lease the Gallery once again and to put on a show. The response was encouraging. Four hundred people crowded the Gallery for the opening reception. Plans for using the place for lectures, discussions, and classes were announced. The exhibition of September was described as a first step in the "rejuvenation" of the Artists Association. To avoid country-gentry criticism non-members' work would have to be approved by a jury of members, while the work of members would be hung without jurying.[12]

The summer of 1942 saw a full program of exhibitions and other events at the Gallery. The twenty-fourth annual show, which opened in August, dimly reflected the existence of the war. Only a social-realism painting showing guerrillas in action, a still life in which scrap metal was dealt with in a romantic-realist manner, and another still life called "Fruits of a Victory Garden" hinted that a war was going on. Nine Association members were then in the armed forces.

In its review of the annual show the *Overlook* rejoiced because "whatever groups there have existed before in the association they are now functioning as one, standing together. Both the older members and talented newcomers indicate their responsibility to produce more and better art in a world at war." Though a curious statement to appear in an account of an art exhibition, the suggestion that the Association was back in successful operation while the war raged was accurate enough.[13]

In 1940 one point about which art-colony debate and conflict had centered was resolved. As planned at its beginnings, the WAA was intended to serve craftspeople as well as artists. Some artists had been none too pleased with the inclusion of craft objects in their shows. After its regular season was over in 1939, the Gallery had presented an exhibition devoted entirely to craft work. It was a success. This stimulated craft workers to revive an old dream of having a craft exhibition and sales shop of their own.

Earlier Byrdcliffe craft workers had held annual exhibitions in the Studio. The building called Varenka had been used for a few years as a shop for the exhibition and sale of Byrdcliffe furniture and other crafts. A briefly functioning "Sloyd Shop" had been established on what is now Whitehead Road.

The new attempt was much more ambitious as far as hopes for sales were concerned. The hope was given visible shape when the Woodstock Guild of Craftsmen was formed. The Guild took space next to the post office on Tinker Street and there opened a shop on May 15. The Guild proposed exerting its influence to maintain high standards of design and workmanship and to show not only the work of art-colony craftspeople but that of workers in crafts of the older Woodstock. "Woodstock is both a rural community and an art center," the Guild told the public, and "one of its basic purposes is to unite these two sources of creative vitality." This marked a departure from Byrdcliffe and Artists Association policy, which had seen art-colony craftspeople distinctly separated from those working outside. A short-lived group called the Craft Co-operative of Ulster County had been set up in the Nook, and this may have influenced Guild policy.[14]

The Guild shop did well. In a few years it moved into its own building first lent and later given by Mrs. Blanche Rosett, widow of Dr. Joshua Rosett, an authority on the human brain (The doctor ran a Brain Institute on top of Ohayo Mountain). The building which the Guild still occupies had been the home of a succession of early Woodstock tanners, a general store, the home of craftsman Hunt Dietrick and other art-colony people, and finally the Jack Horner Shop.

The Artists Association and the Guild were both responding to the growth of Woodstock. Between 1930 and 1940 the town's population had increased by seventeen per cent; in 1940 there were close to two thousand year-round residents. It seemed to some art-colony people that this would be a good time to join in the movement toward town planning and zoning which was rapidly developing in many parts of the country. In 1916 only six American communities had made any attempt at planning; ten years later over five hundred had joined the rush.

In 1929 the New York State Commission for Housing and Regional Planning made public a far-reaching state plan. Early in 1940 a small group of Woodstock people, restricted to propertyowners, began sketching a town plan and a zoning ordinance. This organization, called the Woodstock Township Association, held public meetings, consulted the Regional Planning Association of New York, and published a bulletin which called for the adoption of planning and zoning, not to create "a town beautiful" but to use "business methods" to protect the investment of propertyowners. "Planning pays," the *Bulletin* declared in its effort to turn aside criticism from people who felt that they had a right to do as they pleased with their land and buildings regardless of negative effects on neighbors.

Local organizations such as the newly formed Fish and Game Club, the Winter Sports Association and the American Legion were urged to join the effort. Henry R. Bright, a summer resident who was assistant corporation counsel of the City of New York, was the group's chairman. Ben Webster, who had been so active in projects for reviving Byrdcliffe, was secretary and the major force in the movement.

The planning and zoning project depended for success upon propertyowners. Large propertyowners in the hamlet of Woodstock viewed the whole scheme with loathing. Town officials made no secret of their disapproval. The Township Association slid into extinction.[15]

In the summer of 1940 Woodstock continued to be troubled by many problems which had resulted in large part from almost twenty years of unplanned growth. Sewage disposal, inadequate design of highways, and polluted streams and water supply were all the subject of much concern but little action. The center of the hamlet of Woodstock which had so charmed early Woodstock art colonists by its agreeable scale and lack of crowding stepped up the pace of change as the approaching war began chasing the Great Depression away.

Storefronts aspired to be recognized by the shopping public as "Colonial," and so in good taste and suitable to the hamlet of Woodstock, which, in fact, had only managed to bring together two or three simple structures by the time Colonial days ended. In 1938 the new brick town hall and firehouse of an acceptable Colonial aspect had taken the place of the former frame Fireman's Hall, whose vigorously intersecting planes and square tower had made it a model for many painters who felt the power of Cezanne and the Cubists.[16]

The lack of a railroad had long held back commercial expansion in Woodstock. By 1940 trucks and automobiles had taken the place of railroads as boosters of small towns. The longing for a railroad, which had so haunted the dreams of local landowners, businessmen and speculators, died away and was replaced by agitation for highways better adapted to the age of the automobile. With the help of the shortened distance to the outside world by automobile, real-estate values were again rising.

Farming was becoming less profitable in valuable Woodstock areas and was dying out. The town's last yoke of oxen would soon disappear and horses, except for those in the town's riding academies, would become rarities. The flocks of chickens which had once clucked in every backyard vanished. Automobiles had come to be depended upon year round. With the erection against the old barn occupied by The Nook, and later by The Cafe Espresso, of a concrete block warehouse used by a milk dealer and for frozen-food lockers, some art-colony people saw a disturbing use of the power of businessmen and speculators in real estate to unbalance the face of the hamlet. Others saw the structure as welcome evidence of progress.[17]

In October 1944 Woodstock learned that American troops had at last entered Germany and Russian troops had crossed into East Germany. They heard bad news, too. Hervey White, next-to-the-last surviving member of the group which had founded their art colony in 1902, was dead.

During the night of October 20 Hervey White had died in his sleep in the Maverick cabin called as Six by Eight, so known for its approximate dimensions in feet. The day before he had visited friends and said goodbye because he was about to take off for a winter in St. Mary's. Neighbors recalled hearing him chopping wood for cooking his dinner while singing what they took to be a folk song. There was a memorial service in the Maverick Hall where Hervey had so often acted as a "priest of music." Martin Schuetze read four of Hervey's poems.

Schuetze paid tribute to Hervey by saying in part, "We are here to do the last honors to a man of a rare unity of simplicity and richness, warmth and patient detachment, and of quiet unfailing goodness and love of his fellows. . . . Hervey's greatest achievement is this: where others who were endowed with all the resources of wealth and position failed in similar projects, Hervey alone succeeded by the sheer unaided force of his vision, integrity and love of his fellows. He alone has furnished the final proof that the spirit is mightier than all the material forces. . . . We stand following in our mind's eye this man, young and completely himself to the last, as he goes on his way. . . ." [18]

Hervey's death left only one survivor of the little group which had founded Byrdcliffe with such high hopes in 1902. That survivor was Jane Byrd Whitehead. As she grew increasingly subject to spells of irrationality, Mrs. Whitehead lived on at Byrdcliffe in the midst of an unexpected influx of tenants, refugees from Hitler's Germany and other Central European countries. The refugees were intellectual and creative people who were delighted at finding so congenial a place to live as Byrdcliffe. Among them were the Von Kahlers of Prague, the New York representative of Tass, the Soviet News Agency, a former Polish diplomat, and others. Many remained after the War had ended.

"Madness is overtaking the world," Jane Whitehead sometimes remarked. From time to time during the war Father Francis left town to make appeals for help for the tormented people of Poland and other European countries and to plead for help for European Jews victimized by Germany.[19]

While the War roared ahead St. Dunstan's was attracting devoted parishioners especially among art-colony people. Many of these gave the church objects of ecclesiastical design. Some worked with their own hands to help decorate the church. Mrs. Carl Eric Lindin worked on a wall hanging designed by the Archbishop himself. Into it she wove black yarn made from the hair of the Archbishop's poodle.

On Easter Sunday 1945, a few weeks before Hitler committed suicide and Germany surrendered, St. Dunstan's Church was totally destroyed by fire, with only part of its furnishings saved. It was generally believed in Woodstock that the fire had been caused by the tipping over of one of the many portable kerosene heaters used to warm the church for the Easter services. But Father Francis believed that the fire was the work of agents of his old foe, Archbishop Carfora.[20]

For a time the ruins of St. Dunstan's served to remind Woodstock people of the thousands of fire- and bomb-ravaged buildings of Europe. Father Francis retreated to the Church of Christ on the Mount and there he carried on.

53

AFTER THE WAR
WAS OVER

Wars have affected Woodstock
ever since the French and Indian War hindered the founding of the
first white settlement. The American Revolution, the War of 1812,
the Mexican War, the Civil War, the Spanish-American War and the
two World Wars in turn had both obvious and subtle effects on
Woodstock. The early European phase of the Second World War sent
refugees for absorption into Woodstock life. Later, the temporary
American alliance with the Soviet Union checked, if only for a while,
Russo-American tensions which had been building up since 1917. The
war also steered fresh young people active in the arts to Woodstock—
and the place hasn't been the same since.

For one thing, the population has soared. Between 1940 and 1960
the year-round population of Woodstock almost doubled, going from a
total of 1983 to 3836. Even as the Second World War ended, the
effects of this growth were easy to see. One oldtimer liked to point to
a vacant piece of commercial property on Tinker Street. When he had
first moved down to Woodstock from Mink Hollow half a century
before, he said, he'd been offered the land for four hundred dollars. In
the late Forties it had changed hands for more than ten times that
amount. When asked why he hadn't bought it when it was first offered
to him, he replied, "Why, they wanted too much money."

The increase in the value of business property was caused not
only by the growth of the permanent population of the town but also
by the increase in the number of out-of-towners who came to

Woodstock, especially on summer weekends. It was estimated locally that on Memorial Day weekend in 1948 the town was accommodating two thousand extra overnight people, much as it had in the booming Twenties. As the Woodstock *Weekly Window* commented in 1948, many of these people "trudged purposefully about the village in search of something or other which they never seem to find."[1]

Some of the trudgers were hunting for a sense of freedom they had been told was in the Woodstock air. Some were simply curious about this community, which was so different from the ones they knew. One man who although he had lived only ten miles away had never visited Woodstock said during the 1940s, "All my life I've ben hearing about what this fellow, Hervey Whiteman or whoever he was, has been doing in Woodstock, and by God some day I'll go there and see what it's all about." This man was ripe for becoming a trudger.

Others were more definite about what they expected to find. They'd heard stories about wild artists and nude models lurking in the woods, and of the past orgies known as the Maverick Festivals, and they were on the lookout for sexual surprises. A good many visitors were simply doing what Hudson Valley people had been doing even before the Twenties, "going to Woodstock to look at the crazy artists."

As in the Twenties, a few trudgers found what they valued and wanted in Woodstock. Some returned to join the art colony. Most of them, disappointed in the search, found consolation in spending money in the little shops which had been a feature of Woodstock's Tinker Street since the Twenties and now that the war was over were multiplying. While shopkeepers generally welcomed the trudgers, many other residents did not. As in the anti-tourist agitation of the Twenties, an outcry was raised against an invasion of the town by tourists and against the changes that were taking place to snare more tourist dollars.[2]

A conspicuous leader of anti-trudgism was Holley Cantine, son of a prosperous Saugerties paper-coating family. Holley was a thorough rebel. His magazine, *Retort*, 1942-1951, promoted pacifism and anarchism. Cantine had a deep devotion to the Woodstock in which he had been brought up (his mother was Woodstock painter Jo Cantine). In his weekly publication *The Wasp* Cantine struck out against tourism. One issue of his paper was headlined with the words "TOURISTS GO HOME!" The local news shop (run by Leon Carey, past president of the Chamber of Commerce) refused to carry *The Wasp*, and customers were discouraged from buying it in other shops.

Speaking up in his *Wasp* against the changes in the appearance of the center of Woodstock brought about by business pressure rooted in trudgerism as well as in the growing year-round population, Cantine further antagonized the business layer of Woodstock society. In 1952 he battled against the trustees of the Woodstock Library when they discharged aging Alice Thompson, who had served the library well for many years. Cantine had become devoted to her when he was a library user in his boyhood.[3]

Seen by the trudgers of the late Forties and early Fifties, Woodstock was giving many signs as the *Wasp* noted of moving out of its former small-town look toward a more exalted level of community existence. An example of this was the war memorial. Earlier wars had not brought a memorial to the Village Green. Larger towns might have their statues of a Civil War soldier or bronze tablets memorializing Revolutionary heroes, but Woodstock had been too small and poor and too much lacking in a strong community spirit to do likewise. But the Second World War had not yet quite ended when both local and art-colony people began discussing the possibility of a war memorial.

In 1945 a War Memorial Association arose. It quickly asked for the submission of proposals. Two were selected. Painter-actress Wilna Hervey had suggested and painter Marianne Mecklem had designed a plan for a circle of bluestone flagstones on the Green with a flagpole rising from a circular plantholder. A bronze tablet wrapped around the base of the flagpole carried the names of those killed in all American wars from the Civil War on. This was called the "Visual Memorial."

A "Living Memorial" took the form of an "athletic field and supervised playground" on land on the Rock City Road which the Woodstock Fish and Game Club had taken over from the Outdoor Recreational Association, which had come apart soon after its beginning in 1924. This was the field on which Woodstock baseball teams had long met their opponents. Now it was officially named the Woodstock War Memorial Recreation Center. Financed by local contributions of one thousand dollars matched by the State of New York, the Visual Memorial listed the names of thirteen Civil War, one Spanish-American and twelve Second World War dead. The memorial was dedicated as part of the Memorial Day ceremonies of 1948.[4]

Every man listed had brought sorrow by his death to many Woodstock people. Two in particular had touched a wide range of the town's people. Charles Pierpont, who had enlisted with his twin brother on their eighteenth birthday, was the first local soldier to die in the Second World War. He died in the attack on the Solomon Islands on October 14, 1942. Caleb Milne, who died while serving as an ambulance driver in North Africa in May 1943, had once put Woodstock on the front pages of metropolitan newspapers by staging a fake kidnapping to the great embarrassment of his country-gentry family. In the eyes of Woodstock people, townspeople and art-colony people alike, his war service redeemed him.

In a book of his letters published in 1944 by his mother, Milne conveyed a sharp image of the sands, plants and moods of the African desert and its people. He wrote with deep feelings about the ugliness and waste of war. He wrote, "I dream of the day when one may say 'I am a citizen of the world.' I have never had a provincial sense to much degree, and it seems stupider and blinder than ever now to shout the old nationalistic battle-hymns when they have brought the world into such artificial and complicated chaos. Are people so strange to one another as all that? Is the human soul, the minds of men, so alien to one another, that there is no place where the gods may meet? No, I cannot believe that."

Eventually the name of the War Memorial Recreation Center was changed to Andy Lee Field in memory of a popular young man killed in a shooting accident. The Visual Memorial too shed its original name and lost much of its poignancy as the war receded into the past.[5]

The War Memorial Association was only one sign of an increased civic consciousness to appear in the Woodstock of postwar days. For one thing, many art-colony and summer people were taking a closer and more critical look at the workings of their town government, suggesting or even demanding changes. Before the Second World War few artists or summer people had showed much interest in how and by whom their town was governed. They saw government as a privilege of men of old local families, who had a strong Republican organization. Though most art-colony and a few business people were Democrats, some had enrolled as Republicans in order to be able to vote at Republican caucuses and so exert some influence on the choice of town officials. The art-colony people often left town in the fall before Election Day and so did not vote in Woodstock. Those who lived on the Maverick voted in Hurley and not in Woodstock.

During the Depression years a few artists had become involved as New Dealers in local politics. Sculptor Bruno Zimm had run for supervisor, Nancy Schoonmaker for Congress and Mrs. Charles

Gradwell for the town board. All had been thoroughly overwhelmed. The artists were concentrated in the first election district, which took in Zena and the hamlet of Woodstock; the second district (the so-called upper district, where incomes and contacts with a wider world were lower) was so solidly conservative as to overwhelm any first-district liberal upsurge.

Though more art-colony people were remaining in Woodstock the year round, their voting strength was not significant. Yet because they were vocal and dedicated to the struggle for the ideals of a better and freer life which was part of the Woodstock art colony, they exerted some influence and brought about a few reforms. A notable reform was the ending of the traditional way of holding town board meetings with no advance public notice and an undisguised determination to keep public and press from attending.

Among the leaders in the attempt at reforming town board procedure was Marion Bullard, artist and writer of successful children's books. She had come to Woodstock in 1908 as an art student and from 1930 to 1950 conducted a page of Woodstock news and comment in the weekly *Ulster County News*, the Democratic paper published in Kingston. Before his paper went out of business in the Second World War, Charles Gradwell of the *Overlook* was also active in fighting for many reforms. At one point of discouragement he proposed that the hamlet of Woodstock organize as a village in order to unburden itself of the power of veto over all town actions held by the upper district.

At the war's end Marion Bullard was reflecting art-colony feelings when she crusaded for more responsible ways of handling the town's finances, for a public water supply, for public town board meetings, for a modern central school, and for an airport. After 1947 she also served as a voice for reform on a radio program of Woodstock news and comment on a Kingston radio station.[6]

Some art-colony reformers were encouraged when Kenneth Wilson, stepson of Stanley Longyear, defeated popular garage-owner Albert Cashdollar, who was running for reelection as town supervisor in 1943. Wilson, who had been a political protege of Cashdollar, had managed the tavern known as the Irvington Inn and then for eight years the Woodstock Inn, both owned by his stepfather. He had studied art and had come to know a good many Woodstock artists. Prepossessing in appearance and affable in manner, Wilson was more willing than any previous supervisor to listen to the suggestions of art-colony people.

Wilson rose in the Republican hierachy to become right-hand man of county boss Senator Wicks. He was elected to the State Assembly and eventually was to take Wicks' place. With Wilson as supervisor during the mid and late Forties, a water supply for the hamlet of Woodstock was constructed, town board meetings were opened to the public, and financial record-keeping was improved. Street names began to be given official recognition in the late 1940s and before long previously unnamed roads and streets were given the dignity of names.[7]

Active in the street-naming project was town board member John Pike. Pike was a watercolor painter and teacher who had carried into our own day the dashing manner associated with Winslow Homer. Pike's illustrations appearing in popular magazines were well-known and admired by Woodstock townspeople. Pike became the first Woodstock artist to hold town office. It was his influence that caused some streets and roads to be named for artists—among them Bellows Lane and Speare Road—and caused some older names to be forgotten. At this time Tinker Street, which had been known in official documents as Main Street, was recognized as the name of Woodstock's principal thoroughfare. Pike as a kind of semi-offical designer made sketches for new commercial buildings on Tinker Street.

An organized attempt at helping along the obvious growth and changing of the town was made by a group of businessmen under the revived name of the Woodstock Township Association. They proposed launching drives to clean up the town's streams and to initiate sewage and public garbage disposal systems. In order to attract tourists—this was the Association's principal objective—they favored a strong publicity program and advocated building a museum of Woodstock arts and crafts. This, the Association members felt, would help head off the tendency feared so strongly back in the boom of the Twenties for the town to lose its drawing power as an art colony and become no more than another unprofitable summer resort. Begun with much enthusiasm, the Association quickly collapsed. The art colony revived without it.[8]

New artists settled in postwar Woodstock, notably a contingent of Westerners. Fletcher Martin, Edward Millman, the Magafan twins, Bruce Currie, Edward Chavez as well as Manuel Bromberg, Walter Plate, Reginald Wilson, James Turnbull and others gave new life to the colony. In 1947 the Art Students League Summer School once again became a central fact in the art colony. Its new quarters, the buildings built by the National Youth Administration to house their Center, were admirably suited to its purpose. The Youth Administration by this time had been absorbed into other agencies.[9]

As in its early years the League brought well-known teachers and many students to the town. The most serious problem, however, in the rebirth of the school and colony was the lack of affordable housing. In the early years of the century local housing had been cheap and plentiful. Barns, stables, corn cribs and tents had all done duty, and a dinner might be had at many places for twenty-five cents. By the mid-Forties the town's old farm buildings had been reborn as dwellings, often for non-artists or as studios for the more prosperous among art-colony people. Standards of living for young Americans had risen and fewer were willing to live as simply as the colony's art pioneers have done. Although inexpensive housing for students was often discussed, nothing was actually accomplished. Yet both mature artists and students arrived and remained.

The art colony's revival of the mid-1940s was a response to developments in American art and in the ways in which artists related to the public. European avant-garde movements had diminished under the stress of war. In New York City Arshile Gorki, Willem de Kooning, Jackson Pollock and others were evolving the soon-to-be-famous and influential New York School of action painting or Abstract Expressionism.

In Woodstock Judson Smith turned to vigorous abstractionism. So too did Smith's friend and neighbor, Bradley Walker Tomlin. Herman Cherry and others took up making stabiles and mobiles. Painters who had worked in figurative ways, among them Philip Guston, now agonized as they strove to convert to the new approach. Painters with strong liberal convictions such as Anton Refregier expressed political and reformist ideas in ways which owed something to Diego Rivera or Picasso's Guernica manner.

Underlying the broader interest in the arts which began during the Second World War and expanded during the Forties was the rise of collecting and sponsorship of contemporary painting by corporations and collectors. Earlier Woodstock painters had sometimes experienced the benefit of corporate support. Frank Swift Chase had painted vigorously-brushed and cheerfully-colored views of large American estates for a national corporation which cared for the trees of the rich.

By the Forties similar commissions were available to painters from a variety of corporations making and selling drugs, diamonds, canned fruit and so on. Art had become more respectable and heads of large corporations were seeing themselves as following in the footsteps of such business heroes as Old-Master collector J. P. Morgan. Pepsi-Cola staged annual competitive exhibitions with substantial prizes. International Business Machines Corporation took similar action. Newly-rich executives in large corporations began buying contemporary paintings and sculptures to display in their own penthouses and country retreats. The Container Corporation of America broke new ground in these respects by buying and printing abstract paintings in magazine advertisements. They bought contemporary American paintings and had them reproduced with advertising copy in magazines of wide circulation.[10]

All this helped Woodstock expand as an art colony. It helped bring to the art colony as summer residents more people involved in the business side of art, such as dealers, promotional geniuses for corporations, and so on. The fresh wave of artists was not content simply to work day after day in the way of the earlier artists of the colony and let dealers and collectors come to them if they chose.

During the Thirties most of these artists had been involved in federal projects and in the protests and political activity which had accompanied them. They played a prominent part in the organization of the Artists Equity Association, through which it was hoped artists might be better paid and better accepted by their society. Woodstock's Yasuo Kuniyoshi became its president. In 1947 the Artists Equity Association and the Woodstock Artists Association jointly sponsored the first Woodstock Art Conference.

Theater producer Harold Clurman, Kuniyoshi, Whitney Museum head Juliana Force, Heywood Hale Broun, sculptor David Smith, painter Mitchell Siporin and others took part in this lively event. Speakers and questioners from the audience expressed nostalgia for the federal-project days when artists felt wanted. They discussed ways by which American society might arrive at the same place without the spur of a depression. The proceedings were published and attracted wide attention. After several annual Conferences the sponsors ran out of subjects suited to public discussion and found financing the meetings difficult.

The second Conference showed that the young artists who sponsored it hoped to widen its scope to include contemporary music. Music like this had only occasionally been played at local concerts such as the Maverick. The Society for New Music offered its first public offering as the initial session of the Woodstock Art Conference. Distinguished Shady composer Henry Cowell was featured. Cowell had led the way into new musical fields which greatly influenced the younger composers whom he had taught and encouraged. Six hundred people turned out for the initial concert, but attendance sharply declined at three additional performances.

Musical events formed part of each of the three conferences. Under the direction of Frank Mele the concerts gave readings of works by a wide range of contemporary composers. They went on for several more years after the Conferences were discontinued. Though it had been hoped that the Conferences would focus attention on Woodstock as a center of activity for contemporary music, this hope was not realized.[11]

The Woodstock Art Conferences gave visible expression in Woodstock to the growth of public interest in the arts and the expansion of institutions aimed at serving the arts. In the beginning of the art colony Bolton Brown, who had a university degree in painting, had been an oddity; but by the Forties university courses in art were rapidly multiplying. A painter with a degree was no longer a novelty. In the colony's early years art teachers from many American cities had found a summer in Woodstock a stimulating and profitable experience. Now the flow set in the other way. Woodstock artists left in large numbers each fall to teach at colleges or universities or to become artists in residence.

In 1949 the Woodstock Artists Association announced with obvious pride in the one and only issue of Woodstock *Gargoyles* that member-painters were engaged to teach at Vassar, Hunter and Wesleyan Colleges and at Washington, New York, Iowa and Minnesota Universities. Also, Abbott Laboratories of Chicago had commissioned Fletcher Martin, Edward Chavez and Edward Millman to paint "a series of documentary pictures of North American Indians" in their native environment. Many Woodstock artists were making larger incomes than ever. New galleries were opening and some, like the Rudolph Gallery, were making frequent sales; art dealers from New York and those responsible for important museum exhibitions were coming to choose paintings in Woodstock.[12]

While the Artists Association was the exhibiting and social center for the majority of the colony's artists, a good number of artists worked and lived apart. Raoul Hague, then becoming recognized as an important sculptor, stayed close to the little brick house on the Maverick which had been put together largely by eye by Hervey White. George Ault, who had settled permanently in Woodstock in 1937, had little to do with Woodstock's art society as he worked on his eerie precisionist paintings often involving local barns and street lights. Ault sometimes drank heavily in the town's bars. One night in 1948 he fell into the storm-swollen Tannery Brook. His body was found in the stream five days later.

Sculptor Harvey Fite went his own personal way while remaining close to the center of art-colony social life. In 1940 Fite bought an abandoned bluestone quarry in High Woods adjoining the town of Woodstock. There he began building *Opus 40*, a huge and imposing sculptural landscape which shaped the disorderly heaps of quarry waste into a great composition which was beginning to attract visitors by the late 1940s.

Van Deering Perrine painted and experimented with color music in his old farmhouse in Wittenberg but ignored the existence of the art colony.

Alexander Archipenko worked and taught in his Wittenberg studio, emerging now and then to take part in art-colony social events. Pat Collins, a very gregarious man, painted his urban streetscapes crowded with hundreds of tiny figures. Here and there in Woodstock other artists, conservative, advanced and some whose work defied easy classification, worked in various degrees of isolation or gregariousness.[13]

Not only art but Woodstock theater revived at the war's end. A student production of *Blithe Spirit* was performed in 1945 at the Playhouse, where Alex E. Segal was managing director. The following year Michael Linenthal, a Boston lawyer and actor, took Segal's place. He ran the theater with the kind of mixture of Broadway successes, high-quality plays and occasional new ones which experience had shown able to keep the house from losing money. He also had chamber music performances by well-known Woodstock musicians.

Once gas rationing ended in 1945 the Maverick Theater's prospects had become bright enough to draw aspirants to reviving it. None of the immediate postwar years were notably successful, although some good modern plays such as Sartre's *No Exit* were given. Losses reached a point at which a lawyer for creditors was stationed in the box office to bear off the receipts after each performance. The pressure of officials for modern fire and safety precautions became insistent.

The Maverick Theater had a season of decided vitality in 1950, even in the shadow of Margaret Webster's ambitious competition of Shakespeare's plays at the Playhouse. Some of the people involved had formed the Villetta Players in 1946. They lived in Byrdcliffe's Villetta and used the studio-theater next door, free of rent because of the interest of landlord Peter Whitehead. There they produced Cocteau's *Infernal Machine,* rousing considerable approval among art-colony people. Internal disagreements broke up the project.[14]

In 1949 some of the players returned to Woodstock as the Loft Players. One of these was Jose Quintero. A local girl, Aileen Cramer, daughter of painters Konrad and Florence Ballin Cramer, was also a Loft player. The group offered good productions of the kind of plays that appealed to art-colony people. Its promotional efforts were energetic. As other little theaters had done during the Depression it advertised a "barter night" when a can of beans would buy standing room and a steak the best seat in the house.

Though the Loft Players seemed well adapted to the theatrical interests of the art colony, after their first season they left for New York, where they won success as the Circle in the Square. After that the Maverick Theater, in spite of a number of brave attempts to revive it, sank toward extinction. For a while it was used as an artist's studio and then, as the roof leaked more and more, was torn down.[15]

While the death of Hervey White had thrown doubt on the survival of such Maverick institutions as the theater and the concerts, the concerts survived. Unlike the theater, with its frequent changes in management and quality, the quality of the concerts remained consistently high enough to build up a devoted following. Kees van der Loo, son of Hervey's original partner in buying the Maverick, and Hervey's sons Caleb and Dan repaired roofs and windows and sold some cottages to tenants.

Van der Loo, who had inherited the theater and concert hall as well as some cottages, was faced with a hard task. He set about trying to put his share of the Maverick on a businesslike basis by trying without notable success to collect arrears of back rents piled up under Hervey's kindly reign. He made efforts to keep the theater and the concert hall going.

In the case of the concert hall he was successful. Maverick violinist and conductor Pierre Henrotte, long a popular leader of the musical colony, agreed to direct the concert series. William (Fritz) Kroll, a leading American violinist and chamber-music player who had appeared at the Maverick Concerts ever since about 1930, agreed to play. Mrs. van der Loo managed the box office and publicity. Though audiences were sometimes thin, the concerts went on. A factor in their survival was the presence in Woodstock of refugees from Eastern Europe to whom chamber music was a valued part of a good life.[16]

As the postwar art colony of Woodstock took shape under the spur of an influx of young artists, businessmen modernized and expanded in the growing town. Two new forces, IBM and Rotron, were working to influence the whole town's character. More than a century earlier Woodstock's glassmaking had been a powerful influence for change. Now modern industrial developments exerted their economic strength to mold aspects of Woodstock life into new forms.

During the mid-Forties Dutch refugee engineer J. C. Van Rijn had settled in Woodstock, which he had visited and liked earlier. During the war years he had been a consultant to industry. Now that source of employment dwindled. Van Rijn, working in a rented garage, developed a small electric fan for cooling the electronic systems which were then moving into public and industrial acceptance. Soon he was manufacturing the fans at an ever-accelerating pace. Woodstock artists of all sorts were finding Rotron an understanding employer, even though working in the Rotron plant gave them less time for their work in the arts.[17]

Some other industrial corporations were finding it profitable to set up plants away from large cities. IBM bought land in the Town of Ulster close to Woodstock and by 1955 began operations. Speculative builders bought up level valley lands in Woodstock and there erected housing developments for IBM and Rotron employees. The buildings were set close together and were often of minimal sturdiness. Sales prices were low enough to provide the largest possible number of customers. Better-paid employees of both Rotron and IBM built more elaborate houses on landscaped sites. While this increased the tax base it also put pressure upon town services. And this pressure in turn had many effects on the town.

With land values and taxes rising, farming virtually disappeared. The number of small shops increased. A supermarket came to Mill Hill Road, located on the site of the former elementary school, which it pushed back up Pine Grove Street. Demand for a local bank was heard.

Assemblyman Kenneth L. Wilson and lawyer John Egan, a power in local politics, did a good deal of maneuvering behind the scenes in

Albany. In 1952 the bank appeared. To the surprise of many local people it was a branch of the Bank of Orange County and not of a Kingston bank. The building was located on land on Rock City Road belonging to the family of Assemblyman Wilson, who became one of the bank's trustees. The presence of the bank gave a strong impetus to the Woodstock boom of the 1950s.[18]

On other levels new institutions arrived. The Episcopalian St. Gregory's Church began in a corncrib close to the site of the barn which had been St. Dunstan's. Within five years the church, with a membership of about one hundred, moved to the modern A-frame building which it now occupies. The architect, William Van Benschoten of West Park in Ulster County, was related to the old Woodstock family which gave its name to Van Benschoten's Hill on the Glasco Turnpike.

During the Forties and Fifties Tom Shultis, another member of an old Woodstock family, emerged into considerable countywide prominence. He operated a sawmill powered by a water turbine at the outlet of Yankeetown Pond. Shultis' weather predictions, called "uncannily accurate," were eagerly looked forward to. Reluctant to discuss the basis for his predictions, Shultis hinted when pressed that they owed something to the movements of the planets and the moon.[19]

In 1948 a familiar Woodstock hotel changed hands. Mead's, or the Overlook Mountain Home (as it was called to distinguish it from its big brother higher on the mountain), was sold to Captain Savo Milo, a Yugoslavian architect and aviator who ran the place for some years and featured excellent Balkan cooking. It was rumored in Woodstock that the place had been bought as a possible refuge for exiled King Peter of Yugoslavia, who was said to have visited the hotel.

The huge Overlook Mountain House continued to be a favorite target of hikers and vandals and served as a romantic symbol of Woodstock's days as a hopeful 19th-century summer resort.

The growth and prosperity of the Rotron and IBM plants was caused in large measure by the existence of what came to be known by 1948 as the Cold War. The world's two major power groups, headed by the United States and the Soviet Union, were immersed in a period of fierce hostility marked by rearmament and threatening gestures.

In the United States hidden Communist agents were being "exposed" and "rooted out" from high posts in government. Richard Nixon was taking his first big step toward the Presidency by pursuing

Alger Hiss, a State Department official who had succeeded Woodstock's James T. Shotwell as the head of the Carnegie Endowment for Peace. Under banner-size front-page headlines Kingston newspapers told of the discovery by Congressional committees of Communists "in high places." In March 1948 a fiery cross was burned on the Bearsville Flats in order to express sympathy with the official anti-Russian policy. Less than two weeks later a more unusual manifestation, a fiery hammer-and-sickle flag composed of oil-soaked rags on a pipe frame, was touched off on Route 212 between Deming and Pine Grove Streets.

In Hollywood well-known figures in the entertainment world were blacklisted, including Kingston-born Howard Koch, whom Hervey White had helped and encouraged. Koch's first play was produced at the Maverick Theater. He went on to become famous as a writer of the script for *Casablanca* and many other films. Koch wrote the script for the version of H.G. Wells' *War of the Worlds,* which caused a panic when produced on radio in 1938 by Orson Welles.[20]

It is not to be wondered at in this edgy atmosphere that Woodstock experienced one of its periodic spells of increased antagonism between artists-leftist and townspeople-rightist groups. The antagonism was honed to a keen edge during the Presidential campaign of 1948.

That year President Harry Truman was running against Governor Thomas E. Dewey of New York. Ex-vice-president Henry A. Wallace opposed both on the New Progressive ticket. Wallace drew support from Woodstock New-Deal sympathizers, opponents of the Cold War, a few Communists and many teenagers. The newspapers read in Woodstock predicted a Dewey victory and kept up an unrelenting fire against Wallace.

On August 8 folk singer Pete Seeger brought "something new in Woodstock entertainment" to town. Seeger had married a daughter of Woodstock's Takashi Ohta, the designer who had helped stage Maverick festivals. What Seeger brought was a folk music event called a "hootenanny," which was held at the house of the head of the local Wallace Club. Seeger, who had been wandering around the country collecting and singing songs and organizing groups known as People's Songs, played the five-string banjo. He led two hundred people in singing and playing. He had encouraged them to bring their guitars to the event.

Soon Seeger was staging further hootenannies for the Wallace cause. One was a "swimming hootenanny" around the pool high above Shady of Dr. John Kingsbury, a passionate Wallace supporter who was held up to scorn by the New York *Daily News* as "the Red Doctor of Shady." Kingsbury had a degree of Ph. D. in public health. The *News* encouraged a public image of him as a sinister figure masquerading as an M.D. to further a Communist plot.[21]

The Cold War had many manifestations in Woodstock. For a time the Wallace campaign was a target for strong local hostility. Vigorous protests followed the burning of a fiery cross close to a Wallace meeting. A petition asked Supervisor Wilson to investigate the incident. Wilson refused, saying that while he was opposed to violence he had no authority to act.

Summer resident Isidore Halpern, a prosperous New York trial lawyer, made an impassioned speech to the town board suggesting in forcible words that if action were not taken to uncover the cross-burners art-colony and summer people would register to vote in Woodstock and would turn the officials out of office. Though Halpern said he did not see the burning as aimed at any race or political party, it was evident that he and many of the other Jews now well-established in Woodstock felt that as in the 1920s the burning was aimed at them. Supervisor Wilson again stated that he and the board had no authority to take action.

Registration for the coming election spurted to the highest rate in history, alarming some local politicians. Yet on Election Day Dewey swept the town. He had almost 1100 votes, Truman a bit less than 200. Wallace, for all the folk singing and demonstrating in his favor, had only 110 votes.

The surge in singing and guitar-carrying and playing in Woodstock continued after the election was over. So too did the increase in the number of art-colony and summer people who made Woodstock their legal residence for voting purposes.[22]

The Wallace campaign in Woodstock had an effect on the Discussion Group, which had been set up in Woodstock in the 1930s at the suggestion of Dr. Shotwell. Its purpose was to provide a place in which discussions, especially of art, might be held apart from the meetings of the Woodstock Historical Society, which its founder, Dr. Schuetze, had seen as properly having the function of dealing with the arts and trying to shape the course of the art colony. Dr. Shotwell wanted the group to confine itself to local history alone.

Opponents of the forums organized a rival and conservative

association and held meetings addressed by a safely patriotic speaker. In an atmosphere of fear and suspicion the Woodstock Forum people offered to merge with their rival and to alternate speakers. The offer was accepted. Agreement on speakers proved difficult to reach, however, and both forums went out of existence.[23]

Folk music had been of interest in Woodstock since the early days at Byrdcliffe. When it was gaining a national following during the late Thirties the radio and record industry took it up and commercialized it. In the mid-Forties some of the new artists coming to Woodstock from the West brought with them their own devotion to folk music. Painter Edward Chavez sang and played on the guitar the Mexican songs he had learned from his mother. Sam Eskin, collector and singer of folk songs, was a friend of the new artists. A performance by him in the Woodstock Artists Association Gallery drew an overflow audience.

Some local classical-music players and listeners found the growing fashion for folk music distasteful. Maverick pianist and composer Forrest Goodenough wrote in the Woodstock *Weekly Window* (which gave up in September 1948 after twenty-four numbers) that folk songs were "the simple expressions of an uneducated people . . . rather quaint and charming but for the most part crude and extremely repetitious. . . ." Goodenough expressed wonder at the popularity of folk music, which he conceded had "become quite a fad during recent years." [24]

In spite of the disapproval of some professional classical musicians, folk music after the election year of 1948 became ever more solidly based in Woodstock. Interest in it expanded from year to year. As anti-Communist investigations grew in scope and culminated in the McCarthy years of 1953-1954, however, conservative Woodstock townspeople remained convinced that folk music was a manifestation of the creeping Communism which threatened to engulf their town and nation.

FOLKLORE, FOLKWAYS AND HARD CIDER

When Professor Dixon Ryan Fox of Columbia University, president of the New York State Historical Association and a former student of Dr. James Shotwell, came to Woodstock in the summer of 1932 he expressed amazement at the furious activity of members of the Woodstock Historical Society in collecting and preserving the history and folklore of their town. What especially amazed Fox was that unlike most local history groups, which were made up of descendants of early settlers and were primarily interested in their own genealogy and family histories, almost all the members of the Woodstock Society had no family roots in the town. They were art-colony people who had, as Dr. Fox put it, "adopted a background" and made the Woodstock past their own.

While much of the credit for the flourishing of the Woodstock Historical Society was due to the zeal of Dr. Martin Schuetze, the success of the organization was firmly based on the desire of creative and intelligent art-colony people to tie themselves securely to the landscape they so much loved and to the local people who seemed to them to be an expression of the spirit of their mountains, trees, streams and meadows. Most of the 160 people who had gathered to listen to Dr. Fox had known the alienation which came from their choosing to be artists in a society dedicated to commerce and industry. When they eagerly adopted Woodstock as their own country, they were choosing long before the phrase had been invented to become members of a "Woodstock nation." [1]

By 1932 the Historical Society had published seven little booklets dealing with their town's past. Anita M. Smith had begun collecting and presenting in charming form the local history and folklore which eventually grew into her *Woodstock History and Hearsay* of 1959. Other members found themselves listening more closely to the tales of local people and trying to establish warmer relations with them than they had aimed at before.

From the early days at Byrdcliffe, of course, local people and their ways had been sources of interest to art-colony people. Then and later these people liked to repeat local phrases which were new to them and had a quaint and delightful sound in their ears. "It don't bother my time none," a carpenter might remark when asked what he thought of a speech in a current Presidential campaign. If the man were asked for his opinion as to the cause of a leak in the roof, he might say, "I wouldn't wonder if I mightn't go up on that roof some day and look in*to* it and see what there *is* of it."

Art-colony people saw in these phrases an expression of a commitment to being surprised at nothing, a sort of Ulster County version of Horace's *nil admirari*. They were struck too with the succinctness with which old Woodstock people could make a statement. A boy arriving at a social event asked an old lady if a certain friend of his was there. "He's been and went," the lady answered. Local pronunciations were a source of wonder. Why did the numerous members of the Shultis family pronounce their name Sheltis, and why did "nothing" in the mouths of oldtimers become "nathin" and "hen" change to "hin"?

The local people were just as much interested in the way the new people spoke and behaved. Among themselves they discussed the oddities of the artists with amusement and gusto. Among the local people only an occasional young person allowed speech and habits to be affected by those of the artists. To do so would have been seen as disloyal to one's own people. And Woodstock people took an obvious pride in emphasing the details of their own culture. When an artist called the attention of the local woman who was cleaning her house to the sound of an early cicada or locust the woman might say, "Ma'am, that's what *we* call a harvest fly." [2]

Some artists, for example Ned Thatcher, showed snobbery in

their attitudes toward local people. Most regarded them with respect for the way they had preserved their own complex of customs in a world rapidly hastening toward dull uniformity.

Writing in 1932 of the Woodstock landscape as it was when he first saw it, Carl Eric Lindin paid tribute to some of the people who had come to seem to him parts of that landscape: "Old Ford Herrick, who built so many of our houses, sturdy, temperamental, telling a good story while he made his men work at full speed. His brother-in-law Kiersted: one of the best farmers in the county—silent, untiring and loving his soil as only an artist could love his work. Henry Peper, the blacksmith . . . unchanging through all these years, strong and faithful like the iron he hammers. Sherman Elwyn, who takes a righteous pride in his well-tilled and well-ordered farm. . . . Old Mrs. Magee, now dead and gone, but who fed and mothered that whole early generation of poets and painters, always cheerful and kind."

Many painters expressed their admiration for the strong individual characters among local people. Bellows, Speicher, Arnold Blanch and others painted Woodstock men and women against their own backgrounds in ways that showed respect and understanding. Looking back on the early days at Byrdcliffe, Lucy Fletcher Brown told of a woman who made an unforgettable impression on her. "Mrs. Dubois (she was not one whom you would call by her first name) wove the residual rags of the countryside into strips of gay carpet, good, but just, measure, battering it out on her great and ancient handhewn loom. A tall, rawboned figure, with intelligent and powerful visage—it wasn't just a 'face'—of prodigious memory and trenchant tongue. . . . She and her ancient frosted husband who 'carried' everything that was carried between Woodstock and West Hurley . . . were clean with a radiant idealism that simply awestruck me. Mrs. Dubois remains with me to this day as the epitome of all the fundamental virtues." [3]

While art-colony people were seldom on terms of social intimacy with local people, many came to feel close to the men and women who worked for them at such tasks as housecleaning, cooking, carpentry and gardening, or whom they often met in the course of daily life. Through these people they came to feel an understanding (if a very limited one) of local ways. Artists who had the habit of dropping in for drinks at Woodstock taverns met oldtimers there. They listened eagerly to their tales, seeing in them a rugged and admirable simplicity.

By reason of his relaxed operation of the Twaddell House, his willingness to talk to strangers and his look of an oldtime countryman, Jim Twaddell became a favorite among the artists. Winold Riess, painter, illustrator, decorator and operator of an art school, used Twaddell as a model for a cover for the magazine *Survey Graphic* in July 1926. Twaddell's penetrating gray eyes, his weather-beaten hat and his face lined by sun and wind summed up what artists took to be the vigorous, daring, pioneering qualities which distinguished nineteenth-century American males.

With the birth of the art colony Twaddell came into his own as a Woodstock personality. He enjoyed reminiscing. He told of his youth as a drover, of his feats of horsemanship, of his years in Texas, and of his father-in-law, Assemblyman Charles Krack. Twaddell enjoyed telling of the visit of President Grant to Woodstock in 1873; like a number of other local oldtimers he claimed credit for having driven the Presidential carriage from the railroad station at West Hurley to Woodstock and on to the Overlook Mountain House. In more expansive moments he claimed that Grant had actually entered the Twaddell House and chatted for a few moments. Twaddell, when faced with a credulous art-colony listener, was more an inspired inventor of tall tales than a mere raconteur. The *Overlook* printed his splendid fantasy of a morning with General Grant on Overlook Mountain. The *Overlook's* reporter was new to Woodstock and so easily taken in.[4]

Though capable of soaring feats of inventiveness as a storyteller Twaddell was critical of the efforts of others in stretching the truth. Art-colony people sometimes asked him to tell the story of how their town's Tinker Street got its name. The widely-repeated story held that one spring morning (back in 1832, one woman said) a wandering tin peddler or tinker came to town, his wagon jingling with the many pots and pans hanging from its sides. Woodstock's main street was deep in its usual springtime mud. The tinker's horse and wagon started to sink and his shouts and curses only seemed to send horse and wagon deeper. Eventually the wagon, horse and tinker vanished in the mud, and to this day when conditions are right the jingling of the tinware may be heard rising from beneath the street. The story, Twaddell insisted, was a complete fabrication.

The tale of the tinker had first seen print as far as is now known in the Kingston *Argus* of March 29, 1899, probably intended to celebrate the impending eve of April Fools' Day. Twaddell claimed that the street got its name from its numerous "tinker shops." And it was true enough that the street, as it passed through the hamlet of

Woodstock, was lined with hotels, taverns, blacksmith and tinker shops set there for the convenience of teamsters who passed through the town from the up-country on their way to Hudson River ports.

A colorful character named John Brandow worked when the artists first came to town at mending anything at all in his little shop at the west end of the village. Brandow claimed he could mend any imaginable object by what he called "the tinker process," which consisted of trying this and that until something worked. Houst's Department Store began as Henry Houst's tinker shop, where lawnmowers and household gadgets got repaired.

And there is another aspect of the name of which Twaddell was aware. The word tinker, far back in the past of the English language, was used as a generic term for not only tinkers by trade but also for gypsies and vagabonds. The verb "to tinker" meant among other things—to botch or mend badly. In giving the name tinker to their principal street Woodstock people were probably indulging in the kind of humorous self-denigration which gave rise to such American place names as Hardscrabble, Poverty Hollow and Skunk's Misery.

When Twaddell died in 1939 local newspapers described him as the oldest man in Woodstock, possibly the oldest in all Ulster County, His age, the newspapers stated, was between one hundred and one hundred four. Records in the Town of Hunter, where Twaddell was born, show conclusively that he was only ninety. He had probably added ten years to his age in order to bask in the kind of admiration we like to give to picturesque survivors.[5]

Cambridge Lasher (known to all as "Came") was a local man through whom art-colony people felt that they might get in touch with the very essence of old Woodstock. Came's father, John Lasher, had worked for Livingston agent Henry P. Shultis and in the course of his duties had been pushed over a rocky ledge in the incident which gave Woodstock its moment of fame in the Anti-Rent War of 1845. Came, left an orphan when he was only eight, was "bound out" or apprenticed to Henry P. Shultis.

In later life Came liked to tell how he had begun a career as a drover, buying geese and turkeys in Ulster and adjoining counties and driving flocks of the birds to market. He advanced to dealing in cattle and became known far and wide for his skill in judging and managing oxen. He claimed to have been able to judge the weight of an ox to within ten pounds, quite a feat since oxen often weighed over two thousand pounds.

Louise Ault, widow of painter George Ault, wrote a sketch of Came in her *Artist in Woodstock*, "Illiterate, shrewd, wise, kind, rugged and individual, Cambridge was a man after the artist George Ault's heart, whose own spirit was reflected in a remark the old man made to him one day, 'I ain't after nobody's hide, but if anybody's after mine I'll get his'n.'"

By the early 1940s Jim Twaddell, Came Lasher and all the other men and women of old Woodstock who had been in the prime of their lives when Byrdcliffe was founded were gone. A younger generation of local people who still preserved an earlier local culture, if in diluted form, was taking the place of their elders.[6]

Among these was Charles Herrick, a short, sturdily put-together man who earned art-colony respect and affection by his wit, his cheerfulness, his stock of local tales and phrases, and his willingness to tackle any job at all with energy and inventiveness. Charley, as he was known, worked as a gardener and handyman for many art-colony people at Byrdcliffe, Lewis Hollow and elsewhere. When called for jury duty he held up a big bunch of keys to the various houses he guarded while their owners were away. He rattled the keys before the judge and the lawyers and said, "I'm responsible for the safety of all this." He was excused.[7]

Many art-colony people who knew Charley Herrick appreciated the wit and saltiness of his humor. Once a woman saw Charley perched on the roof of a derelict old barn, hard at work disassembling the building. "Charley," the woman called out. "Are you safe up there?" "No, ma'am," Charley answered. "But I'm just as happy as if I was."

Charley liked to reassure newcomers to Lewis Hollow who expressed fear of the rattlesnakes which sometimes wandered there. "A rattlesnake is like a jug of whiskey," he'd say. "You leave it alone and it'll leave you alone. When I first come to work in the Hollow I thought a rattler would jump out from every bush and bite me dead. But I've found out that if a Lewis Hollow man has to wait to die until he's bit to death by a rattler, he'll live so long they'll have to shoot him before they can resurrect him on the Judgement Day."

He had his own adaptation of a familiar American saying, once used by nineteenth-century humorist Josh Billings. "There are an awful lot of these intellectuals here in Woodstock," he'd say. "Sure an intellectual knows a lot. Trouble is what he knows ain't so."

Charley had a way of playing with words and ideas as a magician does with cards, making them appear and disappear and change positions to the astonishment of his listeners. An employer complained that the tomatoes Charley had planted for her didn't live up to the description on the seed package, Charley explained, "Ma'am, you can't believe what you read on the bag seeds come in. Why, them bags just lay there and let them print anything they want on them."

Charley once kept a cow at his home place on the Glasco Turnpike. He'd cut grass from a mountainside field, load it into his pickup truck and deliver it to the cow. A man living near the field asked why he didn't bring the cow up and let her cut the grass for herself. Said Charley, "Why, that's a valuable cow. She's so valuable it wouldn't take a thief to steal her, an honest man might." Then he added, "Now, neighbor, don't get me wrong. I'm not saying you or I would do a thing like that. But b'Jesus, an honest man might."

Well known as Charley Herrick was for his stories and his sayings, he was best known for his skill in making hard cider and his possession of an astonishing treasure of cider lore. He sold his cider during Prohibition, sometimes storing his barrels in the cellars of employers safely away in Europe for the winter. "I make twenty barrels of cider a year," he used to say, "twelve barrels for me and eight for my friends. When my friends drink up their eight barrels they don't get no more. Used to keep coons in a cage by the henhouse. Every Sunday my friends used to come to see them coons, said they was the cutest little fellas they ever saw. But when their eight barrels of cider was drunk up they didn't come to see them coons no more." [8]

"There's this about hard cider," Charley confided. "It puts the fear of God in you and keeps your bowels open."

The fear of God must have hung heavily over Woodstock ever since its first apple trees reached bearing age. Old Woodstock was a cider-drinking town. Before the 1830s men, women and children drank hard cider. Pitchers of it were set on the table at every meal. But as the Prohibition movement gained strength in the 1830s women turned against cider. Prohibition sentiment was centered around the churches, which had a greater appeal to women than to men. Then women began to object to the sour, appley odor which penetrated their houses after their husbands put their year's supply of cider down the cellar to harden. Cider became more a man's drink and less a family one.

Cider flowed bountifully at Woodstock's many taverns, at which the town's men congregated in hours of leisure and at which teamsters from the up-country paused to refresh themselves. And cider had the advantage in a part of the world where apple trees flourished of being cheap.

"A man can get through the winter cheap on hard cider," Charley Herrick used to say. "He fills his jug down the cellar early in the morning and then he sets by the stove emptying it. When his wife has breakfast ready he's feeling so good he don't want any. After a while he gets in his wife's way and she chases him out of the house. He goes to his neighbor's with his jug and the two of them work at cider all day. When night comes a man goes home so full of cider he gets right into bed without needing any dinner. Yessir, a man can get through the winter cheap on hard cider."

A barrel of cider went through many stages until it ended up as vinegar, when women finally approved of it, for they needed it at pickling time. Both men and women favored cider as a medicine, however. It was believed that no cider-drinker ever suffered from kidney stones, unless of course he or she didn't drink enough. Since hard cider was an ingredient in remedies poured down the throats of horses as well as humans, it was entitled to additional respect. Sweet cider was boiled down and used as a pancake syrup. Because of the quantity of maple syrup usually made in Woodstock each year, it was not plentifully made except in years when the flow of maple sap was sluggish.

Twenty barrels a year was the amount many oldtime Woodstock farmers stowed away in their cellars each fall. The quality of the cider varied with the character of the maker. Some men thought nothing of using half-rotten apples or those in which worms predominated over apple. Others, Charley Herrick among them, made a skilled and conscientious craft of cider-making. No muddy or partly rotten apples went into Charley's cider. He examined each apple as he picked it up from beneath a Baldwin tree (his favorite). If it was dirty he'd scour it with a piece of burlap. He contemptuously rejected all unripe or neurotic-looking apples and he'd rejoice when he came upon a tree which had deposited ruddy and sound apples on the grass beneath its branches in October.

Charley made heaps of his cider apples here and there in the orchard. There they rested until they gave off an indescribably aromatic odor and developed a tangibly waxy surface. Then they'd be bagged and taken to the mill. Charley would watch as his apples were ground and pressed lest some scoundrel substitute unsound apples for

Charley's carefully selected ones. Safely enclosed in a clean oak whiskey barrel, the new cider had to be put in a cool cellar and go through a process of maturing. Once the barrel was opened the cider began its progress toward a state of vinegar. It had to be drunk before it became too clearly no longer cider but vinegar.

Charley scorned all attempts to improve cider by adding other substances to the original apple juice. Raisins, honey, cayenne pepper, mustard and brandy simply ruined cider, Charley believed. "Give me plain apple," he like to say. In accordance with an old tradition a barrel of cider called "the mowin' bar'l" would be set aside in the coolest part of the cellar in the fall, not to be opened until mowing began the following summer.

Charley reached the high point of his career as a cider-maker when he worked the Lewis Hollow orchard of Euphemia (Effie) Whittredge on shares. He acted as Miss Whittredge's rattlesnake executioner, handyman and rural philosopher as well. Effie Whittredge, the vigorous, eccentric daughter of renowned nineteenth-century landscape painter Worthington Whittredge, had done well as an interior decorator in New York. She had remained unmarried and without amorous adventures until well into her thirties. Then on a ship bound for Bermuda she met an upstate utilities executive. From that moment until Harry died the two were happy yet discreet lovers, their relationship kept hidden from all but a few close friends. In order to establish a convenient place at which they might meet without fear of discovery by censorious relatives, Effie bought an old quarryman's cottage at the end of a road in Lewis Hollow.

Harry died leaving Effie well off ("I'm one woman who made sin pay" she confided to a friend). She then turned her affections on the place in Lewis Hollow, enlarged her holdings to include the orchard planted some twenty years earlier. She remodelled her house, entertained often and with imagination, and threw herself into the role of orchard owner. Clad in orange britches and the high leather boots she had formerly used in mountain climbing, she'd stride about her farm with Charley in tow, giving instructions and absorbing Charley's wisdom. She extended the color scheme of her house to the orchard and had a truck painted Dutch blue, emblazoned with the legend "Euphemia's Apples." From the truck Charley sold apples in Saugerties, Kingston and Woodstock.

Hard cider, of course, was a central theme on Effie's place. It was served lavishly at her parties. Despite Charley's disapproval she experimented with making additions to cider and bottling it.

Eventually Effie became involved in an affair with a young man named Nathan, an aviator. Effie helped Nathan buy a plane, with which he hoped to make a living. From time to time Nathan would fly over Effie's house and sound an eerie noisemaker to let her know that he was coming down at the Kingston airport. If she could meet him at the airport Effie would stand on her lawn and wave a large white cloth before dashing into her car and making for the airport.

Expecting Nathan one day, Effie wanted to surprise him. She asked a friend to listen for the plane and then to wave the cloth. Nathan wouldn't be able to make out who was doing the waving. Then she eagerly left her house so she could meet him when he landed. But as the friend shook a tablecloth the plane seemed to drop from the sky and crashed on the mountainside. Nathan was found dead in his plane. A note in his pocket asked that he be buried where he fell or that his body be donated to medical research.

The owner of the land where Nathan had crashed refused to permit burial. With Charley's help Effie had Nathan buried on a corner of her land beside the Lewis Hollow Road. When the owner of a nearby house objected, Effie asked Charley to prepare a little stone-walled enclosure near her house. There Nathan was buried under a stone cut by sculptor Bruno Zimm.

By 1940 Effie was gone from the Hollow. Her place was sold to a respectable retired savings banker and his wife. Charley worked for them. He remained devoted to the memory of Effie Whittredge. When anyone criticized her in his presence he would say, "Miss Whittredge was a mighty fine woman," and then with the realistic punning humor that was part of him, ". . . only thing was she read too many of these here sectional books." [9]

After Effie's death Charley went on making cider, though in smaller quantities than formerly. He stored his cider in the cool cellar of the green-painted apple house set in the Whittredge orchard. There he had his mowin' bar'l set aside for this season and in the hot summer mowing days he would pause from swinging his scythe along stone walls and other places the mowing machine couldn't reach. With his helper beside him would make frequent pilgrimages to the apple house and the mowin' bar'l. Under the place's new owner Charley also mowed the enclosure in which Nathan lay, accompanied by a pet dog whose stone reads simply "Davy." One day after he had been mowing the burying ground a neighbor asked Charley what he had been doing. "Been shavin' Nate," he answered.

By the mid-1950s mills which did "custom cider-making" were vanishing. The mills still in business were large commercial establishments too grand for twenty-barrel-a-year men. Over the years Woodstock had had many cider mills, portable hand-operated ones, horse-powered ones, and water-powered mills like the one whose remains still stand beside a bridge in Shady. The last Woodstock mill to press apples was Dave Mazetti's on the Bearsville Flats. Nearby Dave had grown vegetables, run a roadside stand and worked as a bootlegger. He took to running Chauncey De Vall's mill close to the Jonathan Apple monument on the Bearsville Flats.

One fall word got around that the current season ending after Election Day would be the last. The building was tottering. The old Dodge truck engine which furnished power was close to wearing out. In spite of the belief that cider drinking promoted longevity, cidermakers were dying out and young men were not stepping forward to take their places. That last season those drawing their apples to the mill were aware that the event was an historic one, marking the end of what had once been a vital part of old Woodstock.

For ten years before that Charley had helped me make cider each year on the part of Effie's orchard which I had come to own. We took our place in line at the cider mill and Charley joined in the conversation of the predominantly white-haired men stamping to keep their feet warm in the chilling wind.

"There's been enough cider made in this mill to fill the Ashokan Reservoir twice over," said Charley. "But there won't be no more. This is the end."

Several oldtimers standing nearby nodded in agreement. I asked Charley why this was the end. "It's them water heaters," he explained fiercely. "It's the water heaters and the oil burners that the women have to have down there in the cellar. How can you keep your cider cool down a cellar when it's all heated up with the stuff the women have to put down there?"

Charley went on to develop a theme I'd often heard from him. "There's always something the women have to have," he said. "Once it was pianos. At first they played them all day long and then they let them set there and get filled up with dust. Then it was phonographs, then it was radios. Now it's this here television. You'll see what's going to happen. Pretty soon the women will get tired of television and then they'll have to have something else."

A young woman squiring a shaky cane-propped cider-maker stepped beside us and made a face at Charley. "You and your hard cider," she said. "Ugh, I hate the stuff." She looked at him and giggled. Her giggle became a raucous laugh. "It's no laughing matter," said Charley. "There's been enough cider made in this mill to fill the Ashokan Reservoir twice over. But this is the end. This is the end."

It wasn't quite the end. During the next two decades young guitar-carrying people often new to Woodstock held apple pressings in the fall and in a party atmosphere drank the fresh apple juice in an effort to carry on an old Woodstock tradition. But putting twenty barrels of hard cider down your cellar was a thing of the past. Even as the last juice was dripping from the horse-hair strainers in Dave Mazetti's cider mill, within earshot carpenters were hammering together houses for workers at IBM and Rotron. The houses had no cellars at all. Twenty barrels of hard cider would have filled their living rooms from floor to ceiling. Apple orchards were vanishing. A way of life which had been slipping away from Woodstock ever since the twentieth century dawned was ending.[10]

THE BOOMING FIFTIES

In August 1949 a new Woodstock magazine called *Woodstock Gargoyles* spoke its mind about the town. In its premier and only issue, *Gargoyles* presented words and pictures by diverse art-colony personalities such as Maverick editor, poet and novelist Henry Morton Robinson; novelist and fish and game columnist Edmund Gilligan; artists Raoul Hague, Paul Burlin, Carl Walters, Judson Smith, Lucile Blanch and Josef Presser; poet, anarchist and novelist Dachine Rainer; Michael Linenthal, who at that time owned and managed the Playhouse; Frank Meyer, who had turned from being a devoted Communist to using his very substantial talents in the service of the anti-Communist side of the Cold War; and painter Anna Carolan, who was starting a Woodstock museum of art.

The magazine included a symposium titled "Has Woodstock a Past?—Or a Future?" Participants varied in their answers. Fernando Martinez said that the spirit of Woodstock had died with Hervey White. "Woodstock has neither present nor future," he said. Eugene O'Neill, Jr., a classical scholar, felt that the town needed year-round residence by its artists and intellectuals. The summer, with its hordes of tourists, O'Neill believed, was a "necessary evil." Old-time artist Konrad Cramer saw reasons for predicting a fine future. So too did John Pike. Writer Robert Phelps, the first of many members of the art colony to become a part-time Rotron employee, wrote that while Woodstock might have had a past and "conceivably even a future, what it lacks is anything like a lively present."

The Symposium was led by 71-year-old Marion Bullard, who had arrived in Woodstock before anyone else represented in *Gargoyles*. She had observed the change from the "dirt-road and horse-and-buggy days" to "this present of chaotic social change." As painter, crusader for kindness to animals, Woodstock reporter for press and radio, agitator for improvement in local government, foe of the Ku Klux Klan, and an advocate of better schools and an airport on the Bearsville Flats, Marion Bullard had been in the thick of half a century of Woodstock change. She had taken every new twist with an open mind. But with the 1950s about to dawn she confessed herself dazed and uncertain. "The future in Woodstock seems to me anybody's guess" was the best she could say.

Other Woodstock people who thought they had a sharp image of that future looked foward to it with eager anticipation. They were speculators who saw the approach of many forces which might make Woodstock a source of higher profits. The New York Thruway and the Kingston-Rhinecliffe Bridge would bring Woodstock within little more than two hours' driving time of New York City. Route 28 leading from Kingston was being widened and resurfaced. Woodstock's first street signs were put up to help guide strangers by courtesy of the Woodstock Business Association, newly organized and active in promoting its members' welfare. The Association kept pressuring the town board to provide a more favorable climate for business.

One business which was then getting beyond help was the Newgolds' Overlook Mountain House. The buildings were too battered and ravaged to be worth repairing. The world was no longer interested in mountaintop hotels, however fine the views they offered. Those Newgold heirs who had come out on top in the family litigation tried to prevent hikers and others from climbing the washed-out road that led upward from Mead's. They could not hope to accomplish this without hiring round-the-clock guards, and this they did not do. Overlook Mountain remained a major goal of young and old Wooodstock people who found a visit to the mountaintop as exhilarating and inspiring as their great-grandparents had done.

Eventually much of the Newgolds' land was sold to New York State to become part of the Catskill Forest Preserve. A tract incuding the hotel building was sold to a group of prosperous downstate businessmen who put up a cabin which they used in hunting season. The club was named the Be-No Club from a phrase in its bylaws which stated that there would be no sexual activity on the premises.

Though they tried, the Be-No members could not shut out the thieves and vandals who attacked their clubhouse. In 1969 they forbade use of the road that led to the mountaintop from Mead's, claiming to have acquired with the Newgold land the right to control of the road. They permitted use of the road by none but employees of the State Conservation Department. The state set up a tower for its forest-fire observer's use close to the site of the old hotel's observation tower near what had once been called Hopper's Rock. The tower had formerly stood on Gallis Hill near Kingston. A cabin for the observer stood near the base.

Restricting the use of the road to state employees and a few woodlot owners proved impossible even after the Be-No people put up fences and locked gates near Mead's. For years anger bubbled over the issue of free access to the state lands on Overlook. But the road did not become open to pedestrians until years later. The plateau on which the succession of Overlook Mountain Houses had been built was a desolate spot by the 1950s, the ground littered with bits of glass and china, with remnants of lighting and plumbing fixtures, and with beer cans.[1]

Down in Woodstock the note among business people was one of hope. As Rotron and soon IBM prospered and expanded, local business people and politicians saw their town as having a future. They assured the voters that additional industry would "widen the tax base" and lessen the taxes on individual homes. New shops appeared on Tinker Street. New housing developments were built on level flood plains where modern machinery made construction easiest. The hilly parts of town remained for the time without these developments. Construction was more expensive there, and Rotron and IBM employees might have problems getting to and from work in icy winter weather.

Little League baseball arrived in 1956. The next year saw the first meeting of the new Senior Citizens' Club. Dial telephones came into use. Television sets and automobiles multiplied. In 1950 Supervisor Wilson appointed a committee to inquire into "the type of architecture . . . which would best suit the interests of the community." The committee, dominated by businessmen, favored what they called "Colonial architecture," and although their recommendations could have no force under law their decision left marks upon the hamlet of Woodstock.

A large house trailer made its appearance on Orchard Lane: As Richard Thibaut, Jr. the Kingston *Freeman's* Woodstock correspondent, put it, the dwelling, "the first of its kind ever to be seen here," became "the cause of considerable excitement and wonder in the village." Existing buildings on Tinker Street were pushed out close to the sidewalk. The addition of Colonial facades became popular. Among others to receive this treatment was the former Lutheran parsonage near the Woodstock Garage. This building, then used by the Catskill Book and Record Shop, acquired an aggressively Colonial doorway designed by Frederick Gross of New York and fit for an urban apartment house.[2]

The anti-Communist drive of the late 1940s continued into the early Fifties. The period when Senator Joseph McCarthy seized the headlines was marked in Woodstock by sharp conflict. Woodstock educator-sociologist Harold Rugg was then seeing his pioneer series of social-studies school texts being widely attacked as designed to make the American educational system "the handmaiden" of Communism. In the new elementary school across Riseley's bridge on Route 375 teachers warned students that Communists were lurking in the town. Fiery crosses burned elsewhere in Ulster County were sometimes interpreted as warnings to Woodstock left-wingers. Rumors remained active that undercover F.B.I. agents were on the job in Woodstock.

During the Cold War pressures were exerted by government agencies to persuade local people to build shelters against expected Russian nuclear attacks. No one started digging, however, and local Cold-War activity remained confined to verbal battling. In the summer of 1950 a rumor ran around town that "a big Communist was coming to Woodstock to read his poems." The American Legion and Supervisor Wilson immediately looked into the matter. Wilson said he was afraid of another "Peekskill incident." He was referring to a riot which had prevented Paul Robeson from singing at a veterans' rally in Peekskill two years earlier. There had been much bitterness and a suit for heavy damages by Robeson and others, who charged that local police and Governor Dewey had not done their duty in protecting them.

It was true that the Playhouse had scheduled a musical play, *The Barrier*, by black poet Langston Hughes, a revision of Hughes' *The Mulatto* of 1935. Hughes was then being denounced for leftist positions detected in his poems. The performnce of the play was cancelled amid denials that the cancellation had anything at all to do with the rumor. The excitement died away.[3]

Emotional upheavals like these were part of Woodstock life during the Cold-War years. But at the same time the townspeople and the artists usually got along well in the symbiotic side of their relationship. Both took pride in their town. When local illustrators used Woodstock scenes and people in their work everyone was delighted. In 1951 the nationally popular magazine *Collier's* used as the cover of its Christmas number a watercolor by John Pike showing the Village Green during the customary Christmas Eve celebration, when baskets of food were handed out to the poor and children were given gifts.

The Christmas Eve event, which had begun many years earlier as the sort of gesture usual with political organizations, had by that time widened to include much general support. In Pike's cover the center of the hamlet, with the Dutch Reformed Church rising above it, was given the pleasant nineteenth-century look so appealing in Norman Rockwell's covers for *Collier's* rival, the *Saturday Evening Post*.

All Woodstock groups could unite in sorrow at the death of some respected local person. Such a person, for example, was the "village baker," Lenhard Scholl, a kindly man who took pleasure in giving children cookies and who made fruit cakes during the First World War and sent them to Woodstock men in the armed forces (his own son died in that war). In 1952 three sugar maples were planted on the Village Green as a memorial to Marion Bullard. Earlier an evergreen had been placed there to keep alive the memory of the much-loved Dr. Downer.[4]

The image of Woodstock as a warm, friendly, small American town was given additional strength in 1951 by an incident that sent a wave of pride around the town. As the Thanksgiving turkey was roasting in the kitchen of the home of Mr. and Mrs. Joseph Holdridge of Woodstock, a sound truck pulled up at their door. It was there to record the Holdridges' celebration for the Voice of America. Mr. Holdridge, a local speculator-businessman then operating a motel, often played the part of Santa Claus in the Christmas Eve program on the Village Green. He spoke for the Voice of America of his town's charms, explaining that "in the summer here natives cease to own the town because thousands of city people flock to the village, bringing the population up to about 9,000." The Voice, started in 1942 as a wartime propaganda agency, continued to function as an arm of the Cold War. The Holdridge family was an excellent choice for its purpose of presenting the United States as a happy society functioning well under capitalism.[5]

The warm, friendly, small-town side of Woodstock as seen by John Pike and the Voice of America formed a real part of the town's charm. Ever since the art colony began disturbing older ways of local life, people had urged that steps be taken to preserve it. Yet little had been done until the 1950s to retain the visual and cultural appeal of the older Woodstock. Ben Webster's Township Association of 1940 had come to nothing largely because of the conviction of local landowners and politicians that any sort of control over land use would mean lessened opportunity for profit.

By 1950 pressure for planning and zoning was being felt by the town board, which discussed the subject but took no action. That same year a Women's Civic Group (dedicated to "the welfare and progress of the community") and the Business Association were formed. Supervisor Wilson appointed a committee at a meeting of the Association whose duty would be "to help preserve the qualities that have made Woodstock what it is by emphasizing cleanliness, well being, and the preservation of the village trees."

Action was soon being taken under the leadership of Rotron's J. C. Van Rijn and Ben Webster. Van Rijn had become uneasily convinced that the growth of his own company was contributing to local changes of which he didn't approve. In the 1960s an interviewer wrote that Van Rijn loved the town because of its ". . . continued ability . . . to continually renew and regenerate itself as a place of creation. It had, he believed, the ability to inspire; and this must be due in good part to the deep natural beauty of the area. This is why he is so concerned about its being inundated by commercialism. He was proud of giving employment to so many artists and intellectuals; he displayed many works by art-colony painters, sculptors and craftspeople in his handsome headquarters. . . ."

In 1958 Van Rijn had brought into being the Woodstock Association for the Conservation and Development of the Town. Two years later town supervisor Abram Molyneaux appointed the town's first planning board. Though local politicians were still opposed to effective town planning, they recognized that many Woodstock people led by Van Rijn and Webster were eager for it.[6]

At this time Ulster County was experiencing its greatest political scandal, known as the "kick-back scandal." Among other things county politicians had set up a corporation to supply the county highway department with the road oil which was coming into heavy use. Though this was a violation of the law, the local political machine seemed strong enough to be able to ride out the storm, especially as a few Democrats were involved in the scheme. It succeeded thanks to delaying tactics which made it possible to invoke the statute of limitations. But before it was over Boss Wicks had fled the state to avoid testifying and Woodstock's Kenneth L. Wilson had taken his place.

The scandal did much to weaken the hold on the county of the Wicks machine. Woodstock Republican politicians felt less secure. In 1957 newspaperwoman Tobie Geertsema made local history by becoming the first woman elected a member of the town board. She was a Republican running as a Democrat but with an Independent Party endorsement. The next year Democrat Dixon McGrath was elected a justice of the peace. By the late Fifties the local Democrats were including in their platforms planks calling for a town planning board, an end to pollution of streams, and better facilities for outdoor recreation.[7]

The town was moving into an era when public opinion could be more effective and changes might be brought about if enough voters pushed for them. Though citizens did not always take advantage of the new openness of town board meetings, hundreds could show up for a subject about which they had strong feelings.

Because of the presence in the town of new people and the continuing interest in Woodstock of people living within twenty miles or so of the town, the Playhouse was able to keep going. Its management changed from time to time, but it still kept up its policies of balancing presentations to bring in as large an audience as possible. Art-colony people formed only a small part of its patrons. On the Maverick, too, plays were given by hopeful groups until the deterioration of the theater building and stricter official safety rules caused it to close.

Into the 1940s and early 1950s life went on not too differently at Byrdcliffe from the way it had since Ralph Whitehead's death. Tenants of the cottages, many active in the arts, came and went. William Kroll and his music students lived at Byrdcliffe by summer, using as a rehearsal studio the loom room of White Pines (which also housed the handsomely bound if timeworn "Gentleman's Library" of Jane Whitehead's father, onetime mayor of Philadelphia).

Upkeep of the buildings was kept to a minimum. The farm ceased to be operated. Now and then the studio-theater was briefly used. The Villetta became the French Camp, run by Mr. and Mrs. Max

Angiel, with the Whiteheads sometimes spending the winter there. Painters worked in the studios of Skylights. In the East Riding landowners had settled down into living pleasant summer lives after the failure of their attempted reform of the Byrdcliffe system in the 1930s.

As Jane Whitehead approached her ninetieth birthday, she still clung to the ideals which had inspired the founding of Byrdcliffe in 1902. Her will made known after her death in 1955 provided, should her son Peter die before her, that a "self perpetuating committee" be set up to manage and own Byrdcliffe "for the purpose of promoting among the residents of the Town of Woodstock . . . the study, practice and development of skill in the fine arts and crafts, as well as a true appreciation thereof. . . ." The eight trustees of the Byrdcliffe estate would be her friends, six women and two men: Blanche Rosette, Bertha Weyl, Alice Henderson, Zulma Parker, Louise Lindin, Katherine Boyd plus Ben Webster and Mishka Petersham. Most of the trustees were active in the Woodstock Guild of Craftsmen.[8]

When Peter Whitehead took possession of Byrdcliffe he tried to carry out the wishes of his mother as best he could. During the twenty years of his ownership he sold more parcels of land, nearly all on the periphery of Byrdcliffe, to raise enough cash to maintain the rest in a minimal way and to reduce his taxes.

After his mother's death he welcomed the proposal of a company of opera players to establish themselves in the studio-theater. The Turnau Opera Players gave Byrdcliffe some of the brightest moments in its history. They had come together as a group of former students of Josef Turnau, a Central European opera director, and had started out as the Turnau Opera Workshop at New York's Hunter College.

By 1955 they were presenting opera in a former skating rink in the summer resort village of Pine Hill. Pine Hill did not respond with encouragement, and the following year saw the Players delighting audiences at the Byrdcliffe building. With Peter Whitehead's cooperation the theater was enlarged. The operas were skillfully suited in scale to the theater set amid the oaks of Byrdcliffe.

The Turnau group went on to produce operas by winter in many parts of the United State—at colleges and universities, at the 18th-century Asolo Theater in Florida, and elsewhere. Into the Sixties they remained a high point of the Woodstock summer season. Then economic considerations and lack of local financial support made it necessary for the group to give up the theater at Byrdcliffe. After that they sometimes came back to give performances at the Playhouse, but during the Seventies their Woodstock period finally came to an end.[9]

Though Peter Whitehead sold much of Byrdcliffe he maintained its heart as an arts-and-crafts center. He encouraged theater and dancing groups to use the theater, and artists, musicians and writers to occupy the cottages.

From the terrace in front of White Pines, on which his mother had watched as students in the Byrdcliffe School of Art performed morris dances, Peter could see the valley of the Sawkill thickening with houses built for industrial employees. And more uneasily he was aware that another "element," as it was called, was building up strength in Woodstock. The element was made up of the young people known to most local people as "the hippies."

56

BEATS
AND HIPPIES

The "chaotic social change" which had baffled Marion Bullard in 1949 was a mere beginning of what was to come to Woodstock during the next three decades. Woodstock was to experience a taste of what its older people saw as an unexpected decline in the quality of life around them. The sense of constant progress Woodstock boosters had always foreseen had to contend with the disillusionment caused by the Second World War, the nagging uneasiness that followed the explosion of the first atomic bombs over Hiroshima and Nagasaki, the continued Cold War, the rise in agitation for civil rights for blacks, the restlessness of young people in a society which seemed to deny free play to their minds and emotions, and the increasing use of drugs other than alcohol.

An anonymous columnist in the Ulster County *Townsman* in 1964 deplored what he (or she) took to be the fact that "there was nothing to do" in Woodstock. The place, said the reporter, "is losing its aura and color and something MUST BE DONE to protect its quaintness, its charm and winning ways." The reporter threw out a suggestion that was being bandied about among Tinker Street businesspeople. "Why not build a replica of the Paris 'Left Bank' as a tourist attraction?" Artists at work in public, French book stalls, novelty and curio shops might draw three or four hundred thousand tourists a year, the columnist estimated.[1]

But it was not necessary to spend capital trying to bring an imitation Left Bank to Woodstock. By 1965 local business boosters were awakening to a realization that without any effort at all on their part a persistent flow of new people was arriving in Woodstock and gaining strength. But the new people, alas, were not of the kind the businessmen longed for. They did not buy the usual odds and ends in gift shops. Nor did they settle down in the neat new houses provided by speculative builders on the flood plains. Bringing with them their own way of life, they made few concessions to the ways of the older Woodstock. These people were known as "the hippies."

A modest number of forerunners of the hippies, the members of the Beat Generation called the Beatniks, had already begun to seep into town. Their dishevelled appearance, their beards (beards had been on the decline since the Civil War generation), and their rejection of the beliefs of their parents proclaimed their rebelliousness. San Francisco became a center of Beat beliefs and activities in the 1950s. Beat colonies were crystallizing in other places, including Greenwich Village.

By the late 1950s Beat poets were emerging with some compelling ideas. In 1957 Allen Ginsberg's *Howl* and Jack Kerouac's *On the Road* expressed the conviction that young Americans were the victims of a social structure which stifled intuition and denied or perverted basic human urges in order to uphold a rigid money-oriented structure. Ginsberg had spent part of a summer in Woodstock in his boyhood with his mother Naomi, for whom his *Kaddish* is a moving lament. But Beat influence was not strong in Woodstock; it was not until the emergence of the hippies that this movement became a force in Woodstock life.[2]

Most groups of humans tend to see members of other groups with differing ways as being all pretty much alike. Yet all individuals differ from one another in many ways. It was so with the people called hippies who rode the buses from New York City and spread out from the Village Green in ever-greater numbers. Some were "flower children" who exalted love and peace; they wore clean robes, beads, bare feet, beards and often tucked a flower behind one ear. Another category of hippies had a hard, aggressive manner; they seemed to old Woodstock hands to radiate hostility and contempt. And there were all sorts of gradations in between.

One common factor which seemed to knit all the hippies together was the kind of drugs they used to alter consciousness. Older Woodstock people had long used hard cider, whiskey and beer for the same purpose. This was accepted with little grumbling—it was the way things were. But the newcomers with their marijuana and LSD were a different story, one with especially sinister implications when it was added to the openness with which hippies seemed to carry on their sex lives. Though their sexual practices were not too different from those of the older Woodstock, the guilt-free way in which they were carried out shocked many townspeople.

The Beat movement had been small. Those who had joined it were likely to be musicians, writers and assorted intellectuals. But as the word "hippies" began to be used in the 1960s, the movement widened. Restless and dissatisfied young people in all parts of the country were feeling its influence. They were often the children of doctors, dentists and businesspeople, many had dropped out of college. Heroes of the generation included James Dean, the movie actor who died young in an automobile crash after embodying the ideal of the rebel, and Elvis Presley of the wriggling hips, who modified one kind of black music for a white audience.[3]

Music was important to these changes. Beat poets had read their works to the sound of jazz. Folk music had risen and been commercialized on records and radio. Rock music followed. It was to these sounds that the hippies and near-hippies marched into Woodstock carrying their guitars.

During the early Sixties folk and rock musicians were taking up residence in Woodstock. Albert Grossman, the most successful of all managers for popular folk singers, settled in Bearsville. His and other recording studios followed. Bob Dylan bought the big former Stoehr place in the East Riding of Byrdcliffe. Joan Baez, Peter, Paul and Mary and other folk singers became part of Woodstock life after 1962, singing at the Espresso, the former gift shop-soda fountain known since the 1920s as The Nook.

Soon local people accustomed to having strangers ask where they could see the crazy artists were being asked where Bob Dylan lived. Dylan lived in seclusion in Byrdcliffe in the old house which Joan Baez and other musicians believed was haunted. Few Woodstock people saw Dylan. Young people from all over the country tried to break through Dylan's wall of privacy. Eventually he moved to the former Weyl house on Ohayo Mountain where, unlike at his Byrdcliffe hideout, he had ample land to make privacy easier. But even so he sometimes called upon the local police to eject admirers.

In the summer of 1966 Dylan was injured in a motorcycle

accident about which few details were made public. Rumors spread among his fans that he had become a "human vegetable" and would never again appear in public. It was also said that he might succumb to his injuries. For a while it seemed possible that Dylan would join the group of heroes of the hippie and near-hippie pantheon and take a place beside James Dean. But he recovered and went back to performing and writing songs again, although none with the power to stir young emotions of his "Blowin' in the Wind" of 1962.[4]

By the late 1960s the Beat and hippie movements had merged into a far broader and more inclusive one beginning to be referred to as the counterculture. The use of the drugs which the Beats and hippies had favored was seeping into less extreme groups, and the style of dress of Beats and hippies was being produced and sold commercially on a national scale. Timothy Leary, the former Harvard psychologist, was becoming conspicuous as a leader in the rush toward the counterculture, helping to swell the ranks of young people who "tuned in, turned on and dropped out" and came to Woodstock. Runaway boys and girls caught up in the ferment of the times arrived in Woodstock and, dazed and confused, put a strain on local social services. Finally a private organization called Family was formed in Woodstock in the early 1970s to come to their rescue.[5]

The hippie culture and counterculture involved what was commonly called a kind of togetherness. Hippies liked to gather in groups. They rented houses designed for two or three people and packed in a dozen or more. They sat in groups on the Village Green and on Tinker Street sidewalks, and complied reluctantly when police urged them to move on.

In 1965 the town board adopted a lengthy and detailed zoning ordinance under which land use and building were subjected to regulations far more strict than anything ever imposed before. The adoption of the zoning ordinance was a landmark in Woodstock history. The place (if you ignored the hippies) had been moving, some said, toward becoming a bland suburb. Speeded-up means of transportation, increased commercial pressures and the transforming effect of big new local industries had helped bring local ways of living closer to urban ones. It was recognized that Woodstock could never return to its old simplicities. But with the help of an alert public and the new planning methods it was being said that the most highly valued aspects of old Woodstock had a chance of being preserved and the quality of life maintained amid change.

It was in the late 1950s that the efforts of the Woodstock Association had begun the process that led to the acceptance of a town plan and culminated in the adoption of the zoning ordinance. The process had included educational efforts to overcome the natural reluctance of most people to take cheerfully restrictions on their freedom to do as they chose with the land and buildings to which the law gave them title.

Though a majority of Woodstock people favored the adoption of planning and zoning, some continued to oppose it and to object whenever changes in the Town Master Plan and town zoning had to be considered because Woodstock itself was changing. And Woodstock was indeed changing. In the face of strong protests a Kingston ex-politician built the Bradley Meadows shopping center on what had been one of the scenic glories of Woodstock. Rotron and IBM continued to expand.[6]

Local people protested the bombing of North Vietnam by the United States. Some young Woodstockers headed south to join in the civil-rights struggle then reaching a climax. Rumors about the arrival of rock stars set real-estate dealers to predict that Woodstock would become "the Nashville of the north." Painters kept on painting.

Woodstock appeared on occasion in almost unrecognizable form in the media. In New York a leering, titillating story about Woodstock appeared in a sleazy publication called *All Men*. It told, in a way reminiscent of newspaper tales about the Maverick Festivals of the 1920s, of bachannalian orgies taking place in Woodstock. Walter Winchell, leading columnist and gossip-monger of the time, chimed in with a story in the New York *Journal-American* about "British rock and roll stars and touring recording people" gathering at a palatial hideaway in Woodstock and being treated to Rolls Royces and free young women.

In February 1965 Woodstock was discussing, often with heat, a proposal to bring the Newport Jazz Festival to the Johnson-McEvoy place on the Bearsville Flats. The owner, who had been running the place as a resort, was agreeable. The local Chamber of Commerce was interested. But as in the days of the late Maverick Festivals opposition rose and grew until the promoter backed out. The jazz festival, begun in Newport as a gathering of jazz buffs, had acquired a reputation for rowdiness not dissimilar to that which had helped lead to the end of the Maverick Festivals.[7]

By 1965 the town, with its large representation of industrial employees and businesspeople, had become less adventurous. Publicity like that in *All Men* and by Winchell was reviving after a long lull and was chilling to official and unofficial Woodstock.

The sense of relief at having escaped the jazz festival was not to be enjoyed by cautious Woodstockers for very long. Shivers coursed down Woodstock backs in June 1965 as Woodstockers took in a horror story that showed their town in a very unpleasant light. The story that burst upon Woodstock seemed to confirm in many minds all the recent hints, innuendoes and outright claims that Woodstock was becoming the combined Sodom and Gomorrah if not of the state at least of Ulster County.

A 23-year-old man with a record of instability and clashes with the law made public a lurid tale of how he had been tortured while tied in a wheelchair. The scene of the torture was the vacant and neglected old Will Reynolds summer boardinghouse on Mead's Mountain Road. Details of the torture charges raced through Woodstock and Kingston. Harry Thayer, the aggressive manager of the Kingston radio station WGHQ, put the complainant on the air.

The charges stirred up hostility to Woodstock and Woodstock officials. WGHQ's interviewer drew from the young man claims that he knew of 200 Woodstock drug users and 20 pushers, this in addition to chilling details of his alleged torture in the lonely house. The "sadistic torture" charges which WGHQ aired could not be substantiated. The police dropped the case. Yet the picture of Woodstock as a sink of iniquity remained to add tension to the already-troubled air of both Woodstock and Kingston. By this time police agents on several levels had sought out drug users in Woodstock and many arrests had been made.

If it was true that the newly popular drugs were widely used in Woodstock, so too they were in Kingston and many other places throughout the country. The view of Woodstock as a wicked spot had grown through its two generations of existence as an art colony. This helped it to be seen as a suspicious place in the Sixties.[8]

In 1967 this view led to a ludicrous incident. An investigator for a state drug unit arrived in Woodstock naively convinced that the artists were at the heart of the town's drug problem. Posing as an art dealer acting for the head of the Cunard line of steamships, he called on painters and led them to hope he would buy some of their works at high prices to decorate the public rooms of Cunarders. He returned later with a young man whom he introduced as a nephew of his principal. The young man, he explained, wanted a bit of marijuana. Could the artist get him some?

Woodstock painters on whom the agent called were not drug users. At the mention of marijuana they grew suspicious and refused to cooperate. On one such occasion the smiling agent and his smiling "nephew" were photographed without their knowledge. The photograph was printed on the front page of the *Woodstock Week*.

Other incidents on the part of government agents showed how little officialdom understood the nature of the growing drug-using culture. Agitation for setting up a youth center increased. Protection of the town's young people from hippie drug-using influence was an important consideration.

As hippies moved in and population grew a prolonged drought made necessary five additional wells on the Bearsville Flats to maintain a water supply for the water district. In the absence of public means of transportation, hitchikers multiplied. Young people unable to afford life in the center of town took to living in Shady, Willow, Wittenberg and Lake Hill or Shandaken. Though much of the Maverick became filled with suburban dwellings, a few Maverick artists and musicians clung to their footholds.[9]

In 1959 the Woodstock Artists Association as its contribution to the statewide Hudson-Champlain celebration had put together a notable exhibition of Woodstock art of the past. In 1969 the Association celebrated with a fiftieth anniversary exhibit. These two events helped rouse a sense of the historical role of art in the colony. An ambitious project to enlarge and improve the Association's gallery and to form a permanent collection of Woodstock art began being discussed.[10]

Exhibition followed exhibition through the Sixties at the various galleries in town. Reputations rose and fell. Artists came and went.

What created the most locally-caused excitement in the art world of the late Fifites and early Sixties was the work of a tall, burly and bearded plasterer and mason turned sculptor named Clarence Schmidt. For many years Schmidt had been putting together what some called a "crazy castle" from castoff objects of modern American life such as chrome-plated trimmings of cars, refrigerators and so on, discarded toys and kitchen gadgets, lawnmowers, signs and washing machines, furniture, glass, and odds and ends of metal, wood and plastic.

The castle rose from a former bluestone quarry on Ohayo Mountain a bit over the town line in Hurley. It abounded in winding subterranean passages in which colored lights, mirrors and artificial flowers ornamented shrine-like assemblages. Above rose a many-storied and many-roomed structure which suggested a glittering fairy castle, an Arabian-Nights palace designed by a Dada architect or, to the very literally minded, a heap of junk. The structure was glued together with a roofing cement which Clarence called "ashfault."

Much of the material Clarence used had been drawn from the junk collection of eccentric Wittenberg sawmill owner and wood carver Bill Spanhake, who claimed to be a survivor of the sinking of the *Titanic* in 1912. For years Clarence had worked at his construction without attracting much notice. Then Zena painter Sal Sirugo brought a Chicago millionaire to whom he had sold a painting to see Schmidt's castle. The millionaire expressed his admiration by giving Clarence a regular stipend in order to make it possible for him to continue his work.

At this time people in many parts of the United States who had never heard of the junk sculptors of the early twentieth century were assembling such discarded modern artifacts as bottles, cans, wornout tires and bits of discarded metal and glass into naive constructions around their houses. Very quickly Clarence became heralded as the greatest of them all and "the grand-daddy of pop art." In 1964 popular magazines such as *Life* and *The Saturday Evening Post* devoted pages of text and pictures in glowing color to Clarence and his work. The castle was photographed on still and movie film.

Inevitably sightseers and art lovers climbed Ohayo Mountain and made their way to the Junk Castle. Not everyone appreciated or understood what Clarence had accomplished. Neighbors showed their annoyance at the conversion of what had been a secluded neighborhood into a tourist goal. One neighbor, a music teacher and composer, made his indignation public in communications to the local newspapers. He had nothing against Clarence (by then known as The Man of the Mountain), he wrote. Yet he was appalled. While Woodstock had such fine attractions as the Maverick Festivals, the Turnau Opera and its art galleries, the tourists, dazed by the blast of publicity given Clarence's work, had ignored the true intellectual treats of the colony and trooped to what he saw as "a tragic symptom of a decadent society."

Mrs. Schmidt, who lived with the couple's son in a house beside Clarence's which she had built with the proceeds of her earnings as a houseworker, detested the castle. So did her relatives whose land adjoined Clarence's. Disputes with his in-laws mounted into violence, and Clarence spent a night in the county jail after he was charged with aiming a shotgun at a brother-in-law.

After 1964, art experts arrived and pronounced the castle the greatest achievement of its kind. Psychiatrists came, admired and categorized the structure as a love-trap. Indeed, the obvious pleasure with which Clarence welcomed the praise and publicity poured out upon him seemed to bear out this view. Eventually the castle, which because of hasty workmanship was beginning to collapse, ended in flames. Clarence went on. This time he emphasized wrapping the trunks and branches of trees in aluminum foil of which a benefactor had given him an endless supply.

Finally his health failed and he was taken to a Kingston sanitarium. There, dressed in a Santa Claus suit, he like to wave from the verandah at passersby. After a time he was taken off to another sanitarium, where he died.[11]

While Clarence's castle and the steady growth of what Father David Arnold of St. Gregory's called in his parish paper a "hippie flavor" dominated Woodstock minds, art-colony life continued along familiar lines. The Playhouse remained an important element in Woodstock's economy. In 1964 a new group called Performing Arts of Woodstock added its vitality and innovation to Woodstock acting and playwrighting.

Although the Art Students League kept up its schedule of summer classes, its students were finding it harder and harder to locate inexpensive living accommodations in Woodstock. A bequest from Mrs. Fred Dana Marsh for the enlargement of the library was interpreted as making it possible to tear down the old house in which Dr. Larry Gilbert Hall had lived and replace it by another described as Colonial.

In 1961 Ulster County Community College opened, providing a two-year college facility for the county. In the Sixties the Onteora Central School began to function. Hardly had the new district-wide system begun when an English teacher drew criticism for using in class the well-known poem called "The Coney Island of the Mind" by Beat poet Lawrence Ferlinghetti. The teacher narrowly escaped dismissal, resuming his duties, as he put it, "a chastened and wiser man." [12]

Criticism also was heard when town officials provided a few benches on the Village Green. These, often used by what was called by cautious speakers "the undesirable element," were removed, it was explained, "for repairs" but were not returned. Vigorous protest caused them to be reluctantly replaced.[13]

During the Fifties many Woodstock features attractive to tourists had been brought together for promotional purposes as "The Woodstock Festival." This approach was pursued throughout the Sixties. A festival booklet was printed and distributed each year. At the time the word Festival was popular; young people were thronging to music festivals of pop music here and there throughout the country.

In Woodstock folk and rock music events were doing well. A series of very lively weekly ones with performers like Richie Havens provided "hippie music until the wee hours of the morning," as a neighboring resident put it. The supervisor of Saugerties (the events escaped Woodstock hostility by being held across the town line in Saugerties) visited what were called the Soundouts but said he could find nothing wrong with them and had actually enjoyed them. But charges continued that "dope pushers and dope users" were thick as blackberries on the grounds. In the hamlet of Woodstock arrests for possession of small quantities of marijuana and stronger consciousness-altering substances increased. So did arrests for trespassing and burglary.

Older Woodstock people baffled by the new ideas and ways of living penetrating their town expressed anguish. One man wrote in June 1968 to the *Record-Press* to denounce a rock concert at the Woodstock Playhouse. What it actually was, the man wrote, was "a cruel exhibition of senseless noise, a relentless and brutal attack on the human ear. . . ." The audience ". . . was composed of nearly 100 per cent young people clad in grotesque and miscellaneous trappings who applauded with evident pleasure this infernal racket. This is not music. It is nothing else but an invocation to the devil." The music, the writer charged, was a symptom of "the same lawless spirit which was causing riots, murder, rape, robbery and general contempt for the law."

Less than a year after the Playhouse's musical invocation to the devil Woodstock's simmering anti-hippie feeling came to what cookbooks call a rolling boil. A certain long-popular pool in the Sawkill known as the Big Deep showed evidence of boiling early in the year. The spot had been given to the town as a public bathing place by its owner, Mrs. Neilson Parker (she had been talented craftswoman Zulma Steele in the early days of Byrdcliffe). By 1964 the Big Deep had been discovered by the hippies. It had become littered and occasionally rowdy.[14]

At the same time low water by summer had concentrated the

pollution caused upstream by inadequate sanitary facilities and crowding in the hamlet of Woodstock. Early in 1969 the town's officials closed the Big Deep. They also closed Mallory Grove, a streamside public area on the Bearsville Flats, and the California Quarry, owned by the town and used as a source of stone for highway department needs. An ordinance forbade camping on town properties.

The hippies who had taken to camping out in the town, which had no inexpensive housing, were not happy. As late spring warmed the town, more hippies arrived, rucksacks on their backs and their heads full of the praises of Woodstock of which they had read in their underground papers. Woodstock had been pictured there as a tolerant Arcadia, with free camping and swimming places. The hippies now sprawled more noticeably on the sidewalks of Tinker Street. Local citizens wrote letters to their newspapers in which they demanded that something be done to end the flow into town of "the undesirable element."

A Woodstock woman with close family connections to the upper level of local Republican political life assumed leadership of the anti-hippie forces. Arrests of hippies were then reaching as many as fifteen per day. Most of those arrested were appearing for sentence before the town's Democratic justice of the peace, who imposed the usual fines of ten dollars or so. The anti-hippie leader charged that these fines were outrageously low and that the Democratic justice's low fines were largely responsible for the hippie problem. She threatened to phone Governor Nelson Rockefeller and ask him to declare a state of emergency in Woodstock and to call out the National Guard to keep order.

The town justice responded in a press release which, according to the local papers, stated, "Our town is rapidly being overrun with hippies during the day and into the night. They sit everywhere, crowd our sidewalks, ignore cars on the streets, and insult those who ask them to move. Our citizens are afraid to go shopping in the village and our children are intimidated or corrupted by them."

A meeting was called on June 22 at the anti-hippie leader's place. At the meeting Dr. Paul LePaige defined hippies in this way: "A hippie is a creature that walks on two legs, full of lice of the head and pubic section, full of communicable diseases, who speaks an illiterate language." Here the doctor was referring to the novel words and phrases used by hippies and near-hippies, words often borrowed from the speech of American blacks.[15]

The anti-hippie meeting gave some Woodstockers a chance to vent their frustration in words, but it did nothing to contribute to a solution of the problem. It is easy to understand the sense of crisis and fear which brought the anti-hippies together.

The counterculture was gaining ground throughout America. Although in Woodstock hippies increased in numbers almost day by day, they were far from overrunning the town. On June 19 the Kingston *Daily Freeman's* Tobie Geertsema, a former member of the town board, had recognized Woodstock's predicament in a lengthy story under the caption, "The Scene at Woodstock, New Mecca for Rucksackers."

"A Rucksack Revolution was being fought in the name of Youth," wrote Geertsema, "as revolt has swelled into upstate New York and proclaimed Woodstock as its capital. Woodstock as *the scene* and Tinker Street as *the strip* have been building for the past few summer seasons." Geertsema predicted that Woodstock, which had survived similar invasions in the past, would survive this one. "One can visualize Woodstockers learning to live with the newcomers of the 60s just as their grand-parents learned to live with the artists. . . ."

Hippie merchants, the article continued, must also be prepared to learn to live with Woodstockers and to accept the fact that "frantic consumers of their rabbit skins, leather sandals, incense and candles will fade away in September." Geertsema wrote that hippies would never displace Woodstock's art colony "but they could become a permanent and interesting part of the skyline." The hippie invasion would not last, said Geertsema, because "Woodstock is not an inexpensive place to live" and "once this was realized the flood would move on." These views were too rational to be applauded at a time of near-hysteria. They were angrily denounced as inflammatory.[16]

On June 24 the Chamber of Commerce sponsored a meeting in the Town Hall to discuss "The Hippie Impact on Woodstock as a Community." Among six panelists was Michael Green, who called himself a "true hippie." Tobie Geertsema reported that Green, wearing "baggy orange pants, purple shirt, two strands of beads, a sprig of flowers behind his ear," sat "yoga fashion with one foot in his lap."

Green said that non-violence, love of nature, humanity and God were true hippie beliefs. The hippie movement, he admitted, had also drawn less idealistic people "looking for the action." He and his "tribe" felt that some positive step should be taken. He recommended using "a meditation center" like one he had established and making the village center "off limits to loiterers."

The meeting left the people who crowded the Town Hall more puzzled than ever. It did nothing to curb the extremists among the anti-hippies. A few days after the meeting Green's meditation center was vandalized and burned. Green and his "communal family" had set up their center on state land with a permit from forest ranger Aaron Van De Bogart. Its purpose, the tribe members said, "was to re-establish contact with nature and natural ryhthms and to serve as a retreat and a means of offering our services to the community." [17]

The commune in the woods took the American Indian as a model and a source of inspiration. The members believed that they might live off the land without cultivating it. "The heavy violent thing is starting to recede," said Michael Green, referring to the many riots and other violent acts that had marked the 1960s—Haight-Asbury, Chicago, deaths of civil-rights demonstrators in the South. "Indian magic has seeped into the consciousness of the country. The magical forces of the country are converging. . . . Woodstock can be the model for how to save the country from napalm on the one hand and the Black Panthers on the other."

In accordance with their commitment to non-violence, Green and his colleagues refused to cooperate with the police in tracking down the vandals who had destroyed their center. He said that he hoped some day to invite the vandals to dinner.[18]

Woodstock was indeed in confusion and turmoil over its hippie problem. Behind the scenes, only glimpsed now and then by local people, some shrewd young businessmen incorporated as Woodstock Ventures, Inc. were devising means of turning the town's troubles to profit. By this time a few local businesspeople had realized that the hippies whom they had first seen as unprofitable drones might be sources of profit. Shops selling hippie goods were proliferating on Tinker Street. Real-estate values were rising higher than ever even to the sound of hippie guitars and flutes and amid the scent of marijuana which often hung over Tinker Street.

It was becoming clear that hippies, like other humans, had certain needs and requirements that could be profitably satisfied by entrepreneurs knowledgeable in hippie fashions of clothing, food, personal ornaments, and sex and drug paraphernalia. But the Woodstock Ventures people had an eye on more than a mere retailing of merchandise. They hoped to capture the counterculture movement for profit in the temporary form of a festival.

Ever since the Art Students League people had first shocked old Woodstock by their vitality and unconventional ways, the town had been the scene of events at which art-colony people had joined in celebration, giving free rein to the intuitive side of their natures. The Maverick Festivals had been the most conspicuous of these. Throughout the Fifties and Sixties folk and rock gatherings had been local successes.

In 1967 the events called Soundouts had done well, drawing audiences of as much as one thousand to their weekends of music, sleeping bags, marijuana smoking and the pleasant sense of togetherness in a natural setting. Held across the town line in Saugerties on the farm of Pan Copeland, who then operated a Woodstock delicatessen, the Soundouts were organized in a relaxed apparently non-commercial way by Jocko Mofit, whose health-food store was a sign of the times in Woodstock.[18]

By the time the Soundouts came along the phrase "Woodstock Festival" was a familiar one. In the 1950s the name had been originated to describe the promotional effort which included local events which might draw tourists. Enlisting the help of local artists and writers, the festival promoters published an annual guide to the attractions of Woodstock. In 1967 the promoters changed their name to the Woodstock Council for the Arts. Since the word "festival" had suggested to some the kind of hippie orientation which had frightened so many local citizens, they played down the festival aspect by putting the word in small type.

In 1969, however, they returned to displaying the word boldly on the cover of their annual guide. By then the behind-the-scenes businesspeople had taken up the word. Rumors of a proposed "Woodstock Festival" which had nothing to do with the promotional committee began circulating. As in the case of the jazz festival, Woodstock officials were firmly opposed to permitting any such thing. With horror, anti-hippies saw the proposal as marking the peak of hippie penetration of their town. More sensible Woodstockers thought that their town was too small and ill-equipped to handle a huge festival and were relieved when the festival backers gave up and moved on. For a while Woodstock Ventures gave signs of pitching on this place or that for holding their festival. Stone Ridge was rumored as a site for a time and then Wallkill was settled upon with the consent of that town's officials.

In Woodstock people awakened to the fact that the festival, while bypassing their town, was taking its name with it to Wallkill. And then, after Wallkill had second thoughts, it moved from there to White Lake in the town of Bethel. There Woodstock Ventures Inc. promised to stage a Woodstock Music and Art Fair, "Three Days of Peace and Music." This was what would become better known as the Woodstock Festival.

As publicity for the event mounted in the media, a sense of grievance was in the air of Woodstock at what was being called a brazen theft of the town's name. As the time of the festival drew near young people turned up in Woodstock, asking to be directed to the site. Local people told them that the festival would be held some sixty mile away, but that they had been lucky enough to have reached the "true" or "real" Woodstock and not the imitation.[17]

57

A VIEW
FROM THE GREEN

Woodstock people eagerly followed the progress of the three days of peace and music at White Lake as reported by newspapers, on the air, and by refugees from the Festival. They heard of traffic jams, arrests, widespread use of drugs, and rains which turned the grounds on Max Yasgur's Sullivan County farm into a crowded temporary city whose inhabitants lived up to their knees in mud. So vast was the throng reported to be that some people were unable to get close enough to the heart of the action to hear the great rock stars whom they idolized. Woodstockers heard of the warm sense of brotherhood and the conviction that a turning point in planetary life had been reached. As the astrologers had forseen, a new age, the Age of Aquarius, was dawning.

Woodstock people have long been divided into a number of layers, each with its own understanding of what constitutes a good life. By some the Festival was hailed with joy, by others denounced. Some descendants of older Woodstock families, some newer but equally conservative neighbors in Wittenberg, Willow, Shady and Lake Hill, and many inhabitants of the shiny new dwellings in the housing developments of Bearsville and Zena saw the Festival as still another dreadful example of what the permissiveness of modern parents, added to suspected left-wing political movements, had led to. But in the hamlet of Woodstock, with its large young and hippie concentration and its tourist-oriented businesspeople, the Festival was accepted as indeed the jumping-off place for a new kind of society.

After the Festival many young Americans trooped off to places where the Aquarian life might be established and where Aquarian business enterprises might be started. Woodstock seemed one promising place, Taos in New Mexico another. In June 1970 the first number of The Woodstock *Aquarian* was published. Its psychedelically-designed cover pictured a marijuana plant and carried the slogan "Blessed are the peacemakers."

The editor, Allen Gordon, began like this: "Welcome to Woodstock and the Aquarian Age . . . Woodstock a town, but more a name that symbolizes a state of consciousness . . . this valley rumored by the Indians who lived here many moons ago to be haunted with strange spirits, a sacred kind of place . . . Woodstock a Mecca for the culture of the new age . . . Poet-prophet Bob Dylan brought attention to this area when he first came. The pop heroes who either live, or have lived here are many. The Band, Tim Hardin, Paul Butterfield, Jimmy Hendrix. . . ."

In 1967 the vision of the Age of Aquarius had been unveiled in a song in the rock musical "Hair." The vision had been universalized until the editor of the *Aquarian* could write: "Now is the time for intuitive understanding and sharing of the truth . . . the truth that we are all one . . . this is Our Thing . . . this is the magic. . . ." Like Michael Green a few years earlier, The *Aquarian* encouraged a mystical return to the ways of the American Indian as a feature of Aquarian life. In 1971 the *Aquarian* published a full-page composite drawing showing the Catskills as a sacred place to which Indians went only to meditate or perform their ritual dances.[1]

Communes were organized in town. The hippie culture took on more intensively religious overtones, with Buddhism and especially Zen taking hold of members of hippiedom. In its joyous confidence and in its vision of a better and happier world a-coming the movement shared something with the one Ralph Whitehead had brought to Byrdcliffe in 1902.

Though the Byrdcliffe and Aquarian visions differed greatly, both were expressions of a faith that the problems of society might be solved and mankind might move on into an era of joy and fulfillment. But the Aquarian vision, like the Byrdcliffe one in its day, could not always be kept clearly in focus, although both survived.

Harsh contact with the realities of the existing social system began to lessen the joyousness of Aquarians in Woodstock. Minor brushes with the existing system kept cropping up. Town officials pored over their ordinances, wrestling with such problems as whether tipis were permanent or temporary structures. Were tipis required to have flush toilets and other un-Indian gadgets?

Aquarians wondered why it had turned out to be impossible to "live off the land," as had been promised on the bounty nature provided in the form of nuts, leaves, berries and nutritious roots. Divisions arose among Aquarians. Forming into splinter groups, they lost something of the sense of oneness with nature and each other with which the movement had begun.

Contributing most of all to Aquarian difficulties was the economic recession creeping over the nation as the war in Vietnam ended. The Fifties and Sixties had been decades of business and industrial prosperity, with the benefits spread to many but by no means all layers of the country's people. Now that era was ending. Parents and relatives who had been coaxed into financing the Aquarian lifestyle now asked if it were not time for the young to get down to honest work.[2]

Some were indeed working in Woodstock—many at crafts. Never had the colony had so many craftspeople of all sorts. Weaving, leather-working, pottery, furniture-making and metalwork were all being followed. Young men and some women too hired out as carpenters and aspired to build for themselves houses suited to Aquarian aspirations. Domes of the kind designed by Buckminster Fuller multiplied as suited to an Aquarian future.

Craft shops, however, did not handle many local craft wares. The owner of one shop explained why. Woodstock craftspeople, he said, had too much of the "Woodstock character." They worked when they felt like it but when they didn't stopped working and devoted themselves to enjoying life. They were not "reliable."

By 1976 a fair number of people who had come to Woodstock in the cloud of euphoria which rose from the Woodstock Festival were leaving. They said they were not able to make a living in Woodstock. They felt little sense of camaraderie in the town in those times of economic pressure. Too often craftspeople and artists were competitive rather than loving and supportive in the true Aquarian way. Shopkeepers dealing in objects used by the Aquarians were feeling the economic pinch and shops were changing hands.[3]

An emphasis on looking inward to root out the causes of individual difficulties gained strength. And ways of improving relations between people were taught—aikido, tai chi ch'uan, and Creative Movement, yoga exercises, gestalt groups, primal scream and Esalen massage were offered. Private schools for young children increased as Woodstock's large population of single parents found schools like these to ease the burden of singleness. Meditation became popular. Mead's, the old summer hotel in the Wide Clove near which Ralph Whitehead had made the decision to found the art colony, became a Tibetan Buddhist retreat center called Karma Tryana Dharmachakra. Father Francis' church of Christ-on-the-Mount adjoined the retreat center. Father Francis was then approaching his ninetieth birthday. Woodstock's old churches attracted business and industrial people to their services but no counterculturists.[4]

Although some Aquarian-minded people had drifted away from Woodstock by the mid-Seventies, others still aglow with the Aquarian flame were arriving. When added to the effects of the nationwide recession, the presence in town of so many young people with no marketable skills brought the number of Woodstock people on relief to sixty or so. County and local attempts to relieve unemployment had little effect.

Family, Woodstock's Aquarian social-services organization, increased its services. It set up a Free Store and took steps toward giving help to a Free University. Conflict between Family and town officials continued until a partial truce was reached in 1977. The handling of runaways who came to Woodstock had been a chief cause of disagreement.

For a while the Bank of Orange County had permitted use of the old Longyear House beside its facility by the Woodstock Historical Society and later by Family. Bank officials then threatened to tear down the building, which did so much to give grace and dignity to the hamlet. In response to objections by Woodstockers the bank agreed to take no drastic action without advance warning. In violation of this promise bulldozers quickly reduced the building to rubble in an early-morning blitz. The remains were carted off to the town dump.[5]

The counterculturists who looked to a coming Age of Aquarius usually confined their ecological efforts toward preserving the natural environment. But many joined with people on other levels in a sense of outrage at the bank's action. They joined resistance to other profit-motivated attempts to alter the look of the town to which they had become devoted. While still keeping up their Oriental- and American Indian-inspired religious practices they opposed such local changes as the transformation of an especially charming farming area of the town into what was eventually named the Kenneth L. Wilson State Park, the construction of nuclear plants in the Hudson Valley, and the placing of concrete sidewalks along Route 212 in the center of the hamlet of Woodstock.

An alliance of old and new people got behind the purchase by the town of the 76 acres of scenic fields, woodland and Sawkill frontage on the Eames-Comeau place. By 1979 the house was being used for town offices.

By the late Seventies the kind of young people who had caused such fear in the late Sixties had lost their power to arouse emotion, in part because their ways had mellowed with time and in part because the older Woodstock people had become accustomed to them. It was in the 1970s that official concern for the natural and man-made environment led to the creation of an Environmental Commission and a Commission for Civic Design. Both, however, had only advisory powers.

A proposal for a conventional sewage system for the hamlet to be largely funded by federal money was rejected at a referendum. It would have resulted in torn-up streets, much blasted bedrock and the destruction of roadside trees as well as a prolonged period when Tinker Street shops would find it hard to function. After many meetings and much debate a more innovative system also eligible for funding from federal sources was adopted in the late Seventies. In late 1985 it began to function, although in a less innovative form.[6]

By 1980 Woodstock's year-round population had risen to 6823, an increase of nineteen per cent from 1970.

Of significance between the two censuses was a new wave of emergence of Woodstock women into public and business life. Women owned and worked in Tinker Street shops, women took jobs as plumbers, electricians, editors, reporters and carpenters. Three women wielded top political power in local government as town supervisor and members of the Woodstock town board. Though in accordance with a national trend, this change owed much to the energetic young men and women who had come to town in the wake of the Woodstock Festival.

Though the Sixties and Seventies had brought a greater emphasis on both popular and classical music and less on painting, artists remained numerous. Old-time painters and sculptors remained active alongside newer people to whom Woodstock in its familiar role of a glamorous art colony was still attractive. Musicians came to abound as never before. Recording studios proliferated. Albert Grossman, with his restaurants and studios at Bearsville, went on planning to expand his activities even after a slashing attack on him and Woodstock musical ambitions called "Woodstock Was—Dylan's Dream is Dying Hard" in *Harper's* magazine.

A good number of adherents of the counterculture found outlets for their energies as the Aquarian enthusiasm lessened, not only in a variety of the many therapies available in town, but also in supporting environmental projects such as the recycling of materials, and in attending meetings opposed to nuclear-energy use or to foreign policy.

With the death of Peter Whitehead in 1976 the West Riding of Byrdcliffe had become with the exception of a few buildings the property of the Woodstock Guild of Craftsmen. Byrdcliffe as a whole was soon placed on the Register of Historic Places. Much Byrdcliffe furniture, tools and old farm equipment was sold. Woods were lumbered by the Guild in order to raise cash.[7]

The road leading to the top of Overlook Mountain was at last permanently opened to hikers, although not to cars. The rattlesnakes which had been so plentiful on the mountain appeared by this time to have grown fewer. With so much valley land subdivided, mountainside acres began to be sold for the building of weekend homes. This met opposition from the increasingly vocal advocates of stricter zoning.

The middle-of-the-road literary quarterly called *Bluestone* published its last number as the Seventies began. A number of attempts at similar publications and newspapers soon faltered and failed. Neither the Woodstock *Record-Press* (successor to the Woodstock *Press*) nor the Woodstock *Weekly* survived into the Seventies. The Ulster County *Townsman* founded in 1957 did and was joined in 1972 by Woodstock *Times*. In 1972 the Overlook Press was founded in Lewis Hollow. Graphic artists, including some leaders in the field, moved to Woodstock. Television and radio people multiplied in the town.

Woodstock grew in complexity and in the public services thought necessary by its people. Tinker Street approached closer and closer to the condition of a tourist strip which squeezed out businesses which had once served local residents. Visitors might now buy exotic merchandise brought in from the ends of the earth, enjoy drinks or unusual meals, or spend an evening at a night place similar to those at other tourist-minded locations throughout the country.

Local people bought their daily necessities at the shopping centers at the eastern end of the hamlet. There once-numerous gas stations were giving way to encroaching tourist shops. Opponents of the concrete sidewalks laid down on Tinker Street and Mill Hill Road were taking some comfort in the late Seventies in observing the concrete mellow in color and even to crack here and there. The Village Green, once suggested as a solemn memorial grove to departed leading citizens (each one represented by a tree with a memorial tablet attached), became the scene especially on weekends of lively musical or dancing events or social gatherings.

The hotel built by Morris Newgold in the late 1920s on Overlook grew ever more ramshackle. Its tower developed a slant greater then that of the leaning tower of Pisa. The structure was felt to be unsafe for its many visitors, and the Woodstock Fire Department obliged when asked to burn it out. The heavy concrete shell of the building remains to tell of Woodstock's hotel ambitions of the past. The hotel building's closest year-round neighbors now are a television tower, the thriving Tibetan Buddhist retreat center in the Wide Clove and the impressive monastery which has risen beside it.

Less prosperous since Father Francis' death is the Church of Christ-on-the-Mount. Disputes over possession of the church and the right to hold services there have lessened its once-considerable importance to Woodstock.

Ever since the coming of age of its art colony in the late 1920s Woodstock had been marked by animated disputes over almost all matters which affected the welfare of the town and its people. When such disputes raged the townspeople lined up on opposing sides and went through an almost-ritual dance of hostility, conflict, concession and compromise. During the 1980s a proposal to build a huge hotel and convention center on the former Johnson-McEvoy place, changes in plans for a sewerage district, the best use for the Comeau house and its surrounding fields and forests, the building of sidewalks along Route 212, the discovery that asbestos was finding its way into the water supply of Woodstock, the proposed bringing up to date of the town's zoning ordinance—all these and more bought peaks in the town's communal dance.[8]

This book began on top of Overlook Mountain with a look at the landscape of Woodstock and a quick run along the boundaries which do their best to enclose the town and to set it apart from the rest of the world. Now the book ends, hundreds of pages later and some twenty-five hundred feet lower on the Village Green, with a glance at the procession of people who have adapted the Woodstock landscape to human use in ways sanctioned by their society.

It is a long procession that we see, taking more then a thousand years to pass the Green. It begins with the Indians, whose trail as far as we can determine led up the Sawkill Valley and along the Tannery Brook's eastern branch to the rock shelters on Overlook's side, which served as bases for Indian hunting expeditions. Trappers, displaced Indians, squatters and soldiers in the French and Indian War come next, followed by a variety of land speculators and surveyors. Robert Livingston of Clermont appears with tenants to whom he leased land to be cleared and farmed near Cooper Lake, Bearsville and his sawmill in the hamlet of Woodstock. The Revolutionary War's Whigs and Tories file past the Village Green, the Tories sheltered by the dark of night as they pass from the house of one secret sympathizer to another.

An especially sensitive or credulous observer might even catch a glimpse of George Washington talking earnestly with a group of Iroquois Indians. For a Woodstock man, Clowry Chapman, found evidence which convinced him, at any rate, that Washington and the Indian allies of the British had met and made peace near this very spot as the American Revolution approached its end.

For a while after settlers were evacuated by the orders of the military, few people pass what was to become the Village Green. But with the war's end new settlers pour in from the Hudson Valley, New England and farther away. Before long glassworkers and tannery employees appear. As the Anti-Rent War comes to town, occasional tenant farmers in Indian disguises may walk past the Green, cautiously, for this was a predominantly Up-Rent neighborhood.

By 1850 the stream of people increases—teamsters hauling forest and farm products from far back in the Catskills; drovers with their cattle, geese and turkeys; local farmers and their wives and children. So do the number of taverns and blacksmith shops within sight of the Green. Irish-born quarry workers walk by. Young draftees of the Civil War walk soberly past on their way to induction.

Once the Overlook Mountain House is in business, summer visitors stroll on the Green. On Sundays people dressed in their best make their way to church.

In 1902 Ralph Radcliffe Whitehead and his assistants in founding a new Utopia in Woodstock catch their first glimpse of the Green. By then the Green has lost the ragged look of its early years (it was often littered with bluestone from local quarries) in deference to the tastes of summer people. Soon arts-and-crafts enthusiasts stop on the edge of the Green and leave the horsedrawn stages which have brought them from the railroad station at West Hurley. Young men and women enrolled at the summer school of the Art Students League walk by with their easels and paintboxes, pausing to do handsprings on the Green and to astonish passersby with their bizarre costumes. The aged veterans of the Civil War parade past on Decoration Day. Soldiers in succeeding wars take their last look at the Green before leaving town, some forever.

An observer on the Green can easily conjure up in his imagination the people of the 1920s, tourists strolling up and down, painters and near-painters, men and a growing number of women in khaki and denim, descendants of old Woodstock hill families come to do their shopping and looking with amazement at the strange people they see, at the profusion of automobiles and the scarcity of horses, and often at a group of costumed revellers on their way to the Maverick Festival.

The Great Depression years of the Thirties send people passing the Green with hoes and other implements of subsistence farming in their hands. By the 1950s newly arrived artists and more and more musicians join the procession mingled with employees of industries like Rotron and then IBM. The procession thickens and changes during the Sixties. The young people called hippies get off buses from New York and sit, dressed in their robes and beads, in groups on the Village Green. Backpackers trudge by. Winter people with skis on top of their cars whiz past the Green.

In the procession marching past into history the Village Green observer might pick out modern speculators in land and housing alert for favorable sites, and prosperous New York businesspeople looking for second homes, preferably with a magnificent distant view and with no close neighbors. Other businesspeople look the town over with the hope of establishing a business there. Young poets go by. So do actors, assassinologists, therapists, policemen, politicians, Rastafarians and an occasional smiling Buddhist monk. Actors, dancers, people who applaud every action of the town government and people who disapprove of everything, older people grumbling that Woodstock is on the skids and people who look foward to a glorious future for the town.

Organized parades past the Green have long been a pleasant feature of Woodstock life: patriotic parades, parades directed against nuclear facilities, against war, in favor of women's rights and gay rights. A parade celebrating the bicentennial of the American Revolution goes by, including a float depicting B rsy Ross, and ends on the recreation field on Rock City Road with a balloon ascension, a tobacco-juice spitting contest and other appropriate events.

It seems likely that future observers of Woodstock life from the vantage point of the Village Green will see a procession to which new kinds of people will be added, mingled with the older kinds.

In the late 1940s New York State Historian Albert Corey visited Woodstock for the first time. He was told that he should have come earlier, that Woodstock was losing its distinction, and that the art colony was disintegrating. Whimsical Corey replied, "I'm not so sure of that. Its been my observation that while it's very easy to start an art colony, once it's established its almost impossible to root it out."

It is unlikely that the distinctive unit of social life we call Woodstock can easily be rooted out. It has survived many blows and after each one has risen in added strength. And because of the creative vitality that has kept the Woodstock spirit alive future observers looking out from the Village Green and from the top of Overlook may find what they see stirring to their imagination and emotions in ways we cannot dream of.

NOTES

Abbreviations used:

DAB	Dictionary of American Biography
NYHL	New-York Historical Society
NYPL	New York (City) Public Library
NYSL	New York State Library
SUNY	State University of New York

CHAPTER 1

1. Maps used here were the Phoenicia, Bearsville, Woodstock and Kingston West Quadrangles of the *U.S. Geological Survey Topographical Maps*, 7.5 Minute Series, Washington D.C., 1945.
2. Crystal, Roy et al., *New Dimensions in Land Use Planning for Woodstock, New York* (Master of Regional Planning thesis, University of Pennsylvania, 1974), pp. 13–64. The population figure given in the *Ulster County Data Book* as determined by the U.S. Bureau of the Census in 1980 is 6823.

CHAPTER 2

1. Indian artifacts examined include those found in Woodstock by L. H. Zimm, Ludwig Baumgarten, C. A. Berry (this last in photographs) and pottery fragments owned by the Woodstock Historical Society. The notes, plans and maps in the Schrabisch Collection, New York State Museum, were useful. Printed sources used were William A. Ritchie and Robert E. Funk, *Aboriginal Settlement Patterns in the Northeast*, Albany, 1973, pp. 333-358; Robert E. Funk, *Recent Contributions to Hudson Valley Prehistory*, Albany, 1976, pp. 305-313; Leonard Eisenberg, *Paleo-Indian Settlement Pattern in the Hudson and Delaware River Drainages*, Rindge, N.H., 1978, pp. 1-36, 120-122.
2. William A. Ritchie, *Indian History of New York State, Part III, The Algonkian Tribes*, Albany, n.d., passim.
3. William Cronon, *Changes in the Land*, N.Y.C., 1983, esp. pp. 34-55. For Indian trails, personal communication from Harry Siemsen, historian, Town of Kingston. For variants of the name Awaghgonk, Albert Rosa's Petition, Indorsed Land Papers, v. 3, p. 40, New York State Library, hereafter NYSL; Marius Schoonmaker, *History of Kingston N.Y.*, p. 187; N. B. Sylvester, *History of Ulster County N.Y.*, Philadelphia, 1880, Part I, p. 258.
4. For Waughkonk Road, personal communication from Harry Siemsen, May 4, 1972; Henry Ramsay, Memorandum Book of Survey in Ulster County (1844-46), NYSL, p. 23.

5. For "foot path," Woodstock Town Clerk's Minute Book (1787-1804) for December 1789.

6. Events leading up to the Esopus Wars are covered in Mark B. Fried, *Early History of Kingston and Ulster County*, Marbletown and Kingston, 1975. Sources in early printed records are amply cited. The quotation is in E. B. O'Callaghan, *Documents Relating to the Colonial History of the State of New York*, 15 vols., Albany, n.d., passim (1856-1857), Vol. XIII, p. 321. Hereafter referred to as *New York Colonial Documents*.

7. Gladys Feeley and Martin MacDaniel, personal communications; R. Lionel DeLisser, *Picturesque Ulster*, Kingston, 1897, pp. 236-237; 231 and 240; Bruno Louis Zimm, "A Chain of Woodstock Land Titles," in *Publications of the Woodstock Historical Society*, no. 5, August 1931, pp. 6-7.

8. Max Schrabish, ms., "Indian Rock Shelters of Southern New York," N.Y. State Museum, pp. 84-89; Robert E. Funk and William A. Ritchie, personal communications; for the spy incident, Kingston *Daily Freeman*, September 20, 1917 and September 24, 1917.

9. Herbert H. Cutler, personal communication.

10. Dexter A. Hawkins. The New York Public Library and the Woodstock Library have copies of his *The Traditions*.

11. *The Aquarian*, Woodstock, N.Y., 1971, v. 2, no. 1, p. 16.

CHAPTER 3

1. For wheat, *New York Colonial Documents*, v. III, p. 261; for a Brabanter, Schoonmaker, *History of Kingston*, p. 485.

2. *New York Colonial Documents*, v. XIII, p. 451-452.

3. Harry Siemsen, personal communication; late Indian occupancy of rock shelters suggested by presence of trade goods; Schrabisch, "Rock Shelters."

4. Albert Rosa's petition of 1701, Schoonmaker, *History of Kingston*, p. 187; Hardenbergh petition, Indorsed Land Papers, v. 3, p. 41.

5. Petition Cornelis Cool, NYSL, *Calendar of Council Minutes, 1668-1783*, Albany, 1902, v. 9, p. 481; Petition of C. Cool and Adrian Gerritse, Indorsed Land Papers, v. 4, p. 26; for details of granting of lands to Cool and Hardenbergh see Alf Evers, *The Catskills*, Garden City, New York, pp. 33-39.

6. Ulster County Deed Book Liber AA, p. 494 for recital of purposes of Hurley people.

7. Old copy of Indian deed, 1705, Cockburn Papers 11:37.

8. For Hendrik Hekan, Evers, *The Catskills*, pp. 57, 60, 63, 70, 117, 598.

9. Advertisement in New York *Gazette*, April 8, 1771.

10. For Hardenbergh Patent granting ms., Book of Patents, 1664-1786, N.Y. Secretary of State's Office, Albany, vol. 7, p. 363; for further details of the granting see Evers, *The Catskills*, pp. 33-38.

11. Hardenbergh Patentees' conveyance to Cool and Associates, Deed Book AA, p. 494, Ulster County Clerk's office; for trespassing on Kingston Commons, Kingston Trustees Minutes, Dec. 31, 1720; for Kingston-Hardenbergh Patent lawsuit, Schoonmaker, *History of Kingston*, p. 194; for arbitration of the suit, Ulster County Deed Book EE, p. 300.

CHAPTER 4

1. M. Schoonmaker, *History of Kingston*, pp. 129-144.

2. For R. Livingston's acquisition of lands in Catskills see Evers, *The Catskills*, pp. 53-58.

3. Thomas Streatfield Clarkson, *A Biographical History of Clermont or Livingston Manor*, Clermont, N.Y., 1869, p. 24.

4. E. Wooster's map of the Patent on parchment, NYSL; the advertisement of 1749 RRLP, "Methods of

forming...," RRLP; map of
Woodstock with streams, Cockburn
Papers, NYSL, 5:26.
5. Wooster map and survey, NYSL;
map by Charles Clinton, Map Book 3,
p. 50, Ulster County Clerk's office.
6. Map of part of Great Lot 8,
Hardenbergh Patent, 1750s, NYSL.
7. Map with streams ut. supra, mss.,
"Relating to the division of the estate
of Philip Livingston," New-York
Historical Society, hereafter NYHS;
Mrs. Stephen Gitnick, personal
communication.
8. Ms. relating to the Estate of Philip
Livingston for division of Thomas
Wenham lands in Great Lot 26,
Hardenbergh Patent.
9. Letter R. G. Livingston-Henry
Livingston, Adriance Memorial
Library, Poughkeepsie.
10. Schoonmaker, *History of
Kingston*, pp. 134, 139 and passim.

CHAPTER 5

1. Letter Robert Livingston-Robert R.
Livingston, 17 March 1762, RRLP
Series 1, 000035.
2. Ms. "Relating to the estate of Philip
Livingston," NYHS; Evers, *The
Catskills*, pp. 103-109.
3. Letter Robert Livingston-Robert R.
Livingston, 1 March 1762, RRLP
Series 1, 000033.
4. Edwin B. Livingston, *The
Livingstons of Livingston Manor*,
N.Y.C., 1910, pp. 144-145; A. Evers,
"Cornelius Tiebout was a White Collar
Pioneer," in Woodstock *Record-Press*,
October 4, 1962.
5. The map in Cockburn Papers, 5:26,
shows "Livingston's twelve hundred
acres."
6. Letter, 1 March 1762.
7. William Cockburn, lease and survey
book 1762-1790, n.p., Cockburn
Papers, 15:5.
8. Letter March 1, 1762 Robert
Livingston-Robert R. Livingston,
RRLP Series 1, 000033.
9. W. Cockburn, lease and survey
book, NYSL.

10. Map by William Cockburn, 1765,
showing proposed new Albany County-
Ulster County line.
11. New Hampshire Historical Society,
Historical New Hampshire, November
1950, p. 254; "Bentinck, William Henry
Cavendish," in *Dictionary of National
Biography*; J. K. Wallenberg, *Place-
Names of Kent*, Upsala, 1934, p. 272
and 264; The *Diary of Samuel Sewall*,
ed. M. Halsey Thomas, 2 vols. N.Y.C.,
1973, vol. 1, p. 254; letter Robert R.
Livingston-Robert Livingston, 2
February 1764, RRLP Series 1,
000049.
12. W. Cockburn, lease and survey
book.

CHAPTER 6

1. George Dangerfield, *Chancellor
Robert R. Livingston of New York,
1746-1813*, N.Y.C., 1960, pp. 29-30;
Evers, *The Catskills*, Garden City,
N.Y., pp. 102-103.
2. Letter Robert R. Livingston-Robert
Livingston, December 24, 1762, RRLP
Series 1, 000035; George Dangerfield,
*Chancellor Robert R. Livingston of
New York 1746-1813*, N.Y.C., 1960,
pp. 25-30.
3. Letter Robert R. Livingston-Robert
Livingston, 12 April 1766, RRLP
Series 1, 000035.
4. Letter Robert R. Livingston-Robert
Livingston, 12 April 1766, RRLP
Series 1, 000064.
5. Ibid., Dangerfield, *Chancellor
Robert...*, pp. 25-26.
6. The terms of the conveyance of
January 22, 1768 are recited in a deed
Margaret B. Livingston-Robert R.
Livingston, February 22, 1790, not
recorded until 6 May 1840, Ulster
County Deed Book 54, pp. 316-317.
7. E. B. Livingston, *The Livingstons of
Livingston Manor*, N.Y.C., 1910, p. 7.
8. Map of the Division Line Between
the Counties of Albany and Ulster...
by William Cockburn, 1765, map and
print room, NYHS; map "of the
Northerly part of the Great or
Hardenbergh's Patent... made for

Messrs. Ludlow and McEvers," 1773, by W. Cockburn. Ulster County Historical Society, Marbletown, New York. While the above maps are not accurate as to topography, they show existing buildings with fair accuracy.
9. The Cockburn lease and survey book, NYSL, supplied details of terms of leases, supplemented by the many copies of Woodstock leases scattered among the RRLP, NYHS; suggested use of land from Indian artifacts found in Zena by Ludwig Baumgarten, in Lake Hill by Gladys Feeley and in Willow by Ray Van Wagner.
10. The Longyear lease on a printed form, RRLP, NYHS, an abstract with survey in W. Cockburn's lease and survey book.
11. The Winne and Ferris leases are among the RRLP, NYHS, and are abstracted in the W. Cockburn lease and survey book, NYSL.
12. The Hubner lease is among the RRLP, NYHS.
13. Anita M. Smith, *Woodstock History and Hearsay*, Saugerties, 1959, gives the folklore of the Winne lease.
14. The pine tree story is from Richard LeGallienne, *Woodstock an Essay*, Woodstock, N.Y., 1923.

CHAPTER 7

1. Benjamin Snyder Daybook, December 30, 1770, lists amount owed by tenants; Dutch personal and family names are found in the records of the Dutch Reformed Church, Kingston, published in Roswell Randall Hoes, *Baptismal and Marriage Registers of the Old Dutch Church of Kingston, N.Y.*, Kingston, 1891, and similar record of the Katsbaan Church, Saugerties, 1730-1801, published in *Olde Ulster*, vols. 7, 8, 9 (1905-1914), Kingston, N.Y. and in *Katsbaan and Saugerties Reformed Church, 1730-1785*, ed. Jean Worden, Franklin, Ohio.
2. Deed of Release, Garret Newkerk-Evert Wynkoop, April 10, 1771, Ulster County Deed Book.
3. Deed; C. Tiebout to John Read, 1774, mentions "One Newkerk"; deed, John

Read to William Eltinge 1778, mentions "Garett Newkerk"; Ulster County Deed Books, Joseph D. Short, *Short Lineage* (typescript), n.p., 1974.
4. William Cockburn, lease and survey book, Cockburn Papers, NYSL, *passim;* Benjamin Snyder account books; Senate House Library; NYSL; and NYHS; the reference to Thomas Chadwick as "arrested" is in Charles DeWitt's copy book under December 3, 1751, Senate House Museum, Kingston.
5. William Strickland, *Journal of a Tour in the United States of America*, ed. Rev. E. J. Strickland, N.Y.C., 1971, pp. 117-118, gives an account of Great Lot 24 before settlement; for Ludlow land dealings, *Report of the Bureau of Archives*, Toronto, 1905, no. 49, pp. 260-269; for Carle and Ludlow families, George Carle, *A Carl Family History*, privately printed, Baldwin, L.I., 1974, n.p., Chapter 4.
6. The Ben Snyder account books used here are divided between the New York Historical Society 1768-1775, 1768-1795 and 1774-1777 and the Senate House Museum Library, Kingston.
7. My sources for the details of daily life in Woodstock which follow are the Snyder books, which may be located by the dates given.
8. Some of Snyder's words which may not be readily recognized today are: oznabruck, a rough linen or cotton cloth; ell, a measure of 45 inches; cars, kersey or carson, a woolen often used for work clothes; stoof, stuff, a woolen or worsted; pase borte, pasteboard; everlastin, a durable woolen cloth; frieze, a heavy woolen and shoddy cloth often used for overcoats; and cambric, a thin linen or cotton cloth.
9. For the flaxseed trade see Ulysses P. Hedrick, *A History of Agriculture in the State of New York*, 1933, reprinted, N.Y.C., 1966, pp. 163-164.
10. For clearing land, account of "the Practice of Clearing Forests," uncat. ms., RRLP, NYHS; U. P. Hedrick, op. cit., pp. 96-101.

11. "Wigwam" is an Algonkian word applied by early settlers to any structure of bark, branches, etc. Thomas Cole described the building of what he called a wigwam on top of Overlook Mountain in his journal for August 1846.

12. Leases and other papers in the RRLP and the Snyder account books helped supply details of Woodstock life during the 1760s and early 1770s. The estimate of the number of farms on the eve of the Revolution are based on the maps cited earlier, on surviving leases and on the many rent rolls and account books of the Livingstons of Clermont, NYHS.

CHAPTER 8

1. Marius Schoonmaker, *History of Kingston*, N.Y.C., 1888, pp. 168-169, and Appendix, "Agreement to Maintain Constitutional Rights with names of signers and non-signers."
2. Evers, *The Catskills*, pp. 130-131; ibid, pp. 190-191, for Peter Short's house.
3. *New York Genealogical and Biographical Record*, vol. 67, p. 347; Kingston *Daily Freeman*, March 29, 1886.
4. B. Snyder Sloop Account Book, 1776; "Hasbrouck's Rangers," ed. Peter Force, *American Archives*, 5th Series, Washington, 1843, p. 283. Billetting roll for 28 men, order for payment, payroll, Ben Snyder Sloop Book, 1776; for minute men saltpeter, sale of sloop for use as fireboat, B. M. Brink, *Early History of Saugerties*, Saugerties, 1902, p. 262.
5. The sloop's canoe, Snyder Daybook, 1768-1795. NYHS, January 30, 1776, Snyder Daybook, 1776, 3, economic stagnation, Snyder account books.
6 *Public Papers of George Clinton*, first governor of New York, 1777-1795, 1801-1804, 10 vols., Albany, N.Y., 1899-1914, vol. VI, pp. 673-674.
7. Gold under floorboards reported in conversation with Louis H. Zimm, c.1950.

8. Staughton Lynd, "Tenant Uprising . . ," in *New-York Historical Society Quarterly*, April 1964.
9. Whig-Tory animosities are made clear in *N.Y. Calendar of Historical Manuscripts Relating to the War of the Revolution, in the Office of the Secretary of State*, vol. II, pp. 72-74.
10. Ibid, for the capture of Newkirk.
11. Minutes of the Kingston Committee of Safety & Observation, April 9, 1777.

CHAPTER 9

1. The tradition of the Continental Army in Mink Hollow, Anita M. Smith, "Stories of Mink Hollow, History and Hearsay," in *Publications of the Woodstock Historical Society*, no. 2, August 1932, p. 20-21; of the Tory, the bayonet and the baby, ibid, p. 21.
2. Marius Schoonmaker, *History of Kingston, N.Y.*, June 1907, pp. 167-171.
3. B. M. Brink, *Early History of Saugerties*, p. 106; hidden treasure, Wilna Hervey in conversation, c. 1968; Anita M. Smith, "Hearsay and History," in *Publications of the Woodstock Historical Society*, no. 4, July 1938, p. 5.
4. Fear of Indian raids, *Public Papers of George Clinton*, vol. 4, pp. 807-808, 818-19.
5. Traditional image of Brant, Anita M. Smith, *Woodstock History and Hearsay*, Saugerties, 1959, p. 11; and J. T. Kelsay, *Joseph Brant, 1743-1807*, Syracuse, 1984, pp. 653-658.
6. Overlook summit in Revolution and objects found there, Gladys Feeley in conversation, c. 1975.
7. Letter John Butler-A. C. Flick, "New Sources on the Sullivan-Clinton Campaign in 1779," in *N.Y. State Historical Association Proceedings*, July-October 1929, pp. 271-272.
8. Kingston *Daily Freeman*, October 19, 1878; Ruth R. Glunt in conversation, c. 1958.
9. *Public Papers of George Clinton*, vol. 4, pp. 164-165.

10. Davis-Clinton letter, *Calendar of Manuscripts Relating to the War of the Revolution,* Albany, N.Y., 2 vols., vol. 1, pp. 469, 593-594, vol. 2, p. 71.

11. *Public Papers of George Clinton,* vol. 4, pp. 807, 830.

12. *Public Papers of George Clinton,* vol. 4, p. 829.

13. A. C. Flick, "New Sources on the Sullivan-Clinton Campaign 1779," *N.Y. State Historical Association Proceedings,* pp. 188-194.

14. For John Burch, Evers, *The Catskills;* Commins ms. petition, NYHS.

15. *Public Papers of George Clinton,* vol. 6, p. 456.

16. "The Loyalist Problem," in *Olde Ulster,* 3:6, June 1907, p. 170.

17. Andrew McFarland Davis, "The Indian and Border Warfare of the Revolution," in Justin Winsor, *Narrative and Critical History of America,* Boston, 1887, vol. 8, p. 639.

18. Kingston *Daily Freeman,* April 1, 1886.

19. B. M. Brink, "Pioneer Life in Woodstock," in *Early History of Saugerties,* p. 161.

20. L. H. Zimm, *Papers Read to the Woodstock Historical Society,* July 8, 1930, p. 3; John Almon, *The Remembrancer,* vol. 7, London, 1778, reported the order of Congress of October to move settlers back from frontiers. "Toreyfied" used here.

21. *Public Papers of George Clinton,* vol. 6, p. 812; "The Loyalist Problem" in *Olde Ulster,* Vol. 3, p. 6, June 1907, p. 171.

22. "The Loyalist Problem" in *Olde Ulster,* Vol. 3, June 1907, pp. 169-171.

CHAPTER 10

1. Until 1763 what is now Woodstock was an undivided part of Ulster County in which only "towns, villages, neighborhoods and Christian habitations" were distinguished by the charter of 1683.

2. William Smith, *History of the Late Province of New York,* NYHS, 1830, p. 200, characterizes colonial lowland Ulster; Dangerfield, *Chancellor Robert R. . . .,* pp. 424-425, sums up the view of Ulster's back country in the Hardenbergh Patent and of land agent Dr. William Wilson.

3. Col. Charles DeWitt, Supervisor of Hurley and member of Provincial Convention, was of a lowland Ulster family and close to the Livingstons who controlled much of the Hardenbergh Patent.

4. *Public Papers of George Clinton,* vol. 6, pp. 562-563; Peter Short, Woodstock Town Clerk's Minute Book, 1787-1804, passim.

5. L. H. Zimm, in *Southeastern New York,* 1946, vol. 1, p. 74; Schohariekill Road Papers, Senate House Library, Kingston, N.Y.

6. L. H. Zimm, "Captain Elias Hasbrouck, 1741-1791," in *Publications of the Woodstock Historical Society,* no. 16, September 1951, pp. 25-36.

7. N. B. Sylvester, *History of Ulster County, N.Y.,* Philadelphia, 1880, Part 2., p. 144-145; for summary of title to Patentee Woods and its division, Cockburn Papers, New York State Library, Box 8. Cockburn's papers relating to the border survey include many letters, maps and references to the Beekman claim.

8. Here I used the papers relating to the survey in the Cockburn Papers, NYSL.

9. Statute of April 11, 1787 summarizes the petition, *Laws of the State of New York, 1785, 1798,* Albany, 1886, Vol. II, Chapter 80, pp. 508-509.

10. Woodstock Town Clerk's Minute Book on "first Tuesday in June" (June 5): Woodstock Town Clerk's Minute Book, June 5, 1787.

11. Ibid.

12. L. H. Zimm.

CHAPTER 11

1. For election of Rowe, Woodstock Town Clerk's Minute Book, meeting of April 1799; for Wilhelmus Rowe's

possessions and moneylending, Ulster County Surrogate's office, file box 33; for Livingston-Rowe sale with map, Ulster Deed Book; for Winne ejection, Cockburn lease and survey book.

2. For persistence of Dutch speech, "The Reynolds Family," in E. V. Rowe, *The Story of our Family Heritage*, 1956, n.p., privately printed.

3. For Tiebout, NYHS Quarterly Bulletin, 16:4 (January 1933), pp. 112-114, with portrait; "notes relative to Cornelius Tiebout," in Dr. John E. Stilwell collection of Stilwell and other family ms., annotated books, etc., 1650-1850, 6 vols., NYHS; Robert Livingston's view of Tiebout's character expressed in letter Robert Livingston-Robert R. Livingston, May 1, 1762, RRLP, NYHS; Tiebout-Read deed, Ulster Deed Book 32, p. 533; this deed has good details of early settlement of the hamlet of Woodstock.

4. For Hunter-Desbrosses lands, Cockburn Papers, esp. 6:57, NYSL, Box 6; Hunter field notes and rent roll in Durham Center Museum, East Durham, N.Y., and photostats of Hunter land records in NYSL; a map of Great Lot 24 showing John Carl's sawmill etc. is among the RRLP, NYHS, titled "A sketch of the Easterly part of Great Lot no. 24 in the Hardenbergh Patent," August 8, 1794, by John Cox. The Lot as seen by Chancellor Livingston is described in William Strickland, *Journal of a Tour in the United States of America, 1794-1795*, N.Y.C., 1971, pp. 117-118; for Gabriel Ludlow, Lorenzo Sabine, *Loyalists of the American Revolution*, 2 vols., 1966 reprint, Port Washington, N.Y., vol. 2, pp. 34-37; American Loyalists Transcripts, NYPL, vol. 29, p. 36; vol. 19, pp. 405-417; personal communications from Clinton Metz, Village Historian, Freeport, N.Y.; the Ludlow-Carle conveyance is recorded in Ulster Deed Book, GG, April 16, 1774; the Carle-R. R. Livingston conveyance, Deed Book 17.

5. October 8, 1779 for Ludlow claim to half of Great Lot 24, *Second Report* of the Bureau of Archives for the Province of Ontario, Toronto, 1905, pp. 266-270.

6. For Wilhelmus Rowe, file box 33, Ulster Surrogate's office, mentory of the estate of Wilhelmus Rowe, November 8, 1803; The mentory lists 43 locus, received by notes.

7. I could find no conveyance recorded or note of Robert Livingston's Great Lot 8 lands to his son; the terms of the conveyance were recited in the deed Margaret B. Livingston-(Chancellor) Robert R. Livingston, January 22, 1768, in Margaret B. Livingston-Robert R. Livingston, dated February 22, 1790 and not recorded until 1840, all in Ulster County Deed Books; quotations about Judge and Margaret Beekman Livingston from Dangerfield, *Chancellor Robert R. . . .*, pp. 28-29.

8. For Woodstock traditions about Madame Livingston, Allen Updegraff in *The Plowshare*; see also T. S. Clarkson, *A Biographical History of Clermont or Livingston Manor*. Clermont 1869, p. 27; for manumission of Margaret B. Livingston's slaves, her will, photocopy NYHS from original in Will Book B, Office of Surrogate of Columbia County, pp. 70-71; for rebuilding of Clermont and conflict with "Lower class," letters Margaret B. Livingston-Robert R. Livingston, February 4, 1780, December 30, 1779, RRLP, NYHS.

9. For care of Woodstock farms, Margaret B. Livingston-Robert R. Livingston, April 14, 1780; letter Margaret B. Livingston-Robert R. Livingston, 1789, RRLP, NYHS.

10. Quotation from letter, Margaret B. Livingston-Robert R. Livingston, 1789, RRLP, NYHS; for Margaret Livingston-Town of Hurley boundary settlement I relied on the Cockburn Papers, NYSL, Box 8. These include many lists of expenses and people, maps, field notes, letters, etc. The division of the Hardenbergh Patent among the children of Margaret B. and Robert R. Livingston was recorded in Ulster Deed Book 18, pp. 354-358.

11. For Elias Hasbrouck as first supervisor of Woodstock, L. H. Zimm, "Captain Elias Hasbrouck, 1741-1791," in *Publications of the Woodstock Historical Society*, no. 16, September 1951, pp. 24-36; "Woodstock account book, 1791-1811," contains some mention of earlier tenant accounts, NYHS; "R. R. Livingston's Account Book, Clermont, N.Y.," RRLP, NYHS, has some material on earlier Woodstock tenants; the Livingston record of tenants is in the NYHS; Woodstock traditions about Madame Livingston are from Allen Updegraff in *The Plowshare*.

12. For lowland Ulster County in the early nineteenth century I used Washington Irving, *Tour of Ulster*; Stuart M. Blumin, *The Urban Threshold*, Chicago, 1976; Marius Schoonmaker, *History of Kingston, N.Y.*, 1888. The Charles DeWitt letters are in the *Public Papers of George Clinton*; I used here the Schoharie Road papers cited in the previous chapter; details of the boundary survey of the Hurley-Woodstock line are in Box 15 of the Cockburn Papers, NYSL; the petition for creating a town of Woodstock "of Johannes Van B. Bunschoten and Others," *Journal of the Assembly of the State of New York* N.Y.C., 1787, p. 140. The town's first town meeting occupies the first page of the Town Clerk's Minute Book, 1787-1804.

13. Ms. Journals of Thomas Cole in NYSL; Jane Van De Bogart, "An Illustrated History of the Woodstock Glass Company," term paper; New Paltz College, SUNY; letter, G. Seaman, L. Clark and D. Elliot and Co. to NYHS; Pearce David, *The Development of the American Glass Industry*, Cambridge, Mass., 1949; for F. DeZeng, biographical account, *N.Y. Genealogical and Biographic Record*, vol. 11, N.Y.C., 1871; Deed Books, Ulster County Clerk's office.

14. George S. and Helen McKearin, *American Glass*, N.Y.C., 1941; S. S.

Doughty, *Life of Samuel Stilwell*, N.Y.C., 1877; Stilwell Family genealogical publications, NYHS; the Ulster *Plebeian*, July 1808; list of glass company stockholders, NYHS; ledgers and journals of Woodstock glass companies, 1817-1821, Woodstock Historical Society; *Journal*, Woodstock Glass Company store, 1824, in author's possession; Irving Lowens, "The Musical Edsons of Shady. Early American Tunesmiths," in *Bulletin*, NYPL, 65:4, April 1961; ms. song book of Lewis Edson, Jr., Music Collection, NYPL, Cora Van Aken, oral informant, c. 1966, Lincoln Center; Samuel Stilwell in DAB.

CHAPTER 12

1. The "setting off" of parts of the original Woodstock was authorized by the state legislature. See the statutes of the years given. The town meeting of April 1796 was recorded in the Town Clerk's Minute Book, 1887-1804.

2. *Heads of Families at the first Census taken in the year 1790*, Washington, 1908, pp. 170-173, 185-186; the two black settlers are mentioned in the Cockburn lease and survey book, 15:5, Cockburn Papers, NYSL, as on Great Lot 25, also in misc. field book, Cockburn Papers, 6:30; the black settler named Mink was reported on p. 20.

3. Anita M. Smith, *Woodstock History and Hearsay*, as Henry Gridley, aged 86, recalled the tradition. Victor Lasher, Woodstock, told me of black people living near the old Lutheran Church. Scipio's thirty acres are mentioned in the deed Michael Smith-John Wigram, April 19, 1806, Ulster Deed Book. The "Minutes of the Ulster County Court of Sessions . . ." used here are in the NYSL.

4. Martin MacDaniel told me of his family traditions of Indians in Woodstock. Charles Lanman in his *Adventures in the Wilds of the United States*, 2 vol., Philadelphia, 1856 (a collection of pieces published earlier in a half-dozen serials), vol. 1, p. 134, records

being told by an oldtimer that the lake was "discovered by a hunter named Shew." Numerous mentions of Teunis or Dennis Shew occur in accounts of the part of Saugerties close to the base of Overlook Mountain. An agreement in the FDR Library, Hyde Park, N.Y. among the misc. Hudson Valley mss. dated October 14, 1765 mentions Teunis Shew; William Strickland, *Journal of a Tour in the United States of America 1794-1795*. N.Y.C., 1971, p. 116.

5. "Jacob the Jew" is mentioned in the "Great Patent Memoranda," in R. R. Livingston Account Book, NYHS; the Katsbaan Church records, in *Olde Ulster*, 10 vols., Kingston, N.Y., 1905-1914, vols. 7, 8, 9, contain records of Katsbaan-Woodstock relations. Bits of information about the beginnings of the Dutch Reformed Church in Woodstock are in Ulster Deed Book 29, p. 482; for Schohariekill Road, L. H. Zimm in *Southeastern New York*, eds. L. H. Zimm, A. E. Corning, J. W. Emsley and W. C. Jewell, 3 vols., N.Y.C., 1946, p. 74, and in Senate House Library, Kingston, N.Y.

6. For Woodstock Road surveys, I relied on the Town Clerk's Minute Book in the office of the Town Clerk of Shandaken. Tavern licenses are recorded in the same Minute Book. The quotation of notes written by Elias Hasbrouck is from an envelope formerly among the John E. Hasbrouck papers in the library of the N.Y. Genealogical and Biographical Society, New York City (but now recalled by the lender). The widow Hasbrouck's (here spelled Horsebrack) tavern is mentioned in John Lincklaen, *Travels in the Year 1791 and 1792*, N.Y.C., 1897, pp. 118, 125; for Elias Hasbrouck and his descendants in Woodstock, "Captain Elias Hasbrouck, 1741-1791," in *Publications of the Woodstock Historical Society*, no. 16, September 1951, pp. 25-36.

7. Bruno Louis Zimm, "A Chain of Woodstock Land Titles," in *Publications of the Woodstock Historical Society*,

August 1931, pp. 6-27; the "Journal of Hasbrouck and Jensen, Kingston Landing," Senate House Library, Kingston, supplied records of the delivery of slaves, hoop poles, etc. by J. Hunt and other Woodstock men during the 1790s; for tannery, advertisement in Ulster *Plebeian*, August 22, 1809.

CHAPTER 13

1. For Thomas Cole in Woodstock, Thomas Cole mss., Journal 6, NYSL.
2. W. Strickland, *Journal of a Tour. . .*, pp. 161-163, NYSL; for glassmaking background, G.J. and H. McKearin, *American Glass*, N.Y.C., 1941, pp. 7-21 and pp. 180, 181, 212; for Woodstock glassmaking, Pearce Davis, *The Development of the American Glass Industry*, Cambridge, Mass., 1949, pp. 35-63.
3. "Baron de Zeng" for F. A. DeZeng, Edward F. DeLancey, in *N.Y. Genealogical and Biographical Record*, 2:2, April 1871, 4-12.
4. Letters, F. A. DeZeng- R. R. Livingston, April 8, 1802 and November 30, 1802, NYHS, were my chief sources for DeZeng's glassmaking, iron processing and turnpike beginnings as they affect Woodstock. I examined material about DeZeng's many activities outside Woodstock in the libraries of the NYSL, NYHS, Senate House, Kingston. The Glasco Turnpike was incorporated 1807 as the Ulster and Delaware First Branch Turnpike but was being called by its present name in W. Riseley account book, 1813.
5. De Zeng-R. R. Livingston letters cited above for Woodstock ironmaking; James Pierce, "Memoir on the Catskill Mountains," in *American Journal of Science*, Series 1, vol. 6, 1823, p. 95; H. G. Spafford, *A Gazetteer of the State of New York*, Albany, 1813, p. 331, mentions a "bloomery" as in business in Woodstock.

CHAPTER 14

1. S. S. Doughty, *The Life of Samuel Stilwell. . .*, N.Y.C., n.d., pp. 6-7; John E.

Stilwell, *The History of Captain Nicholas Stilwell*, 4 vols., N.Y.C., 1930, vol. 3, pp. 84-87, with portrait. *The Arts and Crafts in New York 1777-1799*, comp. R.S. Gottesman, N.Y.C., 1954, p. 54. *The Arts and Craft Crafts, 1800-18*, Gottesman, N.Y.C., p. 19.
2. Advertisement of sheriff's sale, *Plebeian*, July 26, 1808.
3. For Samuel Stilwell, Historical Committee of the New York Annual Conference of the Methodist Church, *The Onward Way*, Saugerties, N.Y., 1949, pp. 52-54; "Ulster County, N.Y., Woodstock Glass Manufacturing Society, Record of Transfer of Shares, 1809-1815," misc. mss., NYHS.
4. Woodstock Town Clerk's Minute Book, 1805-1870, under date given. Advertisement for wood, *Plebeian*, February 19, 1811; glass for sale, *Plebeian*, December 19, 1811; Stilwell Secession, The *Onward Way*, pp. 53-54; Glasco, N. B. Sylvester, *History of Ulster County N.Y.*, Philadelphia, 1880, part 2, pp. 42-43; for forced sale, B. M. Brink, *The Early History of Saugerties, N.Y.*, 1902, pp. 288-289.
5. Ebenezer Hall, Jonathan Blake, *History of the Town of Warwick, Mass.*, 1873, pp. 94-97.
6. For sand, letter, Daniel Elliot and Co.-R. L. Livingston, July 8, 1817, RRLP, NYHS; "James Pierce on the Catskills," *American Journal of Science*, 1823.
7. Ibid.
8. Advertisement, A. A. Mott, Kingston *Democratic Journal*, January 3, 1849.
9. For the Edsons, Irving Loewens, "The Musical Edsons of Shady, Early American Tunesmiths," in *Bulletin*, NYPL, 65:4, April 1961. A copy of Lewis Edson, Jr. *Social Harmonist* is in the Music Division, NYPL, as is the notebook cited, Woodstock Poormaster's Book, disbursement dated February 3, 1846, Woodstock Historical Society.
10. A. N. Smith, "History and Hearsay," in *Publications of the Woodstock Historical Society*, no. 4, July 1931, p.

14; for Jem Day, S. S. Doughty cited above, pp. 38-40.
11. "Picking pot shells" is used in account books of Bristol Glass Company, 1817-1821, collection of Woodstock Historical Society; Cora Van Aken, personal communication.
12. Jonathan Blake, *History of the Town of Warwick*, Warwick, Mass., 1812; notes copied from the diary of William Cobb (1806-1817) in Warwick, Mass. library by Mrs. Eleanore Morris, the librarian at the Warwick Library.
13. Joseph D. Short, Cravan Aken and Anita N. Smith, personal communications; Rev. H. H. Prout, *Old Times In Windham, Reprinted from Windham Journal*, February 18, 1869-March 31, 1871, Cornwallville, N.Y., 1970, p. 71.

CHAPTER 15

1. Charles Herrick, personal communications, 1942-1950; Evers, *The Catskills*, p. 16.
2. Petition, Lord Cornbury, to Letter, R. Livingston-R. R. Livingston, May 1, 1762, RRLP, NYHS.
3. The Smedes and Cockburn papers relating to mines are in the Cockburn Papers, Box 10, NYSL.
4. S. L. Mitchill and coal, see Evers, *The Catskills*, pp. 271, 277.
5. *Minutes of the Common Council of the City of New York*, 1784-1831, N.Y.C., 1917-1930, 21 vols., vol. 4, pp. 663, 664, 675, 676.
6. *Transactions, Society for the Promotion of the Useful Arts*, vol. 3, Appendix B, February 23, 1814; James Pierce, p. 97.
7. B. L. Zimm "Some History. . .," *Publications of the Woodstock Historical Society*, no. 7, July 1932, pp. 7-13.
8. Kingston *Weekly Leader*, September 13, 1889, under "Bearsville Brevities"; B. L. Zimm, cited above, pp. 7-8.
9. B. L. Zimm, cited above, p. 13.
10. Letter, W. E. Hasbrouck-"Uncle Woolvin," author's collection.
11. Craig Vosburgh, Cora Van Aken, personal communications.

CHAPTER 16

1. For details of Chancellor Livingston credited I have relied in this chapter on George Dangerfield, *Chancellor Robert R. Livingston. . . ."*

2. Marius Schoonmaker, *The History of Kingston*, p. 443; *Plebeian*, July 29, 1805 and December 20, 1805. Cynthia Owen Philip, *Robert Fulton, A Biography*, N.Y.C., 1985; the Robert L. Livingston papers in RRLP, NYHS, too numerous to list here, gave me the materials for his life and activities.

3. For trespassers, letters, S. Hawkens-Robert L. Livingston, December 27, 1805, endorsed "trespassers taken in Woodstock tract," RRLP, NYHS; "Account C. H. Ruggles wt. The Estate of R.R.L.," 1814-1817, expenses incurred in prosecuting trespassers listed; "Account Robert L. Livingston to Cockburn and Sickles," 1832, includes costs and payments in trespassing proceedings.

4. L.H. Zimm, "The Wigrams of Woodstock" in *Publications of the Woodstock Historical Society*, no. 4, 1931, based on John Wigram's diary in 1931 in the possession of Wigram descendant Walter Scott of Tivoli, N.Y. but which I have not yet located. Wigram's activities as Livingston land agent used here are based on the letters and accounts, John Wigram-Robert L. Livingston, 1806-1825, RRLP, NYHS. A much-used map is that of the James B. Murray, Francis Barretto, Junr. tract, dated July 24 and credited to John and his son John S., Ulster County Clerk's office. Others of individual Woodstock farms include those in "John Wigram, Description of Lots Surveyed etc.," October 1822, and many others scattered among the RRLP, NYHS.

5. John Wigram-Robert L. Livingston, January 1, 1806; *Plebeian*, May 24, 1808.

6. Woodstock-Saugerties Turnpike, letter John Wigram-Robert L. Livingston, January 1, 1806; advertisement in *Plebeian*, May 24, 1808 for post office petition; letter John

Wigram-Robert L. Livingston, March 21, 1814.

7. L. H. Zimm, "The Wigrams. . .," cited above, pp. 28-29; for carpeting award, *Plebeian*, November 25, 1820.

8. Philip Bonesteel's bill for "victuals, lodging and horsekeeping, etc." on four occasions in 1813, RRLP, NYHS; notebook marked "1830 Memorandum," under date of July 2, 1811, "Went to Woodstock . . . to settle with tenants," RRLP, NYHS.

9. By 1834 Robert L. Livingston's papers indicate a realization he was living beyond his income. On April 8 of that year he wrote, "My income being insufficient for my establishment—and for my children—and poor Relatives I am busily employed in making my real estate more productive. . . ." Robert L. Livingston's Journal begun April 9, 1834 is in RRLP, NYHS. A memorandum book circa 1817 estimates his income at $10,405 including the "Steam Boats," an entry of May 1, 1816 estimates income from Woodstock rent at $2000. The minutes of the first meeting of the trustees of the Company after its first authorization by the legislature, April 6, 1814, are among the Robert L. Livingston materials, RRLP, NYHS, date missing. "An Act to Incorporate the Woodstock and Saugerties General Manufacturing Company," in *Laws of New York, Thirty-Seventh Session*, vol. 3, ch. CIV, Albany, N.Y., 1815, p. 111.

10. The instructions to agent Eldredge dated March 10, 1825 are in RRLP, NYHS; Beverly McAnear, "Mr. Robert R. Livingston's Reasons Against a Land Tax," in *Journal of Political Economy*, February 1940, pp. 63-90.

CHAPTER 17

1. I relied for rent payments on the many annual rent rolls among the RRLP, NYHS, chiefly on that in the Robert L. Livingston account book, the separate lists of tenants and rents paid or unpaid for 1802, 1816, 1817, 1824, 1840 and on up to 1864 as well

as on the list of rents paid during this period in cattle, wheat, fowls and days riding. I also studied lists and letters dealing with the payment and non-payment of notes, all amonf the RRLP, NYHS. I was helped too by account books of land agent Henry P. Shultis, lent me by his descendant, Lawrence Shultis of Bearsville.

2. The flood of 1818 was reported in the *Plebeian*, March 17, 1818.

3. Here I have used the account books of B. Snyder, W. Riseley, Janson and Hasbrouck, the stores of the two glass factories, New York State and federal census figures after 1825, all cited above; Martin MacDaniel, personal communication, gave me details of shingle-making.

4. "Shingle weaver's shantee," Kingston *Democratic Journal*, April 1, 1846; Hosea Wood, "An Act to Regulate the Culling of Staves and Headings," *Laws of New York*, 11th edition, Chapter LVI, pp. 128-130; Bristol Glass Company store day book, 1824.

5. "An Act to Regulate . . .," cited above; R. G. Albion, *The Rise of New York Port, 1815-1860*, p. 281.

6. Hoop shaving, R. L. De Lisser, *Picturesque Ulster*, 1896-1905, Kingston, N.Y., pp. 167-168, reprinted Cornwallville, N.Y., 1968.

7. Benjamin Force, Bristol Glass Company store day book, October 3, 1819.

8. Martin MacDaniel and Ethel DeGraff, personal communications; Robert L. Livingston and charcoal, notes, October 1832, 8 pp. receipt, February 23, 1828, RRLP, NYHS.

9. "A Map of the Division Line Between the Countys of Albany and Ulster from the Mouth of the Sawyer Kill . . . May and June, 1765," by William Cockburn, Print Room, NYHS; B. L. Zimm, "A Chain of Woodstock Land Titles," in *Publications of the Woodstock Historical Society*, no. 5, August 1931, pp. 16-17.

10. Receipts, 1790-1813, formerly tucked in Robert R. Livingston accounts book, NYHS.

11. "Sherwoods Mill" is referred to in an agreement to operate it, February 2, 1814, between N. Briggs on behalf of Robert L. Livingston and Henry and Jacob Bogardus, RRLP, NYHS.

12. The "Sawmill account," January 1811, between tenant John Montross and "Mr. L." lists white wood planks sawn, Bristol Glass Company store day book; letter Bogardus-R. R. Livingston, July 29, 1806, RRLP, NYHS; Tunis Brizee's "Sawmill at Woodstock," Robert R. Livingston's account book, account 38, RRLP, NYHS.

13. Bogardus-R. R. Livingston letter, July 29, 1806, cited above.

14. Letter, Christian Happy-Robert L. Livingston, February 12, 1822. Many records of sawmill operations are mong the RRLP; especially useful here were the accounts between Rufus Briggs, agent of Robert L. Livingston, and Samuel Perry of Woodstock, March 11, 1811-November 16, 1811. "Amount of Lumber sent from the Saw Mill at Woodstock in the occupation of [Tunis] Brissie January 1807."

15. Petition, June 3, 1822, by Jacob Bogardus, Henry Bogardus, Joseph Miller, Daniel Sherwood, Elias Vangasbeek, Michael Smith, Elijah Freemen, Robert Freeman, Henry Miller, John Quinlan, John Wagner, Peter Wagner, Andrew Rion, Daniel Devall and John Eldridge, RRLP.

16. Ibid, memorandum in hand of R.L.L., n.d., c. 1830, RRLP; Ladew-Robert L. Livingston, August 16, 1833; letter, A.D. Ladew-Robert L. Livingston, August 26, 1833.

17. Cockburn and Sickles' bill for services in trespassing cases, July 19, 1828; letter A.D. Ladew-Robert L. Livingston, RRLP; J.W. Kiersted, account book, 1807-1862, p. 53, NYSL.

18. Letter Jonathan Hasbrouck-Richard M. Hasbrouck, June 20, 1832, Senate House Library, Kingston, N.Y.

CHAPTER 18

1. Lists of trees and uses copied from Francois Michauz, *Histoire des Arbres Foresteriers de L'Amerique*, RRLP, n.d.
2. Leslie C. Wood, *Rafting on the Delaware*, Livingston Manor, 1934, pp. 127-128; statement by Robert L. Livingston chartering, capitalization and prospects of the Esopus Creek Navigation Company, May 1831, uniforms of raftsmen, etc., RRLP.
3. "The Building of Plank Roads" in *Olde Ulster*, 8:10, October 1912, p. 292; *Gazetteer of the State of New York*, Syracuse, 1860, pp. 76-79.
4. Robert L. Livingston statement, cited above, RRLP.
5. Letter E. Miner-Robert L. Livingston, May 27, 1835, RRLP.
6. Letter Robert L. Livingston-Memorandum book of Robert L. Livingston, October 1, 1833, "Employ only tenants. . ."; letter Robert L. Livingston-E. Miner (copy), May 27, 1835, RRLP.
7. Robert L. Livingston-Robert Livingston, cited above; Robert L. Livingston with account of floating of logs downstream with suggestions for changes, letter, Faulkner-Robert L. Livingston, April 17, 1834, RRLP.
8. Ibid. List of wood products of Esopus Creek Navigation Co.
9. Certificate of George B. Smith, Street Commissioner of City of New York (copy), April 22, 1836; letter J. Gale-Robert L. Livingston, October 30, 1836, RRLP.
10. Letter, J. Gale-Robert L. Livingston, 1837, RRLP.
11. Letter H. P. Shultis-Robert L. Livingston, RRLP.
12. Letter W.M. Edwards-J. Gale, Agent, April 1, 1839; letter J. Gale-Robert L. Livingston, July 25, 1839, RRLP; tanbark was also sold to R.L.L. agent A. D. Ladew, see letter April 14, 1832, "Account of Bark, A. D. Ladew, 1833," RRLP.
13. Robert L. Livingston, "Evening Journal for my Private Use," March 16-19, 1835; memorandum book, January 1, 1836, RRLP.
14. R. L. Livingston, memorandum book, RRLP.
15. Letter Wm. Coats Sons-R.L.L., June 1, 1838, RRLP.
16. "In the matter of Robert L. Livingston, a Supposed lunatic," August 30, 1842, p. 10, RRLP.

CHAPTER 19

1. For one of several statements by Robert L. that his income was not "sufficient" for his "establishment," Journal of Robert L. Livingston, 1834, in volume beginning April 8, 1831; Robert L.'s plans for his sons, letter Robert L. L.-Montgomery Livingston, April 9, 1832; letter Robert L. L.-Montgomery Livingston quoted, March 1832, RRLP.
2. For Rodolphe Topffer, E. Benezit, *Dictionaire Critique et Documentaire des Peintres, Sculpteurs, Dessinateurs et Graveurs*, Paris, 1911-1923. Montgomery Livingston's letters between 1832 and 1838 to his father give much information about his life in Europe during these years, RRLP; Bishop John Dubois-Matilda Livingston, September 23, 1836.
3. Montgomery Livingston, May 31, 1837, RRLP.
4. Montgomery Livingston kept the letters printed materials which marked his career as a painter between 1832 and 1855. These are among the RRLP and were used here. For a summary of Livingston's life and work see Ruth Piwonka, *The Landscape Art of Montgomery Livingston*, Kinderhook, N.Y., 1979.
5. The letter R.L.L.-M.L., March 26, 1834. The declining state of Robert L. Livingston is based in part on the ms., "In the matter of Robert L. Livingston, a Supposed Lunatic," p. 7, August 30, 1842, RRLP; for the Reynolds incident, letter J. Gale-Robert L. Livingston, July 7 1838, RRLP.
6. Letter A. D. Ladew-Robert L. Livingston, June 30, 1838, RRLP.

7. Letter H. M. Romeyn-Robert L. Livingston, June 3, 1839, RRLP.

8. Draft of offer to sell 15,000 acres, including most of Woodstock, under heading "For Sale" and signed Radcliff and Adams, n.d., RRLP.

9. Letter J. Livingston-Montgomery Livingston, April 21, 1834, RRLP.

10. Eugene A. and Montgomery Livingston began selling farms as conservators for their father's estate in the spring of 1841, Ulster County Deed Books; John Cochran appointed "lawful attorney and agent" for the Hardenbergh Patent lands of Eugene A. and Montgomery Livingston, articles of agreement, May 20, 1844; for obituary of Henry P. Shultis, RRLP; for services of Henry P. Shultis, "account of Henry Shultis with Eugene A. and Montgomery Livingston," executors of estate of Robert L. Livingston, beginning May 9, 1843, June 2, 1847, RRLP.

11. Henry Ramsay, field notes, no. 548, NYSL, gives a good account of his survey with sketch maps here and there; John W. Davis' account with Eugene A. and Montgomery Livingston, August 11, 1845-September 12, 1846, includes surveying, mapping, expenses, etc.; in "The Down Rent War," by A. W. Hoffman in R. L. De Lisser, *Picturesque Ulster*, Kingston, N.Y., 1897-1905, p. 243, memories of Ramsay having been frightened away still persist; "mendacious" for Shultis' election, Woodstock Town Clerk's Minute Book B.

12. Henry Ramsay field book, no. 5480, Manuscript Room, NYSL, p. 31.

CHAPTER 20

1. New York *Tribune*, 1844.

2. *Democratic Journal*, July 24, 1844.

3. A. W. Hoffman in *Picturesque Ulster*, p. 245. Much Woodstock lore of the Anti-Rent War is handed down in Hoffman's account, pp. 243-251.

4. Letter John Cochran-Livingston.

5. *Democratic Journal*, January 1, 1845.

6. Albany *Argus*, February 10, 1845.

7. *Democratic Journal*, March 5, 1845; letter John Cochran-Eugene A. Livingston, 1845; letter John Cochran-Eugene A. Livingston, March 14, 1845.

8. Letter John Cochran-Montgomery Livingston, March 1845.

9. *Democratic Journal*, March 12, 1845.

10. Ibid.

11. *Democratic Journal*, March 19, 1845; "Hurley Greens," in *Olde Ulster*, vol. 10, p. 78 (1914).

12. *Democratic Journal*, March 19, 1845.

13. Lore of the demonstration has been collected by Anita M. Smith in "Woodstock History and Hearsay," in *Publications of the Woodstock Historical Society*, no. 4, July 1931, and by A.W. Hoffman in *Picturesque Ulster*, p 14.

14. Anita M. Smith, cited above, p. 12; Neva Shultis, *From Sunset to Cock's Crow*, Woodstock, 1957, p. 29.

15. Ulster *Republican*, March 19, 1845.

16. Judge Ruggles' charge, *Democratic Journal*, March 26, 1845.

17. Letter John Cochran-Montgomery Livingston, March 1845, RRLP.

18. Letter John Cochran-Montgomery Livingston, March 21, 1845, RRLP; letter Henry P. Shultis-Robert L. Livingston, April 2, 1845, RRLP.

19. Democratic *Journal*, 1845, various dates.

20. Details on the Livingston farms in Woodstock in tabular form listing names of lives then living in leases, number of acres, value, etc., circa 1846, are among the RRLP, NYHS; a copy of a map of these farms (the original made by John B. Davis and redrawn about 1880) was given to me by Martin Comeau, Ulster County lawyer; Woodstock farms sold are recorded in the Ulster County Deed Books under "List of 15th May, 1864, collected by D. Queen," RRLP.

21. A note to Account 35 (Michael Smith) in Robert R. Livingston's Woodstock Account Book, RRLP, gives the information about this farm to 1805; letter Christian Happy-Eugean (sic), April 19, 1847, RRLP; deed Eugene A. Livingston-Elwin L. Elting, 1872.

22. Albany *Argus*, August 18, 1845, "Land Proprietors" offer to sell; letter, John Hunter-James Powers and John Kiersted, March 31, 1847, Durham Center Museum; deed Elias D. Hunter-Isaac Mosher, March 1854; preceding lease, Cockburn Papers, Box 6, no. 30, NYSL.

23. Woodstock Town Clerk's Minute Book B, 1855; Marius Schoonmaker, *History of Kingston*, pp. 100-101, Cockburn and Rathbun account with Livingston.

24. I relied for details of Montgomery Livingston's life at Clermont on his letters, accounts and property lists among the RRLP. William Kiessel, Bearsville, genealogist of the Shultis family, supplied me with material on the life of Henry P. Shultis.

25. M. Schoonmaker, *History of Kingston*, pp. 100-101.

CHAPTER 21

1. New York State Census, 1855, microfilm edition.

2. *Democratic Journal*, July 24, 1851.

3. For Larry G. Hall, Neva Shultis, *From Sunset to Cock's Crow*, Woodstock, 1957, pp. 12-13.

4. Here I relied on Dr. L. G. Hall's book of accounts and memoranda, formerly owned by Alma Simpkins, present whereabouts unknown, and the inventory of his estate, Ulster Surrogate's office.

5. Drs. Fiero and Heath appear in the Woodstock Town Clerk's Minute Book passim.

6. The Thatcher Dispensatory and the note referred to belong to Towar Boggs, New Brunswick, N.J.

7. Martin MacDaniel of Shady told me of the Indian doctor in Woodstock and of the "penny doctor" William H. Lake of the Town of Kingston mentioned in the Kingston *Freeman*, September 12, 1876.

8. Anita M. Smith, "Herbalist of Woodstock," *As True as the Barnacle Tree*, pp. 27-30; Neva Shultis cited above, pp. 38-39.

9. Betsey Booth, based on many conversations with her grandson, Martin MacDaniel, and on Anita Smith, cited above, p. 17; Douglas Braik, Lewis Hollow, personal communication.

10. The Quitman book is rare; I used the copy in the NYSL.

11. William Boyse, *Writings of the Rev. William Boyse, A Year of Jubilee*, N.Y.C., 1840, pp. 569-563.

12. Saugerties *Evening Post*, January 20, 1879.

13. "Allan Updegraff," in *The Plowshare*, vol. 6, no. 1, (December 1916); vol 6, no. 2; vol. 6, no. 4.

14. Neva Shultis, from *Sundown . . .*; Anita M. Smith, *Woodstock History. . .*, pp. 114-115; A. M. Smith, "History and Hearsay," in *Proceedings of the Ulster County Historical Society*, Marbletown, 1933-1934, pp. 40-51; "Witches Dance," Kingston *Argus*, December 19, 1883.

15. Philip Whitaker's Book (ms.), N.Y. Genealogical and Biographic Society Library; New Paltz *Independent*, May 7, 1897 (reprinted from Kingston *Leader*, n.d.); the July 4 inscription is on a ledge bordering a small spring to the north of the site of the former caretaker's cottage.

16. John Bennet and Seth Masia, *Walks in the Catskills*, N.Y.C., 1974.

17. "The Overlook," Kingston *Press*, May 12, 1939; R. L. De Lisser, *Picturesque Ulster*, Kingston, 1897, pp. 226-227; postcard in author's collection.

18. Variants of this tale are given in F. G. Clough, *Follow the Hudson*, Laramie, Wyo., 1968, p. 25; A. M. Smith, "Hearsay and History," in *Proceedings of the New York Historical Association*, vol. 34, 1936, pp. 67-68; Jim Twaddell, Richard Sharp, personal communications.

CHAPTER 22

1. Woodstock Town Clerk's Minute Book, 1805-1870.

2. "Record of the Dutch Reformed Church of Woodstock N.Y.," in *Publications of the Woodstock Historical*

Society, no. 14, April 1939, pp. 13-14; E. F. Corwin, *A Manual of the Reformed Church of America*, third edition, 1879, pp. 399, 646.

3. *Woodstock Methodist Church*, 125th Anniversary, 1832-1957, n.d., pp. 11, 18-19; A. N. Sylvester, *History of Ulster County. . .*, part 2, p. 322; Chester H. Traver, Church Record, Christ's Lutheran Church, Woodstock, 1906; a condensation of the 1786-1886 centennial address by the Rev. J. J. Earnest, D.D., edited by C.H. Traver, 1901 pp. 7-8; J. F. H. Claiborne, *The Life and Correspondence of John A. Quitman*, 2 vols., N.Y.C., 1860, pp. 16-24; W. Boyse, *The Writings of Plebeian*, December 4, 1819.

4. W. Boyse, *The Writings of. . .*, pp. 541-544, 546-548, 555-556, 557-558.

5. J. J. Earnest, centennial address, 1906; A. N. Sylvester, *History of Ulster County*, 1880, pp. 321-324; Richard Dillon, chairperson, 125th Celebration at St. John's, Letter in Ulster *Townsman*, October 24, 1985; papers in cornerstone box of former Chapel of St. Joan, Woodstock.

6. Accounts of the lives of Woodstock's Reformed Church pastors are found in E. T. Corwin, *Manual of the Reformed Church in America*, under "The Ministry"; ballad quoted from broadside owned by the late Mandeville Diaz, Saugerties.

7. Donations, Bide Snyder, "Woodstock in Olden Days," in the Woodstock *Weekly*, October 11, 1924; camp meeting, Rondout *Courier*, August 20, 1858; *Writings of William Boyse*, p. 95, urges legislation against intoxicating liquors.

8. *Plebeian*, February 1, 1817, February 28, 1821; editorials about "House for Poor," *The Whig*, December 10, 1834.

9. Mrs. Thomas G. S. Hooke, aged 93 c. 1955, personal communication; B. Snyder day book, May 26, for a "bea"; Kingston *Daily Freeman*, July 28, 1879, "Woodstock" signed "Guy"; list and names of quilts and their patterns made

by Louise H. Zimm, author's collection.

10. Louise H. Zimm, "Captain Elias Hasbrouck 1741-1791," in *Publications of the Woodstock Historical Society*, 1952, p. 31; *Plebeian*, March 14, 21, 18, May 9, 1809; Ulster *Palladium*, letter signed "Ariel"; Ulster *Sentinel*, October 18, 1826; letter in reply from Ebenezer Hall, Ulster *Sentinel*, October 25, 1826; Ulster *Palladium*, November 1, 1830.

CHAPTER 23

1. Lease, Margaret B. Livingston-Peter Short, Jr., May 1, 1794, RRLP.

2. John Armstrong, *Memoirs of the Board of Agriculture of the State of New York*, vol. 111, 1826.

3. U. P. Hedrick, *A History of Agriculture in the State of New York*, reprinted, N.Y.C., 1966, p. 321.

4. George R. Stewart, *American Given Names*, N.Y.C., 1979, pp. 160-161; Oxford English Dictionary.

5. Letter, H. H. Reynolds, *The Horticulturist*, New Series, vol. VII, Albany, 1857, p. 51.

6. Letter October 7, 1958 Nam Kyu Chung, Director of the Institute of Agriculture, Suwon, South Korea; Kingston *Daily Freeman*, August 12, 1927.

7. R. W. Howard, *The Two Billion Acre Farm*, N.Y.C., p. 100; *Baptism and Marriage Registers of the Old Dutch Church of Kingston*, R. R. Hoes ed., N.Y.C., 1891, p. 447.

8. Philip Rick, will, Will Book G, 1828, executor's accounts, etc., file box 33, Ulster County Surrogate's office. See also for this chapter Alf Evers, "We call it the Rickey," in *N.Y. Folklore Quarterly*, vol. XV, no. 1 (Spring 1959).

CHAPTER 24

1. Marjorie Hope Nicolson, *Mountain Gloom and Mountain Glory*, Ithaca, 1979, passim.

2. Ulster *Palladium*, October 12, 1831; Peter De Labigarre, "Excursions on Our Blue Mountains," in *Transactions of the N.Y. Society for the Promotion of*

Agriculture, Arts and Manufactures and the Founding of Tivoli, vol. 1, part 2, 1794, pp. 128-139; H. W. Reynolds, "Peter De Labigarre," in *Year Book, Dutchess County Historical Society*, 1972, pp. 45-60, 351-365.
3. A. Evers, *The Catskills*; Roland Van Zandt, *The Catskill Mountain House*, New Brunswick, 1966, pp. 28-36.
4. L. L. Noble, Letters to Charles Lanman, September 22, 1840, August 5, 1841, August 7, 1842, NYHS; Charles Lanman, *Adventures in the Wilds of the United States and British American Provinces*, 2 vols., Philadelphia, 1856, vol. 1, pp. 171-178; A. Evers, "Catskill Cloves and Catskill Painters," in *Catskill Center News*, Summer 1981.
5. Lanman, ibid.
6. Thomas Cole, *Journals*, no. 6, under August 12, 1846.
7. L. L. Noble, *The Course of Empire and other Pictures of Thomas Cole N.A. . .*, N.Y.C., 1853, pp. 339-340.
8. H. T. M., "A Trip to the Mountains," in the Kingston *Journal*, October 16, 1849; "A Trip to Mount Overlook," in Kingston *Argus*, October 30, 1860; "W" and "Overlook Mountain," in Kingston *Journal*, August 22, 1855, are among many regional newspaper accounts of climbs of Overlook.

CHAPTER 25

1. Quoted from the Kingston *Journal*, August 17, 1878; taken by the *Journal* from "several interesting letters" published in the New York *Herald*.
2. Erastus O. Haven, *Autobiography*, N.Y.C., 1883, pp. 98-99.
3. Will Plank, *Banners and Bugles*, Marlborough, N.Y., 1963, pp. 94-99, for Ulster County attitude toward the war; Craig Vosburgh, personal communication, October 21, 1975, about his great-uncle Barney Hoyt.
4. Anita M. Smith, "Hearsay and History," in *Publications of the Woodstock Historical Society*, no. 8, August 1932, p. 25; no. 4, July 1931, p.

17; Kingston *Democratic Journal*, August 16, 1865.
5. *Banners and Bugles*, pp. 101-102, Kingston Democratic *Journal*, May 10, 1865, *Banners and Bugles*, p. 87, 116, Kingston *Democratic Journal*, March 22, 1865.
6. "Letters From the Civil War," in *Publications of the Woodstock Historical Society*, no. 14, April 1939, pp. 10-13.
7. Mrs. Robert Bradley, personal communication, October 19, 1979; Kingston *Daily Leader*, September 11, 1884; "Civil War Records of Woodstock Township, Town Clerk's Office," L. H. Zimm, ed.; *Publications of the Woodstock Historical Society*, no. 17, December 1955, pp. 19-31.
8. *The Hue and Cry*, July 7, 1923, p. 5; The Woodstock *Weekly*, September 27, October 4, October 11, 1924.

CHAPTER 26

1. Frederick Edward Darrow, *Historical Sketches, The Old Senate House*, Kingston, 1883, pp. 36-37.
2. Letter signed "W" in Kingston *Journal*, August 22, 1855.
3. Saugerties *Telegraph*, July 1849.
4. Greene County *Whig*, August 29, 1857, reprinted from Rondout *Courier*, n.d.
5. Kingston *Democratic Journal*, October 8, 1862.
6. Kingston *Argus* and Ulster *Republican*, October 30, 1861; Kingston *Democratic Journal*, January 3, 1866.
7. Kingston *Democratic Journal*, September 7, 1864; for Mead's opening, G. M. Best, *The Ulster and Delaware. . . Railroad Through the Catskills*, San Marino, Cal., 1972, pp. 19-33; Kingston *Press*, August 7, 1871; Saugerties *Telegraph*, July 24, 1878; quoted from Rondout *Courier*, Kingston *Press*.
8. November 4, 25, 1869; Kingston *Press*, stockholders and their shares, incorporation papers of the Woodstock Overlook Mountain House filed February 25, 1870, Box 1, page 44; incorporation records, Ulster County

Clerk's office; Kingston *Press*, December 1, 1870 (story signed "Mail boy"); Kingston *Press*, November 18, 1869; ibid, December 1, 1869; "Charles H. Krack," in *Life Sketches*, Albany, 1870, pp. 257-258; Kingston *Press*, November 18, 1869; Kingston *Argus*, August 17, 1870, May 26, 1869, stereographs of the hotel and surroundings by Ed Lewis of Kingston, July 1871 (author's collection). 9. For waiters, New York *Times*, August 2, 1873; Kingston *Press*, July 13, 1871; New York *Times*, August 2, 1873. 10. June 29, 1871, "Letter from Overlook," in Kingston *Press*, July 8, 1871; "Kingston and its Overlook Mountain House," in F. E. Westbrook, *Historical Sketches, the Old Senate House 1777*, pp. 33-34; "Large Party at the Overlook," Kingston *Press*, July 20, 1871.
11. July 27, 1871; arrivals at the Overlook, Kingston *Daily Freeman*, July 17, 18, August 14, 1871.
12. Register of Mead's Mountain House, in possession of Karma Triyana Dharmaachakra, Woodstock; G. W. Sheldon, *American Painters*, N.Y.C., 1879, p. 52.
13. Kingston *Press*, August 3, 1871, July 20, 1871; Poughkeepsie *Eagle*, August 21, 1873.
14. Letters Fannie L. Lawton-William and George Lawton, June-September 1871 (days of week but not months and days given), author's collection.
15. Kingston *Daily Freeman*, August 23, 1872.

CHAPTER 27

1. Dexter A. Hawkins, *The Traditions of Overlook Mountain*, Islip, N.Y., 1873, p. 21, passim.
2. Kingston *Daily Freeman*, August 15, 1872.
3. Kingston *Daily Freeman*, July 17, 1873.
4. Here I have used many regional and metropolitan newspaper stories chiefly, Kingston *Daily Freeman*, July 30 and 31 1873; New York *Tribune*, July 29, 31,

1873; Kingston *Press*, July 31, 1873; New York *Times*, August 2, 1873, p. 114.
5. *A Visit to the States, a Reprint of Letters from A special Correspondent of the Times*, 2nd Ser., London, 1883.
6. Kingston *Journal* and *Freeman*, August 14, 1883.
7. Rhinebeck *Gazette*, quoted in Kingston *Press*, August 7, 1873; Kingston *Daily Freeman*, August 4, 1873.

CHAPTER 28

1. Ulster *Republican*, May 24, 1843; Kingston *Daily Freeman*, April 21, 1875; Kingston *Daily Freeman*, August 2, 1883; Kingston *Journal*, November 11, 1874; writings of William Boyse, p. 23, 95; Records of the Dutch Reformed Church of Woodstock, under August 11, 1864.
2. Woodstock Reformed Church, Consistory Proceedings, August 11, 1864.
3. The lore used here was given to me in conversations with Monroe Longendyke, Jim Twaddell and Charles Herrick.
4. Monroe Longendyke, Mead's Register, courtesy of its former owner, Capt. Savo Milo.
5. The story was told to me by Henry Wilgus, High Woods.
6. A version of this tale was told to me by Dick Sharp, who heard it told by a man named Ostrander in a Woodstock tavern.
7. Springfield (Mass.) *Republican*, reprinted in Kingston *Daily Freeman*, 1873; Rochester *Democratic* and *Chronicle*, reprinted in the *Argus*, August 6, 1873.
8. Kingston, August 1873.
9. Charles Rockwell, *The Catskill Mountains and the Region Around*, N.Y.C., 1867, p. 35.
10. New York *Times*, July 19, 1875, under "Summer Resorts." The fire was widely reported in the press; New York *Times*, April 2, 1875; Kingston *Daily Freeman* of April 2, 1875 carried a very

long story, continued on April 3; among newspaper accounts used here are those in the Kingston *Weekly Freeman*, July 16, 1875, Kingston *Journal*, August 7, 1878.

11. Kingston *Weekly Freeman*, July 2, 1875; Kingston *Daily Freeman*, August 21, 1877; The *Argus*, June 30, 1875, Kingston *Daily Freeman*, May 1, 1875, Saugerties *Daily Post*, December 12, 1877.

12. Kingston *Weekly Freeman*, July 16, 1875; Kingston *Daily Freeman*, April 21, 1875; Saugerties *Daily Post*, December 27, 1877, January 8, January 10, January 18, January 29, February 1, February 14, February 20, February 28, and at frequent internals until the hotel opened on June 26, 1878.

13. Saugerties *Daily Post*, June 11, 1877, and almost daily until June 28 dealt with the opening of the hotel. In July I have used the *Daily Post's* frequent stories; the *Daily Post* continued to cover the story of the hotel up to its closing September 23.

14. Sources used here were largely from the Saugerties *Evening Post* with a few from the Saugerties *Telegraph*. Other newspapers used include the Poughkeepsie *Eagle*, July 9 and August 12, 1879.

15. The Kingston *Argus*, July 30, 1879; Poughkeepsie *Eagle*, August 25, 1879, the Saugerties *Telegraph* and *Evening Post*, passim.

16. Saugerties *Telegraph* and *Evening Post*, summer of 1879, passim.

17. Saugerties *Telegraph* and *Evening Post*, 1881, passim; A.E.P. Searing, *The Land of Rip Van Winkle*, N.Y.C., 1884; *The Epoch Life of Steele MacKaye*, N.Y.C., 1927, vol. 1, p. 465.

18. Kingston *Daily Freeman*, September 10, 1879; Catskill *Examiner*, August 31, 1889; Kingston *Argus*, July 22, 1896, April 21, 1897; *Ulster Commemorative Biographical Record*, Chicago, 1896, p. 1274; Stamford *Mirror*, May 25, 1897; Kingston *Argus*, July 5, 1899; A.T. Clearwater, *History of Ulster County*

N.Y., Kingston, New York, 1907, p. 407. Here as elsewhere in the story of the story of the Overlook Mountain House, I have consulted the Deed and Mortgage Books in the office of the Ulster County Clerk.

CHAPTER 29

1. Kathleen Maxwell, in *The History of Ulster County, with Emphasis Upon the Last Hundred Years, 1883-1984*, compiled by the Historians of Ulster County, 1984, pp. 144-146.

2. A. N. Sylvester, *History of Ulster County N.Y.*, Part 2, p. 317; copy of contract between Jnó. Rowley (Agent of Eugene A. Livingston) and Henry Lewis, May 11, 1849, RRLP; agreement between Ira S. Herrick and Jno. and William H. Lewis for E. A. Livingston for bluestone quarrying rights, March 9, 1853, RRLP.

3. A. Evers, "Bluestone Lore and Bluestone Men," in *N.Y. Folklore Quarterly*.

4. Cy Keegan, Victor Lasher and Sam Wiley, personal communications.

5. Kathleen Maxwell, op. cit.; Harry Siemsen, personal communication.

6. The chief source here was *Supreme Court* (State of New York), *Testimony on Appeal, Lucius Lawson vs. the Town of Woodstock*, Margaretville, N.Y. 1881, p. 294, passim; Ben Snyder, personal communication. Typical of "big stone" items are Stamford *Mirror*, February 1, 1887, Kingston *Weekly Leader*, March 28, 1890; Kingston *Daily Freeman*, February 18, 1881.

7. *Testimony on Appeal*, passim.

8. Harry Siemsen, Cy Keegan and Henry Wilgus, personal communications; Kingston *Daily Freeman*, July 20, 1880; Pine Hill *Sentinel*, April 23, 1898; Abram Hoffman, "Ulster County Bluestone," in R. L. de Lisser, *Picturesque Ulster*, Kingston, 1897-1905, pp. 119-122, 126-129.

9. Tomas Penning, Walter Kruesi and Cy Keegan, personal communication.

CHAPTER 30

1. Bruce Herrick in Will Rose, *The Vanishing Village*, N.Y.C., 1963, passim, useful in suggesting the character of Woodstock in the eyes of pre-art colony people.

2. Woodstock Assessment Roll, 1896, author's collection; New York State census records (microfilm edition), 1845 and 1875.

3. Kingston *Daily Freeman*, September 17, 1880; Kingston *Daily Freeman*, September 21, 1880.

4. On Arthur Peper, personal communication, John Herrick.

5. Louise Jonas (Ault), "Woodstock Resident First to Hail Cleveland Victory," in Ulster County *Press* updated clipping, c. 1937; Louise Ault, *Artist in Woodstock*, pp. 40-42.

6. For a different version of this story see Neva Shultis, *From Sunset to Cock's Crow*, Woodstock, 1957, pp. 8-9.

7. New Paltz *Independent*, December 3, 1868; Craig Vosburgh.

8. Mrs. T. G. Hooke and Bertha Elwyn, personal communications.

9. Cy Keegan and Walter Kruesi, personal communications; "The Binnewater Class" in *Courier*, November 7, 1851; Stuart M. Blumin, *The Urban Threshold*, Chicago, 1976, pp. 101-102; Anita N. Smith, *Woodstock History and Hearsay*, pp. 101-102; Rose Oxhandler, "The Story of Yankeetown, now Wittenberg," p. 14, in *Publications of the Woodstock Historical Society*, no. 16, September 1951; Kingston *Daily Freeman*, January 8, 1881.

10. The *Argus*, July 30, 1879; Mrs. Bruce Herrick, personal communication; Mrs. Newton Shultis, personal communication.

11. Fred Reynolds, personal communications; Kingston *Weekly Leader*, August 1888; "Stabbed with an Awl," in Kingston *Daily Freeman*, April 18, 1881; Kingston *Argus*, March 22, 1876.

12. "Homicide in Woodstock," in the *Press*, Kingston, N.Y., September 16, 1869; Kingston *Argus*, October 1, 1879, The *Argus*, January 10, 1876.

13. The *Argus*, January 10, 1876; Kingston *Journal*, July 28, 1874.

14. Kingston *Daily Freeman*, September 21, 1880.

15. A. T. Clearwater, *History of Ulster County N.Y.*, pp. 442-444; Kingston *Weekly Leader*, October 26, 1888; September 11, 1884; the *Argus*, September 6, 1879.

16. Will Rose, *The Vanishing Village*, pp. 162-166.

17. Kingston *Daily Freeman*, February 8, 1881; Woodstock *Press*, October 20, 1960; Neva Shultis, personal communication. Figures given here are from the *Annual Reports of the Superintendent of Common Schools*, Albany, 1841, 1880, 1881.

18. Kingston *Daily Freeman*, April 15, 1879; Victor Lasher and the Rev. Harvey Todd, personal communications.

19. Autograph album of Zella Wolven, Lake Hill, 1883, containing calligraphic drawings by John Sickler and John E. Hasbrouck; A. Evers. "Some Ulster Flyleaf Rhymes and Games," in *N.Y. Folklore Quarterly*.

20. Bertha Elwyn, "The Gay Nineties in Woodstock," in *Publications of the Woodstock Historical Society*, no. 6, September 1931, pp. 15-20.

21. Hannah Catherine Cooper Vosburgh, "Fifty Years Ago in a Farmhouse," in *Publications of the Woodstock Historical Society*, no. 6, September 1931, pp. 15-20.

CHAPTER 31

1. The *Argus*, June 23, 1875; Kingston *Daily Freeman*, October 26, 1880; Kingston *Daily Leader*, September 3, 1884.

2. Kingston *Press*, 1871.

3. N.B. Sylvester, *History of Ulster County. . .* part 2, pp. 321-322.

4. Among newspaper stories about projected railroads to Woodstock used here were Saugerties *Daily Post*, July 24, 1878, August 4, 1881; Saugerties *Weekly*

Post, April 2, September 17, October 1, 1891; Kingston *Daily Leader*, August 22, 1881, October 10, 1889, October 25, 1889, August 1, 1903.

5. Pine Hill *Sentinel*, May 29, 1909, February 10, 1912; Gerald M. Best, *The Ulster and Delaware*, San Marino, Calif., 1972, pp. 14, 142; Harris Gordon and Eugene Dauner, personal communications.

6. Leila James Roney and Paul Domville, personal communications.

7. Kingston *Daily Freeman*, April 18, 1881.

8. Kingston *Daily Freeman*, April 18, 1881.

9. M. S. Forde, interview with Oscar Howland in "Lore of the Catskills," Harold W. Thompson Archive, New York State Historical Association; Charles Herrick, personal communication; Kingston *Journal*, December 10, 1878.

10. Kingston *Daily Freeman*, December 15, 1880; Charles Herrick, personal communication.

11. Lists and advertisements of Woodstock boardinghouses with numbers accommodated, prices, etc. were included in guides to the Catskills, cited below.

12. Kingston *Daily Freeman*, July 15, 1881; Register of Overlook Mountain Home, (Mead's), 1869-1930; Mrs. Robert Bradley, Mrs. Victor Lasher and Martin MacDaniel, personal communications; booklet advertising Riseley's, author's collection. Used here were Walton Van Loan, *Catskill Mountain Guide*, 1882 and 1887; R. Ferris, *The Catskills, An Illustrated Handbook*, June 1897; Ulster and Delaware Railroad, *The Catskill Mountains*, 1890, 1900, 1903; Kingston *Weekly Leader*, October 19, 1888; the *Argus*, July 16, 1879.

13. The *Argus*, July 19, 1876; Kingston *Daily Freeman*, August 1, 1878; Kingston *Daily Freeman*, August 21, 1877.

14. Woodstock *Press*, February 12, 1932.

15. Used here were the Dan Sully materials in the Billy Rose and Locke Collections, NYPL, Lincoln Center Branch. These consist in part of promotional materials and so were used with caution. *Commemorative Biographical Record, Ulster County, N.Y.*, Chicago, 1896, pp. 805-806; "Daniel Sully Dead," in New York *Mirror*, July 2, 1910; "A visit to Dan Sully's Farm," in New York *Dramatic Mirror*, September 8, 1900, August 1, 1903; *Dramatic News*, July 2, 1910.

16. Among Ulster County newspaper stories, used were Kingston *Argus*, October 7, 1890, June 28, 1893; Kingston *Daily Freeman*, August 3, 1889; Pine Hill *Sentinel*, July 6, 1895; Kingston *Daily Freeman*, August 10, 1906, August 20, 1907; also Anita M. Smith, *Woodstock History and Hearsay*, p. 117; federal census records, 1870-1900.

17. Materials on George Fox, Tony Denier, Theater Collection, NYPL, Lincoln Center Branch; Mrs. T. G. Hooke, Victor Lasher and the following Sully relations: Mrs. Irving Lasher, Mr. and Mrs. George Wilbur, Mrs. Charles E. Cross, personal communications; *Gazetteer and Business Directory of Ulster County, N.Y., 1871-1872*, Syracuse N.Y., 1871, p. 297. Typescript of "the Old Mill Stream" in NYPL, Lincoln Center Branch.

CHAPTER 32

1. Charles Lanman, *Adventures in the Wilds of the United States of North America, and British American Provinces*, 2 vols., Philadelphia, 1856, vol. 1, pp. 173-174.

2. Ruth Reynolds Glunt, personal communication.

3. Kingston *Daily Freeman*, October 19, 1878.

4. Griffin Herrick, Elsworth MacDaniel, Aaron Vandebogart, personal communications; Kingston *Weekly Freeman*, October 10, 1879.

5. New York *Times*, June 1, 1874.

6. Kingston *Daily Freeman*, July 28, 1879, May 24, 1875; Kingston *Weekly Freeman*, July 16, 1875.

7. Kingston *Daily Freeman*, April 30, 1879.

8. Kingston *Daily Freeman*, April 30, 1879.

9. Evers, *The Catskills*, pp. 590-591; Charles H. Weidner, *Water for a City*, New Brunswick, N.J., 1974, pp. 140-145; the Kingston *Journal*, August 21, 1861; Kingston *Weekly Journal*, March 2, 1882.

10. Kingston *Argus*, August 1, September 5, 1894.

11. *Report of Committee on New Water Supply, City of Kingston, N.Y.*; Kingston *Argus*, October 31, 1894; Weidner, *Water*, pp. 148-149; Martin Comeau, Craig Vosburgh, George Shultis and Mary Snyder, personal communications; Woodstock *Times*.

CHAPTER 33

1. Bertha F. Elwyn, "The Gay Nineties in Woodstock," in *Publications of the Woodstock Historical Society*, no. 12, April 1935, pp. 19-27.

2. Young people leaving, Martin Comeau, personal communication; Dr. Mortimer Downer in Town Clerk's Minute Book; "Woodstock Where People Seldom Die," in Kingston *Freeman*, clipping datelined January 30, no year; "Abram Cole Dead aged 104 Years," Kingston *Freeman*, April 3, 1917, with photo.

3. For Arkville, *Journal of Fine Arts*; Mrs. Lawrence of Arkville, personal communication; Evers, *The Catskills*.

4. Candace Wheeler, *Yesterdays in a Busy Life*, N.Y.C., 1918, pp. 209-257.

5. *The Balliol College Register, 2nd Ed., 1833-1933*, Jno. Elliot, Oxford, 1934, p. 83; Hervey White, "Ralph Radcliffe Whitehead," in *Publications of the Woodstock Historical Society*, no. 10, July 1933, pp. 14-29; Anita M. Smith, *Woodstock History*, pp. 40-43.

6. The R. R. Whitehead collection of letters, photographs and other materials formerly in White Pines,

Byrdcliffe, with permission of owner, Mark Willcox, Wawayanda, Pa.; Mark Willcox, Kenneth Downer and Isabel Byman, personal communications.

7. For the R. R. Whitehead-Jane Byrd McCall letters, 1890s, Mark Willcox; *Grass of the Desert*, London 1892, pp. 57-74.

8. John Ruskin, *Modern Painters*, vol. 7, library edition of Ruskin's Works, N.Y.C., n.d., pp. 175-179.

CHAPTER 34

1. Hervey White, "Ralph Radcliffe Whitehead," in *Publications of the Woodstock Historical Society*, no. 10, July 1933, pp. 14-29; transcripts of tape recordings made by W.E. Gledhill, Santa Barbara Historical Society and Constance Ealing, Arthur Ogilvy, Gail Harrison, Helen Weedon, and Mrs. Alfred M. Smith, April-May 1960; newspaper items in the Santa Barbara *Morning Press* about R. R. Whitehead, October 23, 1894-April 16, 1911, courtesy of Allen Staley, now in the Woodstock Historical Society Collection.

2. Hervey White, *Autobiography*, a typescript in the Iowa Authors Collection, University of Iowa Library, pp. 5-8 and passim; Hervey White, "Ralph Radcliffe Whitehead," in *Publication of the Woodstock Historical Society*, no. 10, July 1933. Hervey White, *Man Overboard*, Maverick Press, 1922 (a novel set at Arcady), of which pp. 5-8 describes Whitehead garden, Whitehead's musical activities; Hervey White, "Ralph Radcliffe Whitehead," cited above, p. 22; *Birds of God*, N.Y.C., 1902.

3. Transcript of Gledhill interview with Gail Harrison, p. 6.

4. Life at Arcady, Hervey White, *Autobiography*, pp. 116-129.

5. For Oregon, Hervey White, *Autobiography*, pp. 127-129; "Ralph Radcliffe Whitehead," pp. 23-25.

6. Statement of W.E. Gledhill; "Louise McCurdy Hart," May 1960; Gail Harrison transcript, p. 8.

7. For Bolton Brown, Hervey White, *Autobiography*, pp. 145-146; Bolton Brown, "Early Days at Woodstock," in *Publications of the Woodstock Historical Society*, no. 13, August-September, 1937, pp. 3-4.
8. Carl Eric Lindin, "Bolton Brown," in *Publications of the Woodstock Historical Society*, no. 13, August-September. 1937, pp. 15-16; Hervey White, "Woodstock in 1902, Enter the Art Immigrants" (ms. of lecture, 1937), Woodstock Historical Society Collection.
9. John Ruskin, op. cit.; Bolton Brown, op. cit.
10. Hervey White, "Woodstock in 1902, Enter the Art Immigrants," Woodstock Historical Society, and Bolton Brown, op. cit., give differing accounts of the purchase of the land.
11. Bolton Brown, op. cit.
12. Ralph Radcliffe Whitehead, "A Plea for Manual Work," in *Handicraft*, June 1903; prospectus for the Byrdcliffe Summer School of Art in the Art Room, NYPL.
13. Hervey White, "Woodstock in 1902," op. cit.

CHAPTER 35

1. Hervey White, "Ralph Radcliffe Whitehead," in *Publications of the Woodstock Historical Society*, no. 10, July 1933, p. 27.
2. W. E. Gledhill, transcript of telephone interview with Mrs. Harwood White; Hervey White, *Autobiography*, pp. 150, 161, 162.
3. Lucy Brown, "The First Summer in Byrdcliffe," in *Publications of the Woodstock Historical Society*, no. 2, August 1930, pp. 16-17.
4. Lucy Brown, op. cit.; Hervey White, *Autobiography*, p. 161; Bolton Brown, "Early Days," in *Publications of the Woodstock Historical Society*, no. 13, August-September, 1937, pp. 13-14; Hervey White and Anita M. Smith, personal communications; Hervey White, *Autobiography*, p. 162; Bertha Thompson, "The Craftsmen of Byrdcliffe," in *Publications of the Woodstock Historical Society*, no. 10, July 1933, pp. 8-13.
5. Whitehead as "dictator," Poultney Bigelow, "The Byrdcliffe Colony of Arts and Crafts," in *American Homes and Gardens*, October 1909; Alvin F. Sanborn, "Leaders in American Arts and Crafts," in *Good Housekeeping*, February 1907, p. 390, p. 148.
6. For Birge Harrison, Harry Leith-Ross, "Birge Harrison, 1855-1929" in *Publications of the Woodstock Historical Society*, no. 4, July 1931, pp. 30-34; New *Times*, May 11, 1929; letter from Poulteney Bigelow, May 15, 1929; Arthur Hoeber, "Birge Harrison, N.A., Landscape Painter," in *The International Studio*, vol. XLIV, no. 173, July 1911, pp. 111-V; John E. E. Trask, "Birge Harrison," in *Scribner's Magazine*, November 1907, vol. XLII, no. 5, pp. 576-583.
7. Carl Eric Lindin, "The Woodstock Landscape," in *Publications of the Woodstock Historical Society*, no. 7, July 1932, pp. 14-25; Bertha Thompson, op. cit., p. 11. For lithographic press, Hervey White, *Autobiography*, p. 111; framemaking, Alvin F. Sanborn, "Leaders in American Arts and Crafts," op. cit., p. 152; Zulma Parker, personal communication.
8. "The Hotel," by Hervey White, in *Maverick Hoot*, vol. 1, no. 2.
9. Bolton Brown, "Early Days at Woodstock," op. cit.
10. Ibid.
11. Bertha Thompson, op. cit.
12. Ibid.
13. Hervey White, "Ralph Radcliffe Whitehead," op. cit., pp. 27-29.
14. Ibid.
15. Ibid.
16. Hervey White, *Autobiography*, pp. 157, 164, 165-166; Gelett Burgess, "The Late Charles H. Hinton, Philosopher of the Fourth Dimension, Inventor of the Baseball Gun," in New York *Times*, May 5, 1907, p. 8; Lucy Brown, op. cit.

CHAPTER 36

1. *The Art Students League of New York, Summer 1959* (the school's catalog), pp. 3-7; John F. Carlson, "The Art Students League in Woodstock," in *Publications of the Woodstock Historical Society*, no. 9, September 1932, pp. 11-18 (some errors in dates, etc.); Margaret Ruff, "League Summer School Opened 1902" in Ulster County *Townsman*.
2. Evers, *The Catskills*, p. 633.
3. Rosie Magee, Anita N. Smith, *Woodstock History and Hearsay*, pp. 70-76; Richard LeGallienne, *Woodstock An Essay*, Woodstock, 1932, p. 14.
4. Town Historian of Milan, Dutchess County, 1982.
5. For barnacles, Anita N. Smith, *Woodstock. . .*, pp. 70-76.
6. Edward L. Chase, personal communication.
7. Edward L. Chase and Sam Wiley, personal communications.
8. Edward L. Chase, personal communication.
9. Sam Wiley, personal communication; Kingston *Daily Freeman*.
10. Birge Harrison, "Painting at Woodstock," in *Arts and Decoration*, 2:7, May 1912, pp. 245-248.
11. Birge Harrison, "The Appeal of the Winter Landscape," in *Fine Arts Journal*, 1914, vol. XXX, pp. 191-196.
12. J. Nilsen Laurvik, "The Arts Students League Summer School," in *International Studio*, May 1911, pp. 61-64.
13. Richard LeGallienne, op. cit., p. 16; Alexander Brook, "Andrew Dasburg," in the *Art*, vol. 6, July 1924, pp. 19-20; Jerry Bywaters, "Andrew Dasburg," in *American Federation of Arts*, p. 19; Richard LeGallienne, op. cit; for "slop brown" painting before Sunflower Club, Elizabeth M. Loder, *D. Putnam Brinley, 1879-1963, Impressionist and Mural Painter*, Yarmouth, Me., 1983, p. 13.
14. Alice Wardwell, personal communication; Hervey White, *Autobiography*, p. 192.
15. For Konrad Cramer, diaries of Florence B. and Konrad Cramer, in Archives of American Art, passim; Milton Wolf Brown, *The Story of the Armory Show*, N.Y.C., 1963; Hervey White, "The Hawk's Nest," in *The Wild Hawk*, 2:4, February 1913, n.p.
16. Robert LeGallienne, op. cit., pp. 15-16.

CHAPTER 37

1. "Byrdcliffe 1907," a promotional booklet, copy in Woodstock Library; Diary of Olaf Westerling, 1904-1905, courtesy of Mildred Andersen, Chicago; Aileen Webster Payne, personal communication.
2. Ralph Radcliffe Whitehead, "A Plea for Manual Work," op. cit., Byrdcliffe, 1907.
3. Aileen Webster Payne and Peter Whitehead, personal communications; Deed Books, Ulster County Clerk's office.
4. "Byrdcliffe 1907"; Aileen Webster Payne and Mark Willcox, personal communications.
5. Poulteney Bigelow, op. cit.
6. Four programs of the Dolmetsch concerts, Mark Willcox collection.
7. Anita M. Smith, *Woodstock History and Hearsay*, p. 43; Elizabeth Burroughs Kelly, personal communication.
8. Hervey White, *Autobiography*; Eva Beard, personal communication.
9. Paul Evans, *Art Pottery of the United States*, N.Y.C., 1974, pp. 38-39; Bertha Thompson, "The Craftsmen of Byrdcliffe," op. cit., p. 12.
10. Leonard Ochtman, Birge Harrison, "Painting at Woodstock," in *Arts and Decoration*, May 1912, pp. 247-248.
11. Kingston *Freeman*, 1914.
12. Letter Hervey White-Ralph R. Whitehead, October 9, 1914, Willcox collection.
13. Frances Rogers, *The Story of a Small Town Library*, Woodstock, 1974, pp. 16-25 and passim.

CHAPTER 38

1. Hervey White, *Autobiography*, p.

190; catalog of Blue Dome Frat, N.Y.C., November 1914.
2. Hervey White, *Autobiography*, p. 190; New York *Tribune*, February 27, 1916.
3. J.F. Carlson, op. cit.
4. Hervey White, *Autobiography*, pp. 170-175.
5. Hervey White, "Our Rural Slums," in *The Independent*, vol. 65, 1908, pp. 819-821.
6. For Thorstein Veblen, Hervey White, *Autobiography*, p. 172.
7. Hervey White, *Autobiography*, p. 114, 188.
8. Ibid. p. 115.
9. Ibid. p. 175.
10. Ibid. "An Unrecorded Private Press," in *The Book Collector's Packet* (June-July), 1933, p. 21-25.
11. Some Maverick Press ephemera in the NYSHL, Kingston, and in the Rare Book Room, NYPL.
12. Hervey White, "Untitled Poem," in *The Wild Hawk*, January 1912.

CHAPTER 39

1. Kingston *Daily Freeman*, August-September 1914, passim; Martin Schuetze, *Byrdcliffe Afternoons*, Woodstock, 1938.
2. Hervey White, *Autobiography*, pp. 200-202; Kingston *Daily Freeman*, June 19, 1917.
3. Sam Wiley, personal communication.
4. Hervey White, "Fire and Water, an Incident of the War," in *The Wild Hawk*, December 1914, vol. 4, no. 2, n.p.; Hervey White, "Friends and Enemies," New York *Times*, October 5, 1915. "A Farce from the Trenches," in *The Wild Hawk*, July 1915, vol. 4, no. 9, deals with a similar situation.
5. Hervey White, *Autobiography*, pp. 201-202.
6. Hervey White, *Autobiography*, p. 201; Paul Domville, personal communication.
7. Ruth Reynolds Glunt, personal communication.
8. Louise Lindin, personal communication.

9. For Ned Thatcher, *The Overlook*, June 20, 1933; Kingston *Daily Freeman*, August 18, 1950.
10. Hervey White, *Autobiography*, p. 187.
11. Florence Cramer diary, Archives of American Art (microfilm).
12. Sam Wiley, personal communication; Hervey White, *Autobiography*, p. 203.
13. Kingston *Daily Freeman*, November 6, 1918.
14. For telephones, Kingston *Daily Freeman*, July 6, 1879; Kingston *Weekly Leader*, September 12, 1903; "Mildred Jones, Woodstock Telephone Operation for 30 Years," in Ulster *News* and Kingston *Leader*, January 5, 1950; Telephone Directory, Kingston District, May 1917, courtesy of Jane Vandebogart.
15. Louella Stewart, New York *Evening Post Magazine*, May 29, 1915.
16. Newspaper clipping, in Mark Willcox collection, the paper not identified; Jane Perkins Claney, "White Pines Pottery, the Continuing Arts and Crafts Experiment," in *The Byrdcliffe Arts and Crafts Colony, Life By Design*, Wilmington, Del. 1984, n.p.

CHAPTER 40

1. Hervey White, *Autobiography*, pp. 124-125.
2. Ibid., pp. 188-189, 197-199; for origin of the name, p. 115.
3. Ibid., p. 198.
4. Maverick music, ibid, pp. 193-194, 214-216; Paul Kefer in *The Overlook*, July 23, 1933, p. 7; Hervey White, "Birth of the Maverick Concert Hall," in *The Hue and Cry*, September 1, 1933 (reprinted from *The Wild Hawk*, October 1915).
5. Hervey White, *Autobiography*, pp. 207-209; for the well, ibid., pp. 188-189.
6. Promotional materials printed at Maverick Press, NYSHL, folder 2581; Kingston *Daily Freeman*, September 4, 1915.
7. Flyer advertising Maverick Festival ca. 1915. SHL, Kingston.

NOTES

8. Hervey White, *Autobiography*, pp. 207-212.
9. Ibid., p. 209.
10. Hervey White, "Art and the Community, Outline of a Scheme of Co-operation Between Artists and Farmers," in *The Wild Hawk*, 5:5, March 1916, n.p.
11. Hervey White, "Birth of the Maverick Concert Hall," op. cit.
12. Leonard D. Abbott, "An Impression of Woodstock," in *The Overlook*, July 25, 1931.
13. Hervey White, *Autobiography*, p. 223; Raoul Hague and Walter Steinhilber, personal communications; and letter W. Steinhilber-A. Evers, July 16, 1979, author's collection.
14. Hervey White, *Autobiography*, p. 223-224; A. Walter Kramer, "Community Participation, the Soul of Maverick Festival at Woodstock," in *Musical America*, September 15, 1917; letter, W. Steinhilber-A. Evers, July 16, 1979, author's collection; letter, W. Steinhilber-Editor, Woodstock *Times*, May 2, 1976.
15. Virginia Holdridge, personal communication; Hervey White, *Autobiography*, pp. 225, 235; Kingston *Daily Freeman*, August 25, 1920.
16. Walt Peters and Walter Steinhilber, personal communications.
17. Hervey White, *Autobiography*, pp. 225, 240-243.
18. Raoul Hague, Walter Steinhilber and Carl Walters, personal communications; Helen Appleton Read, "Woodstock, Where Art Finds Atmosphere," in *Christian Science Monitor* (clipping circa 1923).

CHAPTER 41

1. Charles Herrick, Albert Cashdollar, Victor Lasher, Ruth R. Glunt (formerly Mrs. Tristram Tupper), personal communications.
2. A copy of the booklet is in the author's collection.
3. Ruth Reynolds Glunt, personal communication; Ruth R. Glunt, "The

Overlook Mountain House," in *The Catskills*, 1-3, pp. 1-43.
4. Bill Newgold "My Grandfather and the Mountain," in *The Conservationist*; Gabriel Newgold, personal communication.
5. Benjamin Stolber, *Tailor's Progress*, Garden City, N.Y., 1940, p. 287; Will Hutty and Martin MacDaniel, personal communications.
6. Julian J. Jaffe, *Crusade Against Radicalism*, Port Washington, N.Y., 1977, pp. 192-193, 7.
7. "The U.C.P. and the C.P. United, An Account of the Joint Unity Convention," in *The Communist*, vol. 1, no. 1, July 1921, pp. 1-3; "An Attempt by Communists to Seize the American Labor Movement," United Mine Workers of America, Indianapolis, 1922, pp. 46-47.
8. J. M. Longendyke, Walter Steinhilber, Charles Herrick, Hanno Schraeder and Will Hutty, personal communications; letters W. Steinhilber-A. Evers, August 11, 13, 1979, author's collection.
9. "An Attempt by Communists. . . ," pp. 44-46.
10. "Orphan Asylum at Woodstock," in Kingston *Daily Freeman*, September 14, 1914; Ulster County Deed Book, p. Andrew Kohl-Woodstock Lodge, Inc.; Bill Newgold and Victor Lasher, personal communications.
11. *The Hue and Cry*, August 30, 1924, p. 9; Kingston *Daily Freeman*, September 14, 1923; New York *Times*, editorial, "A Case for Investigation," September 14, 1923; Lamont Simpkins, personal communication.
12. Newgold heirs, Gabriel and Wilbert, denied that the Communist meeting had been held at their hotel, personal communication.
13. J. Edgar Hoover, *Masters of Deceit, the Story of Communism in America and How to Fight It*, N.Y.C., 1958, p. 60.
14. A copy of the anonymous broadside is in the author's collection; letter, W. Steinhilber-A. Evers, August 13, 1979, author's collection.

CHAPTER 42

1. Postmaster W. S. Elwyn, personal communication; also quoted in Woodstock *Press*, January 2, 1931, as to growth based on postal business.
2. J. P. McEvoy, personal communication.
3. Ralph Radcliffe Whitehead, "A Plea for Manual Work," in *Handicraft*, 2:3, June 1903, p. 67; Hughes Mearns, "Summer Resorters, Welcome to Woodstock," in *The Woodstock Bulletin*, September 1, 1929.
4. Bill Newgold in *The Conservationist*, op. cit.; Martin MacDaniel, personal communication.
5. Broadside, author's collection.
6. "Certificate of Classification of Woodstock Valley Hotel," in Incorporation Reports, Ulster County Clerk's office, 1927-1929, pp. 36-38; Shagbark Colony advertisement, *The Hue and Cry*, June 19-July 17, 1926.
7. *The Saturday Morning*, various dates, 1928; *The Hue and Cry*, July 27, 1929; Kingston *Daily Freeman*, August 6, 1929.
8. Bill Newgold, op. cit.; Gabriel Newgold and J. M. Longendyke, personal communications; Stephen B. Ayres obit., New York *Times*, June 3, 1929; "Old Woodstock Inn Has New Owner" in Woodstock *Bulletin*, October 15, 1929.
9. Kingston *Daily Freeman*, October 27, 1930; Hervey White, *Autobiography*, p. 258 and passim; advertisement in *The Hue and Cry*, July 25, 1925, "Dancing Classes, Alexis Kosloff. . ."; *The Woodstock Bulletin*, September 1, 1929.
10. Program, "Concert of Old Music by the Ambrose Choir of Woodstock," August 21, 1925, author's collection; David Robison, *Maverick Concerts*, 1975.
11. Alf Evers, "A Half Century of Theater in Woodstock," in *Fifty Years of Theater*, pp. 2-5, Woodstock Playhouse, 1975.
12. Hervey White, *Autobiography*; Dudley Digges, "The New Maverick

Theater," in *The Hue and Cry*, 2:2, July 5, 1924; Harry Gottlieb, personal communication.
13. Hervey White, "The Maverick Theater," in *The Hue and Cry* (Annual), v. 3, 1925, p. 47.
14. "The Phoenix Players," in *The Hue and Cry* (Annual), v. 3, 1925, p. 48; Ridgely Torrence, "The Phoenix Theatre," in *The Hue and Cry* (Annual), v. 4, no. 10, 1926, pp. 71-72.
15. Hervey White, *Autobiography*, pp. 207-209; Anita M. Smith, *Woodstock History and Hearsay*, pp. 59-60; A. Evers, "A Half Century of Woodstock Theater," pp. 2-5 and passim.
16. Anita M. Smith, *Woodstock History and Hearsay*, pp. 62-64. The weekly Woodstock *Bulletin*, July-October 1929, supplied details of the theatrical summer written by theater publicity people. *The Hue and Cry* that summer contained often lengthy reviews and much theatrical gossip.
17. Used here were photographs 1890-1940 of Woodstock buildings in author's collection and personal inspection. "Agriculture Retreats, Easels Advance," in New York *Herald*, July 1, 1923.
18. Ibid.
19. Hervey White, Walter Steinhilber and Howard Barnes, personal communications.
20. Hervey White, *Autobiography*, p. 220; Christopher Evers, personal communication.
21. The beginnings of the chapel of St. Joan of Arc are documented by means of clippings and ms. records in the copper box in the church's cornerstone, photographed 1985 (in author's collection); Martin Comeau and Victor Lasher, personal communications.

CHAPTER 43

1. Karal Ann Marling, introduction to *Woodstock, an American Art Colony, 1902-1970*, Poughkeepsie, 1977, n.p.
2. Karal Ann Marling, "Birge Harrison"; C. E. Lindin, "Gallery Reflections," in *The Hue and Cry*,

August 3, 1929; Harry Leith-Ross, "Birge Harrison 1855-1929," in *Publications of the Woodstock Historical Society*, no. 4, July 31, 1931, pp. 30-34.

3. William Innes Homer, *Robert Henri and His Circle*, Ithaca, 1969, p. 264 and passim; Anita M. Smith, *Woodstock History and Hearsay*, pp. 78-81 and passim; Hanno Schraeder, personal communication.

4. Charles Rosen and Sam Wiley, personal communications.

5. *Woodstock, an American Art Colony*, n.p.; Anita M. Smith, *Woodstock History and Hearsay*, pp. 77-78 and passim; Helen Appleton Read, "Eugene Speicher," in *Creative Art*, January 1929, pp. 11-16.

6. New York *Sun and Globe* review reprinted in Kingston *Daily Freeman*, November 1923.

7. *Avon Charles Rosen, 1878-1950*, p. 47 passim; Alexander Brook, "Robert Chanler," in *Creative Art*, 4:3, March 1928; *Yasuo Kuniyoshi*, N.Y.C., 1986; Henry Lee McFee, "My Painting and its Development," in *Creative Art*, 4:3, March 1929; "The Happy Valley," in *The Arts*, 10-2, August 1926.

8. Anita M. Smith, *Woodstock History and Hearsay*, pp. 59, 74; Alexander Archipenko and Alfeo Faggi, personal communications; *Archipenko, International Visionary*, Donald H. Haishan, ed., Washington D.C., 1969, passim; obituary, Woodstock *Record-Press*, March 5, 1964; Ralph Flint, "Art in the Catskills," in *Christian Science Monitor*, September 17, 1924; Raoul Hague, Walter Steinhilber and Emmet Edwards, personal communications.

9. Clinton Adams, *The Woodstock Ambience 1917-1939*, Albuquerque, N.M., 1982; Richard LeGallienne, *Woodstock, an Essay*, Woodstock, 1923; *The Hue and Cry* (Annuals), 1925 and 1926, text, illustrations and advertising place Woodstock artists and others in the Woodstock of the twenties. Karal Ann Marling, "The New Woodstock," op. cit.

10. *Bolton Brown, Lithographer*, Syracuse University, 1981; John Taylor Arma, *Bolton Brown, the Artist and the Man*, Woodstock, 1937.

11. For crafts in the 1920s the following were helpful: editorial and "The Recent Craft Exhibition at the Gallery of the Woodstock Art Association," in *The Hue and Cry*, August 2, 1924; "Second Art Exhibition," in *The Hue and Cry*, August 30, 1924, reprinted from Catskill Mountain *Reflector*; Hervey White, *Autobiography*, pp. 195-196; and scattered items in *The Hue and Cry* and the Woodstock *Bulletin* through the 1920s; obituary of Edward Thatcher, Kingston *Daily Freeman*, August 18, 1950; Zulma Parker and Bertha Thompson, personal communications; obituary, Ulster *Townsman*, May 25, 1972.

12. Hervey White, *Autobiography*, pp. 336-338; Ernest Brace, "Carl Walters," in *Creative Art*; Carl Walters, personal communication.

13. "The King's Daughters," in *100th Anniversary Shady United Methodist Church 1871-1971*, n.p.; Arthur Stone, personal communication.

14. Edward T. Chase and Sam Wiley, personal communication; Louella Stewart reprinted Ulster *Townsman*, April 18, 1968 from the *Evening Post Saturday Magazine*, May 29, 1915.

15. Woodstock *Bulletin*, 1929, p. 13. Ibid.

CHAPTER 44

1. Woodstock *Weekly*, September 27, 1924; Leon Carey and Virginia Holdridge, personal communications.

2. Hervey White, *Autobiography*; Walter Steinhilber, letter to Woodstock *Times*, May 2, 1976; photocopy of original, New York *Times*, August 22, 23, 1926.

3. Kingston *Daily Freeman*, August 9, 13, 1927; Woodstock *Bulletin*, August

12, 1928, reprinted from *Knickerbock Press*; New York *Herald Tribune*, September 1, 1928.

4. "Catskills Moon Sets Maverick Festival Aglow" in New York *Herald Tribune*, September 1, 1928; "Public Characters, No. 2," *The Hue and Cry*, July 28, 1928.

5. Hervey White, "Criticism," in Woodstock *Bulletin*, September 1, 1929; "Maverick Festival Number" of *The Hue and Cry*, August 30, 1929, with Festival Program.

6. Photocopy of broadside, "To the citizens of Woodstock, August 23, 1929," signed "Committee of Fifty," author's collection; R.L. Duffus, "A Serpent Invades an Eden," in New York *Times Sunday Magazine*, August 25, 1929.

7. Hervey White, "Criticism," in Woodstock *Bulletin*, September 1, 1929.

8. Here I used "How the Issue Was Decided" in Woodstock *Bulletin*, September 15, 1929, which quotes New York newspapers reports on the Festival of that year; and "Todd Claims Hale's Article Was Anonymous," ibid., which deals with the Committee of Fifty confrontation.

9. Comerford death notice, *The Hue and Cry*, July 21, 1933; "The Big Brother of the Maverick," "Press Echoes of Festival," op. cit.

10. Hervey White, "The Maverick Festival," "A Word of Explanation to New Revelers," "Press Echoes of the Festival," op. cit., in *Souvenir Program, Maverick Festival, 1930*.

11. Kingston *Daily Freeman*, October 27, 1930, July 30, 1931; *The Overlook*, August 8, 22, 1931; *Art Notes*, September 4, 1931; "Woodstock Plans Gayest Festival," in Kingston *Daily Freeman*, September 4, 1931.

12. "Maverick Fete Was a Mild Party," in Kingston *Daily Freeman*, September 8, 1931; *Art Notes*, August 29, 1931; Hervey White, *Autobiography*, p. 288.

CHAPTER 45

1. Lucy Brown, "The First Summer in Byrdcliffe," in *Publications of the Woodstock Historical Society*, no. 2, August 1930, pp. 16-17 and passim.

2. Martin Schuetze, "As I Knew Him in Woodstock"; Howard Brubacker, "In His Workshop," in *Walter Weyl, An Appreciation*, privately printed, 1922, pp. 54-83, 110-133.

3. John Unterecker, *Voyager, A Life of Hart Crane*, N.Y.C., 1969, pp. 327-328, 330-331.

4. Ibid. and p. 335; *Letters of Hart Crane 1916-1932*, ed. Brom Weber, N.Y.C., 1952, pp. 158-159.

5. William Murrell, "Fragments of a Broken Lyre," in the *Plowshare*, n.p.

6. John Unterecker, op. cit., p. 331; Brom Weber, op. cit., p. 161; Sam Wiley, personal communication.

7. Woodstock Town Clerk's Minute Book, 1915-1935, p. 92; Woodstock Electric and Power Co., corporation records; Ulster County Clerk's office, 443 Box 36; Craig Vosburgh and Victor Lasher, personal communications.

8. Advertisement for radios, Woodstock *Weekly*, December 26, 1924; "Woodstock Radio Night," in Woodstock *Weekly*, January 9, 1925.

9. Karl Cousins, Craig Vosburgh and Martin MacDaniel, personal communications.

10. Prospectuses for "The Woodstock Athletic Club" and "The Athletic Holding Co., Inc.," and John F. Carlson, "In Praise of the Woodstock Athletic Association the Challenge of our Time," all in program *Vaudeville and Dance for the Benefit of the Woodstock Athletic Club*, pp. 2-3, 1924.

11. Kingston *Argus*, July 26, 1899, for safety of dam; Craig Vosburgh and Fordyce Burhans, personal communications; "Is Cooper Lake a Menace to Woodstock?" in Ulster County *News*, October 1, 1942; Woodstock *Times*, March 28, 1985.

12. Martin Comeau, personal

communication; Kingston *Daily Freeman*, July 5, 1922.

CHAPTER 46

1. Kingston *Daily Freeman*, June 19, 29, July 5, 1922; F. G. Clough, *Follow the Hudson*, Laramie, Wyo., 1968, pp. 25-26.
2. Kingston *Daily Freeman*, ibid.
3. Kingston *Daily Freeman*, August 3, 6, 1912; "Water Rights Are Granted Woodstock," in Woodstock *Bulletin*, July 1, 1929.
4. J. P. McEvoy and Charles Herrick, personal communications.
5. J. P. McEvoy and Sam Wiley, personal communications; Anita M. Smith, *Woodstock History and Hearsay*, p. 171.
6. William C. Kiessel, Shultis genealogical chart, Ulster County Deed Books, 470, p. 7; 464, pp. 26, 342; Ulster Surrogate's Office Wills, 1890, p. 112, Thomas Johnson in Town of Woodstock Assessment Roll 1827, 1897; "Civil War Records of Woodstock Township," in *Publications of the Woodstock Historical Society*, no. 17, December 1955, pp. 22-23.
7. Norbert and Elizabeth Heerman, personal communication; "New Yorker Buys Large Zena Estate" in Woodstock *Bulletin*, March 1, 1930.
8. Changes mentioned in buildings in the hamlet of Woodstock are documented by photographs in the author's collection and in that of the Woodstock Historical Society.
9. For prizes won see the biographical sketches in the *American Art Annual* under the painters mentioned, 1920s and 1930s.
10. Kenneth Wilson obituary, Kingston *Daily Freeman*.
11. Ethel Boggs, Sam Wiley and Gretchen Mount, personal communications.
12. A. Evers, *The Catskills*, pp. 646-648.
13. Hughes Mearns, "Summer Resorters Welcome to Woodstock," in

Woodstock *Bulletin*, September 1, 1920.
14. A copy of *The Pochade* is in the Woodstock Library.

CHAPTER 47

1. Runs of *The Plebeian* are in the Kingston Area Library and the New-York Historical Society Library.
2. Ulster County newspapers used in this chapter are microfilm editions in the Kingston Area Library unless otherwise noted. Pine Hill *Sentinel*, Ulster County Community College Library, December 6, 1905, December 7, 1905, December 16, 1905, March 24, 1906; Kingston Daily *Freeman*, October 9, 1914, October 18, 1914.
3. Hervey White, *Autobiography*, pp. 228, 288.
4. A complete run of *The Plowshare* is in the Woodstock Library; for Gustav Hellstrom, *Svenska Man och Kvinnen Biografisk Uppelslagbok*, Stockholm, 1940, pp. 403-404.
5. William Murrell, "Fragments of a Broken Lyre," in *The Plowshare*, January 1920.
6. The Woodstock Library and Woodstock Historical Society have files of *The Hue and Cry*; Hervey White, *Autobiography*, pp. 228-229; Henry Morton Robinson and John Pasciutti, personal communications.
7. Editorials in *The Hue and Cry* (Annual), 4:10, 1926; an incomplete file of the Woodstock *Weekly* is in the author's collection.
8. "From an Old Cocker," in *Woodstock Almanac*, Ernest Brace and Rudolf Wetterau, eds., 1924, p. 29.
9. Hervey White, *Autobiography*, pp. 247-248; Kingston *Daily Leader*, advertisement in *Hue and Cry* (Annual), 1925.
10. A file of the Woodstock *Bulletin* is in the Woodstock Library.
11. I have seen only nos. 1, 3 and 7 of the Maverick *Hoot*, photocopies in author's collection; Joe Gould, personal communication; F.G. Clough, *Follow the Hudson*, pp. 48-50.

12. A file of the Woodstock *Press* is in the Woodstock Library.

13. Malcolm Cowley, *Exiles Return*, N.Y.C., 1934, pp. 265-267.

14. For 1924, F. J. Hoffman et al., *The Little Magazine*, Princeton, N.J., 1947, p. 274; three nos. in author's collection.

15. Martin Schuetze, "A History of Woodstock," in Woodstock *Bulletin*, September 1, 1929, p. 22; ibid., "To Write History of Woodstock," p. 1.

16. Martin Schuetze, "The President's Address," in *Papers Read to the Woodstock Historical Society*, July 8, 1930, pp. 3-7.

17. Martin Schuetze, "Our View of History," in *Publications of the Woodstock Historical Society*, no. 2, August 1930, pp. 3-7.

18. Martin Schutze, "Our Project of a Museum," in *Publications of the Woodstock Historical Society*, no. 3, September 1930, pp. 3-7.

CHAPTER 48

1. Woodstock Town Clerk's Minute Book, 1915-1935, p. 440, December 3, 1929.

2. Ibid., July 30, October 1932; Albert Cashdollar, personal communication.

3. Woodstock Town Clerk's Minute Book, 1915-1935, May 2, 1933; *The Overlook*, October 4, 1935, pp. 1 and 4; Woodstock *Press*, January 8, 1932.

4. Here I am using my own observations of Woodstock people during the Depression. Louise Ault, *Artist in Woodstock, George Ault the Independent Years*, Philadelphia, 1978, pp. 1-75, is informative for the Depression era.

5. Ibid; advertisement Harry B. Merritt, *The Overlook*, June 25, 1932; Dyrus Cook, *Donkeying Through Seven States*, privately printed, 1933; *The Overlook*, July 9, 1932.

6. *The Overlook*, June 11, 1937, December 2, 1938; Woodstock *New Yorker*, April 2, 1938 (a copy is in the local history room, NYPL); May

Wilgus Wetterau and Tom Penning, personal communications.

7. George Layman, Dr. George Lambert, Lorenz Stowall and Victor Lasher, personal communications.

8. Tom Wolf, Konrad Cramer and Robert Brinkman, personal communications.

9. *The Overlook*, June 13, 1931, June 25, 1932, July 25, 1932.

10. Ibid; Irving Kalish, personal communication; *The Overlook*, June 25, 1932.

11. *The Overlook*, November 13, 1936.

CHAPTER 49

1. *Woodstock Sesquicentennial Celebration*, May 30 to June 5, 1937, Woodstock, 35 pp. (the official program); New York *Herald Tribune*, May 31, 1937.

2. Album of photographs of the various features of the celebration taken by Konrad Cramer, in Woodstock Library.

3. "Chamber of commerce to promote toboggan slide and rink and advertise," Woodstock *Bulletin*, September 15, 1928; "Snow Train Announced by N.Y. Central," in *The Overlook*, November 29, 1935.

4. Woodstock *Press*, January 15, 1932; J. F. O'Connor and Leon Carey, personal communications.

5. Miss Evens, Kingston *Argus*, October 4, 1899; Woodstock *Weekly*, October 4, 11, 1924; Woodstock Town Clerk's Minute Book, 1915-1935, pp. 432, 433.

6. The floods mentioned here were reported in Kingston and Saugerties by newspapers, among them the *Argus*, December 25, 1878; The Catskill *Examiner*, July 13, 1889; and Woodstock newspapers of the dates given; Howard Mayer, Craig Vosburgh, Charlotte Reynolds and Hanno Schrader, personal communications.

7. "The Villetta Inn," an advertising booklet, author's collection; Eugene Patterson and Jean Gaede, personal communications.

8. Here I used the Benjamin Webster Papers, Woodstock Library, consisting of drafts headed "The Dream Purpose Fulfillment, A Five Year Plan For Byrdcliffe, Investment Schedule," not dated or page numbered; letters Francis Smyth-Peter Whitehead, November 24, 1933, Jane Whitehead-Benjamin L. Webster, December 20, 1933.

9. Webster Papers, Woodstock Library.

10. Here I have used the "Byrdcliffe Afternoons" file box of Martin Schuetze with the letters that passed between the organizers and speakers, newspaper clippings, and broadsides as well as the *Byrdcliffe Afternoons*, Woodstock 1938 and 1939.

11. Ibid. Letters J. T. Shotwell-Martin Schuetze, March 3, 1939; Martin Schuetze, May 9, 1939 (retained copy); *Byrdcliffe Afternoons*, 1940, broadside; Schuetze file, clippings from *The Overlook*; reporting on the Afternoons, Schuetze file.

12. Flora and Gene Patterson, personal communication; U.S. Department of Commerce, Bureau of the Census, *Religious Bodies*, 1936, vol. 11, part 2; Denominations, Wash. 1941, pp. 1297-1312; "In America," in Victor James Horton, *The Old Catholic Church*, Saugerties, 1941, pp. 27-31.

13. "Handicraft of Local Monks" in New York *Telegram*, October 23, 1937; Deed, The Board of Missions of the Protestant Episcopal Church in the Diocese of Albany-The Board of Managers of the Diosecan Missionary and Church Extension Society of the Protestant Episcopal Church in the Diocese of New York, May 22, 1931; Ulster County Deed Book 551, p. 491; Board of Managers of the Diocesan Missionary and Church Extension Society of the Protestant Episcopal Church in the Diocese of New York-Jane Byrd Whitehead, Ulster County Ulster County Deed Book 692, pp. 375-376; December 4, 1941 for St. Dunstan's.

14. Kingston *Daily Freeman*, April 14, 1941; Ulster County *News*, November 27, 1941; Sylvia Day, "Don Quixote with a Collar," in the Woodstock *Week*, April 7, 1966; V. J. Horton, op. cit., pp. 22-27; Father Francis, Patricia Pick, Darryl Parham and Captain Savo Milo, personal communications.

CHAPTER 50

1. Anita Philips, "Our Theatre," in *The Hue and Cry*, June 16, 1933.

2. Woodstock *Press*, October 24, 1930, November and December 1931, passim.

3. Kingston *Weekly Leader*, November 9, 1888; Pine Hill *Sentinel*, May 5, 1900; Fire Company, Ulster Book of Incorporation, Book 4, p. 207; "Fireman! Save My Child" in *The Hue and Cry*, June 30, 1945.

4. Woodstock Town Record Book, 1915-1935, pp. 36-367; "The Story of the Woodstock Playhouse," in *Fifty Years of Theater*, Woodstock, 1957, p. 13, statement by Albert E. Milliken, inside back cover.

5. *The Hue and Cry*, June 30, July 28, August 18, August 4, 1945; Alf Evers, in *Fifty Years of Theater*," Story of the Woodstock Playhouse," p. 13.

6. K. A. R. Marling, "Federal Patronage and the Woodstock Colony," Ph. D. dissertation, Bryn Mawr College, 1971, pp. 36-39; *The Hue and Cry*, September 1, 1933, full page advertisement with program, humorous story, August 28, 1933.

7. New York *Times*, August 3, 1933; *The Hue and Cry*, September 1, 1933; Marling, pp. 52-58, op. cit.

8. Marling, "After the Crash," in *Woodstock, An American Art Colony, 1902-1977*, Vassar College Art Gallery, Poughkeepsie, 1977, n.p.

9. Marling, ibid; the total Ulster County vote for Thomas was 762. Legislation Manual, New York State, 1937, p. 1032.

10. Carl Eric Lindin, "Bolton Brown," in *Publications of the Woodstock Historical Society*, no. 13, August to September 1937, pp. 15-17; Clinton

Anderson, *The Woodstock Ambience*, Albuquerque, N.M., 1981.

CHAPTER 51

1. Kingston *Daily Freeman*, October 16, 1936.
2. *The Overlook*, May 28, 1937.
3. *The Overlook*, March 4, 1938.
4. "After the Crash," in *Woodstock, An American Art Colony, 1902-1907*, n.p., Poughkeepsie, 1977.
5. Ibid.
6. Ibid.
7. Ibid; *The Story of the Woodstock Craft Center from March 15, 1939*, Federal Security Agency, National Youth Administration; a scrapbook containing newspaper clippings, photographs, rules, constitution and other materials, courtesy of D. J. Stern.
8. Ibid, *The Story of the Woodstock Craft Center*.
9. *Order*, vol. 1, November 1, 1936-August 15, 1937, passim, N. T. Boggs; John Pascuitti, personal communication.
10. Hervey White, *Autobiography*, pp. 228-229.
11. Kingston *Daily Freeman*, June 9, 1933; H. M. Robinson, "The Maverick," in *Publications of the Woodstock Historical Society*, no. 11, August to September 1933, pp. 10-11.
12. White, *Autobiography*, p. 287; John Pasciutti, personal communication; Hervey White, *Autobiography*, pp. 216-217; undated "Special to the Press" newspaper clipping quoting extensively from letter, Hervey White-Fritizie Smith, describes White's *Passion Play*, author's collection.
13. J. P. C., "An Open Letter," in *The Phoenix*, 1-1, Spring 1938; Cooney, pp. 20-32; Cooney gives the broad philosophical base for his venture in an advertisement, "The Maverick Carpentry and Woodcraft Shop," in *The Phoenix*, 2-1, Spring 1939. The craft work of the colony is also described.

14. The Woodstock Library has an incomplete run of *The Phoenix*.
15. For Cooney's pacifist views, see James Peter Cooney, "Swords into Plowshares," in *The Phoenix*, Easter, 1940, pp. 136-145; Hervey White, Adolph Heckeroth and John Pasiutti, personal communications.

CHAPTER 52

1. Nat Austin and Walter Steinhilber, personal communications.
2. "Woodstock Today," in Charles E. Gradwell, *Woodstock*, N.Y.C., n.p., 1941.
3. The Woodstock *Press* covered home-front activities in detail. See December 30, 1941, April 9, June 11, 26, July 3, 10, 17, August 21, October 23, 1942. Anita M. Smith, *Woodstock History and Hearsay*, pp. 119-197, gives a good account of home-front and military experiences of local people.
4. Anita M. Smith, *Woodstock History and Hearsay*.
5. "Local Family Servant Unmasked as Spy," in Woodstock *Press*, July 17, 1942.
6. W. W. Farr Jr., Ardmore, Pa.; school paper, author's collection.
7. Editorial in *Retort*, 1:1, Winter, 1942, n.p.
8. Woodstock *Press*, August 14, 1942.
9. Wilbert Newgold, personal communication; Alf Evers, "Overlook Mountain," in *The Conservationist*, March 1958.
10. "Servicemen Return, Village Rejoices," in *The Hue and Cry*, July 21, 1945; *The Overlook*, September 13, 1940 for Lindin quotation.
11. Woodstock *Press*, September 19, 1941.
12. Woodstock *Press*, September 19, 1941.
13. "24th Annual Show Tells Story of Woodstock Art in Wartime," in Woodstock *Press*, August 14, 1942.
14. The Woodstock Guild of Craftsmen, *A Woodstock Center for Woodstock Crafts*, Woodstock, 1940, an eight-page pamphlet.

15. *The Overlook*, May 17, 29, June 14, 1940.
16. Photographs of buildings in hamlet of Woodstock, 1940s and 1950s, author's collection.
17. "Architectural Notes," in *The Wasp*, June 28, 1952; "Fireman's Hall," in Permanent Collection, Woodstock Artists Association.
18. Martin Schuetze, "Hervey White, November 26, 1866 to October 20, 1944 (Spoken at his Funeral, October 23, 1944)," Bearsville, N.Y., 1944.
19. Peter Whitehead, Father W. H. Francis, and Gene and Flora Patterson, personal communications.
20. Ulster County *News*, November 27, 1941; Darryl Parham, personal communication.

CHAPTER 53

1. Oscar Mosher, personal communication; "Summer Season Starts With a Real Roar," in The Woodstock *Weekly Window*, June 3, 1948.
2. Ibid.
3. "Tourists Go Home," in *The Wasp*, July 10, 1954.
4. "Memorial Ass'n Receives Thanks," in Woodstock *Weekly Window*, June 3, 1948.
5. Caleb Milne, "I Dream of the Day," Woodstock, 1944, pp. 4-5, passim.
6. Sherman Short, Charles Rosen and Nancy Schoonmaker, personal communications; "Marion Bullard, 1878-1915," in *Publications of the Woodstock Historical Society*, no. 17, December 1955, pp. 10-18, headed "Woodstock Years" by Rose Oxhandler.
7. "Kenneth L. Wilson" in *The New York Red Book*, M. D. Hartman, ed., Albany, 1966-1967, pp. 288-289; "Woodstock Profiles," No. 4, Ken Wilson, in *The Hue and Cry*, July 7, 1945.
8. Sylvia Day, "The Charmed Life of John Pike," in Ulster County *Townsman*, November 11, 1976; John Pike, personal communication; "Civic

Leaders Organize," in *The Hue and Cry*, June 9, 1945.
9. A differing view of postwar Woodstock art is in the Marling dissertation, 1976, under "After the Crash"; personal communication with the Woodstock artists mentioned.
10. Fletcher Martin and Edward Milman, personal communications.
11. *The First Woodstock Art Conference*, ed. John D. Morse, Woodstock and New York, 1947, passim; Kingston *Daily Freeman*, August 13, 31, September 2, 1948.
12. Woodstock Artists Association Bulletin, "Fall Plans for Artists," in Woodstock *Gargoyles*, 1949, n.p.; Rudolph Fiolic, personal communication.
13. Louise Ault, *Artist in Woodstock*, Philadelphia, 1978, passim; "Actor into Sculptor, Teacher, Harvey Fite," in *Record-Press*, Section 11, p. 3, February 14, 1963, contains a good account of the evolution of Opus 40. Ms. Leeb-Lundberg, owner of Perrine's house, personal communication; *Archipenko, International Visionary*, ed. Donald H. Karshar, Washington, 1969.
14. Alf Evers, "A Half Century of Woodstock Theater," in *Fifty Years of Theater*, Woodstock, 1975; Jean Mele, "Reporter About Town," in Kingston *Daily Freeman*, August 26, 1950.
15. Lillian Heermann and Aileen Cramer, personal communications.
16. *Maverick Sunday Concerts, 1916-1975, 60th Season*, Woodstock 1975, n.p.; Kees van der Loo, personal communication.
17. "A Dutchman in the Catskills," in *Fortune*, May 1964.
18. Kingston *Daily Freeman*, January 28, 1952, May 15, 1957, July 10, June 10, 1975.
19. Kingston *Daily Freeman* August 3, 1957; Woodstock *Times*, May 15, 1957; Kingston *Daily Freeman*, April 5, December 31, 1957.
20. Kingston *Daily Freeman*, August 28, 1948; "Fiery Cross Disturbs

Woodstock Last Friday Night," in
Ulster County *News*, March 28, 1948;
ibid, December 30, 1948.
21. Kingston *Daily Freeman*, June 16,
June 17, July 2, July 27, 1948; for
biog. sketch John A. Kingsbury, Anita
M. Smith, *Woodstock*, p. 110.
22. Kingston *Daily Freeman*, August
30, September 7, 1948.
23. Kingston *Daily Freeman*, June 14,
1948; Ulster County *News*, June 17,
1948.
24. Forrest Goodenough, "Cadenzas,"
in Woodstock *Weekly Window*, June
3, 1948.

CHAPTER 54

1. Dixon Ryan Fox, "On Adopting a
Background," in *Publications of the
Woodstock Historical Society*, no. 8,
August 1932, pp. 3-10.
2. I have heard the words and phrases
quoted here many times during half a
century in Woodstock. Among those
reporting these and similar word uses
were Anita M. Smith, Louise Hasbrouck
Zinn and Charles Rosen.
3. Edward T. Chase, Carl Eric Lindin,
"The Woodstock Landscape," in *Fallen
Leaves*, Woodstock, n.d., n.p., reprinted
from *Publications of the Woodstock
Historical Society*, no. 7, July 1932,
quotation p. 20; Lucy Fletcher Brown,
"The First Summer in Byrdcliffe," in
*Publications of the Woodstock Historical
Society*, no. 2, August 1930, pp. 14-15.
4. Stanley Kimmel, "When Grant Came
to Overlook," in *The Overlook*, July 30,
1932.
5. Kingston *Argus*, March 29, 1899;
unidentified newspaper clipping, c. 1937,
author's collection, quotes Twaddell,
Kenneth Downer; "Dr. Downer" in
*Publications of the Woodstock Historical
Society*, no. 5, August 1931, p. 35;
Kenneth Downer, personal
communication; *The Overlook*, June 30,
1932; J. M. Longendyke and Stanley
Kimmel, personal communications; obit.,
James Twaddell, *The Overlook*, June 30,
1939; *New York State Census, 1855*
gives Twaddell's age as twelve.

6. Louise Ault, *Artist in Woodstock*,
Philadelphia, 1978, pp. 40-42.
7. Unless otherwise noted stories and
phrases attributed to Charley Herrick in
this chapter were told to me in person.
8. Paul Domville, personal
communication.
9. Douglas Braik, Paul Domville and
Aileen Webster Payne, personal
communications.
10. Paul Domville, personal
communication; Alf Evers, "No More
Cider," in Woodstock *Times*, October 5,
1972.

CHAPTER 55

1. Tobie Geertsema, "Be-No Lodge. . .
Maybe No Barricade, Either," in
Kingston *Daily Freeman*, February 14,
1972; David Bird, "Private Fence Bars
Access to State Park," in New York
Times, April 6, 1973.
2. Hughes Mearns, "A Scholar With
Vision," in *The Overlook*, June 27, 1931;
Margaret Gibbs, *The D.A.R.*, N.Y.C.,
1969, p. 197; Harold Rugg, personal
communication; Kingston *Daily
Freeman*, November 25, 1950.
3. Kingston *Daily Freeman*, August 22, 1950.
4. Ulster County *News* and Kingston
Leader, March 23, 1950; Kingston *Daily
Freeman*, January 22, 1952.
5. "Holdridges Chosen as Real
American Family in Holiday" in
Kingston *Daily Freeman*, November 20,
1951.
6. Ulster County *News* and Kingston
Leader, June 15, 1950; Kingston *Daily
Freeman*, June 10, 1950; Ulster *News*
and Kingston *Leader*, June 15, 1950;
clipping (undated), Woodstock *Week*, c.
January 1968.
7. Peter Whitehead, Max Angiel and
Gene and Flora Patterson, personal
communications; Jane McCall
Whitehead, will, Ulster County
Surrogate's office, file box 1078, vol. 29.
8. Program, Turnau Opera Players, July
4-September 1, 1958, author's collection;
Jack Marquardt, Ward Pinner and
Yehudi Wyner, personal
communications.

9. Paul Domville and Douglas Braik, personal communications.

10. Alf Evers, "No More Cider," in Woodstock *Times*, October 5, 1972.

CHAPTER 56

1. Ulster *Townsman*, 1964

2. Allen Ginsburg, personal communication.

3. A view of hippies is included in Ruth Brady, "A Reader's Thoughts on Everything . . . ," vol. 4, no. 35, in Woodstock *Week*, August 1968.

4. Anthony Scaduto, *Bob Dylan, An Intimate Biography*, N.Y.C., 1971, pp. 245-247 and passim; effect of Dylan on Woodstock, Bill Konach in New York *Times*, July 9, 1969, pp. 45 and 87.

5. "The Scene at Woodstock," Kingston *Daily Freeman*, June 10, 1962; "Family is Ten Years Old" in Woodstock *Times*, May 22, 1980; the hippie impact on Woodstock is well reported in Tobie Geertsema, op. cit.

6. The ordinance was published in the Ulster *Townsman*, December 31, 1964, accepted by the Town Board, December 28, 1965. The events leading up to the adoption are reported in the publications of the Woodstock Association for the Conservation and Improvement of the Township, from their *Woodstock Speaks Up*, February 1960, through the ten *Bulletins* published through 1965.

7. Real estate dealer Mrs. B. B. Matteson, personal communication; "Woodstock Becoming Middletown U.S.A.?" and "Will Jazz Festival Bring This?," letters from Paul and Marie Arndt and anon. in *The Record-Press*, January 14, 1965.

8. "Torture Case to Grand Jury," in *The Record-Press*, June 10, 1965.

9. Woodstock *Week*, August 3, 1967.

10. "Artists Mad at Fuzz Mo.," in the Woodstock *Week*, August 3, 1967.

11. "Clarence, Woodstock's Legendary Old Man of the Mountain," in *The Record-Press*, July 1964; ibid., "Big Wrangle Over Clarence," in July 23, 1964; "King Jugged for Assault," in

Ulster *Townsman*, September 24, 1964; William C. Lipke and Gregg Blasdel, *Schmidt*, University of Vermont, Burlington, 1974, biblio, 212 pp. passim; Clarence Schmidt, Dr. A. E. Solomon and Hanus Schimmerling, personal communications.

12. "Olive Post Censures Use of Poem at OCS," "Teacher Clarifies," in Ulster *Townsman*, March 15, 1962.

13. Village Green benches, Marion Bullard in Ulster County *News*, November 18, 1948. The Woodstock Festival booklets were published annually, 1956-1969, by the Woodstock Festival Committee. The activities of the committee are summarized in the booklet for 1960.

14. Edgar Leaycraft, "Woodstock during 1967," in Ulster *Townsman*, February 8, 1968 (Edward Leaycraft is given in the source incorrectly), summarizes the Sound-in; Bill Kovach, "Woodstock's a Stage, But Many Don't Care for the Show," in New York *Times*, July 9, 1959, is a good report on Woodstock and its conflicts in the late 1960s; letter, Laurence E. Shultis, Ulster *Townsman*, June 12, April 17.

15. Ellen Jacob, "It Can't Happen Here," in Ulster County *Townsman*, June 19, 1969; "Between Me and the Lamppost," in Ulster County *Townsman*, April 12, June 19, 1969 (this regular column is invaluable for giving the anti-hippie side through the latter half of the 1960s).

16. Tobie Geertsema, "Woodstock Situation-A Touch of Violence," in Kingston *Daily Freeman*, June 17, 1969; "Violence No Answer to Hippie Problem," in Ulster *Townsman*, June 26, 1969.

17. Tobie Geertsema, "The Hippie Movement and its Impact on Woodstock," in Kingston *Daily Freeman*, June 16, 1969.

18. For Woodstock Festival and Soundouts, Evers, *The Catskills*, 710-715.

CHAPTER 57

1. The Woodstock *Aquarian*, vol. I, no. 2, passim, vol. II, no. 1, passim.
2. "You Should Never Throw Away the Past," in Woodstock *Times*, March 4, 1976, looks back at sixties and changes; letter Kenny O'Brien, in Woodstock *Times*, October 2, 1975.
3. "Good Jobs for All," in Woodstock *Times*, July 1, 1976 quotes Ken Traub on "unreliability," others on other aspects of work for young people.
4. The Woodstock *Aquarian*, vol. II, no. 1, deals with the interests to which young people of the sixties were turning.
5. "Sounding Board" in Ulster County *Townsman*, August 30, 1973, summarizes Longyear controversy.
6. "Woodstock Sewage System on Horizon," in Ulster County *Townsman*, June 16, 1977; "Central Sewage Defeated. . . ," September 14, 1978; problems of projected innovative sewerage system stated in "Our Sewer Plan Needs Drano," in Woodstock *Record*, August 1, 1983.
7. "End of an Era," in Woodstock *Times*, December 31, 1975.
8. Disputes over the matters mentioned here are still in progress and may be followed by means of reports in the Woodstock newspapers.

INDEX

Abbot, Leonard D., 477
Abbott Laboratories, 623
Abby, Aunt, 216
Abstract Expressionism, 621
Adams, Evangeline, 475
Adams, John Quincy, 429
Adams Express Company, 296
Addams, Jane, 410, 425–26, 454, 456
Adirondack Mountains, 400, 418
Adventures of Young Maverick, The (White), 456, 457
Africana, 525
Age of Aquarius, 667–71; *see also* Hippies
Airplanes, 486, 640
Albany, city of, 142, 194, 239, 313, 350, 626–627
Albany *Argus*, 192, 194, 195, 196, 239
Albany County, 97, 129, 139
Albany Glass Factory, 116–17, 119
Alcohol, 186, 49, 101–102, 232, 233, 354, 378, 653–54; bees and, 232, 367; bootleggers, 525, 530, 571; cider, 354, 359, 385; drunkenness, *see* Drunkenness; Prohibition, 466, 525, 536, 572; sale of, 299, 302, 307–308, 310; temperance movement, 298–99, 307, 310, 312, 359; wine, 536
Alderbark Mountain, 2
Alexander, William, 26
Alfred University, 453
Algonkian Indians, 7, 8
Alida, 276
Allen, Augusta, 518
Allen, Willard, 569

Allencrest Hotel, 569, 598
All Men, 656, 657
Almanacs, 217
Almon, John, 72
Alsea, Oregon, 411
Altenberg, Alexander, 513
Amato, Frank P., 499
Ambrose choir, 502
American Art Union, 182
American Communist Party, 591
American Journal of Science, 129, 142–43, 248
American Laboratory Theater, 584
American Legion, 574, 605, 611, 646
American Scene style of painting, 589–90, 608, 609
Amoucht, 19
Anarchism, 606, 616
Anderson, Margaret, 556
Andes, 199
Andy Lee Field, 541, 618
Angelus, 417
Angiel, Mr. and Mrs. Max, 649–50
Anglican Church, 583
Anguagekonk, 8, 17, 20
Animals: bewitching of, 210, 211, 213–14, 216; farm, 105, 158–59, 220, 362–63, 598, 612, 635; horses, 359–61; oxen 360–61; wild, 4, 91, 106, 219–20, 248, 381–82
Anne, Queen, 45, 139
Ansonia, 308, 359
Anti-Catholicism, 100, 490
Anti-Federalist party, 235
Anti-Masonism, 235

714

INDEX

INDEX

INDEX

INDEX

Middletown, Town of, 84, 97, 108
Mijer, Pieter, 517, 559
Militia, 27, 31, 57, 116; Anti-Rent and, 190–91, 193–96, 197; Revolutionary War and, 58–59
Millay, Edna St. Vincent, 479, 480
Millay, Norma, 479
Miller, Annatje, 73–74
Miller, David, 169
Miller, Henry, 601
Miller, Kenneth Hayes, 594
Miller, Lillie, 372
Miller, Peter, 49, 59, 60, 82, 83; Tory capture of, 72–75, 100, 219, 378
Miller, Petrus, 74
Miller, Willie, 373
Mill Hill Road, 192, 228, 280, 354, 364, 368, 436, 497, 509, 548, 571, 576, 626, 673
Mill House, 71
Milliken Albert Edward, 587
Millman, Edward, 620, 623
Mill Stream Lodge, 385, 388
Millstream Road, 576
Milne, Caleb, 618
Milo, Captain Savo, 627
Miner, E., 174
Mine Workers Union, 491–92
Mining, 30, 41, 89, 136–46, 156, 171; coal, 139, 140–44, 145, 249; gold and silver, 137–40, 144–46; oil and gas, 144
Minister's Face, 3, 30, 139, 249, 252, 255, 284, 312
Mink Hollow, 16, 19, 24, 39, 47, 64, 81, 82, 90, 98, 101, 102, 131, 168, 201–202, 205, 207, 228, 363, 364, 381, 383, 384, 394, 396, 397, 545, 567, 598; Sully and, 385–88; witchcraft and, 211, 215–16
Mink Hollow barn, 387
Mink Hollow Road, 48, 365, 384
Minklaer, Cornelis, 127
Minnehaha Spring, 257, 311
Minute men, 57
"Miramont Gallery," 499
Mirbeau, Octave, 457
Mission furniture, 387–88, 428
Mitchell, Stewart, 535
Mitchill, Dr. Samuel Latham, 140
Mixed-media art, 516
Modern art, 442, 43; Woodstock School of, 400, 512–15, 608, 609
Modern painters, 511–15
Modern Painters (Ruskin), 403, 406, 413
Mofit, Jocko, 665
Moholy-Nagy, L., 579
Molasses, 268
Molyneaux, Abram, 648
Moncure, Gabrielle, 543
Monet, Claude, 400

Moneylenders, 88
Monroe, Harriet, 456
Monroe, Kirk, 384
Montessori, Maria, 550
Montessori School, 550
Montgomery, Janet Livingston, 38, 92, 95
Montgomery, Richard, 92, 95
Montgomery, Dr. Thomas E., 366, 381, 383
Montgomery, Mrs. Thomas E., 381
Montoma, 211
Montross, Jacob, 152
Moore, Anne, 559
Moore, Charles Herbert, 284
Moore, Isabel, 534
Moore, Lou Wall, 432
Moran, Thomas, 400
More, Hermon, 513
Morgan, J. P., 622
Morgan, William, 235
Morning Star, 417
Morris, William, 401, 406, 408, 409, 417, 422, 428, 447, 517
Mortgage foreclosures, 575
Mosher, Isaac, 202
Mosher, Oscar, 363
Mosher, Phoebe Perry, 207
Mosher, S. A., 367
Mosher, Wilson, 372
Motion pictures, 449
Mott, Alfred A., 130
Mott, Jacob, 125
Mott, John, 128
Mott, William, 128
Mountain laurel, 509
Mountains, 246
Mountain View House, 311
Mount Nebo, 275
Mount Pleasant, 278, 364, 383, 394
Mount Tobias, 2
Mount Tremper, 2, 39, 82, 118, 169
Mount Tremper, village of, 9, 228, 277, 368
Mower's store, 548
Mud, 267–68; tinker legend and, 267–68, 634
Mulatto, The (Hughes), 646
Mullersruh, 417
Munson, Gorham B., 537, 562, 564; fight between Josephson and, 562–63
Mural painting, 595
Murder, 232, 365, 367, 553
Murphy, Fitzgerald, 387
Murphy, Herman Dudley, 425
Murphy, J. Francis, 401
Murray's quarry, 350
Murrell, William, 480, 536, 556, 563
Musical concerts, 461; chamber music, 469–70, 475, 476, 501, 506, 624, 625, 626; rock and folk, 661, 665, Woodstock Festival, 665–68; *see also* Maverick Concerts

INDEX

INDEX

INDEX

MAP

OF THE

PLACES OF INTEREST

IN THE VICINITY OF

"OVERLOOK"

Drawn by M? Logan Lashur,

Compliments of
M? Logan Lashur

INDIAN HEAD

Farm Hou

Deserte
Coalkil

Lillie Spring

ZIGZAG PATH

OLD GLASS ROAD

BROOK

Farm House

THE
PLAINS

BROOK

Saw Mill

SAWKILL CREEK

Spring Valley House

Ruins of Glass Factory

Farm House.

Stable

Minnehaha
Spring

OLDEST PATH ON MT. 50 YEARS OLD.

Anderson
Rock

Spring

SHORT CUT

ROAD FROM WEST HURLEY.

Half Way Rock

Plaza

Gorge View

GORG

MEADS

HURLEY.

ROAD FROM WEST

Shandakin View

California
Rock

Terrace
Rock